Beef Porterhouse Steak

1. Hold steak steady with fork. Use tip of knife to cut closely around bone. Lift bone to one side of platter.

2. Carve across full width of steak, cutting through both top loin and tenderloin. Diagonal slicing (instead of perpendicular) is recommended for thick steaks. (See *Corned Beef, page 708*, for description of diagonal slices.)

Pork Loin Roast

1. Before roast is brought to table, remove back bone leaving as little meat on it as possible. Place roast on platter with rib side facing carver so he can see angle of ribs and can make his slices accordingly.

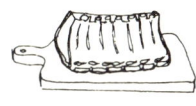

2. Insert fork in top of roast. Make slices by cutting closely along each side of rib bone. One slice will contain the rib; the next will be boneless.

Whole Ham

1. Ham is placed on platter with decorated or fat side up and shank to carver's right. Location of bones in right and left hams may be confusing so double-check location of knee cap which may be on near or far side of ham. Remove two or three lengthwise slices from thin side of ham which contains knee cap.

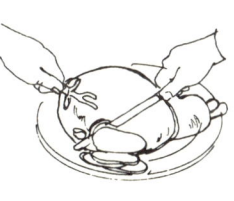

2. Make perpendicular slices down to leg bone or lift off boneless cushion similar to method illustrated for Picnic Shoulder.

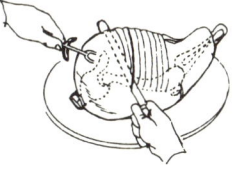

3. Release slices by cutting along leg bone.

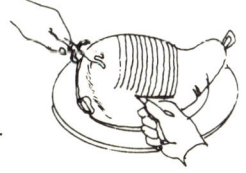

Picnic Shoulder

Carving is the same for both a roasted (baked) smoked picnic and a roasted (baked) fresh picnic.

1. Remove a lengthwise slice as shown here. Turn picnic so that it rests on surface just cut. Cut down to arm bone at a point near elbow bone. Turn knife and cut along arm bone to remove boneless arm meat.

2. Carve boneless arm meat by making perpendicular slices from top of meat down to cutting board.

3. Remove the meat from each side of the arm bone. Then carve the two boneless pieces.

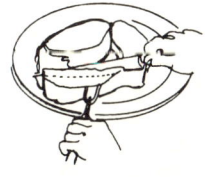

Continued on back cover

REGENCY FAMILY COOKBOOK

REGENCY
FAMILY
COOKBOOK

The complete cookbook for
the American home

THOMAS NELSON PUBLISHERS, INC.
NASHVILLE   NEW YORK

Copyright © 1978 by Thomas Nelson, Inc., Publishers

All rights reserved under International and Pan-American Conventions. Published in Nashville, Tennessee, by Thomas Nelson, Inc., Publishers and simultaneously in Don Mills, Ontario, by Thomas Nelson & Sons (Canada) Limited. Permission granted by Consolidated Book Publishers to reprint some recipes from *The American Family Cookbook*, copyright © 1971, 1974, by Processing & Books, Inc.

Manufactured in the United States of America.

Contents

Culinary Know-How — 1
Equipping Your Kitchen • Use Correct Techniques • Measurements & Equivalent Ingredients • Culinary Terms • Oven Temperatures • High Altitude Cooking • Helpful Hints for the Cook • Foreign Words and Phrases • How to Do It

Chapter 1 **APPETIZERS—HOT & COLD** — 12
Planning • Hot Appetizers • Cold Appetizers • Sit-Down Appetizers

Chapter 2 **SOUPS—HOT & COLD** — 25
Helpful Hints about Soups • Soup Garnishes • Soups to Serve Hot • Chowders & Fish Soups • Soups to Serve Cold

Chapter 3 **BREADS—YEAST, QUICK, & THE KIND YOU BUY** — 36
Helpful Hints about Breads • Storage • Yeast Loaves • Yeast Sweet Breads & Coffee Cakes • Yeast Dinner Rolls • Yeast Sweet Rolls and Doughnuts • Quick Breads • Quick Tea Breads & Coffee Cakes • Biscuits & Muffins • Breads from Mixes • Dough from the Dairy Case • Bakers's Breads

Chapter 4 **EGG & CHEESE DISHES** — 63
About Eggs • About Cheese • Egg Dishes • Cheese Dishes • Souffles

Chapter 5 **MEATS** — 77
Storage • Methods of Cooking • Beef • Pork • Lamb • Veal • Variety Meats • Ground Meat Cookery

Chapter 6 **POULTRY & STUFFINGS** — 133
Classes • Styles • Storage • Cooking Poultry • Chicken • Turkey • Duckling • Goose • Rock Cornish Game Hens • Stuffings for Poultry

Chapter 7 **FISH & SHELLFISH** — 151
Availability • Storage • Fish • Shellfish

Chapter 8 **VEGETABLES** — 167
Selection • Storage • Preparation • Vegetables A to Z

Chapter 9 **SAUCES & GRAVIES** — 195

Chapter 10 **SALADS & SALAD DRESSINGS** — 201
Salad Pointers • Green & Vegetable Salads • Fruit Salads • Molded Salads • Main-Dish Salads • Salad Dressings

Chapter 11 **CAKES & TORTES—FROSTINGS AND FILLINGS** 221
  Helpful Hints about Cakes • Conventional Cakes • One-Bowl & Quick Cakes • Angel Food & Sponge Cakes • Chiffon Cakes • Frostings & Fillings

Chapter 12 **PIES** 251
  Techniques for Making Pies • Pastry Crusts • Pie Shells • Pies • Tarts

Chapter 13 **DESSERTS & DESSERT SAUCES** 273
  Cake Desserts • Pastries • Custards & Puddings • Refrigerator Desserts • Ice Cream Desserts • Ice Cream, Sherbets, & Ices • Fruit Desserts • Dessert Sauces

Chapter 14 **COOKIES** 305
  Bar Cookies • Drop Cookies • Molded Cookies • Refrigerator Cookies • Rolled Cookies

Chapter 15 **BEVERAGES—HOT & COLD**

Bonus Chapters
  PRESERVING & FREEZING 335
    Methods of canning • Equipment • Canning Procedure • Home Canning • Preserving • Jellies • Jams • Marmalades • Preserves • Conserves • Fruit Butters

  OUTDOOR COOKING 363
    Meats on the Grill • Chicken on the Grill • Fish & Shellfish on the Grill • Cooking in Aluminum Foil • Skillet Cooking

Foreword

American cooking has always had a spirit of discovery. Each new group to arrive on our shores has brought new and different recipies for special dishes. Holiday delicacies, unusual spices, and ingredients from many parts of the world have all found their way into common usage as new neighbors discovered each other's ways of preparing and serving food. In addition, the resources of the new country have changed the traditional menus to create meals unique to the new land. Corn bread, succotash, pumpkin pie—all strange at first—have become lasting favorites. Virginia Oysters, Louisiana Shrimp, and Florida Oranges were all discovered and incorporated as settlers spread across the land.

Of course, modern techniques of freezing, refrigerating, and transporting the abundance of our farms and fields make possible the availability of a variety of foods year-round that would have seemed impossible only a generation ago. Fresh fruits, which once had only a very limited season, are now taken for granted all year. In this sense, the discoveries of technology have changed our ways of cooking and eating.

The increase in overseas travel has exposed many Americans to a great variety of the world's foods. Returning from tours abroad, many home cooks are tempted to duplicate at home the tastes discovered abroad. These discoveries then become a permanent part of our American cooking.

The *Regency Family Cookbook* draws on this almost overwhelming variety of American cuisine to help you make every meal interesting, wholesome, and tasty. Some recipes reflect the regional specialties of this and other countries. Others have their origins in the pioneer's need to make the most of the land's bounty. Old favorites appear too, often with new and easier ways to produce the familiar tastes. Many recipes may be new to you, inviting the personal discovery that has always marked American cooking.

For the veteran home chef or the person just learning to cook, the *Regency Family Cookbook* provides a source of successful, kitchen-tested recipes spanning the entire range of foods. Soups, appetizers, baked goods, main courses, salads, and desserts are all explored through broad-ranging selections of recipes accompanied with special hints to make the cooking process easier and the results enjoyable.

If you are planning a "bringing-the-boss-home" dinner party or just looking for something a little different for the family supper, the *Regency Family Cookbook* has what you want. Each recipe has been carefully kitchen-tested and has been written in a clear, concise outline form to make it easy to follow and understand. The range of ideas in each category offers plenty of variety for any occasion.

This is truly a cook's book, and we hope it will become a favorite companion as you discover the excitement of new dishes.
Bon Apetit!

Gordon Stone

Culinary Know-How

Presented here are basic information for food preparation and reference material. Before you begin to cook, read especially Use Correct Techniques, Culinary Terms, and How To Do It. Become familiar with the other information given and refer to it as needed.

EQUIPPING YOUR KITCHEN

Your choice of equipment often depends upon the amount of cupboard and other storage space available. With a minimum of space one must choose essential items wisely, making sure that a bulky item such as a large saucepot or skillet can serve more than one purpose. The following list should help in making a wise choice of equipment.

For food preparation:
Set of measuring spoons — ¼ teaspoon, ½ teaspoon, 1 teaspoon, 1 tablespoon
Set (or nest) of measuring cups — ¼ cup, ⅓ cup, ½ cup, 1 cup
Glass measuring cups for liquids — 1 cup, 2 cups (1 pint), 4 cups (1 quart)
Mixing bowls — 1 pint, 1 quart, 3 quarts
Knives — butcher knife, serrated bread knife, slicing knife (with long, thin blade), chopping knife (French), paring knives, grapefruit knife
Forks — long-handled fork, two-tined fork, two or three small forks, blending fork
Spoons — three wooden spoons of various sizes and lengths, slotted metal spoon, slotted wooden spoon, two metal tablespoons, three metal teaspoons
Spatulas — small, medium
Rubber scrapers — two plate and bowl scrapers (wide), one bottle and jar scraper (narrow)
Beater — hand rotary type
Strainers — small, medium
Colander
Cookie cutters — assorted sizes and shapes
Juicer or reamer
Vegetable parer
Vegetable brush (stiff)
Kitchen shears
Apple corer
Graters — small hand grater, set of larger graters for fine and coarse grating and shredding
Cutting board
Wire cooling racks — two or three
Pancake turner
Pastry blender
Rolling pin (stockinette cover)
Pastry brush
Pastry canvas
Flour sifter

For baking and top-of-range cooking:
Custard cups — six (6 ounce)
Muffin (or cupcake) pans — two sets of six (one set 1¾ x 1 inch, one set 2½ x 1¼ inch)
Casseroles with covers — 1½, 2, and 3 quarts
Individual casseroles or ramekins — six
Pie pans — 8 inch, 9 inch
Cake pan (square) — 8 inch, 9 inch
Cake pans (round) — two or three 8 or 9 inch
Cake pan (tubed) — 9 or 10 inch
Baking pan — 11 x 7 x 1½ inch
Food mill
Garlic press
Meat grinder
Timer
Wooden chopping bowl and chopper
Potato masher or ricer
Flour shaker
Salt and pepper shakers
Can opener (wall-type or electric)
Funnels
Ladle
Tongs
Loaf pan — 9 x 5 x 3 inch
Open roasting pan — 13 x 9 x 2 inch
Double boiler — 1½ quarts
Saucepans with tight-fitting covers — 1, 2, and 3 quarts
Dutch oven — 3 quarts
Coffee maker — 4 or 6 cups
Teakettle
Teapot — 6 cups
Toaster
Skillets with tight-fitting covers — two (one small 6 or 8 inch, one large deep 10 inch)
Molds — two or three, including a ring mold

Miscellaneous items (handy to have):
Melon ball cutter
Steam cooker
Ice cream scoop
Corkscrew and bottle opener
Knife sharpener — wall-type or electric

Use Correct Techniques

Tea ball
Thermometers—meat, candy, deep frying, portable oven thermometer (if oven is unreliable)
Sink strainer
Juice can opener
Biscuit and bun warmer
Jars with screw-top covers (for storing foods in refrigerator and on cupboard shelves)
Canister set
Hot pads, tiles, or stands (for hot dishes)
Pot holders
Garbage can
Freezer storage containers and moisture-vaporproof bags
Refrigerator storage dishes with covers
Aluminum foil
Paper baking cups
Waxed paper
Paper towels

Nice-to-have appliances:
Coffee maker
Waffle baker
Blender
Electric mixer—table-type or portable
Electric skillet

USE CORRECT TECHNIQUES

Read recipe carefully.
Assemble all ingredients and utensils.
Select pans of proper kind and size. Measure pans inside, from rim to rim.
Use standard measuring cups and spoons. Use liquid measuring cups (rim above 1-cup line) for liquids. Use nested or dry measuring cups (1-cup line even with top) for dry ingredients. When measuring with a tablespoon, use a standard one which holds 1/16 of a cup.
Check liquid measurements at eye level.
Level dry measurements with a straight-edged knife or spatula. Fill the cup, spoon, or other measure to overflowing before passing spatula or knife over top. *To measure flour*, fill cup lightly; do not dip measuring cup into container with flour. *To measure regular brown sugar*, pack into measuring cup so that sugar will hold the shape of cup when turned out.
Level fats with a spatula or straight edge of knife after pressing fat firmly into nested-type measuring cup. To measure amounts of fat less than 1 cup, use individual cups (¼, ⅓, or ½), or measure in tablespoons. The water-displacement method may be used if the water that clings to the fat will not affect the product. To measure ¼ cup fat, for example, pour ¾ cup cold water into a standard measuring cup for liquids. Then add the fat to water until the water level rises to the 1-cup mark in the cup. (Be sure water entirely covers the fat.) Drain off the water thoroughly.

Sift regular all-purpose flour before measuring if you so desire. Milling processes have improved considerably through the years until today's all-purpose flour is of such high quality that sifting is not always necessary. Follow miller's directions on the package, if available. Spoon, without sifting, the whole-grained types of flour (whole wheat, buckwheat, etc.) into measuring cup.
Beat whole eggs until thick and piled softly when recipe calls for well-beaten eggs.
Beat egg whites as follows: *Frothy*—entire mass forms bubbles; *Rounded peaks*—peaks turn over slightly when beater is slowly lifted upright; *Stiff peaks*—peaks remain standing when beater is slowly lifted upright.
Beat egg yolks until very thick when recipe calls for well-beaten egg yolks.
Place oven rack so top of product will be almost at center of oven. Stagger pans so no pan is directly over another and they do not touch each other or the walls of oven. Place single pan so that center of product is near center of oven.
Covering foods to be stored in the refrigerator will depend upon the type of refrigerator used.

MEASUREMENTS & EQUIVALENTS

Dash, speck, or few grains . less than ⅛ teaspoon
60 drops .... 1 teaspoon
3 teaspoons (½ fluid ounce) ...... 1 tablespoon
⅛ cup (1 fluid ounce) .... 2 tablespoons
¼ cup (2 fluid ounces) .... 4 tablespoons
⅓ cup .... 5 tablespoons plus 1 teaspoon
½ cup (4 fluid ounces) .... 8 tablespoons
⅔ cup ...... 10 tablespoons plus 2 teaspoons
¾ cup (6 fluid ounces) .... 12 tablespoons
1 cup (8 fluid ounces) .... 16 tablespoons
2 cups (16 fluid ounces) .... 1 pint
4 cups (32 fluid ounces) .... 1 quart
2 pints .... 1 quart
2 quarts .... ½ gallon
4 quarts (liquid) .... 1 gallon
8 quarts (dry) .... 1 peck
4 pecks .... 1 bushel
16 ounces (dry measure) .... 1 pound
1 ounce .... 28.35 grams
1 pound .... 453.59 grams

Additional Equivalents & Substitutions

Baking powder, 1 teaspoon ... 1 teaspoon cream of tartar plus ¼ teaspoon baking soda
Baking powder, double-acting ... 1 teaspoon will leaven 1 cup flour

Baking soda .... ½ teaspoon with 1 cup fully soured milk	will neutralize the acid in that amount of milk and leaven 1 cup flour
Bread, 1 to 2 slices (soft)	1 cup crumbs
1 pound loaf	10 cups small bread cubes
Butter, 1 cup ..	⅞ to 1 cup vegetable shortening or lard plus ½ teaspoon salt
Butter or margarine, 2 tablespoons	1 ounce
½ cup (4 ounces)	1 stick
Chocolate, unsweetened, 1 square	1 ounce
1 square	3 to 4 tablespoons cocoa plus 1 tablespoon shortening
Cornstarch, 1 tablespoon	2 tablespoons all-purpose flour
Cream, light (20%), 1 cup	⅞ cup milk plus 3 tablespoons butter
Cream, heavy (40%), 1 cup	¾ cup milk plus ⅓ cup butter
1 cup	2 cups whipped
Eggs, whole, 4 to 6	1 cup
whites, 8 to 10	1 cup
yolks, 10 to 14	1 cup
Flour, cake, 1 cup sifted	⅞ cup (or 1 cup minus 2 tablespoons) all-purpose flour
Garlic, 1 clove	¼ teaspoon garlic powder
Marshmallows, 10 miniature	1 large
16 large	¼ pound (4 ounces)
Onion, ¼ cup chopped	1 tablespoon instant minced onion or 1 teaspoon onion powder
Sugar, granulated, 2¼ cups	1 pound
superfine, 2⅓ cups	1 pound
brown, about 2¼ cups firmly packed .	1 pound
granulated brown, about 3⅛ cups ...	1 pound
confectioners', 3½ cups	1 pound
Syrup, corn, about 1½ cups	1 pound
maple, about 1½ cups	1 pound

INGREDIENTS

Baking powder—double-acting type.

Bread crumbs—two slices fresh bread equals about 1 cup soft bread crumbs or ¼-inch cubes. One slice dry or toasted bread equals about ½ cup dry cubes or ¼ to ⅓ cup fine dry crumbs. *Buttered crumbs* are soft or dry bread or cracker crumbs tossed in melted butter or margarine. Use 1 to 2 tablespoons butter or margarine for 1 cup soft crumbs and 2 to 4 tablespoons butter or margarine for 1 cup dry crumbs.

Catsup—See *Ketchup*.

Chocolate—the term chocolate refers to *unsweetened chocolate*. *Sweet chocolate* is chocolate with sugar added. It may also contain cocoa butter and flavorings. It is used for dipping candies and other confections. *Semisweet chocolate* is small pieces or 1-ounce squares formed from slightly sweetened chocolate and used for candymaking or baked products, or eaten as a confection. (Also available in the form of bars.) *Cocoa* is a powdered chocolate product from which some of the cocoa butter has been removed. The fat content varies from 10% to 22%. *Breakfast cocoa* is a high-fat cocoa which contains at least 22% cocoa fat. *Dutch process cocoa* can be either "cocoa" or "breakfast cocoa" which is processed with one or more alkaline materials as permitted under government regulations. *Instant cocoa* is a mixture of cocoa, sugar, and an emulsifier. It can be prepared for use by dissolving in hot liquid with no cooking necessary.

Cornstarch—thickening agent. 1 tablespoon has the thickening power of 2 tablespoons flour.

Fats and Oils—Butter is fat from sour or sweet cream gathered in a mass, sometimes salted and colored. It contains not less than 80% by weight of milk fat. *Unsalted butter* is butter made from sweet cream. Also called sweet butter. *Whipped butter* is butter into which air has been whipped. *Cooking or salad oils* include: corn oil, refined from the dried, crushed corn germ; cottonseed oil, refined from the crushed seed of the cotton plant; peanut oil, the oil extracted from peanuts, a by-product of peanut butter; safflower oil, the oil extracted from the seed of the safflower plant, used for cooking purposes and also used commercially for the manufacture of safflower margarine. *Cracklings* are the residue from rendered fat of meat. *Hard fats* are coconut or palm oils in solid form used mostly in candymaking. *Lard* is fat rendered from the fatty tissues of the hog. *Margarine* is made by the emulsification of various oils with cultured milk and further processing to produce a consistency similar to that of butter; contains 80% fat; usually colored; may or may not have salt added. Soft-type and whipped margarine are also available. *Olive oil* is oil from the flesh of ripe olives. Virgin olive oil is that which is first extracted and is better in flavor and appearance than the oil produced by the second or third pressing. Use olive oil when specified in a recipe. *Poultry fat* is a

Ingredients

cooking fat made commercially by rendering the leaf fat removed from the body cavities of chickens and turkeys and sometimes from the fat that is skimmed from vats of poultry being cooked for canning. *Shortening* is a general term used for cooking fats. May be meat fats or vegetable oils. Or, may be a blend of animal fats; or a blend of vegetable oils; or a blend of animal and vegetable. *Suet* is the clear, white fat of beef and mutton.

Flour—the term flour when used in recipes with no other qualifications as to special purpose or preparation (bread, cake, self-rising flour) usually refers to all-purpose or general-purpose flour. *Bread flour* is milled from blends of spring and winter hard wheats or from either type alone. It has a fairly high protein content and is slightly granular to the touch. It may be bleached or unbleached and is milled mostly for commercial bakers. *All-purpose flour* is a blend of hard or soft wheat flours which are lower in protein content than bread flour, but higher than cake flour. It can usually be used with good results for most home-baked products. Blends are prepared to satisfy the demands of different areas. In the South, for instance, a softer blend is available to make satisfactory quick breads, while in the North a harder blend is marketed for use in making yeast breads and rolls. *Instant-blending flour* is an all-purpose flour which some associate with the term "instantized" to indicate that the flour dissolves readily in liquids without forming lumps. *Self-rising flour* is flour to which leavening agents and salt have been added in proper proportions for home-baking. The leavening agent most often used, with soda, is calcium phosphate. *Whole-wheat flour* (also graham flour) is flour milled so that the natural constituents of the wheat kernel remain unaltered. *Pastry flour* is made of either hard or soft wheats, but usually the latter. It is fairly low in protein and finely milled though not as fine as cake flour. It is used chiefly by bakers and biscuit manufacturers. *Cake flour* is milled from soft wheats. The protein content is low and the granulation so fine that the flour feels soft and satiny.

Fruit pectin—a substance in fruit which, when used in the right proportions with sugar and acid, forms a jelly. *Liquid or bottled pectin* is refined from apple juice. *Powdered pectin* is made from citrus or apple pectin, then dried and packaged.

Gelatin—a granulated animal product used to thicken salads, desserts, and some soups. Available unflavored or in packaged form with sugar, color, and flavoring.

Grated peel—whole citrus fruit peel finely grated through colored part only (white is bitter).

Herb bouquet (bouquet garni)—a bunch of aromatic herbs (such as a piece of celery with leaves, a sprig of thyme, 3 or 4 sprigs of parsley, and sometimes a bay leaf) tied neatly together and used to flavor soups, stews, braised dishes, and sauces. Enclose fine, dry herbs in a cheesecloth bag.

Julienne strips—vegetables, meats, poultry, or cheese, cut into narrow strips.

Ketchup—a smooth, well-seasoned tomato relish.

Milk and Milk Products—Fresh fluid milk contains not less than 3.25% milk fat and not less than 8.25% milk solids other than fat. *Vitamin D milk* is whole or skim milk in which the vitamin D content has been increased. *Homogenized milk* is fresh milk in which the size of the fat globules is reduced so that the cream does not rise to the top. *Evaporated milk* is sterilized homogenized milk containing about 60% less water than whole milk. When diluted with an equal amount of water, it is used as fresh whole milk. It is also used, undiluted, as cream. *Sweetened condensed milk* is milk from which about half the water has been removed. It contains a large amount of added sugar which acts as a preservative. *Skim milk* is milk from which most of the fat has been removed thereby reducing its vitamin A content. Some skim milks are fortified by adding a water-soluble vitamin A and D concentrate. *Sour milk*, see *To sour milk, page 12*. *Buttermilk* as sold in retail markets is usually a cultured (fermented) product made of fresh skim milk. (It is also the by-product from churning cream into butter.) The bacterial culture used converts the milk sugar into lactic acid. Cultured buttermilk may also be made from fresh fluid whole milk, concentrated fluid milk, or reconstituted nonfat dry milk. *Dry milk (whole) and dry milk (nonfat)* are made from fresh whole milk and skim milk respectively. After most of the water has been removed from them they are dried until a fine-textured powder results. The process has no appreciable effect on the nutritive value and when mixed with water these products have the original composition of pasteurized milk. *Yogurt* is a cultured product (with a consistency resembling custard) usually made from fresh partially skimmed milk enriched with added milk solids other than fats. Fermentation is accomplished by a mixed bacterial culture. *Half and half* is a mixture of milk and cream, usually 10% to 12% fat. *Light cream*, sometimes referred to as table or coffee cream, contains 18% to 20% fat. *Heavy (or whipping) cream* contains between 30% and 36% fat. *Dairy sour cream* is a cultured product sold commercially and made by adding bacterial cultures to pasteurized and homogenized cream. (See *To sour cream, page 12.*)

Monosodium glutamate (Accent, MSG, and others) — a basic seasoning produced from natural sources and added to foods to enhance their characteristic flavors without adding a flavor of its own.

Packaged mixes — flour combined with other ingredients such as shortening, baking powder or other leavening agent, sugar, and dry milk; marketed in packages. They require only the addition of liquid and sometimes eggs to prepare a batter from them.

Sugars and Syrups — *Granulated sugar* is a highly refined white sugar composed of almost pure sucrose which is found in large quantities in sugar cane and sugar beets. *Superfine granulated sugar* is a specially screened, uniformly fine-grained sugar used in cakes and in mixing drinks. *Confectioners' (powdered) sugar* is granulated sugar crushed and screened to desired fineness. A small amount of cornstarch is added to prevent caking. Confectioners' sugar is used in frostings and icings and for dusting doughnuts, pastries, etc. *Brown sugar* is unrefined cane sugar which varies in color from very light to very dark. It contains various amounts of molasses, some non-sugars (ash) naturally present in molasses, and moisture. *Granulated brown sugar* is a specially processed brown sugar which does not harden and can be poured from the package. To substitute for regular brown sugar, see manufacturer's equivalents table. *Maple sugar* is a solid product obtained by evaporating maple sap or maple syrup to the point where crystallization occurs. *Molasses* is the liquor remaining after the crystallization of raw sugar from the concentrated sap of the sugar cane. Sometimes a second and third crystallization is made, resulting in two grades of molasses known as "light" and "dark" molasses. When a large proportion of the sugar has been removed, the resulting product has a strong flavor and is called "black strap." It is used for fermentation purposes. *Sorghum (or sorgo)* is a syrup somewhat resembling molasses produced from a cane-like grass. It has a mild flavor appealing to many people especially in the Southwest where the grass is grown. *Corn syrup* is a product resulting from the partial hydrolysis of cornstarch with coloring and flavoring usually added to the syrup. Light and dark corn syrups are marketed. Many table syrups contain some corn syrup combined with such sweeteners as sorghum, cane syrup, or honey and butterscotch or vanilla for flavoring. *Honey* is defined as "the nectar and saccharine exudations of plants gathered, modified, and stored by the honey bee." Honey must contain not more than 25% water. The flavor and color of honey depends upon the source of the nectar. Orange blossoms, clover, buckwheat, and basswood are common sources. *Maple syrup* comes from the sap of the maple tree collected in early spring and concentrated to the desired consistency. Pure maple syrup contains not over 35% water. *Sugar substitutes* are non-caloric sweetening agents. *Sugar syrup* is a solution of sugar and water used to sweeten beverages.

Tenderizer, Instant Meat — powdered product, seasoned and unseasoned, used on less tender cuts of meat; follow label directions.

Vinegar — usually refers to cider vinegar when the type of vinegar is not specified in recipe.

CULINARY TERMS

Bake — To cook in a container (covered or uncovered) in an oven or oven-type appliance. Usually called roasting when applied to meats, see *Roast, page 17.*

Barbecue — To roast or broil on a rack over hot coals or on a revolving spit in front of or over heat source.

Baste — To spoon liquid (or use baster) over cooking food to add moisture and flavor.

Beat — To make a mixture smooth by introducing air with a brisk motion that lifts the mixture over and over, or with a rotary motion as with a hand rotary beater or electric mixer.

Blanch — To preheat or precook in boiling water or steam. This process is used to inactivate enzymes and shrink food for canning, freezing, and drying. The blanching process is also used to aid in the removal of skins from nuts, see *page 11*, fruits, and vegetables.

Culinary Terms

Blend — To mix two or more ingredients so that each loses its identity.

Boil — To cook in liquid in which bubbles rise continually and break on the surface. Boiling temperature of water at sea level is 212°F.

Braise — To cook slowly in a covered utensil in a small amount of liquid or in steam. (Meat may or may not be browned in small amount of fat before braising.)

Bread — To coat with bread crumbs alone or to coat with bread crumbs, then with diluted slightly beaten egg or evaporated milk, and again with crumbs.

Broil — To cook by direct heat.

Candy — To cook fruit (also citrus fruit peel and ginger) in a heavy syrup until plump and transparent, then drain and dry. Candied product is also known as crystallized fruit, peel, or ginger. Term also applies to vegetables cooked in a syrup or sugar and fat mixture (i.e. candied sweet potatoes or carrots). Candy is synonymous with glaze (*i.e.* glazed or candied cherries).

Caramelize — To heat dry sugar or foods containing sugar until a brown color and characteristic flavor develop.

Chop — To cut into pieces with a knife or other sharp tool. (Also see *Mince, below.*)

Coddle — To cook slowly just below the boiling point (as applied to eggs and fruit).

Combine — To mix ingredients.

Cream — To mix one or more foods together until soft and creamy. Usually applied to shortening and sugar.

Cube — See *Dice, below.*

Cut in — To distribute solid fat in dry ingredients by chopping with pastry blender or knives until finely divided.

Devil — To mix with hot seasoning as pepper, mustard.

Dice — To cut into small cubes.

Dissolve — To cause a liquid and a dry substance to pass into solution.

Dredge — To coat or sprinkle with flour or other fine substance.

Flake fish (freshly cooked or canned) — Gently separating the fish into flakes, using a fork. Remove the bony tissue from crab meat while flaking it. (Bones of salmon are edible and need not be removed.)

Fold — To combine by using two motions, one which cuts vertically through the mixture (using a flexible metal or rubber spatula or wire whisk) and the other which turns the mixture over by sliding the implement across the bottom of the mixing bowl.

Fricassee — To cook by braising (usually applied to poultry, rabbit, and veal).

Fry — To cook in fat; called *sauté* or *panfry* when cooking with a small amount of fat; called *deep-fat frying* when cooking in a deep layer of fat.

Glacé — To coat with a thin sugar syrup cooked to the crack stage. When used for pies and certain types of bread the mixture may contain a thickening, but it is not cooked to such a concentrated form as for a glacé; or it may be uncooked.

Grate — To reduce to small particles by rubbing on anything rough and indented. Use a rotary-type grater with hand-operated crank for grating chocolate and nuts, following manufacturer's directions. Grated chocolate and nuts should be fine and light.

Grind — To reduce food to particles by cutting, crushing (electric blender may be used), or by forcing through a food chopper.

Knead — To manipulate with a pressing motion plus folding and stretching.

Lard — To insert matchlike strips of fat, called lardoons, into gashes in side of uncooked lean meat by means of a larding needle or skewer; or to place on top of meat.

Marinate — To allow food to stand in liquid (usually a seasoned oil and acid mixture) to impart additional flavor.

Mask — To cover completely; usually applied to the use of mayonnaise or other thick sauce but may refer to forcemeat or jelly.

Mince — To cut or chop into small, fine pieces.

Mix — To combine ingredients in any way that effects a distribution.

Panbroil — To cook uncovered on a hot surface, usually in a skillet. (For meat, see *page 79.*)

Parboil — To boil uncooked food until partially cooked. The cooking is usually completed by another method.

Parch — To brown by means of dry heat. Applied to grains.

Pare — To cut off the outside covering. Applied to potatoes, apples, etc.

Pasteurize — To preserve food by heating to a temperature (140° to 180°F) which will destroy certain microorganisms and arrest fermentation. Applied to milk and fruit juices.

Peel — To strip off the outer covering. Applied to oranges, grapefruit, etc.

Poach — To cook in a hot liquid using precautions to retain shape. The temperature used varies with the food.

Purée — To force through a fine sieve or food mill or to blend in an electric blender until a smooth thick mixture is obtained.

Reconstitute — To restore concentrated foods to their normal state, usually by adding water. Applied to such foods as nonfat dry milk or frozen fruit juices.

Reduce liquid — To continue cooking the liquid until the amount is sufficiently decreased, thus concentrating flavor and sometimes thickening the original liquid. Simmer when wine is used; boil rapidly for other liquids.

Render — To remove fat from connective tissue over low heat.

Rice — To force food through ricer, sieve, or food mill.

Roast — To cook by dry heat, usually in an oven.

Scald milk — To heat in top of a double boiler over simmering water or in a heavy saucepan over direct heat just until a thin film appears. The term scald is also used when simmering certain foods in boiling water for a few seconds, see *Blanch, page* **15**.

Scallop — To bake food, usually with sauce or other liquid. The top may be covered with crumbs. The food and sauce may be mixed in the baking dish or arranged in alternate layers with or without crumbs.

Score — To make cuts in the surface of meat before roasting, usually making a diamond pattern (example roast ham).

Sear — To brown meat quickly with intense heat.

Sieve — To force through a sieve.

Simmer — To cook in a liquid just below boiling point; bubbles form slowly and break below surface.

Steam — To cook in steam with or without pressure. The steam may be applied directly to food (*i.e.*, pressure cooker).

Steep — To allow a substance to stand in liquid below the boiling point for the purpose of extracting flavor, color, or other qualities.

Sterilize — To destroy microorganisms. For culinary purposes this is usually done at a high temperature with steam, dry heat, or by boiling in a liquid.

Stew — To cook slowly in a small amount of liquid.

Stir — To mix food ingredients with a circular motion in order to blend them.

Truss — To fasten the cavity of stuffed poultry or meat with skewers and/or cord.

Whip — To beat rapidly to produce expansion due to incorporation of air as applied to eggs, gelatin mixtures, and cream, see *To whip cream, page* **12**.

OVEN TEMPERATURES

Very slow	250° to 275°F
Slow	300° to 325°F
Moderate	350° to 375°F
Hot	400° to 425°F
Very hot	450° to 475°F
Extremely hot*	500° to 525°F

*When you broil, set regulator at *Broil*. Distance from top of food to source of heat determines the intensity of heat upon food.

NOTE: Use a portable oven thermometer for double checking oven temperatures. When baking in glass, decrease oven temperature by about 25°F.

HIGH ALTITUDE COOKING

The homemaker who lives in a high-altitude region, or moves to one, soon realizes that changes must be made in many of her recipes. These changes usually involve a slight adjustment in cooking temperatures and, in the case of some baked goods, an adjustment in ingredients. Most basic recipes are adaptable without changes in areas where the altitude is not more than 3000 feet above sea level. The difference in atmospheric pressure (it decreases at higher altitude) makes it necessary to cook vegetables longer than at sea level, to use a lower final temperature when cooking candy mixtures and cake frosting, and to make adjustments in recipes for cakes and other baked products.

Water — As altitude increases and the atmospheric pressure decreases, water boils at a lower temperature because the pressure of resistance of the water surface is less. At sea level, water boils at

Cake Baking

212°F, but for each additional 500 feet of altitude the boiling point lowers one degree. At 5000 feet the boiling point is 202°F — a decrease of 10° from the boiling point of water at sea level.

Vegetables — As altitude increases and the boiling point of water decreases, the cooking period will increase. Thus, when boiling vegetables this extra cooking time will range from 2 to 10 minutes except for beets, beans, turnips, and onions, which require considerably more time.

Frozen vegetables — Most frozen vegetables need very little additional time when cooked at a high altitude. Vegetables such as broccoli, green and wax beans, and mixed vegetables may require up to 12 minutes extra time.

Baked vegetables — The time required for baked potatoes, squash, etc., at high altitude is about the same as for low altitude.

Deep Frying — Foods such as French-fried potatoes, doughnuts, and croquettes may be prepared as easily at a high altitude as at low. Suitable temperatures for deep frying are from 350° to 375°F. Avoid much higher temperatures as the product fried is apt to be over-brown. For the best results with doughnuts modify a "sea-level recipe" by reducing the leavening agent and fat in the recipe. A recipe calling for a very rich mixture might be modified by reducing the sugar or using a proportion of hard wheat flour with the regular flour.

Liquid — The liquid content may be increased from 1 to 4 tablespoons per cup in direct proportion to the altitude above 2500 feet.

Baking Temperatures — In general, 360° to 370°F gives the best results for layer cakes and cupcakes. When paper cups are used, the oven temperature should be increased 15° to 25°F. Above 5000 feet the oven temperature might need to be increased 3° to 4° for every 1000 feet.

Yeast Breads — see *page 36*.

For more information about adjustments required in using sea-level baking recipes at high altitudes, write to the home economics department of your state university or college.

Cake Baking

In general, cake recipes which call for half as much shortening as sugar and half as much sugar as flour are best for high altitude cake baking. Recipes with these proportions may be more easily adjusted to high altitudes, and frequently require little if any modification up to 5000 feet except in the leavening agent. Sponge cake and angel food cake recipes require less modification than do some butter cakes.

Sugar — As a general rule, recipes that call for a maximum amount of sugar at sea level should be decreased approximately ½ tablespoon per cup for every 1000 feet above 3000 feet.

Leavening agent — At elevations above 3000 feet, it may be necessary to decrease the leavening agent. There can be no set rule for adjusting the amount of baking powder as the modification depends upon the type of baking powder, the number of eggs, and the amount of flour. In recipes calling for a maximum amount of baking powder, it may be decreased as much as half a teaspoon at 5000 feet. In soda and sour milk recipes, the soda must remain in proportion to the sour milk and other acid ingredients. (½ teaspoon soda will neutralize 1 cup sour milk.)

Flour — In some recipes at high altitudes an increase of one level tablespoon for each cup of flour improves the texture of the cake. This modification is easier and produces the same result as decreasing the shortening.

Shortening — For best results, the shortening should not exceed one quarter of the flour. Above 5000 feet, a decrease of about ½ teaspoon per 1000

How to Modify Baking Recipes

	ALTITUDE		
	2500-4000 ft.	4000-6000 ft.	over 6000 ft.
Reduce baking powder: for each teaspoon use	⅞ teaspoon	¾ teaspoon	½ teaspoon
Reduce double-acting baking powder: for each teaspoon use	¾ teaspoon	½ teaspoon	¼ teaspoon
Reduce sugar: for each cup use	no change	⅞ cup	¾ cup
Increase liquid: for each cup add	no change	3-6 teaspoons	6-12 teaspoons

feet may improve some recipes.
Eggs — The addition of an egg may prevent a too-rich cake from falling. Eggs also increase the capacity of the batter to hold liquid.

HELPFUL HINTS FOR THE COOK

- To keep bacon from curling while broiling or panfrying, snip edges with shears before cooking.
- To make a smooth mixture of flour (or cornstarch) and water to be used to thicken a sauce or gravy, combine ingredients in a glass jar, cover tightly, and shake well. Sauces thickened with flour or cornstarch must be cooked rapidly and thoroughly to overcome the raw starch taste.
- When adding whole eggs or egg yolks to a sauce, always stir a little of the hot sauce into the slightly beaten eggs; immediately blend into the remaining hot sauce. Cook 3 to 5 minutes, stirring to keep the mixture cooking evenly.
- To keep cornmeal from lumping, moisten it thoroughly with cold water before pouring in the boiling water.
- To make poached fish firm and white, add a little lemon juice to the cooking liquid.
- To make applesauce with an extra-fine flavor, do not pare or core the apples. Wash and quarter them, removing stems and blossom ends. Put apples into a deep saucepan with several tablespoons of water to start the cooking. Cover and cook until apples are soft, but not mushy. Force through a colander or food mill; add sugar and spices as desired. Heat only until sugar is dissolved.
- To make a flavorful gravy from pot roast drippings, add canned consommé (instead of water) to the meat during cooking.
- To keep a mixing bowl from slipping on working surface, place a folded moist towel under it.
- To test the heat of a griddle, sprinkle several drops of water on the surface and if water "dances" in small beads the griddle is hot enough to brown the food.
- To keep a metal skillet or saucepan from warping (becoming rounded on bottom), avoid pouring cold water into the utensil while hot. The sudden change of temperature causes the warping.
- To remove fish odors from utensils, add 2 tablespoons baking soda to the dishwashing water.
- To avoid "boilovers" while cooking macaroni, spaghetti, or rice, add 1 tablespoon cooking oil or shortening to the cooking liquid.

FOREIGN WORDS & PHRASES

Ala, au, aux — Dressed in a certain style.
A la mode — In the style of.
Al dente — A term used to refer to not-quite tender pasta. In Italian it means "to the tooth."
Artichaut — Artichoke.
Asperge — Asparagus.
Aspic — Any jellied dish or a jellied glaze.
Au gratin — Baked with a topping of crumbs, and often with grated or shredded cheese.
Au jus — Served with natural juice or gravy.
Au naturel — Plainly cooked.
Beurre — Butter; *beurre fondu*, melted butter; *beurre noir*, butter browned until almost black.
Bisque — A thick soup, usually made from shellfish; or an ice cream containing ground or pulverized nuts or macaroons.
Blanquette — White meat in cream sauce that has been thickened with egg yolks.
Bombe glacée — A mold of ice cream filled with a different kind of ice cream or a water ice.
Bouchées — Small pastry shells or pepper cases filled with creamed meat or fish. The French word means "a mouthful."
Bouquet garni — See *Herb bouquet, page 4.*
Café noir — Black coffee.
Canapé — A small piece of bread, toasted or fried, spread with some highly flavored mixture and served as an appetizer.
Canard — Duck.
Cannelon — Meat stuffed, rolled up, and roasted or braised.
Cassoulet — A hearty white bean and meat mixture often with goose or duckling. The dish originated in Languedoc, France.
Caviar — The salted roe of the sturgeon.
Champignons — Mushrooms.
Chaud-froid — Literally "hot-cold." In cooking, a jellied sauce.
Chiffonade — Designates any dish served with shredded vegetables.
Chou — Cabbage.
Chou-fleur — Cauliflower.
Compote — A stew; often applied to fruits stewed in syrup.
Court bouillon — Liquid used for poaching fish.
Crème — Cream.
Croustade — Case for creamed meat, fish, poultry, and other mixtures, made of bread, rice, or pastry.
Croutons — Small cubes of fried or toasted bread served with soup or tossed with salads.

De, d' — Of.
Demitasse — Literally "half a cup." Used to signify a small cup of black coffee generally served at the close of a luncheon or dinner.
Diable — Deviled.
Dragées (silver) — Tiny edible, round silver-colored candies.
Duchesse — Whipped potatoes mixed with egg and forced through a pastry tube.
Éclair — An oblong choux pastry filled with whipped cream or custard; usually chocolate glazed.
En brochette — Impaled on a skewer.
En coquilles — In the shell.
En gelée — In jelly.
En papillote — Baked in an oiled paper case.
Entrée — The main dish of an informal meal or a subordinate dish served between main courses.
Farce — Forcemeat. A well-seasoned stuffing with chopped meat, fish, poultry or nuts.
Farci — Stuffed.
Fillets — Long, thin pieces of boneless meat or fish.
Fines herbes — Minced parsley, chives, chervil, etc. (See also *Bouquet garni, page* **9,** or *Herb bouquet, page* **4.**)
Flambé — A food served with lighted spirits poured over.
Fondant — A sugar and water mixture cooked to the softball stage (234°F), cooled, and kneaded.
Fondue — Literally "melted"; usually applied to cheese, eggs, and crumbs.
Fraises — Strawberries.
Frappé — Iced or semifrozen.
Fricassée — Braised meats or poultry.
Fromage — Cheese.
Gâteau — Cake.
Gelée — Jelly.
Glacé — Frozen dessert (ice or ice cream); also glazed (see *Candy* and *Glacé, page* **6**).
Goulash — A thick Hungarian meat stew.
Haricots verts — Small green beans.
Huîtres — Oysters.
Jambon — Ham.
Jardinière — Mixed vegetables served in their own sauce.
Laitue — Lettuce.
Légumes — Vegetables.
Lyonnaise — Cooked with onions.
Macédoine — A mixture; usually vegetables, with or without meat. Sometimes fruit mixtures.

Marrons — Chestnuts.
Marzipan — A paste of almonds and sugar molded in various forms (realistic colors and shapes).
Meringue — Whites of eggs whipped with sugar to the stiff peak stage.
Mousse — A light appetizer, main dish, or dessert mixture containing whipped cream, flavorings or seasonings, sugar (if dessert), gelatin, and other ingredients. It is usually turned into a mold and then chilled or frozen.
Noir — Black.
Oeufs — Eggs.
Pain — Bread.
Pâté — a) Seasoned ground cooked meat including liver, poultry or fish mixture chilled before serving; b) meat mixture baked in a covered pan or casserole set in a larger pan of boiling water, cooled thoroughly, and sliced (also called *terrine*); c) meat, fish, or vegetable filling baked in a pastry case.
Pâté de foie gras — A paste of goose livers.
Pâtisserie — Pastry.
Pêche — Peach.
Petits pois — Small green peas.
Pièce de résistance — The main dish in a meal; usually the roasted meat, but also poultry or game served with sauces and stuffing.
Pois — Peas.
Polonaise, À la — Served with a topping of bread crumbs browned in butter and sieved hard-cooked egg yolk.
Pommes — Apples.
Pommes de terre — Potatoes. Literally, "apples of the earth."
Potage — Soup.
Poulet — Chicken.
Purée — Mashed or sieved food.
Ragoût — A thick, highly seasoned stew.
Ratatouille — A mixed vegetable stew that usually includes eggplant and tomatoes cooked in olive oil and is typical of the cooking in southern France.
Réchauffé — Reheated or warmed-over.
Ris de veau — Sweetbreads.
Rissoles — Minced fish or meat rolled in thin pastry and fried.
Rôti — Roast.
Roux — A mixture of butter and flour used for thickening soups or sauces.
Sauté — Fried lightly in a little fat.
Sorbet — Frozen punch. This name is often given to water-ice when several kinds of fruit are used.
Soufflé — Literally "puffed up." A delicate baked

custard which may contain fruit, cheese, flaked fish, minced poultry, meat, or vegetables.
Tarte — Tart.
Tartelette — A little tart.
Timbale — An unsweetened custard, usually seasoned with fish, meat, or vegetables, baked in a mold or molds.
Timbale case — A small case of deep-fried batter in which creamed mixtures and desserts are served.
Tourte — A tart; a pie.
Truffles — A species of fungi, similar to mushrooms, growing in clusters some inches below ground. Used in seasoning and for a garnish.
Tutti-frutti — Mixed fruits.
Vapeur, À la — Steamed.
Velouté — Velvety; smooth.
Vichyssoise — A cream soup of puréed potatoes, chicken stock, and leeks. Best served icy cold.
Vinaigrette — A marinade or salad sauce of oil, vinegar, pepper, and herbs.

HOW TO DO IT

To blanch nuts — Cover nuts with rapidly boiling water and allow them to remain in the water only until the skins are loosened. Drain off the water immediately and spread nuts on absorbent paper to dry. Remove the skins by squeezing the nuts between the thumb and index finger. Dry nuts thoroughly by spreading them on absorbent paper. Avoid loss of flavor in nuts by blanching only about ½ cup at a time and allowing them to stand in the water the shortest time possible.

To deep-fat fry — About 20 minutes before ready to deep fry, fill a deep saucepan one-half to three-fourths full with vegetable shortening, all-purpose shortening, lard, or cooking oil for deep frying. Heat slowly to temperature given in recipe. A deep frying thermometer is an accurate guide for deep frying temperatures.

If thermometer is not available, the following bread cube method may be used: A 1-inch cube of bread will brown in 60 seconds at 350° to 375°F. If using an electric deep fryer, follow manufacturer's directions for fat and timing.

To clarify fats — Strain lightly cooled fat such as lard and vegetable shortening which have been used for deep frying through several thicknesses of cheesecloth to remove foreign material. Then add several slices of pared raw potato to cooled fat in a heavy saucepot and heat slowly until potato will absorb any foreign flavors in the fat and also attract some of the sediment floating in the fat.

To make butter balls — Scald, then chill butter paddles in a bowl of ice and water. Measure butter by tablespoonfuls (for uniformity) and drop into the icy water. For each ball, place a portion of butter on the grooved side of one paddle. Using the second paddle, grooved side down, work paddles lightly in a rolling motion until a ball is formed. Drop into icy water. Later pile into a serving dish and refrigerate until ready to use.

To make butter curls — Lightly draw a special butter curler (available at most department stores) across a quarter-pound print of butter. Drop each curl into a bowl of ice and water to chill. Allow several curls for each serving.

To clean mushrooms — Wash mushrooms quickly under running cold water, spread on absorbent paper, dry completely, and cut off the tips of stems. Leave caps whole, or slice mushrooms lengthwise through stems and caps, or chop, as directed in recipe.

To cut marshmallows or dried fruits (uncooked) — Use scissors dipped frequently in water to avoid stickiness.

To melt chocolate — Melt unsweetened chocolate over simmering water or over very low heat in a heavy saucepan; sweet or semisweet over hot (not simmering) water.

To plump raisins — Place raisins in a strainer over simmering water for a few minutes, or pour boiling water over them and let stand a few minutes before draining. Then spread raisins on absorbent paper to remove excess moisture before using.

To cook wild rice — Put 1 cup wild rice into a colander or sieve and wash thoroughly with running cold water. Bring 3 cups water and 1 teaspoon salt to boiling in a large saucepan. Gradually add the rice. Cook, uncovered, 25 minutes, or until rice is tender when a kernel is pressed between fingers; drain. (1½ cups cooked rice)

To prepare crumbs — Place cookies, crackers, zwieback, or the like on a long length of heavy waxed paper. Loosely fold paper around material to be crushed, tucking under open ends. With a rolling pin, gently crush to make fine crumbs. Or place crackers in a plastic bag and crush.

To use an electric blender — Cover blender container before starting and stopping motor to avoid splashing. To aid in even mixing, frequently scrape down sides of container with a rubber spatula, first stopping motor.

To grind, put in blender container enough food at one time to cover blades. Cover; turn on motor and grind until very fine. Turning motor off and on helps to throw food back on blades. Empty container and grind next batch of food.

If using the electric blender for preparing crumbs, break 5 or 6 crackers, cookies, pieces of dry bread, or the like into blender container. Cover container. Blend as directed by manufacturer until crumbs are medium fine. Empty container and repeat blending until desired amount of crumbs is obtained.

To prepare garlic—Separate desired number of cloves from garlic root and remove outer (thin, papery) skin from cloves.

To prepare quick broth—Dissolve 1 chicken bouillon cube in 1 cup boiling water for quick chicken broth or 1 beef bouillon cube or ½ teaspoon concentrated meat extract for quick meat broth. Instant bouillon granules are also available for preparing quick broth.

To roast chestnuts—Wash chestnuts and make a slit in both sides of each shell. Turn chestnuts into a shallow pan and mix in cooking oil (about 1 tablespoon per pound). Roast in a 450°F oven 20 minutes. Cool. Remove shells and all inner skins with a sharp knife.

To toast nuts—Spread nuts in a shallow baking dish or pie pan and heat in a 350°F oven until delicately browned; move and turn nuts occasionally. Or, if desired, nuts may be browned lightly in a heavy skillet in a small amount of butter, margarine, or cooking oil over medium heat, moving nuts constantly while browning.

To salt nuts—Sprinkle salt over hot toasted nuts (brushed lightly with butter or margarine before or after toasting).

To sour milk—Add 2 tablespoons vinegar or lemon juice to each 1 pint milk. Allow to stand at room temperature 30 minutes, then return to refrigerator. To sour evaporated milk (after it has been diluted with water) follow directions for fresh milk.

To sour cream—Add 1 tablespoon vinegar or lemon juice to 1 cup cream or 1 cup undiluted evaporated milk.

To whip cream (for use as topping or filling or as an ingredient in a cake)—Pour chilled heavy (whipping) cream into a chilled bowl and beat (on medium speed at first, then on high, if using electric mixer) until soft peaks are formed when beater is slowly lifted upright. If whipped cream is to be incorporated into a frozen or refrigerator dessert or salad, beat until of medium consistency (piles softly).

The maximum amount of cream that should be whipped at one time is 1½ cups. If recipe calls for more than 1½ cups, whip 1 cup at a time. Heavy cream doubles in volume when whipped.

To whip evaporated milk—Chill undiluted evaporated milk before whipping. To chill the milk, pour the amount called for in recipe into a dry refrigerator tray. Place in freezer until ice crystals form around edges. Then turn into a chilled bowl and beat with electric beater on medium speed until stiff peaks are formed. Use immediately. If whipped milk is to be refrigerated for several hours before using, stabilize it with lemon juice in this manner: Whip the milk as directed, then add 1 tablespoon lemon juice for each cup of milk (measured before whipping). Continue beating until thoroughly blended.

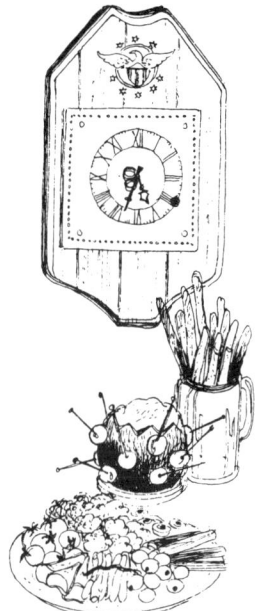

Chapter 1

APPETIZERS—Hot & Cold

Appetizers are dainty, attractive contrivances served for the purpose of putting party guests in a company mood and to *arouse* the appetite—not *satisfy* it. These morsels are usually so delicious and eye-appealing in their artful variety that it is sometimes difficult for hostess and guests alike to remember to use restraint where they are concerned.

The occasion sets the stage for the kind of appetizers offered to guests. For "stand-up" occasions when served in the living room or patio, they are usually of one- or two-bite size. They should be distinctive in flavor, zesty, and nippy, to put a sharp edge on the appetite. They should be easy to eat, not too fragile, not too "drippy."

For "sit-down" occasions, when appetizers are served at the table, generally for the first course of a meal, they may be larger in size and are eaten with a fork.

PLANNING APPETIZERS

There is no limit to the kinds of meat, poultry, fish, cheese, vegetables, and fruits that can be used. Though imagination and ingenuity are the only limiting factors in selecting appetizers, there is one rule that should be followed—*avoid repeating any food in the main part of the meal that has been used in the appetizers.* Remember that they are a part of the whole menu; select them to harmonize with the rest of the meal. Choose them for complementary flavors, for contrast of texture and color and variety of shape. Picture the serving dishes, trays, and other appointments as you plan the menu.

Avoid a last-minute rush by wise selection (do not include too many appetizers that require last-minute doing), by careful buying, and beforehand preparation. Take cues from assembly-line production techniques for organizing your work. For example, use large sandwich loaves, cut in lengthwise slices, for canapé bases and finger sandwiches; stack several slices together and cut several identical shapes at one time; spread canapé bases all at one time.

Hors d'Oeuvres—Hot or cold, simple or elaborate, hors d'oeuvres are savory tidbits about one bite in size and are eaten with the fingers from wooden or plastic picks. Almost anything that can be presented in an interesting manner can be offered. Many good leftovers can be transformed into culinary gems. They may be single items such as marinated shrimp or a combination of foods. Every nation has specialties, but all are intended to stimulate the appetite.

Hors d'oeuvres are usually served to a gathering of people at a party or before dinner. A continental custom is to serve the hors d'oeuvres at the table as the first course of a luncheon or dinner. Here the use of a fork is acceptable.

Fill miniature shells made from puff paste or choux paste or spread waffle squares, thin griddlecakes, or crêpes with piquant mixtures—delectable!

Holders for pick-type hors d'oeuvres are available in housewares departments or can be made from a molded cheese (such as Edam), grapefruit, oranges, apples, a small head of red or green cabbage, a melon, eggplant, cucumbers, or a cauliflower. If necessary, level base by removing a thin slice from the underside. Put hors d'oeuvres on wooden or plastic picks and insert into the holder.

Canapés—Finger foods too, canapés are thin slices of fancy-cut bread or toast, or some other "base" spread with a flavored butter, then topped with a well-seasoned food (meat, fish, or vegetable) or a piquant mixture, not sweet in flavor. They are dainty "bites," fresh in appearance and easy to handle.

Bases for canapés are the many breads, used plain, toasted, or deep-fried, along with the packaged commercial products such as crackers, Melba toast, and potato chips. Brown breads, nut breads, rye, wheat, white, and pumpernickel bread give variety to canapés. The bread slices, never more than ¼ inch thick, can be cut into many shapes—rounds, squares, diamonds, ovals, rectangles, and crescents.

Spread canapé bases with butter or margarine, seasoned with herbs, prepared horseradish, or prepared mustard, if desired, then with the filling or "spread," and finally topped with a garnish. Garnishes should be scaled to the dainty size of the canapés and should be as good to eat as they are to behold.

Canapés may be sealed with a clear aspic to hold the garnishes in place, to add a gloss, and to prolong their freshness.

Take time to arrange canapés in an attractive design on the serving tray—the effect will be gratifying. Prepare enough to replenish the tray, re-creating the original arrangement.

Garnishes for Canapés:

Anchovies—fillets or rolled
Bacon (crisp cooked)—crumbled or small pieces
Carrots—thin notched rounds
Caviar (black or red)
Cheese (sharp) shredded slices, half slices, or thin unpared slices
Eggs (hard-cooked)—rings, slices, sieved egg yolk, or egg-white cutouts
Green pepper—cutouts or narrow strips
Lobster—pieces of clawmeat
Mint—sprigs or chopped
Mushrooms (slices)—cooked in butter
Nuts (plain, toasted, or salted)—chopped, ground, or whole
Olives (green or ripe)
Chives—minced or chopped
Cream cheese—softened, plain or tinted and forced through pastry bag and decorating tubes to form rosettes, designs, or borders
Cucumbers—notched—slivered, chopped, rings of pitted olives, or sliced pimiento-stuffed olives
Parsley-sprigs or snipped
Paprika
Pickles—chopped or slices
Pimiento—strips or chopped
Radishes—thin slices
Shrimp (cooked, fresh)—whole
Tomato—cutouts
Watercress-sprigs or snipped

HOT APPETIZERS

FONTAINEBLEAU HORS D'OEUVRE PIE
This unique anchovy-latticed pie is served at the Fontainebleau Hotel in Miami Beach, Florida.

2 cups peeled, diced ripe tomatoes
1 tablespoon olive oil
½ teaspoon rosemary
½ teaspoon oregano
⅛ teaspoon garlic powder
⅛ teaspoon pepper
¼ cup sliced pitted ripe olives
1½ cups thinly sliced onions
2 tablespoons butter
1 unbaked 9-in. pastry shell (pastry rolled about ¼ in. thick)
⅓ cup shredded Parmesan cheese
2 cans (2 oz. each) anchovies, drained
9 pimiento-stuffed olives
Olive oil

1. Mix tomatoes with olive oil, rosemary, oregano, garlic powder, pepper, and ripe olives in a large skillet; cook uncovered over medium heat about 10 minutes, or until sauce is thickened.
2. Meanwhile, in a separate pan, cook onions with butter until tender and golden; cool in pan.
3. Sprinkle bottom of pastry with half of the cheese; cover with cooled onion-butter mixture. Spread thickened tomato mixture over onions and sprinkle with remaining cheese.
4. Arrange anchovies over top, lattice fashion, making crisscross strips about 1 inch apart. Cut each olive in 3 slices and place one slice in each lattice square; brush olives lightly with olive oil.
5. Bake at 350°F 30 to 40 minutes, or until crust is well browned. Serve warm. 6 OR 12 SERVINGS

Hot Appetizers

AVOCADO TOAST FINGERS

Mississippi belle Mary McKay parlayed a second-hand cookstove and a deft way with fine food into Vicksburg's now famous Old Southern Tea Room. These hot appetizers are one of her claims to fame.

1 very ripe avocado	½ teaspoon salt
1 teaspoon lemon juice	6 slices white bread, toasted and crusts removed
1 teaspoon grated onion	
1 teaspoon paprika	Bacon slices

1. Peel avocado; mash pulp with a fork. Then beat in lemon juice, onion, paprika, and salt. Beat until smooth.
2. Spread mixture over toast slices. Cut each slice into 3×1-inch strips. Place narrow strips of bacon on each toast finger.
3. Put on a baking sheet and broil until bacon is crisp. Serve immediately. 18 APPETIZERS

TERIYAKI

An oriental appetizer of Japanese origin.

1 teaspoon ground ginger	3 tablespoons cooking or salad oil
⅓ cup soy sauce	1 tablespoon cornstarch
¼ cup honey	
1 clove garlic, minced	½ cup water
1 teaspoon grated onion	⅛ teaspoon red food coloring
1 lb. beef sirloin tip, cut in 2×½×¼-in. strips	

1. Blend ginger, soy sauce, honey, garlic, and onion in a bowl. Add meat; marinate about 1 hour.
2. Remove meat, reserving marinade, and brown quickly on all sides in the hot oil in a skillet.
3. Stir a blend of cornstarch, water, and food coloring into the reserved marinade in a saucepan. Bring rapidly to boiling and cook 2 to 3 minutes, stirring constantly.
4. Add meat to thickened marinade to glaze; remove and drain on wire rack.
5. Insert a frilled wooden pick into each meat strip and serve with the sauce.

ABOUT 24 APPETIZERS

FLASH UN KAS

These melt-in-your-mouth morsels of flaky filled pastry claim a Pennsylvania Dutch heritage.

1 cup butter, softened	Filling: goose liver pâté or ground ham, *below*
8 oz. cream cheese, softened	
2 cups sifted all-purpose flour	

1. Cream butter and cream cheese together until well blended. Add the flour and mix until smooth. Chill pastry thoroughly (overnight if possible).
2. Using a small portion of pastry at a time, roll pastry about ⅛ inch thick on a lightly floured surface; cut out rounds with a 2-inch cookie cutter.
3. Spoon a rounded one-fourth teaspoonful of filling onto half of each round. Fold dough over filling and press edges together with a fork. Transfer to baking sheets.
4. Bake at 400°F 8 to 10 minutes, or until lightly browned. Serve hot. ABOUT 9 DOZEN APPETIZERS

FILLING: Mix thoroughly *2 ounces goose liver pâté, 1 teaspoon Worcestershire sauce,* and *1 teaspoon steak sauce;* or mix *2 ounces ground country-style ham, 1 teaspoon steak sauce,* and *1 teaspoon ketchup.* (Each filling is enough for about 4½ dozen appetizers.)

NOTE: This pastry will keep for several weeks if wrapped tightly in moisture-vaporproof material and stored in the refrigerator.

SWISS CHEESE PASTRY MORSELS

2 cups finely shredded Swiss cheese	1 to 1¼ cup sifted all-purpose flour
½ cup butter or margarine, softened	Liverwurst spread
	Deviled ham
	Cocktail onions

1. Mix cheese and butter; blend in flour.
2. For each pastry morsel shape 1 teaspoon of the dough into a ball; set balls 1 inch apart on a baking sheet.
3. For liverwurst or deviled ham appetizers, make an indentation in center of each ball before baking and fill with ½ teaspoon of the spread or ham.
4. For onion appetizers, mold 1 teaspoon of the pastry dough around a cocktail onion covering it completely.
5. Bake at 400°F 15 minutes, or until golden. Serve warm. 4 DOZEN APPETIZERS

Hot Appetizers

BROILED BACON-CHEESE CANAPÉS

4 oz. sharp Cheddar cheese, cut in pieces
3 slices bacon
¼ medium-sized green pepper
2 teaspoons grated onion
2 teaspoons mayonnaise
2 doz. 2-in. bread rounds

1. Put cheese, bacon, and green pepper through the coarse blade of a food chopper. Blend in the onion and mayonnaise.
2. Arrange bread rounds on a baking sheet or broiler rack. Toast on one side. Spread the topping on untoasted side. Broil 3 inches from source of heat until topping is bubbly and light golden.

2 DOZEN CANAPÉS

CHEDDAR PUFFS

¼ cup butter or margarine, softened
8 oz. shredded sharp Cheddar cheese (about 2 cups)
1¼ cups sifted all-purpose flour
¾ teaspoon paprika
¼ teaspoon dry mustard
⅛ teaspoon cayenne pepper

1. Blend butter and cheese until smooth. Mix in a blend of the flour, paprika, dry mustard, and cayenne pepper.
2. Shape dough into rolls about 1¼ inches in diameter. Wrap in waxed paper and chill.
3. Cut into ¼ inch slices. Place about 1 inch apart on lightly greased baking sheets.
4. Bake at 400°F about 8 minutes. Serve hot.

ABOUT 4 DOZEN PUFFS

ON-THE-WING APPETIZERS

30 chicken wing-drums (2½ to 3½ lbs.)
½ teaspoon salt
¼ cup soy sauce
¼ cup spiced peach syrup
2 tablespoons sugar
¼ teaspoon monosodium glutamate
½ teaspoon ground ginger
1 tablespoon lemon juice
5 drops Tabasco
1 clove garlic, crushed

1. Disjoint the wings; use thickest wing portions for appetizers and remaining wing portions for chicken broth.
2. Place the wing-drums on rack on a foil-lined baking sheet or broiler pan; sprinkle with salt.
3. Mix remaining ingredients thoroughly; brush marinade generously on wing-drums.
4. Place in 350°F oven about 1 hour, or until wing-drums are golden brown and tender, brushing frequently with the marinade.

ABOUT 10 SERVINGS

BROILED BACON BUNS

4 frankfurter rolls
¾ lb. sliced bacon, crisply cooked
1 cup shredded sharp Cheddar cheese (4 ozs.)

1. Preheat broiler.
2. Place rolls in a shallow pan; toast in broiler. Top each half with bacon and cheese.
3. Broil 3 minutes, or until cheese melts.

4 SERVINGS

BROILED DATE APPETIZERS

2 cups (1 lb.) pitted fresh dates
½ cup water
½ cup orange juice
3 tablespoons wine vinegar
½ teaspoon ground cinnamon
¼ teaspoon ground nutmeg
½ cup lightly packed brown sugar
⅛ teaspoon salt
Bacon slices, cut in thirds

1. Put dates into a bowl. Blend water, orange juice, vinegar, cinnamon, nutmeg, brown sugar, and salt in a saucepan. Bring to boiling, reduce heat and simmer 5 minutes.
2. Pour mixture over dates; cover and let stand until cool. Refrigerate at least 24 hours to allow flavors to blend.
3. Wrap 2 dates in one-third slice of bacon and skewer with a pick; repeat, using all dates.
4. Broil 6 inches from source of heat 6 to 8 minutes, or until bacon is crisp, turning once.

ABOUT 2 DOZEN APPETIZERS

SAUCY COCKTAIL FRANKS

1 jar (10 oz.) currant jelly
⅓ cup prepared mustard
1 lb. frankfurters, cut diagonally in 1-in. pieces

1. Melt jelly and blend in mustard; heat thoroughly.
2. Stir in the frankfurters, coating each piece; simmer about 30 minutes, stirring occasionally.
3. Serve with wooden picks.

8 TO 12 SERVINGS

Hot Appetizers

HAM-CHEESE PUFFS

6 to 9 slices bread, toasted
1 cup firmly packed ground cooked ham
3 tablespoons finely chopped green pepper
1 tablespoon prepared mustard
¼ teaspoon Worcestershire sauce
½ cup Thick White Sauce, *page 196*
3 oz. cream cheese, softened
1 egg yolk
1 teaspoon grated onion
¼ teaspoon baking powder

1. Cut eighteen 2-inch rounds from the toast.
2. Combine ham with green pepper, mustard, and Worcestershire sauce; mix well and stir in the white sauce.
3. Beat the cream cheese with remaining ingredients until thoroughly blended.
4. Spread toast rounds generously with ham mixture and top with cheese mixture.
5. Place under broiler about 5 inches from source of heat and broil until cheese topping is golden brown. Serve immediately.   1½ DOZEN PUFFS

SI SI PASTRIES
A south-of-the-border appetizer.

1 can (4½ oz.) deviled ham
¼ cup tomato sauce
¼ cup chopped green pepper
¼ cup chopped celery
½ teaspoon chili powder
Pastry for a 1-crust pie
Yellow cornmeal

1. Blend the deviled ham, tomato sauce, green pepper, celery, and chili powder. Cover and chill.
2. Prepare pastry and roll very thin, using cornmeal instead of flour for rolling. Cut the pastry into twenty 3-inch rounds.
3. Spoon about 1 tablespoon of the chilled deviled ham mixture onto each round. Moisten half the edge of each round with water. Fold pastry in half and press edges together with a fork to seal. Place on an ungreased baking sheet.
4. Bake at 425°F 10 to 12 minutes, or until golden brown. Serve immediately.   20 PASTRIES

HOT MUSHROOM APPETIZERS

1 lb. large fresh mushrooms
1 cup crushed wheat wafers
½ teaspoon fresh onion juice
½ lb. chicken livers
3 tablespoons butter or margarine
1 chicken bouillon cube
½ cup boiling water
½ teaspoon salt
⅛ teaspoon tarragon leaves, crushed
Garlic butter

1. Wash mushrooms; remove stems and set caps aside.
2. Chop stems and combine with onion juice and chicken livers. Cook in heated butter in a skillet 10 minutes, stirring occasionally to cook evenly. Remove livers and chop.
3. Return chopped livers to skillet with crumbs, bouillon cube dissolved in water, the salt, and tarragon. Blend thoroughly.
4. Generously brush mushroom caps, inside and out, with garlic butter; fill with the chicken liver mixture. Place in a shallow baking pan.
5. Bake at 375°F about 20 minutes. Garnish with *sieved hard-cooked egg yolk*. Serve hot.
   ABOUT 2 DOZEN APPETIZERS

SARDINE FINGER CANAPÉS

7 slices white bread
Herbed Mayonnaise, *page 23*
1 can (3¾ oz.) Norwegian sardines
½ cup shredded Parmesan cheese

1. Toast bread slices on one side. Remove crusts and cut each slice into 3 strips. Spread untoasted sides generously with Herbed Mayonnaise.
2. Coat sardines with shredded cheese. Place 1 sardine on each toast strip.
3. Broil 3 inches from source of heat until lightly browned. Garnish each canapé with a tiny sprig of *parsley* at each end. Serve hot.   21 CANAPÉS

OLIVE BITES

25 pitted ripe olives
2 to 3 tablespoons minced green onion
½ cup all-purpose flour
¼ teaspoon salt
⅛ teaspoon dry mustard
4 oz. sharp Cheddar cheese, shredded (about 1 cup)
3 tablespoons butter or margarine, melted
1 teaspoon milk
1 or 2 drops Tabasco

1. Stuff olives with the onion and set aside.
2. Combine flour, salt, and mustard in a bowl. Mix

in the cheese and a blend of the remaining ingredients.
3. Using about 1 teaspoonful of dough for each, shape dough around olives and place on a baking sheet.
4. Bake at 400°F 10 to 12 minutes. Serve at once. 25 OLIVE BITES

BACON-WRAPPED SHRIMP APPETIZERS

Chili Dip, *below*
16 cooked shrimp
½ cup butter or margarine, melted
1½ teaspoons chili powder
1 clove garlic, minced
8 bacon slices

1. Prepare Chili Dip; chill.
2. Meanwhile, dip shrimp into a mixture of melted butter, chili powder, and garlic. Wrap shrimp in half slices of bacon and fasten with small skewers or wooden picks.
3. Place on rack in broiler pan and broil 3 inches from source of heat about 5 minutes. Brush with butter sauce and continue broiling about 5 minutes. Serve with chilled dip. 16 APPETIZERS

CHILI DIP: Mix ¾ *cup mayonnaise, 3 tablespoons chopped sweet pickle, 1 tablespoon chopped pimiento-stuffed olives, 1½ teaspoons grated onion, 1 tablespoon chili powder,* and *1 hard-cooked egg,* chopped, in a bowl. Turn dip into a chilled serving bowl and serve with the shrimp. ABOUT 1 CUP DIP

"VEAL-LETS" PARMIGIANA

Cut *1 small loaf French bread* into ½-inch slices. Lightly brown slices in *¼ cup olive or other cooking oil* heated with *1 halved garlic clove* in a skillet. Drain on absorbent paper. Brown *2 veal cutlets* (pounded flat) in hot oil remaining in skillet. Drain off excess oil. Cover; cook 8 minutes, turning once or twice. Cut veal in small pieces and put on bread slices. Top each with *tomato sauce,* a square of sliced *mozzarella cheese,* a strip of *pimiento,* and a sprinkling of *seasoned pepper, oregano,* or *Italian seasoning.* Broil until cheese is melted.

COLD APPETIZERS

Dip-Its

CHILI AND BEAN DIP

1 cup pork and beans with tomato sauce
¼ cup mayonnaise
2 tablespoons dry onion soup mix
1 tablespoon chili powder
1 wedge onion
Dairy sour cream

1. Put all ingredients except sour cream into an electric blender container. Cover and blend.
2. Transfer mixture to a serving dish and stir in sour cream to taste, about ½ cup.
3. Serve *potato chips* and *corn chips* as dippers.
ABOUT 2 CUPS DIP

BLUE CHEESE DIP WITH MUSHROOMS

½ cup crumbled blue cheese
½ cup dairy sour cream
½ cup mayonnaise
½ cup finely chopped celery
½ teaspoon salt
2 drops Tabasco
Mushrooms, fresh or canned

1. Mix cheese, sour cream, mayonnaise, celery, salt, and Tabasco in a bowl. Chill thoroughly.
2. Spear mushrooms with cocktail picks and use as dippers. ABOUT 1½ CUPS DIP

MULTI-CHEESE BLENDIP

2 oz. Cheddar cheese, shredded
2 oz. blue cheese, crumbled
2 oz. Port du Salut (Trappist cheese), cut in pieces
2 oz. cream cheese, cut in pieces
¼ cup butter, cut in pieces
½ cup dairy sour cream
⅛ teaspoon salt
1 tablespoon sherry
¼ teaspoon Tabasco
⅛ teaspoon Worcestershire sauce
1 small clove garlic, minced

1. Using an electric mixer or blender, blend all ingredients together until light and creamy; chill thoroughly.
2. Serve with a tray of assorted *crackers.*
ABOUT 2¼ CUPS DIP

TUNA SENSATION

8 oz. cream cheese, softened
2 tablespoons minced onion
½ clove garlic, minced
1 tablespoon prepared horseradish
1 teaspoon Worcestershire sauce
½ teaspoon salt
Few grains black pepper
⅛ teaspoon crushed chervil
½ cup dairy sour cream
1 can (6½ or 7 oz.) tuna, drained and flaked

1. Mix into cream cheese the onion, garlic, horseradish, Worcestershire sauce, salt, pepper, and chervil. Blend in sour cream. Add tuna and mix thoroughly.
2. Turn dip into a serving bowl and ring with finely snipped *parsley*. Serve with a tray of *crackers*.

ABOUT 1⅔ CUPS DIP

PUNGENT PATE SPREAD

½ lb. liverwurst
1 package (8 ozs.) Neufchatel cheese, softened
1 tablespoon crumbled blue cheese
½ cup chopped celery
1 tablespoon finely chopped onion
2 tablespoons chopped parsley
¼ cup dairy sour cream
¼ teaspoon salt
2 teaspoons Worcestershire sauce
Rye crackers

1. Peel casing from liverwurst; mash liverwurst well with a fork in a medium bowl. Beat in Neufchâtel and blue cheeses until smooth.
2. Stir in celery, onion, parsley, sour cream, salt, and Worcestershire sauce. Chill.
3. When ready to serve, spoon into a small bowl; garnish with parsley. Place bowl on a large serving plate or tray; surround with crisp rye crackers.

2½ CUPS SPREAD

GUACAMOLE

1 chilled large ripe avocado
1 chilled large ripe tomato, peeled and chopped
¼ cup finely chopped onion
¾ teaspoon salt
4 teaspoons wine vinegar
1 tablespoon lemon juice
½ teaspoon finely chopped hot chili pepper

1. Peel avocado; cut in pieces. Crush avocado with a fork. Add remaining ingredients; mix well.
2. Serve with *crisp crackers, potato chips, or corn chips, page 34.*

ABOUT 2 CUPS

BRAUNSCHWEIGER CANAPÉ SPREAD

½ cup Braunschweiger (smoked liver sausage)
1 to 2 teaspoons grated onion

1. Beat Braunschweiger with a fork until soft; mix in onion.
2. Spread on *buttered toast rounds*. Garnish with *caviar* and *sieved hard-cooked egg yolk*.

ABOUT ½ CUP

NUT-COATED CHEESE LOG

8 oz. cream cheese, softened
4 oz. Roquefort cheese
1 jar (5 oz.) pasteurized process sharp Cheddar cheese spread
1 tablespoon Worcestershire sauce
1 tablespoon grated onion
½ teaspoon salt
¼ cup minced parsley
¼ cup chopped pecans

1. Thoroughly blend cheeses, Worcestershire sauce, onion, and salt. Chill several hours.
2. Shape cheese mixture into a log or mound; coat evenly with the parsley and pecans. Chill until ready to serve with *crisp crackers*.

ABOUT 2 CUPS

CUCUMBER DIP

1 large cucumber
1 package (8 ozs.) cream cheese
3 tablespoons finely chopped green onions
2 tablespoons lemon juice
¼ teaspoon salt

1. Trim 3 thin slices from cucumber and set aside for garnish.
2. Pare remaining cucumber; grate into a bowl, then drain well. Beat cucumber into cream cheese until smooth; stir in onions, lemon juice, and salt; cover. Chill several hours.
3. Spoon into a small serving bowl; garnish with cucumber slices. Place bowl on a large plate or tray; surround with cherry tomatoes, carrot sticks, and celery chunks.

1½ CUPS

NOTE: If chilled dip seems too thick at serving time, thin with 1 to 2 tablespoons milk.

HOMEMADE POT CHEESE

1 "Baby" Gouda cheese
2 tablespoons red wine

Cold Appetizers

(remove wax coating), finely shredded
3 oz. blue cheese
¼ cup butter or margarine, softened
vinegar
½ cup dairy sour cream
1½ tablespoons chopped chives
Few grains cayenne pepper

1. Mix cheeses with butter in a heavy saucepan. Add remaining ingredients; blend thoroughly.
2. Cook over low heat, stirring vigorously, until cheese is melted. Cool slightly.
3. Spoon into small pots and store in refrigerator.
ABOUT 2½ CUPS

SHRIMP CRISPS

2 dozen medium-sized fresh shrimp, shelled and deveined
1 slice onion
1 slice lemon
1 teaspoon mixed pickling spices
1 teaspoon salt
1 can (8 ozs.) water chestnuts, drained
½ cup mayonnaise or salad dressing
2 tablespoons sweet pickle relish
¼ teaspoon red-pepper seasoning
2 dozen sesame crackers
Parsley

1. Half-fill a large skillet with water; heat to simmering. Add shrimp, onion, lemon, pickling spices, and salt. Heat just to simmering again; cook 5 minutes, or until shrimp are tender. Lift from water with a slotted spoon; drain; chill.
2. Slice water chestnuts thin. Blend ¼ cup of the mayonnaise with pickle relish and red-pepper seasoning in a bowl.
3. Spread remaining ¼ cup mayonnaise on crackers; overlap water chestnut slices, dividing evenly, around edge on each. Spoon a heaping ½ teaspoon relish mixture onto center of each cracker; top with a shrimp and parsley. 2 DOZEN

NOTE: Assemble appetizers no sooner than an hour before serving so crackers stay crisp.

CHEESE BALL

Prepare this cheese ball well ahead of serving time.

2 pkgs. (8 oz. each) cream cheese
½ lb. sharp Cheddar cheese, shredded
2 teaspoons grated onion
½ teaspoon seasoned salt
¼ teaspoon salt
1 can (2¼ oz.) deviled ham
2 tablespoons finely chopped parsley
2 teaspoons Worcestershire sauce
1 teaspoon lemon juice
1 teaspoon dry mustard
½ teaspoon paprika
2 tablespoons finely chopped pimiento, thoroughly drained
Finely chopped pecans (about ⅔ cup)

1. Soften the cream cheese in a small mixer bowl, beating with electric beater. Beat in the Cheddar cheese, onion, Worcestershire sauce, lemon juice, dry mustard, paprika, seasoned salt, salt, and deviled ham until mixture is creamy.
2. Stir in the parsley and pimiento. Cover and refrigerate several hours, or until cheese mixture is firm enough to handle.
3. Shape into a ball and coat evenly with the chopped pecans. Wrap in moisture-vaporproof material and refrigerate until ready to serve. Or blend nuts with snipped *parsley* or snipped slices of *dried smoked beef* before coating. Serve with assorted *crackers* and small thin *cocktail rye-bread slices.* 1 CHEESE BALL (ABOUT 3 CUPS)

CAMEMBERT MOUSSE

This delicate mousse provides a pleasant contrast to an assortment of highly seasoned appetizers.

1 env. unflavored gelatin
½ cup cold milk
8 oz. Camembert cheese, forced through a fine sieve
2 tablespoons sieved pimiento
2 tablespoons minced parsley
½ teaspoon paprika
1 egg white, beaten to stiff, not dry, peaks
½ cup chilled heavy cream, whipped

1. Soften gelatin in milk in a heavy saucepan. Stir over low heat until gelatin is dissolved. Add the cheese and stir until melted.
2. Remove from heat and mix in pimiento, parsley, and paprika. Turn into bowl, cover, and refrigerate until cool.
3. Fold egg white and cream into the cooled cheese mixture. Turn into a 2-cup fancy mold; chill several hours, or until firm.
4. Unmold onto a large serving dish or tray. Surround with assorted crisp relishes such as *celery curls, carrot* and *zucchini sticks, radish roses, green pepper strips, cucumber slices, green onions,* and *green* and *ripe olives.* Serve with a tray of assorted *crackers.* ONE 2-CUP MOLD

LIVER PÂTÉ EXCEPTIONALE

This excellent and quite different recipe from Charlie's Café Exceptionale in Minneapolis, Minnesota, is large enough to serve a crowd.

Pâté:
1 lb. onions, sliced
1 clove garlic, finely minced
¼ cup rendered chicken fat
1 lb. chicken livers, coarsely diced
1 teaspoon salt
Few grains freshly ground black pepper
Sauce:
1¼ cups olive oil
¾ cup horseradish mustard
¼ cup vinegar
½ cup finely diced celery
½ cup finely diced onion
¼ cup snipped parsley
1 tablespoon paprika
1 teaspoon salt
½ teaspoon freshly ground black pepper

1. For pâté, add the onions and garlic to hot chicken fat in a skillet. Cook, stirring occasionally, until onion is golden.
2. Add chicken livers, salt, and pepper. Cook the livers until cooked through, but not browned.
3. Put the onion-liver mixture through a food chopper; turn into a bowl and whip to a smooth paste with rotary beater. If pâté is too thick, add *chicken broth* until of desired consistency.
4. For sauce, combine the olive oil in a bowl with the remaining ingredients; mix well. Serve with the liver pâté.   2 CUPS PÂTÉ AND 3 CUPS SAUCE

Canapés & Hors d'Oeuvres

WINE-CHEESE

Whip together *½ cup whipped unsalted butter* and *4 teaspoons Roquefort cheese*. Spread onto *toasted bread rounds*. Whip *2 packages (3 ounces each) cream cheese* with *2 tablespoons sauterne*. Pipe a swirl of the mixture onto each canapé. Roll edges in minced *parsley*. Top with *pimiento-stuffed olive slice*; sprinkle with *paprika*. Glaze and chill.

CARCIOFI ALLA GRECA GEORGE'S

These Greek-style artichokes are included on the menu at George's on Via Marche in Rome.

6 artichokes
4 oz. fresh mushrooms, sliced
⅔ cup coarsely chopped onion
½ cup olive oil
½ cup dry white wine
Juice of 1 lemon
30 fennel seeds
¼ teaspoon coriander
Salt and pepper to taste

1. Rinse artichokes and discard the hard outer leaves. Quarter artichokes, remove and discard "choke" or fuzzy part, and arrange the pieces in a large baking pan or shallow heatproof casserole having a cover. Allow plenty of space for the artichokes.
2. Cover artichoke pieces with the mushrooms and onion. Then pour over them a mixture of the remaining ingredients.
3. Cover and place over medium heat. Bring to a rapid boil and cook about 1 minute.
4. Transfer the pan to a 350°F oven for about 30 minutes, or until artichokes are tender.
5. Remove from oven; cool at room temperature, then refrigerate to chill thoroughly. Serve cold.
   ABOUT 8 SERVINGS

CHEESY SESAME-STUFFED CELERY

3 oz. cream cheese, softened
1 tablespoon milk
1 teaspoon grated onion
2 teaspoons butter
¼ cup sesame seed
2 tablespoons shredded Parmesan cheese
Celery stalks

1. Beat cream cheese, milk, and onion together until fluffy; chill in refrigerator.
2. Melt butter in a skillet over medium heat. Add sesame seed and stir constantly until delicately browned. Remove from heat and stir in the Parmesan cheese; cool.
3. To serve, fill crisp celery stalks with cheese mixture; sprinkle sesame-seed mixture generously over top. Cut crosswise into 2-inch lengths.

CUCUMBER-CHICKEN CANAPÉS

1 cup finely chopped cooked chicken
⅔ cup chopped salted pecans
⅓ cup chopped seeded pared cucumber
1 teaspoon monosodium glutamate
Few grains white pepper
½ cup mayonnaise
Thinly sliced white bread (crusts removed), cut in 1½-in. rounds
Whipped butter or margarine
Unpared cucumber slices

1. Combine chicken with pecans, chopped cu-

Cold Appetizers

cumber, monosodium glutamate, pepper, and mayonnaise. Chill the mixture thoroughly.

2. When ready to make canapés, spread bread with whipped butter. Cover with cucumber slice and spread chicken mixture over cucumber, leaving green edge showing.

3. Cut thin slices of cucumber in half and remove seeds. Sprinkle with *paprika*. Twist cucumber and set on canapé. Place *pimiento-stuffed olive slices* or sprigs of *parsley* along side of cucumber.

ABOUT 2½ DOZEN CANAPÉS

CRAB-AVOCADO CANAPÉS

1 pkg. (6 oz.) frozen crab meat, thawed, drained, and flaked	1 teaspoon capers Mayonnaise Avocado Spread, *below*
Italian salad dressing	Thinly sliced bread
¼ cup diced celery	(crusts removed), cut
1½ teaspoons diced pimiento	in fancy shapes

1. Toss crab meat with a small amount of the salad dressing. Chill well.

2. When ready to make canapés, combine crab meat with celery, pimiento, and capers; mix well. Blend with enough mayonnaise to just moisten.

3. Spread avocado mixture over bread and cover with crab mixture. Garnish each canapé with sprigs of *watercress*.

ABOUT 1½ DOZEN CANAPES

AVOCADO SPREAD: Scoop out the pulp from *1 medium-sized avocado* and mash. Blend in *1 teaspoon Italian salad dressing mix, 1 teaspoon lemon juice*, and only enough *dairy sour cream* to make of good spreading consistency. Chill until ready to use.

ABOUT ½ CUP SPREAD

SAVORY MINIATURE CROUSTADES

Miniature Croustades, page 116	3 tablespoons finely crumbled blue cheese
1 can (2¼ oz.) deviled ham	1 cup dairy sour cream

1. Mix the deviled ham with blue cheese and gently blend in sour cream.

2. Shortly before serving, fill Miniature Croustades with sour cream mixture. Garnish with tiny *parsley sprigs* or *pimiento pieces*.

ABOUT 4 DOZEN APPETIZERS

DEVILED HAM CANAPÉS

1 can (4½ oz.) deviled ham	¼ cup butter or margarine
¼ cup dairy sour cream	2 teaspoons lemon juice
¼ teaspoon dill weed	
3 tablespoons chopped cucumber pickle	

1. Mix deviled ham, sour cream, dill weed, and pickle. Chill thoroughly.

2. Cream the butter with the lemon juice until fluffy. Spread on toast rounds. Cover with deviled ham spread and garnish with slices of *pimiento-stuffed olives*.

ABOUT ¾ CUP SPREAD

LOBSTER APPETIZER TIDBITS

6 frozen South African rock lobster tails (about 5 oz. each)	1 teaspoon prepared mustard
1 cup mayonnaise	½ teaspoon onion salt
1 teaspoon curry powder	½ teaspoon paprika
	1 teaspoon Angostura bitters

1. Drop frozen lobster tails into boiling *salted water*; cover, bring to boiling, lower heat and simmer only until lobster meat turns white (6 to 8 minutes). Drain and rinse with cold water.

2. Using scissors, remove thin membrane on underside of each tail, cutting close to shell; insert fingers under meat and remove from shell in one piece; chill thoroughly.

3. Blend mayonnaise with the remaining ingredients; chill.

4. At serving time, cut lobster into bite-size pieces, insert a wooden pick into each piece, and arrange on a platter with chilled dip in center.

APPETIZERS FOR 12

BUTTER TARTS WITH MUSHROOM CREAM

A prize-winning recipe truly worthy of its blue ribbon.

Butter Pastry for Tarts, page 254	½ lb. fresh mushrooms, chopped
2 beef bouillon cubes	¼ cup minced onion
⅓ cup boiling water	2 tablespoons flour
½ cup butter or margarine	1 cup heavy cream, whipped

1. Prepare tart shells. Cool.

2. Meanwhile, dissolve bouillon cubes in the boiling water; set aside to cool.
3. Heat butter in a skillet; add the mushrooms and onion and cook, stirring occasionally, until mushrooms are tender, about 8 minutes.
4. Put flour into a small saucepan. Add the cooled broth gradually, stirring constantly. Continue to stir and bring to boiling; boil 1 minute. Blend sauce with the mushrooms; set aside to cool.
5. When ready to serve, blend whipped cream with mushroom mixture. Spoon mushroom cream into tart shells. Garnish with sprigs of *watercress*.

ABOUT 2 DOZEN TARTS

SARDINE CARTWHEEL
The enchanting fjord city of Stavanger, Norway, is noted not only for its beauty and friendly people, but for its world-famous sardines. The catch is held in nets in the cool waters of the fjords for three days before being prepared for smoking, drenching with pure olive oil, and packing into cans.

1 slice pumpernickel or rye bread cut from a round loaf (bread slice about 8 in. in diameter and ¼ in. thick)	1 chilled hard-cooked egg
	½ teaspoon grated lemon peel
	⅛ teaspoon salt
	1 to 3 cans (3¾ oz. each) Norwegian sardines, about 22
Herbed Mayonnaise, *page 23*	

1. For a perfect round, invert an 8-inch bowl over bread slice and cut with pointed knife around edge to remove crust. Spread bread generously with Herbed Mayonnaise.
2. Separate yolk from white of egg; finely chop white and sprinkle over mayonnaise. Sieve yolk; toss with lemon peel and salt; sprinkle lightly over white, reserving about 1 teaspoon for garnish.
3. Arrange sardines spoke-fashion over egg with large ends of sardines placed about ½ inch from outer edge of bread and tails toward the center. Turn sardines once, so a little egg yolk will adhere. Spoon reserved egg yolk in center.
4. Break wooden picks into various lengths; thread *1, 2, or 3 cocktail onions* onto each pick, depending upon length of pick. Insert picks into center of canapé in a cluster.
5. Arrange *watercress leaves* around outer edge of sardines on canapé to make a ½-inch border.
6. Using a broad spatula or turner, transfer cartwheel to serving plate. Squeeze a few drops of *lemon juice* over each sardine.
7. To serve, cut into pie-shaped wedges with a whole sardine on each wedge.

20 TO 22 CANAPÉS

HERBED MAYONNAISE: Blend *½ cup mayonnaise, 1 teaspoon grated onion, ¼ teaspoon dill weed, ½ teaspoon crushed tarragon,* and *2 teaspoons finely snipped parsley* thoroughly. Cover and chill.

SIT-DOWN APPETIZERS

OYSTERS ROCKEFELLER
This delectable appetizer originated at Antoine's restaurant in New Orleans where a patron tasted it and exclaimed, "Why, this is as rich as Rockefeller!"

1 egg, well beaten	1 lb. fresh spinach, cooked, drained, and finely chopped
2 cups Medium White Sauce, *page 196*	
2 doz. shell oysters	1 tablespoon minced parsley
2 tablespoons sherry	½ teaspoon Worcestershire sauce
2 tablespoons butter or margarine	6 drops Tabasco
1 tablespoon finely chopped onion	¼ teaspoon salt
Few grains ground nutmeg	¼ cup shredded Parmesan cheese

1. Stir the egg into white sauce; set aside.
2. Pour *coarse salt* into a 15x10x1-inch jelly roll pan to a ¼-inch depth. Open oysters and arrange the oysters-in-the-shells on the salt; sprinkle ¼ teaspoon sherry over each.
3. Heat the butter in a heavy skillet. Add the onion and cook until partially tender. Add the chopped spinach, 2 tablespoons of the white sauce, parsley, Worcestershire sauce, and Tabasco to the skillet along with a mixture of the salt and nutmeg; mix thoroughly. Heat 2 to 3 minutes.

Sit-Down Appetizers

4. Spoon spinach mixture over all of the oysters. Spoon remaining white sauce over spinach. Sprinkle each oyster with cheese.
5. Bake at 375°F 15 to 20 minutes, or until tops are lightly browned.

4 TO 6 SERVINGS

SHRIMP COCKTAIL, SEVICHE STYLE
Seviche is a popular marinated raw fish dish served as an appetizer south of the border.

1½ lbs. cooked shrimp, shelled, deveined, and chilled	½ cup lime juice
	1½ teaspoons salt
	½ teaspoon monosodium glutamate
1 firm ripe tomato, peeled and diced	2 to 3 teaspoons soy sauce
¼ cup thinly sliced green onions with tops	¼ teaspoon Worcestershire sauce
¼ cup thinly sliced celery	½ clove garlic, minced

1. Dice the chilled shrimp into a bowl and combine with remaining ingredients; toss lightly to mix well. Chill in refrigerator, covered, about 8 hours.
2. Serve very cold on cocktail sea shells lined with *leaf lettuce*. Or, if desired, spoon cocktail mixture into ripe *avocado halves* brushed with *lime juice*.

6 SERVINGS

ROSY SAUCE
(Salsa Rosata)
From Antico Martini, a famous restaurant on St. Mark's Square in Venice, Italy, comes this delightfully smooth and piquant dressing for seafood.

¾ cup ketchup	1½ teaspoons Worcestershire sauce
½ cup mayonnaise	
½ cup heavy cream	1 teaspoon prepared horseradish
2 tablespoons cognac	
	4 drops Tabasco

1. Mix all ingredients; chill thoroughly.
2. Arrange chilled *seafood* on *lettuce*, drizzle with *lemon juice* and spoon on sauce.

ABOUT 1½ CUPS SAUCE

SHRIMP REMOULADE
Here is a best-liked Creole cocktail sauce to enhance shrimp or crab meat.

2 cups mayonnaise	1 teaspoon finely crushed chervil
1 tablespoon prepared mustard	
	1 teaspoon tarragon leaves, finely crushed
1 tablespoon finely chopped sweet pickle	
1 tablespoon chopped capers	½ teaspoon anchovy paste
1 tablespoon minced parsley	1 to 2 drops Tabasco
	Deveined cooked shrimp, chilled

1. Blend all ingredients except shrimp. Refrigerate until thoroughly chilled.
2. Allowing 4 or 5 shrimp for each appetizer, spoon onto crisp *lettuce* with sauce over all.

6 TO 8 SERVINGS

LOMI LOMI SALMON
There are several versions of this fish preparation, some of them using smoked or salted salmon.

1 lb. raw salmon steaks	2 tablespoons lemon juice
½ cup cider vinegar	
¾ cup finely sliced green onions	1 tablespoon soy sauce
	1 tablespoon peanut oil
3 large ripe tomatoes, peeled and diced	1 teaspoon salt

1. Remove bones and skin from salmon and cut into small pieces (about 2 cups). Marinate in the vinegar about 2 hours.
2. Drain salmon and mix with the green onions and tomatoes.
3. Blend remaining ingredients. Pour over salmon and vegetables; toss lightly to mix. Chill mixture thoroughly before serving.

ABOUT 6 SERVINGS

CRAB LOUIS

1 hard-cooked egg, chopped	1 tablespoon prepared horseradish
1 green onion, trimmed and chopped	1 can (7½ ozs.) crab meat
	2 medium avocados
½ cup mayonnaise or salad dressing	1 tablespoon lemon juice
	Boston lettuce
¼ cup chili sauce	

1. Blend egg, onion, mayonnaise, chili sauce, and horseradish in a small bowl. Chill.
2. Drain liquid from crab meat; pick over meat and remove any bony tissue; cut meat into small pieces. Chill.
3. When ready to serve, cut avocados in half and pit; brush with lemon juice. Place each half on a lettuce-lined salad plate. Spoon crab evenly into avocados; spoon dressing over crab. Garnish each plate with a lemon wedge if you like. Serve as an appetizer.

4 SERVINGS

* Broiled Bacon Buns (page 16)

Chapter 2
SOUPS—Hot & Cold

Gone is the fire-blackened iron soup kettle of yesteryear that bubbled on the kitchen stove the livelong day. But its legacy remains, and soup is still a national favorite—a fine test of a homemaker's skill in striking a harmonious balance of flavors.

Soups may be roughly divided into two groups. In the first group belong the soups made from meat stock. These are the various modifications of the brown and white stocks, the bouillons, consommés, and broths. In the second group belong the soups that may be made either with or without meat stock. These are the various modifications of cream soups, purées and bisques, of chowders and stews, and of vegetable soups.

An unthickened clear soup (bouillon, consommé, broth) is appropriately served at the beginning of a hearty meal while a cream soup may well begin a light meal. Soups may be main-dish fare, too. Here the hearty, thick varieties are appropriate—chowders, bisques, stews, and some fruit soups.

With the perfecting of modern commercial processing of soups, more time-consuming methods of preparing soup stock at home have become less common. Available to homemakers today are not only soups in cans, but also variety in packaged soup mixes. Convenience, quality, and flavor are appealing factors built into both types. Bouillon cubes also belong to the convenience group.

HELPFUL HINTS ABOUT SOUPS

• When preparing cream soups, a thorough blending of fat and flour and cooking with the milk or cream (see recipe for white sauce) help prevent a film of fat appearing on the surface of the soup. This film often forms when the soup is too thin.
• To avoid curdling of cream of tomato soup, thicken the sieved tomatoes before adding (hot) to the cold milk, stirring constantly.
• Cream soups usually have the consistency of a thin sauce. The vegetable used will determine the amount of flour needed to thicken the soup. At least ¼ cup chopped or ⅓ cup sieved vegetable per cup of thin white sauce will give a most satisfactory soup; 2 to 3 tablespoons sieved spinach per cup is a desirable proportion for cream of spinach soup. Add a little hot milk or cream if the soup is too thick, or thicken with a flour-water mixture if the soup is too thin.
• Instructions for clarifying soups are given in *Consommé, page 26.*
• The electric blender is the modern way to quick-and-easy blending of everything and anything into savory soups. Remember, when using it, to pour the liquid into container first, usually ½ to 1 cup, then gradually add the other ingredients.
• Cool soups to lukewarm before storing in covered container in the refrigerator; keep several days only. Store in freezer for longer periods.

SOUP GARNISHES

Garnishes are to soup as jewels are to the costume—a glamorous accent. They need not be elaborate. The normally stocked refrigerator will usually yield the wherewithal for many of the garnishes suggested on page 26.

* *Chunky Corn Chowder (page 28)*

Apples (red or golden) — unpared and diced
Bacon — crisp and crumbled; prepared baconlike pieces
Croutons — plain; buttered; herbed
Eggs, hard-cooked — chopped; chopped or sieved whites; sieved yolks; combined with bacon
Lemons — thinly sliced and notched or cut in fancy shapes; shredded lemon peel
Nuts (walnuts, peanuts, pecans, cashews, filberts, and pistachios) — toasted and salted or dry roasted, finely or coarsely chopped; (toasted almonds) unsalted, salted or dry roasted and slivered or coarsely chopped
Olives — sliced pimiento-stuffed olives; quartered (or wedges) ripe olives
Vegetables (fresh) — thinly sliced notched carrots; thinly sliced scored cucumbers; snipped chives; snipped parsley; snipped green onion tops; sprigs of watercress; slivered or chopped green or red peppers
Whipped Cream — unsalted, salted, seasoned or herbed; topped with caviar, sieved pimiento or hard-cooked egg yolk, black pepper, nutmeg, or shredded cheese

SOUPS TO SERVE HOT

BEEF STOCK

The simmering soup pot . . . pot-au-feu in French . . . that bubbled on the old cook stove the livelong day, is part of French-American cooking tradition and the source of many eating pleasures. Even today modern cooks continue to simmer the broth for hours to obtain flavorful and rich stock.

3 lbs. lean beef (chuck or plate), cut in 1-in. pieces	5 carrots, pared and cut in large pieces
1 soup bone, cracked	2 turnips, pared and cut in large pieces
3 qts. cold water	3 stalks celery with leaves, sliced
1½ tablespoons salt	4 leeks, sliced
2 large onions	Herb bouquet, *page 4*
2 whole cloves	

1. Put meat and soup bone into a large saucepot; add water and salt. Cover and bring to boiling. Remove foam. Cover saucepot and simmer about 4 hours, removing foam as necessary.
2. Slice 1 onion; insert the cloves into second onion. Add onions, remaining vegetables, and herb bouquet to saucepot. Cover and bring to boiling. Reduce heat and simmer about 1½ hours.
3. Remove from heat; remove soup bone and strain stock through a fine sieve. Allow to cool. (The meat and vegetables strained from stock may be served as desired.)
4. Remove fat that rises to surface (reserve for use in other food preparation). Store stock in a covered container in refrigerator for future use, or reheat and serve with slices of crisp *toast*.

ABOUT 2½ QUARTS STOCK

BROWN STOCK: Follow recipe for Beef Stock. Cut any meat from soup bone and brown the meat along with beef pieces in *¼ cup fat* in saucepot before cooking. Proceed as in Beef Stock.

WHITE STOCK: Follow recipe for Beef Stock. Substitute *veal shank and breast* for beef. Add one half of a disjointed ready-to-cook *stewing chicken*.

CONSOMMÉ: Follow recipe for White Stock. Cool stock and stir in *2 egg whites*, slightly beaten, *crushed shells of the eggs*, and *4 teaspoons water*. Heat slowly to boiling, stirring constantly. Remove from heat and let stand 25 minutes. Strain through two thicknesses of cheesecloth.

BOUILLON: Follow recipe for Consommé. Substitute Brown Stock for White Stock.

BEEF BOUILLON WITH BROILED ORANGE

Vermont House, located in Newbury, Vermont, serves hot beef bouillon with a flair.

Thick orange slices	3 tablespoons sherry
2 tablespoons melted butter	Beef bouillon

1. Brush tops of orange slices with a mixture of butter and sherry. Broil with tops 2 to 3 inches from source of heat about 8 minutes, brushing occasionally with butter mixture.

2. To serve, place an orange slice in bottom of each soup dish. Pour hot beef bouillon over orange slices. Serve immediately.

ONION SOUP LES HALLES

In this quickly prepared version of the onion soup made famous by Les Halles (former Paris market), canned vegetable juice and consommé are substituted for the long-cooking meat and vegetable stock used in the traditional recipe.

2 tablespoons butter	2 teaspoons tarragon vinegar
2 large onions, coarsely chopped	1 can (10½ oz.) condensed beef consommé
1 clove garlic, finely chopped	1⅓ cups water
½ teaspoon salt	1 can (12 oz.) cocktail vegetable juice
⅛ teaspoon black pepper	
⅛ teaspoon thyme	
1 large sprig parsley, snipped	

1. Heat butter in a saucepan; add onions and garlic and cook about 5 minutes.
2. Stir in salt, pepper, thyme, parsley, vinegar, consommé, water, and vegetable juice. Simmer about 10 minutes.
3. Serve piping hot, floating a *buttered toast round*, topped with *shredded Parmesan cheese*, in each bowl of soup. ABOUT 1 QUART SOUP

BEEF SOUP

This hearty soup is a favorite recipe from Mrs. Hubert Humphrey, wife of the former Vice President.

1½ lbs. beef for stew	½ cup chopped onion
1 soup bone	1 can (15 oz.) Italian-style tomatoes
1½ to 2 teaspoons salt	1 tablespoon Worcestershire sauce
½ teaspoon pepper	
2 bay leaves	1 beef bouillon cube
4 medium-sized carrots, pared and sliced	Pinch oregano (or other herb desired)
1 cup chopped cabbage	
1 cup chopped celery	

1. Put meat and soup bone in a heavy 3-quart kettle; cover with cold water (about 4 cups). Add salt, pepper, and bay leaves. Bring rapidly to boiling. Reduce heat. Add carrots, cabbage, celery, and onion; cover and simmer until meat is tender, about 2½ hours.
2. Remove and discard bone and bay leaves. Cut meat into bite-size pieces and return to soup. Mix in tomatoes, Worcestershire sauce, bouillon cube, and oregano. Cover and simmer 30 minutes.

6 SERVINGS

CUBAN BLACK BEAN SOUP

This soup is a specialty created by Executive Chef Robert Halberg and was featured in the Salon Reál of the Executive House's Condado Beach Hotel in San Juan, Puerto Rico.

1 lb. black beans, washed	10 tablespoons olive oil
2 quarts boiling water	½ lb. onions, peeled, trimmed, and chopped
2 tablespoons salt	
5 cloves garlic	½ lb. green peppers, peeled, trimmed, and chopped
1½ teaspoons cumin	
1½ teaspoons oregano	
2 tablespoons white vinegar	

1. Put beans into a large heavy saucepot or Dutch oven and add boiling water; boil rapidly 2 minutes. Cover tightly, remove from heat, and set aside 1 hour. Add salt to beans and liquid; bring to boiling and simmer, covered, until beans are soft.
2. Put the garlic, cumin, oregano, and vinegar into a mortar and crush to a paste.
3. Heat olive oil in a large skillet. Mix in onion and green pepper and fry until onion is browned, stirring occasionally. Thoroughly blend in the paste, then stir the skillet mixture into the beans. Cook over low heat until ready to serve.
4. Meanwhile, mix a small portion of *cooked rice*, *minced onion*, *olive oil*, and *vinegar* in a bowl, set aside to marinate. Add a soup spoon of rice mixture to each serving of soup. ABOUT 2 QUARTS SOUP

NOTE: For a combination soup and salad course served before the entrée, set out chilled ripe *avocado halves* and spoon the piping hot bean soup into the cavities. (The blend of flavors is subtle, elegant, and distinctive.)

WHOLE-MEAL BARLEY BROTH

2 small lamb shanks, weighing about 1 lb.	2 medium carrots, pared and diced
½ cup medium barley	1 medium onion, diced (½ cup)
2½ teaspoons salt	

Soups to Serve Hot

½ teaspoon dried rosemary, crushed
6 cups water
1 cup diced celery
1 can (10¾ ozs.) condensed tomato soup

1. Trim any excess fat from lamb. Combine shanks with barley, salt, rosemary, and water in a kettle; heat to boiling; cover. Simmer 1½ hours, or until lamb is tender. Remove shanks from kettle to a plate.
2. Stir carrots, onion, and celery into barley mixture; cover. Simmer 15 minutes, or until vegetables are tender.
3. While vegetables cook, take lamb from bones, discarding bones and fat; dice meat.
4. Let barley mixture stand a minute or two, then skim off fat; stir tomato soup and lamb into kettle. Heat again just to boiling. (If you prefer a thinner soup, stir in a little more water.) Ladle into soup bowls.
6 SERVINGS

CHINESE CABBAGE SOUP

1 chicken breast (¾ lb.), cooked
7 cups chicken broth
6 cups sliced Chinese cabbage (celery cabbage)
1 teaspoon soy sauce
1¼ teaspoons salt
¼ teaspoon black pepper

1. Cut chicken into strips about ⅛ inch wide and 1½ to 2 inches long. Combine with chicken broth and heat only until hot. Add Chinese cabbage and cook 3 to 4 minutes (only until cabbage is crisp-tender; do not overcook).
2. Stir in the soy sauce and a mixture of the salt and pepper. Serve hot.
6 SERVINGS
NOTE: If desired, *lettuce* may be substituted for the cabbage. Reduce cooking time to 1 minute.

LUMBERJACK BURGOO

1 smoked pork hock, weighing about ¾ lb.
2 teaspoons salt
¼ teaspoon pepper
Water
4 chicken thighs
2 large potatoes, pared and diced (about 2 cups)
1 large onion, chopped (1 cup)
½ cup diced celery
½ cup chopped green pepper
1 can (16 oz.) tomato puree
1 teaspoon leaf thyme, crushed
2 tablespoons Worcestershire sauce
6 slices French bread, cut ¼-inch thick
1 package (10 ozs.) frozen whole-kernel corn
Butter or margarine
1½ teaspoons sesame seeds

1. Combine pork hock, salt, pepper, and water to cover in a kettle; heat to boiling; cover. Simmer 1½ hours; add chicken to kettle. Simmer ½ hour longer, or until meats are tender. Remove from broth and cool until easy to handle.
2. Stir potatoes, onion, corn, celery, green pepper, tomato purée, and thyme into broth; heat to boiling; cover again. Simmer 30 minutes, or until vegetables are tender.
3. While vegetables cook, peel skin from pork hock and chicken; take meat from bones and dice. Stir into kettle with Worcestershire sauce; heat just to boiling.
4. Spread French bread with butter; sprinkle sesame seeds over slices; place on a cookie sheet. Toast in 350° oven.
5. Spoon soup mixture into bowls; place a slice of toast on top of each.
6 SERVINGS

CHUNKY CORN SOUP

¼ cup diced salt pork
1 large onion, chopped (1 cup)
1 cup coarsely chopped celery
2 large potatoes, pared and diced (2 cups)
2 cups water
1½ teaspoons dillweed
1 teaspoon salt
2 knockwurst (½ lb.)
1 large can evaporated milk (1⅔ cups)
1 can (12 ozs.) whole-kernel corn
1 can (16 ozs.) cream-style corn

1. Sauté salt pork slowly until almost crisp in a kettle; push to one side.
2. Stir onion and celery into drippings; sauté until soft. Stir in potatoes, water, dillweed, and salt; heat to boiling; cover. Simmer 12 minutes, or until potatoes are tender.
3. While potatoes cook, peel skin from knockwurst; slice meat in thin rounds.
4. Stir milk, whole-kernel corn and liquid, cream-style corn, and knockwurst into mixture in kettle; heat slowly, stirring several times, just to boiling.
5. Ladle into soup bowls. Serve with Sesame Sticks (recipe on page 46).
8 SERVINGS

SOUP MEXICANA

1 chicken breast
6 cups chicken broth
2 onions, chopped
1 teaspoon monosodium glutamate
1 tablespoon butter or margarine
1½ teaspoons grated onion
2 cups chopped zucchini
1 cup drained canned whole kernel corn
⅓ cup tomato purée
2 oz. cream cheese, cut in small cubes
2 avocados, sliced

1. Cook chicken breast 30 minutes, or until tender, in the broth with the chopped onion and monosodium glutamate. Remove chicken; dice and set aside. Reserve broth.
2. Heat butter and grated onion in a large saucepan; blend in zucchini and corn. Cook about 5 minutes, stirring occasionally. Mix in the broth and tomato purée. Cover and simmer about 20 minutes.
3. Just before serving, mix in diced chicken, cream cheese, and avocados.   6 TO 8 SERVINGS

NOTE: Any remaining soup may be stored, covered, in the refrigerator.

CUCUMBER SOUP

A featured treat served at the Copper Kettle in Aspen, Colorado.

1 tablespoon butter
½ cup chopped onion
½ cup sliced carrot
4 cups chopped celery (with leaves)
3 cucumbers, pared and diced
¼ teaspoon thyme
½ teaspoon tarragon leaves, crushed
6 cups chicken broth
2 eggs, slightly beaten
1 cup heavy cream
2 tablespoons dry sherry
1 teaspoon lemon juice

1. In a kettle, cook onion, carrot, and celery with butter until vegetables are soft, about 5 minutes.
2. Add cucumber, thyme, tarragon, and chicken broth; cover and cook 10 minutes. Cool slightly.
3. Pour half of mixture into an electric blender container; blend until smooth. Repeat with remaining half. Pour purée back into kettle; heat thoroughly.
4. Blend beaten eggs with cream. Slowly stir in about ½ cup of hot purée, then stir into remaining hot purée. Heat 5 minutes, stirring constantly. Blend in sherry and lemon juice. Serve sprinkled with *paprika* and *toasted sesame seed*.

ABOUT 2 QUARTS SOUP

BAYOU CHOWDER

1 medium onion, chopped (½ cup)
1 small green pepper, quartered, seeded, and chopped (½ cup)
2 tablespoons salad oil
1 can (13¾ ozs.) chicken broth
1 can (16 ozs.) stewed tomatoes
1 bay leaf
½ teaspoon dried basil, crushed
3 cups water
1 can (4½ ozs.) deveined shrimp, drained and rinsed
1 can (5 or 6 ozs.) boned chicken, cut up
1 can (12 ozs.) pork luncheon meat, diced
¾ cup packaged precooked rice

1. Sauté onion and green pepper in salad oil until soft in a kettle. Stir in chicken broth, tomatoes, bay leaf, basil, and water; heat to boiling; cover. Simmer 10 minutes.
2. Stir in shrimp, chicken, and luncheon meat; heat to boiling. Stir in rice; cover; remove from heat. Let stand 5 minutes. Remove bay leaf.
3. Ladle into soup bowls; serve with thick slices of toasted French bread.   6 SERVINGS

CREAMY MUSHROOM SOUP

¼ cup butter or margarine
1 lb. fresh mushrooms, coarsely chopped
4 green onions with tops, sliced (reserve one half of green tops)
¼ cup flour
2 teaspoons salt
4½ cups milk
1 cup beef broth (dissolve 1 beef bouillon cube in 1 cup boiling water)

1. Heat butter in a saucepan. Stir in the mushrooms and green onions; cook about 5 minutes, or until just tender. With a slotted spoon, remove vegetables to a bowl; set aside.
2. Blend a mixture of the flour and salt into the butter in saucepan; heat until mixture bubbles. Gradually add the milk and broth, stirring constantly. Bring to boiling and cook until thickened.
3. Remove from heat and stir in the vegetables.
4. Garnish each serving with a spoonful of *dairy sour cream* and the reserved green onion tops.

6 TO 8 SERVINGS

COCK-A-LEEKIE SOUP

1 stewing chicken, weighing about 4 lbs., cut up
4 teaspoons seasoned salt
3 bunches of leeks
1 cup chopped celery
¾ cup packaged precooked rice

Soups to Serve Hot

2 bay leaves
8 cups water
2 tablespoons chopped parsley

1. Combine chicken, seasoned salt, bay leaves, and water in a kettle. Heat to boiling; cover. Simmer 1½ hours, or until chicken is tender. Remove from broth and cool until easy to handle, then take meat from bones and dice. Remove bay leaves from broth; reheat broth to boiling.
2. While chicken cooks, trim leeks; slice white part thin. (There should be about 5 cups.) Stir leeks and celery into broth; cover again. Simmer 20 minutes.
3. Stir in rice; cover; turn off heat. Let stand 5 minutes. Stir in diced chicken; reheat to boiling.
4. Ladle into soup bowls; sprinkle parsley over each serving.   8 SERVINGS

TOMATO CREAM
A recipe from the Jockey Club in Madrid, Spain.

2 tablespoons butter
2 leeks, chopped (about 2½ cups)
2 carrots, diced (about 1 cup)
2 tablespoons flour
2½ cups beef broth
1 to 2 teaspoons sugar
¼ teaspoon salt
4 large ripe tomatoes (2 lbs.), cut in pieces

1. Heat butter in a saucepan. Add leeks and carrots; cook, stirring occasionally, until lightly browned. Stir in the flour and heat until bubbly.
2. Blend in the broth; bring to boiling, stirring constantly, and cook for 3 minutes.
3. Stir in sugar, salt, and tomatoes; simmer 1 hour.
4. Force mixture through a coarse sieve or food mill. Serve very hot.   4 SERVINGS

PASTA E FAGIOLI

1 large onion, chopped (1 cup)
2 tablespoons salad oil
1 can (13¾ ozs.) chicken broth
3½ cups water
1 package (8 ozs.) elbow macaroni
1 teaspoon garlic powder
1 teaspoon dried basil, crushed
1 teaspoon salt
2 cups diced cooked pork
1 can (15 ozs.) tomato sauce with onions, celery, and green peppers
1 can (16 ozs.) red kidney beans
Grated Romano cheese

1. Sauté onion in salad oil in a kettle until soft. Stir in chicken broth and water; heat to boiling. Stir in macaroni, garlic powder, basil, and salt. Reheat to boiling; cook 7 minutes, or until macaroni is almost tender.
2. Stir in pork, tomato sauce, and kidney beans and liquid; heat to boiling. Simmer 10 minutes longer.
3. Ladle into soup bowls; sprinkle Romano cheese over each serving. Serve with toasted Italian bread if you like.   6 TO 8 SERVINGS

YELLOW PEA SOUP WITH PORK
(Ärter med Fläsk)
It is said that every Thursday pea soup is served throughout Sweden, from fisher's cottage to Royal Palace.

¾ lb. (about 1⅔ cups) yellow peas, rinsed
2½ qts. cold water
1 lb. smoked shoulder butt
3 qts. water
¾ cup coarsely chopped onion
1 teaspoon salt
½ teaspoon monosodium glutamate
¼ teaspoon sugar
1 teaspoon leaf thyme

1. Cover the peas with the cold water in a large saucepan; let stand overnight.
2. Put smoked shoulder butt into a large saucepot with the 3 quarts water and onion. Simmer 1½ to 2 hours, or until meat is tender.
3. Remove meat and set aside. Skim fat from liquid, leaving about 2 tablespoons. Drain the peas and add to the broth with the remaining ingredients. Cook slowly until peas are tender.
4. Serve soup with thin slices of the smoked butt.   ABOUT 2½ QUARTS SOUP

EGG DROP SOUP

2 lbs. chicken wings or backs
1 small onion, peeled and sliced
Few celery tops
6 peppercorns
1 teaspoon salt
6 cups water
2 tablespoons cornstarch
1 egg
2 green onions, trimmed and sliced thin

1. Wash chicken; combine with onion, celery tops, peppercorns, salt, and water in a kettle; heat to boiling; cover. Simmer 1½ hours.
2. Remove chicken from broth and set aside to use in a casserole or sandwich filling. Strain broth into a

bowl. Measure out ½ cup, then return remainder to kettle; cook rapidly until it measures 4 cups.
3. Mix the ½ cup broth and cornstarch in a small bowl until smooth; stir into kettle. Cook, stirring constantly, until mixture thickens slightly and boils 1 minute. Turn off heat.
4. Beat egg well (but not until foamy) in a small bowl; pour into hot soup in a thin stream, stirring constantly, so egg forms thin shreds.
5. Ladle soup into bowls; sprinkle green onions over each serving. 4 TO 6 SERVINGS

2. Stir in carrots, potatoes, cabbage, corn, green beans, and herbs; heat to boiling again; cover. Simmer 1 hour longer, or until meat is tender.
3. Remove meat from kettle; cool until easy to handle, then take meat from bones, discarding bones and fat. Dice meat and return to kettle with tomatoes and parsley. Heat to boiling.
4. Ladle into soup bowls. Serve with toasted French bread or your favorite crackers. 10 SERVINGS

Chowders & Fish Soups

CREAM OF TURKEY SOUP

½ cup butter
6 tablespoons flour
½ teaspoon salt
Few grains black pepper
2 cups cream
3 cups turkey or chicken broth
¾ cup coarsely chopped cooked turkey

1. Heat butter in a saucepan. Blend in a mixture of the flour, salt, and pepper. Heat until mixture bubbles.
2. Gradually add the cream and 1 cup of the broth, stirring constantly. Bring to boiling; cook and stir 1 to 2 minutes.
3. Blend in remaining broth and turkey. Heat thoroughly (do not boil). Garnish with slivers of *carrot*. ABOUT 6 SERVINGS

OLD-FASHIONED VEGETABLE SOUP

2½ lbs. beef shank crosscuts
1 large onion, peeled, quartered, and sliced
1 cup sliced celery
3 teaspoons salt
¼ teaspoon pepper
10 cups water
6 medium carrots, pared and sliced
2 large potatoes, pared and diced
2 cups coarsely shredded green cabbage
1 package (10 ozs.) frozen whole-kernel corn
1 package (10 ozs.) frozen cut green beans
2 teaspons mixed Italian herbs
1 can (16 ozs.) stewed tomatoes
¼ cup chopped parsley

1. Combine beef, onion, celery, salt, pepper, and water in a large kettle; heat to boiling. Skim top; cover. Simmer 2 hours.

BRENNAN'S GUMBO À LA CREOLE
Brennan's in New Orleans, Louisiana includes this taste-tempter among their popular dishes.

4 small onions, chopped
⅔ cup butter
¼ cup flour
2 qts. rich chicken stock
2½ cups cooked tomatoes
½ lb. okra
Bouquet garni, *page 29*
Salt
Pepper
Cayenne pepper
6 hard-shelled crabs
24 large peeled shrimp
24 oysters

1. Sauté the onions until lightly browned in heated butter in a large saucepan. Add flour and cook 5 minutes, stirring constantly.
2. Gradually add chicken stock, tomatoes, okra, bouquet garni, salt, and peppers to taste; add crabs. Simmer 1 hour.
3. Add shrimp and oysters and cook slowly 5 minutes.
4. Put a spoonful of *cooked rice* into each soup bowl and ladle in hot gumbo. ABOUT 8 SERVINGS

SEAFOOD BISQUE

1 small onion, chopped (¼ cup)
2 tablespoons butter or margarine
2 cans (10¾ ozs. each) condensed cream of shrimp soup
2 cups milk
⅛ teaspoon red-pepper seasoning
1 cup light cream
1 can (7½ ozs.) crab meat, drained and cut into small chunks
1 lemon, cut into 8 slices

1. Sauté onion in butter in a kettle until soft; stir in soup, milk, and red-pepper seasoning. Heat slowly,

stirring several times, to boiling.
2. Sir in cream and crab meat; heat again just until hot. (Do not boil.)
3. Ladle into soup cups or bowls; float a slice of lemon on each serving. 8 SERVINGS

NEW ENGLAND CLAM CHOWDER

2 tablespoons butter or margarine
½ cup finely diced celery
¼ cup thinly sliced leek (white part only)
¼ cup minced onion
¼ cup minced green pepper
1¾ cups milk
1 cup cream
3 tablespoons flour
½ cup finely diced potato
12 large hard-shelled clams (to prepare, see note), or 2 cans (7½ oz. each) minced clams, drained (reserve liquid)
½ teaspoon Worcestershire sauce
½ teaspoon salt
⅛ teaspoon thyme
3 drops Tabasco
Few grains white pepper
Finely chopped parsley

1. In a heavy 3-quart saucepan melt butter over low heat. Add the celery, leek, onion, and green pepper; stirring occasionally, cook 6 to 8 minutes, or until partially tender.
2. Meanwhile, combine milk and cream and scald.
3. Blend flour into the vegetable-butter mixture; heat until mixture bubbles. Gradually add the scalded milk and cream, stirring constantly. Bring to boiling, stirring constantly; cook 1 to 2 minutes.
4. Stir in the potato, reserved clam liquid, salt, thyme, Tabasco, and pepper. Bring to boiling and simmer 25 to 35 minutes, stirring frequently. Add minced clams and Worcestershire sauce. Reheat.
5. Pour soup into a tureen or individual soup bowls. Garnish with parsley. Serve with *chowder biscuits* or *crackers*. 4 TO 6 SERVINGS
NOTE: To prepare clams and broth, rinse clams thoroughly under cold running water. Place clams in a saucepan and add *3 cups water*. Cook over medium heat until shells open completely. Drain the clams, reserving 2 cups of broth for chowder. Remove clams from shells. Cut off the hard outsides (combs) and chop clams into small, fine pieces. Decrease milk in chowder to 1 cup.

ZUPPA DI PESCE: ROYAL DANIELI

This fish soup recipe is from the Danieli Royal Excelsior, a hotel in Venice, Italy.

3 lbs. skinned and boned fish (haddock, trout, cod, salmon, and red snapper)
1-lb. lobster
1 lb. shrimp with shells
½ cup coarsely cut onion
1 stalk celery with leaves, coarsely cut
2 tablespoons cider vinegar
2 teaspoons salt
¼ cup olive oil
2 garlic cloves, minced
1 bay leaf, crumbled
1 teaspoon basil
½ teaspoon thyme
2 tablespoons minced parsley
½ to 1 cup dry white wine
½ cup chopped peeled tomatoes
8 shreds saffron
1 teaspoon salt
½ teaspoon freshly ground black pepper
6 slices French bread
¼ cup olive oil

1. Reserve heads and tails of fish. Cut fish into bite-size pieces.
2. In covered saucepot, simmer lobster and shrimp 5 minutes in 1 quart water with onion, celery, vinegar, and 2 teaspoons salt.
3. Remove and shell lobster and shrimp; devein shrimp. Cut lobster into bite-size pieces. Set lobster and shrimp aside.
4. Return shells to the broth and add heads and tails of fish. Simmer 20 minutes.
5. Strain broth, pour into saucepot and set aside.
6. Sauté all of the fish in ¼ cup oil with garlic, bay leaf, basil, thyme, and parsley 5 minutes, stirring constantly.
7. Add to reserved broth along with wine, tomatoes, saffron, 1 teaspoon salt, and the pepper. Bring to boiling; cover and simmer 10 minutes, stirring occasionally.
8. Serve with slices of bread sautéed in the remaining ¼ cup olive oil. ABOUT 2½ QUARTS SOUP

SHELLFISH CHOWDER

Tradition has it that French fishermen returning to port would toss some of their catch into a huge copper pot, "la chaudière," to be used later as part of a community feast of thanksgiving for their safe return. When the custom reached New England "la chaudière" became "chowder."

1 pt. oysters
1 cup shucked clams
½ lb. scallops, diced
3 cups cold chicken broth
3 tablespoons quick-cooking tapioca
3 egg yolks
¾ cup cream or milk
½ teaspoon monosodium glutamate
¼ teaspoon celery salt
⅛ teaspoon salt
⅛ teaspoon pepper

1. Heat oysters with liquor, clams, and scallops in a saucepan 5 minutes; drain, reserving liquid. Mix broth and tapioca; let stand 5 minutes.
2. Pour reserved liquid and chicken broth with tapioca into saucepan. Bring to boiling, stirring constantly, and cook until soup is thickened.
3. Beat egg yolks in a bowl and gradually beat in cream. Quickly stir about 3 tablespoons hot soup into egg yolk mixture. Immediately stir into soup. Stir constantly about 5 minutes (do not boil).
4. Add the oysters, clams, scallops, monosodium glutamate, celery salt, salt, and pepper. Heat thoroughly.

ABOUT 6 SERVINGS

SALMON CHOWDER

3 tablespoons butter
½ cup chopped onion
1½ cups diced pared potatoes, cooked
2 tablespoons chopped green pepper
1 can (10½ oz.) condensed cream of celery soup
3 cups milk
1 can (16 oz.) pink salmon, drained, skin and bones discarded, and meat separated in chunks
1 cup diced pared carrots, cooked
1 can (16 oz.) tomatoes, drained
1 teaspoon salt
½ teaspoon monosodium glutamate
¼ teaspoon pepper

1. Heat butter in a large saucepan. Add onion and green pepper; cook until tender.
2. Stir in soup and milk. Mix in salmon and remaining ingredients. Heat thoroughly, stirring occasionally (do not boil).
3. Ladle chowder into heated soup bowls and serve immediately.

8 TO 10 SERVINGS

SOUPS TO SERVE COLD

JELLIED CONSOMMÉ MADRILÈNE

3 cups tomato juice
1 cup strong chicken broth (dissolve 2 chicken bouillon cubes in 1 cup boiling water)
½ cup chopped green pepper
1 teaspoon sugar
2 env. unflavored gelatin
¾ cup cold water
2 teaspoons lemon juice
2 teaspoons Angostura bitters

1. Blend in a saucepan the tomato juice, chicken broth, green pepper, and sugar. Cover and simmer 6 to 8 minutes, or until green pepper is tender.
2. Soften gelatin in the cold water in a bowl.
3. Strain tomato juice mixture into bowl with gelatin and stir until dissolved. Blend in the lemon juice and bitters. Cool. Chill until firm.
4. Just before serving, stir mixture lightly with a fork. Spoon into chilled bowls. Garnish servings with notched slices of *lemon*, if desired.

4 TO 6 SERVINGS

AVOCADO SOUP

4 fully ripe avocados, peeled and pitted
3 cups cold chicken broth
2 teaspoons lime juice
½ teaspoon salt
⅛ teaspoon garlic powder
2 cups chilled cream

1. Put all ingredients except cream into an electric blender container. Cover and blend until smooth. Mix with the cream and chill thoroughly.
2. Serve with *lemon slices* or garnish as desired.

6 SERVINGS

JELLIED BORSCH

1 can (10½ oz.) condensed consommé
1 soup can water
½ clove garlic
2 stalks celery, cut in pieces
1 tablespoon brown sugar
¼ teaspoon ground ginger
⅛ teaspoon cayenne pepper
1 jar (16 oz.) pickled sliced beets, drained (reserve liquid)
1½ env. unflavored gelatin
¼ cup lemon juice
1 cup dairy sour cream

1. Heat consommé and water to boiling in a saucepan. Stir in garlic, celery, brown sugar, ginger, and cayenne pepper. Remove from heat, cover, and let stand 30 minutes.
2. Meanwhile, soften gelatin in reserved beet liquid in a saucepan. Stir over low heat until gelatin is completely dissolved.
3. Strain the consommé; stir in dissolved gelatin. Chill until the consistency of unbeaten egg white,

stirring occasionally.
4. Put beets and lemon juice into an electric blender container. Cover and blend thoroughly. Add to gelatin mixture along with the sour cream; blend thoroughly.
5. Pour into a shallow 3-quart dish; depth of mixture will be about ¾ inch. Chill until firm.
6. To serve, cut into cubes. Spoon into bouillon cups and garnish each with *dairy sour cream.*
ABOUT 1½ QUARTS SOUP

CREME SENEGALESE
The curry flavor typifies West African cuisine.

2 tablespoons butter or margarine	2 qts. chicken broth, cooled
2 stalks celery, finely chopped	½ cup finely cut fresh pineapple
2 tablespoons grated onion	1 canned pineapple slice, finely cut
1 to 2 tablespoons curry powder	1½ cups finely diced cooked chicken
2 tablespoons flour	2 cups cream

1. Heat butter in a large saucepan. Add celery and onion; cover and cook until celery is tender, stirring occasionally; remove from heat.
2. Blend curry powder and flour in a bowl; slowly add 1 cup of the chicken broth, stirring until smooth after each addition.
3. Adding gradually and stirring constantly, pour into mixture in saucepan. Bring to boiling; continue cooking 5 minutes, stirring constantly.
4. Continue stirring and gradually add remaining broth; simmer, uncovered, 30 minutes, stirring occasionally.
5. Remove from heat; sieve mixture. Stir in the fresh and canned pineapple and the diced chicken. Cool soup.
6. Blend cream into cooled soup; chill thoroughly.
7. Top each serving of chilled soup with *whipped cream.*
ABOUT 2 QUARTS SOUP

JELLIED CHICKEN APPETIZER

1 envelope unflavored gelatin	6 drops red-pepper seasoning
2 cans (13¾ ozs. each) chicken broth	Yellow food coloring
	8 radishes

1. Soften gelatin in 1 cup of the chicken broth in a small saucepan. Heat, stirring constantly, until gelatin dissolves; stir into remaining chicken broth in a medium bowl, then stir in red-pepper seasoning and several drops food coloring to tint bright yellow. Chill several hours, or overnight, until softly set.
2. When ready to serve, spoon into 8 small soup cups or parfait glasses; garnish each serving with a radish which has been cut into a rose shape. Serve with crisp wheat wafers if you like.
8 SERVINGS

CUCUMBER SOUP, DANISH STYLE

2 medium cucumbers, pared	3 cups chicken broth
2 tablespoons butter	1 medium cucumber, pared and grated (discard seeds)
1 medium leek, sliced	1 cup chilled light cream
2 bay leaves	
1 tablespoon flour	Juice of ½ lemon
1 teaspoon salt	

1. Slice 2 cucumbers; cook slowly in butter with the leek and bay leaves until tender but not brown. Stir in flour and salt. Heat until bubbly.
2. Stir in the broth. Simmer 20 to 30 minutes. Press mixture through a sieve and chill.
3. Add grated cucumber, cream, lemon juice, and a bit of *chopped fresh dill.* Correct seasoning.
4. Serve in chilled cups with a dollop of *dairy sour cream* on top of each.
6 SERVINGS

VICHYSSOISE
From the quaint, colonial Lord Jeffery Inn at Amherst, Massachusetts, comes this version of leek and potato soup.

4 to 6 leeks	1 cup light cream
3 medium-sized (1 lb.) potatoes, thinly sliced	1 cup chilled heavy cream
4 cups chicken broth (dissolve 6 chicken bouillon cubes in 4 cups boiling water)	Snipped chives

1. Finely slice the white part and about an inch of the green part of each leek to measure about 1 cup.
2. Cover; simmer the leeks and potatoes in broth until very soft, about 40 minutes.
3. Sieve the cooked vegetables or blend until smooth in electric blender. Mix in the light cream; chill thoroughly.
4. Just before serving, stir in heavy cream. Garnish with chives.
ABOUT 2 QUARTS SOUP

Chapter 3
BREADS—Yeast, Quick & the Kind You Buy

Bread and life, home, and hospitality are inextricably associated in the human imagination and experience. As old as history, breadmaking was one of the first culinary arts practiced—and at a time when home itself was little more than a few flat stones arranged round a fire. Now most of the peoples of the earth have breads characteristically their own.

In our country we have no single traditional bread. We have, instead, welcomed the traditions of all the peoples who have come here and made them our own.

Made with or without leavening, bread appears in a hundred different delightful guises—as soft loaves and crusty loaves, holiday breads and coffee cakes, waffles, griddlecakes, popovers, muffins and doughnuts, and in other forms too numerous to mention.

HELPFUL HINTS ABOUT BREADS

- To glaze tops of fancy breads and rolls brush before baking with slightly beaten egg white mixed with 1 tablespoon milk or water; or egg yolk slightly beaten with a little milk or water.
- To slice newly baked bread, cut with a hot knife.
- To butter bread for thin sandwiches, spread end of loaf with softened butter, then cut off a slice as thin as possible. Repeat buttering and slicing.
- To freshen rolls, place them in a heavy paper bag. Twist top of bag and place in a 400°F oven 10 to 15 minutes. (Or wrap securely in aluminum foil.)
- Use a 1-quart glass measuring cup for mixing pancake and waffle batters, muffin and quick-bread batters. Start by measuring the liquid ingredients into the cup; mix well and beat in the combined dry ingredients. Now the batter is in a "pouring" container ready to pour onto waffle baker, griddle, or into a baking pan.
- When making baking powder biscuits, roll dough or pat to ¼-inch thickness; then fold one half of dough over the other half. Then cut out biscuit rounds. (The hot baked biscuits will split open easily for spreading with butter or margarine.)
- To prepare crumbs from dry bread, force through the fine blade of food chopper or place dry bread in a small plastic bag and crush with a rolling pin. Crush in an electric blender, if available. If using the food chopper, tie a paper bag onto end of food chopper to keep crumbs from scattering.
- Use a slotted pancake turner to transfer uncooked cut doughnuts from pastry canvas to hot fat. Fry only as many doughnuts at one time as will float uncrowded one layer deep in the fat. Drain over fat a few seconds on turner, or use a long-handled two-tined fork; put onto absorbent paper.

STORAGE

Store bread in a cool dry place. If a loaf is not consumed in several days, keep it fresh by placing in a moisture-vaporproof bag and storing it in the refrigerator. If you bake or purchase more than one loaf at a time, keep one loaf in the refrigerator and wrap the other loaf in freezer wrap and place it in the freezer. If loaf has been sliced before freezing, remove only the number of slices required for a single meal and thaw at room temperature. Baked rolls and biscuits are stored in a similar manner.

Yeast Loaves

BASIC WHITE BREAD

6½ cups sifted all-purpose flour
3 tablespoons sugar
2 teaspoons salt
1 envelope active dry yeast
1 cup milk
1 cup water
3 tablespoons shortening

1. Mix 2 cups of the flour, sugar, salt, and yeast in a large bowl.
2. Combine milk, water, and shortening in a small saucepan; heat until warm. Very slowly beat into yeast mixture; continue beating 2 minutes, scraping side of bowl once or twice. Beat in 1 cup flour; beat 2 minutes. By hand, stir in 3 cups more flour to make a stiff dough.
3. Turn out onto a lightly floured board; knead 8 minutes until smooth and elastic, adding only enough of the remaining ½ cup flour to keep dough from sticking. Shape into a ball; place in a greased large bowl; turn to coat all over with shortening; cover. Let rise in a warm place, away from drafts, 1 hour, or until dough is doubled.
4. Punch dough down; knead a few times; divide in half; cover. Let stand 15 minutes.
5. Roll out each half on a lightly floured board to a rectangle, 14x9 inches. Starting at a short end, roll up tightly, jelly-roll fashion. Fold ends of loaves under; place each, seam side down, in a greased baking pan, 8½x4½x2¾ inches, cover. Let rise again 45 minutes, or until doubled.
6. Preheat oven to 400°F.
7. Bake 30 minutes, or until golden and loaves sound hollow when tapped with finger. Loosen around edges with a knife; turn out onto wire racks. Brush tops with melted butter or margarine if you prefer a soft crust; cool completely.   2 LOAVES

WHITE BREAD
(Straight Dough Method)

1 pkg. active dry yeast
¼ cup warm water
1 cup milk, scalded
2 tablespoons sugar
2 tablespoons shortening
1 tablespoon salt
¾ cup cold water
6 cups (about) all-purpose flour

1. Soften yeast in the warm water.
2. In a large bowl combine the scalded milk, sugar, shortening, and salt. Add the cold water and cool until lukewarm. Blend in the yeast.
3. Beat in about 3 cups of the flour gradually until batter is smooth. Then stir in enough remaining flour to form a dough stiff enough to form into a ball. Turn dough onto a lightly floured surface and let rest 5 to 10 minutes.
4. Knead until dough is smooth and satiny, 5 to 10 minutes. Put into a greased deep bowl; turn dough to bring greased surface to top. Cover; let rise in a warm place until doubled, 45 to 60 minutes.
5. Turn onto a lightly floured surface and divide dough into halves. Form each into a smooth ball; cover and let rest 5 to 10 minutes.
6. Shape into loaves and place in 2 greased 9x5x3-inch loaf pans. Cover; let rise again until doubled, 45 to 60 minutes.
7. Bake at 400°F 45 to 50 minutes.   2 LOAVES BREAD

OLD-FASHIONED HERB BREAD
Sage gives this bread its distinctive flavor.

1 pkg. active dry yeast
¼ cup warm water
¾ cup milk, scalded
3 tablespoons butter
3 tablespoons sugar
1½ teaspoons salt
3 to 3½ cups all-purpose flour
1 egg, beaten
¼ teaspoon ground nutmeg
2 to 3 teaspoons crushed sage

1. Soften yeast in the warm water.
2. Blend milk, butter, sugar, and salt thoroughly in a large bowl; cool to warm. Add 1 cup flour and beat thoroughly. Beat in egg, nutmeg, and sage, then the yeast. Mix in enough remaining flour to make a soft (but not sticky) dough.
3. Turn onto a lightly floured surface and knead until smooth and elastic. Put into a greased deep bowl; turn dough to bring greased surface to top. Cover; let rise in a warm place until doubled, 1 hour.
4. Punch down dough and let rest about 10 minutes.
5. Shape dough into a round loaf. Place in a greased 9-inch pie pan and let rise again until doubled, about 45 minutes.
6. Brush lightly with slightly beaten *egg white*. Sprinkle with *caraway seed*.
7. Bake at 400°F 10 minutes; reduce oven temperature to 375°F and bake 20 to 25 minutes, or until bread is well browned.
     ONE 9-INCH ROUND LOAF BREAD

NOTE: If desired, add *1 teaspoon caraway seed* to the dough and top loaf with additional seed.

LUCIA BUNS

5½ cups sifted all-purpose flour
½ cup sugar
½ teaspoon salt
⅛ teaspoon powdered saffron
3 packages active dry yeast
½ cup butter or margarine, softened
1 cup very warm water
2 eggs
Dark raisins

1. Mix 1 cup of the flour, sugar, salt, saffron, and yeast in large bowl of electric mixer; add butter.
2. Beat in water slowly; continue beating, scraping side of bowl, 2 minutes.
3. Beat eggs in a small bowl; measure 1 tablespoonful into a cup and set aside for brushing buns. Beat remainder into yeast mixture with another ¼ cup flour; beat 2 minutes. Stir in 4 cups of the flour to make a stiff dough. Turn out onto a lightly floured board; knead 8 to 10 minutes, or until smooth and elastic, adding only enough of the remaining ¼ cup flour to keep dough from sticking.
4. Divide dough in half, then cut each half into 16 even pieces. Roll each into a 12-inch-long log with palms of hands; coil ends of strips toward center to form an "S." Place on greased cookie sheets.
5. Stir 1 tablespoon water into egg in cup; brush over buns; place a raisin in center of each coil. Cover with foil; freeze until firm, then place in transparent bags; seal, date, and return to freezer. (Plan to use within a month.)
6. When ready to finish buns, place on ungreased cookie sheets; cover with a clean towel. Let stand about 2 hours, or until completely thawed, then let rise in a warm place, away from drafts, 45 minutes, or until doubled.
7. Preheat oven to 350°F.
8. Bake 15 minutes, or until buns are golden and sound hollow when tapped with finger. Remove from cookie sheets to wire racks. Serve warm. 32 BUNS

ANADAMA BREAD

½ cup yellow cornmeal
2 cups boiling water
2 tablespoons shortening
½ cup molasses
1½ teaspoons salt
1 pkg. active dry yeast
½ cup warm water
6 cups all-purpose flour

1. Stirring constantly, add the cornmeal to the boiling water in a large bowl. Stir in the shortening, molasses, and salt. Set aside to cool to lukewarm.
2. Meanwhile, soften yeast in the warm water.
3. Blend 1 cup of the flour into lukewarm cornmeal mixture; beat until very smooth. Mix in yeast. Add about half of the remaining flour and beat until very smooth. Then mix in enough of the remaining flour to make a soft dough.
4. Turn onto a lightly floured surface. Cover and let rest 5 to 10 minutes.
5. Knead dough until satiny and smooth. Form into a ball and put into a greased deep bowl. Turn dough to bring greased surface to top. Cover; let rise in a warm place until doubled, about 1 hour.
6. Punch down dough and turn onto a lightly floured surface. Divide into halves and form into smooth balls. Shape into loaves. Place in 2 greased 9x5x3-inch loaf pans. Cover; let rise again until doubled, about 1 hour.
7. Bake at 375°F 40 to 45 minutes, or until bread tests done. Remove from pans, brush tops with *melted butter or margarine* and cool on wire racks.
2 LOAVES BREAD

GRANNY'S TEXAS BRAN BREAD

1½ cups boiling water
3 tablespoons shortening
3 tablespoons brown sugar
2 tablespoons molasses
2 teaspoons salt
1 cup whole bran
1 pkg. active dry yeast
½ cup warm water
5 to 5½ cups all-purpose flour

1. Pour boiling water over shortening, brown sugar, molasses, salt, and bran in a large bowl. Blend well and set aside to cool to lukewarm.
2. Soften yeast in the warm water.
3. Beat 1 cup flour into bran mixture. Stir yeast into batter until thoroughly blended. Continue beating while gradually adding about half of the remaining flour. Beat vigorously, then mix in enough remaining flour to make a soft (not sticky) dough.
4. Lightly grease top of dough. Cover; let rise in a warm place until doubled, about 2 hours.
5. Turn onto a lightly floured surface and divide into halves. Knead gently until dough is smooth and "springy."
6. Shape dough into loaves. Place in 2 greased 8x4x2-inch loaf pans. Cover; let rise again until almost doubled, about 45 minutes.
7. Bake in a 325°F oven (*not preheated*) 50 to 55

minutes. Remove from oven; turn out of pans onto wire rack and lightly brush loaves with *melted butter.* 2 LOAVES BREAD

RAISIN-OATMEAL BREAD

4 tablespoons butter or margarine
2 cups milk
2 tablespoons sugar
1½ teaspoons salt
2 envelopes active dry yeast
½ cup very warm water
5½ cups sifted all-purpose flour
2 cups quick-cooking rolled oats
1 cup dark raisins

1. Combine butter, milk, sugar, and salt in a small saucepan; heat to scalding; cool to lukewarm.
2. Dissolve yeast in very warm water in a large bowl. (Very warm water should feel comfortably warm when dropped on wrist.) Beat in cooled milk mixture and 2 cups of the flour until smooth. Stir in rolled oats, raisins, and 3¼ cups flour to make a soft dough.
3. Turn out onto a lightly floured board; knead 8 minutes until smooth and elastic, adding only enough of the remaining ¼ cup flour to keep dough from sticking. Shape into a ball; place in a greased large bowl; turn to coat all over with shortening; cover. Let rise in a warm place, away from drafts, 1 hour, or until dough is doubled.
4. Punch dough down; knead a few times; divide in half.
5. Roll out each half on a lightly floured board to a rectangle, 14x9 inches. Starting at a short end, roll up tightly, jelly-roll fashion. Fold ends of loaves under; place each, seam side down, in a greased baking pan, 8½x4½x2¾; cover. Let rise again 40 minutes, or until dough is doubled.
6. Preheat oven to **375°F.**
7. Bake 45 minutes, or until golden and loaves sound hollow when tapped with finger. Loosen around edges with a knife; turn out onto wire racks. Brush tops with melted butter or margarine if you prefer a soft crust; cool completely. 2 LOAVES

JULEKAKE

½ cup milk
½ cup granulated sugar
1 teaspoon salt
½ cup butter or margarine
½ cup mixed candied fruits, finely chopped
½ cup dark raisins
½ cup chopped California walnuts
2 envelopes active dry yeast
½ cup very warm water
3 eggs
5½ cups sifted all-purpose flour
1½ teaspoons ground cardamom
1¾ cups sifted confectioners' powdered sugar
½ teaspoon vanilla
Red and green candied cherries, slivered

1. Combine milk with granulated sugar, salt, and butter in a small saucepan; heat just until butter melts. Cool to lukewarm.
2. Dissolve yeast in very warm water in a large bowl.
3. Beat eggs in a small bowl; measure 2 tablespoons into a cup and set aside for brushing loaves. Beat remaining eggs and milk mixture into yeast mixture, then beat in 2 cups of the flour and cardamom until smooth. Beat in fruits, raisins, and walnuts.
4. Beat in 3 cups flour to make a soft, sticky dough.
5. Turn out onto a lightly floured board; knead until smooth and elastic, adding only enough of the remaining ½ cup flour to prevent sticking. Place in a greased large bowl; turn to coat all over with shortening; cover with a towel. Let rise in a warm place, away from drafts, 1½ hours, or until double.
6. Punch dough down; knead a few times; divide in half. Shape each half into a ball; place several inches apart on a greased large cookie sheet; flatten tops slightly; cover. Let rise again 1½ hours, or until double.
7. Preheat oven to **350°F.**
8. Stir 1 teaspoon water into remaining beaten egg; brush over raised dough.
9. Bake 35 minutes, or until loaves are golden and sound hollow when tapped with finger. Loosen from cookie sheet; remove to wire racks; cool.
10. Blend confectioners' sugar, vanilla, and just enough water to make a medium thin frosting; spread over loaves. Decorate with cut cherries to resemble Christmas trees or holly wreaths. 2 LOAVES

SWEDISH RYE BREAD
(Limpa)

Anise seed, orange peel, molasses, brown sugar, and rye flour all contribute to the exceptional flavor of this bread.

2 pkgs. active dry yeast
½ cup warm water
½ cup packed dark brown sugar
4 teaspoons grated orange peel
¾ teaspoon anise seed
1½ cups hot water

⅓ cup molasses	2½ cups medium rye flour
2 tablespoons butter or margarine	3½ to 4 cups all-purpose flour
1 tablespoon salt	

1. Soften yeast in the warm water.
2. Combine the brown sugar, molasses, butter, salt, orange peel, and anise in a large bowl. Add the hot water and blend. Cool to lukewarm.
3. Beat in 1 cup of the rye flour until smooth. Stir in yeast. Gradually add all of the rye flour, beating vigorously. Mix in enough of the all-purpose flour (2½ to 3 cups) to make a soft dough, beating until the dough comes away from the sides of bowl.
4. Turn onto a lightly floured surface and let rest about 10 minutes.
5. Knead in enough remaining flour to make a smooth elastic dough which does not stick to kneading surface. Form into a ball and put into a greased deep bowl. Turn dough to bring greased surface to top. Cover; let rise in a warm place until doubled.
6. Punch down dough; pull edges into center and turn dough completely over in bowl. Cover; let rise again until almost doubled.
7. Punch down again and turn onto a lightly floured surface. Divide dough into halves and shape into smooth balls. Place on a greased baking sheet sprinkled with cornmeal. Cover; let rise again until doubled, about 30 minutes.
8. Bake at 375°F 25 to 30 minutes. Remove to a wire rack and immediately brush lightly with *milk.* Cool. 2 LOAVES BREAD

NOTE: *2 teaspoons caraway seed may be substituted for orange peel. Decrease anise to ½ teaspoon.*

CHERRY-COCONUT BABKA

2¼ cups sifted all-purpose flour	3 eggs
¾ cup sugar	1 container (3½ ozs.) candied red cherries, chopped (½ cup)
1 envelope active dry yeast	½ cup flaked coconut
½ cup milk	¼ cup water
⅓ cup butter or margarine	2 tablespoons lemon juice

1. Combine ¾ cup of the flour, ¼ cup of the sugar, and yeast in large bowl of electric mixer.
2. Combine milk and butter in a small saucepan; heat until warm. (Butter need not melt.) Very slowly beat into yeast mixture; continue beating for 2 minutes at medium speed, scraping side of bowl once or twice.
3. Add eggs and ½ cup flour; beat 2 minutes to form a thick batter. By hand, beat in remaining 1 cup flour; cover. Let rise in a warm place, away from drafts, 1 hour, or until doubled.
4. Stir cherries and coconut into batter. Spoon into a greased 2-quart tube mold; cover. Let rise again 1 hour, or until doubled.
5. Preheat oven to **350°F**.
6. Bake 40 minutes, or until loaf is golden and a long metal skewer inserted near center comes out clean. Cool in mold on a wire rack 5 minutes; loosen around edges and tube with a knife; turn out onto rack.
7. While loaf cools, combine remaining ½ cup sugar and water in a small saucepan; heat to boiling; simmer 2 minutes. Remove from heat; stir in lemon juice. While hot, brush over warm loaf until all is absorbed. Slice loaf into wedges. Serve warm or cold.

1 EIGHT-INCH ROUND LOAF

SALLY LUNN

This bread, named after an eighteenth century pastry cook, has many variations, some made with yeast and others with baking powder. It can be baked in a loaf or cake pan or in muffin pans and is served warm from the oven with plenty of butter.

1 pkg. active dry yeast	2 tablespoons sugar
¼ cup warm water	¾ teaspoon salt
½ cup milk, scalded	2 cups all-purpose flour
⅔ cup butter or margarine, softened	2 eggs, well beaten

1. Soften yeast in the warm water.
2. Pour scalded milk over butter, sugar, and salt in a large bowl; cool to lukewarm. Add about ½ cup flour and beat until smooth.
3. Stir the yeast into the batter; mix well. Add about half of the remaining flour and beat until very smooth. Add eggs; beat until smooth. Blend in the remaining flour; beat thoroughly at least 5 minutes. Scrape down from sides of bowl. Cover; let rise in a warm place until doubled, about 45 minutes.
4. When doubled, beat again at least 5 minutes.
5. Turn into a greased 1½-quart ring mold or Turk's-head mold. Cover; let rise again until doubled, about 45 minutes.
6. Bake at 350°F 25 to 30 minutes, or until golden brown. Run knife around edge of mold to loosen the loaf and gently remove to wire rack. Serve warm.

1 RING LOAF

Yeast Loaves

SALLY LUNN WITH STRAWBERRIES

1 cup milk, scalded	3 eggs, beaten
½ cup sugar	5 cups all-purpose flour
2 teaspoons salt	½ teaspoon ground nutmeg
½ cup butter or margarine, melted	3 pts. fresh strawberries, sliced and sweetened
1 pkg. active dry yeast	
½ cup warm water	

1. Combine milk, ¼ cup of the sugar, salt, and butter; cool to lukewarm.
2. Soften yeast in the warm water in a large bowl. Blend with the milk mixture and eggs.
3. Gradually beat in the flour until smooth. Cover; let rise in a warm place until doubled, about 1 hour.
4. Stir dough down and turn into a greased and sugared 10-inch tubed pan. Cover; let rise again until doubled, about 30 minutes.
5. Mix remaining ¼ cup sugar with the nutmeg and sprinkle over top of dough.
6. Bake at 400°F about 40 minutes. Remove from oven and cool 5 minutes. Turn out Sally Lunn and serve warm or cooled with the strawberries mounded in the center of the ring. Accompany with a bowl of *whipped cream* or a pitcher of *cream*.

ONE 10-INCH RING LOAF

NOTE: If desired, the strawberries may be left whole and unhulled to be dipped into the cream as they are eaten.

EASTER EGG BREAD

Shaped in the form of a wreath and decorated with colorful Easter eggs, this bread is probably of Italian origin. However, other countries which celebrate Easter also prepare it to add a festive touch to the Easter breakfast or dinner.

2 pkgs. active dry yeast	1½ tablespoons lemon juice
½ cup warm water	¾ cup sugar
1 cup all-purpose flour	1 teaspoon salt
⅓ cup water	2 eggs, well beaten
¾ cup butter or margarine	3¾ to 4¼ cups all-purpose flour
1 tablespoon grated lemon peel	6 colored eggs (uncooked)

1. Soften yeast in the warm water in a bowl. Mix in the 1 cup flour, then the ⅓ cup water. Beat until smooth. Cover; let rise in a warm place until doubled, about 1 hour.
2. Cream butter with lemon peel and juice. Add sugar and salt gradually, beating until fluffy. Add eggs in halves, beating thoroughly after each addition.
3. Add yeast mixture and beat until blended. Add about half of the remaining flour and beat thoroughly. Beat in enough flour to make a soft dough.
4. Knead on floured surface until smooth. Put into a greased deep bowl; turn dough to bring greased surface to top. Cover; let rise in a warm place until doubled.
5. Punch down dough; divide into thirds. Cover; let rest about 10 minutes.
6. With hands, roll and stretch each piece into a roll about 26 inches long and ¾ inch thick. Loosely braid rolls together. On a lightly greased baking sheet or jelly roll pan shape into a ring, pressing ends together. At even intervals, gently spread dough apart and tuck in a colored egg. Cover; let rise again until doubled.
7. Bake at 375°F about 30 minutes. During baking check bread for browning, and when sufficiently browned, cover loosely with aluminum foil.
8. Transfer coffee cake to a wire rack. If desired, spread a *confectioners' sugar icing* over top of warm bread.

1 LARGE WREATH

CANDIED FRUIT COBBLECAKE

5¼ cups sifted all-purpose flour	½ cup butter or margarine
½ cup granulated sugar	2 eggs
1 teaspoon salt	1 cup chopped mixed candied fruits
1 teaspoon ground cinnamon	1 tablespoon butter or margarine, melted
2 envelopes active dry yeast	1 cup sifted confectioners' powdered sugar
¾ cup milk	2 tablespoons orange juice
½ cup water	

1. Mix 2 cups of the flour, granulated sugar, salt, cinnamon, and yeast in large bowl of electric mixer.
2. Combine milk, water, and the ½ cup butter in a small saucepan; heat until warm. Very slowly beat into yeast mixture; continue beating for 2 minutes at medium speed, scraping side of bowl once or twice.
3. Beat in eggs and 1 cup flour; beat 2 minutes. By hand, beat in candied fruits and 2 cups flour until completely blended.
4. Sprinkle remaining ¼ cup flour onto a pastry board; turn dough out onto board. Knead 8 to 10 min-

utes, or until smooth and elastic. Shape into a ball; place in a greased large bowl; turn to coat all over with shortening; cover. Let rise in a warm place, away from drafts, 1½ hours, or until doubled.
5. Punch dough down; knead a few times; divide in half. With palms of hands, roll each half on a lightly floured board to an even log 9 inches long. Cut into 1-inch slices; shape each into a ball. Place balls in 3 rows of 3 each in 2 greased baking pans, 8x8x2 inches; cover. Let rise again 1¼ hours, or until doubled.
6. Preheat oven to 375°F. Brush melted butter over raised dough.
7. Bake 30 minutes, or until cakes are golden and sound hollow when tapped with finger. Cool in pans on wire racks 10 minutes; turn out onto racks.
8. Combine confectioners' sugar and orange juice in a small bowl; beat until smooth. Drizzle over coffee cakes. Break apart into rolls. Serve warm or cold.

8 TO 10 SERVINGS

(Dough will not rise.)
4. When ready to roll out, divide dough into halves. On a lightly floured surface, roll each to an 18x12-inch rectangle. Brush with half of the melted butter; sprinkle evenly with a mixture of the sugar, cinnamon, and raisins. Roll lengthwise as for a jelly roll.
5. Put each roll, seam edge down, onto an ungreased baking sheet or jelly roll pan, form into a ring and press ends together to seal. (Or each ring may be placed in a 10-inch tubed springform pan.) Cover lightly; let rise in a warm place until doubled, about 1½ hours.
6. Bake at 375°F 30 minutes, or until well browned. Remove from oven and cool slightly on wire rack. If desired, rings may be drizzled with *Glaze, below.* Serve warm. 2 COFFEE RINGS

GLAZE: Combine ¾ *cup confectioners' sugar* and ½ *teaspoon vanilla extract.* Stir in *1 to 1½ tablespoons milk or cream* until of spreading consistency.

TEA RINGS: Follow recipe for Coffee Rings. After shaping into rings, snip each ring at 2-inch intervals almost to center and turn each section on its side.

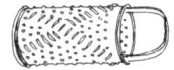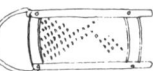

Yeast Sweet Breads & Coffee Cakes

COFFEE RINGS

1 pkg. active dry yeast
¼ cup warm water
¾ cup butter
¾ cup sugar
1 teaspoon salt
3 eggs, well beaten
5¾ to 6 cups all-purpose flour
¼ cup milk, scalded and cooled to lukewarm
1 cup dairy sour cream
¼ cup melted butter
1 cup sugar
1 tablespoon ground cinnamon
1 cup raisins

1. Soften yeast in the warm water.
2. Beat the butter with the ¾ cup sugar and salt until thoroughly blended. Add the eggs, beating constantly until light and fluffy. Beat in 2 cups of the flour until smooth. Blend in yeast and milk, then sour cream. Beat in enough of the remaining flour to make a soft dough.
3. Turn onto a lightly floured surface and knead until smooth and elastic. Form into a ball and put into a greased deep bowl; turn dough to bring greased surface to top. Cover with moisture-vaporproof material; place in refrigerator overnight.

DANISH PASTRY COFFEE CAKE

1 pkg. active dry yeast
¼ cup warm water
1 cup butter or margarine
2 tablespoons sugar
3 egg yolks, well beaten
1½ teaspoons grated orange peel
1 teaspoon vanilla extract
2¼ cups all-purpose flour
3 egg whites
¾ cup sugar
1 teaspoon ground cinnamon
1 cup finely chopped nuts

1. Soften yeast in the warm water.
2. Cream butter with 2 tablespoons sugar. Beat in the yeast, beaten egg yolks, grated peel, and extract. Continue beating until well blended.
3. Add the flour, about a fourth at a time, beating until blended after each addition. Divide the dough into thirds; wrap separately in moisture-vaporproof material and refrigerate several hours or overnight.
4. When ready to roll out the pastry, prepare the filling. Beat egg whites until frothy; add a mixture of the sugar and cinnamon, 2 tablespoons at a time, beating well after each addition. Continue beating until stiff peaks are formed. Fold in the nuts.
5. Removing one portion of pastry from refrigera-

Yeast Sweet Breads & Coffee Cakes

tor at a time, roll out on floured surface into a 16x12-inch rectangle. Spread a third of the filling evenly over rectangle, then roll up starting wit long side.
6. Repeat twice using remaining pastry and place rolls several inches apart in a jelly roll pan or on a baking sheet. Cover lightly and set aside at room temperature 1 hour. (Dough will rise only slightly.)
7. Bake at 350°F 25 to 30 minutes, or until lightly browned. Let cool in pan on wire rack. While still warm, glaze with a *confectioners' sugar icing*, if desired. 3 COFFEE CAKES

CINNAMON PINWHEEL LOAF

1/3 cup shortening	3¾ cups sifted all-purpose flour
Milk	
1/3 cup granulated sugar (for dough)	3 tablespoons granulated sugar (for filling)
1 teaspoon salt	1 teaspoon ground cinnamon
1 envelope active dry yeast	½ cup sifted confectioners' powdered sugar
¼ cup very warm water	
1 egg	½ teaspoon vanilla

1. Combine shortening, ¾ cut milk, the ⅓ cup sugar, and salt in a small saucepan; heat to scalding; cool to lukewarm.
2. Dissolve yeast in very warm water in a large bowl. Beat in egg, cooled milk mixture, and 2 cups flour until smooth. Beat in 1½ cups more flour to make a stiff dough.
3. Turn out onto a lightly floured board; knead 5 minutes until smooth and elastic, adding only enough of the remaining ¼ cup flour to keep dough from sticking. Shape into a ball; place in a greased large bowl; turn to coat all over with shortening; cover. Let rise in a warm place, away from drafts, 1 hour, or until dough is doubled. .
4. Punch dough down; knead a few times. Roll out on a lightly floured board to a rectangle, 16x9 inches.
5. Mix the 3 tablespoons sugar and cinnamon in a cup; sprinkle evenly over rectangle. Starting at a short end, roll up tightly, jelly-roll fashion. Fold ends of loaf under; place, seam side down, in a greased baking pan, 9x5x3 inches; cover. Let rise again 45 minutes, or until doubled.
6. Preheat oven to 375°F.
7. Bake 45 minutes, or until golden and loaf sounds hollow when tapped with finger. Loosen around edges with a knife; turn out onto a wire rack; cool.
8. Blend confectioners' sugar, vanilla, and 1 to 2 teaspoons milk in a cup to make a smooth, thin glaze; drizzle over loaf. Let stand until glaze is firm. 1 LOAF

HONEY BUN COFFEE RING

½ recipe for Yeast Rolls, *page 44*	½ cup honey
	1 tablespoon melted butter or margarine
½ cup melted butter or margarine	¼ cup firmly packed brown sugar
½ cup finely chopped nuts	2 tablespoons flour
6 tablespoons seedless raisins	1 teaspoon ground cinnamon

1. Follow recipe for Yeast Rolls to shaping process.
2. Divide into small pieces about the size of walnuts and shape into balls. First coat with the ½ cup melted butter, then roll in nuts. Place one layer of balls about ¼ inch apart in well-greased 9-inch tubed pan. Sprinkle with 3 tablespoons of the raisins. Arrange second layer on top of first. Sprinkle with remaining raisins. Press down slightly.
3. Combine honey and 1 tablespoon melted butter with remaining ingredients; spoon over dough.
4. Cover; let rise in a warm place 45 to 60 minutes, or until doubled.
5. Bake at 375°F 35 to 40 minutes. Allow to stand in pan 5 minutes before removing. Cover with a wire rack. Invert and remove pan. Turn right-side up immediately. ONE 9-INCH TUBED COFFEE CAKE

RAISIN-NUT LOAF

3 cups sifted all-purpose flour	1½ teaspoons ground cinnamon
¾ cup sugar	1 cup dark raisins
1 teaspoon salt	1 cup finely chopped filberts
1½ teaspoons baking soda	
1½ teaspoons baking powder	1 egg
	1½ cups sour milk
	¼ cup salad oil

1. Preheat oven to 350°F.
2. Sift flour, sugar, salt, baking soda, baking powder, and cinnamon into a large bowl; stir in raisins and filberts.
3. Beat egg in a small bowl: stir in sour milk and salad oil. Add all at once to flour mixture; stir just until mixture is evenly moist. Spoon into a greased

baking pan, 9x5x3 inches.

4. Bake 1 hour, or until a wooden pick inserted into center comes out clean. Cool in pan on a wire rack 10 minutes. Loosen loaf around edges with a knife; turn out onto rack; cool completely.

5. For easy, neat slicing, wrap loaf in foil and store overnight.   1 LOAF

NORWEGIAN CHRISTMAS BREAD
(Julekake)

1 cup milk, scalded
½ cup butter, softened
½ cup sugar
1 teaspoon salt
1 teaspoon ground cardamom
2 pkgs. active dry yeast
½ cup warm water
½ cup currants
½ cup coarsely chopped almonds
½ cup mixed candied fruit
1 tablespoon flour
4½ to 5 cups all-purpose flour
1 egg, beaten
1 tablespoon sugar
⅛ teaspoon ground cinnamon

1. Pour scalded milk over butter, ½ cup sugar, salt, and cardamom in a bowl. Stir until butter is melted. Cool to lukewarm.
2. Soften yeast in the warm water.
3. Toss currants, almonds, and mixed fruit with the 1 tablespoon flour; set aside.
4. Add about 2 cups of the flour to milk mixture and beat until smooth. Stir in yeast, egg, and then the fruit-nut mixture. Beat in enough of the remaining flour to make a soft dough.
5. Turn onto a lightly floured surface. Knead dough until smooth and elastic, 5 to 8 minutes. Form into a ball and place in a greased deep bowl. Turn dough to bring greased surface to top. Cover; let rise in a warm place until doubled, about 1½ hours.
6. Punch down dough and turn onto a lightly floured surface. Divide dough into halves and shape each into a round loaf. Place on a greased baking sheet. Cover; let rise again until doubled, about 1 hour.
7. Bake at 350°F 25 minutes. Brush tops with *softened butter* and sprinkle with a mixture of the sugar and cinnamon. Remove to wire racks to cool.
    2 LOAVES BREAD

KULICH

This traditional Russian Easter bread is baked in mushroom or mosque-like shapes.

1 pkg. active dry yeast
¼ cup warm water
¼ cup butter or margarine, softened
¼ cup sugar
1 teaspoon salt
¼ cup milk, scalded
2¼ cups all-purpose flour
1 egg, slightly beaten
½ teaspoon vanilla extract
¼ teaspoon ground cardamom
¼ cup chopped candied red cherries
¼ cup chopped candied green cherries
2 tablespoons chopped toasted almonds
¾ cup confectioners' sugar
4 teaspoons milk

1. Soften yeast in the warm water.
2. Put butter, sugar, and salt into a bowl; add the scalded milk and stir until butter is melted. Cool to lukewarm.
3. Beat ½ cup of the flour into milk mixture. Stir in the yeast, then beat in egg, extract, and cardamom. Add remaining flour gradually, beating thoroughly after each addition. Cover; let rise in a warm place until doubled, 1½ to 2 hours.
4. Punch down dough; let rise again until almost doubled, 30 to 45 minutes.
5. Turn dough onto a lightly floured surface. Distribute cherries and almonds evenly over dough; knead about 15 times. Shape dough into a ball and put into a well-greased 1-pound coffee can. Cover; let rise again until doubled, 30 to 40 minutes. Place can on a baking sheet, if desired.
6. Bake at 350°F 45 minutes, or until bread is well browned. Cool in can 10 to 15 minutes, then turn out onto a wire rack to cool completely.
7. Blend the confectioners' sugar and milk until smooth. Spoon icing over Kulich and allow it to drip down sides. Garnish top with a whole *candied red cherry*.
    1 LOAF KULICH

STOLLEN

A German sweet bread shaped in long loaves, this recipe is rich with almonds, candied citron, raisins, and currants.

1⅓ cups toasted blanched almonds, chopped
1 cup golden raisins
½ cup currants
1 cup (about 7 oz.) chopped citron
1 tablespoon grated lemon peel
2 teaspoons salt
1 cup all-purpose flour
1 teaspoon ground nutmeg
6 to 7 cups all-purpose flour
3 eggs, well beaten
Melted butter

2 pkgs. active dry yeast
½ cup warm water
1 cup milk, scalded
1 cup sugar
1 cup butter, softened
1½ cups confectioners' sugar
¾ teaspoon vanilla extract
2 to 3 tablespoons milk or cream

1. Reserve ⅓ cup of the almonds for topping. Mix the remaining 1 cup almonds with the raisins, currants, citron, and lemon peel; set aside.
2. Soften yeast in the warm water.
3. Pour scalded milk over sugar, butter, and salt in a large bowl. Stir until butter is melted. Cool to lukewarm.
4. Blend in a mixture of the 1 cup flour and the nutmeg; beat until smooth. Stir in yeast.
5. Add about half of the remaining flour and beat until very smooth. Add beaten eggs in thirds, beating well after each addition. Mix in the reserved fruit-nut mixture. Mix in enough of the remaining flour to make a soft dough.
6. Turn dough onto a lightly floured surface; cover and let rest 5 to 10 minutes.
7. Knead until smooth and elastic. Form into a ball and put into a greased deep bowl; turn dough to bring greased surface to top. Cover; let rise in a warm place until doubled, about 2½ hours.
8. Punch down dough; pull edges to center and turn dough completely over in bowl. Cover; let rise again until nearly doubled, about 1½ hours.
9. Punch down dough and turn onto a lightly floured surface. Divide into halves and shape into smooth balls. Shape each ball into an oval 13 inches long and about 1 inch thick. With rolling pin, flatten and press one lengthwise half of oval about ½ inch thick. Turn unflattened half of dough over flattened half; lightly press edges together. Press the fold down firmly with palm of hand; this helps to prevent dough from springing open during rising.
10. Place each stollen on a lightly greased baking sheet. Brush tops with melted butter. Cover; let rise in a warm place until doubled, about 1½ hours.
11. Bake at 325°F about 30 minutes, or until light golden brown.
12. Meanwhile, blend confectioners' sugar, extract, and enough milk to make a thin frosting.
13. Remove Stollen to wire racks. Immediately spread frosting over tops and sprinkle with reserved almonds.

2 LARGE STOLLEN

Yeast Dinner Rolls

YEAST ROLLS

2 pkgs. active dry yeast
½ cup warm water
2 cups milk, scalded
½ cup sugar
6 tablespoons shortening
2 teaspoons salt
6 to 7 cups all-purpose flour
2 eggs, well beaten
Melted butter or margarine

1. Soften yeast in the warm water.
2. Pour hot milk over sugar, shortening, and salt in a large bowl. Cool to lukewarm.
3. Blend in 1 cup flour and beat until smooth. Stir in yeast. Add about half of remaining flour and beat until very smooth. Beat in the eggs. Beat in enough remaining flour to make a soft dough.
4. Turn dough onto a lightly floured surface; cover and let rest 5 to 10 minutes.
5. Knead dough until smooth and elastic. Form into a ball and put into a greased deep bowl; turn dough to bring greased surface to top. Cover; let rise in warm place until doubled, about 1 hour.
6. Punch down dough; pull edges to center and turn completely over in bowl. Cover; let rise again until almost doubled, about 45 minutes.
7. Again punch down the dough and turn onto a lightly floured surface.
8. Follow suggestions for shaping rolls, using amount needed for a single baking. Place rolls about 1 inch apart on lightly greased baking sheets or as directed. Brush tops with melted butter. Cover; let rise again until rolls are light, 15 to 25 minutes.
9. Bake at 425°F 15 to 20 minutes.

ABOUT 5 DOZEN ROLLS

NOTE: This dough may be kept 3 days in the refrigerator. Grease top of dough and cover. Punch down occasionally as it rises. Remove amount needed for a single baking and return remainder to refrigerator. When ready to use, shape rolls and let stand at room temperature for 1 hour, or until light.

BUTTERY YEAST ROLLS

¾ cup butter or margarine, softened
1 cup boiling water
2 teaspoons salt
½ cup sugar
2 pkgs. active dry yeast
½ cup warm water
2 eggs, beaten
¾ cup icy cold water
6½ to 7½ cups all-purpose flour

1. Mix butter, boiling water, salt, and sugar in a large bowl until thoroughly blended. Cool to warm.
2. Soften yeast in the warm water. Blend in the eggs and cold water. Beat into warm mixture in large bowl. Add 3 cups flour, ½ cup at a time, beating vigorously after each addition until batter is smooth. Mix in enough remaining flour to make a soft dough that does not stick to sides of bowl.
3. Turn dough onto a lightly floured surface; let rest 5 to 10 minutes.
4. Knead until satiny and smooth. Form into a ball and put into a greased deep bowl; turn dough to bring greased surface to top. Cover tightly and refrigerate overnight or for several days.
5. Remove dough and punch down. Brush top with *oil*. Cover; let rise in a warm place until doubled. (This can take from 1 to 2½ hours.)
6. Shape as desired. Place rolls on greased baking sheets and let rise again until light.
7. Bake at 425° to 450°F 12 to 18 minutes. (Temperature and timing depend on the size of rolls.)   5 TO 6 DOZEN ROLLS

CRESCENT ROLLS
(Croissants)
These flaky morsels will be recognized by any traveler to France as the traditional breakfast roll served with coffee—a duo familiarly known as the continental breakfast.

1 pkg. active dry yeast	1 cup milk, scalded
¼ cup warm water	2½ cups all-purpose flour
1 tablespoon sugar	
¾ teaspoon salt	1 cup butter

1. Soften yeast in the warm water.
2. Combine the sugar, salt, and scalded milk in a large bowl; stir until sugar is dissolved. Cool to lukewarm.
3. Beat in ½ cup of the flour. Stir in the yeast, then beat in remaining flour. Turn dough onto a lightly floured surface and let rest 5 to 10 minutes.
4. Knead until dough is smooth and elastic. Form into a ball and put into a greased deep bowl. Turn dough to bring greased surface to top. Cover; let rise in a warm place until doubled, about 1 hour.
5. When doubled, chill dough 2 hours.
6. Cream butter until softened. Turn chilled dough onto a lightly floured surface; roll into a ¼ inch thick rectangle. Spread surface with ¼ cup creamed butter and fold dough from each end over center, making three layers. Turn a quarter of the way around. Repeat rolling, spreading with butter, folding and turning three more times. Chill dough 2 hours or longer.
7. Divide dough into halves. Roll each half on a lightly floured surface into a round, ¼ inch thick. Cut each round into 12 wedge-shaped pieces. Roll up each piece beginning at outer edge.

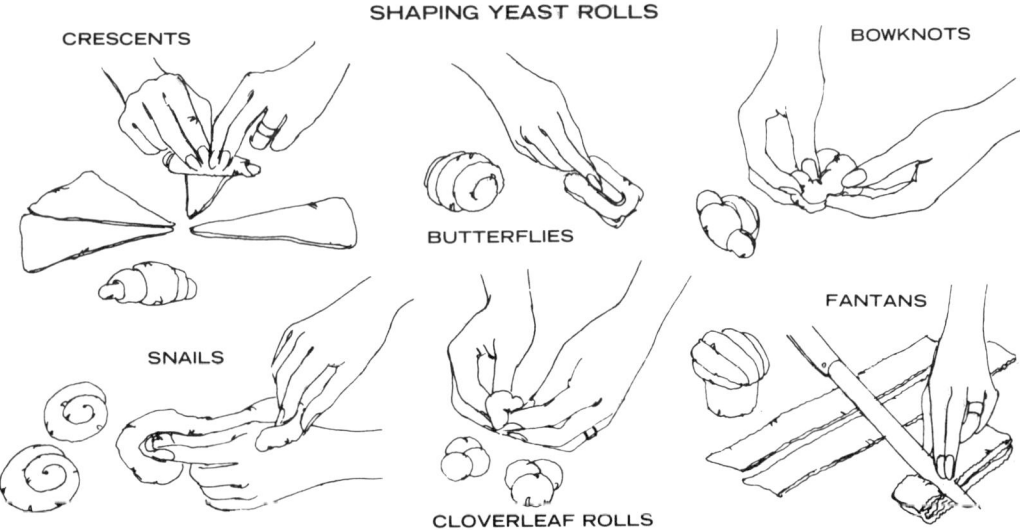

SHAPING YEAST ROLLS

CRESCENTS — BUTTERFLIES — BOWKNOTS — SNAILS — CLOVERLEAF ROLLS — FANTANS

Yeast Dinner Rolls

Place with points underneath on baking sheets covered with brown paper. Curve into crescents. Chill 20 minutes. Brush tops lightly with *cream*.
8. Bake at 400°F 15 minutes; reduce oven temperature to 350°F and continue baking 15 minutes longer, or until golden brown.   2 DOZEN ROLLS

BUTTER SEMMELS

1 pkg. active dry yeast	1½ teaspoons salt
¼ cup warm water	2 cups milk, scalded
½ cup mashed potato (unseasoned)	8 to 8½ cups all-purpose flour
½ cup sugar	2 eggs
½ cup butter	Melted butter
½ cup sugar	Sesame or poppy seed

1. Soften yeast in the warm water. Mix in the mashed potato and ½ cup sugar. Cover; let rise in a warm place until doubled, about 1½ hours.
2. Put butter, ½ cup sugar, and the salt into a bowl. Add scalded milk and stir until butter is melted; cool.
3. Add 1 cup of the flour and beat until smooth. Beat in the eggs, one at a time, then the yeast mixture. Add remaining flour gradually, beating in enough to form a soft dough.
4. Turn onto a lightly floured surface and knead until smooth. Put into a greased deep bowl; turn dough to bring greased surface to top. Cover; let rise in a warm place until doubled, about 1½ hours.
5. Punch down dough. Using about a fourth of the dough at a time, put onto a lightly floured surface and shape as desired into braids, snails, crescents, or twists. (To shape into braids, roll a portion of dough ¼ inch thick; cut into 3x¾-inch strips. With hands, roll and stretch each strip; braid three strips together, tuck ends under, and place on greased baking sheet.)
6. Brush with melted butter and sprinkle with sesame or poppy seed. Cover; let rise again until doubled, about 1 hour.
7. Bake at 400°F 8 minutes, or until delicately browned.   ABOUT 6 DOZEN ROLLS

HERBED PARMESAN ROLLS

2 pkgs. active dry yeast	2 eggs, slightly beaten
1 cup warm water	1 cup grated Parmesan cheese
½ cup butter or margarine	½ teaspoon marjoram, crushed
¼ cup sugar	½ teaspoon oregano, crushed
2½ teaspoons salt	
2 cups milk, scalded	
7 to 7½ cups all-purpose flour	½ teaspoon rosemary, crushed

1. Soften yeast in the warm water.
2. Put butter, sugar, and salt into a large bowl; pour the scalded milk over all and stir until butter is melted. Beat in about 1 cup of the flour. Stir in yeast.
3. Gradually add about one half of the remaining flour, beating until smooth. Beat in eggs. Mix in a blend of cheese, marjoram, oregano, and rosemary.
4. Gradually add enough remaining flour to make a stiff dough, beating until smooth and dough comes away from sides of bowl.
5. Turn dough onto a lightly floured surface and let rest about 10 minutes.
6. Knead, adding more flour if dough seems too sticky, until satiny smooth and small blisters appear under the surface of dough. Form into a ball and put into a greased deep bowl. Turn dough to bring greased surface to top. Cover; let rise in a warm place until doubled.
7. Punch down dough; turn onto a lightly floured surface. Shape as desired (see *Suggestions for Shaping Rolls, page 45*). Cover; let rise again until doubled.
8. Bake at 425°F 10 to 12 minutes. Remove to wire racks, brush tops lightly with *melted butter or margarine*, and cool.   ABOUT 5 DOZEN ROLLS

NOTE: The dough may be divided to yield both rolls and 9x5x3-inch loaves of bread. Bake bread at 375°F 30 to 40 minutes.

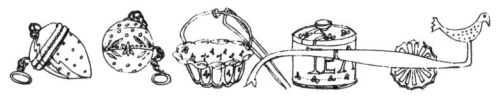

SESAME STICKS

1 package refrigerated crescent rolls	1 egg Sesame seeds

1. Preheat oven to 375°F.
2. Separate rolls into 4 rectangles; pinch together at diagonal perforations.
3. Roll each to a 10-inch-long rectangle on a lightly

floured board. Starting at a long side, roll up tightly, jelly-roll fashion. Cut in half; place, seam side down, on a large cookie sheet.
4. Beat egg in a small bowl; brush over shaped dough; sprinkle sesame seeds on each.
5. Bake 12 minutes, or until sticks are golden. Remove from cookie sheet to a wire rack. Serve warm.

8 STICKS

Yeast Sweet Rolls & Doughnuts

SWEET-TOOTH BREAKFAST ROLLS
Follow recipe for *Yeast Rolls, page 44* Use all of dough or divide as needed. Try any of the given sweet fillings or toppings in one of the following ways: 1) Spread a filling on buttered crescents before rolling up. 2) Brush snails or large rolls with melted butter or margarine and spread with topping before baking. 3) Glaze or frost plain baked rolls and top with nuts. 4) Put a spoonful of filling in center of 4-inch squares of ½-inch thick dough. Then fold in corners, press together and brush tops with melted butter or margarine. 5) Into bottom of greased muffin-pan well put ½ teaspoon butter or margarine and cover with filling and unbaked roll. Bake at 350°F 25 to 30 minutes. After baking, invert and allow to stand 5 minutes. Lift off pan.

Fillings
The amount of spread or filling needed will depend upon variation used and the number of rolls prepared.

Pineapple Spread: Mix in a saucepan ¼ *cup packed brown sugar, 1 tablespoon cornstarch,* and ¼ *teaspoon salt.* Blend in *1 can (8½ ounces) crushed pineapple* and syrup. Bring rapidly to boiling, stirring constantly, and cook 2 minutes, or until thickened. Blend in *1 teaspoon butter or margarine.* Cool before spreading on unbaked rolls.

1 CUP SPREAD

Orange Cube: Into each unbaked roll press a small *sugar cube* which has been dipped in *orange or lemon juice.* Sprinkle with *grated peel.*

Marmalade Spread: Spread *marmalade or jam* on baked or unbaked rolls.

Apricot Spread: Put through a sieve or food mill *1 cup drained cooked apricots.* Add ¼ *cup sugar* and ¼ *teaspoon ground nutmeg;* mix well.

1 CUP SPREAD

Almond Filling: Blend ⅔ *cup finely chopped blanched almonds,* ¼ *cup confectioners' sugar,* and *1 slightly beaten egg white.* Spread on unbaked dough and roll as for a jelly roll.

1 CUP FILLING

DANISH PASTRY
"Practice makes perfect" is a good adage to remember when preparing Danish pastry. Unrivaled as accompaniments for morning or afternoon coffee, Danish pastries — flaky, rich, and delicious — well worth the time spent in perfecting one's techniques.

1½ pkgs. (1½ tablespoons) active dry yeast
½ cup warm water
¾ cup milk, scalded and cooled to lukewarm
2 eggs, beaten
¼ cup sugar
½ teaspoon salt
4 cups all-purpose flour
1⅓ cups firm butter
⅓ cup all-purpose flour
Vanilla Cream Filling, See below
Almond Paste Filling, page 48

1. Soften yeast in the warm water in a large bowl.
2. Stir the milk, eggs, sugar, and salt into the yeast. Add the 4 cups flour in fourths, beating until batter is smooth after each addition.
3. Using a pastry blender, cut butter into the ⅓ cup flour until mixture is well blended; set aside.
4. Turn dough onto a lightly floured surface; roll into a 14-inch square. Spread butter-flour mixture evenly over half of dough, leaving a 2-inch border.
5. Fold dough in half and roll about ¼-inch thick. Fold in thirds and roll out; repeat this procedure 3 times. Wrap in moisture-vaporproof material and refrigerate for 30 minutes.
6. Meanwhile, prepare desired filling.
7. Remove dough from refrigerator; working quickly, roll out dough into a 20-inch square. Shape as desired (see *Shapes, below*).
8. Place on ungreased baking sheets and let rise in a warm place about 15 minutes. Brush plain tops with *beaten egg.*
9. Bake at 450°F 6 to 10 minutes, or until golden brown. Immediately remove from baking sheets to wire racks. Serve warm.

20 TO 20 FILLED PASTRIES

VANILLA CREAM FILLING: Beat *2 egg yolks* slightly in the top of a double boiler. Stir in *1 cup milk* and a mixture of *2 tablespoons flour* and *2 tablespoons sugar*. Cook over simmering water, stirring constantly until thick. Cool, stirring occasionally. Blend in *1 tablespoon vanilla extract*.

ALMOND PASTE FILLING: Combine ⅓ *pound ground almonds* and ½ *cup sugar*. Gradually add *1 slightly beaten egg*, mixing until smooth.

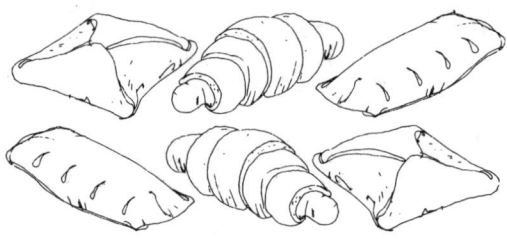

Shapes

Combs: Cut dough into 4 equal strips. On each of the strips, place about a fourth of the filling lengthwise down the center. Bring sides together at center. Coat each 20-inch strip on both sides with a mixture of 6 tablespoons finely chopped almonds and 2 tablespoons sugar. Cut each strip into five 4-inch pieces and make 4 cuts on one side of each piece about a third of the way across. Place, folded side down, on baking sheet.

Crescents: Cut dough into 4 equal strips. Cut each of the strips into 7 triangles. Spread some filling on each triangle, roll up beginning at base, curve ends slightly, and place on baking sheet with point underneath.

Envelopes: Cut dough into 4-inch squares. Spread center of each with about 1 tablespoon filling. Fold corners toward center and press edges to seal.

SEMLOR

A Shrove Tuesday Scandinavian specialty, there will be demands from your family to make these delicious almond buns at any time of the year.

1 pkg. active dry yeast	1 egg
¼ cup warm water	3 to 3¼ cups all-purpose flour
½ cup butter	
¼ teaspoon almond extract	¾ teaspoon salt
½ teaspoon vanilla extract	½ cup heavy cream
	¼ cup water
¼ cup sugar	½ cup (4 oz.) almond paste
2 tablespoons ground blanched almonds	1 tablespoon heavy cream

1. Soften yeast in the warm water.
2. Cream butter with the extracts until softened; add the sugar and almonds and beat thoroughly. Add the egg and beat until fluffy.
3. Blend in 1 cup of the flour and the salt, then the ½ cup cream and the water; beat vigorously until smooth.
4. Stir the yeast into the batter. Beat in enough remaining flour to make a soft (not sticky) dough.
5. Turn dough onto a lightly floured surface; cover and let rest 5 to 10 minutes.
6. Knead until satiny and elastic. Form into a ball and put into a greased bowl; turn dough to bring greased surface to top. Cover; let rise in a warm place until doubled, about 1 hour.
7. Meanwhile, mix almond paste with 1 tablespoon cream and blend until paste is slightly softened; set aside.
8. Punch down dough. Turn out and divide into 12 equal portions (or 18 portions for medium-sized buns). Shape each into a ball and flatten slightly. Place 1 very generous teaspoonful of the almond paste in center (slightly less for smaller buns), bring dough up over filling and seal in filling.
9. Place balls 2 inches apart on greased baking sheet. Cover; let rise again until light, 35 to 45 minutes.
10. Brush tops of buns lightly with *beaten egg*.
11. Bake at 400°F 12 to 15 minutes. Serve warm or cooled.   1 DOZEN LARGE (OR 1½ DOZEN MEDIUM-SIZED) SEMLOR

HOT CROSS BUNS: Follow recipe for Semlor, preparing the dough only. Omit the extracts and almonds. Cream ¼ *teaspoon ground cinnamon* and a *few grains ground mace* with the butter. Mix ½ *cup currants* and, if desired, *2 tablespoons finely chopped candied citron* into dough before the final addition of flour. Proceed as directed. Shape dough into 20 buns. With lightly greased sharp knife or scissors, cut a *deep* cross in top of each bun. Bake. Prepare *Confectioners' Sugar Icing, below,* **and drizzle into crosses on warm buns.**   20 BUNS

CONFECTIONERS' SUGAR ICING: Blend until smooth ½ *cup plus 2 tablespoons confectioners' sugar, 2 teaspoons water*, and ¼ *teaspoon vanilla extract*.

MINIATURE ORANGE SWEET ROLLS

1 pkg. active dry yeast	2 eggs
1/4 cup warm water	2 tablespoons butter, melted
1 cup milk, scalded	1/2 cup sugar
1/3 cup sugar	3 tablespoons grated orange peel
3/4 teaspoon salt	Orange Glaze, *below*
1/3 cup butter or margarine	Confectioners' Sugar Icing *page 48*
4 to 4 1/2 cups all-purpose flour	

1. Soften yeast in the warm water.
2. Pour hot milk over sugar, salt, and butter in a large bowl and stir until butter is melted; add 1 cup flour and beat thoroughly. Stir in yeast.
3. Add the eggs, one at a time, beating vigorously after each addition.
4. Mix in enough flour to form a soft dough. Turn onto a lightly floured surface; let rest 5 to 10 minutes.
5. Knead dough until satiny and smooth. Put into a greased deep bowl; turn dough to bring greased surface to top. Cover; let rise in a warm place until doubled.
6. Using one half of dough at a time, roll each half on a lightly floured surface into a rectangle 1/4 inch thick. Brush 1 tablespoon of the melted butter over dough.
7. Blend the 1/2 cup sugar and grated peel; sprinkle half of mixture evenly over dough.
8. Beginning with longer side, roll up dough and press edges together; cut into 1-inch slices.
9. Place, cut side up, in greased muffin-pan wells; brush lightly with melted butter. Let rise again until doubled, about 30 minutes.
10. Bake at 375°F for 12 to 15 minutes. Remove rolls to wire racks. While warm, drizzle with Orange Glaze, then with Confectioners' Sugar Icing. ABOUT 5 DOZEN ROLLS

ORANGE GLAZE: Stir together in a saucepan 1/2 cup sugar, 1/4 cup light corn syrup, 1/4 cup hot water, and 1 tablespoon grated orange peel. Bring to boiling and cook 2 minutes, stirring occasionally.

PUMPKIN ROLLS

Here's a unique way and a rewarding one, too, for using a little leftover canned pumpkin.

3/4 cup milk, scalded	1/4 teaspoon ground nutmeg
1/4 cup shortening	1/8 teaspoon ground allspice
1/4 cup sugar	
3/4 teaspoon salt	
3/4 cup canned pumpkin	1/8 teaspoon ground cloves
1 pkg. active dry yeast	1/8 teaspoon ground ginger
1/2 cup warm water	1 egg
3 1/2 to 4 1/2 cups all-purpose flour	
1/2 teaspoon ground cinnamon	

1. Combine scalded milk, shortening, sugar, and salt in a large mixer bowl; stir in the pumpkin. Cool to lukewarm.
2. Soften yeast in the warm water.
3. Blend 1 cup of the flour and the spices thoroughly; add to cooled milk mixture and beat until smooth. Stir in yeast.
4. Beating constantly, add another cup of flour and the egg. Beat until smooth, then mix in enough remaining flour to make a soft, smooth dough. Cover; let rise in a warm place until doubled, about 1 hour.
5. Stir dough down and let rise until doubled.
6. Turn onto a lightly floured surface. Shape dough into 2-inch balls; brush with *melted butter or margarine.* Place 1 ball in each greased 2 1/2-inch muffin-pan well. Cover; let rise again until doubled, about 30 minutes.
7. Bake at 375°F 20 minutes. 2 DOZEN ROLLS

CREOLE DOUGHNUTS
(Beignets)

Here's one of many versions of those famous melt-in-your-mouth morsels served freshly fried in the French quarter of New Orleans, where tourists and natives alike flock each day to enjoy them with cups of New Orleans coffee.

1 pkg. active dry yeast	2 cups milk, scalded
1/4 cup warm water	6 1/2 to 7 cups all-purpose flour
1/2 cup sugar	
1/2 cup cooking or salad oil	2 eggs, well beaten
1 1/2 teaspoons salt	Fat for deep frying heated to 365°F

1. Soften yeast in the warm water.
2. Put sugar, oil, and salt into a large bowl. Immediately pour scalded milk over ingredients in bowl; stir until sugar is dissolved. Cool to lukewarm.
3. Blend in 1 cup flour, beating until smooth. Stir in yeast. Add about half of the remaining flour to yeast mixture and beat until very smooth. Beat in the eggs.
4. Beat in enough of the remaining flour to make a soft dough. Turn dough onto a lightly floured surface; cover and let rest 5 to 10 minutes.

5. Knead until dough is smooth and does not stick to the surface, about 5 minutes. Form into a ball and put into a lightly greased deep bowl; turn dough to bring greased surface to top. Cover; let rise in a warm place until doubled, about 2 hours.
6. Punch down dough. Turn onto a lightly floured surface and roll about ¼ inch thick. Cut into 2-inch diamonds or squares. Place on a lightly floured surface, cover with waxed paper, and let rise again until doubled.
7. About 20 minutes before frying, heat fat.
8. Fry pieces in heated fat 2 to 3 minutes, or until lightly browned. Fry only as many at one time as will float uncrowded one layer deep in fat. Turn as they rise to surface and several times during frying. Remove doughnuts with slotted spoon; drain over fat for a few seconds, then put on absorbent paper.
9. Shake 2 or 3 doughnuts at one time in a bag containing *confectioners' sugar*.

ABOUT 6 DOZEN DOUGHNUTS

QUICK BREADS

Quick breads get their name from the relatively short time of preparation as compared with yeast breads. The leavening of quick breads is usually achieved by the use of baking powder or baking soda. Popovers are an exception with steam causing them to rise.

Sometimes the term "quick bread" is used in a broad sense so that it includes all baked products made from batters or doughs even though they are not always true breads. Thus, one method of classifying a quick bread is according to the thickness of the batter or dough before baking.

Pour Batter (popovers, timbales, waffles, griddlecakes) — Pour batters are fluid enough to pour.

Drop Batter (muffins, drop biscuits, drop cookies, cream puffs, fruit and nut loaf breads) — Drop batters are thicker than pour batters and break from the spoon instead of pouring in a stream.

Soft Dough (rolled biscuits, doughnuts) — Soft doughs feel soft but not sticky to the touch and can be handled on a lightly floured surface.

Stiff Dough (pastry, rolled cookies) — No true breads fall in this category as stiff doughs are firm and lack the resiliency of soft doughs.

An important reminder — do not overmix a quick bread. This is especially important when all-purpose flour (rather than cake flour) is used in preparing the batter or dough. Too much beating or mixing causes the gluten in flour to become elastic, a development which is desirable in making good yeast bread but should be avoided in quick breads.

TECHNIQUES FOR MAKING QUICK BREADS

(Read also *Use Correct Techniques, page 2.*)

Have all ingredients at room temperature unless recipe specifies otherwise.

Preheat oven at required temperature.

Place oven rack so top of product will be almost at center of oven. Stagger pans (when more than one rack is needed) so no pan is directly over another and they do not touch each other or the walls of the oven. Place a single pan so that the top of product is as near center of oven as possible.

Prepare pans as directed in recipe.

Sift all-purpose flour, or not, as desired. (To measure, see *page 2.*)

Cream shortening (alone or with flavoring and spices) by stirring, rubbing, or beating with spoon or electric beater until softened. Add sugar in small amounts, creaming thoroughly after each addition. Thorough creaming helps to insure a fine-grained product.

Cut in shortening — Mix cold shortening with dry ingredients using a pastry blender, two knives, or tines of fork until the mixture resembles coarse crumbs. Work gently and do not overmix. (Method is used for mixing baking powder biscuits and some loaf breads.)

Beat eggs — See *page 2.*

Fill pans one-half to two-thirds full.

Apply baking tests when minimum baking time is up. For coffee cakes and quick loaf breads, insert a cake tester or wooden pick in center; if it comes out clean, cake or bread is done.

Remove quick loaf breads and coffee cakes from pans as they come from the oven, unless otherwise directed. Set on wire racks to cool.

Wrap cooled quick loaf breads in aluminum foil or other moisture-vaporproof material.

Quick Tea Breads & Coffee Cakes

APRICOT BREAD
Served at Johnny Cake Inn, Ivoryton, Connecticut.

½ cup hot water
1 cup dried apricots cut fine
2 cups sugar
2 eggs
¼ cup butter or margarine, melted
1 cup orange juice
4 cups sifted all-purpose flour
1 teaspoon baking soda

1. Add hot water to apricots in a bowl; beat in the sugar thoroughly. Add eggs, one at a time, beating well after each addition. Beat in the melted butter, then the orange juice.
2. Sift flour and baking soda together and add about ½ cup at a time to apricot mixture, mixing only until blended after each addition. Turn into 4 greased 7x4x2-inch loaf pans and spread evenly.
3. Bake at 350°F about 30 minutes.
4. Cool bread 10 minutes in pans on wire rack; remove from pans and cool completely. To store, wrap and refrigerate.   4 SMALL LOAVES BREAD

OAT FLAKE BANANA BREAD

1¼ cups sifted all-purpose flour
⅔ cup lightly packed brown sugar
2½ teaspoons baking powder
½ teaspoon salt
1 large egg
1 cup mashed banana (2 to 3 bananas with brown-flecked peel)
⅓ cup butter or margarine, melted and cooled
1 teaspoon vanilla extract
⅔ cup water
1 tablespoon orange-flavored instant drink granules
2 cups ready-to-eat oat flakes
½ cup chopped nuts

1. Mix the flour, brown sugar, baking powder, and salt together in a bowl; set aside.
2. Beat egg until thick and piled softly. Mix in banana, cooled butter, extract, and then a mixture of the water and drink granules.
3. Add liquid ingredients all at one time to the dry ingredients. Stir just enough to moisten flour. Mix in oat flakes and nuts. Turn into a greased 8x4x2-inch loaf pan and spread evenly.

4. Bake at 350°F 55 minutes, or until bread tests done.
5. Cool in pan on wire rack 10 minutes. Remove from pan and cool completely on rack.   1 LOAF BREAD

BANANA BREAD
A favorite of former President Lyndon B. Johnson.

½ cup butter
1 cup sugar
2 eggs, well beaten
3 medium-sized ripe bananas with brown-flecked peel, mashed
2 cups all-purpose flour
1 teaspoon baking soda
¼ teaspoon salt
1 cup sour milk

1. Cream butter and sugar together thoroughly. Add the eggs and beat well. Mix in bananas.
2. Sift flour, baking soda, and salt together. Add alternately with sour milk to banana mixture. Turn into a greased 9x5x3-inch loaf pan and spread evenly.
3. Bake at 350°F about 1 hour, or until bread tests done.   1 LOAF BANANA BREAD

CHEESE-CRANBERRY BREAD

1½ cups cranberries, cut in halves
½ cup sugar
2¼ cups sifted all-purpose flour
¾ cup sugar
3 teaspoons baking powder
½ teaspoon salt
½ cup coarsely chopped walnuts
2 teaspoons grated orange peel
1½ cups finely shredded sharp Cheddar cheese
1 egg, slightly beaten
1 cup milk
¼ cup butter, melted and cooled

1. Mix cranberries and ½ cup sugar well.
2. Sift flour, sugar, baking powder, and salt together into a large bowl. Mix in the sugared cranberries, walnuts, orange peel, and cheese.
3. Beat the egg, milk, and butter together. Add to mixture in bowl; stir just until dry ingredients are moistened. Turn into a greased 9x5x3-inch loaf pan and spread evenly.
4. Bake at 350°F about 1 hour, or until bread tests done.
5. Cool bread 10 minutes in pan on wire rack; remove from pan and cool completely before slicing. To store, wrap and refrigerate.   1 LOAF BREAD

CALIFORNIA FRUIT-NUT BREAD

2½ cups sifted all-purpose flour
3 teaspoons baking powder
¾ cup sugar
½ teaspoon baking soda
1 teaspoon salt
1 medium-sized orange
1 cup (about 7 oz.) pitted dates
½ cup walnuts
Buttermilk
1 egg, well beaten
3 tablespoons shortening, melted and cooled

1. Sift flour, baking powder, sugar, baking soda, and salt together into a large bowl.
2. Cut the orange into pieces; discard any seeds. Force through the medium blade of a food chopper with dates and nuts. Reserve orange juice in a measuring cup; add enough buttermilk to make 1 cup liquid. Combine with egg and shortening.
3. Add the liquid ingredients and orange-date mixture to dry ingredients; mix only until blended. Turn into a well greased 9x5x3-inch loaf pan and spread evenly.
4. Bake at 350°F about 1¼ hours, or until bread tests done.
5. Cool 10 minutes on wire rack. Remove loaf from pan; cool completely. To store, wrap tightly in aluminum foil or moisture-vaporproof material.

1 LOAF BREAD

LEMON NUT-BREAD

2½ cups sifted all-purpose flour
1 cup sugar
3 teaspoons baking powder
½ teaspoon salt
1 cup chopped nuts
1 egg
2 teaspoons grated lemon peel
¾ cup undiluted evaporated milk
½ cup water
¼ cup butter, melted

1. Sift flour, sugar, baking powder, and salt together. Mix in the nuts; set aside.
2. Thoroughly beat egg with lemon peel, then beat in the remaining ingredients in order.
3. Add the liquid mixture all at one time to the dry ingredients and stir just until the dry ingredients are moistened. Turn into 2 greased 7x4x2-inch loaf pans or one 9x5x3-inch loaf pan and spread evenly.
4. Bake at 375°F about 40 minutes, or until bread tests done.
5. Cool 10 minutes in pans on wire rack; remove from pans and cool completely.

2 LOAVES BREAD

SWISS WHIPPED CREAM-NUT LOAF

1 cup heavy cream
1 egg
1 cup sugar
1 teaspoon grated lemon peel
1 cup chopped walnuts
1 cup golden raisins, plumped
1¾ cups sifted all-purpose flour
1½ teaspoons baking powder
¼ teaspoon salt

1. Beat cream until very soft peaks are formed; beat in egg and sugar until thoroughly blended. Mix in the lemon peel, walnuts, and raisins.
2. Sift the flour, baking powder, and salt together; fold into the cream-sugar mixture. Turn into a greased 9x5x3-inch loaf pan and spread evenly.
3. Bake at 325°F 70 minutes, or until bread tests done.
4. Cool bread 15 minutes in pan on wire rack; remove from pan and cool completely. 1 LOAF BREAD

IRISH SODA BREAD WITH CURRANTS

4 cups sifted all-purpose flour
2 tablespoons sugar
2 teaspoons baking soda
1½ teaspoons salt
¼ cup butter or margarine
⅔ cup dried currants, plumped
½ cup white vinegar
1 cup milk

1. Mix flour, sugar, baking soda, and salt in a bowl. Cut in the butter with pastry blender or two knives until particles resemble rice kernels. Lightly mix in currants.
2. Mix vinegar and milk. Add half of the liquid to dry ingredients; blend quickly. Add remaining liquid and stir only until blended.
3. Turn dough onto floured surface. Lightly knead dough about 10 times and shape into a round loaf. Place on greased baking sheet.
4. Bake at 375°F 35 to 40 minutes.

1 LARGE LOAF SODA BREAD

DUTCH APPLE CAKE

2 cups sifted all-purpose flour
3 tablespoons sugar
3 teaspoons baking powder
1 teaspoon salt
1 cup chilled heavy cream
3 medium-sized apples, washed, quartered, cored and pared
¼ cup sugar
½ teaspoon ground cinnamon
2 tablespoons butter or margarine, melted

1. Sift flour, 3 tablespoons sugar, baking powder, and salt together into a bowl.
2. Beat cream until it piles softly. With a fork, lightly blend whipped cream into dry ingredients. Turn into a greased 9x9x2-inch baking pan and spread evenly.
3. Cut each apple quarter into 3 slices. Arrange slices in parallel rows on batter; press into batter. Combine ¼ cup sugar and cinnamon and sprinkle evenly over apples. Pour melted butter over top.
4. Bake at 400°F about 25 minutes, or until cake tests done. Cut into squares. 9 SERVINGS

QUICK COFFEE CAKE
(Blitzkuchen)

1⅓ cups sifted all-purpose flour	1 teaspoon vanilla extract
1½ teaspoons baking powder	⅔ cup sugar
¼ teaspoon salt	2 eggs, beaten
¼ cup butter	½ cup milk
	Topping, *below*

1. Mix flour, baking powder, and salt thoroughly and set aside.
2. Cream the butter with extract; gradually add the sugar, creaming until fluffy. Add the eggs in thirds, beating thoroughly after each addition.
3. Alternately add dry ingredients in thirds and milk in halves to creamed mixture, mixing until blended after each addition. Turn into a well greased 9x9x2-inch pan. Sprinkle with Topping.
4. Bake at 350°F about 25 minutes.
ONE 9-INCH SQUARE COFFEE CAKE
TOPPING: Mix *¼ cup sugar, ½ teaspoon ground cinnamon,* and *¼ cup chopped walnuts.*

BLUEBERRY COFFEE CAKE

2 cups sifted all-purpose flour	4 egg yolks (½ cup)
2 teaspoons baking powder	1 cup mashed potato, cooled to room temperature
1 cup butter or margarine	4 egg whites (⅔ cup)
2 teaspoons orange extract	¾ teaspoon salt
1 teaspoon grated orange peel	2 cups blueberries, fresh or thawed frozen
2 cups sugar	Orange Cream Icing, page 53

1. Blend the flour and baking powder; set aside.
2. Cream butter, extract, and orange peel. Add sugar gradually, beating vigorously. Add egg yolks, one at a time, beating until light and fluffy after each addition. Mix in mashed potato.
3. Add dry ingredients in thirds, beating only until blended after each addition.
4. Beat egg whites and salt until stiff, not dry, peaks are formed. Gently fold into the batter.
5. Rinse (if fresh) and thoroughly drain blueberries on absorbent paper; dredge with about 2 tablespoons flour. Using as few strokes as possible, fold berries into batter. Turn into greased and floured 3-quart (13x8-inch) shallow baking dish.
6. Bake at 350°F 35 to 40 minutes, or until cake tests done.
7. Cool in baking dish on wire rack. Spread with Orange Cream Icing. To serve, cut cake into squares, rectangles, or diamond-shaped pieces.
ONE 13x8-INCH COFFEE CAKE
ORANGE CREAM ICING: Combine *1 cup confectioners' sugar, 1 teaspoon butter,* softened, *1 teaspoon grated orange peel, 1 teaspoon light corn syrup,* and *2 tablespoons dairy sour cream.* Beat until smooth. ABOUT ½ CUP ICING

TOASTED FILBERT COFFEE CAKE

2 cups sifted all-purpose flour	1 teaspoon vanilla extract
2 teaspoons baking powder	1 cup sugar
½ teaspoon baking soda	2 eggs
½ teaspoon salt	1 cup dairy sour cream
½ cup butter or margarine	Toasted Filbert Topping, *below*

1. Blend the flour, baking powder, baking soda, and salt; set aside.
2. Cream the butter and extract. Add sugar gradually, beating constantly until thoroughly creamed. Add the eggs, one at a time, beating until light and fluffy after each addition.
3. Alternately add dry ingredients in thirds and sour cream in halves, mixing only until blended after each addition.
4. Spoon half of the batter into a greased and floured 9x9x2-inch baking pan; evenly sprinkle half of the filbert topping over batter. Spoon on remaining batter and top with filbert mixture.
5. Bake at 325°F about 40 minutes, or until coffee cake tests done. Set pan on wire rack to cool.
ONE 9 INCH SQUARE COFFEE CAKE

TOASTED FILBERT TOPPING: Mix *1 cup finely chopped toasted filberts, ⅓ cup packed brown sugar, ¼ cup sugar,* and *1 teaspoon ground cinnamon.*
NOTE: To toast filberts, see *To toast nuts, page 12.*

JOHNNYCAKE

1 cup sifted all-
   purpose flour
1 cup yellow cornmeal
½ teaspoon baking soda
¼ to ½ teaspoon salt

¾ cup firmly packed
   light brown sugar
1 egg, well beaten
½ cup buttermilk or
   sour milk
⅓ cup dairy sour cream

1. Blend flour, cornmeal, baking soda, and salt in a bowl. Mix in brown sugar.
2. Add a mixture of egg, buttermilk, and sour cream all at one time to dry ingredients. Beat with a rotary beater until *just* smooth. Turn into a greased 11x7x1½-inch baking pan; spread evenly.
3. Bake at 425°F about 20 minutes.
4. Break or cut johnnycake into squares. Serve hot with *butter* and warm *maple syrup.*

ONE 11x7 INCH JOHNNYCAKE

HERMITAGE SPOON BREAD

Spoon bread was a favorite of Andrew Jackson whose Tennessee home was called the Hermitage.

1 cup white hominy
   grits, or water-
   ground white cornmeal
1½ teaspoons salt
1 cup cold water

2 cups hot milk
2 eggs, beaten
3 tablespoons butter
   or margarine

1. Combine hominy grits with the salt and cold water in a heavy saucepan. Stir until smooth, then stir in the hot milk. Cook and stir over low heat until mixture begins to thicken.
2. Remove from heat; add eggs and butter. Beat until well blended. Turn into a well greased 1-quart casserole.
3. Bake at 350°F 45 minutes, or until center is "set." Serve hot with plenty of *butter.*

ABOUT 6 SERVINGS

BACON-NUT CORN STICKS

1 cup sifted all-
   purpose flour
1 cup yellow cornmeal
¼ cup sugar
1 teaspoon baking
   powder
½ teaspoon baking soda
½ teaspoon salt
⅓ cup coarsely chopped
   pecans

6 to 8 slices crisply
   fried bacon, drained
   on absorbent paper
   and crumbled
1 egg, well beaten
1 cup buttermilk
5 tablespoons melted
   shortening

1. Combine the flour, cornmeal, sugar, baking powder, baking soda, and salt in a bowl, mix well and stir in the pecans and bacon.
2. Add a mixture of the remaining ingredients and stir only until flour is moistened. Spoon mixture into 12 preheated greased corn-stick pan sections (5½x1½ inches).
3. Bake at 425°F 10 to 15 minutes.

1 DOZEN CORN STICKS

CORN-CHEESE TWISTS

½ cup sifted all-
   purpose flour
¼ cup yellow cornmeal
½ teaspoon salt
¼ to ⅓ cup (about ½
   5-oz. jar) pasteur-
   ized process sharp
   Cheddar cheese
   spread

2 tablespoons
   shortening
2 tablespoons cold
   water

1. Mix flour, cornmeal, and salt in a bowl. Cut in the cheese spread and shortening with a pastry blender or two knives until pieces resemble coarse crumbs.
2. Gradually add the water, stirring with a fork until mixture forms a ball and leaves sides of bowl.
3. Roll between two sheets of waxed paper to ⅛-inch thickness. Using a pastry wheel, cut dough into 3x½-inch strips. Twist each strip by holding both ends and turning in opposite directions; press ends onto ungreased baking sheets.
4. Bake at 425°F about 5 minutes, or until golden brown. Cool the twists on wire racks.

ABOUT 5 DOZEN TWISTS

Biscuits & Muffins

BUTTERMILK BISCUITS

2 cups sifted all-purpose flour
2½ teaspoons baking powder
¼ teaspoon baking soda
1 teaspoon salt
⅓ cup lard or vegetable shortening
¾ cup buttermilk

1. Blend flour, baking powder, baking soda, and salt in a bowl. Cut in lard with a pastry blender or two knives until particles are the size of rice kernels. Add buttermilk and stir with a fork only until dough follows fork.
2. Gently form dough into a ball and put on a lightly floured surface. Knead lightly with fingertips 10 to 15 times. Gently roll dough ½ inch thick.
3. Cut with a floured biscuit cutter or knife, using an even pressure to keep sides of biscuits straight. Place on ungreased baking sheet, close together for soft-sided biscuits or 1 inch apart for crusty ones. Brush tops lightly with *buttermilk*.
4. Bake at 450°F 10 to 15 minutes, or until biscuits are golden brown.   ABOUT 1 DOZEN BISCUITS

BAKING POWDER BISCUITS: Follow recipe for Buttermilk Biscuits. Omit the baking soda, increase baking powder to 3 teaspoons, and substitute ¾ *cup milk* for buttermilk.

IRISH SCONES

1¾ cups sifted all-purpose flour
1 tablespoon sugar
1½ teaspoons baking powder
½ teaspoon baking soda
½ teaspoon salt
½ cup shortening
½ cup buttermilk

1. Mix flour, sugar, baking powder, baking soda, and salt in a bowl. Cut in shortening with a pastry blender or two knives until particles are the size of rice kernels.
2. Add the buttermilk and stir with a fork until dough follows fork and forms a ball.
3. Turn dough onto a floured surface and knead lightly with fingertips about 8 times. Divide dough in half and shape each into a round about ½ inch thick. Cut each round into 6 wedge-shaped pieces. Place on an ungreased baking sheet.
4. Bake at 450°F 8 to 10 minutes. Serve warm.
   1 DOZEN SCONES

ITALIAN CHEESE CRESCENTS

1 cup pot cheese or uncreamed cottage cheese
3 tablespoons all-purpose flour
½ teaspoon salt
1 egg
¼ teaspoon Italian herbs
2 packages refrigerated crescent rolls
2 tablespoons butter or margarine, melted
1 teaspoon sesame seeds

1. Preheat oven to 375°F.
2. Combine cheese, flour, salt, egg, and Italian herbs in a small bowl; beat until well blended.
3. Separate crescent rolls into triangles as label directs; spoon 1 tablespoon of the cheese mixture on wide end of each. Roll up; place, point up, on a cookie sheet. Brush melted butter over rolls; sprinkle sesame seeds on top.
4. Bake 18 minutes, or until rolls are golden. Remove from cookie sheet. Serve hot.   16 ROLLS

BRAN PUFFS

½ cup milk
½ cup shortening
⅓ cup sugar
1 teaspoon salt
1 cup whole bran cereal
2 envelopes active dry yeast
½ cup warm water
1 egg
3 cups sifted all-purpose flour
½ cup dark raisins

1. Scald milk with shortening, sugar, and salt in a small saucepan; pour over bran in a large bowl. Let stand until liquid is almost absorbed and mixture is lukewarm.
2. Dissolve yeast in warm water in a medium bowl. Beat egg into bran mixture, then beat in yeast mixture and 2 cups of the flour until smooth. Stir in just enough of the remaining 1 cup flour to make a soft dough; stir in raisins.
3. Turn dough out onto a lightly floured board; knead about 5 minutes until smooth and elastic, adding only enough of any remaining flour to keep dough from sticking. Shape into a ball; place in a greased large bowl, turning to coat all over with shortening; cover. Let rise in a warm place, away from drafts, 1 hour, or until doubled.
4. Punch dough down; cut into 18 equal pieces. Shape each into a ball; place in a greased medium-sized muffin-pan cup; cover. Let rise again 1 hour, or until doubled.

5. Preheat oven to 375°F.
6. Bake 25 minutes, or until rolls are golden and sound hollow when tapped with finger. Remove from pans to wire racks. Serve warm or cold.   18 ROLLS

GINGER-DATE MUFFINS

- 2 cups sifted all-purpose flour
- 1/3 cup sugar
- 3 teaspoons baking powder
- 1/2 teaspoon salt
- 1 egg, well beaten
- 1 cup milk
- 1/4 cup butter, melted
- 1/2 cup sliced fresh dates
- 2 tablespoons finely slivered, preserved ginger
- Spiced sugar (use 2 tablespoons sugar mixed with 1/8 teaspoon each ground cinnamon, ground ginger, and nutmeg)

1. Mix flour, sugar, baking powder, and salt in a bowl. Add a mixture of beaten egg, milk, and melted butter. Quickly and lightly stir until dry ingredients are barely moistened, adding the dates and ginger with the last few strokes.
2. Spoon batter into greased 2½-inch muffin-pan wells. Sprinkle spiced sugar over batter.
3. Bake at 425°F about 15 minutes.   15 MUFFINS

MUFFINS: Follow recipe for Ginger-Date Muffins. Omit dates, ginger, and spiced sugar. Bake 20 to 25 minutes.   1 DOZEN MUFFINS

BLUEBERRY MUFFINS: Follow recipe for Muffins. With a final few strokes, gently mix *1 cup rinsed and drained fresh blueberries* into batter.

STOUFFER'S PUMPKIN MUFFINS
A favorite from the Stouffer Restaurant chain.

- 1½ cups all-purpose flour
- 1/2 cup sugar
- 2 teaspoons baking powder
- 3/4 teaspoon salt
- 1/2 teaspoon ground cinnamon
- 1/2 teaspoon ground nutmeg
- 1/4 cup butter
- 1/2 cup seeded raisins
- 1 egg, beaten
- 1/2 cup milk
- 1/2 cup canned pumpkin
- 1 tablespoon sugar

1. Sift the flour, 1/2 cup sugar, baking powder, salt, cinnamon, and nutmeg together. Cut in butter until particles are the size of rice kernels. Mix in raisins and set aside.
2. Blend egg, milk, and pumpkin; add to dry ingredients and lightly stir until dry ingredients are barely moistened (batter will be lumpy).
3. Spoon batter into greased muffin-pan wells, filling each about 2/3 full. Sprinkle 1/4 teaspoon sugar over each.
4. Bake at 400°F 18 to 20 minutes. Serve at once.
   1 DOZEN MUFFINS

ORANGE-PRUNE MUFFINS

- 1¾ cups sifted all-purpose flour
- 1/2 cup regular wheat germ
- 1/3 cup sugar (for batter)
- 3 teaspoons baking powder
- 1/2 teaspoon mace
- 1/2 teaspoon salt
- 1 cup snipped dried prunes
- 2 eggs
- 1/4 cup salad oil
- 2/3 cup milk
- 1/4 cup sugar (for topping)
- 1 teaspoon grated orange rind
- 2 tablespoons orange juice

1. Preheat oven to 400°F.
2. Mix flour, wheat germ, the 1/3 cup sugar, baking powder, mace, and salt in a large bowl; stir in prunes.
3. Beat eggs slightly in a small bowl; stir in salad oil and milk. Add all at once to flour mixture; stir just until mixture is evenly moist. Spoon into greased medium-sized muffin-pan cups.
4. Bake 20 minutes, or until muffins are puffed and golden. Cool in pan on a wire rack 10 minutes; remove from pan.
5. While muffins cool, combine the 1/4 cup sugar, orange rind, and juice in a small saucepan. Heat, stirring constantly, to boiling; cook 1 minute. Brush hot glaze over muffins. (Mixture will soak in.) Serve muffins warm.   1 DOZEN MUFFINS

BREADS FROM MIXES

FRUIT-FILLED COFFEE RING

- 1 pkg. hot roll mix
- 1½ teaspoons grated lemon peel
- 1/3 cup chopped dried apricots
- 1/3 cup chopped prunes
- 1/2 cup chopped walnuts
- 1/4 cup butter or margarine, melted
- 3 tablespoons sugar
- 1 cup golden raisins
- Melted butter or margarine
- Orange Glaze, *page 57*

1. Prepare hot roll mix according to package

* Breads (pages 35-62)

directions; add lemon peel with the dry mix. Let dough rise according to directions.
2. Mix butter with the sugar, raisins, apricots, prunes, and walnuts; set aside.
3. When dough is doubled, punch down and turn onto a lightly floured surface; roll into a 16x12-inch rectangle. Top dough evenly with fruit filling; roll up, starting with long edge. Snip off both ends on a diagonal; reserve end pieces for center.
4. Cut the roll diagonally into 12 slices; arrange slices in a circle on a large greased baking sheet with pointed ends out and each slice overlapping slightly. Place reserved ends in center; brush top with melted butter. Cover; let rise in a warm place until doubled.
5. Bake at 350°F about 30 minutes, or until golden brown. While still warm, spread with Orange Glaze and, if desired, sprinkle with *grated orange peel*.
1 LARGE COFFEE RING

ORANGE GLAZE: Blend *1 cup confectioners' sugar* with *2 tablespoons orange juice* until smooth.

PETITE ORANGE-CURRANT LOAVES

1 pkg. hot roll mix	⅓ cup dried currants
⅔ cup chopped candied orange peel	Melted butter or margarine

1. Prepare hot roll mix according to package directions adding orange peel and currants with the dry mix. Let dough rise according to directions.
2. When dough is doubled, punch down, turn onto a lightly floured surface and divide into 4 equal portions.
3. Roll each portion into a 7x4-inch rectangle; beginning with shorter side, roll up dough; pinch edges and ends to seal. Place sealed-edge down in 4 greased 5x3x2-inch loaf pans; brush tops with *melted butter*. Cover; let rise in a warm place until doubled.
4. Bake at 375°F 20 to 25 minutes, or until golden brown. Remove loaves from pans to wire racks; turn right side up. While still hot, spread tops with desired *glaze*.
4 SMALL LOAVES

MINIATURE BUTTER CREAM LOAVES

Serve individual loaves on small bread boards with knives for morning coffee or a special brunch.

1 pkg. hot roll mix	1 cup chopped nuts
Butter Cream Filling, See Below	

Sally Lunn with Strawberries (page 40)

1. Follow hot roll mix directions on package through first rising.
2. Meanwhile, prepare Butter Cream Filling and spread about 1 tablespoon of the filling over bottom and sides of each of four 5x3x2-inch loaf pans. Cover remaining filling; set aside.
3. When dough is doubled, punch down, turn onto a lightly floured surface and divide into 4 equal portions. Roll each portion into an 8x4-inch rectangle.
4. Reserve ¼ cup filling for topping. Spread one fourth of remaining filling over each dough rectangle and sprinkle with one fourth of the nuts. Beginning with a shorter side, tightly roll up dough; pinch edges and ends to seal.
5. Place sealed edge down in prepared pans. Brush tops with *melted butter or margarine.* Cover; let rise in a warm place until doubled.
6. Bake at 375°F 20 to 25 minutes, or until golden brown.
7. Immediately remove loaves from pans and set on wire racks. Spread reserved filling over hot loaves.
4 SMALL LOAVES

BUTTER CREAM FILLING: Prepare 1 *package vanilla-* or *chocolate-flavored butter cream frosting mix* according to package directions adding an additional *2 tablespoons butter* and *½ teaspoon vanilla extract* with the butter.

FROSTED BROWN SUGAR BUBBLE LOAF

4 cups biscuit mix	2 tablespoons grated lemon peel
¼ cup firmly packed brown sugar	1 cup milk
1 teaspoon ground cinnamon	1 egg, well beaten
½ teaspoon ground mace	½ cup butter or margarine, melted
Few grains salt	½ teaspoon vanilla extract
¼ cup coarsely chopped toasted almonds	Coffee Glaze, *page 58*
¼ cup firmly packed brown sugar	

1. Mix biscuit mix with ¼ cup brown sugar, cinnamon, mace, and salt thoroughly; set aside.
2. Combine almonds, remaining ¼ cup brown sugar, and lemon peel; mix well.
3. Blend milk, egg, ¼ cup melted butter, and the extract. Make a well in the center of the dry ingredients and add the liquid. Stir with a fork until dough follows fork. Gently form dough into a ball and turn onto a lightly floured surface. Knead light-

Breads from Mixes

ly 10 to 15 times.

4. Shape dough into 52 small balls, about 1 inch in diameter. Form three layers of balls, 18 in each of the first two and 12 in the third, in a greased 9x5x3-inch loaf pan, brushing each layer with some of remaining melted butter and sprinkling with a third of the nut mixture. Place 4 balls down the center and brush with any remaining butter.

5. Bake at 350°F about 45 minutes, or until loaf is golden brown.

6. Remove from pan and drizzle with Coffee Glaze. Serve hot; pull apart with two forks.

ONE 9x5-INCH LOAF

COFFEE GLAZE: Stir about *2½ teaspoons double or triple strength coffee* into *¾ cup confectioners' sugar* until smooth and of desired consistency.

PRUNE BRAID

1 package hot roll mix	½ teaspoon ground cardamom
Egg	
Warm water	½ cup water
½ cup chopped pitted prunes	½ cup chopped pecans
	1 tablespoon butter or margarine, melted
Sugar	

1. Prepare hot roll mix with egg and warm water and let rise as label directs.
2. While dough rises, combine prunes, ½ cup sugar, cardamom, and the ½ cup water in a small saucepan. Heat to boiling; simmer 5 minutes, or until thick. Cool; stir in pecans.
3. Punch dough down; divide into thirds. Roll out each third on a lightly floured board to a rectangle, 14x4 inches; spread one third of the prune mixture over each rectangle. Starting at a long side, roll up dough, jelly-roll fashion. Place rolls side by side on a greased large cookie sheet; pinch at one end to seal, then braid and seal other end; cover. Let rise 45 minutes, or until doubled.
4. Preheat oven to 375°F.
5. Brush melted butter over raised dough; sprinkle sugar generously over top.
6. Bake 30 minutes, or until braid is golden and sounds hollow when tapped with finger. Remove from cookie sheet to a wire rack; cool. Serve warm or cold.

1 SIXTEEN-INCH BRAID

QUICK 'N' EASY JAM BRAID

2 cups biscuit mix	¼ cup milk
¼ cup butter, cut in small pieces	⅔ cup whole strawberry preserves
3 oz. cream cheese, cut in small pieces	

1. Put biscuit mix into a bowl; using a pastry blender, cut in butter and cheese until pieces are the size of peas.
2. Gradually add milk, blending with a fork. (Mixture will be lumpy and crumbly.) Turn dough onto a lightly greased baking sheet and roll into a 14x8-inch rectangle.
3. Evenly spread strawberry preserves through center of rectangle in a 2-inch wide, lengthwise strip. Cut dough with a knife into 1-inch strips from the outside edges to the filling. Braid the strips over filling by lifting one strip from each side and crossing diagonally in center.
4. Bake at 425°F about 15 minutes, or until lightly browned. Serve warm.

6 SERVINGS

PARMESAN QUICK BREAD

3 cups biscuit mix	¾ cup shredded Parmesan cheese
¾ cup yellow cornmeal	1¼ cups buttermilk
¼ cup sugar	2 eggs, beaten

1. Combine biscuit mix, cornmeal, sugar, and cheese in a large bowl.
2. Mix buttermilk and eggs; add to dry ingredients and stir only until blended. Turn into a buttered 9x5x3-inch loaf pan; spread evenly to edges.
3. Bake at 350°F 40 to 50 minutes, or until bread tests done.
4. Remove from pan set on a wire rack to cool completely.

1 LOAF BREAD

CHEDDAR CHEESE QUICK BREAD: Follow recipe for Parmesan Quick Bread. Increase biscuit mix to 3¾ cups. Substitute *1½ cups shredded sharp Cheddar cheese* for Parmesan. Cook *6 slices bacon* until crisp. Drain and crumble. Add bacon to the bowl with dry ingredients.

NEW MOON YEAST ROLLS

1 pkg. active dry yeast	2 tablespoons butter, softened
⅔ cup warm water	
3 cups biscuit mix	4 oz. (about ½ cup) almond paste
2 tablespoons sugar	
1 egg, beaten	

1. Soften yeast in the warm water in a large bowl. Add biscuit mix, sugar, and egg; beat vigorously until well mixed.
2. Turn dough onto a lightly floured surface and knead until smooth (about 20 times). Roll dough into a 10-inch square and spread softened butter over half of dough. Fold unbuttered half over buttered portion; press edges to seal.
3. Roll dough into a 12-inch round and crumble almond paste evenly over surface. Cut dough into 16 wedge-shaped pieces. Beginning at wide end, roll toward point.
4. Place each on a greased baking sheet with point underneath; curve into a crescent. Cover; let rise in a warm place until doubled, about 1 hour.
5. Bake at 375°F 12 to 15 minutes, or until golden brown. If desired, brush with *melted butter* immediately after removing from oven. Serve warm.

16 ROLLS

CRESCENT CHEESE ROLLS: Follow recipe for New Moon Yeast Rolls. Add *¼ to ½ cup finely shredded Cheddar cheese* with the biscuit mix.

SESAME SEED TWISTS

2 cups biscuit mix
¼ cup butter, chilled
Melted butter
2 tablespoons toasted sesame seed

1. Prepare biscuit mix as directed on package for rolled biscuits. Roll on lightly floured surface into a 12-inch square about ⅛ inch thick.
2. Thinly slice and quickly place about 3 tablespoons of the chilled butter onto half of dough; fold other half over it. With rolling pin gently press down and seal the open edges. Repeat procedure using remaining chilled butter; fold other half over forming a 6-inch square. Chill about 1 hour.
3. Roll dough into a 12-inch square. Divide into halves and set one half in refrigerator.
4. Brush surface with melted butter. Sprinkle with some of the sesame seed. Cut into twelve 6x1-inch strips. Twist each strip and place on an ungreased baking sheet, pressing ends. Brush with a mixture of *1 egg yolk* and *1 teaspoon milk*. Sprinkle with sesame seed. Repeat.
5. Bake at 425°F about 10 minutes.

2 DOZEN TWISTS

HOT CROSS FRUIT MUFFINS

These quick-to-mix muffins resemble the traditional hot cross buns in flavor and appearance.

2 cups biscuit mix
3 tablespoons sugar
½ to ¾ teaspoon ground cardamom
½ cup dark or golden raisins
¼ cup chopped citron
1 egg, well beaten
⅔ cup milk
2 tablespoons melted shortening, or cooking or salad oil
Frosting, *below*

1. Mix the biscuit mix, sugar, and cardamom in a bowl; stir in the raisins and citron.
2. Blend the egg, milk, and shortening thoroughly. Add to dry ingredients; stir quickly and lightly until dry ingredients are barely moistened. Spoon batter into greased 2½-inch muffin-pan wells.
3. Bake at 400°F about 15 minutes.
4. Meanwhile, prepare Frosting.
5. Remove muffins from pan to wire rack; cool slightly. Then form a cross on each muffin, using the frosting.

1 DOZEN MUFFINS

FROSTING: Beat together until smooth *½ cup plus 2 tablespoons confectioners' sugar, 2 teaspoons water, ¼ teaspoon vanilla extract,* and *1 tablespoon almond paste.*

PEACHY RICH BREAKFAST SLICES

3 cups biscuit mix
1 cup flour or biscuit mix
1 cup lightly packed dark brown sugar
¾ cup butter or margarine
1 can (29 oz.) cling peach slices, drained
6 egg yolks
3 tablespoons sugar
6 tablespoons cream

1. Prepare biscuit mix for biscuit dough as directed on the package. Spread dough evenly over bottom and slightly up sides of a lightly greased 15x10x1-inch jelly roll pan.
2. With fork, mix flour with brown sugar and cut in butter. Spoon evenly over dough in pan. Arrange peach slices in rows over crumb mixture.
3. Bake at 375°F about 20 minutes, or until lightly browned around edge.
4. Meanwhile, beat together the egg yolks, sugar, and cream. Pour evenly over peaches and continue baking about 10 minutes, or until custard is set. Serve warm, cut into slices.

ABOUT 24 SLICES

BANANA CORNBREAD

1 pkg. corn muffin or cornbread mix
⅓ cup sugar
⅛ teaspoon baking powder
2 medium-sized bananas having brown-flecked peel, peeled and mashed (about 1¾ cups)
2⅔ tablespoons lukewarm water
1 egg, well beaten
¼ teaspoon vanilla extract

1. Combine mix, sugar, baking powder, and a *few grains salt* in a bowl. Mix well and stir in remaining ingredients. Turn into a greased 8x8x2-inch baking pan and spread evenly.
2. Bake at 425°F about 20 minutes.

ONE 8-INCH SQUARE CORNBREAD

BANANA CORN MUFFINS: Follow recipe for Banana Cornbread. Spoon batter into greased 2½-inch muffin pan wells; fill each ¾ full. Bake at 425°F 15 to 18 minutes. ABOUT 1 DOZEN MUFFINS

Things to do with
DOUGH FROM THE DAIRY CASE

CORNMEAL-KIST BISCUITS

1 pkg. (8 oz.) refrigerated fresh dough for biscuits
Yellow cornmeal

Separate biscuits and coat each with cornmeal. Place about 2 inches apart on an ungreased baking sheet. Bake as directed on package.

10 BISCUITS

MACE 'N' CHEESE BISCUITS

1 pkg. (8 oz.) refrigerated fresh dough for biscuits
12 thin 1¾-inch squares sharp Cheddar cheese
2 tablespoons butter, softened
½ teaspoon ground mace
¼ teaspoon dry mustard

1. Separate biscuits into halves; put bottom halves on ungreased baking sheet. Top each biscuit half with a square of cheese.
2. Blend the butter, mace, and dry mustard; spread on both sides of the remaining biscuit halves and place onto cheese squares. Sprinkle tops with *poppy seed*.
3. Bake at 400°F about 8 minutes, or until biscuits are lightly browned.

10 OR 12 BISCUITS

WATERCRESS BISCUITS: Follow recipe for Mace 'n' Cheese biscuits. Omit mace and dry mustard. Blend thoroughly the butter, ⅛ *teaspoon ground allspice*, and ¼ teaspoon chervil. Mix in ⅓ *cup finely chopped watercress.* Spread underside of biscuit tops with the seasoned butter; place, butter side down, onto cheese squares. Brush biscuit tops with *melted butter* and sprinkle with *poppy seed.*

PAN O' ROLLS

¼ cup butter or margarine
1 clove garlic, minced
2 tablespoons finely snipped parsley
2 pkgs. (8 oz. each) refrigerated fresh dough for biscuits
½ cup shredded Parmesan cheese

1. Heat butter and garlic in a small skillet; stir in parsley. Remove from heat.
2. Separate biscuits; dip each in the garlic butter to coat. Overlap 15 biscuits around the outer edge of a 9-inch round layer-cake pan; form an inner circle by overlapping remaining biscuits.
3. Drizzle any remaining butter over top of biscuits and sprinkle evenly with Parmesan cheese.
4. Bake at 425°F 15 to 20 minutes, or until golden brown. Serve hot.

20 ROLLS

DOUBLE ONION BISCUITS

1 pkg. (8 oz) refrigerated fresh dough for biscuits
¼ cup butter or margarine, softened
2 tablespoons snipped parsley
1½ tablespoons dry onion salad dressing mix

1. Separate and slightly flatten biscuits. Spread

half of them with a mixture of the remaining ingredients. Top with remaining biscuits.
2. Cut center from each double biscuit with a doughnut cutter. Gently stretch and twist each ring into a figure eight and place on a baking sheet.
3. Bake at 425°F 10 minutes. 10 BISCUITS

PINEAPPLE-PECAN COFFEE CAKE

¼ cup firmly packed brown sugar	1 teaspoon grated orange peel
3 tablespoons butter	2 pkgs. (8 oz. each) refrigerated fresh dough for biscuits
¼ cup light corn syrup	
20 pecan halves	
1 can (8¾ oz.) crushed pineapple, well drained	¼ cup butter, melted

1. Mix in a 9-inch layer cake pan the brown sugar, butter, and corn syrup. Arrange pecan halves, flat side up, in the pan. Spoon a mixture of crushed pineapple and orange peel over pecans.
2. Set pan in a 425°F oven for 10 minutes.
3. Dip each biscuit in the melted butter. Overlap 15 of the biscuits around the outer edge of the pan; form an inner circle by overlapping remaining biscuits.
4. Return to oven and bake at 425°F 20 minutes.
5. Remove from oven. Cover with a serving plate and invert; allow pan to remain over cake 1 to 2 minutes. Lift off pan. Serve warm.

ONE 9-INCH COFFEE CAKE

FLAKY CHEESE-FILLED ROLLS

1 pkg. refrigerated fresh dough for fantan rolls	½ teaspoon Worcestershire sauce
	¼ teaspoon paprika
2 slices (about 2 oz.) pasteurized process Cheddar cheese, cut in 1½-in. squares	Few grains ground cinnamon
	Few grains cayenne pepper
1 tablespoon prepared mustard	

1. Remove roll dough from package and divide into 36 rounds, each round consisting of 2 layers of dough. Place a square of cheese on half the rounds.
2. Combine remaining ingredients; mix well. Spread a thin coating of the mixture over cheese. Cover with remaining rounds of dough and press edges together lightly to seal in the filling. Transfer to ungreased baking sheet.
3. Bake at 400°F about 10 minutes.

1½ DOZEN ROLLS

ORANGE STICKY BUNS
Here's a modern version of the sticky buns reputed to have been served fresh every day at breakfast, teatime, and dinner in 19th century Philadelphia.

1 medium-sized orange	1 pkg. refrigerated fresh dough for fantan rolls
1 cup sugar	

1. Put orange peel and pulp through fine blade of food chopper. Mix orange with sugar in a saucepan and bring to boiling; boil 5 minutes.
2. Spoon about 2 teaspoons of orange-sugar mixture into each of 12 greased small muffin-pan wells.
3. Separate roll dough into 12 pieces and put one in each well. Pull sections of each roll apart slightly and drizzle remaining orange-sugar mixture between the sections.
4. Bake rolls as directed on package.
5. Remove from oven and turn pan upside down on wire rack; let cool 1 to 2 minutes; remove pan. If desired, frost with a *confectioners' sugar icing* while warm. 12 SMALL BUNS

Bakers' Breads

FRENCH TOAST

2 eggs, slightly beaten	3 to 4 tablespoons butter or margarine
⅔ cup milk or cream	
1 tablespoon sugar	8 slices bread, white or whole wheat
½ teaspoon salt	

1. Combine eggs with milk, sugar, and salt in a shallow dish or pie pan.
2. Dip bread slices one at a time into egg mixture, coating each side well. Transfer to a skillet which has been preheated with some of the butter. Brown slices over medium heat, turning once. Add butter as needed to keep slices from sticking.
3. Serve with *butter, maple syrup, honey, jam,* or *confectioners' sugar.* 8 SLICES FRENCH TOAST

NOTE: To brown French toast in the oven, place bread slices on a well greased baking sheet. Place in a 450°F oven; allow about 10 minutes for each side.

Baker's Breads

OAHU TOAST: Drain contents of *1 can (8½ ounces) pineapple slices;* reserve syrup. Follow recipe for French Toast. Omit sugar and substitute for milk pineapple syrup and *water* to make ⅔ cup liquid. Lightly brown pineapple slices in *2 to 3 tablespoons butter or margarine.* Serve half of a pineapple slice with each slice of toast.

CINNAMON-ORANGE FRENCH TOAST: Follow recipe for French Toast. Substitute *⅔ cup orange juice* for milk and add *½ teaspoon ground cinnamon.* Or, add *2 teaspoons grated orange peel* and *½ teaspoon ground cinnamon* to egg mixture.

ORANGE TOAST "BLINTZES"

You'll appreciate this modern approach to preparing the ever-popular Jewish blintze. Thin slices of bread are used instead of the thin pancakes to hold the cottage cheese filling. Not exactly a traditional blintze, but a very tasty brunch or luncheon dish.

12 thin slices white bread	1 tablespoon grated orange peel
⅓ cup milk	Few grains salt
1 egg, slightly beaten	3 tablespoons butter or margarine, melted
¾ cup small curd creamed cottage cheese	2 tablespoons sugar
1 tablespoon sugar	1 teaspoon ground cinnamon

1. Trim crusts from bread; brush tops and sides of bread with milk.
2. Combine the egg, cottage cheese, 1 tablespoon sugar, orange peel, and salt; mix well.
3. Spread 2 tablespoons of the mixture evenly over each of 6 bread slices. Place remaining slices, milk-side down, on filling. Press edges together.
4. Brush tops with melted butter and sprinkle with a mixture of sugar and cinnamon. Place "blintzes" on a greased baking sheet.
5. Toast in a 400°F oven 10 minutes.   6 SERVINGS

BUTTERED FRENCH BREAD

Cut *1 loaf French bread* on the diagonal into ¾-inch slices almost through to the bottom. Place in center of a piece of aluminum foil large enough to cover loaf. Generously spread desired *Seasoned Butter, below,* onto cut surfaces and over top of loaf. If desired, sprinkle with *paprika.* Twist ends of foil securely, leaving top partially open so steam can escape. Set in a 400°F oven 15 to 20 minutes.

SEASONED BUTTERS: Into *½ cup softened butter* blend one of the following—

⅓ cup finely chopped pimiento-stuffed olives and ¼ teaspoon oregano	2 tablespoons finely chopped parsley, 1 minced clove garlic, ¼ teaspoon ground coriander, ⅛ teaspoon ground ginger, and ½ teaspoon celery seed
1 teaspoon lemon or lime juice, and 1 tablespoon minced chives	

RINGLET CROUSTADES

12 slices day-old bread, about ¾ in. thick	¼ cup butter or margarine, melted
	2 tablespoons grated Parmesan cheese

1. Using a scalloped-edge cookie cutter, cut bread slices into rounds. Set 6 rounds aside.
2. With a sharp, pointed knife or cookie cutter, cut out center of the 6 remaining shapes to make rings at least ¾-inch wide.
3. Lightly brush rounds (for bases), rings, and centers with melted butter. Arrange on a baking sheet, buttered-side down.
4. Mix cheese with remaining butter. Brush sides and tops of bases, rings, and centers with butter-cheese mixture.
5. Toast in a 325°F oven 15 to 20 minutes, or until golden brown and crisp.
6. For each ringlet shell, place a ring on a base. Fill with a creamed mixture and top with a center round.   6 SERVINGS

ALMOND RINGLET CROUSTADES: Follow recipe for Ringlet Croustades. Substitute *½ cup finely chopped, toasted blanched almonds* for the Parmesan cheese. Generously brush bases, rings, and centers with the melted butter and sprinkle each piece with the almonds.

SESAME RINGLET CROUSTADES: Follow recipe for Ringlet Croustades. Omit cheese. Lightly brown *2 to 3 tablespoons sesame seed* in 2 tablespoons of the melted butter. Mix *½ teaspoon onion salt* with remaining 2 tablespoons melted butter. Brush bottoms of bases, rings, and centers with the butter and tops with toasted sesame seed.

Chapter 4

EGG & CHEESE DISHES

ABOUT EGGS The perfection of an egg is one of nature's miracles, for here is an object lovely in form, filled with nourishment, and so versatile that few foods can match it. Served alone or in combination with other foods, eggs are equally appealing in the morning, at noon, and at night.

Grading — Graded eggs in cartons kept in a clean, cold refrigerator by the dealer are safe buys.

Eggs may be graded according to federal, state, or private standards. U.S. grades refer to interior quality; sizes refer to weight per dozen.

Grade AA and A eggs are top quality. They have a large amount of thick white and a high, firm yolk. Good for all uses, they are the best choice for poaching, frying, or cooking in the shell. Grade B and C eggs have thinner whites and somewhat flatter yolks which may break easily. Offering the same food values as top-grade eggs, these less expensive eggs are a practical buy for scrambling, thickening sauces, making salad dressings, and combining with other foods. Quality of eggs should be checked before using by breaking each egg in a small dish.

Whether the color of the egg shell is brown or white makes no difference in the quality or food value of the egg, though in some localities it does influence price. Eggs with brown shells sometimes have yolks of deeper yellow color than those with white shells.

Most eggs are grouped according to these sizes: jumbo, extra large, large, medium, and small — with a minimum weight per dozen of 30, 27, 24, 21, and 18 ounces respectively. Small eggs were at one time more plentiful in late summer and fall and at that time were likely to be a good buy. However, this marketing pattern is changing to reflect the growing tendency to year-round baby chick production. Nowadays egg production is geared so that young pullets (less than a year old) come into their laying period throughout the entire year. Their first eggs are small, increasing in size as the hen grows to maturity. Weight for weight the nutritive value and cooking performance of small eggs equal those of large eggs of the same quality grade. Only because of their smaller size is the price per dozen less than that of large eggs.

Nutrients — Eggs are an important food for children and adults alike because they contain many important nutrients — complete protein, vitamins A and D, the B vitamins, iron, and phosphorous.

Storing — As soon as possible after purchasing, store eggs in the refrigerator in their own egg container to keep them upright, or store on the egg shelf of the refrigerator door, small ends down. Remove only as many eggs as needed at one time.

Do not buy cracked or soiled eggs. If some eggs have been cracked bringing them from the market, cook those as soon as possible. If ever necessary to remove soil from eggs, wipe them with a damp cloth before storing them or wash them just before using. Washing them before storing removes the film or "bloom" which seals the pores of the shell and keeps out bacteria and odors.

Food Preparation — The fundamental rule in egg cookery is: *Cook eggs with low to medium, even heat.* This applies to all methods of cooking eggs. Too high a temperature and overcooking toughen the protein in eggs and egg dishes, making them leathery and/or curdled.

In combining hot mixtures with whole eggs or egg yolks, always *slowly* add the hot mixture (3 or 4 spoonfuls or entire amount) to the beaten egg, stirring or beating constantly.

Separating egg yolks from egg whites is quicker

and easier if done soon after eggs are removed from refrigerator. However, eggs at room temperature, especially egg whites, beat to a greater volume than eggs taken directly from the refrigerator. (For stages of beating eggs, see *page 2*.)

Leftover egg whites may be refrigerated (in covered containers) about one week. For longer periods they should be frozen. Uses for egg whites: angel food or white cake, seven-minute frosting, meringue. Store leftover egg yolks in refrigerator; use within 2 or 3 days. Freeze them for longer storage periods.

HELPFUL HINTS ABOUT EGGS
- To divide a raw egg, beat well before measuring with a tablespoon.
- To hard-cook egg yolks, use only unbroken yolks and slip them gently into simmering water. Keep below boiling point until yolks are firm. Remove with a slotted spoon.
- To slice hard-cooked eggs without breaking the yolk, dip knife into water before slicing.

SOFT-COOKED EGGS
Put eggs into a saucepan and cover with cold or warm water. Cover. Bring water rapidly to boiling. Turn off heat. If necessary to prevent further boiling, remove saucepan from heat source. Let stand, covered, 2 to 4 minutes, depending upon firmness desired. Cool eggs promptly in cold water for several seconds to prevent further cooking. Serve hot. NOTE: When cooking more than four eggs, do not turn off heat but reduce heat to keep water below simmering. (Eggs are a protein food and therefore should never be boiled.) Hold 4 to 6 minutes.

HARD-COOKED EGGS: Follow method for Soft-Cooked Eggs. After bringing water to boiling, let eggs stand, covered, 20 to 22 minutes. Cool cooked eggs promptly under running cold water and crackle the shells. Roll eggs between hands to loosen shell, then start peeling at large end.

ABOUT CHEESE

For the fullest enjoyment of most cheeses, remove them from the refrigerator at least 1 hour before serving; the interior of Camembert and Brie should be almost runny. Serve Neufchâtel, cottage, and cream cheeses chilled.

The joy of cheese is in the tasting. An English gourmet once said that "the only way to learn about cheese is to eat it," and for some 4,000 years of recorded history people have been doing just that.

No one knows just how or when cheese was discovered. The ancient Greeks esteemed it so highly that they believed it to be a gift of the gods. Legend has it that it was discovered quite by accident when an Arab traveler carried as part of his food supply on a journey across the desert some milk in a crude container fashioned from a sheep's stomach. By some happy chance the heat of the day and the rennet still remaining in the container caused the milk to separate into curds and whey. The whey satisfied the traveler's thirst and the curd his appetite — and so cheese was born.

Few foods equal cheese for nutritive value and variety of flavor and texture. More than 350 different cheeses have been catalogued and described, oftentimes in accents of rapture. Cheese is produced and prized around the world. It serves more purposes than can be listed here. It can be used as an appetizer, entrée, or dessert, and the magic of its flavor — its many flavors — combines enchantingly with many other foods. Cooking with cheese is a fascinating and rewarding adventure. Success is certain if two simple rules are kept in mind. Cheese requires a low temperature, since it is a protein food and it must not be overcooked.

In different parts of the world, different kinds of milk and different methods of handling cheese have produced many different and distinctive types. As people of many lands came to the United States, they brought the knowledge of and the taste for native cheeses with them. As a result, many kinds of cheese which originated abroad are today being produced in this country, and a good many of them are also imported from their native lands and made available to American homemakers.

A few, such as Roquefort or blue, Swiss, Parmesan, and most of all, Cheddar, have become so thoroughly domesticated here that almost everyone knows them and has used them at some time. But others, which also offer a great deal of eating pleasure, are not as widely known.

These cheese varieties are *natural cheeses*, made directly from milk, with or without aging and "ripening" by bacterial action or molds. Natural cheese is purchased in cuts made from the big "wheels" and other forms; it is also available precut into slices, wedges, and convenient-shaped pieces and prewrapped in airtight packages. Natural cheeses made domestically are often made in loaves or bricks which would not be recognized in the native lands of the cheeses.

There are four types of natural cheeses: Soft, semisoft, hard, and very hard. The *soft cheeses* include the unripened cream and cottage cheese as well as the ripened Camemberts and Bries (both table rather than cooking cheeses). The *semisoft cheeses* are Roquefort and other blue-veined cheeses which are often used in dressings and spreads. The *hard cheeses* include Swiss and Cheddar and these are the most commonly used cooking cheeses. *Very hard cheeses* like Parmesan and Romano are generally grated and used as toppings for cooked foods.

In the United States various other forms of cheese have been developed through the years, such as: *Process cheese* — Produced from natural cheeses blended for uniformity of flavor, texture, and cooking quality. The cheeses are ground together, melted, pasteurized, and poured into molds lined with moisture-vaporproof packaging material; the packages are sealed and the cheese, virtually sterilized, is cooled in the packages. Process cheese has typically a perfectly smooth consistency and good keeping quality.

Cheese food — May either be process, made like process cheese but with certain dairy products added; or cold-pack, with the same additions but not pasteurized. The process type is perfectly smooth; the cold-pack type is somewhat granular and crumbly because it is not homogenized.

Process cheese spreads — Cheese foods of a slightly higher moisture content to produce a more spreadable consistency at room temperature.

EGG DISHES

Poached Eggs

POACHED EGGS

Grease bottom of a skillet. Pour in *water* to a depth of 2 inches. Bring water to boiling; reduce heat to keep water at simmering point. Break each *egg* into a saucer or small dish and quickly slip into water, holding the saucer close to the surface of the water. Cook 3 to 5 minutes, depending upon firmness desired. Carefully remove egg with a slotted spoon or pancake turner. Drain by holding spoon on absorbent paper for a few seconds. Season with *salt* and *pepper*. Serve immediately.

EGGS AU GRATIN
(Oeufs Gratines Laperouse)
A recipe from Restaurant Laperouse in Paris.

1 cup finely chopped mushrooms	8 poached eggs, *above*
2 tablespoons butter	1 cup Hollandaise Sauce, *page 197*
1 to 1½ cups Béchamel Sauce, *page 196*	¼ cup grated Parmesan cheese

1. Cook mushrooms in butter until very dry.
2. Mix in the desired amount of Béchamel Sauce.
3. Spread the mushroom sauce in 4 ovenproof ramekins. Put 2 poached eggs in each dish and cover with Hollandaise Sauce. Sprinkle with Parmesan cheese and brown under the broiler.

4 SERVINGS

POACHED EGGS "DUCHESSE ANNE"
A breakfast or luncheon treat from the Grand Hotel de la Place in Dinan, France.

3 large tomatoes, cut in halves	½ cup strong beef broth
2 cups chopped mushrooms	¼ cup port wine
	6 bread rounds, 4 in. each
¼ cup chopped onion	3 tablespoons butter, softened
3 tablespoons butter	
⅓ cup chopped parsley	6 poached eggs, *above*
¼ cup soft bread crumbs	12 slices bacon, fried

1. Scoop out seeds from tomato halves. Put tomatoes into a shallow baking pan; set aside.
2. Add mushrooms and onion to 3 tablespoons hot butter in a skillet; cook until just tender. Mix in parsley and bread crumbs; heat 2 minutes.
3. Season tomato halves with *salt* and *pepper*; spoon in mushroom mixture.
4. Bake at 350°F about 20 minutes, or until toma-

Egg Dishes

toes are just tender.
5. Meanwhile, simmer broth to reduce by one half; mix in the wine; simmer 5 minutes.
6. Spread the butter on both sides of the bread rounds; heat rounds in skillet until golden brown.
7. Arrange toast rounds on preheated platter. Place a tomato half on each round and drizzle with wine sauce. Top each with a poached egg and 2 bacon strips. 6 SERVINGS

EGGS BENEDICT

4 English muffin halves, buttered and toasted	4 poached eggs, *above* Hollandaise Sauce, *page 197*
4 thin slices cooked ham, heated	

Top each toasted English muffin with a ham slice. Place one poached egg on each ham slice. Season with *salt* and *pepper*. Spoon Hollandaise Sauce over each serving. 4 SERVINGS

Scrambled Eggs

SCRAMBLED EGGS

6 eggs	¾ teaspoon salt
6 tablespoons milk, cream, or undiluted evaporated milk	⅛ teaspoon pepper
	3 tablespoons butter or margarine

1. Beat the eggs, milk, salt, and pepper together until blended.
2. Heat an 8- or 10-inch skillet until hot enough to sizzle a drop of water. Melt butter in skillet.
3. Pour egg mixture into skillet and cook over low heat. With a spatula, lift mixture from bottom and sides of skillet as it thickens, allowing uncooked portion to flow to bottom. Cook until eggs are thick and creamy. 4 SERVINGS

SCRAMBLED EGGS DE LUXE: Follow recipe for Scrambled Eggs. Add ½ *teaspoon Worcestershire sauce* and ¼ *cup finely shredded Cheddar cheese* to egg mixture in skillet. Cook as directed. Before removing from heat, gently stir in *1 medium-sized firm ripe tomato*, cut in small cubes, and *1 cup croutons*, ¼ to ½ inch. 4 TO 6 SERVINGS

BACON AND CREAM CHEESE SCRAMBLE

6 tablespoons milk, cream, or undiluted evaporated milk	¼ teaspoon salt
	⅛ teaspoon black pepper
3 oz. cream cheese, cubed	3 tablespoons butter or margarine
2 tablespoons butter or margarine	½ cup diced cooked bacon
6 eggs	

1. Put the milk, cream cheese, and 2 tablespoons butter into top of a double boiler. Heat over simmering water until cheese is softened. Stir to blend.
2. Beat the eggs, salt, and pepper until blended. Stir into the cheese mixture.
3. Heat a skillet until hot enough to sizzle a drop of water. Melt the 3 tablespoons butter. Add a mixture of eggs and cooked bacon. Cook over low heat. With a spatula, lift mixture from bottom and sides of skillet as it thickens, allowing uncooked portion to flow to bottom. Cook until thick and creamy. 4 SERVINGS

HAM AND CREAM CHEESE SCRAMBLE: Follow recipe for Bacon and Cream Cheese Scramble. Substitute ½ *cup diced cooked ham* for bacon.

SCRAMBLED EGGS WITH CHEESE
After a busy day Jerry Lewis finds that eggs with cheese hit the spot, so he heads for the kitchen and takes matters into his own hands.

4 eggs	¼ cup grated American cheese
¼ teaspoon salt	
Few grains pepper	1½ tablespoons butter

1. Break eggs, one at a time, into a cup; then turn each into a medium bowl before adding the next.
2. Add salt, pepper, and cheese, then beat with a fork just enough to blend.
3. Melt butter in an 8-inch skillet, tilting it so bottom and sides are covered. When butter is hot, pour in egg mixture.
4. Cook over low heat, scraping gently as eggs set, so they will cook uniformly. Cook until done, but still moist—eggs will continue to cook in the hot pan on the way to the plate. Serve immediately. ABOUT 2 SERVINGS

Egg Dishes

CHILI-EGG

- 1 lb. ground beef
- 1 medium-sized green pepper, quartered, seeded, and diced (¾ cup)
- 1 medium onion, chopped (½ cup)
- ½ cup diced celery
- 1 tablespoon chili powder
- 1½ teaspoons salt
- ⅛ teaspoon pepper
- 1 can (16 ozs.) tomatoes
- 1 can (16 ozs.) red kidney beans
- 8 eggs
- ⅓ cup milk
- 3 tablespoons butter or margarine
- 2 tablespoons chopped parsley

1. Shape ground beef into a large patty; place in a kettle. Brown in its own fat, turning once; break up into chunks; push to one side.
2. Stir green pepper, onion, celery, and chili powder into drippings; sauté until onion is soft. Stir in 1 teaspoon of the salt, pepper, tomatoes, and kidney beans and liquid. Heat to boiling; cover. Simmer 30 minutes; uncover. Simmer 30 minutes longer, or until thick.
3. While chili simmers, beat eggs with milk and remaining ½ teaspoon salt in a medium bowl until well blended.
4. Melt butter in a medium skillet; pour in egg mixture. Cook slowly, lifting mixture around edge of pan as it cooks to let soft part run to bottom; continue cooking just until eggs are softly set but still creamy moist on top.
5. Spoon chili mixture into 6 individual serving bowls; spoon eggs in a ring around edge on each. Sprinkle parsley over all. 6 SERVINGS

PISTO A LA "EL CHICO"

A favorite main-dish egg scramble from Señor Benito Collada, impresario of New York City's smart El Chico Spanish Restaurant.

- 1 large clove garlic
- 1 cup thinly sliced onion
- 1 cup slivered green pepper
- ½ cup olive oil
- 1 cup thin raw potato strips
- 1 tablespoon chopped parsley
- ⅓ cup (2 oz.) diced cooked ham
- 2 cups small cubes yellow summer squash
- 2 cups peeled, finely cut, ripe tomatoes
- 2 teaspoons salt
- 1 teaspoon sugar
- ⅛ teaspoon pepper
- 6 eggs, beaten

1. Add garlic, onion, and green pepper to heated olive oil in a large skillet; cook until softened, then remove garlic.
2. Add remaining ingredients except eggs to skillet; cook over medium heat, stirring frequently, about 10 minutes, or until squash is just tender.
3. Pour beaten eggs into vegetables and cook as for *Scrambled Eggs, page 66* 6 SERVINGS

LEMON CUSTARD FRENCH TOAST

- 8 slices French bread, cut 1 inch thick
- 4 eggs
- 2 teaspoons sugar
- 1 teaspoon grated lemon rind
- Dash of salt
- 1 cup milk
- ¾ cup coarsely crushed bite-sized corn cereal squares
- Golden Apricot Syrup (recipe follows)

1. Place bread in a single layer in a shallow glass baking dish.
2. Beat eggs in a medium bowl until blended; stir in sugar, lemon rind, salt, and milk; pour over bread. Let stand 2 minutes, then turn slices. Let stand 15 minutes longer at room temperature, or overnight in refrigerator, until milk is absorbed completely.
3. Preheat oven to 400°F.
4. Sprinkle cereal on a sheet of waxed paper. Lift bread slices from dish and dip in cereal to coat both sides generously; place in a single layer on a lightly greased large cookie sheet.
5. Bake 20 minutes, or until puffed and crisp. Serve hot with Golden Apricot Syrup. 4 SERVINGS

GOLDEN APRICOT SYRUP

- 1 can (12 ozs.) apricot nectar
- ¼ cup honey
- 1 tablespoon lemon juice
- 1 teaspoon grated orange rind
- 2 tablespoons butter or margarine

1. Combine apricot nectar, honey, lemon juice, and orange rind in a small saucepan. Heat slowly, stirring constantly, to boiling; simmer, stirring once or twice, 15 minutes, or until syrupy-thick. Stir in butter until melted.
2. Pour into a pitcher; serve hot. ABOUT 1 CUP

Omelets

FRENCH OMELET

- 6 eggs
- 6 tablespoons milk or water
- ¾ teaspoon salt
- ⅛ teaspoon black pepper
- 3 tablespoons butter or margarine

Egg Dishes

1. Beat the eggs, milk, salt, and pepper together until blended.
2. Heat an 8- to 10-inch skillet until just hot enough to sizzle a drop of water; melt butter in the skillet.
3. Pour egg mixture into skillet. As edges of omelet begin to thicken, draw cooked portions toward center with spoon or fork to allow uncooked mixture to flow to bottom of skillet, tilting skillet as necessary; do not stir.
4. When eggs are thickened but surface is still moist, increase heat to quickly brown the bottom of omelet. Loosen edges carefully and fold in half; slide onto a warm serving platter. If desired, garnish with sprigs of *watercress*. 4 TO 6 SERVINGS

CITRUS OMELET: Follow recipe for French Omelet. Substitute *3 tablespoons lemon or orange juice* and *3 tablespoons water* for liquid.

CHICKEN LIVER OMELET: Follow recipe for French Omelet. Just before serving, enclose in omelet *¼ pound chicken livers* which have been coated with *seasoned flour* and browned in *butter or margarine* with *minced onion*.

BACON OMELET: Unwrap *½ pound sliced bacon*, do not separate, and cut crosswise into fine thin strips. Put into an unheated 8- to 10-inch skillet and fry until crisp. Drain bacon fat from skillet and return about 2 tablespoons fat to skillet. Follow recipe for French Omelet. Decrease salt to ½ teaspoon, omit butter, and pour egg mixture over bacon in skillet.

ROQUEFORT OMELET

At the Fleur de Lis Restaurant in San Francisco, California, Roquefort Omelet is a featured dish. Follow recipe for French Omelet. Substitute *¼ cup heavy cream* and *1 tablespoon melted butter* for the milk, decrease salt to ¼ teaspoon, omit pepper, and add a *few grains cayenne pepper*. Before browning bottom of omelet, sprinkle with about *¼ pound crumbled Roquefort cheese* (reserve a little for garnish). Top the omelet with the cheese and snipped *parsley*.

SAUCY HAM OMELET

1 can (12 oz.) chopped ham, cut in sticks	2 tablespoons milk
2 tablespoons butter or margarine	1 tablespoon flour
4 eggs	⅛ teaspoon salt
	Apple Sauce, *next column*

1. Brown ham sticks in a skillet.
2. Add butter to skillet, then a blend of the eggs, milk, flour, and salt. Arrange ham sticks spoke-fashion; cook until egg mixture is set.
3. Cut into wedges and serve with warm Apple Sauce. ABOUT 4 SERVINGS

APPLE SAUCE: Heat *1 can (12 ounce) apple juice* in a saucepan until hot. Stir in a mixture of *2 tablespoons brown sugar, 1 tablespoon cornstarch, ¼ teaspoon ground cinnamon*, and *2 tablespoons lemon juice*. Bring to boiling, stirring constantly; simmer about 10 minutes, or until slightly thickened. Remove from heat and stir in *1 tablespoon butter or margarine* until melted.

ABOUT 1¼ CUPS SAUCE

MUSHROOM OMELET

¾ lb. fresh mushrooms, sliced lengthwise	⅛ teaspoon pepper
½ cup butter or margarine	1 cup milk
¼ cup flour	3 eggs, slightly beaten
½ teaspoon salt	4 teaspoons butter or margarine

1. Cook mushrooms in ¼ cup hot butter in a large skillet until lightly browned and tender. Reserve 8 slices for garnish. Put remaining mushrooms into a bowl; cover and set aside in a warm place.
2. Blend flour, salt, and pepper into remaining ¼ cup butter heated in a saucepan. Heat until bubbly. Gradually add the milk, stirring constantly.
3. Remove from heat and vigorously stir about ⅓ cup hot mixture into the beaten eggs. Blend into remaining hot mixture. Cover and set aside.
4. Heat an 8-inch skillet until hot enough to sizzle a drop of water; melt 1 teaspoon butter. Pour about a fourth of the egg mixture into the skillet and cook until lightly browned on bottom and firm but slightly moist on top. Loosen edges carefully with spatula and slide omelet layer into a shallow round baking dish.
5. Spoon a third of mushrooms over omelet layer. Repeat process with remaining egg mixture, alternating omelet and mushroom layers. Top the last omelet layer with reserved mushroom slices.
6. Bake at 350°F 10 to 15 minutes, or until thoroughly heated. Cut into wedges and garnish with *parsley*. 4 SERVINGS

ZUCCHINI OMELET

4 small zucchini
¼ cup butter or margarine
¾ teaspoon salt
Few grains pepper
½ cup shredded Parmesan cheese
½ teaspoon marjoram
4 eggs, beaten

1. Wash zucchini and trim off ends. Cut crosswise into ⅛-inch slices.
2. Heat the butter in a skillet over low heat; add zucchini and sprinkle with a mixture of the salt and pepper. Cook slowly, turning slices occasionally, until lightly browned.
3. Blend Parmesan cheese and marjoram into eggs. Pour mixture over zucchini in skillet and cook until egg mixture is set.
4. Remove skillet from heat and set under broiler about 4 inches from source of heat for 2 minutes, or until top is lightly browned. Serve cut in wedges.
4 SERVINGS

Hard-Cooked-Egg Dishes

EGGS STUFFED WITH CHICKEN LIVER PASTE

¼ lb. chicken livers
5 hard-cooked eggs
4 slices bacon, diced and fried until crisp
1 tablespoon chopped parsley
1½ teaspoons minced chives
½ teaspoon onion salt
¼ teaspoon tarragon leaves, crushed
¼ teaspoon salt
¼ teaspoon pepper
Few grains cayenne pepper
1½ to 2 tablespoons mayonnaise

1. Rinse chicken livers with cold water and drain; put livers into a saucepan and add enough hot water to barely cover. Cover saucepan and simmer 10 to 15 minutes, or until livers are tender when pierced with a fork; drain and set aside to cool.
2. Cut each hard-cooked egg into halves; remove egg yolks to a bowl and mash with a fork. Sieve the chicken livers into the bowl. Mix in bacon and remaining ingredients.
3. Fill egg whites with liver mixture and sprinkle with *paprika*. Chill thoroughly.
4. To serve, cut into halves and spear each on a frilly pick.
20 STUFFED EGG QUARTERS

CRAB-STUFFED EGGS

12 hard-cooked eggs, cut in halves lengthwise
1 can (6½ oz.) crab meat, drained and flaked
2 tablespoons melted butter
¼ cup dairy sour cream
2 to 3 tablespoons mayonnaise
4 drops Tabasco
4 teaspoons grated onion
½ teaspoon Worcestershire sauce
½ teaspoon salt
⅛ teaspoon white pepper

1. Remove egg yolks from whites. Sieve yolks; toss with crab meat.
2. Blend in a mixture of the remaining ingredients. Stuff egg whites. Garnish each with *pimiento* or *parsley*.
24 STUFFED EGG HALVES

STUFFED EGGS SOPHISTICATE

12 hard-cooked eggs
3 oz. cream cheese, softened
½ cup dairy sour cream
2 tablespoons melted butter
¼ teaspoon Tabasco
¾ to 1 teaspoon salt
¼ teaspoon dry mustard

1. Cut eggs lengthwise into quarters and remove egg yolks, leaving egg whites intact. Put egg yolks through a sieve. Set aside.
2. Beat cream cheese until fluffy; blend in sour cream, butter, Tabasco, and a mixture of the salt and dry mustard. Add egg yolks; mix lightly.
3. Fill egg whites by piping the mixture through a pastry bag and tube. Sprinkle with *paprika*.
4 DOZEN STUFFED EGG QUARTERS

CURRY-ALMOND-STUFFED EGGS: Follow recipe for Stuffed Eggs Sophisticate. Mix *½ teaspoon curry powder* with salt and dry mustard. Blend *½ cup toasted blanched almonds*, finely chopped, into the egg yolk mixture.

DILLY BACON-STUFFED EGGS: Follow recipe for Stuffed Eggs Sophisticate. Omit Tabasco and dry mustard. Blend into the cream cheese *½ teaspoon dill weed*, *1 tablespoon chopped capers*, and *2 teaspoons caper liquid*. Mix in *6 slices diced cooked bacon*.

PERKY STUFFED EGGS

12 hard-cooked eggs
⅓ cup finely chopped green pepper
2 tablespoons mayonnaise

Egg Dishes

¼ cup chopped pimiento-stuffed olives
3 tablespoons finely chopped onion
2 tablespoons finely chopped parsley
¼ cup tomato sauce
2 tablespoons dairy sour cream
2 teaspoons lemon juice
6 drops Tabasco
¼ teaspoon salt
Few grains pepper
½ teaspoon dry mustard

1. Using a sharp-pointed knife, cut a saw-toothed line lengthwise around each egg. Gently pull halves apart and remove egg yolks. Set whites aside.
2. Sieve egg yolks or mash them with a fork. Add the green pepper, olives, onion, parsley, and a mixture of the remaining ingredients; mix well. Fill the egg whites with egg yolk mixture. Cover; chill thoroughly.   24 STUFFED EGG HALVES

SCOTCH EGGS

1½ lbs. ground beef
1 tablespoon instant minced onion
1 teaspoon seasoned salt
⅛ teaspoon pepper
6 hard-cooked eggs, shelled
2 tablespoons milk
¼ cup dry bread crumbs
1 tablespoon salad oil
1 can (6 ozs.) tomato paste
1½ cups water
3 cups hot cooked noodles
1 tablespoon butter or margarine
1 tablespoon chopped parsley
1 envelope spaghetti sauce mix with mushrooms

1. Preheat oven to 400°F.
2. Combine ground beef, onion, salt, and pepper in a large bowl; mix lightly. Divide into 6 mounds; shape each mound around a hard-cooked egg to cover completely.
3. Measure milk into a pie plate; sprinkle bread crumbs on waxed paper. Roll meat in milk, then in bread crumbs to coat well. Place in a greased shallow pan.
4. Bake 30 minutes, or until beef is as done as you like it.
5. While meat cooks, prepare spaghetti sauce mix with salad oil, tomato paste, and water as label directs.
6. Toss noodles with butter and parsley in a medium bowl; spoon in center of a large serving platter. Cut each meatball in half; arrange around edge. Pass sauce separately.   6 SERVINGS

EGGS FARCI

In this casserole stuffed eggs and sausages are topped with a rich mushroom and ripe olive sauce, creating a tempting dish to offer guests.

8 hard-cooked eggs, cut in halves
1 cup cream
½ cup all-purpose flour
1 can (13¾ oz.) clear chicken broth
2 cans (6 oz. each) chopped or sliced broiled-in-butter mushrooms, drained (reserve liquid)
4 teaspoons instant minced onion softened in 4 to 6 teaspoons water
1 teaspoon Worcestershire sauce
1 cup pitted ripe olives, quartered lengthwise
1 lb. pork sausage links or smokie link sausages, browned
1 large tomato, cut in thin wedges*

1. Fill the egg white halves with a deviled mixture of *mayonnaise*, sieved egg yolks, *Worcestershire sauce*, *dry mustard*, *salt*, and *pepper* to taste. Arrange deviled egg halves in an ungreased 2-quart shallow baking dish; set aside.
2. Meanwhile, blend enough cream with flour in a saucepan to make a paste. Set over heat. Stirring constantly to keep mixture smooth, gradually add remaining cream, then chicken broth and reserved mushroom liquid. Stir occasionally until mixture begins to thicken, then stir constantly until it bubbles; continue to cook 2 to 3 minutes.
3. Blend in the onion, Worcestershire sauce, mushrooms, and olives. Heat thoroughly and pour over stuffed eggs in the baking dish.
4. Alternate browned sausage links and tomato wedges over top; brush tomatoes with *oil*, and sprinkle with *monosodium glutamate* and *seasoned pepper*. Spoon coarse *buttered bread crumbs* (about ½ cup crumbs mixed with 1 tablespoon melted butter or margarine) over all.
5. Set under broiler about 5 inches from source of heat until crumbs are browned. Garnish with snipped *parsley*.   8 TO 10 SERVINGS

*If desired, use drained canned sliced tomatoes or tomato wedges.

NOTE: *Celery*, thinly sliced on the diagonal, may be cooked until crisp-tender in a small amount of the chicken broth and mixed into the sauce.

DEVILED EGGS

8 hard-cooked eggs
2 tablespoons milk
1 tablespoon lemon juice
1½ teaspoons prepared mustard
½ teaspoon salt
Dash of pepper
1 tablespoon chopped pimiento-stuffed green olives
Parsley

1. Cut eggs in half lengthwise; scoop out yolks into a small bowl; mash well.
2. Stir in milk, lemon juice, mustard, salt, pepper, and olives; pile back into whites. Trim each half with a small tuft of parsley. **8 SERVINGS**

EGG-AND-TREASURE TUNA BAKE

4 hard-cooked eggs
2 tablespoons mayonnaise or salad dressing
1 teaspoon prepared mustard
1 can (10¾ ozs.) condensed cream of mushroom soup
¼ cup milk
⅛ teaspoon salt
⅛ teaspoon pepper
2 cups uncooked medium noodles
1 package (3 ozs.) cream cheese with chives
1 can (3 ozs.) tuna, drained and broken up
2 tablespoons chopped onion
½ cup crushed potato chips

1. Preheat oven to 375°F.
2. Cut eggs in half lengthwise; scoop out yolks into a small bowl; mash well. Stir in mayonnaise, mustard, salt, and pepper; pile back into whites.
3. Cook noodles as label directs; drain; return to kettle.
4. Blend cream cheese with mushroom soup and milk in a medium bowl; stir in tuna and onion. Spoon over noodles; toss lightly to mix.
5. Spoon one third of the noodle mixture into a 1-quart baking dish; top with half of the deviled eggs. Repeat layers; spoon remaining tuna mixture on top. Sprinkle potato chips around edge in dish.
6. Bake 30 minutes, or until bubbly in the center. **4 SERVINGS**

CHEESE DISHES

CHEESE CASSEROLE ROYALE

1 cup dairy sour cream
⅔ cup shredded Swiss cheese
4 egg yolks, well beaten
1 cup browned buttered soft bread crumbs
4 egg whites (½ cup)
¾ teaspoon seasoned salt
½ to ¾ cup ground walnuts

1. Blend sour cream and cheese into beaten egg yolks. Turn into a greased 1½-quart shallow baking dish that has been sprinkled with the crumbs.
2. Set dish in a pan in a 375°F oven. Pour boiling water into pan to a depth of 1 inch. Bake 20 minutes, or until a knife inserted near center comes out clean.
3. Meanwhile, beat egg whites with salt until stiff, not dry, peaks are formed. Fold in walnuts.
4. Remove baking dish from oven and top with meringue. Return to oven and bake 8 minutes, or until meringue is browned. **ABOUT 6 SERVINGS**

DUTCH CHEESE CROQUETTES

1 cup milk
½ cup chopped carrot
⅓ cup chopped onion
1 teaspoon salt
¼ teaspoon thyme
3 sprigs parsley
3 peppercorns
1 bay leaf
1½ teaspoons unflavored gelatin
¼ cup cold water
4½ tablespoons flour
2 tablespoons butter
1 egg yolk, slightly beaten
¾ lb. Gouda cheese, finely shredded
1½ teaspoons lemon juice
½ teaspoon ground nutmeg
⅛ teaspoon black pepper
1 cup fine dry bread crumbs
1 egg, slightly beaten
Fat for deep frying heated to 375°F

1. Mix milk, carrot, onion, salt, thyme, parsley, peppercorns, and bay leaf in top of double boiler; heat 20 minutes over boiling water. Strain the mix-

Cheese Dishes

ture, reserving milk for sauce.
2. Soften gelatin in cold water and dissolve over hot water; set aside.
3. Blend flour into hot butter in a heavy saucepan; heat until bubbly. Add reserved milk gradually, stirring constantly. Bring to boiling; stir and cook 1 to 2 minutes.
4. Vigorously stir about 3 tablespoons hot mixture into egg yolk; immediately blend into mixture in saucepan. Cook and stir over low heat 2 minutes. Stir in cheese and heat just until melted.
5. Remove from heat. Stir in dissolved gelatin, then lemon juice, nutmeg, and pepper. Pour mixture into a shallow pan and chill about 4 hours.
6. Shape chilled mixture into balls, cones, or cylinders. Roll in bread crumbs, then dip into egg and again roll in bread crumbs, shaking off loose crumbs.
7. Deep fry in the hot fat, turning often to brown evenly. Remove with slotted spoon to absorbent paper. Serve hot.   ABOUT 6 SERVINGS

GREEN ENCHILADAS

1 carton (8 ozs.) cream-style cottage cheese	4 tablespoons butter or margarine
1 package (8 ozs.) sharp Cheddar cheese, shredded (2 cups)	4 tablespoons all-purpose flour
	Water
1 medium onion, chopped (½ cup)	1 can (13¾ ozs.) chicken broth
¼ cup chopped ripe olives	1 can (4 ozs.) green chili peppers, drained, seeded, and chopped
1¼ teaspoons salt	
½ cup salad oil	1 cup (8-oz. carton) dairy sour cream
12 tortillas	

1. Combine cottage cheese, 1½ cups of the Cheddar cheese, onion, olives, and ½ teaspoon of the salt in a medium bowl; mix well.
2. Heat salad oil in a medium skillet; place tortillas, only 1 at a time, in oil and heat for about 15 seconds on each side; remove from skillet and drain on paper toweling. As each is heated, measure about 2 tablespoons of the cheese mixture onto one edge; roll up, jelly roll fashion. Place, seam side down, in a 11¾x7½x1¾-inch baking dish.
3. Preheat oven to 375°F.
4. Melt butter in a medium saucepan; stir in flour and remaining ¾ teaspoon salt; heat, stirring constantly, until bubbly.

5. Add enough water to chicken broth to measure 2 cups; stir into flour mixture. Continue cooking and stirring until sauce thickens and boils 1 minute; stir in chili peppers.
6. Slowly stir about 1 cup of the hot sauce into sour cream in a small bowl, then stir back into saucepan; heat just until hot. (Do not boil.) Pour over filled tortillas; sprinkle remaining ½ cup Cheddar cheese in a ribbon down center.
7. Bake 20 minutes, or until bubbly. 4 TO 6 SERVINGS

MONTEREY TAMALE BUSY-DAY DINNER

2 cans (16 ozs. each) barbecued beans	1 cup shredded Monterey Jack cheese (4 ozs.)
1 can condensed chili-beef soup	1½ cups shredded iceberg lettuce
1 can (15 ozs.) tamales in chili gravy	

1. Preheat oven to 375°F.
2. Combine beans and soup in a 2-quart shallow baking dish. Remove wrappings from tamales; arrange tamales, chevron style, on top of bean mixture; sprinkle cheese all over.
3. Bake 45 minutes, or until bubbly and cheese melts. Sprinkle shredded lettuce around edge in dish.
                                                            6 SERVINGS

ALL-AMERICAN POTATO SCALLOP

4 large potatoes	1 package (8 ozs.) process American cheese, cut up
5 tablespoons butter or margarine	Few drops red-pepper seasoning
¼ cup all-purpose flour	
1½ teaspoons salt	1 jar (2 ozs.) pimientos, drained and chopped
1 teaspoon dry mustard	
1½ cups milk	½ cup fine bread crumbs

1. Scrub potatoes. Cook, covered, in boiling salted water in a large saucepan 30 minutes, or until tender; drain. Cool, then peel and slice ⅛ inch thick.
2. Preheat oven to 350°F.
3. Melt 4 tablespoons of the butter in a medium saucepan; stir in flour, salt, and mustard. Cook, stirring constantly, until bubbly. Stir in milk; continue cooking and stirring until sauce thickens and boils 1 minute. Stir in cheese until melted, then red-pepper seasoning and pimientos.

4. Layer one third of the potatoes into a deep 1½-quart baking dish; top with one third of the sauce. Repeat layers.
5. Melt remaining 1 tablespoon butter in a small saucepan; stir in bread crumbs; sprinkle over potato mixture.
6. Bake 45 minutes, or until sauce bubbles up.

8 SERVINGS

Quiches, Pies & Tarts

QUICHE LORRAINE
Andre Pittet, Chef at the Hotel Saskatchewan of the Canadian Pacific Railway, contributed this recipe.

½ cup diced bacon
1 cup chopped onion
½ cup diced mushrooms
1 unbaked 10-in. pastry shell
3 cups shredded white Cheddar cheese
2 eggs, slightly beaten
1 cup milk
½ teaspoon salt
⅛ teaspoon pepper
¼ teaspoon nutmeg

1. Fry the bacon for 5 minutes in a skillet and pour off about half of the fat. Add onion and mushrooms and cook until onion is soft.
2. Turn contents of skillet into the pastry shell and sprinkle with cheese. Pour a mixture of eggs, milk, salt, pepper, and nutmeg over cheese.
3. Bake at 350°F 30 to 35 minutes, or until lightly browned.
4. Serve hot as an appetizer or main dish.

ONE 10-INCH PIE

SWISS AND TUNA PIE

3 eggs
½ teaspoon salt
½ teaspoon dry mustard
Few grains cayenne pepper
1 cup heavy cream
½ cup ale
1 unbaked 9-in. pastry shell, chilled
2 cans (6½ or 7 oz. each) tuna, drained and flaked
8 oz. Swiss cheese, shredded
1 tablespoon flour

1. Beat eggs, salt, dry mustard, and cayenne pepper together until foamy. Beat in cream and ale.
2. Cover bottom of pastry shell with a layer of tuna. Sprinkle half of the cheese over the tuna.

Repeat layering. Sprinkle flour over cheese. Pour egg mixture over all.
3. Bake at 425°F 15 minutes. Reduce oven temperature to 300°F and bake 25 minutes, or until a knife inserted halfway between center and edge of filling comes out clean.

4 TO 6 SERVINGS

OLIVE-CHEESE TART

1½ cups sliced leek or onion
2 tablespoons butter or margarine
1 cup sliced pimiento-stuffed olives
1 9-in. unbaked pastry shell, chilled
½ cup shredded Swiss cheese
½ cup shredded Parmesan cheese
4 teaspoons flour
3 eggs (about ¾ cup)
⅛ teaspoon white pepper
⅛ teaspoon ground nutmeg
1½ cups light cream

1. Cook leek until tender in hot butter. Mix in olives and turn into the chilled pastry shell, distributing mixture evenly. Blend cheeses and flour; sprinkle over leek mixture.
2. Beat eggs, pepper, and nutmeg together. Beat in cream; pour over cheese mixture in pastry shell.
3. Bake at 425°F 15 minutes. Reduce oven temperature to 300°F and bake 20 minutes, or until a knife comes out clean when inserted halfway between center and edge of filling. Let stand 10 minutes before serving.
4. Garnish center with slices of *pimiento-stuffed olives*. Serve hot as an appetizer cut in small wedges or as a main dish cut in large wedges.

ONE 9-INCH TART

SWISS CHEESE-BACON PIE

1½ cups all-purpose flour
½ teaspoon garlic salt
½ teaspoon seasoned salt
½ teaspoon paprika
⅔ cup vegetable shortening
¼ cup cold water
6 to 8 oz. sliced Swiss cheese
9 slices bacon, diced and fried until crisp
4 eggs, slightly beaten
1 teaspoon Worcestershire sauce
2 cups light cream
1 tablespoon butter, melted
1½ tablespoons flour
½ teaspoon dry mustard
½ teaspoon celery salt
¼ teaspoon basil
1 tablespoon butter
½ cup chopped onion
1 teaspoon poppy seed

1. Blend flour, garlic salt, seasoned salt, and paprika in a bowl. Using a pastry blender or two knives, cut in shortening until pieces are size of small peas. Sprinkle water over mixture, a small amount at a time; mix lightly with a fork after each addition. Add only enough water to hold pastry together. Roll out pastry and fit into a 9-inch pie pan; flute edge.
2. Cover pastry with overlapping slices of Swiss cheese and sprinkle evenly with bacon.
3. Combine in a bowl the eggs, Worcestershire sauce, cream, melted butter, and a mixture of the flour, mustard, celery salt, and basil; beat slightly to blend thoroughly. Pour over bacon and cheese.
4. Bake at 350°F 45 minutes, or until custard is set and top is lightly browned. Remove from oven.
5. Meanwhile, heat 1 tablespoon butter in a small skillet; add onion and cook until soft.
6. Top custard evenly with onion and poppy seed. Cut into wedge-shaped pieces and serve at once.

6 TO 8 SERVINGS

Fondues & Rabbits

BAKED CHEESE FONDUE

3 cups soft bread cubes	3 tablespoons grated onion
1 tablespoon melted butter or margarine	½ teaspoon salt
	¼ teaspoon pepper
1 teaspoon poppy seed	½ teaspoon dry mustard
2 cups milk	¼ teaspoon paprika
1 or 2 drops Tabasco	4 egg yolks, well beaten
12 oz. sharp Cheddar cheese, shredded	
	4 egg whites

1. Lightly toss 1 cup of the bread cubes with the melted butter and poppy seed. Set aside.
2. Scald milk and pour into a large bowl. Mix in Tabasco. Add remaining bread cubes, the shredded cheese, onion, and a mixture of salt, pepper, dry mustard, and paprika. Mix lightly but thoroughly until cheese is melted. Add beaten egg yolks gradually, stirring constantly.
3. Beat egg whites until stiff, not dry, peaks are formed. Gently fold with cheese mixture.
4. Turn into a lightly buttered 2-quart casserole. Top with poppy seed-coated bread cubes.
5. Set casserole in a pan in a 325°F oven. Pour boiling water into pan to a depth of 1 inch. Bake 50 to 60 minutes, or until a knife inserted halfway between center and edge comes out clean.

ABOUT 6 SERVINGS

SWISS CHEESE FONDUE

Fondue is more than a gourmet's delight; it is a food tradition, one of the few foods that must be prepared and served just so to be truly itself. It is a dish for friends dining intimately, for all must eat literally from the same pot. No harsh metal must ever come in contact with a fondue. It is a recipe for a chafing dish with an earthenware pan and a little cheerful flame to keep the fondue barely bubbling. When the time comes for eating the fondue, all must be prepared to dunk—for here dunking is smiled upon. Do it with cubes of French bread or hard French rolls, cut so each cube has crust on at least one side. Spear the bread cubes from the soft side, and be sure your fork penetrates the sturdy opposite crust securely, for he whose bread first falls off into the fondue traditionally pays the reckoning by purchasing a bottle of wine. Only ladies are free of this ruling. They must forfeit a kiss for every piece of bread they lose. (Special long-tined forks make the process easier.) When you dip into the pot, stir the fondue gently, thus helping to keep it well blended as well as accumulating more of the delectable cheese mixture on your bread cube. Lift it out with a twirling motion and eat—quickly! As the meal progresses, some of the cheese will form a brown crust on the bottom of the pan—this is a special delicacy which should be lifted out and divided among the company.

1 loaf (1 lb.) French bread	2 cups Neuchâtel or other dry white wine
1 tablespoon corn starch	1 lb. natural Swiss cheese, shredded
2 tablespoons kirsch	Freshly ground black pepper to taste
1 clove garlic, halved	Ground nutmeg to taste

1. Cut bread into bite-size pieces each having at least one crusty side; set aside.
2. Mix cornstarch and kirsch in a small bowl; set aside.
3. Rub the inside of a 2-quart flame-resistant casserole or porcelain-finished saucepan with cut surface of garlic. Pour in wine; place over medium heat until wine is about to simmer (*do not boil*).
4. Add the shredded cheese in small amounts to the hot wine, stirring constantly until cheese is melted. Heat cheese-wine mixture until bubbly.
5. Blend in the cornstarch mixture and continue stirring while cooking 5 minutes, or until fondue begins to bubble; add seasoning.

6. Spear bread with forks to use for dipping. Keep the fondue gently bubbling throughout serving time.   ABOUT 10 SERVINGS

NOTE: If desired, a hibachi or grill (with charcoal for fuel) may be used to cook the fondue.

PORK-AND-PINEAPPLE RABBIT RAREBIT

1 can (12 ozs.) pork luncheon meat	Dash of salt
1 can (8 ozs.) sliced pineapple, drained	Dash of pepper
	1 cup milk
¼ cup butter or margarine	4 slices process American cheese, cut up
¼ cup all-purpose flour	4 slices frozen French toast

1. Cut luncheon meat into 8 slices; brown lightly on both sides in a medium skillet; remove from skillet.
2. Brown pineapple lightly in drippings in skillet; keep hot.
3. While meat and pineapple brown, melt butter in a medium saucepan; stir in flour, salt, and pepper; cook, stirring constantly, until bubbly. Stir in milk; continue cooking and stirring until sauce thickens and boils 1 minute. Stir in cheese until melted.
4. Heat French toast as label directs; place each slice on a serving plate. Top with two slices of meat and a slice of pineapple; spoon cheese sauce over all.

4 SERVINGS

WELSH RABBIT IN CHAFING DISH

¼ cup butter	1 teaspoon dry mustard
2 lbs. sharp Cheddar cheese, shredded (about 8 cups)	Few grains cayenne pepper
	4 eggs, slightly beaten
2 teaspoons Worcestershire sauce	1 cup light cream or half and half

1. In a chafing dish blazer over simmering water, melt butter. Add cheese and heat, stirring occasionally, until cheese is melted. Mix in Worcestershire sauce, dry mustard, and cayenne pepper.
2. Blend eggs and cream; strain. Mix into melted cheese. Cook until thick, stirring frequently.
3. Garnish with *parsley sprigs*. Serve over toasted *English muffin halves*.   6 CUPS WELSH RABBIT

NOTE: When reheating mixture, thin with desired amount of *sherry, other white wine*, or *milk*.

WELSH RABBIT WITH EAST INDIAN FLAVOR

1 tablespoon butter	½ teaspoon dry mustard
1 lb. sharp Cheddar cheese, shredded (about 4 cups)	Few grains cayenne pepper
	⅔ cup milk
½ teaspoon Worcestershire sauce	2 tablespoons chutney
	6 slices bread, toasted

1. Heat butter in top of a double boiler over simmering water. Add cheese all at one time and stir occasionally until cheese begins to melt. Blend in the Worcestershire sauce, dry mustard, and cayenne pepper. Add milk gradually, stirring constantly until mixture is smooth and cheese is melted.
2. Spread a teaspoon of chutney over each slice of toast. Top with cheese mixture. Serve immediately. Top each serving with a *poached egg*, if desired.

6 SERVINGS

SOUFFLÉS

CHEESE SOUFFLÉ

¼ cup flour	¼ teaspoon Tabasco
¾ teaspoon salt	8 oz. sharp Cheddar cheese, coarsely shredded
¾ teaspoon monosodium glutamate	
½ teaspoon dry mustard	6 egg yolks, well beaten
⅛ teaspoon paprika	
1⅔ cups (14½-oz. can) evaporated milk	6 egg whites

1. Blend the flour, salt, monosodium glutamate, dry mustard, and paprika in a heavy saucepan. Add the evaporated milk gradually, then the Tabasco, stirring until smooth. Bring to boiling; stir and cook 1 to 2 minutes.
2. Add cheese all at one time and stir until cheese is melted. Remove from heat.
3. Pour sauce slowly into beaten egg yolks, beating constantly.
4. Beat egg whites until stiff, not dry, peaks are

formed. Spoon the sauce over egg whites and fold together until just blended. Turn into an ungreased 2-quart soufflé dish (deep casserole with straight sides). About 1½ inches from edge of dish, draw a circle by inserting the tip of a spoon 1 inch into the mixture to form a "top hat."
5. Bake at 300°F 55 to 60 minutes, or until a knife inserted halfway between center and edge of soufflé comes out clean. ABOUT 6 SERVINGS

SWISS CHEESE SOUFFLÉ

¼ cup butter or margarine	1 cup milk
¼ cup flour	6 oz. natural Swiss cheese, finely shredded (about 1½ cups)
¼ teaspoon salt	
Few grains black pepper	4 egg yolks, well beaten
⅛ teaspoon ground nutmeg	4 egg whites

1. Heat butter in a saucepan. Blend in a mixture of flour, salt, pepper, and nutmeg; heat until bubbly. Add milk gradually, stirring constantly. Bring to boiling; stir and cook 1 to 2 minutes. Remove from heat.
2. Stir in the cheese all at one time. Pour sauce slowly into beaten egg yolks, beating constantly.
3. Beat egg whites until stiff, not dry, peaks are formed. Spoon cheese mixture over egg whites; fold until just blended. Turn into an ungreased 1½-quart soufflé dish (deep casserole with straight sides).
4. Bake at 325°F about 50 minutes, or until a knife inserted halfway between center and edge of soufflé comes out clean. 6 SERVINGS

FRYING PAN SOUFFLÉ

⅓ cup butter or margarine	¼ teaspoon cream of tartar
⅓ cup all-purpose flour	1 cup shredded process American cheese (4 ozs.)
1 teaspoon salt	
Dash of pepper	
1½ cups milk	6 green onions, trimmed and sliced thin
6 eggs, separated	
	1 medium-sized red pepper, quartered, seeded, and chopped

1. Preheat oven to 325°F.
2. Melt butter in a medium saucepan; stir in flour, salt, and pepper. Cook, stirring constantly, until bubbly. Stir in milk; continue cooking and stirring until mixture thickens and boils 1 minute; cool while beating eggs.
3. Beat egg whites in a large bowl until foamy; add cream of tartar and continue beating until mixture forms soft peaks.
4. Beat egg yolks in a second large bowl until creamy; slowly beat in cooled sauce; fold in beaten egg whites. Pour into a buttered 10-inch skillet with ovenproof handle.
5. Bake 35 minutes, or until puffed and golden. Sprinkle cheese over top; return to oven just until cheese starts to melt; remove from oven. Sprinkle green onions and red pepper on top. Cut into wedges; serve at once. 6 SERVINGS

TOP HAT SHRIMP SOUFFLÉ

1 can (about 10 oz.) condensed cream of shrimp soup	¼ teaspoon dry mustard
	Few grains white pepper
	6 oz. sharp Cheddar cheese, shredded (about 1½ cups)
¼ cup dried parsley flakes	
2 tablespoons grated onion	6 egg yolks, well beaten
1 tablespoon flour	6 egg whites

1. Set out a 2-quart soufflé dish (deep casserole with straight sides); do not grease. Fold a 24-inch piece of aluminum foil lengthwise in half. Place around dish, cut side down, overlapping the ends; tie with a string to secure around dish.
2. Turn soup into a saucepan. Blend in the parsley flakes, onion, and a mixture of flour, dry mustard, and white pepper. Heat until bubbly, stirring constantly; cook 3 minutes. Remove from heat.
3. Add the cheese all at one time and stir until cheese is melted.
4. Spoon sauce into beaten egg yolks, stirring vigorously until blended.
5. Beat egg whites until stiff, not dry, peaks are formed. Spoon the egg yolk mixture over the egg whites. Gently fold together until just blended. Turn into the dish. About 1½ inches from edge of dish, draw a circle by inserting the tip of a spoon 1 inch into the mixture to form a "top hat."
6. Bake at 325°F 50 minutes, or until a knife inserted halfway between center and edge comes out clean. ABOUT 6 SERVINGS

Chapter 5
MEATS

Meat is king of the dinner table — the food that holds the center spot in the menu and the hub around which most meals are planned. Prized for its flavor and food value, meat satisfies the appetite as no other food can — not only when it is eaten but for a longer time thereafter.

America is almost unique in the world in the abundance of its meat supply and the manner in which this abundance is taken for granted. Historically there are good reasons why this came to be. The early colonists found an almost untouched supply of game in the American wilderness. As the pioneers pushed westward they encountered even more abundance. Where fruits, grains, and vegetables might be scarce because the land was not yet cultivated, there was no end to the amount of meat to be had for the shooting. No doubt, the high meat diet of the pioneers had much to do with the heartiness, toughness, and spirit which settled our country.

Meat is an excellent source, perhaps the best, of the "complete" proteins used to build and repair body tissue. It is rich in vitamins and minerals and aids in the formation of nitrogen-containing substances which are essential to enzymes, certain hormones, and to other body functions. It can also be a source of energy.

Protein for performing these body functions can also be obtained from milk, cheese, eggs, poultry, and fish, all sources which provide amino acids essential to body growth. Legumes (dry beans, peas, nuts) are another source but are called "incomplete" proteins because the necessary amino acids are present in unfavorable proportions. It is recommended that these proteins be supplemented in the same meal with meat or other animal protein.

STORAGE

The ideal temperature for storing unfrozen meats and meat products to be used in a day or two is as low as possible without actually freezing them.

Fresh Meats (beef, veal, pork, and lamb cuts; hamburger; variety meats such as liver, heart, and tongue) — Prepackaged fresh meat purchased in self-service markets may be refrigerated in the original wrapping providing the meat is to be used within one or two days. If kept longer, the wrapper should be loosened at the ends. Meat not prepackaged should be removed from the market wrapping paper and stored unwrapped or loosely covered with waxed paper or aluminum foil.

Frozen Meats — Meats purchased in retail markets and held more than three days should be wrapped in special freezer material using the "drugstore wrap" and stored in the freezer section of refrigerator. If fresh meat is to be frozen and stored longer than a week it should be done only in a freezer which can maintain a 0°F (or lower) temperature throughout the storage period. Meat purchased frozen must be kept frozen until used, and should be stored in freezer-storage compartment for not more than two weeks. The ice cube compartment of a home refrigerator usually does not maintain a temperature as low as a freezer storage compartment. Individual servings of fresh meat (chops and ground meat patties) to be frozen should be separated by several layers of moisture-vaporproof material before overwrapping into larger packages. This facilitates easy separation of each serving

Meats

before cooking.

Cooked Meats or Leftover Meats—Cool cooked leftover meats quickly, then cover and place in the refrigerator. Meat cooked for future use should be cooled, uncovered, in the refrigerator or in a cool place with good air circulation. Divide large quantities of meat dishes such as stews into smaller amounts for faster cooling.

Cured Meats (ham, bacon, etc.) ***and Ready-to-Serve Meats*** (luncheon meat, frankfurters, etc.)—Store in the fresh food compartment of the refrigerator, not in the freezing compartment. Freezing is not advisable for longer than one month as the salt present in these meats favors the development of rancidity when meats are frozen. Store these meat products in their original wrappers.

Canned Hams (and other perishable canned meats)—Store these meats in the unopened can in the fresh food compartment of the refrigerator unless otherwise indicated on label. Do not freeze.

STORAGE TIME

For top quality, fresh meats should be used in 2 or 3 days, ground meat and variety meats should be used in 24 hours.

METHODS OF COOKING

Since the first cave family discovered that meat tasted better when cooked, only two ways of cooking meat have ever been devised: by dry heat and by moist heat. There are several methods of cooking by dry heat: roasting, broiling, panbroiling, frying, and rotisserie cooking. There are two methods of cooking by moist heat: braising and cooking in liquid. Most of these methods have been used for thousands of years, from cave days to the present, but in the comparatively few years since the experimental method was first applied to cooking, more has been learned about the techniques that give cooked meat the best appearance, texture, and flavor than in all the millennia that went before.

In general, dry-heat methods are used for the more tender cuts of meat with little connective tissue. Exceptions to this rule are the smaller cuts (steaks, chops, and cutlets) of veal, though it is classed as a tender meat. Veal needs longer cooking to develop its flavor and to soften its connective tissue. Long cooking by dry heat tends to dry veal out; therefore a moist-heat method, braising, is the method of choice for veal cuts other than roasts.

During broiling, panbroiling, or frying, when meat is to be turned, if using a fork, insert it into fat rather than the lean portion thus avoiding loss of juices from the lean.

Roasting—To roast, in modern usage, is to cook in an oven, uncovered, and without the addition of any liquid. Thousands of laboratory tests on all kinds of roasts have revealed many facts about roasting methods which today can be stated as rules. These rules have as their objective the desired degree of doneness combined with maximum palatability and juiciness, the most appetizing appearance, and minimum shrinkage.

Rules worth noting

• A constant low temperature should be maintained throughout the cooking period.

It has been proved in test after test that searing a roast at a high temperature for a short period and then reducing heat to complete the cooking does not help "seal in" the juices. Using a constant (low) temperature cooks the meat more uniformly with less shrinkage and loss of juices and fat. In addition, this method has these advantages: It results in more palatable meat with surface fat which is not charred; it involves less work for the homemaker since there is less spattering of the fat on roasting pan and oven racks and walls; it requires less watching during cooking; it makes the final clean-up job easier.

We should add that using a high temperature at the beginning of roasting does result in more pan drippings which are a richer brown and therefore make a richer, more flavorful gravy.

• The only accurate test for doneness is the internal temperature as registered by a meat thermometer. **The shape of the roast, the proportion of lean to fat, the amount of bone, the aging of the meat—all affect the time that will be required to produce the desired degree of doneness. Timetables are useful in estimating about how much total time will be required, but only a meat thermometer will register the temperature at the center of the roast, thus indicating the degree of doneness. To use a meat thermometer, insert the thermometer so the tip is slightly beyond the center of the largest muscle. (It should not contact fat or bone.)**

• Cooked fat side up the roast will be self-basting.

- Covering the roast or adding water produces moist-heat cooking and is not done in roasting.
- Seasoning may be added before or after cooking; penetration is to a depth of only ¼ to ½ inch.
- If the roast is allowed to set 20 minutes after removal from the oven, carving will be easier. The roast must be removed from the oven when the thermometer registers 5° to 10° lower than the desired doneness.

Broiling — To broil is to cook by direct heat. It may be done with a gas flame, an electric unit, or over hot coals. The regulator is set for broiling. The broiler and broiler pan may or may not be preheated. The meat is placed on the rack in broiler pan, then placed in oven or broiler oven at a distance so that a moderate broiler temperature can be maintained at the surface of meat. The distance the meat is placed from the heat is determined by the thickness of the cut and the equipment being used. A 1-inch cut is placed 2 to 3 inches from the heat and a 2-inch cut 3 to 5 inches.

When browned on one side, season the meat, turn, and broil to the desired degree of doneness. Season the second side when cooking is completed.

A roast meat thermometer may be used to test doneness by inserting it in the steak or chop shortly before the end of the estimated total broiling time. Without the thermometer it is easy to check on doneness by cutting into the meat next to the bone and observing the color.

Broiling as a cooking method is reserved for tender steaks and chops of beef, pork, and lamb. Veal, although tender, is not usually broiled for the reasons already explained.

Rotisserie Roasting — Poultry and the tender cuts of meat are used for this type of cooking by dry heat. A spit is inserted through the piece of meat or the bird to be cooked, then it is roasted over an open fire, usually out-of-doors, or under broiler heat in an oven. A rotisserie motor is used to turn the spit slowly during the cooking process. Follow the rotisserie manufacturer's directions for regulating temperature and cooking time.

Panbroiling — To panbroil is to cook by heat transmitted through the hot metal of a skillet, but without added fat or liquid. Panbroiling is used for the same cuts as is broiling. Fat should be poured off as it collects, to insure even cooking; the pan should not be covered. To test for doneness, cut a small gash close to the bone and note the color of the meat at the center. If necessary, return to heat until done.

Frying — To fry is to cook in fat, whether in a large amount (deep frying) or a small amount (panfrying). Meats most often fried are thin steaks, chops, and liver. They are usually floured or breaded to produce a brown, flavorful crust. In panfrying the meat is browned in a small amount of fat and than cooked at moderate temperature until done, turning frequently. If the skillet is covered or water is added, the procedure becomes braising rather then true frying.

Braising — To braise meat is to brown it slowly on all sides in hot fat (meat coated with flour before browning, if desired), then to simmer it gently either in its own juices (by covering the skillet) or in a small amount of added liquid, which may be water, milk, cream, meat stock, vegetable juice, or other liquid. The cooking done after browning (braising) may be done either on top of the range or in the oven.

This method is used in cooking pot roasts, veal and pork chops and steaks. These are all either less tender cuts of meat, such as round or flank steak, or small cuts of veal which lack fat. Chops and steaks are also braised for variety.

Cooking in Liquid — Large, less tender cuts of meat for stews are tenderized by cooking them in liquid. This method is also used for cooking meats for soups and such variety meats as heart and tongue which are much exercised muscles.

Cover meat entirely with either hot or cold liquid. To develop flavor and increase color, brown meat slowly on all sides before adding liquid. (Do not brown corned beef or cured or smoked pork.) Add desired seasonings, cover kettle and cook slowly (do not boil) until meat is tender. If served cold, cool it, then chill in refrigerator in cooking stock. This results in more flavorful, juicy meat with very little shrinkage. If vegetables are to be served with the meat, add them just long enough before meat is tender to cook them. For preparing stews, cut the meat into 1- to 2-inch pieces, cubes, rectangles, or long narrow strips. For added flavor and color, pieces may be coated with flour and browned in hot fat before liquid is added. No fat is necessary if flour is not used. Add just enough hot or cold liquid (water, vegetable juices, or stock) to cover meat. Add seasonings; cook slowly (do not boil) until meat is tender.

To thicken cooking liquid—Pour ½ cup cold water into a screw-top jar; sprinkle ¼ cup flour onto the water (or use amounts specified in recipe). Cover jar tightly and shake until well blended. Slowly pour one half of mixture into cooking liquid, stirring constantly. Bring to boiling. Gradually add only what is needed of remaining mixture for consistency desired. Bring to boiling after each addition. After final addition cook 3 to 5 minutes, stirring occasionally.

COOKING FROZEN MEATS

Frozen meats which have been defrosted before cooking may be cooked in exactly the same way and by the same methods as meats which have not been frozen. Meat that is cooked before defrosting may be cooked by the same methods also, but a longer cooking time is required.

It is especially important to use a roast meat thermometer when cooking frozen meat. Roast unthawed meat about one hour before attempting to insert the thermometer.

BEEF

STANDING RIB ROAST OF BEEF

3-rib (6 to 8 lbs.) standing rib roast of beef (have meat dealer saw across ribs near backbone so it can be removed to make carving easier)

1½ teaspoons salt
1 teaspoon monosodium glutamate
⅛ teaspoon pepper

1. Place roast, fat side up, in a shallow roasting pan. Season with a blend of salt, monosodium glutamate, and pepper. Insert meat thermometer so tip is slightly beyond center of thickest part of lean; be sure tip does not rest on bone or in fat.
2. Roast at 300° to 325°F, allowing 23 to 25 minutes per pound for rare; 27 to 30 minutes per pound for medium; and 32 to 35 minutes per pound for well done meat. Roast is also done when meat thermometer registers 140°F for rare; 160°F for medium; and 170°F for well done.
3. Place roast on a warm serving platter. Remove thermometer.
4. Meat drippings may be used for *Brown Gravy, page 200*. For a special treat, serve with *Yorkshire Pudding,* **next column**.   8 TO 10 SERVINGS

NOTE: A rib roast of beef may be one of three cuts. From the short loin end of the rib section, a first-rib roast is cut. This is mostly choice, tender "rib eye" meat. From the center rib section, the center-rib roast is cut. It has less "rib eye" meat than the first-rib roast and is usually somewhat less expensive. From the shoulder end of the rib section, the sixth-and-seventh rib roast is cut. It has the least "rib eye" meat and is likely to be least tender of the three. It usually is the least expensive. When purchasing a rib roast, buy not less than two ribs for a standing roast; for a rolled rib roast, buy a 4-pound roast.

ROLLED RIB ROAST OF BEEF: Follow recipe for Standing Rib Roast of Beef. Substitute *rolled beef rib roast* (5 to 7 pounds) for the standing rib roast. Roast at 300° to 325°F, allowing 32 minutes per pound for rare; 38 minutes per pound for medium; and 48 minutes per pound for well done meat.

YORKSHIRE PUDDING: Pour ¼ *cup hot drippings* from roast beef into an 11x7x1½-inch baking dish and keep hot. Add *1 cup milk, 1 cup sifted all-purpose flour,* and *½ teaspoon salt* to *2 well-beaten eggs*. Beat with hand rotary or electric beater until smooth. Pour into baking pan over hot drippings. Bake at 400°F 30 to 40 minutes, or until puffed and golden. Cut into squares and serve immediately.

ABOUT 8 SERVINGS

BEEF WELLINGTON

Beef Wellington, juicy rare tenderloin spread with liver pâté and encased in flaky pastry, is symbolic of the finest in elegant dining.

3½- to 4-lb. beef tenderloin
1 can (2 to 3 oz.) liver pâté or spread

Pastry (prepared from pie crust mix or Buttery Pastry, *below*)
1 egg yolk, fork beaten
1 teaspoon water

1. Set beef on a rack in a shallow roasting pan. Roast at 425°F 25 minutes (medium rare). Remove

from oven and cool completely.
2. Discard any fat on roast. Sprinkle with *salt* and *pepper* and spread with liver pâté.
3. Meanwhile, prepare pastry (enought for the equivalent of three 9-inch pie shells).
4. On a lightly floured surface, roll out pastry large enough to wrap around the roast.
5. Place meat on one edge of pastry and bring other edge over meat to cover completely; reserve extra pastry for decorations. Moisten edges with water and pinch together firmly. Place on a baking sheet. Cut out a few small holes on top to allow steam to escape.
6. Cut out decorative shapes from reserved pastry. Moisten underside of each with water and place on top. Brush entire surface of pastry with a mixture of egg yolk and water.
7. Bake at 425°F 30 to 35 minutes, or until pastry is golden brown.
8. Let stand 5 to 10 minutes before carving into thick slices. 6 TO 8 SERVINGS

For Buttery Pastry: Prepare pastry as directed in step 3, roll out on a lightly floured surface into an 18-inch square, and dot the center portion with slivers of *butter* (6 tablespoons). Fold so the two sides meet in center and seal by pressing edges with fingers. Fold ends to center and seal. Wrap and chill 20 minutes. Roll out as directed in step 4.

CHILI CON QUESO BEEF ROAST

1 beef chuck arm-bone roast weighing about 4 lbs. and cut 2½ inches thick	2 canned green chili peppers
	1 envelope instant meat marinade
2 canned whole pimientos	1 cup shredded sharp Cheddar cheese (4 ozs.)

1. With a sharp knife, cut 8 deep slits about 3 inches long in top of roast.
2. Cut pimientos and chili peppers in quarters; fold each piece of pimiento around a strip of chili pepper; stuff deep into slits in roast. Slash fat edge of roast every inch so it will lie flat.
3. Prepare meat marinade as label directs in a shallow dish. Place roast in dish; turn to coat all over with marinade; let stand 15 minutes.
4. When ready to cook, preheat broiler. Remove roast from dish; place on rack in broiler pan. Brush part of the marinade over top.
5. Broil, 8 inches from heat, 20 minutes; turn; brush again with marinade. Broil 20 minutes longer for rare, or until beef is as done as you like it. (To test, cut a small slit near bone.)
6. Sprinkle cheese over roast; heat 1 to 2 minutes until cheese melts.
7. Remove roast to a cutting board; carve diagonally into ¼-inch-thick slices. 6 TO 8 SERVINGS

FILET MIGNON STANLEY

Filet mignon and sautéed bananas enhanced with a piquant horseradish-flavored sauce could be the pièce de résistance of a special dinner—a feature at Brennan's in New Orleans, Louisiana.

2 beef tenderloin steaks (about ¾ lb. each)	1 cup milk
	½ cup prepared horseradish
2 bananas	1½ teaspoons salt
2 tablespoons butter	2 drops Worcestershire sauce
½ cup butter	
1 tablespoon flour	

1. Broil steaks on both sides until well browned. Season to taste with *salt* and *pepper*.
2. Meanwhile, peel bananas and halve lengthwise. Sauté on both sides in the 2 tablespoons butter in a skillet (do not overcook). Lift bananas from skillet; keep warm.
3. Melt the ½ cup butter in the skillet; stir in the flour. Pour in milk, cooking and stirring until sauce comes to boiling.
4. Reduce heat and add horseradish, salt, *pepper* to taste, and Worcestershire sauce. Cook sauce 1 minute longer.
5. Arrange broiled steaks on a platter, surround with bananas, and pour sauce over them.
 2 SERVINGS

PRIME BEEF TOURNEDOS ORLANDO

At La Rue, a well-known Los Angeles restaurant, tournedos are marinated and charcoal broiled to perfection.

4 beef tenderloin steaks (tournedos)	Pepper
	1 teaspoon chopped shallots
Olive oil	
Lemon juice	1 teaspoon chopped chives
Salt	

1. Marinate steaks 1 hour in a mixture of remain-

ing ingredients, using proportions to taste.
2. Remove from marinade and charcoal broil to desired doneness.
3. Serve each filet on a broiled *eggplant* slice. Top with *Bordelaise Sauce, page 196*. 4 SERVINGS
NOTE: Tournedos are slices from the smaller half of a beef tenderloin and usually cut ½ to ¾ inch thick, weighing 3 to 5 ounces.

OYSTERS UP
Hollywood personality Martha Hyer serves this easy-to-prepare, perfectly delicious steak-oyster "bake" as one of her specialties.

1 beef sirloin steak, cut 1¾ in. thick	Freshly ground black pepper
2 tablespoons butter	1 pt. oysters, drained and picked over
Salt	

1. Broil steak 5 minutes on each side; remove to heatproof platter.
2. Spread steak with 1 tablespoon butter and sprinkle with mixture of ½ teaspoon salt and ⅛ teaspoon pepper. Cover steak with oysters; season oysters with ½ teaspoon salt and ⅛ teaspoon pepper and dot with remaining butter.
3. Leaving steak on platter, bake at 425°F 20 minutes, or until oysters are plump with edges curled (do not overcook). 4 TO 6 SERVINGS

STEAK DIANE

¼ cup butter or margarine, softened	Freshly ground black pepper
1 clove garlic, crushed	½ teaspoon Worcestershire sauce
8 thin slices (1 lb.) beef tenderloin	½ lemon
Salt	

1. Blend butter and garlic; set aside 20 minutes.
2. Heat about 1 tablespoon of the garlic butter in a large heavy skillet. When very hot, add as many steaks at a time as will fit uncrowded in bottom; brown quickly on both sides.
3. Transfer steaks to a hot serving platter and season on both sides with salt and pepper.
4. Add remaining butter and Worcestershire sauce to pan; heat until bubbly and lightly browned.
5. Holding the cut lemon over the pan, squeeze in some juice. Insert the tines of a fork through the peel and use to quickly blend in the juice (rubbing sides and bottom of pan with cut side).
6. Immediately pour hot sauce over steak and sprinkle with *snipped chives*. 4 SERVINGS

PARMESAN STEAK

1 beef sirloin steak, weighing about 4 lbs. and cut 2 inches thick	⅓ cup bottled Italian salad dressing
	⅓ cup grated Parmesan cheese

1. Trim any excess fat from steak; slash remaining fat edge to prevent curling. Place steak in a large shallow dish; pour salad dressing over top. Let stand 2 to 3 hours at room temperature, turning several times, to season.
2. When ready to cook, preheat broiler. Remove steak from dish; place on rack in broiler pan. Brush dressing in dish over top.
3. Broil, 8 inches from heat, 15 minutes; turn. Broil 10 minutes; sprinkle Parmesan cheese on top; broil 5 minutes longer for rare meat, or until steak is as done as you like it.
4. Remove to a cutting board; carve into ¼-inch-thick slices. 8 SERVINGS

STEAK À LA BARBARA STANWYCK
Extremely simple in its preparation, yet quite sophisticated in flavor, this is movie-actress Barbara Stanwyck's favorite way with steak.

½ cup soy sauce	1 club steak or small Porterhouse steak, about ¾ in. thick
1 teaspoon brown sugar	
¼ teaspoon freshly ground black pepper	2 tablespoons butter
1 teaspoon olive oil	

1. Mix soy sauce with brown sugar, pepper, and olive oil; pour into shallow pan.
2. Put steak into sauce and spoon a little sauce over top; marinate 30 minutes; turn several times.
3. Heat a large heavy skillet; add butter and when very hot, add the steak to skillet. Cook over high heat until charred on one side; turn and cook quickly until charred on other side. (The result will be steaks charred on the outside, but pink in the middle.) Serve immediately on a well heated platter. 1 OR 2 SERVINGS

DEVILED STEAK

1 beef round steak, weighing 2 lbs. and cut 1 inch thick	1 tablespoon lemon juice
2 tablespoons salad oil	1 teaspoon salt
1 large onion, coarsely chopped (1 cup)	½ teaspoon garlic powder
2 tablespoons prepared hot spicy mustard	½ teaspoon pepper
	½ cup water
	1 large green pepper, cut into rings

1. Preheat oven to 350°F.
2. Cut steak into serving-sized pieces. Brown in salad oil in a large skillet; place pieces in a single layer in a baking dish, 12x8x2 inches.
3. Stir onion into drippings in skillet; sauté until soft; spoon over steak.
4. Mix mustard, lemon juice, salt, garlic powder, pepper, and water in a small bowl; pour over steak; cover tightly.
5. Bake 1 hour and 45 minutes.
6. Overlap green pepper rings around edge in dish; cover again. Bake 15 minutes longer, or until meat is tender.   8 SERVINGS

FONDUE BOURGUIGNONNE

Sauces (3 or more), *below*	Beef tenderloin or sirloin, cut in 1-in. pieces (allow ⅓ to ½ lb. per person)
Cooking oil to half-fill a fondue pot, heated to 375°F	

1. The hot oil in a copper pot (narrower at the top) is set over canned heat or an alcohol burner on a metal tray. This type of beef-fondue cooker and two-pronged forks with long handles are usually available from specialty shops or the housewares section of department stores. (Plates with dividers for the individual sauces are also available and convenient, but not necessary for this service.) One cooker is ample for four persons.
2. Dishes piled with the raw meat are set on the table between guests or at convenient intervals. Pieces of meat are speared with the forks, then plunged into the hot oil and cooked one to two minutes, or to the desired degree of doneness. Meat is transferred to the plate and eaten with a table fork, thus allowing for meat to be cooking at all times.
3. The meat is finally dipped into the sauces which have been spooned into the plate sections.

Chilled crisp relishes such as *radishes, celery* and *carrot sticks*, and slices of *buttered dark rye bread*, along with cups of steaming hot *coffee*, complete the menu.

Jiffy Sauces for Fondue Bourguignonne

ONION-CHILI: Combine ½ envelope (about ¾ ounce) *dry onion soup mix* and ¾ *cup boiling water* in a saucepan. Cover partially and cook 10 minutes. Adding gradually, mix in 1½ *tablespoons flour* and ¼ *cup water*. Bring to boiling, stirring constantly; cook until thickened. Remove from heat; mix in 2 *tablespoons chili sauce*.

ONION-HORSERADISH: Blend ½ *envelope (about ¾ ounce) dry onion soup mix*, 1 *tablespoon milk*, 2 *teaspoons prepared horseradish*, and desired amount of *snipped parsley* into 1 *cup dairy sour cream*.

HORSERADISH: Blend 3 *tablespoons prepared horseradish*, 1 *teaspoon grated onion*, and ½ *teaspoon lemon juice* with 1 *cup mayonnaise*.

CURRY: Blend 1 *tablespoon curry powder*, 1 *teaspoon grated onion*, and ½ *teaspoon lemon juice* with 1 *cup mayonnaise*.

MUSTARD: Blend 1 *tablespoon cream* with 1 *cup mayonnaise* and stir in *prepared mustard* to taste.

CAPER: Mix 1 *tablespoon chopped capers* and 1 *cup bottled tartar sauce*; blend in 1 *tablespoon cream*.

BÉARNAISE: Blend 1 *tablespoon parsley flakes*, ½ *teaspoon grated onion*, ¼ *teaspoon crushed tarragon*, and 1 *teaspoon tarragon vinegar* into *hollandaise sauce* prepared from a mix according to package directions, or *Hollandaise Sauce, page 197*.

PAPRIKA: Prepare 1 *cup medium white sauce*. Blend in 1 *teaspoon minced onion, few grains ground nutmeg*, and 2 to 3 *teaspoons paprika*.

BARBECUE: Blend *prepared horseradish* to taste with a *bottled barbecue sauce*.

VELVET LEMON SAUCE

2 eggs	Few grains white pepper
½ teaspoon salt	½ slice onion
2 tablespoons lemon juice	½ cup hot water
½ cup soft butter	

1. Put eggs, salt, lemon juice, butter, pepper, and onion into an electric blender container. Blend until smooth. Add hot water, a little at a time, while blending.
2. Turn into top of double boiler. Cook over simmering water, stirring constantly until thickened, about 10 minutes. ABOUT 1¼ CUPS SAUCE

RÉMOULADE SAUCE

1 cup mayonnaise
1½ teaspoons prepared mustard
¼ teaspoon anchovy paste
2 tablespoons finely chopped sour pickles
1 tablespoon chopped capers
1½ teaspoons minced parsley
½ teaspoon finely crushed chervil
½ teaspoon crushed tarragon

Blend all ingredients in a small bowl. Cover; chill thoroughly. ABOUT 1 CUP SAUCE

CALYPSO STEAK STICKS

2 lbs. boneless beef (tenderloin, sirloin, or rib), cut 1¼ in. thick
1 cup soy sauce
⅓ cup honey
2 cloves garlic, minced
¼ cup finely chopped crystallized ginger
2 firm bananas with all-yellow peel
¼ cup flaked coconut

1. Slice meat across grain into ¼-inch strips.
2. Combine the soy sauce, honey, garlic, and ginger; mix well and pour over the meat strips in a large shallow dish. Refrigerate about 30 minutes, turning meat once.
3. Remove meat from marinade, reserving marinade. Thread meat onto twelve 8-inch skewers, allowing space at end of each skewer for banana pieces.
4. Peel bananas and cut into ¾-inch pieces; dip pieces into marinade, roll in coconut, and drizzle with *lime juice.*
5. Put 1 or 2 pieces of banana on end of each skewer; brush meat and banana pieces with marinade.
6. Broil 3 inches from source of heat about 3 minutes, turning once and brushing with marinade. (Meat should be rare.) 6 SERVINGS

BEEF STROGANOFF

2 lbs. boneless beef (tenderloin, sirloin, or rib), cut in 2x¼x¼-in. strips
½ cup flour
1 teaspoon salt
½ teaspoon monosodium glutamate
⅛ teaspoon black pepper
⅓ cup butter or margarine
½ cup finely chopped onion
2 cups beef broth
3 tablespoons butter or margarine
½ lb. fresh mushrooms, sliced lengthwise
1 cup dairy sour cream
3 tablespoons tomato paste
1 teaspoon Worcestershire sauce

1. Coat meat strips evenly with a mixture of the flour, salt, monosodium glutamate, and pepper.
2. Heat ⅓ cup butter in a large heavy skillet. Add meat strips and onion. Brown on all sides over medium heat, turning occasionally. Add the broth; cover and simmer about 20 minutes.
3. Heat 3 tablespoons butter in a skillet over medium heat. Add mushrooms and cook until lightly browned and tender. Add mushrooms to the meat and remove skillet from heat.
4. Blending well after each addition, add a mixture of the sour cream, tomato paste, and Worcestershire sauce in small amounts. Return to heat. Continue cooking over low heat, stirring constantly, until thoroughly heated (do not boil).
ABOUT 6 SERVINGS

CAN-CAN STROGANOFF

2 lbs. boneless beef (sirloin)
⅓ cup flour
½ teaspoon monosodium glutamate
¼ teaspoon salt
⅛ teaspoon black pepper
⅓ cup butter or margarine
1 can (10½ oz.) condensed beef broth
1 can (10½ oz.) condensed onion soup
1 can (3 oz.) sliced broiled mushrooms, drained (reserve liquid)
1 cup dairy sour cream
5 drops Tabasco

1. Cut meat into 2x½x½-inch strips. Coat with a mixture of the flour, monosodium glutamate, salt, and pepper.
2. Heat butter in a large heavy skillet over low heat; add the meat and brown slowly and evenly on all sides.
3. Add the beef broth, onion soup, and reserved mushroom liquid; cook and stir until boiling. Re-

duce heat, cover, and simmer 20 to 25 minutes, or until meat is tender.
4. Stir in the mushrooms and heat thoroughly; remove skillet from heat.
5. Combine the sour cream and Tabasco and add in small amounts to the meat in skillet, stirring vigorously after each addition.
6. Return to heat; cook and stir over low heat until thoroughly heated. Turn into a warm serving dish. Serve immediately with *cooked buttered wide noodles*.   ABOUT 8 SERVINGS

SUKIYAKI

A delectable Japanese specialty usually cooked quickly at the table before the guests.

½ cup Japanese soy sauce (shoyu)
¼ cup sake
⅓ cup sugar
3 oz. beef suet, cut in small pieces
1½ lbs. beef tenderloin, sliced 1/16 in. thick and cut in pieces about 2½x1½ in.
12 scallions (including tops), cut in 2-in. lengths
½ head Chinese cabbage (cut lengthwise), cut in 1-in. pieces
½ lb. spinach leaves, cut in 1-in. strips
2 cups drained shirataki (or cold cooked very thin long egg noodles)
12 large mushrooms, sliced lengthwise
12 cubes tofu (soybean curd)
1 can (8½ oz.) whole bamboo shoots, drained and cut in large pieces

1. Mix the soy sauce, sake, and sugar to make the sauce; set aside.
2. To prepare Sukiyaki in the traditional Japanese manner at the table, use a large skillet on a hibachi. (A hot plate or an electric skillet makes a good substitute.) Arrange all ingredients artistically on a large platter or tray and bring to the table. Prepare two servings at a time.
3. Heat beef suet in a skillet until sufficient fat is melted. Remove remaining suet. Add enough sauce to cover bottom of the skillet.
4. Add the beef and cook over high heat, turning once, just until pink color disappears; remove and set aside. Arrange all other ingredients in individual mounds in skillet. Top with beef.
5. Cook until vegetables are just tender. Do not stir. Serve immediately with bowls of *hot cooked rice*.   4 SERVINGS

BEEF CHOW MEIN

¼ cup butter or margarine
1 lb. beef tenderloin or sirloin steak, cut in 3x½x⅛-in. strips
3 tablespoons butter or margarine
½ lb. fresh mushrooms, sliced lengthwise
2 cups sliced celery
2 green onions, sliced ½ in. thick
½ green pepper, cut in narrow strips
1½ cups boiling water
1 teaspoon salt
½ teaspoon monosodium glutamate
⅛ teaspoon pepper
2 tablespoons cold water
2 tablespoons cornstarch
2 teaspoons soy sauce
1 teaspoon sugar
1 can (16 oz.) Chinese mixed vegetables, drained
2 tablespoons coarsely chopped pimiento

1. Heat ¼ cup butter in a large skillet. Add beef and brown evenly. Remove meat; set aside.
2. Heat 3 tablespoons butter in skillet. Stir in mushrooms, celery, green onions, and green pepper; cook and stir 1 minute. Reduce heat and blend in boiling water, salt, monosodium glutamate, and pepper. Bring to boiling; cover and simmer 2 minutes. Remove vegetables; keep warm.
3. Bring liquid in skillet to boiling and stir in a blend of cold water, cornstarch, soy sauce, and sugar. Cook and stir 2 to 3 minutes. Reduce heat; mix in meat and Chinese vegetables and pimiento. Heat thoroughly.
4. Serve piping hot with *chow mein noodles*.
   4 TO 6 SERVINGS

RIPPLED STEAK

1 beef round steak, weighing 2 lbs. and cut 1 inch thick
Instant unseasoned meat tenderizer
4 small zucchini
1 can (16 ozs.) small whole white potatoes, drained
1 cup bottled plain barbecue sauce
16 cherry tomatoes, stemmed

1. Moisten steak; sprinkle tenderizer all over and pierce meat with a fork as label directs. Cut steak across grain into long thin strips.
2. Trim zucchini; cut each crosswise into 4 chunks. Parboil, covered, in boiling water in a small saucepan 3 minutes, or until barely tender; drain.
3. Preheat broiler. Thread steak strips, accordion

style and alternating with zucchini chunks and potatoes, onto 8 long skewers. Place on rack in broiler pan; brush part of the barbecue sauce over all.
4. Broil, 6 inches from heat, turning several times and brushing with remaining sauce, 3 to 5 minutes, or until steak is as done as you like it. Garnish end of each skewer with 2 cherry tomatoes.   8 SERVINGS

LONDON BROIL

2½ lbs. flank steak, scored on both sides
3 tablespoons butter or margarine
2 teaspoons bottled exotic sauce

1. Place flank steak on broiler rack and broil about 3 inches from source of heat 2 to 3 minutes on each side. Season with *salt* and *pepper* before turning.
2. Meanwhile, brown butter in a skillet and add exotic sauce. Blend thoroughly.
3. Brush both sides with sauce; place on heated platter. Cut steak diagonally across grain into very thin slices. Serve with *herb-buttered noodles*.
   6 TO 8 SERVINGS

CHINESE BEEF AND PEA PODS

1½ lbs. flank steak (1 or 2), thinly sliced diagonally across grain
1 to 2 tablespoons cooking oil
1 bunch green onions, chopped
1 or 2 pkgs. (7 oz. each) frozen Chinese pea pods, partially thawed to separate
1 can (10½ oz.) condensed beef consommé
3 tablespoons soy sauce
¼ teaspoon ground ginger
2 tablespoons cornstarch
2 tablespoons cold water
1 can (16 oz.) bean sprouts, drained and rinsed

1. Brown meat in hot oil in a large heavy skillet. Remove and keep warm.
2. Put the green onions and pea pods into skillet. Stir in a mixture of consommé, soy sauce, and ginger. Bring to boiling and cook, covered, about 2 minutes.
3. Mix a blend of cornstarch and water into boiling liquid in skillet. Stirring constantly, boil 2 to 3 minutes. Mix in the meat and bean sprouts; heat thoroughly.
4. Serve over *cooked rice*.   6 SERVINGS

MOCK PEPPER STEAK

3 cups thin strips cooked beef
2 tablespoons salad oil
8 green onions, trimmed and cut into 1-inch lengths
1 envelope instant beef broth
1½ cups water
3 tablespoons soy sauce
1 teaspoon garlic powder
2 medium-sized green peppers, quartered, seeded, and cut into ¾-inch squares
4 teaspoons cornstarch
2 medium tomatoes, each cut in 8 wedges
Chinese noodles (from a 6 oz. package)

1. Brown beef in salad oil in a large skillet; remove from pan with a slotted spoon and set aside.
2. Stir onions into drippings; sauté 1 minute. Stir in beef broth, water, soy sauce, garlic powder, and green peppers; heat to boiling; cover. Simmer 3 minutes, or just until peppers are crisp-tender.
3. Mix cornstarch with a little water until smooth in a cup; stir into mixture in skillet. Cook, stirring constantly, until sauce thickens and boils 1 minute.
4. Stir in beef and tomatoes; cover. Heat just until hot. Serve with Chinese noodles.   4 SERVINGS

HERBED BEEF ROULADES

¼ cup chopped celery
¼ cup chopped red pepper
4 tablespoons butter or margarine
3 cups water
1½ cups packaged herb stuffing mix
6 cube steaks, weighing about 1½ lbs.
2 tablespoons shortening
1 envelope onion soup mix
1 lb. wax beans, tipped and cut in 1-inch pieces
1 pint cherry tomatoes, stemmed
1 tablespoon all-purpose flour

1. Sauté celery and red pepper in butter in a medium saucepan until soft; stir in ½ cup of the water. Heat to boiling; stir in stuffing mix until evenly moist.
2. Place steaks flat on a cutting board; spoon about ¼ cup of the stuffing mixture onto each. Roll up, jelly-roll fashion; tie tightly with string.
3. Brown rolls in shortening in a large skillet.
4. Combine remaining 2½ cups water and soup mix in a 4-cup measure; pour over steak rolls. Heat to

boiling; cover. Simmer, turning rolls once, 1 hour and 10 minutes.
5. Place beans in skillet; cover. Simmer 15 minutes, or until steak is tender and beans are still slightly crisp.
6. Add cherry tomatoes to skillet; cover. Heat 1 to 2 minutes, or just until hot.
7. Lift steak and vegetables from skillet with a slotted spoon and arrange in rows on a large deep platter; keep hot.
8. Mix flour with a little water in a cup until smooth; stir into liquid in pan. Cook, stirring constantly, until gravy thickens and boils 1 minute. Serve separately to spoon over steak rolls. 6 SERVINGS

SAVORY POT ROAST

3- to 4-lb. beef pot roast	⅛ teaspoon black pepper
2 tablespoons flour	
2 tablespoons paprika	3 tablespoons fat
2 teaspoons salt	4 onions, thinly sliced

1. Coat meat with a mixture of the flour, paprika, salt, and pepper. Brown meat on all sides in hot fat in a large skillet or Dutch oven.
2. Lift out meat and put about one third of the onions in a layer in bottom of skillet or Dutch oven. Return meat and cover with remaining onions.
3. Cover tightly and cook over low heat about 3 hours, or until meat is tender. 6 TO 8 SERVINGS

STUFFED STEAK ROLLS

6 beef cube steaks	2 teaspoons ground ginger
½ cup soy sauce	
⅓ cup lemon juice	1 clove garlic, minced
⅓ cup water	Stuffing, *below*
⅓ cup sugar	2 tablespoons butter or margarine

1. Put cube steaks into a large, shallow dish. Pour a mixture of soy sauce, lemon juice, water, sugar, ginger, and garlic over them; marinate 30 minutes.
2. Drain steaks well, reserving marinade. Put a large spoonful of stuffing at end of each cube steak. Roll up as for a jelly roll and secure with metal or wooden picks.
3. Heat butter in a large skillet. Add the steak rolls and brown well on all sides, brushing frequently with marinade. Cover skillet and cook about 5 minutes, or until meat is tender. 6 SERVINGS

STUFFING

12 slices white bread, toasted	¼ teaspoon crushed rosemary
½ cup butter or margarine, melted	3 tablespoons snipped parsley
¼ cup milk	3 tablespoons minced onion
1 teaspoon salt	
⅛ teaspoon pepper	

Soak bread in cold water, squeeze out as much of the water as possible, and pull into fluffy pieces. Pour butter, milk, salt, pepper, and rosemary over the bread. Add parsley and onion; toss lightly.
4 CUPS STUFFING

BEEF POT ROAST À LA PROVINCE

3 lbs. beef bottom round or blade pot roast	1 can (10½ oz.) condensed beef consommé
¼ cup butter or margarine	1 cup dairy sour cream
	½ cup dry red wine
3 carrots, chopped	1 tablespoon drained capers
4 stalks celery, chopped	
	1 teaspoon salt
1 onion, chopped	½ teaspoon paprika
1 clove garlic, minced	⅛ teaspoon black pepper
1 can (6 oz.) sliced mushrooms (undrained)	

1. Brown beef on all sides in heated butter in a heavy skillet having a tight-fitting cover. Add the carrots, celery, onion, and garlic; cook until onion is golden, stirring occasionally. Add mushrooms.
2. Blend thoroughly the consommé and remaining ingredients; pour into skillet. Cover and simmer 2 to 3 hours, or until meat is tender. Remove meat to heated serving platter and keep hot.

Beef

3. Skim any excess fat from gravy. If desired, thicken gravy with flour. Serve with the roast. Garnish plate with *cauliflowerets* and *parsley*.

ABOUT 6 SERVINGS

NOTE: If desired, omit red wine and add a mixture of *⅓ cup red wine vinegar, 2 tablespoons water,* and *2 tablespoons brown sugar.*

MONTEREY BEEF DINNER

6 tablespoons all-purpose flour	1 can condensed (10½ ozs.) consommé
2½ teaspoons salt	2 cans (5½ ozs. each) apple juice
¼ teaspoon pepper	
1 beef chuck roast, weighing about 3½ lbs.	1 teaspoon dried thyme, crushed
2 tablespoons salad oil	1 package (16 ozs.) carrots, pared
1 large onion, chopped (1 cup)	1 lb. fresh green beans, tipped
2 cloves of garlic, chopped	12 small potatoes, pared

1. Mix 2 tablespoons of the flour with salt and pepper in a cup; rub over both sides of roast. Brown roast in salad oil in a Dutch oven; remove and set aside.
2. Add onion and garlic to drippings; sauté until soft. Stir in consommé, apple juice, and thyme; heat to boiling. Place meat in liquid; cover. Simmer, turning several times, 2 hours.
3. Add carrots to Dutch oven, cover again; cook 10 minutes. Add whole green beans and potatoes; cover. Cook 30 minutes longer, or until meat and vegetables are tender.
4. Remove meat to a large serving platter; place vegetables around edge; keep warm. Reheat liquid in Dutch oven to boiling.
5. Mix remaining 4 tablespoons flour with a little water until smooth in a cup; stir into boiling liquid. Cook, stirring constantly, until gravy thickens and boils 1 minute; add salt to taste, if needed. Pass gravy separately to spoon over meat.   6 to 8 SERVINGS

SAUERBRATEN

Potato dumplings and Sauerbraten are a famous German duo.

3- to 4-lb. beef blade pot roast	2 cups water
1 clove garlic, halved	2 onions, sliced
2 teaspoons salt	2 bay leaves
	1 teaspoon peppercorns
¼ teaspoon pepper	¼ cup sugar
2 cups cider vinegar	2 tablespoons lard

1. Rub meat with cut surface of garlic, then with salt and pepper. Put meat and garlic into a deep casserole having a cover.
2. Heat the vinegar, water, onions, bay leaves, peppercorns, and sugar just until boiling; pour over meat and allow to cool. Cover and refrigerate 4 days, turning meat each day.
3. Remove meat; strain and reserve liquid for cooking the meat.
4. Brown meat in heated lard in a Dutch oven, turning to brown evenly. Add half of the reserved liquid; cover and simmer 2 to 3 hours, or until meat is tender, adding additional liquid as needed. Slice meat; serve with *Potato Dumplings, below* and, if desired, *Gingersnap Gravy.*   6 TO 8 SERVINGS

GINGERSNAP GRAVY: Stir *¾ cup crushed gingersnaps* and *1 tablespoon sugar* into cooking liquid in Dutch oven. Simmer 10 minutes; stir occasionally.

POTATO DUMPLINGS
(Kartoffelklösse)

1 to 2 slices bread, cut in ½-in. cubes	1 teaspoon salt
1 to 1½ tablespoons butter or margarine	⅛ teaspoon white pepper
	¼ cup cornstarch
1 egg, well beaten	⅔ to ¾ cup all-purpose flour
6 potatoes, mashed or riced and cooled	

1. Brown bread cubes lightly on all sides in heated butter in a large skillet; set aside.
2. Whip egg into cooled mashed potatoes until fluffy. Stir in salt, pepper, and cornstarch. Mix in enough flour to make a soft dough.
3. Break off pieces of dough and shape into 1-inch balls. Poke one of the bread cubes into the center of each ball.
4. Drop dumplings into boiling *salted water* (2 quarts water and 2 teaspoons salt) only as many as will lie uncrowded one layer deep. Cook about 5 minutes, or until dumplings rise to surface. Using a slotted spoon, remove dumplings; drain over water a few seconds. Put into a heated serving dish. Serve with *melted butter.* Dumplings may be served with sauerkraut, other meat, or poultry.

ABOUT 18 DUMPLINGS

EPICUREAN BEEF À LA FAR EAST

- 3- to 4-lb. beef pot roast, cut in 6 large chunks for individual servings
- 3 tablespoons fat
- 3 onions, halved and sliced
- ½ cup hot water
- ¼ cup soy sauce
- 1¼ cups warm milk
- ½ cup flaked coconut
- 2 teaspoons cornstarch
- 1 teaspoon curry powder
- 3 cups hot cooked rice
- ½ cup chutney
- ½ cup golden raisins, plumped

1. Brown meat evenly on all sides in hot fat in a Dutch oven or saucepot. Mix in onions, hot water, and soy sauce. Cover and simmer 2½ hours, or until meat is just tender.
2. Meanwhile, pour warm milk over coconut in a bowl; let stand about 1 hour or longer.
3. Remove meat and keep warm. If necessary, skim and discard fat from cooking liquid.
4. Drain coconut and reserve; add to coconut milk a mixture of cornstarch and curry powder and blend thoroughly. Stir into boiling liquid in Dutch oven. Cook and stir 2 to 3 minutes.
5. Lightly toss chutney, coconut, and raisins with hot rice. Serve gravy and meat on rice. If desired, accompany with *chutney* and *preserved kumquats*.

6 SERVINGS

STUFFED BEEF PINWHEEL

- ¼ cup finely chopped celery
- 2 tablespoons minced onion
- 4 tablespoons butter or margarine
- 3 cups fresh bread crumbs (6 slices)
- ½ cup regular wheat germ
- 1¾ teaspoons salt
- ¼ teaspoon dried leaf sage, crumbled
- Pepper
- 1½ lbs. lean ground beef
- 1 egg
- ¾ cup milk
- 1 teaspoon prepared hot spicy mustard

1. Sauté celery and onion in butter in a medium skillet until soft; stir in 2 cups of the bread crumbs, ¼ cup of the wheat germ, ¼ teaspoon of the salt, sage, and ⅛ teaspoon pepper; toss lightly to mix.
2. Combine ground beef, remaining 1 cup bread crumbs, ¼ cup wheat germ, egg, milk, mustard, remaining 1½ teaspoons salt, and remaining ¼ teaspoon pepper in a large bowl; mix lightly until well blended.
3. Pat meat mixture into a rectangle, 12x8, on a sheet of waxed paper.
4. Preheat oven to 350°F.
5. Spread stuffing mixture over meat. Starting at an 8-inch side, roll up meat, jelly-roll fashion, using waxed paper as a guide. Place roll, seam side down, in a shallow baking pan.
6. Bake 50 minutes, or until loaf is crusty brown. Lift roll onto a large serving platter; cut crosswise into serving-sized slices.

6 SERVINGS

BEEF BRISKET WITH HORSERADISH SAUCE

- 6- to 7-lb. fresh beef brisket
- 4½ teaspoons seasoned salt
- 4 to 5 tablespoons flour
- ½ cup chili sauce
- ½ cup ketchup
- 1 jar (5 oz.) prepared horseradish
- 1 cup boiling water

1. Sprinkle the beef with seasoned salt; coat evenly with flour. Set on a rack in a roasting pan. Roast at 450°F 30 minutes.
2. Combine the chili sauce, ketchup, and horseradish; mix well and spoon over meat.
3. Pour boiling water into bottom of pan; cover. Reduce oven temperature to 350°F and return meat to oven. Continue roasting about 3 hours, or until meat is tender.
4. If desired, thicken cooking liquid for gravy.

10 TO 12 SERVINGS

MEAL-IN-A-KETTLE

- 4- to 5-lb. fresh beef brisket
- 2 soup bones
- 4 white turnips, pared and diced
- 1 cup chopped celery
- 1 cup chopped onion
- ½ cup chopped parsley
- 2 cloves garlic, quartered
- 1 large bay leaf
- ½ teaspoon thyme, crushed
- 2½ tablespoons salt
- 6 peppercorns
- 1 teaspoon monosodium glutamate
- 1 tablespoon sugar
- 4 lbs. chicken pieces (breasts and legs)
- ½ cup barley
- 1 can (16 oz.) whole tomatoes
- 1 lb. small white onions, peeled
- 1 pkg. (10 oz.) frozen corn
- 1 pkg. (9 oz.) frozen cut green beans

1. Put beef and bones into a large kettle. Cover with cold water. Bring to boiling. Remove foam.

2. Add turnips, celery, chopped onion, parsley, garlic, bay leaf, thyme, salt, peppercorns, monosodium glutamate, and sugar. Return to boiling, cover, and simmer 4 hours.
3. Add chicken and continue cooking 1 hour, or until chicken and beef are tender.
4. Remove chicken and beef; set aside and keep warm. Remove and discard bones, bay leaf, and peppercorns. Skim off fat and bring broth to boiling.
5. Stir in barley; cover, and cook 30 minutes. Cut tomatoes in pieces and add with the tomato liquid and onions; cook, covered, 15 minutes. Mix in corn and beans, cover, and continue cooking until vegetables are just tender, about 15 minutes.
6. Meanwhile, cut chicken and beef in serving-sized pieces, discarding chicken bones and skin and removing fat from beef. Return meat to kettle just before serving. Ladle into soup plates.

ABOUT 10 SERVINGS

TOMATO-SMOTHERED STEAK

3 tablespoons fat
1½ lbs. beef arm or blade steak, cut 1½ in. thick
¼ cup flour
2½ teaspoons salt
¼ teaspoon black pepper
1½ teaspoons chili powder
1 teaspoon celery salt
1 large onion, sliced
¼ cup finely chopped green pepper
1 can (16 oz.) tomatoes
3 drops Tabasco

1. Heat fat in large heavy skillet or in a Dutch oven over medium heat.
2. Coat meat with a mixture of the flour, salt, pepper, chili powder, and celery salt. Brown meat on both sides in hot fat.
3. Add onion, green pepper, tomatoes, and Tabasco. Bring liquid rapidly to boiling; reduce heat, cover tightly, and cook slowly over direct heat or in a 300°F oven about 2 hours, or until meat is tender.

ABOUT 6 SERVINGS

SWISS STEAK IN VEGETABLE SAUCE

¼ cup flour
½ teaspoon monosodium glutamate
¼ teaspoon salt
Few grains pepper
1 can (10½ oz.) condensed beef broth
½ to ¾ cup hot water
½ bay leaf
⅛ teaspoon ground cinnamon
1½ lbs. beef round, blade, or arm steak, cut 1¼ in. thick
2 tablespoons butter or margarine
1 can (10¾ oz.) condensed vegetable soup
⅓ cup ketchup

1. Mix the flour, monosodium glutamate, salt, and pepper and pound into the meat with a meat hammer, using one half of mixture for each side.
2. Heat butter in a Dutch oven or heavy saucepot; add steak and brown evenly on both sides.
3. Add broth, hot water, bay leaf, and cinnamon. Cover pot and bring liquid rapidly to boiling; reduce heat and simmer until steak is tender, 60 to 75 minutes.
4. Remove meat to a platter and keep warm.
5. Pour the vegetable soup and ketchup into the pot; heat thoroughly, stirring to blend in brown residue on bottom. Remove bay leaf; pour sauce over meat and serve immediately.

ABOUT 6 SERVINGS

TERIYAKI BEEF ROLLS

2 lbs. ground beef
1 teaspoon salt
⅓ cup soy sauce
⅓ cup salad oil
⅓ cup orange juice
1 teaspoon sugar
1 teaspoon ground ginger
1 clove garlic, crushed
1 can (8 ozs.) crushed pineapple in juice
Butter or margarine
¼ cup thinly sliced green onions

1. Combine ground beef and salt in a medium bowl; mix lightly. Shape into 6 even logs about 5 inches long.
2. Mix soy sauce, salad oil, orange juice, sugar, ginger, and garlic in a large shallow dish. Place meat logs in mixture, turning to coat all over. Let stand, spooning soy mixture over meat several times, 1 hour to season.
3. Preheat broiler.
4. Remove meat from marinade and place on rack in broiler pan.
5. Broil, 6 inches from heat, turning and brushing several times with marinade, 8 minutes, or until beef is as done as you like it.
6. While meat cooks, heat pineapple in a small saucepan; drain off juice.
7. Place meat logs, spoke fashion, on a large serving platter; spoon fruit over meat; sprinkle green onions on top.

6 SERVINGS

BEEF SAIGON

1½ lbs. thinly sliced beef rump roast	1½ teaspoons curry powder
Unseasoned meat tenderizer	½ teaspoon ginger
	1 tablespoon chili sauce
3 tablespoons butter or margarine	2 teaspoons soy sauce
	¾ cup tomato sauce or canned tomatoes
1 tablespoon chopped scallions	2 teaspoons sugar
1 tablespoon chopped onion	1 tablespoon lemon juice
¼ teaspoon garlic salt	½ cup canned beef gravy

1. Cut beef into 3-inch squares. Treat with meat tenderizer as directed on label of jar.
2. Heat butter in a large skillet; add meat and brown pieces quickly on both sides; transfer meat to a hot platter.
3. Add scallions, onion, and garlic salt to drippings in skillet; cook gently a few minutes. Stir in remaining ingredients.
4. Heat to boiling; place meat in sauce, cover, and cook over low heat until tender, about 30 minutes.
5. To serve, place a mound of *hot cooked rice* (preferably wild rice) on a heated large platter. Cover rice with meat slices and pour gravy over all.
6. Surround meat and rice with alternating mounds of *drained bean sprouts*, heated with *2 tablespoons butter*, and a mixture of *1 cup sliced water chestnuts* and *1 cup canned sliced mushrooms*, which have been heated separately with *2 tablespoons butter*.   4 TO 6 SERVINGS

ITALIAN BEEF BAKE

2 cups uncooked small macaroni shells	1 jar (15 ozs.) meatless spaghetti sauce
½ lb. ground beef	1 can (8 ozs.) cut green beans
1 tablespoon salad oil	
1 medium onion, chopped (½ cup)	1 cup shredded mozzarella cheese (4 ozs.)

1. Cook macaroni as label directs; drain. Place in a 1½-quart baking dish.
2. Preheat oven to 350°F.
3. Shape ground beef into a patty; brown in salad oil, turning once, in a large skillet; break up into chunks and push to one side. Stir onion into drippings; sauté until soft.
4. Stir in spaghetti sauce, beans and liquid, and half of the cheese; heat to boiling; stir into macaroni. Sprinkle remaining cheese on top.
5. Bake 30 minutes, or until bubbly and cheese melts and browns lightly.   4 SERVINGS

GLAZED CORNED BEEF

4 lbs. mild-cure corned beef for oven roasting	2 tablespoons butter or margarine
¼ cup firmly packed brown sugar	1 teaspoon dry mustard
	1 teaspoon prepared horseradish
⅓ cup catsup	
2 tablespoons vinegar	

1. Preheat oven to 325°F.
2. Place corned beef on a rack in roasting pan; roast as label directs.
3. While roast cooks, combine brown sugar, catsup, vinegar, butter, mustard, and horseradish in a small saucepan. Heat slowly, stirring constantly, to boiling; brush half over corned beef.
4. Continue roasting, brushing once again with remaining sauce, 20 minutes, or until meat is tender and richly glazed.
5. Remove roast to a large serving platter. For easier slicing, let stand at least 20 minutes. Slice thin; serve plain or with mustard if you like.   6 SERVINGS

BEEF AND BROCCOLI SKILLET

2 lbs. broccoli	3 cups hot chicken broth
¼ cup olive oil	
2 cloves garlic, minced	4 teaspoons cornstarch
2 lbs. boneless beef (round or chuck), sliced very thin and cut diagonally in 4x½-in. strips	¼ cup cold water
	3 tablespoons soy sauce
	1 teaspoon salt
	2 cans (16 oz. each) bean sprouts

1. Cut broccoli into pieces about 2½ inches long and ¼ inch thick; set aside.
2. Heat 2 tablespoons of the olive oil with garlic in a large skillet; add beef pieces and cook until evenly browned. Remove beef from skillet; set aside.
3. Pour remaining oil into skillet. Add broccoli; cook over high heat ½ minute, tossing constantly. Pour broth slowly into skillet; cover and cook 3 minutes. Remove broccoli; keep warm.

4. Blend in a mixture of cornstarch, cold water, soy sauce, and salt. Bring to boiling, stirring constantly, and cook until mixture thickens. Add bean sprouts, broccoli, and beef; toss to mix, then heat thoroughly. Serve with *hot fluffy rice*. 8 SERVINGS

BEEF, BURGUNDY STYLE
(Boeuf Bourguignon)

Among many interpretations of this famous French beef stew is actor David Janssen's version.

2 lbs. beef round steak, cut in 1½-in. cubes	1 cup chopped onion
	½ cup chopped carrot
	1 clove garlic, minced
2 tablespoons flour	2 tablespoons cognac
1½ teaspoons salt	3 sprigs parsley, chopped
½ teaspoon freshly ground black pepper	
	1 bay leaf
1 tablespoon butter or margarine	¼ teaspoon marjoram
	2 cups dry red wine

1. Coat meat with a mixture of flour, salt, and pepper. Brown meat quickly on all sides in heated butter in a large skillet. Then remove to a 2½-quart casserole.
2. Brown onion, carrot, and garlic in butter remaining in skillet.
3. Heat cognac; ignite and pour over beef. When flame has expired, stir in vegetables and remaining ingredients. Cover casserole and bake at 350°F about 2½ hours. 4 TO 6 SERVINGS

RAGOUT WITH PIQUANT SAUCE

½ to ¾ lb. sliced Canadian-style bacon, cut in strips	6 to 8 carrots, pared and sliced
	1 cup mayonnaise
1½ lbs. beef round steak, cut in 3x¼-in. strips	1 clove garlic, minced
	1 tablespoon lemon juice
3 onions, thinly sliced	Few grains cayenne pepper
4 potatoes, pared and sliced	

1. Arrange bacon strips in an even layer on the bottom of a Dutch oven. Cover with the beef strips. Season to taste with *salt, pepper,* and *monosodium glutamate*. Cover with a layer of onions, potatoes, and carrots, adding more seasoning after each layer. Cover tightly and cook slowly 2 hours, or until vegetables are tender.
2. Meanwhile, blend the remaining ingredients in a bowl. Cover and chill.
3. To serve, arrange each layer separately on a large deep platter. Pour the cooking juices over all. Serve with the mayonnaise sauce.
ABOUT 6 SERVINGS

BEEF WITH ONIONS
(Stifado)

This superbly flavored dish is popular at Smokey Joe's Grecian Terrace in St. Louis.

2 lbs. lean beef or pork, cut in 1½-in. pieces	4 firm ripe tomatoes, quartered
	2 to 3 cloves garlic, minced
2 tablespoons butter	
2 tablespoons olive oil	2 to 3 tablespoons wine vinegar
4 lbs. small white onions	
	2 to 3 bay leaves

1. Brown meat on all sides in hot butter and oil in a large heavy saucepot.
2. Add remaining ingredients and then enough water to half cover ingredients in the pot. Season to taste with *salt* and *pepper*.
3. Bring to boiling, cover and simmer 1½ hours, or until meat is tender and liquid is reduced to a flavorful gravy. 4 TO 6 SERVINGS

QUICK BEEF GOULASH

1 medium onion, chopped (½ cup)	1 can (15 ozs.) spaghetti with tomato sauce and cheese
½ cup chopped celery	
1 tablespoon salad oil	1 can (8 ozs.) cut green beans, drained
1½ cups cubed roast beef	
	½ teaspoon dried basil, crushed
	¼ teaspoon salt

1. Sauté onion and celery in salad oil until soft in a medium skillet. Stir in beef; sauté 3 minutes.
2. Stir in remaining ingredients; cover. Simmer, stirring once or twice, 10 minutes to blend flavors.
4 SERVINGS

GOULASH, GYPSY STYLE

¾ cup butter or margarine
2 teaspoons marjoram, crushed
1 teaspoon caraway seed, crushed
1 teaspoon grated lemon peel
1 clove garlic, crushed
1 teaspoon tomato paste
2 lbs. onions, sliced
1 tablespoon paprika
3 lbs. boneless lean beef for stew, cut in 1-in. cubes
2 teaspoons salt
⅛ teaspoon pepper
½ teaspoon monosodium glutamate
1 cup water
1 green pepper, cut in short strips (about 1½ cups)

1. Heat the butter in a kettle. Combine marjoram, caraway seed, lemon peel, and garlic; add, with tomato paste, to kettle. Mix in the onions and cook, stirring occasionally until soft. Sprinkle the paprika over all and blend in well.
2. Add the beef, a mixture of the salt, pepper, and monosodium glutamate, and the water; stir. Cover and simmer until meat is tender, 1½ to 2 hours.
3. Just before serving, mix in green pepper and cook, uncovered, about 5 minutes, or until crisp-tender. Serve over *hot buttered noodles*.

6 TO 8 SERVINGS

BURGOO

Burgoo — a stew traditionally served on Derby Day at Churchill Downs — gave its name to a colt, Burgoo King, who went on to win the Derby in 1932. Relished by Southerners any time, Burgoo is often served at sporting and political events.

1 lb. boneless beef (chuck or rump), cut in pieces
¼ lb. boneless lamb shoulder, cut in pieces
1 beef soup bone, cracked
1 lb. chicken breasts, thighs, or legs
4 teaspoons salt
¾ teaspoon black pepper
¼ teaspoon cayenne pepper
2 qts. water
1½ cups whole kernel corn
1⅓ cups lima beans
1 cup diced potato
1 cup chopped onion
½ cup chopped green pepper
½ cup diced carrot
1 cup sliced okra
2½ cups canned tomatoes with liquid
1 clove garlic, crushed or minced
½ cup chopped parsley

1. Put the meat, soup bone, chicken, salt, peppers, and water into a saucepot; cover and bring to boiling. Reduce heat and simmer about 2 hours, skimming off foam during first part of cooking.
2. Add corn, lima beans, potato, onion, green pepper, and carrot; cover and simmer 1 hour. Remove cover and cook 1 hour longer, stirring occasionally to prevent sticking on bottom of pot.
3. Add the okra, tomatoes, and garlic; cover and simmer 1 to 1½ hours longer. About 10 minutes before end of cooking period, remove bones and any pieces of fat, then stir constantly for remaining time. (Stew will thicken rapidly and may scorch if not carefully watched at this point.)
4. Remove from heat and stir in the parsley.

ABOUT 3 QUARTS BURGOO

"BOILED" DINNER

4 lbs. corned beef brisket
⅓ to ½ cup (about 1½ oz.) dry onion soup mix
4 peppercorns
1 clove garlic, minced
1 bay leaf
¼ teaspoon rosemary, crushed
3 cups water
6 medium-sized potatoes, pared and quartered
6 medium-sized carrots, pared and cut in 1½-in. pieces
½ cup celery, cut in 1-in. pieces
1 medium-sized head young green cabbage, cut in wedges

1. Put meat into a deep saucepot or Dutch oven having a tight-fitting cover. Add soup mix, peppercorns, garlic, bay leaf, rosemary, and water. Cover, bring to boiling, and simmer 3½ hours.
2. Add vegetables, placing cabbage on top of meat. Cover and cook 1 hour, or until tender.
3. Remove vegetables and meat to a large heated serving platter. If desired, thicken liquid in saucepot and serve in a gravy boat.

6 TO 8 SERVINGS

COOKED CORNED BEEF BRISKET

5 lbs. corned beef brisket
1 onion, halved
1 clove garlic, halved
6 whole cloves
8 peppercorns
2 bay leaves
4 stalks celery, cut in pieces

1. Put corned beef into a large kettle; cover with cold water. Add remaining ingredients and bring to boiling. Cover and simmer 3½ to 4 hours, or until the beef is tender.
2. Remove beef from liquid. Slice and serve hot with *English Mustard Sauce, page 198.*

8 TO 10 SERVINGS

PORK

FIESTA ROAST PORK

4-lb. pork loin roast
1 clove garlic, crushed
1 teaspoon rubbed sage
1 teaspoon oregano
2 teaspoons salt
⅓ cup flour
2 cups tomato purée
1 teaspoon chili powder
1 cup water
½ cup thinly sliced olives
½ cup chopped green pepper
½ cup dark seedless raisins
1 cup sliced fresh mushrooms

1. Rub pork with a mixture of the garlic, sage, oregano, and salt. Place pork, fat side up, in a roasting pan. Insert meat thermometer so tip is slightly beyond center of thickest part of meat, being sure the tip does not rest in fat or on bone.
2. Roast, uncovered, at 325° to 350°F 2 to 2½ hours. (Allow 30 to 35 minutes per pound.) Meat is done when internal temperature reaches 170°F. Remove meat and pour off drippings; return ¼ cup drippings to pan. Reduce oven temperature to 250°F.
3. Blend the flour into drippings in pan. Stirring constantly, heat until mixture bubbles. Remove from heat. Add gradually a mixture of the tomato purée, chili powder, and water, stirring constantly. Return to heat and bring to boiling; continue stirring and cook until sauce thickens; cook 1 to 2 minutes. (Scrape pan to blend in brown residue.) Stir in remaining ingredients and cook 10 minutes.
4. Return pork roast to pan. Basting occasionally with sauce, heat in 250°F oven about 30 minutes. Serve hot.

6 TO 8 SERVINGS

PRUNE-STUFFED PORK ROAST

15 to 20 prunes
3- to 4-lb. pork loin roast
¾ to 1 teaspoon salt
Few grains black pepper
1½ teaspoons ground ginger
Prune Gravy, *below*

1. Rinse prunes, cut into halves, and remove and discard pits.
2. Rub fat side of meat with a mixture of the salt, pepper, and ginger. Lightly mark the fat side at about ½-inch intervals to indicate slices. Cut 2 or 3 pockets along each line and insert prunes so they are completely embedded in meat. (Some prunes come to the top of the meat by the end of the roasting period.)
3. Insert meat thermometer so that tip is slightly beyond center of thickest part of meat, not in fat or on bone. Place roast, fat side up, on a rack in a shallow roasting pan.
4. Roast, uncovered, at 325° to 350°F until internal temperature registers 170°F, about 1½ to 2 hours. (Allow 30 to 35 minutes per pound.)
5. Transfer roast to heated serving platter and keep warm while preparing gravy. Pour off all but ¼ cup of drippings (to be used for gravy). Drizzle some of remaining drippings over roast.
6. To serve, carve roast so that prune design will appear to cut surface on each slice.

ABOUT 6 SERVINGS

PRUNE GRAVY: Add about *2 cups hot water* to the ¼ cup drippings in roasting pan; bring to boiling, stirring constantly to loosen brown residue. Stir in a mixture of *½ cup cold water* and *¼ cup flour*. Season with about *¾ teaspoon salt*. Bring to boiling and boil 1 to 2 minutes, stirring constantly. Stir in *½ cup chopped prunes*; heat thoroughly. Serve with the pork roast and *Franconia Potatoes, page 183.*

DUXBURY PORK

5 lb. pork center-cut loin roast
1 teaspoon salt
¼ teaspoon pepper
½ teaspoon ground ginger
¾ cup currant jelly
½ cup frozen concentrate for cranberry-orange juice, thawed

1. Preheat oven to 325°F.
2. Trim any excess fat from pork.
3. Mix salt, pepper, and ginger in a cup; rub into roast. Place on a rack in a shallow roasting pan. Insert meat thermometer into center of roast without touching bone.
4. Roast 2 hours, or until thermometer registers 160°F.
5. Combine currant jelly and cranberry concentrate in a small saucepan; heat to boiling. Simmer 5 minutes; brush part over roast.
6. Continue roasting, brushing often with remaining sauce, ½ hour, or until thermometer registers 170°F.
7. Remove roast to a large serving plate; carve into chops.

6 TO 8 SERVINGS

PORK ROAST WITH OLIVES AND RICE

7-lb. pork loin roast
3 cloves garlic, slivered
1½ cups chicken broth
¾ cup dry vermouth
½ teaspoon ground sage
¼ teaspoon pepper
¾ cup sliced pimiento-stuffed olives
Special Gravy, *below*
Saffron Rice, *below*

1. Score fat side of pork roast; insert garlic in slits. Place, fat side up, in a shallow roasting pan. Insert a meat thermometer in roast so that tip rests in thickest part of the meat.
2. Combine broth, vermouth, sage, and pepper; pour over meat.
3. Roast at 325°F until meat thermometer registers 170°F, basting occasionally. Total cooking time will be about 2½ hours. The last hour of cooking time, add ½ cup of the sliced olives to liquid in pan.
4. Transfer roast to a heated platter; keep warm.
5. Remove olives; reserve to add to rice along with remaining olives. Use liquid for the gravy.
6. Spoon the Saffron Rice onto platter around the roast. Accompany with the gravy.

ABOUT 12 SERVINGS

SPECIAL GRAVY: Skim excess fat from reserved liquid. Measure liquid and add enough water to make 1¾ cups. Return liquid to pan or pour into a saucepan and bring to boiling. Stir a blend of *2 tablespoons cornstarch* and *¼ cup water* into boiling liquid; boil 1 to 2 minutes, stirring constantly. Pour into a gravy boat.   ABOUT 2 CUPS GRAVY

SAFFRON RICE: In a large saucepan, combine *1 quart chicken broth, 2 cups uncooked white rice, 2 tablespoons butter or margarine, ½ teaspoon salt,* and *¼ teaspoon crushed saffron*. Bring to boiling, stirring with a fork. Cook, covered, over low heat 15 to 20 minutes, or until rice is tender. Toss reserved olives with rice.   ABOUT 8 CUPS

ROAST PORK, PENNSYLVANIA DUTCH STYLE

6-lb. pork loin roast
¼ cup flour
1¼ teaspoons salt
1 teaspoon ground ginger
¼ teaspoon pepper
1 cup hot water
2 onions, thinly sliced
2 tablespoons flour
1½ cups water

1. Have meat dealer loosen chine bone. Rub meat with a mixture of the flour, salt, ginger, and pepper. Place roast, fat side up, in a shallow pan. Insert meat thermometer so tip is slightly beyond center of largest muscle, being sure the tip does not rest in fat or on bone.
2. Roast, uncovered, at 400°F 45 minutes. Turn oven temperature to 350°F and continue roasting about 1¾ hours. After the first hour, add the hot water and sliced onions; baste every 15 minutes. Meat is done when internal temperature reaches 170°F.
3. Place roast on a hot serving platter; remove thermometer and keep roast hot.
4. Stir the remaining flour into drippings in pan. Stirring constantly, add the 1½ cups water, bring rapidly to boiling and cook 1 to 2 minutes. Serve with the roast.   8 TO 12 SERVINGS

HAWAIIAN PORK ROAST

3 lb. pork center-cut loin roast (section C in drawing above)
2 teaspoons ground cinnamon
2 teaspoons parsley-garlic salt
1 teaspoon curry powder
½ cup pineapple preserves
2 tablespoons lemon juice

1. Preheat oven to 325°F.
2. Trim any excess fat from pork roast.
3. Mix cinnamon, garlic salt, and curry powder in a cup; rub into all sides of roast. Place roast on a rack in a shallow baking pan; insert meat thermometer into center of roast without touching bone.
4. Roast 1½ hours, or until thermometer registers 160°F.
5. Combine preserves and lemon juice in a cup; brush half over roast.
6. Continue roasting, brushing again with remaining pineapple mixture, 30 minutes, or until thermometer registers 170°F and meat is richly glazed.
7. Place roast on a large serving platter. To serve, carve roast into chops.   4 SERVINGS

•

ROAST FRESH LEG OF PORK

Score rind of a *12- to 14-lb. fresh leg of pork (ham)*, spacing slits ½ inch apart, and rub with a mixture of *1 tablespoon coarse salt* and *4 teaspoons ground ginger*. Put *bay leaves* in several of the slits. Insert a meat thermometer so tip is slightly beyond center of thickest part of meat, being sure that tip does not rest in fat or on bone. Place on a rack in a shallow roasting pan. Roast, uncovered, at 325° to 350°F until internal temperature registers 170°F. (Allow 22 to 26 minutes per pound.) Remove thermometer and transfer roast to carving board or heated serving platter. For easier carving, allow roast to set 15 to 20 minutes after removing from oven.

16 TO 20 SERVINGS

FRESH LEG OF PORK WITH EXOTIC STUFFING

6- to 8-lb. boned fresh leg of pork (ham) or lean shoulder	1 can (13½ oz.) pineapple tidbits, drained (reserve syrup)
¼ cup butter or margarine	½ cup seedless raisins
1 cup uncooked rice	½ to 1 teaspoon curry powder
2 large onions, chopped (about 1½ cups)	½ teaspoon garlic powder
1 can (10½ oz.) condensed beef broth	½ teaspoon marjoram
1 teaspoon salt	1 teaspoon seasoned salt
2 cups chopped celery	1 teaspoon salt
3 cups small bread cubes	¼ teaspoon pepper
	2 teaspoons ground ginger

1. Have meat dealer bone the leg or shoulder of pork. (If leg is used, have it cut almost through to bottom so it will lie flat.) Have wooden skewers available.
2. Heat butter in a large skillet. Add rice and onion and cook over medium heat, stirring occasionally, until rice is light brown. Stir in broth and 1 teaspoon salt; cover tightly and simmer over very low heat 15 minutes.
3. Combine rice mixture with celery, bread cubes, pineapple, raisins, and a mixture of curry powder, garlic powder, marjoram, and seasoned salt; blend thoroughly by tossing lightly with a fork.
4. Rub inside surface of flattened leg or shoulder with a mixture of 1 teaspoon salt and the pepper. Spread dressing over meat; roll lengthwise, secure firmly with skewers, and lace tightly. (Any leftover stuffing may be baked in a greased casserole; place in oven about 1 hour before meat is done.)
5. Rub meat with the ginger, then place on rack in a large shallow roasting pan. Roast at 325° to 350°F 3¾ to 5 hours (allow 22 to 26 minutes per pound), or until meat thermometer registers 170°F. (Insert thermometer into meat and not into stuffing.) During last 30 minutes of roasting, occasionally spoon reserved pineapple syrup over roast.
6. Remove from oven and let stand at least 20 minutes before slicing. Place on a warm platter and garnish with *pineapple rings* and *spiced crab apples*. If desired, make pan gravy with drippings in roasting pan.

12 TO 16 SERVINGS

DANISH PORK DINNER

1 fresh pork shoulder, weighing about 5 lbs.	1 teaspoon salt
1 medium onion, chopped (½ cup)	4 medium-sized sweet potatoes or yams, pared and cut in half
1 cup apple juice	1 cup dried pitted prunes
2 tablespoons brown sugar	2 tablespoons cornstarch
1 teaspoon pumpkin-pie spice	

1. Trim skin and excess fat from pork.
2. Brown pork on all sides in its own fat in a Dutch oven; remove and set aside.
3. Stir onion into drippings; sauté until soft. Stir in apple juice, brown sugar, pumpkin-pie spice, and salt; heat to boiling. Place pork in Dutch oven; cover. Simmer 1½ hours, or until pork is almost tender.
4. Place potatoes in Dutch oven; cover. Cook 20 minutes; add prunes to Dutch oven; cover again. Cook 1 to 2 minutes longer, or until potatoes and pork are tender.
5. Place pork on a large serving platter; spoon potatoes and prunes around pork; keep warm.
6. Strain liquid from Dutch oven into a 4-cup measure, pressing onion through sieve; let stand a few minutes until fat rises to top, then skim off. Measure 2 cups of the liquid and return to Dutch oven; heat to boiling.
7. Mix cornstarch with a little water until smooth in a cup; stir into boiling liquid. Cook, stirring constantly, until sauce thickens and boils 1 minute; pour into a serving bowl.
8. Carve part of the pork; pass sauce to spoon over meat and potatoes.

4 SERVINGS PLUS ENOUGH MEAT FOR A DIVIDEND DISH

RACK OF PORK FORUM

The Forum of the Twelve Caesars, famous New York restaurant, serves this epicurean pork chop dish.

6 thick pork chops	1 tablespoon butter
½ cup packed brown sugar	¼ cup dry white wine
	½ cup pistachio nuts
½ cup crème de cassis	½ cup chopped preserved ginger
2 red apples, cored (not pared)	

1. Flatten the chops to ¾-inch thickness. Place in a shallow baking dish and set in a 400°F oven until browned on one side.
2. Meanwhile, in a small skillet heat brown sugar until melted, stirring frequently. Stir in crème de cassis and continue to cook until mixture is red.
3. Reduce oven temperature to 350°F. Turn chops and season with *salt*. Spoon syrup over them. Bake chops 20 minutes, or until tender.
4. Meanwhile, cut apples into thick slices. Cook slices until just tender in the butter and wine heated in a saucepan.
5. Arrange the chops in a row overlapping on a hot platter and sprinkle with nuts. Arrange the apple slices at one side and fill centers with preserved ginger. 6 SERVINGS

APRICOT-STUFFED PORK ROAST

1 fully-cooked picnic pork shoulder, weighing 5 to 6 lbs., boned	1 cup chopped dried apricots
	8 cups small fresh bread cubes
1 large onion, chopped (1 cup)	1 teaspoon grated orange rind
½ cup chopped celery	1 cup apricot preserves
4 tablespoons butter or margarine	½ teaspoon dry mustard
1 cup water	½ cup thawed frozen concentrate for pineapple juice

1. Trim skin and excess fat from pork.
2. Preheat oven to 325°F.
3. Sauté onion and celery in butter in a small skillet until soft; stir in water and apricots; heat to boiling. Pour over bread cubes and orange rind in a large bowl; toss lightly until evenly moist.
4. Stuff part into pocket in pork, packing in well to fill and give meat a rounded shape, close opening with skewers and tie roast in several places with string. Place on a rack in a roasting pan. (Spoon remaining stuffing into a small baking dish; cover; bake along with roast for 45 minutes.)
5. Roast meat 1½ hours.
6. Combine apricot preserves, mustard, and pineapple concentrate in a small saucepan; heat to boiling. Brush half over pork.
7. Continue roasting, brushing 2 or 3 more times with preserves mixture, 1 hour, or until pork is richly glazed.
8. Remove roast to a heated large serving platter; take out skewers and cut away string. Garnish platter with small inner celery leaves if you like. Carve roast and serve with extra stuffing. 6 TO 8 SERVINGS

PORK CHOPS GOURMET

This recipe came from an amateur chef who won accolades from his fellow-gourmet-club diners for whom he originated the dish.

Fat for browning	Prepared mustard
8 pork chops, cut ½ in. thick	Dill pickles, thinly sliced
1 teaspoon salt	2 tablespoons dill pickle liquid
½ teaspoon black pepper	¼ cup dry vermouth

1. Heat the fat, add chops and brown well on both sides. Sprinkle with a mixture of salt and pepper. Spread each chop generously with mustard.
2. Arrange one layer of pork chops in a saucepot and cover with dill pickle slices. Repeat layering with chops and pickles.
3. Add pickle liquid; cover and cook over low heat 1 hour; add vermouth 20 minutes before end of cooking time.
4. Remove from heat and place chops on heated serving platter. If desired, drizzle additional vermouth over pickles and chops. 4 SERVINGS

HARVEST PORK

4 pork loin chops, cut 1 inch thick	1 tablespoon lemon juice
1 teaspoon salt	4 medium yams or sweet potatoes, pared and cut in ½-inch-thick slices
⅛ teaspoon pepper	
¼ cup firmly packed brown sugar	2 large seedless oranges, pared and sectioned
1 teaspoon grated orange rind	1 tablespoon cornstarch
1 cup orange juice	

Pork

1. Trim any excess fat from chops; rub salt and pepper into both sides of meat.
2. Sauté enough of the fat trimmings to make about 2 tablespoons drippings in a large skillet; discard trimmings.
3. Place pork in skillet and brown slowly, turning once; drain off any drippings.
4. Mix brown sugar, orange rind and juice, and lemon juice in a small bowl; pour over pork. Heat to boiling; cover. Simmer 45 minutes.
5. Place yam slices in sauce around pork; cover. Cook 15 minutes, or until chops and yams are tender.
6. Place orange sections in skillet; cover. Heat 2 to 3 minutes, or just until hot.
7. Lift pork, yams, and orange sections onto a large deep serving platter with a slotted spoon; keep hot.
8. Mix cornstarch with 1 tablespoon water until smooth in a cup; stir into liquid in skillet. Cook, stirring constantly, until sauce thickens and boils 1 minute. Spoon over pork and yams. 4 SERVINGS

SKILLET ORANGE PORK CHOPS

1 cup orange juice	¼ teaspoon thyme, crushed
3 tablespoons instant minced onion	4 pork chops, cut about 1 in. thick
2 teaspoons grated orange peel	½ teaspoon salt
1 tablespoon brown sugar	½ teaspoon monosodium glutamate
½ teaspoon marjoram, crushed	⅛ teaspoon pepper Cooking oil

1. Combine orange juice, onion, orange peel, brown sugar, marjoram, and thyme; set aside.
2. Season pork chops with a mixture of the salt, monosodium glutamate, and pepper. Brown chops well on both sides in a small amount of oil in a heavy skillet. Drain drippings from pan; add orange juice mixture.
3. Cook, covered, over low heat about 45 minutes, or until chops are very tender. If desired, thicken the sauce slightly with a cornstarch-water mixture.
4. Add sectioned pared *oranges* and heat about 5 minutes. 4 SERVINGS

STUFFED PORK CHOPS

2 teaspoons lemon juice	½ cup chopped onion
1 apple, quartered, cored, pared, and diced	¼ cup butter or margarine
	¼ cup apple cider
2 cups soft bread crumbs	8 pork chops, cut 1 to 1¼ in. thick
1 teaspoon salt	(have meat dealer cut a pocket for stuffing)
1 teaspoon celery seed	
⅛ teaspoon black pepper	2 teaspoons fat

1. Sprinkle lemon juice over apple in a bowl. Mix with bread crumbs, salt, celery seed, and pepper.
2. Cook onion in hot butter in a large skillet until soft. Turn the contents of the skillet into apple mixture; toss lightly with enough of the apple cider to just barely moisten. Fill pockets of each chop with the stuffing.
3. Brown chops on both sides in hot fat in the skillet. Remove to a large shallow baking dish. Cover tightly with aluminum foil.
4. Bake at 350°F 1 hour, or until chops are tender and thoroughly cooked. 8 SERVINGS

GREEN BEAN-PORK CHOP SUPPER

2 teaspoons fat	1 can (8 oz.) tomato sauce
6 pork chops, cut ½ to ¾ in. thick	1 tablespoon finely chopped onion
2 cans (16 oz. each) cut blue lake green beans, drained (reserve 2 tablespoons liquid)	1 teaspoon salt
	¼ teaspoon black pepper
1 can (12 oz.) whole kernel corn	¼ teaspoon chervil, crushed
1 tablespoon cornstarch	1 teaspoon Worcestershire sauce

1. Heat fat in a large heavy skillet. Add chops and brown on all sides.
2. Mix beans and corn in a 2½-quart casserole.
3. Blend the reserved bean liquid with cornstarch; stir in the remaining ingredients. Pour sauce over vegetables and toss until well coated. Arrange chops on top of vegetable mixture.
4. Bake, covered, at 350°F 1 hour, or until pork chops are tender. Uncover and bake 10 minutes longer. 6 SERVINGS

APPLE-STUFFED PORK CHOPS

6 pork chops, each 1 inch thick, with pockets for stuffing
1½ teaspoons salt
1 large tart apple, pared, quartered, cored, and chopped (1 cup)
1 small onion, chopped (¼ cup)
1 tablespoon butter or margarine
½ cup plain wheat germ
½ cup fresh bread cubes (1 small slice)
Water
1 lemon, cut into 6 slices

1. Trim any excess fat from chops; sprinkle salt over both sides.
2. Sauté apple and onion in butter in a medium saucepan until soft; stir in wheat germ, bread cubes, and 1 tablespoon water. Stuff into pockets in chops; fasten each in several places with wooden picks.
3. Melt enough of the fat trimmings in a large skillet to make 2 tablespoons drippings; remove trimmings and discard. Place chops in drippings and brown slowly; top each with a slice of lemon. Pour ¼ cup water into skillet; cover.
4. Cook 45 minutes, or until chops are tender. Lift onto a large serving platter, leaving lemon slices in place. 6 SERVINGS

MIDWESTERN PORK BAKE

4 pork shoulder chops, cut ¾ inch thick
4 large carrots, pared and sliced
¾ teaspoon dried thyme, crushed
1 teaspoon salt
⅛ teaspoon pepper
1 can (16 ozs.) whole-kernel corn
4 green onions, trimmed and sliced

1. Trim any excess fat from chops.
2. Sauté a few of the trimmings in a large skillet until 2 tablespoons fat cook out; discard trimmings. Brown chops, turning once, in drippings; remove from heat.
3. Preheat oven to 350°F.
4. Place carrots in a layer in a shallow baking dish; arrange chops, overlapping if needed, in a row on top.
5. Mix thyme, salt, and pepper in a cup; sprinkle half over chops and carrots.
6. Spoon corn and liquid along sides in dish; sprinkle remaining seasoning mix over top, then sprinkle green onions over all; cover.
7. Bake 1 hour, or until chops are tender. Serve from baking dish. 4 SERVINGS

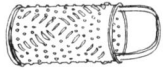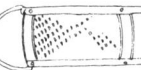

PARTY PORK CHOPS

6 pork chops, cut about 1 in. thick
2 tablespoons flour
2 tablespoons fat
1½ teaspoons salt
⅛ teaspoon pepper
¾ teaspoon dry mustard
½ teaspoon ground cinnamon
¼ teaspoon ground cloves
⅛ teaspoon ground allspice
¼ cup cider vinegar
¼ cup raspberry jam
½ cup hot water
3 large onions, cut in ½-in. slices

1. Coat pork chops with flour. Brown on both sides in heated fat in a large heavy skillet. Transfer browned chops to a shallow baking dish.
2. Mix salt, pepper, dry mustard, cinnamon, cloves, and allspice with the vinegar. Blend in jam and hot water; pour mixture over chops; cover. Bake at 350°F 40 minutes.
3. Arrange onion slices around chops. Cover and continue baking 25 minutes, or until meat is tender.
4. Remove chops and onions to warm platter. If desired, thicken drippings for gravy. 6 SERVINGS

EENYHOW

Hawaiian-born James Shigeta, Hollywood actor, gives this dish a touch of the Orient with the use of soy sauce.

6 loin pork chops
2 bunches watercress, broken in small pieces
1 cup finely chopped green onions
3 medium-sized firm tomatoes, chopped in very small pieces
½ to ¾ cup soy sauce

1. Trim all fat from chops and cut chops in small pieces. Brown in heavy skillet with several pieces of fat to prevent sticking. When meat starts to brown, sprinkle with *soy sauce*, *salt*, and *pepper* and continue browning.
2. Meanwhile, in a large bowl combine the watercress, green onions, and tomatoes. When the pork is thoroughly cooked, toss it with the vegetables and soy sauce like a salad. Serve over *cooked rice*.
6 SERVINGS

Pork

PORK MANDARIN

- 3 tablespoons cooking oil
- 1½ lbs. boneless pork, cut in 2x¼-in. strips
- 2 teaspoons salt
- ¼ cup cornstarch
- ½ cup cold water
- 2 tablespoons soy sauce
- 1 can (13½ oz.) pineapple chunks, drained (reserve syrup)
- 1 can (11 oz.) mandarin oranges, drained (reserve syrup)
- 1 can (12 oz.) apricot nectar
- ½ cup cider vinegar
- ¾ cup lightly packed brown sugar
- 1 cup diced celery
- 1 large green pepper, cut in strips
- 1 can (16 oz.) whole tomatoes, drained and quartered
- 12 blanched almonds, toasted

1. Heat oil in a large heavy skillet. Add pork and brown well on all sides. Season with salt; cover and cook until pork is done, 10 to 15 minutes.
2. Blend cornstarch and water in a saucepan; stir in soy sauce, reserved syrup from fruits, apricot nectar, vinegar, and brown sugar. Bring mixture to boiling, stirring constantly; cook 3 minutes.
3. Add celery and pineapple chunks to meat. Add the sauce and cook over low heat about 5 minutes.
4. Stir in green pepper and tomato pieces and heat about 5 minutes longer.
5. Before serving, add mandarin oranges to mixture. Remove to heated serving dish and top with almonds. Serve with fluffy *cooked rice*.

ABOUT 6 SERVINGS

BAHMIE GORENG

This Indonesian dish was created during the days of Dutch control. The food of Aruba, Netherlands Antilles, shows the influence of Indonesian cookery. This dish is featured at Executive House's Aruba Caribbean Hotel-Casino, and the recipe was adapted for American use by Executive Chef Monsieur Robert Machax and Mr. Maurice Filleul, Director of Foods and Beverages.

- ½ lb. thin egg noodles
- ¼ cup butter, or 3 tablespoons cooking oil
- 1 medium-sized onion, diced
- 2 cloves garlic, minced
- Celery (heart portion only), diced
- ½ or 1 medium-sized cabbage, diced
- 8 leeks, trimmed and diced
- ½ teaspoon ground ginger
- 1 lb. pork loin, diced
- 1 can (16 oz.) bean sprouts, drained
- Cooked shrimp (about 1 lb.)
- 1 omelet (2 eggs)

1. Cook noodles following package directions. Rinse with cold water; drain.
2. Heat butter in a large saucepot or skillet. Mix in onion and garlic and sauté until browned; transfer to a small bowl. Stir the ginger into fat in skillet, and mix in the pork. Brown on all sides.
3. Mix in the vegetables, bean sprouts, onion, and garlic; cook 15 minutes, stirring occasionally. Stir while adding the drained noodles and shrimp; heat thoroughly.
4. Meanwhile, prepare the omelet. Roll up omelet and slice into thin strips for topping.
5. Turn the bahmie onto a large platter. Top with omelet strips. Serve with "sambals" such as *salted peanuts, flaked coconut, mustards*, and *ketchup*.

4 TO 6 SERVINGS

CANTONESE PORK

- 1 piece boneless pork shoulder
- 2 tablespoons salad oil
- 2 envelopes instant chicken broth
- 1½ cups water
- 2 medium-sized green peppers
- 1½ cups diagonally sliced celery
- 1 can (20 ozs.) pineapple chunks in juice
- 3 tablespoons cornstarch
- 2 tablespoons brown sugar
- ½ teaspoon salt
- ⅓ cup white vinegar
- 3 tablespoons catsup
- 4 cups hot cooked rice

1. Trim any fat from pork; cut pork into thin strips. Brown in salad oil in a large skillet; pour off any excess fat.
2. Stir chicken broth and water into skillet; heat to boiling; cover. Simmer 20 minutes, or until pork is almost tender.
3. Cut green peppers in half; seed and cut into 1-inch squares. Stir into pork mixture with celery; cook, stirring once or twice, 5 minutes, or until pork is tender and vegetables are crisp-tender.
4. Drain juice from pineapple into a cup. Mix cornstarch, brown sugar, and salt in a small bowl; stir in pineapple juice and vinegar until mixture is smooth; stir into skillet. Cook, stirring constantly, until mixture thickens and boils 1 minute.

SZEKELY GOULASH

A Hungarian specialty.

1½ lbs. boneless pork shoulder, cut in 1½-in. cubes	2 tablespoons finely chopped onion
2 tablespoons flour	1 can (27 oz.) sauerkraut, drained
2 teaspoons paprika	½ teaspoon caraway seed
1½ teaspoons salt	1½ cups dairy sour cream
2 tablespoons fat	

1. Coat meat evenly with a mixture of flour, paprika, and salt.
2. Heat fat in a Dutch oven or saucepot. Add onion and cook until soft, stirring occasionally.
3. Brown meat evenly on all sides in the hot fat; add *3 tablespoons hot water.* Cover and simmer 1 hour, stirring occasionally; add small amounts of water as needed during cooking.
4. Mix sauerkraut and caraway seed with the meat; add *2 cups hot water.* Cover and simmer 30 minutes, or until meat is tender.
5. Gradually add about 1½ cups of the cooking liquid to sour cream, blending well. Stir into mixture in Dutch oven. Stirring constantly, heat (do not boil) about 5 minutes. Serve in small bowls; accompany with *boiled new potatoes.*   6 TO 8 SERVINGS

BARBECUED SPARERIBS

3 lbs. spareribs, cracked through center	3 tablespoons butter or margarine
1 tablespoon salt	½ cup cider vinegar
1 teaspoon black pepper	¼ cup ketchup
⅔ cup finely chopped green pepper	¼ cup brown sugar
⅓ cup finely chopped onion	1 tablespoon Worcestershire sauce
¼ cup chopped celery	½ teaspoon dry mustard
	½ teaspoon chili powder
	2 lemon slices

1. Cut ribs into serving-sized pieces, season with salt and pepper, and place, meaty side up, in a shallow roasting pan. Bake at 350°F 30 minutes, turning once.
2. Cook vegetables in heated butter in a saucepan until onion is tender, stirring occasionally. Blend in a mixture of the vinegar, ketchup, brown sugar, Worcestershire sauce, dry mustard, and chili powder, then lemon slices. Simmer 5 to 10 minutes, stirring frequently. Remove from heat; set aside.
3. After ribs have baked for 30 minutes, remove from oven. Pour off excess fat. Spoon one half of the sauce over ribs; cover and continue baking, basting frequently, 1 to 1½ hours, or until meat is tender. Uncover pan the last 15 to 20 minutes.
      6 SERVINGS

APPLE-KRAUT STUFFED SPARERIBS

¼ cup butter or margarine	2 cups sauerkraut
¼ cup chopped onion	1 teaspoon caraway seed
4 cups soft ½-in. bread cubes	2 sections spareribs, about 1 lb. each
1 cup diced pared apple	

1. Heat butter in a skillet; add onion and cook until onion is transparent. Toss lightly with bread cubes, apple, sauerkraut, and caraway seed.
2. Sprinkle both sides of sparerib sections with *salt* and *pepper;* place one sparerib section on rack of a shallow roasting pan. Spread stuffing over it; cover with second section. Fasten the sections together with skewers.
3. Roast at 350°F for 1½ hours, or until meat is tender when pierced with a fork. Remove skewers; cut spareribs into serving-sized pieces and serve with the stuffing.   4 SERVINGS

NOTE: If desired, occasionally brush spareribs with *soy sauce* during roasting.

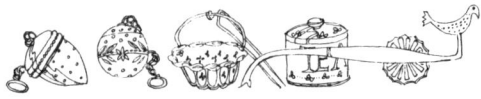

GLAZED PORK SAUSAGE PATTIES

1 lb. bulk pork sausage, shaped in patties about ½ in. thick	½ teaspoon basil
	4 teaspoons cider vinegar
½ cup packed dark brown sugar	½ teaspoon grated onion

1. Put sausage patties into large heavy skillet; add *1 to 2 tablespoons water*, cover, and cook slowly for 5 minutes.
2. Remove cover; pour off liquid. Add a mixture of the remaining ingredients and cook, turning patties frequently, until browned and glazed. Serve immediately.   6 TO 8 SERVINGS

HALF-HOUR MEAL

1 pkg. (10 oz.) frozen lima beans
1 lb. bulk pork sausage
3 tablespoons finely chopped onion
¼ cup water
¼ teaspoon ground nutmeg
¼ teaspoon marjoram
2 tablespoons water
1 tablespoon flour
1 can (4 oz.) sliced ripe olives, drained
1 cup dairy sour cream

1. Cook lima beans following package directions; drain, if necessary.
2. Meanwhile, put sausage into a cold skillet and separate into pieces. Add onion and ¼ cup water; cover, bring to boiling and simmer 10 minutes.
3. Drain off the drippings. Then stir nutmeg and marjoram into skillet mixture. Stir in a blend of *2 tablespoons water* and the flour; bring to boiling and cook 1 to 2 minutes, stirring constantly.
4. Mix in the lima beans and olives. Blend in the sour cream, a small amount at a time. Heat thoroughly (do not boil). Serve at once.
   ABOUT 4 SERVINGS

PORK SAUSAGE LINKS

Cut *link sausages* apart. Place in a cold skillet. Add a small amount of *water*; cover and cook over low heat 5 minutes. Remove cover and pour off fat. Cook, turning to brown on all sides.

CANADIAN-STYLE BACON WITH MUSTARD SAUCE

1½ lbs. Canadian-style bacon (in one piece)
8 to 10 whole cloves
1 cup firmly packed brown sugar
2 tablespoons prepared mustard
3 tablespoons cider vinegar
1 tablespoon butter or margarine

1. Remove casing from bacon. Place bacon, fat side up, on a rack in a shallow roasting pan. Insert whole cloves. Insert a meat thermometer.
2. Roast, uncovered, at 300° to 325°F about 1 hour, or until internal temperature reaches 160°F.
3. Combine remaining ingredients in a saucepan. Stir over low heat until sugar is dissolved and mixture is heated. Serve hot with the bacon.
   ABOUT 6 SERVINGS

SMOKED SHOULDER ROLL WITH MUSTARD SAUCE

1½-lb. cooked smoked pork shoulder roll (butt), *page 102*
⅓ cup packed brown sugar
2 teaspoons flour
1 teaspoon prepared mustard
½ cup water
3 tablespoons cider vinegar
2 egg yolks, slightly beaten
1 tablespoon butter or margarine
1 pkg. (10 oz.) frozen broccoli spears
1 pkg. (10 oz.) frozen cauliflower
½ cup shredded sharp Cheddar cheese

1. Slice cooked shoulder butt.
2. Combine brown sugar and flour in top of double boiler. Stir in mustard, then water and vinegar. Continue stirring and bring to boiling over direct heat and cook 3 minutes.
3. Remove from heat and vigorously stir about 3 tablespoons of hot mixture into beaten egg yolks; immediately blend into mixture in double boiler.
4. Cook over hot water 3 to 5 minutes; stir slowly. Remove from heat and stir in the butter.
5. Cook broccoli and cauliflower according to directions on package; drain, if necessary.
6. Arrange shoulder butt slices in a shallow baking dish. Arrange broccoli spears and cauliflower over meat. Spoon mustard sauce over all and top evenly with cheese.
7. Set in a 350°F oven about 15 minutes, or until thoroughly heated.   4 SERVINGS

SMOKED SHOULDER ROLL: Put smoked shoulder roll (butt) into a large heavy saucepot. Add enough *hot water* to cover meat. Add *1 teaspoon monosodium glutamate, 5 whole cloves, 3 peppercorns*, and *1 clove garlic*. Bring liquid to boiling; reduce heat, cover and simmer (do not boil) about 1 hour, or until meat is tender.

SCHNITZ UN KNEPP
(Apples and Buttons)

Schnitz means "cut" and to the Pennsylvania Dutch the word has come to mean cut dried apples, which when soaked and cooked, are used as stewed fruit, for pie fillings, or in this meat dish.

1 qt. dried apples (about an 8 oz. pkg.)
3-lb. smoked shoulder roll (butt)
2 tablespoons brown sugar
2 cups sifted all-purpose flour
4 teaspoons baking powder
1 teaspoon salt
¼ teaspoon pepper
1 egg, well beaten
3 tablespoons butter, melted
½ cup milk

1. Cover the dried apples with *water*; soak overnight.
2. Next day, cover smoked shoulder roll with water in a large Dutch oven or kettle, cover loosely, and simmer about 30 minutes. Add the apples and water in which they have been soaked and continue to simmer about 1 hour. Stir in the brown sugar.
3. To prepare the dumplings, sift the flour, baking powder, salt, and pepper together into a bowl. Add all at one time a mixture of the beaten egg, melted butter, and milk; mix only until dry ingredients are moistened. Drop by tablespoonfuls onto simmering mixture. Tightly cover the Dutch oven and cook 20 minutes; do not remove cover during cooking.

8 TO 10 SERVINGS

HAM

Glazes for Ham

Remove ham from oven 30 to 40 minutes before time indicated for heating through and spread generously with the desired glaze. Return to oven and continue heating, basting frequently with pan drippings. (If using canned ham, slice it and tie into shape with cord. Remove cord before serving.)

CIDER: Combine and mix thoroughly ¾ *cup packed brown sugar*, ½ *teaspoon dry mustard*, and *2 tablespoons maple syrup*. Spread glaze over ham. Occasionally baste ham with about ¾ *cup apple cider*.

APRICOT (using apricot jam): Combine ¾ *cup apricot jam*, ¾ *cup honey*, and *2 tablespoons lemon juice or cider vinegar*. Spread glaze over ham.

APRICOT (using dried apricots): Pour *1⅓ cups apple cider* over *8 ounces dried apricots* in a bowl. Cover and refrigerate overnight. Purée apricot mixture in an electric blender or force through a food mill. Stir in a mixture of *6 tablespoons brown sugar*, ½ *teaspoon ground cinnamon*, ½ *teaspoon ground allspice*, and ¼ *teaspoon ground cloves*. Spread ham generously with mixture before heating. Heat remaining sauce and serve as an accompaniment to the ham.

MUSTARD GLAZE: Mix thoroughly in a small bowl *1 cup packed brown sugar, 1 tablespoon flour*, and *1 teaspoon dry mustard*. Stir in *2 tablespoons cider vinegar* to form a smooth paste.

JELLY OR JAM: Dilute *1 cup quince or elderberry jelly, jam, or orange marmalade* with ⅓ *cup very hot water*.

BROWN SUGAR: Heat together in a saucepan, stirring until sugar is dissolved, *1 cup packed brown sugar* and ⅔ *cup light corn syrup*. If desired, ⅔ *cup spiced fruit juice or ginger ale* may be substituted for the corn syrup.

GLAZED ROAST HAM

1. Place a *10-lb. whole smoked ham* on a rack in a shallow roasting pan. Roast at 300° to 325°F about 2 hours; remove from oven.
2. Cut off rind (if any) and score fat. Insert a *whole clove* in the center of each diamond.
3. Spread with *one of Glazes for Ham, (above)*, and continue roasting about 1 hour, or until internal temperature reaches 160°F.

ABOUT 20 SERVINGS

FOIL-BAKED FLAVOR-GLAZED HAM

Ham (see Timetable for Baking Ham in Aluminum Foil, *page 104*
Flavor Blends, *page 104*
Cloves
Sauces, *below page 104*

Ham

1. Arrange a large sheet of heavy-duty aluminum foil in a shallow roasting pan; place ham in center.
2. Pour one-half of the desired Flavor Blend over ham and brush it in. Bring foil up, covering ham loosely. Bake according to the timetable.
3. About 30 minutes before baking is finished, open and turn back foil. Spoon out melted fat; remove rind (skin). Score ham in diamond pattern.
4. Stud with cloves. Pour remaining Flavor Blend over ham. Insert meat thermometer and continue baking with foil open, basting with drippings, until browned.
5. Slip a foil frill on bone end of ham after transferring ham to serving platter. Accompany with a fruit or wine sauce.

Flavor Blends for Foil-Baked Ham

ORANGE: Combine one-half of *1 can (6 ounces) frozen orange juice concentrate,* thawed, *1 cup firmly packed brown sugar,* and *½ cup bottled steak sauce.*
PINEAPPLE: Combine *¾ cup unsweetened pineapple juice* with *1 cup firmly packed brown sugar.* Decorate ham with *pineapple slices.*
SHERRY OR MADEIRA: Pour *1 cup wine* over ham before baking. To brown and glaze, sprinkle lightly with *brown sugar* and baste with *1 cup wine.*

Sauces for Foil-Baked Ham

ORANGE: Blend remaining half of orange juice concentrate with *1 cup fruit juice or water.*
PINEAPPLE: Use *1 cup unsweetened pineapple juice.*
WINE: Use *1 cup water.* Stir in any one of the above liquids, blending with the juices and drippings in pan. To thicken, add a mixture of *cornstarch* and *liquid* (about 1 tablespoon per cup of liquid). Bring to boiling, stirring constantly, and cook 1 to 2 minutes.

BAKED HAM SLICE WITH CURRIED FRUIT

1 smoked ham slice, cut 1 in. thick
½ cup lightly packed light brown sugar
1 cup fine, dry bread crumbs
3 tablespoons water
Pepper
2 teaspoons prepared mustard

1. Cut fat from ham. Chop fat and mix with remaining ingredients. Place ham in baking pan. Cover with crumb mixture.
2. Bake at 375°F about 50 minutes. Serve with *Curried Fruit, below.*   6 SERVINGS

CURRIED FRUIT: Use halves of drained canned *apricots, pears,* and *pineapple spears or slices.* Use as many pieces as will fill a deep casserole or approximately 4 pieces fruit per serving. Pour over fruit a mixture of *½ cup butter,* melted, *1 cup lightly packed brown sugar,* and *1 tablespoon curry powder.* Bake 40 minutes in same oven with ham.

TIMETABLE FOR BAKING HAM IN ALUMINUM FOIL
(Oven temperature 350°F)

Kind	Average Weight (Pounds)	Approx. Total Baking Time (Hours)	Internal Temperature of Meat
Fully Cooked			
whole, bone in	8 to 12	3	130°F
half	4 to 6	1½	130°F
whole, partially boned	7 to 11	3	130°F
half	3½ to 5½	1½	130°F
rolled, whole	6 to 10	2½ to 2¾	130°F
half	3 to 5	1 to 1½	130°F
Canned			
small	3 to 6	1	130°F
large	6 to 10	1½ to 1¾	130°F
Cook Before Eating			
whole, bone in	8 to 12	3½ to 4	160°F
half	4 to 6	1¾ to 2	160°F

HAM SLICE IN ORANGE SAUCE

1 smoked ham slice,
  cut 1½ in. thick
  (about 2 lbs.)
2 tablespoons brown
  sugar
½ teaspoon dry mustard
2 teaspoons grated
  orange peel
1 teaspoon grated
  lemon peel
1½ cups orange juice
1 teaspoon cornstarch

1. Put ham slice into a baking dish. Insert *whole cloves* in ham slice at 1-inch intervals. Sprinkle a mixture of the brown sugar, dry mustard, and orange and lemon peels over the surface of the ham. Pour 1 cup of the orange juice over ham.
2. Bake at 300°F about 45 minutes, or until thoroughly heated, spooning the liquid over ham slice occasionally during baking.
3. Blend the remaining orange juice with the cornstarch. Remove ham from oven; pour orange juice mixture into baking dish. Return to oven for about 20 minutes, or until liquid is thickened and clear.
4. Remove cloves from ham slice before serving. Garnish with *lemon slices* and *parsley*.

4 TO 6 SERVINGS

"FRIED" HAM WITH RED GRAVY

A ham slice "fried" in this manner is really pan broiled and produces just enough drippings to make the flavorful "red" gravy dear to all Southerners. To give the palate a real surprise, try using hot coffee instead of water, as some cooks do down South.

Rub a heated large heavy skillet with a piece of *fat* trimmed from a *smoked ham slice*, cut ¼ inch thick (allow ⅓ to ½ pound meat per serving). Place ham slice in skillet and cook over medium heat. Maintain a temperature which allows juices to evaporate rather than collect in skillet. (With too low heat, meat will simmer in its own juices and become dry and less tender when cooked.) Turn meat occasionally for even browning. Remove ham slice to a hot plate; keep hot. Add *½ cup hot water* to skillet and bring to boiling, stirring and scraping bottom of skillet to loosen all drippings. Simmer until some of the water evaporates. Pour gravy over ham or serve with the ham.

HAM À LA CRANBERRY

2 cups sugar
¼ teaspoon salt
2 cups water
1 lb. (about 4 cups)
  cranberries, washed
  and sorted
2 teaspoons grated
  lemon peel
6 cups cubed cooked
  smoked ham or
  luncheon meat
½ cup seedless raisins
  (optional)

1. Combine sugar, salt, and water in a saucepan and heat to boiling; boil, uncovered, 5 minutes. Add cranberries and continue to boil, uncovered, without stirring, about 5 minutes, or until skins pop.
2. Turn cranberry sauce into chafing dish blazer. Blend in the lemon peel, ham, and raisins, if desired. Cook over direct heat until mixture starts to bubble; stir occasionally.
3. Place blazer over simmering water to keep mixture hot. Serve over *toast triangles, patty shells,* or *hot biscuits*.

8 TO 10 SERVINGS

GLAZED HAM AND BANANAS

½ cup orange marmalade
2 tablespoons butter or
  margarine
1 tablespoon lemon juice
4 individual ham steaks,
  weighing about 4 ozs.
  each
2 large green-tipped
  bananas

1. Preheat oven to 350°F.
2. Combine marmalade, butter, and lemon juice in a large skillet with ovenproof handle; heat slowly, stirring constantly, until marmalade melts and sauce is blended.
3. Place ham steaks in skillet; turn to coat well with sauce.
4. Bake 20 minutes. Peel bananas; cut in half lengthwise; place around steaks in skillet. Spoon sauce over bananas to cover.
5. Bake 15 minutes longer, or until bananas and steaks are bubbly and glazed.
6. Cut ham into serving-sized pieces, if necessary. Serve from skillet.

4 SERVINGS

MUSHROOM-HAM CASSEROLE

¼ cup butter
1 lb. fresh mushrooms,
  sliced lengthwise
3 cups julienne strips
  cooked ham

Ham

1 tablespoon minced onion
3 tablespoons flour
1 teaspoon salt
¼ teaspoon dry mustard
1 can (14½ oz.) evaporated milk
⅓ cup water
2 pkgs. (9 oz. each) frozen cut green beans, cooked following pkg. directions and drained
¼ cup pimiento strips
½ lb. sharp Cheddar cheese, shredded

1. Heat butter in a large skillet; add mushrooms and onion and cook over medium heat, stirring occasionally, until mushrooms are lightly browned. Remove mushrooms from skillet and set aside.
2. Blend a mixture of flour, salt, and dry mustard into the skillet. Heat until mixture bubbles, stirring constantly. Remove from heat. Continue stirring, gradually add evaporated milk and water; bring rapidly to boiling; cook 1 to 2 minutes.
3. Add ham, beans, pimiento, and mushrooms; mix well. Turn into a lightly greased, shallow 2-quart baking dish. Top with half of the cheese.
4. Set in a 350°F oven about 20 minutes, or until thoroughly heated and cheese is golden brown. Remove from oven and immediately sprinkle with remaining cheese. Garnish with *mushroom caps browned in butter, a ham slice,* and *parsley.*

6 TO 8 SERVINGS

HAM-OLIVE CRÊPES

⅓ cup butter or margarine
5 oz. fresh mushrooms, coarsely chopped
2 tablespoons grated onion
2 tablespoons butter or margarine
3 tablespoons flour
2 cups cream
⅛ teaspoon pepper
¼ teaspoon oregano, crushed
1 cup (about 6 oz.) thin 1½-in. strips cooked ham
⅓ cup chopped pimiento-stuffed olives
8 Crêpes
¼ cup grated Parmesan cheese

1. Heat ⅓ cup butter in a large skillet; add mushrooms and onion. Cook over medium heat 5 minutes, stirring occasionally. Using a slotted spoon, remove mushrooms; set aside.
2. Add 2 tablespoons butter to skillet; blend in flour and cook until bubbly. Remove from heat and gradually add cream, stirring constantly. Continue to stir and bring mixture to boiling; cook 1 to 2 minutes.
3. Add 1 cup of the sauce to a mixture of the mushrooms, pepper, oregano, ham, and olives. Toss lightly until well mixed.
4. Lightly butter a shallow baking dish. Spoon enough cream sauce over bottom of baking dish to make a thin layer.
5. Spoon 2 to 3 tablespoons of the filling onto the center of each crêpe. Fold one edge of crêpe over filling and roll up. Place filled crêpes in baking dish with open edges down. Spoon remaining sauce over crêpes; sprinkle with Parmesan cheese.
6. Heat, covered, in a 350°F oven for 15 minutes. Remove the dish from oven and uncover.
7. Place baking dish under broiler with top of crêpes 3 to 4 inches from source of heat. Broil 3 to 4 minutes, or until cheese is lightly browned.

8 SERVINGS

HAM JUBILEE

1 two-pound canned ham
2 cans (8¾ ozs. each) fruits for salad
1 tablespoon cornstarch
2 tablespoons brandy
1 teaspoon lemon juice

1. Preheat oven to 350°F.
2. Cut ham into 8 even slices; place slices in a shallow baking dish; cover.
3. Bake 30 minutes, or until heated through.
4. While ham bakes, drain syrup from fruits into a cup; stir into cornstarch in a medium saucepan. Cook slowly, stirring constantly, until mixture thickens and boils 1 minute; stir in brandy and lemon juice. Add fruits; heat slowly just until hot.
5. Spoon over or around ham in baking dish.

8 SERVINGS

HAM 'N' YAMS IN RAISIN-CARAMEL SAUCE

3 tablespoons butter or margarine
1 cup lightly packed light brown sugar
½ cup golden raisins
½ cup cream
6 smoked ham slices (about ½ lb.), cut in halves
6 canned yams or sweet potatoes, cut lengthwise

1. Heat butter in a large skillet. Add brown sugar and raisins; heat, stirring constantly, 10 minutes.
2. Remove from heat; add cream slowly, stirring

until blended. Cook 1 minute.
3. Add ham and yams; spoon sauce over all. Heat thoroughly. Thin the sauce with additional cream, if necessary. 6 SERVINGS

DANISH HAM ROLLS IN SAMSOE CHEESE SAUCE
Leeks, a popular vegetable in Denmark, are featured in this delicious luncheon dish for a party.

6 leeks	4 oz. Samsoe cheese, grated
3 tablespoons butter	6 slices Danish ham
2 tablespoons flour	1 tablespoon bread crumbs
½ teaspoon salt	¾ teaspoon paprika
1¼ cups milk	

1. Cut off and discard the upper green tops of the leeks. Rinse several times in cold water to remove all sand. Place in a saucepan; sprinkle with salt and add *boiling water* to cover. Simmer, covered, for 10 minutes. Drain thoroughly.
2. Meanwhile, melt butter; stir in flour and salt. Add milk gradually, stirring constantly. Bring to boiling; cook and stir 1 to 2 minutes. Add one half of cheese, stirring until blended.
3. Spread ham slices with *mustard*. Wrap a slice around drained leek. Place in a shallow baking dish (open edge down). Pour on sauce.
4. Spoon over a topping mixture of remaining cheese, bread crumbs, and paprika. Dot with *butter* (about 2 tablespoons). Broil with top of dish about 4 inches from source of heat 4 to 5 minutes. 6 SERVINGS

HAM BALLS TROPICALE

2 lbs. ground ready-to-eat ham	2 cans (11 ozs. each) mandarin orange segments
1 lb. ground pork	1 cup firmly packed brown sugar
1 cup regular wheat germ	6 tablespoons cornstarch
1 medium onion, minced (½ cup)	½ cup cider vinegar
¾ cup milk	¼ cup soy sauce
3 eggs	1½ cups halved, seeded green grapes
3 tablespoons salad oil	
1 can (20 ozs.) pineapple chunks in syrup	

1. Combine ham, pork, wheat germ, onion, milk, and eggs in a large bowl; mix lightly until blended. Shape into balls, using 1 level tablespoon for each.
2. Brown meatballs, a few at a time, in salad oil in a kettle; remove to another pan; pour drippings from kettle.
3. Drain syrups from pineapple chunks and mandarin orange segments into a 4-cup measure; add water to make 3 cups.
4. Mix brown sugar and cornstarch in kettle; stir in the 3 cups fruit liquid, vinegar, and soy sauce. Cook, stirring constantly, until sauce thickens and boils 1 minute. Place meatballs in sauce; cover. Simmer 30 minutes.
5. Place pineapple, mandarin orange segments, and grapes on top of meatballs; heat 10 minutes longer, or until fruit is hot.
6. Spoon meatballs and sauce into a large serving bowl. Garnish and serve with hot cooked rice or pilaf if you like. 12 SERVINGS

POTATO-HAM SCALLOP

2 can (16 ozs. each) white whole potatoes	Few drops red-pepper seasoning
3 tablespoons butter or margarine	2 cups milk
¾ cup fresh bread crumbs (1½ slices)	1 cup shredded Swiss cheese (4 ozs.)
3 tablespoons all-purpose flour	½ cup sliced green onions
½ teaspoon salt	¾ teaspoon dillweed
	1 cup minced cooked ham

1. Drain liquid from potatoes; slice potatoes. (There should be about 4 cups.)
2. Melt butter in a medium saucepan; measure out 1 tablespoon and toss with bread crumbs in a small bowl.
3. Stir flour, salt, and red-pepper seasoning into remaining butter in saucepan; cook, stirring constantly, until bubbly. Stir in milk; continue cooking and stirring until sauce thickens and boils 1 minute; remove from heat.
4. Mix cheese, green onions, and dillweed in a small bowl.
5. Preheat oven to 350°F.
6. Layer half of the potatoes into a 1½-quart baking dish; top with half each of the ham, cheese mixture, and sauce; repeat layers, lifting mixture at side of dish with a fork so sauce runs to bottom. Sprinkle buttered crumbs on top.
7. Bake 35 minutes, or until bubbly and topping is toasted. 4 GENEROUS SERVINGS

LAMB

ROAST LEG OF LAMB, FRENCH STYLE

5- to 6-lb. leg of lamb (do not remove fell)
2 teaspoons salt
¼ teaspoon pepper
Garlic cloves, cut in slivers
Melted butter or margarine

1. Rub lamb with a mixture of the salt and pepper. Cut several small slits in surface of meat and insert a sliver of garlic in each.
2. Place lamb, skin side down, on rack in a roasting pan. Insert meat thermometer so tip is slightly beyond center of thickest part of meat; be sure that it does not rest in fat or on bone.
3. Roast, uncovered, at 325°F 2½ to 3½ hours, allowing 30 to 35 minutes per pound. Brush meat frequently with melted butter during roasting. Meat is medium done when thermometer registers 175°F and is well done at 180°F.
4. Remove meat to a warm serving platter and garnish, if you like. Serve with Rice Pilaf.

ABOUT 10 SERVINGS

CUMBERLAND LAMB ROAST

1 leg of lamb, weighing about 8 lbs.
1½ teaspoons seasoned salt
½ teaspoon seasoned pepper
1 cup currant jelly
¼ cup horseradish
2 teaspoons dry mustard
Rice Pilaf (recipe on page 187)

1. Preheat oven to 325°F.
2. Trim excess fat from lamb. Sprinkle salt and pepper over roast; place, fat side up, on a rack in a large roasting pan. Insert meat thermometer into thickest part of roast without touching bone. Do not cover pan or add any water.
3. Roast 3 hours.
4. Beat jelly with horseradish and mustard in a small bowl until blended; brush part over lamb.
5. Continue roasting, brushing every 15 minutes with more jelly mixture, 45 minutes, or until lamb is richly glazed and thermometer registers 170°F for medium. (If you prefer lamb well-done, thermometer should register 180°F.)
6. Place roast on a heated large serving platter; garnish, if you like. Serve with Rice Pilaf (recipe on page 187).

6 SERVINGS PLUS ENOUGH MEAT FOR ONE OR TWO DIVIDEND DISHES

GLAZED ROLLED LEG OF LAMB

5½- to 6-lb. leg of lamb, boned and rolled
2 teaspoons salt
¼ teaspoon pepper
1 cup whole cranberry sauce
1 cup orange juice
½ teaspoon ground ginger
2 medium-sized oranges, quartered, seeded, and ground
1 cup strong vegetable broth (dissolve 2 vegetable bouillon cubes in 1 cup boiling water)

1. Rub lamb with the salt and pepper. Place lamb on rack in a shallow roasting pan.
2. Combine in a saucepan the cranberry sauce (reserving some berries for garnish), orange juice, and ginger; stir in ground orange. Simmer over low heat 5 to 8 minutes, stirring occasionally during cooking. Spoon one half of the sauce over lamb.
3. Roast at 325°F 3½ to 4 hours, allowing 40 to 45 minutes per pound. (A meat thermometer should register 175°F for medium-done lamb.) Baste lamb with broth after each 30 minutes of roasting time. About 20 minutes before lamb is done, baste the meat with remaining orange-cranberry sauce.
4. Transfer roast to a heated platter and garnish with *notched orange slices*, reserved cranberries, and *curly endive*.

8 TO 10 SERVINGS

STUFFED LAMB SHOULDER ROAST WITH HONEY CHUTNEY GLAZE

4- to 5-lb. boned lamb shoulder roast
1 teaspoon salt
¼ teaspoon pepper
⅓ cup chutney
2 medium-sized onions, sliced
1 clove garlic, slivered
¼ cup honey
¼ cup water
3 tablespoons flour

1. Rub the lamb with a mixture of the salt and pepper. Spread the inside surface of the lamb with

about 3 tablespoons chutney. Arrange onion and garlic over chutney and roll meat as for a jelly roll. Secure with cord.
2. Place roast, seam side down, on a rack in a shallow roasting pan. Insert meat thermometer so tip is slightly beyond center of thickest part of meat; be sure that tip does not rest in fat or in stuffing.
3. Roast, uncovered, at 325°F, allowing 35 to 40 minutes per pound. When meat has roasted about 1¾ hours, pour off fat drippings and reserve.
4. Mix the honey, water, and remaining chutney; spoon over roast. Continue roasting until meat has reached the desired degree of doneness, basting occasionally. (Meat is medium done when thermometer registers 175°F and well done at 180°F.) Remove thermometer.
5. Transfer meat to a serving platter; keep hot.
6. Leaving the brown residue in pan, pour honey-chutney mixture into a bowl and allow fat to rise to surface. Skim off fat and return 3 tablespoonfuls to the roasting pan (use reserved drippings, if needed). Blend in the flour until smooth. Stirring constantly, heat until mixture bubbles. Remove from heat and stir in the honey mixture with enough water to make 2 cups liquid. Return to heat, bring to boiling, and boil 1 to 2 minutes, scraping bottom and sides of pan to blend in brown residue. Season to taste with *salt* and *pepper*. 6 TO 8 SERVINGS

LAMB BREAST WITH CARROT STUFFING

2½ cups soft 1-in. bread cubes	1 egg, beaten
3 tablespoons butter or margarine, melted	½ teaspoon salt
	¼ teaspoon crushed marjoram
¾ cup finely shredded carrots	2 tablespoons hot beef bouillon
½ cup finely chopped onion	3-lb. lamb breast (have meat dealer cut a pocket and crack bones)
1 tablespoon finely chopped parsley	

1. Lightly toss bread cubes, butter, carrots, onion, parsley, egg, salt, and marjoram together, blending in bouillon last. Spoon into pocket of breast.
2. Place meat, rib side down, on rack in shallow roasting pan. Roast, uncovered, at 300°F about 2 hours, or until meat is tender. ABOUT 4 SERVINGS

LAMB CHOPS EN BROCHETTE

8 loin lamb chops, cut ¾ to 1 in. thick (allow 2 chops per serving)	4 teaspoons grated onion
	1 teaspoon thyme, crushed
8 green pepper squares (about 1½ in.)	1 teaspoon salt
	¼ teaspoon black pepper
4 small onions	4 cherry tomatoes
¼ cup olive oil	

1. Thread 2 lamb chops onto each of four 15-inch skewers. Alternately thread 2 green pepper squares and 1 onion onto the end of each skewer.
2. Brush chops and vegetables with a mixture of the oil, grated onion, thyme, salt, and pepper.
3. Place skewers on broiler rack and broil 3 inches from source of heat for about 12 minutes, or until chops are evenly browned on both sides; turn and brush frequently. Near end of broiling period, thread 1 cherry tomato onto the tip of each skewer.
4. Arrange the four skewers artistically on a serving platter. Spoon remaining heated marinade onto chops and sprinkle lightly with *lemon juice*.
4 SERVINGS

STUFFED RIB LAMB CHOPS

6 double-rib lamb chops, about 2 in. thick	Few grains pepper
	3 tablespoons butter or margarine, melted
½ cup fine dry bread crumbs	¼ cup finely chopped fresh mushrooms, browned in a small amount of butter or margarine
½ teaspoon crushed basil	
¼ teaspoon salt	

1. Using a sharp knife, make a slit between rib bones into center of meat on each lamb chop; form a pocket. Set aside while preparing the stuffing.
2. Mix the bread crumbs, basil, salt, and pepper; blend in the melted butter. Toss with the mushrooms. Stuff each chop with some of the bread crumb mixture; fasten securely with skewers if necessary.
3. Broil with top of chops about 5 inches from source of heat about 15 minutes on first side. Sprinkle with *salt* and *pepper*, turn, and broil second side. Season. 6 SERVINGS

Lamb

BARBECUED LAMB SHANKS

4 lamb shanks, about 1 lb. each
¼ cup flour
1 teaspoon salt
¼ teaspoon pepper
¼ cup fat
1 cup chopped onion
2 cloves garlic, minced
1 cup ketchup
½ cup water
¼ cup wine vinegar
4 teaspoons Worcestershire sauce
5 drops Tabasco
2 teaspoons sugar
2 teaspoons paprika
1 teaspoon dry mustard
1 teaspoon salt
½ teaspoon pepper

1. Coat the lamb shanks evenly with a mixture of the flour, 1 teaspoon salt, and ¼ teaspoon pepper.
2. Heat fat in a large heavy skillet over medium heat. Add shanks and brown well on all sides. Remove meat to a large shallow baking dish.
3. Meanwhile, combine the onion, garlic, ketchup, water, vinegar, Worcestershire sauce, and Tabasco in a saucepan. Stir in a mixture of sugar, paprika, dry mustard, salt, and pepper and heat to boiling. Pour sauce over lamb.
4. Bake, covered, at 300°F 1½ to 2 hours, or until meat is tender; turn shanks and baste frequently with the sauce. ABOUT 4 SERVINGS

FRUITED LAMB SPARERIBS

3 lbs. lamb spareribs
1 teaspoon salt
¼ teaspoon black pepper
1 teaspoon curry powder
1 cup orange juice
1 teaspoon grated lemon peel
⅓ cup finely chopped celery
¼ cup chopped parsley
1 orange, cut in ¼-in. slices
1 medium-sized lemon, cut in ¼-in. slices
10 canned pineapple slices

1. Put spareribs into a large heavy skillet. Combine salt, pepper, and curry powder; blend in the orange juice, lemon peel, celery, and parsley. Pour over spareribs. Top with orange, lemon, and pineapple slices.
2. Cook, covered, over low heat about 1½ hours, or until meat is tender.
3. Remove spareribs and fruit to a warm serving dish. 4 TO 6 SERVINGS

LAMB-PINEAPPLE KABOBS

1½ lbs. boneless lamb shoulder or leg, cut in 1½-in. cubes
1 can (13½ oz.) pineapple chunks, drained (reserve ½ cup syrup)
½ cup soy sauce
¼ cup lemon juice
2 cloves garlic, minced
½ teaspoon pepper
Orange Barbecue Sauce, page 198

1. Put lamb cubes into a large shallow dish and pour over them a mixture of ½ cup pineapple syrup and remaining ingredients, reserving pineapple chunks. Refrigerate to marinate several hours or overnight; turn occasionally.
2. Remove meat from marinade and drain; reserve marinade for basting kabobs during cooking.
3. Alternately arrange meat pieces and the reserved pineapple chunks on four 8-inch skewers; brush with marinade.
4. Arrange kabobs on broiler rack; broil with tops of kabobs about 3 inches from source of heat 15 to 20 minutes, turning several times and brushing frequently with marinade; test for doneness by cutting a slit in meat cubes and noting color of meat.
5. Serve kabobs on fluffy *cooked rice* with Orange Barbecue Sauce. 4 SERVINGS

LAMB AND COCONUT CURRY

¼ cup butter or margarine
1 lb. boneless lamb shoulder, cut in 1-in. cubes
1 medium-sized onion, sliced
¼ cup flour
1 teaspoon salt
1½ tablespoons curry powder
½ teaspoon ground ginger
1½ cups strong chicken broth
⅓ cup maraschino cherry syrup
¼ cup lemon juice
⅓ cup flaked coconut
⅓ cup golden raisins
8 oz. fine noodles, cooked and drained

1. Heat butter in a large heavy skillet. Add lamb and onion and cook over medium heat until lamb is browned on all sides. Remove meat and onion with a slotted spoon and set aside.
2. Add to the skillet a mixture of the flour, salt, curry powder, and ginger and blend well; allow mixture to bubble. Remove from heat. Add broth, cherry syrup, and lemon juice gradually, stirring

constantly. Return to heat and bring rapidly to boiling, stirring constantly; cook 1 to 2 minutes.
3. Return meat and onion to the skillet; stir in coconut and raisins. Cover and cook over low heat, stirring occasionally, about 40 minutes, or until meat is tender.
4. Serve in a bowl with cooked noodles. Accompany with *toasted coconut* and *chopped mint leaves.*

4 SERVINGS

LAMB STEW PICASSO
An adaptation of an authentic Spanish recipe.

2 lbs. lamb stew meat, cut in 2-in. pieces	3 cloves garlic, minced
¼ cup flour	1 lb. potatoes, pared and sliced
1 teaspoon salt	2 onions, sliced
¼ teaspoon pepper	1 cup chopped celery
¼ cup olive oil	2 tomatoes, cut in wedges
1 cup beef broth	1 cup pimiento-stuffed olives
2 green peppers, chopped	
½ teaspoon marjoram	

1. Coat lamb pieces with a mixture of flour, salt, and pepper.
2. Heat olive oil in a large skillet; add lamb and brown evenly on all sides. Add beef broth slowly, then stir in the green pepper, marjoram, and garlic. Cover and cook over low heat 30 minutes.
3. Add potatoes, onions, and celery; cook, covered, 10 minutes, or until potatoes are tender. Mix in the tomatoes and olives; heat thoroughly.

ABOUT 6 SERVINGS

PERSIAN STEW
The allure of the Middle East is in this hearty dish.

1½ lbs. boneless lean lamb shoulder, cut in 1- to 1½-in. pieces	⅛ teaspoon coarsely ground pepper
1 tablespoon cooking oil	½ teaspoon oregano leaves, crushed
½ cup chopped onion	½ teaspoon thyme leaves, crushed
2 cans (8 oz. each) tomato sauce	½ teaspoon ground turmeric
¼ cup water	¼ teaspoon ground cinnamon
1 tablespoon lemon juice	1¼ cups canned white beans (such as Great Northern)
1 bay leaf	
½ teaspoon salt	

1. In a large heavy skillet, brown lamb on all sides in hot oil. Add onion and cook until tender, stirring occasionally.
2. Mix tomato sauce, water, lemon juice, bay leaf, salt, pepper, oregano, thyme, turmeric, and cinnamon. Pour over meat. Bring to boiling, cover, and simmer 1½ to 2 hours, until meat is tender. Stir in beans during the last half hour of cooking.
3. Remove bay leaf. Ladle into bowls.

4 SERVINGS

MOCK DUCK

3 slices bacon, cut into 1-inch pieces	1 tablespoon curry powder
1 rolled boned lamb shoulder, weighing about 4 lbs.	1 tablespoon sugar
	1 teaspoon salt
	1 envelope instant beef broth
1 small onion, chopped (¼ cup)	¾ cup water
4 tablespoons all-purpose flour	1 jar (4¾ ozs.) baby-pack peaches

1. Sauté bacon until almost crisp in a 4-quart pressure cooker; remove and drain on paper toweling.
2. Brown lamb slowly on all sides in drippings; remove from cooker.
3. Stir in onion; sauté until soft. Stir in 2 tablespoons of the flour, curry powder, sugar, salt, beef broth, water, and peaches; cook, stirring constantly, until bubbly. Add bacon and lamb; cover cooker.
4. Heat to 15 pounds pressure as manufacturer directs; cook 40 minutes. Let pressure fall naturally. Uncover cooker; place roast on a large serving platter; keep warm. Skim fat from liquid; reheat liquid to boiling.
5. Blend remaining 2 tablespoons flour with 2 tablespoons water until smooth in a cup; stir into boiling liquid. Cook, stirring constantly, until sauce thickens slightly and boils 1 minute.
6. Cut strings from lamb; slice part of the meat; serve sauce separately to spoon over meat.

4 SERVINGS PLUS ENOUGH MEAT FOR A DIVIDEND DISH

FRUITED LAMB STEW DE LUXE

1½ lbs. boneless lean lamb, cut in 1½-in. pieces	3 onions, coarsely chopped
½ cup all-purpose flour	¾ cup dried apricots
4 teaspoons salt	½ cup pitted dried prunes

Lamb

¼ teaspoon black pepper
½ teaspoon ground allspice
2 tablespoons butter or margarine
3 cups beef broth
1 tablespoon brown sugar
4 lemon slices, cut in quarters
3 pkgs. (10 oz. each) frozen Brussels sprouts, partially thawed to separate sprouts
Noodle Ring, *below*

1. Coat lamb with a mixture of flour, salt, pepper, and allspice; set remaining flour aside.
2. Brown the meat on all sides in heated butter in a large saucepot. Add 2½ cups of the broth, the brown sugar, onions, apricots, prunes, and lemon slices. Cover and bring to boiling. Reduce heat and simmer about 1 hour.
3. Add Brussels sprouts and continue cooking 15 to 20 minutes, or until sprouts are just tender.
4. Blend remaining ½ cup broth and reserved seasoned flour. Stir into boiling stew. Boil and stir 1 to 2 minutes. Serve in Noodle Ring.
6 TO 8 SERVINGS

NOODLE RING: Add *2 tablespoons salt* to *4 to 6 quarts rapidly boiling water*; gradually add *1 pound medium egg noodles* so boiling does not stop. Cook, uncovered, stirring occasionally, until noodles are tender; drain. Turn into a greased 9-inch ring mold, pressing gently with a spoon. Let stand 5 minutes before unmolding onto a serving plate.

CASSOULET

1 package (16 ozs.) dried Great Northern beans
2 teaspoons salt
6 cups water
4 slices bacon
1 lean boneless lamb shoulder, weighing 1 lb. and cut into 1-inch cubes
1 large onion, chopped (1 cup)
¼ lb. salami, diced
1 can (16 ozs.) stewed tomatoes
1 teaspoon garlic powder
1 teaspoon dried thyme, crushed
¼ teaspoon pepper
1 large bay leaf

1. Rinse beans. Place in a kettle with 1 teaspoon of the salt and water. Heat to boiling; cook 2 minutes; remove from heat; cover. Let stand 1 hour. Reheat to boiling; simmer 2 hours, or until beans are tender but still firm enough to hold their shape.
2. Sauté bacon in a large skillet until fat starts to cook out; remove slices and drain on paper toweling.
3. Preheat oven to 375°F.
4. Stir lamb into drippings and brown; remove with a slotted spoon and add to bean mixture.
5. Pour off all fat, then measure 2 tablespoons and return to skillet; stir in onion and salami; sauté until onion is soft. Stir in tomatoes, garlic powder, remaining 1 teaspoon salt, thyme, pepper, and bay leaf; heat to boiling; stir into bean mixture. Spoon into a 2½-quart baking dish; cover.
6. Bake 1 hour and 30 minutes; uncover. Place bacon slices on top. Bake, uncovered, 30 minutes longer, or until bacon is crisp and lamb is tender. Remove bay leaf before serving.
6 TO 8 SERVINGS

INDONESIAN LAMB

1 lean boneless lamb shoulder, weighing 1½ lbs.
1 tablespoon salad oil
1 medium onion, chopped (½ cup)
2 teaspoons curry powder
1 teaspoon salt
¼ teaspoon ground ginger
⅛ teaspoon ground cardamom
¾ cup light raisins
1 jar (4¾ ozs.) baby-packed applesauce
1 cup water
1 tablespoon lemon juice
4 cups hot cooked rice

1. Trim all fat from lamb; cut lamb into 1-inch cubes. Brown in salad oil in a large skillet; remove meat from skillet. Pour off all fat, then measure 2 tablespoons and return to skillet.
2. Stir onion into drippings; sauté until soft. Stir in curry powder, salt, ginger, and cardamom; cook 1 minute longer. Stir in raisins, applesauce, water, and lamb; heat to boiling; cover.
3. Simmer 1½ hours, or until lamb is tender and sauce thickens slightly. Stir in lemon juice.
4. When ready to serve, spoon in rice around edge of a large shallow serving bowl; spoon lamb mixture in center. Serve with finely diced, pared cucumbers, chopped slivered almonds, chopped preserved kumquats, and crisp diced bacon to sprinkle on top if you like.
6 SERVINGS

LAMB LOAF WITH CURRY SAUCE

⅓ cup milk
2 slices slightly dry white bread, crumbled
1 egg
1½ lbs. ground lamb
1½ teaspoons salt
¼ teaspoon pepper
1 teaspoon curry powder
1 tablespoon butter or margarine

3 medium carrots, pared and shredded (1 cup)
1 large onion, chopped (1 cup)
1 clove garlic, crushed
1 tablespoon all-purpose flour
1 can (5½ ozs.) apple juice
1 jar (7¾ ozs.) junior apricots

1. Preheat oven to 350° F.
2. Combine milk, bread, and egg in a large bowl; let stand a few minutes until liquid is absorbed, then beat with a spoon until blended.
3. Add lamb, carrots, ½ cup of the onion, garlic, salt, and pepper; mix lightly until well blended. Spoon into a greased baking pan, 8x4x2 inches; pack down lightly.
4. Bake 1 hour, or until loaf is firm and browned.
5. While loaf bakes, sauté remaining ½ cup onion with curry powder in butter until onion is soft in a medium saucepan. Stir in flour until blended; stir in apple juice and apricots. Cook, stirring constantly, until sauce thickens and boils 1 minute.
6. Loosen lamb loaf around edges with a knife; turn out onto a large serving platter. Garnish with carrot curls and parsley if you like: Cut crosswise into thick slices; serve with curry sauce. 6 SERVINGS

VEAL

STUFFED BREAST OF VEAL

½ cup butter
⅓ cup finely chopped onion
⅓ cup diced celery
6 slices bread, toasted and cubed
½ cup water
½ cup chopped cooked prunes
1 cup diced unpared apple
1 egg, slightly beaten
1 teaspoon salt
¼ teaspoon pepper
½ teaspoon poultry seasoning
3½-lb. breast of veal, boned and rolled (about 2¼ lbs.)
½ teaspoon salt
¼ cup butter
½ cup water

1. Heat ½ cup butter in a skillet. Add onion and celery; cook about 5 minutes; stir occasionally.
2. Put bread cubes into a large bowl; add ½ cup water, the vegetable mixture, prunes, apple, and egg, and a mixture of the 1 teaspoon salt, pepper, and poultry seasoning; mix lightly and thoroughly.
3. Unroll veal and spread the stuffing to within 1 inch of the edge of the meat. Reroll jelly-roll fashion and tie. If necessary, secure ends with skewers. Rub meat with the ½ teaspoon salt.
4. Heat the ¼ cup butter in a roasting pan. Add the meat and brown well on all sides.
5. Set meat on a rack; slowly add the ½ cup water. Cover pan; roast at 325°F about 2 hours, or until meat is tender.
6. Transfer meat to a platter and keep warm. Prepare *Gingersnap* or *Ginger gravy, page 200*.

ABOUT 6 SERVINGS

VEAL FLORENTINE "21"
A popular veal dish from Jack and Charlie's "21" restaurant in New York City.

3½- to 5-lb. breast of veal with pocket (have meat dealer cut meat away from ribs to form a pocket)
½ lb. bulk pork sausage
2 tablespoons water
3 tablespoons minced onion
3 cups finely chopped cooked spinach
1 cup bread crumbs
4 eggs, fork beaten
1½ to 2 teaspoons salt
¼ teaspoon black pepper

1. Rub veal outside and inside the pocket with *salt* and *pepper*; set aside.
2. Put pork sausage into a cold large skillet, cutting sausage apart with a spoon. Add water; cover and cook slowly 8 to 10 minutes. Remove cover; pour off liquid. Add onion and brown over medium heat, stirring occasionally.
3. Put sausage into a large bowl along with the remaining ingredients; mix well. Lightly spoon stuffing into pocket. Skewer or sew to keep stuffing in place. Put roast, rib side down, on rack in a shallow roasting pan.
4. Roast at 325°F 45 to 50 minutes, or until meat is tender. Transfer roast to a hot serving platter and remove skewers. Garnish with *parsley*.

ABOUT 8 SERVINGS

Veal

BREADED VEAL CUTLETS
(Wiener Schnitzel)

2 lbs. veal round steak (cutlet), cut ½ in. thick	¼ teaspoon pepper
⅓ cup flour	3 eggs, slightly beaten
1½ teaspoons salt	1½ cups French bread crumbs or sour French bread crumbs
1 teaspoon monosodium glutamate	Lard for deep frying heated to 375°F

1. Pound meat on one side with meat hammer. Turn and repeat process until meat is about ¼ inch thick. Cut into 6 serving-size pieces. Coat with a mixture of the flour, salt, monosodium glutamate, and pepper. Dip veal into eggs, then lightly coat with crumbs. Let stand 5 to 10 minutes to "seal."
2. Deep fry only as many pieces at one time as will lie uncrowded one layer deep in the hot lard. Fry until brown on both sides, 3 or 4 minutes; turn slices several times during cooking (do not pierce). Remove meat with tongs and drain over fat for a few seconds before removing to absorbent paper. Serve with *lemon wedges*. 6 SERVINGS

Scaloppine (also spelled scaloppini) is a popular Italian dish made of thin slices of veal—called scaloppine in Italian, escalope in French, scalop in English—sautéed or broiled and served with a well-seasoned sauce containing wine or tomato. Here are various interpretations of this popular dish as it is served in well-known Continental and American restaurants, each recipe exemplifying Italian culinary creativity at its best.

SCALOPPINI EL PRESIDENTE
A recipe from La Scala Restaurant in Beverly Hills, California.

¼ cup flour	1 zucchini, pared and cut in ½-in. slices
1 teaspoon salt	1 egg, slightly beaten
1 teaspoon pepper	2 to 3 tablespoons milk
12 small ¼-in. thick slices veal steak (about 2 lbs.)	3 tablespoons butter or margarine
2 tablespoons clarified butter, see page 11	¼ cup white wine
	Finely chopped parsley

1. Combine flour, salt, and pepper; toss the veal slices in the seasoned flour to coat lightly.
2. Brown veal on both sides in hot clarified butter in a large heavy skillet over medium heat.
3. Meanwhile, coat zucchini slices with flour; dip in a mixture of the beaten egg and milk.
4. Heat butter in a heavy skillet; add zucchini slices and brown quickly on both sides. Drain on absorbent paper.
5. Place scaloppini on a heated serving platter and overlap with zucchini slices; pour the butter left in skillet over them. Set aside in a warm place.
6. Add the wine to the skillet in which the zucchini was cooked; heat, stirring in all the brown bits. Pour the sauce over meat and zucchini and sprinkle with parsley. 4 SERVINGS

SCALOPPINE ALLA MARSALA
A recipe from Rosellini's in Seattle, Washington.

1½ lbs. leg of veal (have meat dealer cut meat into slices less than ½ in. thick)	4 tablespoons olive oil
	2 cups thinly sliced fresh mushrooms
	Juice of 1 lemon
4 tablespoons butter	½ cup Marsala or sherry

1. Flatten each veal slice with a wooden mallet or the side of a cleaver. Dip the slices in *seasoned flour*.
2. Brown veal slices on both sides in hot butter and oil in a skillet. Add mushrooms; cook 10 minutes.
3. Add the lemon juice and wine; simmer 5 minutes. Serve immediately. 4 SERVINGS

VEAL CORDON BLEU

6 even slices veal for scallopini, weighing about 2 lbs.	1 tablespoon milk
	1 package seasoned coating mix for chicken
Salt	2 tablespoons melted butter or margarine
Pepper	
3 long slices boiled ham	2 tablespoons water
2 long slices Swiss cheese	¼ cup dry red wine

1. Preheat oven to 350°F.
2. Spread veal flat on counter; sprinkle each slice lightly on both sides with salt and pepper.
3. Cut ham slices in half crosswise; cut cheese in thirds crosswise. Place a piece of cheese, then a piece of ham on each slice of veal; roll up, jelly-roll fashion; fasten with wooden picks.

4. Brush rolls with milk; shake in coating mix. Place rolls, not touching, in a greased shallow baking pan. Drizzle butter over top.
5. Bake 40 minutes, or until rolls are golden brown and veal is tender. Arrange on a serving platter.
6. Stir water into drippings in pan; stir in wine; heat to boiling. Spoon over veal rolls. 6 SERVINGS

PAPRIKA CREAM SCHNITZEL

1½ lbs. veal round steak (cutlet), cut about ½ in. thick	1½ teaspoons salt
	1 teaspoon paprika
	1 cup dairy sour cream
4 slices bacon, diced	½ cup tomato sauce
2 tablespoons chopped onion	Noodles

1. Cut meat into serving-sized pieces; set aside.
2. Cook bacon until crisp in a large heavy skillet. With slotted spoon, remove bacon to a small dish, leaving the fat in skillet.
3. Put meat and onion into skillet; brown meat on both sides. Sprinkle with a mixture of the salt and paprika. Spoon a blend of the sour cream and tomato sauce over meat. Cover skillet. Cook over low heat about 20 minutes (do not boil).
4. Turn noodles onto a heated serving platter and put sauced meat on noodles. Top with reserved bacon pieces. 4 TO 6 SERVINGS

DON QUIXOTE HORCHER

A favorite at Horcher's famous Madrid restaurant.

½ teaspoon salt	⅓ cup flour
¼ teaspoon pepper	Butter
4 veal scallops, trimmed (about 1¾ lbs.)	4 bananas
	Cream Sauce, *below*
	Grapes or orange sections
2 eggs, fork beaten	

1. Sprinkle salt and pepper over meat. Dip each veal scallop in egg, then coat with flour.
2. Sauté each scallop quickly in 1 tablespoon hot butter in skillet until golden brown on both sides. Remove to heated platter and keep warm.
3. Peel and halve each banana lengthwise. Sauté quickly in 1 tablespoon butter in the skillet until lightly browned on both sides.
4. Prepare Cream Sauce and add grapes.
5. To serve, place 2 banana halves on each veal scallop. Serve the sauce separately. Accompany with *saffron rice*. 4 SERVINGS

CREAM SAUCE: Blend *¼ cup flour* into *½ cup butter or margarine*, heated, in a heavy saucepan. Cook and stir until bubbly. Mix in *2 cups chicken broth* and bring rapidly to boiling, stirring constantly; cook 1 to 2 minutes. Vigorously stir about 3 tablespoons of the hot sauce into *4 fork-beaten egg yolks*. Immediately blend into mixture in saucepan. Cook over low heat 3 to 5 minutes, stirring constantly. Blend in *¼ cup butter or margarine*.
ABOUT 2 CUPS SAUCE

VEAL VIENNESE WITH SOUR CREAM

2 slices (about 1½ lbs.) veal round steak	¼ cup butter or margarine
¼ cup flour	2 cups soft bread crumbs
1 teaspoon salt	
1 teaspoon paprika	½ cup grated Parmesan cheese
½ teaspoon poultry seasoning	½ cup water
¼ teaspoon pepper	1 can (10½ oz.) condensed cream of chicken soup
¼ cup fat	
1 can (16 oz.) small whole onions, drained	1 cup dairy sour cream
	¼ teaspoon seasoned salt
2 tablespoons sesame seed	

1. Coat meat with a mixture of the flour, salt, paprika, poultry seasoning, and pepper. Pound meat on one side with a meat hammer. Turn and repeat process until flour mixture is well pounded in and meat is about ¼ inch thick.
2. Brown meat on both sides in hot fat in a large skillet. Transfer meat to a 1½-quart shallow baking dish. Put onions into dish; set aside.
3. Lightly brown sesame seed in the hot butter in the skillet, stirring frequently. Add bread crumbs and stir until well coated. Remove from heat and add cheese; toss until well mixed. Spoon over the meat. Pour in water.
4. Bake at 350°F 1 hour, or until meat is tender. If necessary, add more water during baking.
5. When meat is almost tender, heat the soup to boiling in a saucepan. Stirring constantly, gradually add the sour cream. Mix in seasoned salt. Heat (do not boil). Serve with the veal. 5 OR 6 SERVINGS

Veal

VEAL BIRDS WITH MUSHROOM STUFFING

2 lbs. veal round steak, about ½ in. thick
1 teaspoon salt
¼ teaspoon pepper
2 slices bacon, diced
1 cup chopped fresh mushrooms
1 tablespoon chopped onion
1 cup soft bread crumbs
¼ cup milk
2 tablespoons fat
½ cup water

1. Pound meat on both sides on a flat working surface with meat hammer; cut into 6 serving-size pieces. Season with a mixture of salt and pepper.
2. Cook bacon in skillet until lightly browned; remove with slotted spoon.
3. Add mushrooms and onion to bacon fat in skillet and cook about 5 minutes.
4. Lightly toss mushrooms, onion, and bacon with bread crumbs; add milk and mix lightly.
5. Spoon some of stuffing onto each piece of veal; roll meat around stuffing and fasten securely with skewer or wooden picks.
6. Heat fat in a large heavy skillet; add the veal rolls and brown on all sides. Transfer rolls to a 2-quart casserole; add the water; cover.
7. Bake at 350°F about 1 hour, or until meat is tender when pierced with a fork. If desired, thicken drippings for gravy. 6 SERVINGS

GOLDEN VEAL RAGOUT

1 large onion, chopped (1 cup)
9 medium carrots, pared and quartered
12 small potatoes, pared
1 piece boneless, veal shoulder weighing 2 lbs. and cut into 1½-inch cubes
1 can (10¾ ozs.) condensed golden mushroom soup
¼ cup dry white wine
½ teaspoon dried oregano, crushed
2 tablespoons all-purpose flour

1. Place onion, carrots, potatoes, and veal in layers in a slow cooker.
2. Mix soup, wine, and oregano in a small bowl; pour over mixture in cooker, covering veal completely; cover. Cook on high 1 hour, then turn temperature setting to low and cook for 8 hours.
3. Remove veal and vegetables from liquid in cooker to a large deep serving platter; keep warm. Return temperature setting to high.
4. Blend flour with a little water in a cup until smooth; stir into liquid in cooker. Cook, stirring constantly, until gravy thickens. Serve separately to spoon over veal and vegetables. 6 SERVINGS

VEAL TARRAGON

1½ lbs. veal steak, cut ¼ in. thick
½ cup all-purpose flour
1½ teaspoons salt
½ teaspoon black pepper
1 teaspoon crushed tarragon leaves
6 tablespoons butter
½ lb. fresh mushrooms, sliced
½ cup chopped onion
1 cup water
1 can (14½ oz.) evaporated milk
¼ cup snipped parsley
12 oz. green noodles, cooked and buttered

1. Trim bone and excess fat from veal and discard. Cut veal into 1½-inch-square pieces. Coat pieces with a mixture of the flour, salt, pepper, and tarragon. Reserve remaining flour mixture.
2. Heat butter in a large skillet; add mushrooms and cook over medium heat until lightly browned, turning occasionally. Remove mushrooms and set aside.
3. Add veal and onion to skillet; cook over medium heat until onion is soft and meat is lightly browned. Add water, cover, and reduce heat; simmer for 30 minutes, or until meat is tender.
4. Stir reserved flour into skillet; heat until mixture bubbles. Remove from heat and add evaporated milk gradually, stirring constantly. Cook over low heat, stirring occasionally, until thickened. Add mushrooms and heat well. Stir in parsley.
5. Serve over the cooked noodles. 4 TO 6 SERVINGS

BUDGET VEAL PARMIGIANO

1 egg
1 tablespoon water
½ cup packaged dry bread crumbs
6 veal cube steaks, weighing 1½ lbs.
2 tablespoons salad oil
1 can (16 ozs.) marinara sauce
1 small onion, chopped (¼ cup)
1 teaspoon garlic salt
½ teaspoon dried Italian herbs
⅛ teaspoon pepper
2 long slices Muenster cheese, cut crosswise into 12 strips
¼ cup grated Romano cheese

1. Beat egg with water in a pie plate; sprinkle bread crumbs on waxed paper.
2. Dip veal into egg mixture, then into bread crumbs to coat well. Brown steaks in salad oil in a large skillet, turning once; place in a shallow baking dish. Pour all drippings from skillet.
3. Preheat oven to 350°F.
4. Combine marinara sauce, onion, garlic salt, Italian herbs, and pepper in same skillet; heat slowly to boiling; pour over veal. Arrange cheese strips, chevron fashion, on top; sprinkle Romano cheese over all.
5. Bake 30 minutes, or until bubbly. 6 SERVINGS

VARIETY MEATS

LIVER AND ONIONS, ITALIAN STYLE

1½ lbs. beef liver, sliced about ¼ to ½ in. thick	½ teaspoon monosodium glutamate
½ cup flour	⅛ teaspoon pepper
1 teaspoon salt	2 onions, thinly sliced
	⅓ cup olive oil
	½ cup Marsala

1. If necessary, remove tubes and membrane from liver; cut liver into serving-sized pieces.
2. Coat liver with a mixture of flour, salt, monosodium glutamate, and pepper; set aside.
3. Cook onions until tender in hot oil in a large skillet. Remove onions and add liver. Brown on both sides over medium heat.
4. Return onions to skillet; add the wine. Bring to boiling and cook 1 minute. Serve at once.

4 OR 5 SERVINGS

CALF'S LIVER ON SKEWERS, ZURICH STYLE
(Brochette de Foie de Veau Zurichoise)

Veltliner - Keller, another famous Swiss restaurant in Zurich, serves this version of liver on skewers.

Season chunks of *calf's liver* with *salt* and *pepper*, place sprigs of *fresh sage* on each piece and roll a strip of *bacon* around each. Spear 6 or 7 pieces on each skewer, brush the pieces with *melted butter*, and grill under a broiler or over an open fire. Serve these on a plate with *cooked green beans, new potatoes with parsley*, and garnish with *lemon slices* and *watercress*. Serve with *red wine*, if desired.

CALF'S LIVER MATIUS

A popular dish served at the famous Forum of the Twelve Caesars, New York City.

1 onion, minced	2 lbs. calf's liver, cut in 2½-inch strips
1 clove garlic, minced	2 tablespoons butter
¼ teaspoon tarragon	⅓ cup applejack (apple brandy)
1 cup dry white wine	
1 cup Brown Sauce Espagnole, *below*	

1. Mix onion, garlic, and tarragon with the wine in a saucepan. Cook the mixture until the liquid is reduced to about half its original volume. Stir in the Brown Sauce Espagnole and heat thoroughly.
2. In a skillet or chafing dish, sauté the liver strips in heated butter about 3 minutes, turning occasionally. The liver should be well browned outside but still pink inside.
3. Warm the applejack, ignite it and pour over the liver strips. When the flame dies, pour the sauce over the liver.

ABOUT 8 SERVINGS

BROWN SAUCE ESPAGNOLE

½ cup beef, veal, or pork drippings	1 stalk celery
1 small carrot, coarsely chopped	3 sprigs parsley
2 onions, coarsely chopped	1 clove garlic, crushed
½ cup all-purpose flour	1 small bay leaf
8 cups hot Beef Stock, page 26	1 pinch thyme
	¼ cup tomato purée or tomato sauce

1. Put drippings in a heavy saucepot; add carrot and onion and cook until onion starts to turn golden, shaking the pan to insure even cooking. Blend

in the flour; cook and stir until flour and vegetables are a rich brown.
2. Add 3 cups beef stock gradually, stirring constantly; add celery, parsley, garlic, bay leaf, and thyme. Cook and stir until sauce thickens.
3. Add 3 cups stock and simmer slowly 1 to 1½ hours, or until sauce is reduced to 3 cups; stir occasionally. Skim off fat as it rises to surface.
4. Add tomato purée, cook several minutes longer and strain through a fine sieve.
5. Add 2 more cups of stock and cook slowly 1 hour longer, skimming the surface occasionally. Continue cooking until reduced to about 4 cups.
6. Cool sauce, stirring occasionally. Store in a covered container in refrigerator. If not used within a few days, store in freezer.   1 QUART SAUCE

LIVER À LA MADAME BEGUE

1 lb. calf's liver, cut in 1-in. cubes	2 small onions, thinly sliced
1 teaspoon salt	3 large sprigs parsley
Few grains pepper	Fat for deep frying heated to 390°F

1. Sprinkle liver with salt and pepper. Put into a bowl; cover with onion and parsley. Cover and refrigerate 2 hours.
2. Fry in the heated fat 40 to 60 seconds. Drain over fat for a few seconds before removing. Serve immediately garnished with *lemon wedges* and *parsley*, if desired.   4 SERVINGS

BEEF TONGUE WITH TOMATO SAUCE

1 fresh beef tongue, 3 to 4 lbs.	2 cans (6 oz. each) tomato paste
1 tablespoon salt	1 can (10¾ oz.) condensed tomato soup
2 or 3 bay leaves	
1 stalk celery with leaves, cut in pieces	½ to ¾ cup water
	¼ to ½ teaspoon thyme
1 small onion	1 pkg. (8 oz.) noodles, cooked and drained
1 teaspoon peppercorns	

1. Wash tongue and put into a 4-quart kettle. Add water to cover, salt, bay leaves, celery, onion, and peppercorns. Cover and simmer about 1 hour per pound, or until tongue is tender.
2. Place tongue on a platter. When cool enough to handle, remove skin; cut away roots, gristle, and small bone at thick end. Diagonally cut tongue into ¼-inch slices. Put slices into a large heavy skillet and set aside.
3. Combine tomato paste, soup, water, and thyme; mix thoroughly and pour over tongue. Cover and heat about 20 minutes.
4. Serve tongue and sauce with noodles.
   ABOUT 12 SERVINGS

CREAMED HAM AND SWEETBREADS
When planning a bridal shower luncheon for 20 to 24 people, consider this for the main course.

2 lbs. sweetbreads, rinsed with cold water	6 cups strong chicken broth
	2 cups cream
2 qts. water	4 cups cubed cooked ham
4 teaspoons lemon juice	
2 teaspoons salt	1 ripe avocado, peeled and cut in cubes
1 lb. fresh mushrooms, sliced	
	1 cup quartered ripe olives
¼ cup chopped onion	
1 cup butter or margarine	½ cup snipped parsley
	2 pimientos, cut in strips
¾ cup flour	
1 teaspoon celery salt	2 tablespoons drained capers
1 teaspoon savory, crushed	
	Baked puff pastry patty shells
⅛ teaspoon cayenne pepper	

1. Put the sweetbreads, water, lemon juice, and salt into a large saucepot. Cover, bring to boiling, reduce heat, and simmer 20 minutes.
2. Drain and cover with cold water. Change water repeatedly until sweetbreads are cool. Drain. Remove tubes and membranes. Cut sweetbreads into bite-size pieces and refrigerate until ready to use. (Sweetbreads should be cooked as soon as possible after purchase.)
3. Cook mushrooms and onion in hot butter or margarine in a large heavy saucepot or Dutch oven, stirring frequently until onion is soft and mushrooms are tender, about 5 minutes. With a slotted spoon, remove mushrooms, allowing butter to drain back into pan. Set mushrooms aside.
4. Blend a mixture of flour, celery salt, savory, and cayenne pepper into hot butter in the sauce pot; heat until bubbly. Gradually add the chicken broth, stirring constantly; bring rapidly to boiling. Cook 2 minutes longer, stirring constantly.

5. Stir in the cream, sweetbreads, mushrooms, ham, avocado, olives, parsley, pimientos, and capers. Heat the mixture thoroughly, stirring occasionally.
6. Spoon sauce into warm patty shells. Replace top of shell and top with a sprig of *watercress*.

20 TO 24 SERVINGS

CREAMED SWEETBREADS

1 qt. water
1 tablespoon lemon juice
1 teaspoon salt
1 lb. sweetbreads
½ lb. fresh mushrooms, sliced lengthwise
¼ cup butter
1 tablespoon chopped onion
⅓ cup butter
½ cup flour
¾ teaspoon salt
½ teaspoon savory
½ teaspoon celery salt
Few grains white pepper
1 cup chicken broth, cooled
2 cups milk
1 cup cream
1 cup cooked chicken pieces
1 pkg. (9 oz.) frozen green beans, cooked and drained

1. In a large saucepan, combine water, lemon juice, and salt. Add sweetbreads, cover and bring to boiling; lower heat and simmer 20 minutes. Drain, cool and remove membrane; cut sweetbreads into pieces and refrigerate.
2. Lightly brown the mushrooms in ¼ cup butter in a heavy skillet; set aside.
3. Cook onion about 5 minutes in ⅓ cup butter in a saucepan over low heat. Stir in a mixture of the flour, salt, savory, celery salt, and white pepper; heat until mixture bubbles. Gradually add chicken broth, milk, and cream, stirring constantly. Bring rapidly to boiling, stirring constantly; cook 1 to 2 minutes longer.
4. Gently mix in the sweetbreads, chicken, green beans, and mushrooms. Continue cooking over low heat until thoroughly heated; stir occasionally.
5. Turn into chafing dish and keep hot over the pan of simmering water.

6 TO 8 SERVINGS

BEEF AND KIDNEY PIE

1 beef kidney
½ cup French dressing
1 lb. boneless lean beef for stew, cut in 1-in. pieces
1 tablespoon Worcestershire sauce
¼ teaspoon basil, crushed
1 bay leaf
⅔ cup all-purpose flour
1½ teaspoons salt
¼ teaspoon pepper
¼ teaspoon paprika
¼ cup chopped onion
3 tablespoons fat
2 cans (10¾ oz. each) condensed tomato soup
1 cup hot water
1 pkg. (10 oz.) frozen green peas
Pastry for a 1-crust pie
1 can (8 oz.) mushrooms, drained
3 tablespoons butter or margarine

1. Remove membrane from kidney and cut kidney lengthwise through center. Remove skin, white tubes, and fat. Thoroughly rinse kidney with cold water. Cut into ¾- to 1-inch cubes. Put cubes into a bowl and pour dressing over all. Turn each piece to coat. Cover and marinate at least 1 hour, turning pieces occasionally.
2. Meanwhile, coat beef pieces with a mixture of the flour, salt, pepper, and paprika.
3. Drain kidney pieces and add along with beef and onion to hot fat in a top-of-range casserole. Brown meat on all sides.
4. Stir in soup, water, Worcestershire sauce, and basil. Add more hot water if needed to cover meat. Add bay leaf. Cover; simmer 45 minutes.
5. Mix in the frozen peas and continue simmering 15 to 45 minutes, or until meat is tender.
6. Prepare pastry and roll into a round about ⅛ inch thick and larger than overall size of casserole top. Fold in quarters; with a knife make slits near center to allow steam to escape; set aside.
7. Heat mushrooms about 5 minutes in hot butter in a small saucepan, stirring constantly.
8. When meat is tender, remove bay leaf. Stir in mushrooms. If necessary, thicken liquid.
9. Moisten rim of casserole with cold water. Lift pastry gently and unfold over hot mixture in casserole. Fold extra pastry under at edge and gently press to rim of casserole to seal. Flute edge.
10. Bake at 425°F 15 to 20 minutes, or until pastry is lightly browned.

6 SERVINGS

LAMB 'N' KIDNEY GRILL

1. For lamb kidneys, remove membrane and split *kidneys* through centers. Using scissors, remove cores and tubes. Marinate kidneys 1 hour in *French dressing* or brush with *melted*

butter. Broil about 5 minutes on each side, or until evenly browned. Season with *salt* and *pepper.*
2. For bacon curls, panbroil *bacon slices* until evenly browned. Remove one slice at a time from skillet and, using a fork, immediately roll into a curl; drain on absorbent paper.
3. For lamb chops, purchase *lamb chops* cut ¾ to 1 inch thick. Broil or panbroil to desired degree of doneness; season with *salt* and *pepper.*
4. To serve, arrange kidneys, bacon curls, and lamb chops in a shallow decorative baking dish and place dish over a warmer. Garnish with *broiled cherry tomatoes.*

TRIPE CREOLE

2 lbs. fresh tripe	6 tomatoes, peeled and coarsely chopped
2 onions, thinly sliced	1 green pepper, thinly sliced
1 large clove garlic, minced	½ teaspoon thyme
4 tablespoons butter or margarine	2 small bay leaves
¼ cup finely chopped lean ham	Few grains cayenne pepper

1. Wash the tripe thoroughly in cold water; drain. Put into a saucepan and add *salted water* to cover (1 teaspoon salt per 1 quart water). Bring to boiling, reduce heat and simmer, covered, about 5 hours, or until tender.
2. Drain tripe and cut into 2x½-inch strips.
3. Cook onion and garlic until golden in heated butter in a saucepan. Add remaining ingredients and season to taste. Bring to boiling and cook 10 minutes, stirring occasionally. Add tripe. Bring to boiling, cover and cook 30 minutes.   6 TO 8 SERVINGS

HEART WITH APPLE-RAISIN DRESSING

2 lbs. heart	½ chopped onion
½ cup flour	½ cup packed brown sugar
2 teaspoons salt	½ cup seedless raisins
1 teaspoon monosodium glutamate	2 tablespoons water
½ teaspoon pepper	¼ cup fat or bacon drippings
3 tablespoons fat	1 qt. bread cubes
1 lemon, sliced	½ cup milk
8 whole cloves	2 tablespoons butter or margarine, melted
1 bay leaf	½ teaspoon salt
1 cup hot water	
3 tart apples, quartered, cored, pared, and diced	

1. Cut arteries, veins, and any hard parts from the heart. Wash and drain on absorbent paper. Cut heart into 1-inch cubes. Coat with a mixture of flour, salt, monosodium glutamate, and pepper.
2. Brown meat on all sides in 3 tablespoons hot fat in a 2-quart top-of-range casserole. Add lemon, cloves, bay leaf, and water; cover and simmer 1½ to 2½ hours, or until meat is tender. If necessary, add hot water during cooking. Drain meat; discard lemon, cloves, and bay leaf.
3. Meanwhile, mix apples, onion, brown sugar, raisins, and water into ¼ cup hot fat in a large skillet; cover and simmer 5 minutes, stirring once or twice.
4. Lightly toss together bread cubes, milk, butter, and salt. Add meat cubes and apple mixture; toss until mixed. Turn into the casserole.
5. Heat in a 350°F oven 15 to 20 minutes, or until browned.   ABOUT 6 SERVINGS

GROUND MEAT COOKERY

Ground meats have a versatility all their own. They are adaptable to the skillet, the casserole, the oven, the open fire. They can be combined deliciously with pastry, with cereal, with fruits and vegetables; piled into molds or broiled on a plank or a skewer; shaped into loaves or balls or patties; add nutrition and flavor to soup.
Purchase ground beef that has been *freshly* ground, either regular (contains not more than 25% fat) or lean (contains not more than 12% fat). Or buy a cut of beef such as chuck, round, flank, plate, brisket, shank, or neck meat and have it ground. If the cut is quite lean, have 2 ounces of suet per pound of beef ground with the cut. A coarse grind helps to insure extra-juicy patties.
Purchase pork that has been *freshly* ground or have pork shoulder meat ground.
Purchase lamb that has been *freshly* ground or have lamb shoulder meat ground.
Store ground meat uncovered or lightly covered in refrigerator. Partial drying on the surface of

* Frying Pan Souffle (page 76)

meat increases its keeping quality. Use within two days of purchase.

Store frozen ground meat in the freezing compartment of the refrigerator or in a freezer, wrapped in freezer wrapping material.

Break ground meat block apart with a wooden spoon when meat is added to skillet. Brown over medium heat. For small pieces, move and turn with a wooden spoon at beginning of browning process. For larger pieces, brown slightly before moving and turning meat.

Shape balls, burgers, and loaves with a light touch. (Excessive handling results in a compact and less juicy product.)

Always cook pork until well done.

Unmold meat loaves. For easier slicing, let meat loaves stand in pan 5 to 10 minutes after removing from oven. With spatula, gently loosen meat from sides of pan. Pour off excess juices; invert onto a platter and remove pan. For meat loaves with topping, pour off excess juices and lift loaf onto platter with two wide spatulas.

Ground Beef

SAUCY GROUND MEAT TOWERS

2 lbs. lean ground beef	½ teaspoon monosodium glutamate
2 tablespoons instant minced onion	½ teaspoon garlic salt
2 eggs, beaten	¼ cup fat
1 teaspoon Worcestershire sauce	Herbed Tomato Sauce, *below*
1½ teaspoons salt	½ pkg. (4 oz.) stuffing mix
¼ teaspoon pepper	

1. Lightly mix the ground beef, onion, eggs, Worcestershire sauce, salt, pepper, monosodium glutamate, and garlic salt. Shape into 12 patties, making 6 of them slightly smaller in diameter.
2. Brown patties on both sides in heated fat in a heavy skillet. Remove to absorbent paper.
3. Prepare Herbed Tomato Sauce.
4. Prepare stuffing mix according to directions on package for moist stuffing. Shape into 6 patties, using about ⅓ cup stuffing for each.
5. Arrange the larger meat patties in skillet; put a stuffing patty on each, and top with smaller patties.
6. Pour sauce over and around the "towers"; heat thoroughly, basting occasionally.   6 SERVINGS

* *Rolled Rib Roast of Beef (page 80)*

HERBED TOMATO SAUCE: Combine in a saucepan *2 cans (8 ounces each) tomato sauce* and *1 can (4 ounce) mushroom stems and pieces, 4 whole cloves, 1 bay leaf, ½ teaspoon salt, ⅛ teaspoon black pepper,* and *¼ teaspoon thyme.* Cover; simmer 10 minutes. Remove cloves and bay leaf.

SAUCE-CROWNED MEAT RING

¾ cup coarse dry bread crumbs	1 cup chopped onion
1 bottle (7 oz.) lemon-lime carbonated beverage	1 clove garlic, crushed
	2 teaspoons salt
	1½ teaspoons dill weed
2 lbs. lean ground beef	⅓ cup Worcestershire sauce
2 eggs, slightly beaten	

1. Soak bread crumbs in lemon-lime carbonated beverage. Add ground beef, eggs, onion, garlic, salt, and dill; mix lightly, but thoroughly.
2. Pack lightly into a deep 1½-quart ring mold. Turn out onto a jelly roll pan or baking sheet. Brush the meat ring with the Worcestershire sauce.
3. Bake at 350°F 45 minutes; baste occasionally.
4. Spoon *Topping, below,* over meat. Bake 15 minutes longer.   ABOUT 6 SERVINGS

TOPPING: Thoroughly blend *½ cup chili sauce* and *1 teaspoon Worcestershire sauce.*

SHEEPHERDER'S STEW

1½ lbs. ground lamb	12 small potatoes, pared
1 clove garlic, minced	1 cup thinly sliced celery
1 teaspoon salt	2 cups water
¼ teaspoon pepper	1 envelope onion soup mix
1 cup fresh bread crumbs (2 slices)	1 can (8 ozs.) stewed tomatoes
⅓ cup milk	½ teaspoon dried thyme, crushed
2 tablespoons salad oil	
9 medium carrots, pared and quartered lengthwise	1 package (10 ozs.) frozen lima beans

1. Combine lamb, garlic, salt, pepper, bread crumbs, and milk in a large bowl. Mix lightly until well blended; shape into 24 balls.
2. Brown in salad oil in a large skillet; remove with a slotted spoon and pile in the center of a 3-quart baking dish. Place carrots, potatoes, and celery around lamb in dish. Pour all drippings from skillet.
3. Preheat oven to 350°F.

4. Stir water, onion soup mix, tomatoes, thyme, and limas into skillet; heat to boiling, breaking up limas with a fork. Spoon over lamb and vegetables; cover.
5. Bake 60 minutes, or until potatoes and carrots are tender. Serve in soup plates.   6 SERVINGS

ITALIAN MEAT PATTIES

1 lb. lean ground beef	1 clove garlic, minced
1 egg, fork beaten	¾ teaspoon salt
3 tablespoons dry bread crumbs	⅛ teaspoon black pepper
2 teaspoons minced parsley	⅛ teaspoon ground nutmeg
1 teaspoon grated lemon peel	

1. Lightly but thoroughly mix all ingredients in a bowl. Shape into 4 patties.
2. Brown patties on both sides in heated *olive oil* in a large skillet, cooking until of desired degree of doneness.   4 SERVINGS

GARLIC CHEESEBURGERS

Flavorful Tomato Sauce	1½ teaspoons seasoned salt
1½ lbs. lean ground beef	¼ teaspoon pepper
1 egg, beaten	1 tablespoon butter or margarine
2 cloves garlic, crushed	6 slices sharp Cheddar cheese

1. Prepare the tomato sauce and keep hot.
2. Lightly mix the ground beef, egg, garlic, seasoned salt, and pepper. Shape mixture into 6 patties about ¾ inch thick.
3. Brown patties on both sides in heated butter in a skillet, allowing about 10 minutes.
4. Cover each patty with a slice of cheese. Cook about 3 minutes longer, or until cheese is slightly melted.
5. Pour hot tomato sauce into a warm serving dish and arrange cheeseburgers in the sauce.   6 SERVINGS

BEEF LINDSTROM

This meat patty, the Scandinavian counterpart of an American hamburger, is usually served with fried eggs and a green salad for lunch.

1½ lbs. lean beef, ground twice	½ teaspoon monosodium glutamate
2 egg yolks, beaten	¼ teaspoon pepper
¼ cup cream	3 medium-sized cooked potatoes, diced
2 tablespoons chopped onion	½ cup finely diced pickled beets
1 tablespoon capers	3 tablespoons butter or margarine
1 teaspoon salt	

1. Lightly toss the ground beef, egg yolks, cream, onion, capers, salt, monosodium glutamate, and pepper in a bowl. Add potatoes and beets and mix well. Refrigerate 1 to 2 hours.
2. Shape the mixture into patties about ¾ inch thick. Brown on both sides in heated butter in a heavy skillet. Serve immediately.   6 TO 8 SERVINGS

FINNISH MEATBALLS

1½ lbs. ground round steak	½ cup finely chopped green pepper
1 egg, slightly beaten	1 to 2 tablespoons butter
2 teaspoons salt	
½ teaspoon pepper	1 can (8 oz.) tomato sauce
½ teaspoon dill weed	
2 cups grated raw potato	⅓ cup cold water
	1 tablespoon flour
½ cup finely chopped onion	1 cup dairy sour cream

1. Combine in a bowl the ground meat, egg, and a mixture of the salt, pepper, and dill, then the vegetables; toss to mix. Lightly shape into 1-inch balls.
2. Brown meatballs evenly on all sides in hot butter in a large skillet. When thoroughly cooked, remove meatballs to a warm serving dish; keep hot.
3. Add tomato sauce to the drippings in skillet and stir in a blend of water and flour. Bring rapidly to boiling, stirring mixture constantly; cook 1 to 2 minutes.
4. Reduce heat. Stirring gravy vigorously with a French whip or spoon, add sour cream in very small amounts. Heat thoroughly, about 3 minutes (do not boil). Pour gravy over meatballs and serve.   ABOUT 6 DOZEN MEATBALLS

GERMAN MEATBALLS
(Koenigsberger Klops)

1 cup soft bread crumbs	3 cups water
¼ cup milk	2 tablespoons chopped onion
½ cup chopped onion	1 bay leaf
2 tablespoons butter or margarine	1 whole clove
1 lb. ground beef	2 peppercorns
¼ lb. ground veal	¼ teaspoon salt
4 anchovy fillets, mashed	2 tablespoons butter or margarine
1 egg, fork beaten	2 tablespoons flour
1 teaspoon salt	2 tablespoons lemon juice
½ teaspoon monosodium glutamate	1 tablespoon chopped capers
¼ teaspoon pepper	

1. Put bread crumbs and milk into a large bowl.
2. Cook ½ cup onion in 2 tablespoons hot butter in a skillet until golden, stirring occasionally.
3. Add the contents of the skillet, the ground meat, anchovies, egg, 1 teaspoon salt, monosodium glutamate, and pepper to the bread crumb mixture; mix lightly. Shape meat mixture into 2-inch balls.
4. Bring water, 2 tablespoons chopped onion, bay leaf, clove, peppercorns, and ¼ teaspoon salt to boiling in a saucepan. Put meatballs into boiling liquid. Return to boiling and simmer 20 minutes. Remove meatballs with a slotted spoon; keep hot. Strain cooking liquid and reserve 2 cups.
5. Heat remaining butter in the saucepan. Mix in flour and heat until bubbly. Stir in reserved liquid, lemon juice, and capers. Bring rapidly to boiling, stirring constantly. Cook and stir 1 to 2 minutes.
6. Return meatballs to gravy and heat thoroughly.

6 TO 8 SERVINGS

SWEDISH MEATBALLS

1 lb. ground round steak	½ teaspoon brown sugar
½ lb. ground pork	¼ teaspoon ground allspice
½ cup instant mashed potatoes	¼ teaspoon ground nutmeg
½ cup fine dry bread crumbs	⅛ teaspoon ground cloves
1 egg, beaten	⅛ teaspoon ground ginger
1 teaspoon salt	½ cup fine dry bread crumbs
½ teaspoon monosodium glutamate	
¼ teaspoon pepper	3 tablespoons butter or margarine

1. Lightly mix in a large bowl the ground meats, potatoes, ½ cup crumbs, egg, and a mixture of the salt, monosodium glutamate, pepper, brown sugar, allspice, nutmeg, cloves, and ginger.
2. Shape mixture lightly into 1-inch balls. Roll balls in remaining crumbs.
3. Heat the butter in a large heavy skillet. Add the meatballs and brown on all sides; shake pan frequently to brown evenly and to keep balls round. Cook, covered, about 15 minutes, or until meatballs are thoroughly cooked.

3 DOZEN MEATBALLS

SAUCED WALNUT BEEF BALLS ORIENTALE

1 lb. lean ground beef	½ cup strong beef broth
⅓ cup milk	3 tablespoons cider vinegar
½ teaspoon salt	1 tablespoon soy sauce
¼ teaspoon seasoned pepper	¼ cup sugar
½ cup fine soft bread crumbs	2 tablespoons cornstarch
½ cup finely chopped walnuts	½ cup water
¼ cup finely chopped onion	1 green pepper, cut in strips
1 egg, beaten	1 firm ripe large tomato, cut in wedges
¼ cup flour	Toasted Soy Walnuts, below
⅓ cup cooking oil	
1 can (8¾ oz.) pineapple tidbits, drained (reserve syrup)	Packaged precooked rice, cooked and kept warm

1. Lightly mix the ground beef and a blend of the milk, salt, seasoned pepper, and crumbs, then mix in the walnuts and onion. Shape into 12 balls.
2. Beat egg with flour. Coat balls with mixture. Drain on wire rack.
3. Brown meatballs evenly on all sides in hot oil in a large (about 10-inch) heavy skillet. Remove all but 1 tablespoon of the oil and push balls to one side of skillet.
4. Pour in the reserved pineapple syrup, beef broth, vinegar, soy sauce, and sugar, and a mixture of cornstarch and water. Stir until blended. Mix in pineapple and green pepper. Bring rapidly to boiling, stirring constantly; cook 3 minutes. Stir in

tomato and move meatballs through mixture; heat thoroughly.

5. To serve, spoon onto warm platter. Garnish with the soy walnuts, reserving enough to top rice. Spoon rice into heated cups. Serve immediately.

4 TO 6 SERVINGS

TOASTED SOY WALNUTS: Blend *1 teaspoon butter or margarine* and *1 teaspoon soy sauce* in small skillet and heat. Stir in *½ cup walnut halves*, turning occasionally until nuts are toasted.

KRAUT AND BEEF PASTIES

2½ cups undrained sauerkraut	1 tablespoon cooking oil
1 lb. ground round steak	½ cup chopped onion
½ lb. lean ground pork	½ cup Italian-style seasoned bread crumbs
½ lb. ground veal	
2 to 2½ teaspoons salt	2 cups sifted all-purpose flour
1 teaspoon monosodium glutamate	½ teaspoon salt
½ teaspoon marjoram leaves, crushed	¼ teaspoon black pepper
¼ teaspoon black pepper	⅔ cup vegetable shortening

1. Drain sauerkraut thoroughly, reserving 2 tablespoons liquid; set aside.
2. Prepare meat filling. Have beef, pork, and veal ground together at the meat market. Put meat into a large bowl and mix with a blend of salt, monosodium glutamate, marjoram, and pepper.
3. Heat oil in a large skillet; add onion and cook until crisp-tender. Turn into bowl and blend with meat mixture.
4. Put meat into hot skillet and, stirring occasionally, cook until meat is no longer pink. Remove from heat and stir in seasoned bread crumbs; cool.
5. Prepare pastry. Sift together flour, salt, and pepper. Using a pastry blender, cut shortening into flour until pieces are the size of small peas.
6. Chop the sauerkraut or snip into short lengths. Add to flour mixture. Toss with a fork until mixed. Adding gradually, drizzle reserved sauerkraut liquid over all while continuing to toss mixture until moistened. Turn onto waxed paper and press together to form a ball.
7. Divide dough into 12 equal pieces. On a well-floured surface, roll out each to a 6-inch round. Put about ⅓ cup meat mixture (slightly off center) onto each pastry round. Overlapping pastry, seal edges (flute, if desired), and prick tops with a fork.
8. Place on ungreased baking sheets; bake at 375°F 35 to 40 minutes, or until lightly browned. Serve hot or cold.

12 MEAT PASTIES

ZESTY KRAUT PASTRY SNACKS: Prepare pastry for Kraut and Beef Pasties. Divide dough into 4 portions for rolling. On a well-floured surface roll each fourth as thin as possible and cut into squares. Transfer to ungreased sheets; brush tops lightly with *butter or margarine* and sprinkle with any of the following: *sesame, caraway, or poppy seeds; garlic or onion salt; grated Parmesan or Cheddar cheese; instant minced onion, dill weed, chili powder, oregano, or curry powder*; or *finely chopped dried beef.* Bake at 425°F 13 minutes. Serve hot.

ABOUT 4 DOZEN SNACKS

BEEF TACOS

Lard	12 canned or frozen tortillas, dried at room temperature about 2 hrs.
1 cup finely chopped onion	
1 clove garlic, minced	
1 lb. lean ground beef	Finely shredded lettuce
1 teaspoon salt	Finely chopped onion
2 teaspoons chili powder	Shredded Cheddar cheese
Pinch ground cumin	

1. Heat 3 tablespoons lard in a large heavy skillet. Add onion and garlic and cook until tender. Blend in ground beef and a mixture of salt, chili powder, and cumin; brown meat lightly.
2. Fry tortillas, one at a time, in ½ inch of lard heated to 375°F in a heavy skillet. When tortilla becomes limp, fold in half with tongs and hold edges apart while frying to allow for filling. Fry 1½ to 2 minutes, or until crisp and golden. Drain on absorbent paper.
3. To serve, spoon 3 to 4 tablespoons of beef mixture into each tortilla; top with lettuce, onion, and cheese. If desired, serve with a *salsa picante* (a Mexican hot sauce).

12 TACOS

BEEF YORKSHIRE PIE

Reminiscent of old-fashioned Yorkshire pudding (usually baked in a roasting pan along with a beef roast), this unique pie stands alone as an excellent main dish.

1½ lbs. lean ground beef
½ cup finely chopped onion
1 teaspoon salt
¼ teaspoon pepper
½ teaspoon ground coriander
⅛ teaspoon ground cumin
⅛ teaspoon garlic powder
1½ cups all-purpose flour
½ teaspoon salt
3 eggs, beaten
1½ cups milk

1. Cook ground beef and onion in hot skillet, cutting meat apart with fork. Remove from heat, drain off fat. Mix in 1 teaspoon salt, pepper, coriander, cumin, and garlic powder; set aside.
2. Place a well-greased 10-inch skillet (heat-resistant handle) in a 400°F oven until very hot.
3. Blend flour and the remaining salt in bowl. Add mixture of eggs and milk; beat until smooth.
4. Pour half of the batter into the hot skillet; cover with the beef mixture and top with remaining batter.
5. Bake at 400°F 40 minutes, or until puffed and golden. Cut into wedges and serve from skillet.

ABOUT 6 SERVINGS

SLOPPY JOE BAKE

1 lb. ground beef
1 small green pepper, quartered, seeded, and chopped (½ cup)
1 medium onion, chopped (½ cup)
1 can (16 ozs.) tomatoes
1 can (8 oz.) tomato sauce
1 teaspoon dried thyme, crushed
½ teaspoon salt
¼ teaspoon pepper
1 package (8 ozs.) mostaccioli (macaroni), cooked and drained
1 package (8 ozs.) sliced process American cheese, shredded
¼ cup grated Romano cheese

1. Preheat oven to 350°F.
2. Shape ground beef into a large patty; place in a large skillet. Brown, turning once, in its own fat; break up into chunks; push to one side.
3. Stir green pepper and onion into drippings in skillet; sauté until soft. Stir in tomatoes, tomato sauce, thyme, salt, and pepper; heat to boiling.
4. Layer half each of the mostaccioli, meat sauce, and American cheese into a 2-quart baking dish; repeat layers. Sprinkle Romano cheese on top.
5. Bake 30 minutes, or until bubbly and cheese melts and browns lightly.

6 SERVINGS

CHILI AND BEANS

Walt Disney's home and heart were in the Southwest as evidenced by one of his favorite recipes.

2 lbs. dry chili beans (pink or red)
2 medium onions, sliced (about 1½ cups)
2 to 3 teaspoons salt
½ cup cooking oil
2 cloves garlic, crushed
2 lbs. coarsely ground beef
1 can (28 oz.) whole red tomatoes
1 cup chopped celery
1 teaspoon chili powder (depending upon taste)
1 teaspoon paprika
1 teaspoon dry mustard
Salt to taste

1. Soak beans overnight in cold water.
2. Drain off water; put beans, onions, and salt into a large kettle; add water to come 2-inches over beans. Simmer about 4 hours, or until tender; add hot water if necessary, to maintain liquid level.
3. Meanwhile, prepare sauce. Heat oil in a large deep skillet or Dutch oven; add garlic and ground beef; cook slowly until meat is lightly browned. Add remaining ingredients; simmer 1 hour.
4. When beans are tender, add sauce to them and simmer 30 minutes.

3 TO 3½ QUARTS CHILI

NOTE: For a very spicy chili, add a pinch of *chili seeds, coriander seeds, cumin seeds, fennel seeds, cinnamon, cloves, ginger, turmeric,* and *1 small yellow Mexican chili pepper.*

BEEF POLYNESIAN

2 tablespoons butter
1 lb. lean ground beef
1 can (4 oz.) mushrooms, drained
½ cup golden raisins
1 pkg. (10 oz.) frozen green peas
½ cup beef broth
1 teaspoon curry powder
1 tablespoon soy sauce
1 orange, sliced
½ cup salted cashew nuts
Fried Rice, *next page*

1. Heat butter in a large heavy skillet. Add ground beef and separate into small pieces; cook until lightly browned.
2. Add mushrooms, raisins, peas, broth, curry powder, and soy sauce. Break block of peas apart and gently toss mixture to blend.
3. Arrange orange slices over top. Cover loosely and cook over low heat 15 minutes.
4. Mix in the cashews and serve with Fried Rice.

ABOUT 4 SERVINGS

FRIED RICE: Cook *½ cup chopped onion* in *2 tablespoons butter* until light golden. Mix in *2 cups cooked rice* and *2 tablespoons soy sauce*. Cook over low heat, stirring occasionally, 5 minutes. Stir in *1 slightly beaten egg* and cook until set.

BEEF-EGGPLANT PATTIES IN CASSEROLE

1 medium-sized eggplant, pared and cut in ½-in. cubes	3 tablespoons water
	4 eggs, beaten
	6 tablespoons olive oil
1 lb. lean ground beef	1 clove garlic
½ cup soft bread crumbs	1 can (28 oz.) Italian-style tomatoes, sieved
¼ cup shredded Parmesan cheese	1 tablespoon chopped parsley
2 tablespoons chopped parsley	1 teaspoon oregano
1 clove garlic, minced	¾ teaspoon basil
¾ teaspoon salt	¾ teaspoon salt
¼ teaspoon black pepper	⅛ teaspoon black pepper

1. Put eggplant into a heavy saucepan with just enough boiling *salted water* to cover bottom of pan; cover tightly and cook until just tender, about 3 minutes. Drain thoroughly in a colander, discarding the liquid.
2. Lightly but thoroughly mix ground beef with the bread crumbs, cheese, 2 tablespoons parsley, minced garlic, and a mixture of ¾ teaspoon salt and ¼ teaspoon pepper. Mix in the water, eggs, and the eggplant. Shape mixture into 8 patties.
3. Heat olive oil in a heavy skillet; add patties and brown on both sides over medium heat. Transfer patties to a shallow baking dish; set aside.
4. Add garlic to oil in skillet and heat 1 minute. Remove garlic and stir in a mixture of the remaining ingredients. Simmer about 10 minutes.
5. Pour sauce over patties in baking dish and set in a 375°F oven 15 minutes, or until thoroughly heated. 6 TO 8 SERVINGS

GROUND BEEF-EGGPLANT CASSEROLE

1 large or 2 small eggplant, pared and cut in ½-in. slices	½ cup chopped green pepper
	2 cans beef gravy-sauce with tomato
1½ lbs. lean ground beef	¾ teaspoon crushed basil
¾ teaspoon salt	¼ lb. thinly sliced mozzarella cheese
½ teaspoon monosodium glutamate	¼ cup fine dry bread crumbs
⅛ teaspoon black pepper	1 tablespoon butter or margarine
¼ cup chopped onion	
1 clove garlic, minced	

1. Brown eggplant slices in a small amount of hot *cooking oil* in a large skillet. Remove from skillet and set aside.
2. Mix the ground beef with salt, monosodium glutamate, and pepper; set aside.
3. Add about 2 tablespoons oil to the skillet. Add onion, garlic, and green pepper to hot oil and cook about 2 minutes, stirring occasionally. Add the meat and cook until it has lost its pink color, stirring occasionally.
4. Remove from heat and stir in a mixture of the gravy-sauce and basil.
5. Spoon about one third of the meat sauce over the bottom of a 2-quart baking dish. Arrange half the eggplant slices in a layer over the sauce. Place slices of cheese over the eggplant. Repeat with meat sauce and eggplant; end with remaining meat sauce. Sprinkle a mixture of the bread crumbs and butter over the top.
6. Set in a 375°F oven about 20 minutes, or until mixture is thoroughly heated and topping is browned. Accompany with *buttered noodles* and a crisp *green salad*. ABOUT 8 SERVINGS

GROUND BEEF À LA STROGANOFF

2 tablespoons butter or margarine	1 can (10½ oz.) condensed beef consommé
½ cup finely chopped onion	1 tablespoon wine vinegar
1 clove garlic, minced	
1 lb. ground beef	1 can (4 oz.) sliced mushrooms, drained
2 tablespoons flour	
2 teaspoons salt	1 cup dairy sour cream
¼ teaspoon pepper	¼ cup snipped parsley
½ teaspoon tarragon	8 oz. noodles, cooked according to pkg. directions and drained
¼ teaspoon basil	
1 can (6 oz.) tomato paste	

1. Heat butter in a skillet; add onion and garlic.

Cook about 5 minutes, stirring occasionally. Add the ground beef, separate into pieces, and brown lightly.
2. Sprinkle a mixture of flour, salt, pepper, tarragon, and basil over the meat. Stir in tomato paste, consommé, and vinegar. Simmer, uncovered, 10 minutes, stirring occasionally. Remove from heat; stir in mushrooms and sour cream. Heat thoroughly, stirring occasionally (do not boil).
3. Toss parsley with noodles and top with sauce.
ABOUT 6 SERVINGS

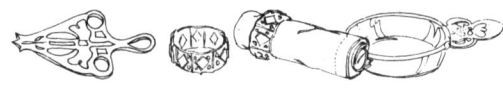

Ground Pork

CHINESE SIZZLED MEATBALLS WITH VEGETABLES AND RICE

1 lb. lean ground pork or beef round steak
1 teaspoon salt
½ teaspoon crushed marjoram leaves
¼ teaspoon garlic powder
1 egg, fork beaten
2 tablespoons bottled sweet and sour sauce
1 tablespoon peanut oil
2 cans (12 to 14 oz. each) fried rice with meat, heated following label directions
2 pkgs. (10 oz. each) frozen cauliflower, cooked
1 divider-pak can (43 oz.) mushroom chow mein or beef chop suey, heated following label directions

1. Lightly and thoroughly mix meat with a blend of salt, marjoram, and garlic powder; mix in egg and sweet and sour sauce. Gently shape into 1-inch balls.
2. Brown meatballs evenly on all sides in hot oil in a skillet. Cover while cooking.
3. To serve, turn hot fried rice onto a serving platter; add the cauliflower, sprinkle with *monosodium glutamate*, drizzle with *sweet and sour sauce or soy sauce*, spoon on chow mein, and top with the meatballs.
4. Garnish with *parsley* and *orange fans* made by cutting navel oranges into ¼-inch slices, cutting each slice into thirds, and overlapping pieces to resemble open fans.
ABOUT 6 SERVINGS

DANISH MEATBALLS
(Frikadeller)

1½ lbs. lean ground pork
1 medium-sized onion, quartered or minced
2 tablespoons flour
1¼ cups milk
1½ teaspoons salt
⅛ teaspoon black pepper
2 egg whites
½ cup butter

1. Force ground pork and onion through the medium blade of a meat grinder three times into a large mixing bowl. Or, have meat market grind the pork three times; mix in the minced onion.
2. Mix in flour. Add milk, about 4 tablespoons at a time, beating thoroughly after each addition. Mix in a blend of salt and pepper.
3. Beat egg whites to stiff, not dry, peaks and fold into meat mixture until blended.
4. Thoroughly heat butter, all at one time, in a large skillet. Spoon meat mixture by tablespoonfuls (keeping oval shape) into hot butter. Fry until browned on all sides.
2½ DOZEN MEATBALLS
NOTE: If using an electric blender, pour half of the milk into the container, add the quartered onion, and about ¼ of the meat. Blend, continuing to add milk and as much meat as container will hold. Empty into a large mixing bowl. Put milk and remainder of meat into container and blend until smooth. Empty into bowl. Mix in flour and seasonings; proceed with steps 3 and 4.

CHEESE BALL CASSEROLE À LA MEXICANA

1 lb. lean ground pork, cooked until lightly browned, drained
½ lb. ground smoked ham
1 green pepper, finely chopped
1 small onion, finely chopped
3 cloves garlic, minced
2 tablespoons snipped parsley
1 can (16 oz.) tomatoes, well drained
2 tablespoons tomato juice
2 teaspoons sugar
½ teaspoon salt
¼ teaspoon pepper
½ cup dark seedless raisins
¼ cup chopped green olives
1 tablespoon capers
Shredded tortillas (enough to make 2 cups)
½ lb. sharp Cheddar cheese, thinly sliced
1 egg, beaten
Tortillas

Ground Ham

1. Mix pork and ham thoroughly; blend in green pepper, onion, garlic, parsley, tomatoes, tomato juice, sugar, salt, pepper, raisins, olives, capers, and shredded tortillas. Heat about 20 minutes in a large saucepan, stirring occasionally.
2. Meanwhile, cover bottom and sides of a 1½-quart casserole with overlapping cheese slices.
3. When meat mixture is hot, quickly stir in egg and spoon into lined casserole. Around edge of dish overlap small pieces (quarters) of tortillas and remaining cheese slices.
4. Set in a 325°F oven 15 minutes, or until cheese is bubbly.
5. Serve with warm tortillas. 8 SERVINGS

Ground Ham

HAM-VEAL LOAF WITH SAUCY TOPPING

1½ lbs. ground cooked ham	¼ teaspoon ground thyme
½ lb. ground veal	¼ cup finely chopped onion
½ lb. ground pork	½ cup finely chopped green pepper
2 eggs, fork beaten	2 tablespoons finely chopped parsley
½ teaspoon salt	¾ cup soft bread crumbs
⅛ teaspoon black pepper	¾ cup apple juice
½ teaspoon ground nutmeg	Topping, *below*
½ teaspoon dry mustard	

1. Combine ground meat with eggs, salt, pepper, nutmeg, dry mustard, and thyme in a large bowl. Add onion, green pepper, and parsley and toss.
2. Add the crumbs and apple juice; mix thoroughly but lightly. Turn into a 9x5x3-inch loaf pan and flatten top.
3. Bake at 350°F 1 hour. Remove from oven; drain and reserve juices. Unmold loaf in a shallow baking pan and spoon some of the juices over loaf. Spoon the Topping over loaf; return to oven 30 minutes.
4. Remove loaf to a warm platter. 1 MEAT LOAF

TOPPING: Blend ⅔ *cup packed light brown sugar, 2 teaspoons cornstarch, 1 teaspoon dry mustard,* and *1 teaspoon ground allspice* in a small saucepan. Add ⅔ *cup apricot nectar, 3 tablespoons lemon juice,* and *2 teaspoons cider vinegar.* Bring rapidly to boiling and cook about 2 minutes, stirring constantly. Reduce heat and simmer 10 minutes.

ABOUT 1¼ CUPS TOPPING

PARTY HAM LOAF

¼ cup pineapple syrup	2 eggs, beaten
¾ cup packed brown sugar	1 teaspoon dry mustard
1 tablespoon cider vinegar	¾ teaspoon salt
24 whole cloves	⅛ teaspoon pepper
24 canned pineapple chunks	½ teaspoon ground nutmeg
4 slices bread, cut in cubes	⅓ cup chopped onion
½ cup milk	1½ lbs. ground cooked ham
	½ lb. ground pork
	½ lb. ground veal

1. Mix the pineapple syrup, brown sugar, and vinegar in a small saucepan; heat until sugar is dissolved, stirring constantly. Pour ¼ cup syrup into a 9x5x3-inch loaf pan.
2. Insert cloves in pineapple chunks; with cloves down, arrange in pan in the shape of a pineapple.
3. Mix bread cubes, milk, and eggs together in a large bowl; lightly mix in, in order, a mixture of the mustard, salt, and pepper, the onion, ground meat, and remaining syrup. Spoon lightly into pan.
4. Bake at 350°F about 1½ hours.
5. To unmold, loosen meat from sides of pan. Pour off excess juices, invert onto warm platter, and remove pan. Form leaves with *green pepper strips* to resemble pineapple crown.

ABOUT 8 SERVINGS

HAM PINWHEEL RING

1½ cups ground ham	Baking Powder Biscuit dough, *page 55*
⅓ cup sweetened condensed milk	1 to 2 tablespoons melted butter or margarine
¼ cup pickle relish	Sauce Par Excellence, *page 129*
2 teaspoons prepared mustard	
2 tablespoons minced parsley	

1. Lightly mix ham with condensed milk, relish, mustard, and parsley; set aside.
2. Prepare biscuit dough. Roll into a rectangle about ¼ inch thick on a lightly floured surface. Spread ham mixture evenly over dough. Starting with long side of dough, roll up and pinch long edge to seal. (Do not pinch ends of roll.)

3. Place roll on a baking sheet, sealed edge down. Bring ends of roll together to form a ring. Brush lightly with the melted butter. With scissors or sharp knife, make cuts at 1 inch intervals around outside of ring to within ¼ inch of center. Slightly pull out and twist each section so that cut sides rest almost flat on baking sheet.
4. Bake at 400°F 20 to 30 minutes, or until ring is golden brown.
5. Meanwhile, prepare sauce and serve with ham ring garnished with *parsley*. 6 TO 8 SERVINGS

SAUCE PAR EXCELLENCE

¾ lb. fresh mushrooms, sliced lengthwise
½ cup butter or margarine
1¾ cups plus 2 tablespoons (1½ 10½-oz. cans) condensed cream of chicken soup
3 tablespoons milk
1½ teaspoons Worcestershire sauce
1½ cups dairy sour cream

1. Cook mushrooms in hot butter in a large skillet until lightly browned, stirring occasionally. Stir a blend of soup, milk, and Worcestershire sauce into skillet. Simmer, stirring constantly until heated.
2. Remove from heat. Add sour cream in very small amounts, blending after each addition. Cook over low heat, stirring constantly, until thoroughly heated (do not boil). ABOUT 4 CUPS SAUCE

Ground Lamb

ARMENIAN MEATBALLS

1 lb. ground lamb
1 egg, beaten
½ teaspoon salt
⅛ teaspoon black pepper
¼ teaspoon garlic salt
1 cup shredded Cheddar cheese
1 cup small soft bread cubes
1 cup chopped parsley
⅓ cup finely chopped onion
2 tablespoons butter
1 can (8 oz.) tomato sauce
¼ cup shredded Parmesan cheese

1. Lightly mix ground lamb and egg in a bowl. Blend in a mixture of the salt, pepper, and garlic salt. Add Cheddar cheese, bread cubes, parsley, and onion; mix lightly to blend. Shape into 18 2-inch balls.
2. Heat butter in a skillet. Add meatballs and brown evenly on all sides, turning gently.
3. Remove meatballs to a 1-quart shallow baking dish. Pour tomato sauce over meatballs and top with the Parmesan cheese. Cover the baking dish.
4. Set in a 350°F oven 20 minutes. Remove cover and heat an additional 10 minutes. 6 SERVINGS

CURRIED LAMB-PRUNE BURGERS
Prunes and ketchup greatly enhance the flavor of these broiled bacon-wrapped patties.

1¼ lbs. ground lamb
½ cup ketchup
⅔ cup snipped dried prunes
¾ teaspoon salt
Few grains pepper
1 teaspoon curry powder
1 cup soft bread crumbs
¼ cup minced parsley
2 tablespoons minced onion
8 slices bacon

1. Lightly mix ground lamb, ketchup, and prunes in a bowl. Blend in a mixture of seasonings. Add bread crumbs, parsley, and onion; toss lightly to blend.
2. Shape into 8 patties, fasten a slice of bacon around each, and place on broiler rack. Broil with top of meat about 5 inches from heat source 6 minutes on each side, or until desired doneness.
3. Serve with *French fries*, *dill pickles*, and a *tossed salad* or *cole slaw* with *cherry tomatoes*.
 8 SERVINGS

MOUSSAKA

1 medium eggplant, weighing about 1¾ lbs.
Salt
Salad oil
2 cups very finely chopped cooked lamb
1 medium onion, chopped (½ cup)
⅓ cup water
1 tablespoon chopped parsley
2 tablespoons tomato paste
⅛ teaspoon pepper
2 eggs
2 tablespoons butter or margarine
2 tablespoons all-purpose flour
Dash of nutmeg
1 cup milk
¼ cup dry bread crumbs
⅛ teaspoon paprika

1. Pare eggplant and cut into ½-inch-thick slices. Sprinkle salt over slices; set aside.
2. Heat 3 tablespoons salad oil in a medium skillet; stir in lamb and onion; sauté until lamb is brown and onion is soft. Stir in water, parsley, tomato paste, 1 teaspoon salt, and pepper. Simmer 10 minutes; cool.
3. Beat 1 of the eggs in a small bowl; stir into lamb mixture.
4. Brown eggplant slices, a few at a time, in salad oil in a large skillet, adding more oil as needed; remove from skillet and drain on paper toweling.
5. Preheat oven to 350°.
6. Melt butter in a small saucepan; stir in flour, nutmeg, and ¼ teaspoon salt. Cook, stirring constantly, until bubbly. Stir in milk; continue cooking and stirring until sauce thickens and boils 1 minute. Beat remaining egg in a small bowl; stir in about half of the hot sauce, then stir back into pan; cook 1 minute longer.
7. Sprinkle bread crumbs into a baking dish, 9x9x2 inches. Top with half of the eggplant, all of the meat sauce, and remaining eggplant. Pour cream sauce over top; sprinkle paprika over sauce.
8. Bake 40 minutes, or until bubbly and lightly browned.

4 SERVINGS

BALKAN LAMB AND EGGPLANT CASSEROLE
(Moussaka)

3 cloves garlic, minced	Freshly ground black pepper
2 large onions, chopped	2 teaspoons paprika
1 large green pepper, chopped	2 large eggplant, pared and cut in ½-in. slices
1 tablespoon olive oil	1 cup yogurt
1½ lbs. lean ground lamb	4 egg yolks
1½ teaspoons salt	½ cup flour

1. Cook garlic, onion, and green pepper 3 minutes in hot oil in a large skillet. Add ground lamb and season with salt, pepper, and paprika. Separate meat and cook until pink color is gone. Using a slotted spoon, remove mixture from skillet; set aside.
2. Coat eggplant with *flour*. Lightly brown slices in hot *butter or margarine* in the skillet.
3. In a 2½-quart casserole, alternate layers of eggplant and meat; cover.
4. Bake at 350°F 45 minutes.

5. Mix remaining ingredients and spoon over mixture in casserole. Cover and continue baking 15 minutes; uncover and brown top under broiler.

8 TO 10 SERVINGS

SOUTH AFRICAN CURRY
(Bobotie)

This distinctive curried lamb recipe is from Chocolate House, Princess Street, Edinburgh, Scotland.

1 thick slice bread, crumbled (about 1 cup)	1 to 2 tablespoons sugar
1 cup milk	⅓ cup seedless raisins
2 medium-sized onions, sliced	8 almonds, finely chopped
1 apple, pared and sliced	1 egg, fork beaten
3 tablespoons butter	2 lbs. cooked lamb or mutton, finely chopped
2 tablespoons curry powder	1 egg, fork beaten

1. Soak bread crumbs in milk. Drain off milk and reserve (about ½ cup); set crumbs aside.
2. Cook onions and apple in heated butter in a large skillet until just tender, stirring occasionally. Mix in curry powder, sugar, raisins, and almonds. Blend in 1 egg, bread crumbs, then lamb. Cook a few minutes over medium heat, stirring constantly. Season to taste with *salt* and *pepper*. Turn into a buttered 2½-quart baking dish.
3. Mix reserved milk and remaining egg; season to taste with *salt* and *white pepper*. Pour over meat mixture.
4. Set in a 350°F oven about 15 minutes, or until custard is set.

ABOUT 8 SERVINGS

Ground Veal

SKILLET VEAL LOAF FIRENZE

1 lb. ground veal	1 medium-sized carrot, finely chopped
¼ lb. ham	1 stalk celery, finely chopped
½ teaspoon salt	
⅛ teaspoon pepper	2 tablespoons finely chopped parsley
⅛ teaspoon ground cinnamon	
1 teaspoon grated lemon peel	¼ cup olive oil
3 eggs, beaten	2 tablespoons butter or margarine

2 tablespoons flour
1 medium-sized onion, finely chopped
1 cup vegetable broth (dissolve 1 vegetable bouillon cube in 1 cup boiling water)

1. Have meat dealer grind veal and ham together three times.
2. Add salt, pepper, cinnamon, and lemon peel to beaten eggs; blend well. Lightly mix in meat. Turn onto waxed paper or aluminum foil and gently shape into a large patty. Coat with flour; set aside.
3. Add the onion, carrot, celery, and parsley to hot oil and butter in a 10-inch skillet. Cook about 5 minutes, stirring occasionally. Add meat and brown on both sides.
4. When meat is browned, add about ½ of the vegetable broth to the skillet. Cover and simmer about 25 minutes, or until meat is cooked. If necessary, add a little more hot broth to keep meat from sticking. Place meat on a hot platter; keep hot.
5. Add remaining broth to skillet; force the mixture through a coarse sieve, or purée in an electric blender. Heat the sauce; pour some over meat loaf and serve the remaining sauce in a gravy boat.

6 SERVINGS

VEAL-OYSTER LOAF

½ pt. oysters, drained
1 lb. ground veal
1¼ cups crushed corn flakes
½ cup minced onion
¾ cup undiluted evaporated milk
1 egg, fork beaten
¾ teaspoon salt
¼ teaspoon paprika
¼ teaspoon marjoram
⅛ teaspoon thyme

1. Pick over oysters to remove any shell particles; finely chop. (If oysters are frozen, thaw before using.) Combine oysters with ground veal, corn flakes, onion, evaporated milk, and egg and a mixture of the remaining ingredients.
2. Pack lightly into a greased 9x5x3-inch loaf pan.
3. Bake at 350°F about 1½ hours.
4. To unmold, loosen loaf gently from sides of pan with a spatula. Invert onto a hot serving platter and remove pan. Garnish with *parsley sprigs*.

6 TO 8 SERVINGS

VEAL-SPINACH PINWHEELS

1 pkg. (12 oz.) frozen chopped spinach
¼ cup shredded Parmesan cheese
1 egg, beaten
1½ teaspoons salt
⅛ teaspoon black pepper
1 lb. ground veal
¼ cup chopped onion
⅔ cup soft bread crumbs
¼ teaspoon marjoram
⅛ teaspoon thyme
2 tablespoons butter or margarine

1. Cook spinach according to directions on package; drain thoroughly. Lightly toss with cheese.
2. Toss lightly the ground veal, onion, bread crumbs, egg, salt, pepper, marjoram, and thyme.
3. Put veal mixture between two pieces of waxed paper; press into a 10x6-inch rectangle. Remove top piece of paper.
4. Spread spinach mixture evenly over meat. Roll up, starting with shorter side. Wrap meat roll and chill about 30 minutes.
5. Cut meat roll into 4 slices; arrange on broiler rack. Dot with 1 tablespoon butter.
6. Broil with top of meat about 4 inches from source of heat about 8 minutes; turn and dot slices with remaining butter; broil about 3 minutes.

4 SERVINGS

CANNELLONI ALLA PIEMONTESE "MAISON"

This interpretation of cannelloni served at Hotel Limone, Limone Piemonte, Italy, differs from the usual cannelloni inasmuch as squares cut from pancakes are used instead of pasta.

6 thin 10-in. pancakes
⅓ cup finely chopped onion
3 tablespoons olive oil
½ lb. ground veal, cooked (or other cooked meat)
1 pkg. (10 oz.) frozen chopped spinach, cooked and drained
1 egg
⅓ cup grated Parmesan cheese
¼ teaspoon salt
Pinch pepper
Pinch nutmeg
1½ cups Béchamel Sauce, *page 196*

1. Cut pancakes into 2½-inch squares; keep warm.
2. Cook onion in heated olive oil in a skillet about 3 minutes. Add ground meat and cook until lightly browned. Mix spinach with meat mixture; force mixture through medium blade of food chopper.
3. Mix egg, cheese, salt, pepper, and nutmeg with meat mixture until thoroughly blended. Place about 1 tablespoon meat mixture on each pancake square and roll each into a sausage shape.
4. Arrange the filled cannelloni in a shallow buttered baking dish; cover with Béchamel Sauce.
5. Heat in a 375°F oven until golden brown. Serve very hot.

4 TO 6 SERVINGS

Ground Veal

PARTY VEAL LOAF WITH SAUCE

- 1½ lbs. ground veal
- 1 lb. ground ham
- 1 cup instant nonfat dry milk
- ¼ cup grated onion
- 1 egg, fork beaten
- 2 cans (29 oz. each) cling peach halves, drained (reserve 3 cups syrup)
- 1 teaspoon dry mustard
- 1 teaspoon water
- 1 cup fine dry bread crumbs
- ½ teaspoon salt
- ⅛ teaspoon pepper
- ¼ teaspoon ground cloves
- Sauce, *below*

1. In a large bowl, mix the veal, ham, and dry milk with a fork. Add onion, egg, 1 cup of the reserved peach syrup, a blend of dry mustard and water, and a mixture of bread crumbs, salt, pepper, and cloves; mix lightly but thoroughly.
2. Shape mixture into a loaf and place on a rack in a large shallow baking pan. Insert *whole cloves* into meat loaf.
3. Bake at 350°F 1½ hours. Generously spoon Sauce over loaf every 20 minutes during baking.
4. About 15 minutes before baking time is up, put the peach halves into pan around the meat loaf and spoon Sauce over them. Continue baking.
5. Let meat loaf stand a few minutes before slicing. Transfer to a serving platter and surround with peaches. Fill cavities with Sauce and pour remainder into a sauceboat. ABOUT 12 SERVINGS

SAUCE: In a saucepan, mix the remaining 2 cups reserved peach syrup, *1 cup packed brown sugar, ¼ cup cider vinegar,* and *12 whole cloves.* Bring to boiling; simmer 5 minutes.

STUFFED CABBAGE ROLLS
(Kaldomar)

- 1 large head cabbage (3 to 3½ lbs.)
- 1 lb. ground veal
- 1 lb. ground beef
- 1¼ cups milk
- 2 teaspoons salt
- 1 teaspoon ground nutmeg
- 2 cans (10½ oz. each) condensed beef broth
- ⅔ cup fine dry bread crumbs
- 4 teaspoons grated onion
- 2 soup cans water
- ¼ cup flour
- ½ cup water

1. Remove and discard wilted outer leaves from head of cabbage; rinse and cut out the core.
2. Put cabbage in kettle; add boiling water to cover and *1 teaspoon salt.* Cover and bring water to boiling; reduce heat and simmer until cabbage leaves are softened, about 5 minutes. Carefully separate the leaves and set aside 16 large and 16 small leaves to drain on absorbent paper.
3. Combine the ground meat and the milk, crumbs, onion, salt, and nutmeg; mix thoroughly.
4. Place a small cabbage leaf in center of a large leaf. Put about ⅓ cup of the meat mixture onto the center of each small leaf. Roll each leaf, tucking ends in toward center. Fasten securely with wooden picks and tie with cord.
5. Combine beef broth and water in a saucepot and bring to boiling. Add cabbage rolls one at a time so that water continues to boil. Reduce heat; cover and cook about 25 minutes, or until the cabbage rolls are tender.
6. Remove rolls with slotted spoon; reserve broth for sauce or gravy. Remove wooden picks and cord from rolls and keep rolls warm.
7. Combine the flour and water in a saucepan and blend thoroughly. Add 2 cups of the reserved broth slowly, stirring constantly. Cook and stir over medium heat until sauce comes to boiling; cook 3 minutes longer until thickened and smooth.
8. Pour sauce over cabbage rolls in a serving dish. If desired, use *Cream Gravy, below,* instead of the sauce. 8 SERVINGS

CREAM GRAVY: Heat *3 tablespoons butter or margarine* in a saucepan; blend in *3 tablespoons flour* and cook over medium heat until bubbly. Stir in 1 cup reserved beef broth and cook, stirring constantly until boiling. Stir in *1 cup milk* and a mixture of *½ teaspoon salt, ¼ teaspoon ground cardamon,* and a *few grains sugar.* Bring to boiling; cook 3 minutes, stirring until thickened.

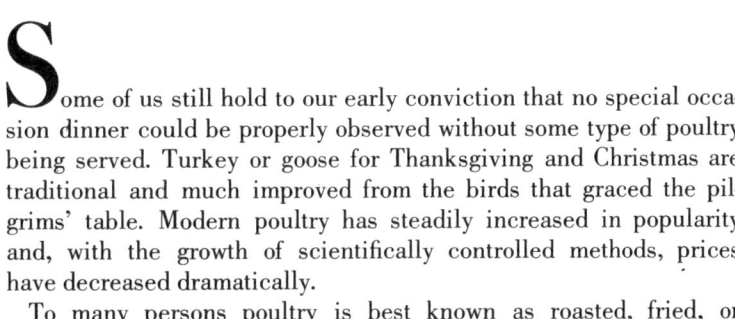

Chapter 6
POULTRY & STUFFINGS

Some of us still hold to our early conviction that no special occasion dinner could be properly observed without some type of poultry being served. Turkey or goose for Thanksgiving and Christmas are traditional and much improved from the birds that graced the pilgrims' table. Modern poultry has steadily increased in popularity and, with the growth of scientifically controlled methods, prices have decreased dramatically.

To many persons poultry is best known as roasted, fried, or broiled. But there are many additional ways, some regional and international, of preparing the favorite bird and many new touches for the time-tested ways.

Poultry includes all domesticated birds used for food: chicken (including capon), turkey, duckling, goose, Rock Cornish game hen (a delicious hybrid), squab, and guinea.

CLASSES

Chicken and turkeys are classified according to size, age, and sex. Age influences tenderness of the meat and therefore determines the cooking method. Size determines the cooking time.

Chicken—Broiler, either sex, 1½ to 2½ pounds ready-to-cook weight, 10 to 12 weeks old; *fryer*, either sex, 2 to 3 pounds ready-to-cook weight, 12 to 16 weeks old; *broiler-fryer*, a meatier, more tender all-purpose young chicken varying in weight from 1½ to 4 pounds ready-to-cook weight; *roaster*, either sex, usually over 3½ pounds, and about 3 months old; *capon*, unsexed male, usually over 10 months old, 4 pounds or over, exceptionally good flavor, especially tender, with large proportion of white meat; *stewing chicken*, female, more than 10 months old, 3 to 5 pounds ready-to-cook weight.

Turkey—Fryer-roaster, either sex, usually under 16 weeks old, 4 to 8 pounds ready-to-cook weight; *young hen or tom*, female or male, usually under 8 months old, 8 to 24 pounds ready-to-cook weight; *mature hen or tom*, over 10 months old, less tender, and seldom found on the consumer market; *frozen boned turkey* (rolls, loaves, or slices in gravy), cooked according to directions on label.

Duckling—Either sex, 8 to 9 weeks old, 3½ to 5 pounds ready-to-cook weight.

Goose—Classifications less well established, but weights range from 4 to 8 pounds ready-to-cook weight for young birds, up to 14 pounds for mature birds.

STYLES

Dressed poultry refers to birds which have been bled and feather-dressed but have head, feet, and viscera intact. *Ready-to-cook poultry* is fully cleaned and ready for cooking. Today almost all chickens, turkeys, and ducklings are completely eviscerated, vacuum-sealed in sturdy plastic bags which eliminate air pockets (and thus freezer burn), then quick-frozen and held at 0°F from processing plant to the consumer. Ready-to-cook poultry is sold fresh or ice-chilled in a few markets, but as a rule it is not easily obtainable.

Since 1953 only ready-to-cook poultry is permitted to carry United States Department of Agriculture grades on individual birds; but the use of official inspection and grading services is entirely voluntary on the part of the packers.

Poultry & Stuffings

STORAGE

Poultry is a perishable food and must be safeguarded against spoilage or deterioration of flavor.

Fresh poultry—To store fresh or ice-chilled ready-to-cook chicken or turkey, remove from store wrappings. Remove neck and giblets. Wrap bird (whole or cut in pieces) loosely in waxed paper or transparent, moisture-vaporproof material, ends open to let in air. Place in a shallow pan and store in the coldest part of the refrigerator. Use within 48 hours. If poultry is to be frozen, wrap securely in freezer wrap and place immediately in freezer.

Quick-frozen poultry must be kept frozen until ready to use and once thawed must not be refrozen. In thawing frozen poultry before cooking, follow directions on the label, if available. Or use one of the following methods: *Refrigerator thawing*—Keep in original wrapping and place on a tray in refrigerator from 1 to 3 days. A 4-pound chicken or turkey requires about 1 day while a 20- to 24-pound turkey may take as long as 3 to 3½ days. *Cold-water thawing*—Place bird in its original wrapper in a large pan or in the sink; cover completely with very cold water. Change water frequently so that it will remain cold. An 8- to 12-pound bird requires 3 to 6 hours; 12- to 20-pound bird 6 to 8 hours; 20- to 24-pound bird 10 to 12 hours. Once it is thawed, refrigerate poultry if not cooking immediately. *Room-temperature thawing*—This method is less satisfactory than other methods. If time permits, refrigerator thawing is the most satisfactory method.

Cooked poultry, gravy, and stuffing should not be left at room temperature for longer than it takes to finish the meal. Never store bird with stuffing; remove stuffing and store it covered in refrigerator; cover gravy and refrigerate. If only one side of a roast bird has been carved, wrap remainder of bird in waxed paper, aluminum foil, or moisture-vaporproof material; store in refrigerator. If more than one half of the meat has been used, remove the remaining meat from the bones and wrap tightly before storing. Cooked pieces should be tightly wrapped and refrigerated. Do not keep cooked poultry, however carefully stored, for more than a few days. If keeping leftover turkey or other poultry for more than several days, immediately remove meat from bones, wrap meat in moisture-vaporproof material, and store in freezer.

COOKING POULTRY

Two general principles apply to the cooking of all kinds of poultry: 1) Cook at low to moderate heat for a suitable length of time. High temperatures shrink the muscle tissue and make the meat tough, dry, and hard. Poultry should always be cooked until well done; the meat should separate easily from the bone and should be tender to the fork. 2) Suit the method of cooking to the age or class of the bird. Young birds of all kinds may be broiled, fried, or roasted in an open pan. Older, less tender birds require cooking by moist heat in a covered casserole or Dutch oven, or in water or steam.

A recommended method of cooking turkey when a moist product is desired is wrapping the bird in heavy-duty aluminum foil and cooking it at a comparatively high oven temperature for a shorter time than is required for roasting, uncovered, at a lower temperature. Directions for roasting in foil are often included on the box in which foil is packed.

Another satisfactory method may be used if one prefers an especially moist bird. Encase the bird securely in a brown carry-out grocery bag and place, seam side of bag up, on the rack in a roasting pan. Use a moderate oven temperature (325°F) for a medium-sized bird and a slow temperature (275° to 300°F) for a bird 20 pounds and up.

Stuffing Poultry for Roasting

Ingredients for a stuffing should be mixed *just before needed* and the bird should be stuffed *just before roasting*. Never stuff a bird a day in advance and store in refrigerator or freezer. These are safety precautions to prevent food poisoning, since stuffing is the perfect medium for disease-producing bacteria. *Immediately* after the meal is served, remove the stuffing from the bird and store, covered, in the refrigerator. Use leftover stuffing within 2 or 3 days; heat thoroughly before serving.

Any extra stuffing which cannot be put into the bird may be put in a greased, covered baking dish or wrapped in aluminum foil and baked in the oven during the last hour of roasting.

Tests for Doneness of Roast Poultry

A meat thermometer used to test doneness should register 180°-185°F when inserted in center of thigh muscle or 165°F when inserted in center of stuffing. Poultry is also done when the thickest part of drumstick feels soft when pressed with fingers protected with clean cloth or paper napkin.

CHICKEN

HONEY-GLAZED FILBERT ROAST CHICKEN
A new flavor twist in the stuffing and the glaze.

- ½ pkg. herb-seasoned stuffing mix (2 cups)
- 1 cup toasted filberts, chopped
- ½ cup chopped celery
- 1 chicken liver, finely chopped
- ½ cup butter or margarine, melted
- ½ cup water
- 1 roaster chicken or capon, about 5 lbs.
- ½ cup honey
- 2 tablespoons soy sauce
- 1 teaspoon grated orange peel
- 2 tablespoons orange juice
- Green grapes

1. Combine stuffing mix with the filberts, celery, chicken liver, butter, and water; toss lightly. Stuff cavity of chicken with the mixture, then tie chicken legs and wings with cord to hold close to body.
2. Place chicken, breast up, on rack in a shallow roasting pan. Roast at 325°F 2½ to 3 hours, or until chicken tests done. (The thickest part of drumstick feels soft when pressed with fingers and meat thermometer registers 180° to 185°F.)
3. Meanwhile, combine honey, soy sauce, and orange peel and juice. Brush chicken frequently with the mixture during last hour of roasting.
4. Place chicken on a serving platter and garnish with grapes.   **6 SERVINGS**

NOTE: To toast filberts, spread in a shallow pan and set in a 400°F oven 10 to 15 minutes, stirring occasionally to toast evenly.

PENNSYLVANIA DUTCH ROAST CHICKEN
This chicken, smothered with a coating which helps to hold in the natural juices, is steamed (not truly roasted) to succulent perfection.

- 1 roaster chicken, 3 to 4 lbs.
- Butter or margarine, softened
- Bread Stuffing, *below*
- 1 cup dairy sour cream

1. Rub inside of chicken with a mixture of *salt* and *pepper*, then rub generously with butter. Fill with stuffing; sew, or skewer and lace with cord.
2. Put chicken into a roasting pan; cover.
3. Roast at 400°F 1½ to 2 hours, or until chicken is tender; about every 15 minutes during roasting spoon some of the sour cream over the chicken. Remove cover for the last 30 minutes of roasting if a darker brown is desired.
4. For a thicker gravy, *1 tablespoon flour* may be stirred into the liquid in pan after removing the chicken. Set pan over heat and bring mixture to boiling, stirring constantly; boil 1 minute.
   4 TO 6 SERVINGS

BREAD STUFFING: Soak *4 slices white bread* in *cold water* and squeeze out all excess moisture. Using a fork, fluff bread and drizzle with *2 tablespoons melted butter or margarine*. Blend into *1 slightly beaten egg* a mixture of *1 teaspoon salt*, *⅛ teaspoon black pepper*, and *¼ teaspoon poultry seasoning*, then *1 teaspoon chopped parsley* and *1 teaspoon grated onion*. Add egg mixture to bread mixture and toss lightly until thoroughly mixed. If desired, finely chopped *cooked giblets* may be added.

ORANGE-GLAZED ROAST CHICKEN

- 1 roasting chicken, weighing about 5½ lbs.
- 5 tablespoons butter or margarine
- 1 small onion, chopped (¼ cup)
- ½ cup water
- 1 can (6 ozs.) frozen concentrate for orange juice (¾ cup)
- 1 package (8 ozs.) herb-seasoned stuffing mix
- ¼ cup light corn syrup
- ½ teaspoon dry mustard

1. Rinse chicken inside and out; pat dry with paper toweling. Salt cavities lightly.
2. Melt butter in a small saucepan; measure out 1 tablespoon and set aside for brushing chicken.
3. Preheat oven to 350°F.
4. Stir onion into rest of melted butter in saucepan; sauté until soft. Stir in water and ½ cup of the orange concentrate; heat to boiling. Pour over stuffing mix in a bowl; toss until evenly moist.
5. Stuff into neck and body cavities of chicken. Skewer neck skin to back; twist wing tips flat against back. Fasten body opening with skewers and string; tie legs to tail. Place chicken, breast side up, on a rack in a small roasting pan. Brush the melted butter over chicken.
6. Roast 2¼ hours.
7. While chicken cooks, combine remaining ¼ cup orange concentrate, corn syrup, and mustard in a small saucepan; heat to boiling; brush part over chicken.

8. Continue roasting, brushing two or three more times with remaining orange mixture, 45 minutes, or until chicken is tender and richly glazed. Lift onto a large serving platter; pull out skewers and cut away string. Carve chicken into serving-sized pieces.

6 TO 8 SERVINGS

OVEN-BARBECUED CHICKEN

3 broiler-fryers, 1½ to 2 lbs. each, quartered
6 tablespoons butter, melted
1½ teaspoons salt
¼ teaspoon freshly ground black pepper
¾ to 1 cup Golden Barbecue Sauce, *below*

1. Put chicken on rack in a roasting pan and brush generously with butter; sprinkle with salt and pepper.
2. Roast at 350°F about 50 minutes, or until golden brown, brushing occasionally with butter.
3. Brush browned chicken with Golden Barbecue Sauce and repeat every 5 minutes; continue to roast about 40 minutes, or until chicken is tender. Serve immediately.

6 SERVINGS

GOLDEN BARBECUE SAUCE: Pour ¾ *cup light molasses* into a bowl; gradually add ½ *cup prepared mustard*, 2 *tablespoons plus* 2 *teaspoons Worcestershire sauce*, ¾ *cup cider vinegar*, 1 *teaspoon Tabasco*, ⅛ *teaspoon marjoram*, and ⅛ *teaspoon oregano*, blending well after each addition. Store, covered, in refrigerator. Mix thoroughly before using.

ABOUT 2 CUPS SAUCE

NOTE: This sauce may also be used in preparing barbecued frankfurters, spareribs, hamburgers, bologna, or canned luncheon meat.

CHICKEN KUMQUAT

1 broiler-fryer, 2½ to 3 lbs., cut up
½ cup flour
1 teaspoon salt
¼ teaspoon pepper
½ teaspoon rosemary leaves, crushed
½ cup butter or margarine
1 jar (8 oz.) kumquats and syrup
3 tablespoons coarsely chopped crystallized ginger
1 cup chicken broth
Sliced almonds, toasted

1. Coat chicken pieces evenly with a mixture of flour, salt, pepper, and rosemary.
2. Heat butter in a skillet. Add chicken pieces and brown evenly over medium heat, about 15 minutes. When chicken is browned, arrange pieces in a shallow baking pan.
3. Put kumquats and syrup into an electric blender container; blend until smooth. Mix kumquat purée, ginger, and chicken broth with drippings in skillet. Heat to boiling. Pour sauce over chicken.
4. Bake at 350°F about 45 minutes, or until tender, basting several times. Garnish with almonds.

ABOUT 4 SERVINGS

CHEF'S CHICKEN

1 broiler-fryer, weighing about 3½ lbs.
1 can (8 ozs.) tomato sauce
⅓ cup salad oil
⅓ cup orange juice
¼ cup lemon juice
1 teaspoon dried thyme, crushed
1 teaspoon salt
½ teaspoon garlic powder
¼ teaspoon pepper
2 tablespoons honey
1 teaspoon prepared hot mustard

1. Rinse chicken inside and out; pat dry with paper toweling. Close body opening with skewers and string; skewer neck skin to back; twist, wing tips flat against back. Place chicken in a transparent bag.
2. Combine tomato sauce, salad oil, orange juice, lemon juice, thyme, salt, garlic powder, and pepper in a small bowl; pour over chicken in bag; fasten bag. For easy handling, place bag in a large bowl. Chill chicken, turning bag several times, overnight to season.
3. When ready to cook chicken, preheat oven to 350°F.
4. Remove chicken from bag and place on a rack in a small roasting pan; for a compact shape, tie legs to tail. Pour marinade from bag into a small bowl.
5. Bake chicken 1 hour; brush generously with marinade. Bake 30 minutes; brush again with marinade; bake 15 minutes.
6. Mix honey and mustard in a cup; brush over chicken. Bake 15 minutes longer, or until chicken is tender.
7. Place on a large serving platter; cut away strings and take out skewers. Garnish platter with parsley and tomato wedges if you like. Carve chicken into serving-sized pieces.

4 TO 6 SERVINGS

CHICKEN AND SWEET POTATOES IN CREAM

4 chicken breasts
1 cup cream
⅛ teaspoon ground cloves

2 tablespoons honey
½ teaspoon salt
½ teaspoon ground nutmeg
¼ teaspoon ground allspice
2 tablespoons butter or margarine
1 can (18 oz.) sweet potatoes

1. Arrange chicken, skin side up, in a shallow baking pan.
2. Mix together cream, honey, salt, nutmeg, allspice, and cloves. Pour over chicken. Dot with butter.
3. Bake at 350°F 30 minutes, basting with cream mixture. Remove from oven and arrange sweet potatoes around chicken; spoon sauce over potatoes, if desired. Return to oven and bake 30 minutes longer, or until chicken is tender.   4 SERVINGS

CANTONESE CHICKEN

4 boneless chicken breasts, weighing about 1½ lbs.
5 tablespoons salad oil
1 large green pepper, quartered, seeded, and cut in thin strips
1 large red pepper, quartered, seeded, and cut in thin strips
2 cups diagonally sliced celery
2 medium onions, peeled, sliced, and separated into rings
1 can (8 ozs.) water chestnuts, drained and sliced
2 tablespoons cornstarch
1 envelope instant chicken broth
1 teaspoon sugar
1 teaspoon ground ginger
½ teaspoon seasoned pepper
1½ cups water
¼ cup soy sauce
Hot cooked rice

1. Rinse chicken and dry on paper toweling; cut into thin strips.
2. Heat 3 tablespoons of the salad oil in a large skillet; add chicken and sauté, stirring often, 10 minutes; push to one side.
3. Add remaining 2 tablespoons salad oil to skillet; heat. Place green and red peppers, celery, onions, and water chestnuts in separate piles in skillet; sauté 3 minutes, or just until vegetables are crisp-tender.
4. While vegetables cook, mix cornstarch, chicken broth, sugar, ginger, and seasoned pepper in a small saucepan; stir in water and soy sauce. Cook, stirring constantly, until sauce thickens and boils 1 minute. Pour over chicken and vegetables; heat slowly just until hot. Serve as is from skillet with cooked rice, or toss all ingredients together first, if you prefer.
6 SERVINGS

ORIENTAL OVEN-FRIED CHICKEN

2 tablespoons soy sauce
2 tablespoons honey
1 tablespoon lemon juice
1 clove garlic, minced
3 lbs. chicken pieces for frying
¾ cup flour
¾ cup all-vegetable shortening, melted in a skillet
2 cans (3 oz. each) chow mein noodles, finely crushed

1. In a large bowl or dish, mix the soy sauce, honey, lemon juice, and garlic. Put chicken into marinade and turn pieces to coat. Cover and refrigerate 2 to 3 hours, turning pieces once or twice.
2. Remove chicken and coat with flour (shake in a plastic bag, if desired). Dip pieces in melted shortening and then coat with crushed noodles. Arrange chicken pieces, skin side down, one layer deep in a large shallow baking dish; pour any remaining shortening over chicken.
3. Bake at 375°F 30 minutes. Turn chicken pieces over and bake about 15 minutes, or until tender.
6 SERVINGS

SESAME CHICKEN

12 chicken drumsticks, weighing about 2 lbs.
4 tablespoons salad oil
2 teaspoons minced pared gingerroot
1 clove garlic, minced
2 tablespoons sesame seeds
1 can (20 ozs.) crushed pineapple in juice
¼ cup firmly packed light brown sugar
⅓ cup soy sauce
2 tablespoons cornstarch
¾ cup water
Hot cooked rice

1. Rinse chicken drumsticks and dry on paper toweling.
2. Measure salad oil into a large skillet; heat; add chicken and brown. Remove from skillet and set aside.
3. Stir gingerroot, garlic, and sesame seeds into drippings; sauté slowly, stirring several times, until seeds are golden.
4. Stir in pineapple and juice, brown sugar, and soy sauce; heat to boiling.
5. Mix cornstarch with water until smooth in a small bowl; stir into mixture in skillet. Cook, stirring constantly, until sauce thickens and boils 1 minute.
6. Place chicken in sauce; heat to boiling; cover. Simmer, stirring several times, 45 minutes, or until chicken is tender.
7. Arrange chicken on a large deep serving platter; spoon part of the sauce over top. Serve the rest separately with cooked rice.
6 SERVINGS

Chicken

FLAVOR-FULL BROILED CHICKEN

Spread *chicken pieces* generously with an *Herb Butter, Lemon Butter,* or *Honey Glaze, below,* spreading some of the butter or glaze between skin and meat. Arrange chicken, skin side down, in a shallow baking pan or broiler pan without rack. Broil about 9 inches from source of heat 25 to 30 minutes, brushing occasionally with butter or glaze. Turn and broil, continuing to brush, 20 minutes longer, or until tender.

HERB BUTTERS

Rosemary: Mix thoroughly with ½ *cup butter or margarine,* softened, *1½ teaspoons crushed rosemary leaves* and *2 teaspoons snipped chives.*

Tarragon: Mix thoroughly with ½ *cup butter or margarine,* softened, *1½ teaspoons crushed tarragon leaves.*

Herb-Garlic: Mix thoroughly with ½ *cup butter or margarine,* softened, *1 clove garlic,* minced, *¾ teaspoon thyme,* and *¼ teaspoon curry powder.*

LEMON BUTTER: Blend ¼ *cup melted butter or margarine,* ¼ *cup cooking oil, 3 tablespoons lemon juice,* ¼ *teaspoon seasoned salt,* and ¼ *teaspoon Tabasco.*

HONEY GLAZE: Blend ½ *cup honey,* ⅓ *cup soy sauce, 6 tablespoons lemon juice, 2 teaspoons dry mustard,* and *2 cloves garlic,* minced.

HERBED CHICKEN

8 chicken thighs, weighing about 1½ lbs.
1 egg
1 tablespoon water
1½ cups herb-seasoned stuffing mix
½ teaspoon salt
¼ teaspoon pepper
¼ cup butter or margarine, melted

1. Rinse chicken and dry on paper toweling.
2. Preheat oven to 400°F.
3. Beat egg with water in a pie plate. Measure stuffing mix into a transparent or paper bag; crush fine with a rolling pin; stir in salt and pepper.
4. Dip chicken pieces, one at a time, into beaten egg, then shake in crumb mixture to coat well. Place in a single layer in a greased shallow baking pan; drizzle melted butter over top.
5. Bake 45 minutes, or until chicken is crisp and tender.

4 SERVINGS

DIETER'S CHICKEN KIEV

4 ozs. Neufchatel cheese
4 teaspoons freeze-dried chives
4 boneless chicken breasts or cutlets, weighing 10 ozs. each
1 teaspoon seasoned salt
2 tablespoons diet margarine
1 envelope instant chicken broth
¼ cup water

1. Blend cheese and chives in a small bowl; spread into a 4x1-inch rectangle on waxed paper; wrap in paper. Place in freezer for 10 to 20 minutes, or until very firm.
2. Rinse chicken breasts and dry in paper toweling. Cut each in half; pound thin between sheets of waxed paper. Sprinkle seasoned salt evenly over chicken. Place flat, skin side down, on counter.
3. Cut cheese into 8 equal pieces; place each on a half chicken breast. Fold edges up over cheese, then roll up meat, jelly roll fashion; fasten in several places with wooden picks.
4. Brown chicken rolls slowly in margarine in a large skillet; stir in chicken broth and water. Heat to boiling; cover. Simmer 40 minutes, or until chicken is tender. Place on a large serving platter; take out picks. Pass sauce separately to spoon over chicken.

8 SERVINGS

SWEET-SOUR CHICKEN

3 chicken breasts, weighing about 10 ozs. each, cut in half
3 tablespoons salad oil
1 large onion, chopped (1 cup)
⅔ cup water
2 envelopes instant chicken broth
1 can (20 ozs.) pineapple chunks in syrup
2 tablespoons cornstarch
2 tablespoons cider vinegar
2 tablespoons soy sauce
1 small green pepper, seeded and cut in rings
¼ cup toasted slivered almonds

1. Rinse chicken breasts and dry on paper towel.
2. Brown in salad oil in a large skillet; remove from skillet and place on a plate.
3. Stir onion into drippings; sauté until soft. Stir in water and chicken broth; return chicken to skillet. Heat to boiling; cover tightly. Simmer 40 minutes, or until chicken is tender. Remove from skillet and arrange on a large deep serving platter; keep hot.
4. Drain syrup from pineapple and stir into cornstarch until smooth in a small bowl; stir in vinegar and soy sauce. Stir into liquid in skillet. Cook, stirring con-

stantly, until sauce thickens and boils 1 minute. Stir in pineapple and green-pepper rings; heat again just until hot. Spoon over chicken on platter; sprinkle almonds on top. Serve with hot cooked rice if you like.

6 SERVINGS

DIXIE CHICKEN PIE

- 1 broiler-fryer, weighing about 2½ lbs., cut up
- Few celery tops
- 1 small onion, peeled and sliced
- 4 peppercorns
- 1¾ teaspoons salt
- 3 cups water
- 1 ham steak, weighing about 1 lb.
- 6 tablespoons butter or margarine
- 6 tablespoons all-purpose flour
- ¼ teaspoon pepper
- 1 can (16 ozs.) whole boiled onions, drained
- 1 package (10 ozs.) frozen mixed vegetables
- ¾ teaspoon dried rosemary, crushed
- ½ package piecrust mix

1. Rinse chicken and dry on paper toweling. Combine chicken, celery tops, onion, peppercorns, 1 teaspoon of the salt, and water in a large skillet; heat to boiling; cover. Simmer 1 hour, or until chicken is tender. Remove from broth and cool until easy to handle. Strain broth into a 4-cup measure; add water, if needed, to make 2½ cups.
2. Pull skin from chicken and take meat from bones; dice chicken and ham.
3. Melt butter in same skillet; stir in flour, remaining ¾ teaspoon salt, and pepper; cook, stirring constantly, until bubbly. Stir in the 2½ cups broth; continue cooking and stirring until sauce thickens and boils 1 minute. Stir in chicken and ham, boiled onions, mixed vegetables, and rosemary; heat, breaking up vegetables with a fork, to boiling; pour into a 1¾-quart baking dish.
4. Preheat oven to 425°F; keep chicken mixture hot in oven as it heats.
5. Prepare piecrust mix as label directs. Roll out to an oval, round, or square 1 inch larger than baking dish; trim even. Using a small cookie cutter, make two or three cutouts in pastry to let steam escape. (Or cut several slits in pastry with a knife.) Place pastry over filling in baking dish; turn overhang under, flush with rim; flute edge.
6. Bake 30 minutes, or until pastry is golden.

6 SERVINGS

CEYLONESE CHICKEN

- 1 broiler-fryer, weighing about 3 lbs., cut in serving-sized pieces
- 2 tablespoons salad oil
- 1 medium onion, chopped (½ cup)
- 1 clove of garlic, minced
- 1½ teaspoons salt
- 1½ teaspoons ground coriander
- 1 teaspoon fennel seeds
- ½ teaspoon ground cardamom
- ½ teaspoon ground cumin
- ⅛ teaspoon ground turmeric
- 1 can (6 ozs.) tomato paste
- 1¼ cups milk

1. Rinse chicken and dry on paper toweling. Brown pieces in salad oil in a large skillet; remove from skillet.
2. Stir onion and garlic into drippings; sauté until soft. Stir in salt, coriander, fennel seeds, cardamom, cumin, turmeric, and tomato paste; very slowly stir in milk. Heat to boiling; place chicken in sauce; cover.
3. Simmer, turning once, 45 minutes, or until chicken is tender. Serve with plain steamed rice if you like.

4 SERVINGS

CHICKEN BENEDICT

- 2 boneless chicken breasts or cutlets, weighing about 8 ozs. each
- 2 tablespoons all-purpose flour
- ½ teaspoon salt
- Dash of pepper
- 2 tablespoons salad oil
- 1 envelope hollandaise sauce mix
- Water
- 1 package (3 ozs.) sliced Canadian bacon
- 2 English muffins, split
- Paprika

1. Rinse chicken and dry on paper toweling. Cut each breast in half; shake with a mixture of flour, salt, and pepper in a transparent bag to coat well.
2. Brown chicken in salad oil in a large skillet; cover. Cook slowly 30 minutes, or until chicken is tender; keep hot.
3. While chicken cooks, prepare hollandaise sauce mix with water as the label directs.
4. Preheat broiler.
5. Sauté Canadian bacon, turning once, in a second skillet until brown; keep hot.
6. Place muffin halves on a cookie sheet; toast in broiler. Top each half with bacon, then chicken; spoon hollandaise sauce over chicken; sprinkle paprika over sauce.
7. Broil, 6 inches from heat, 2 to 3 minutes, or until sauce bubbles up. Serve with spiced peaches and crisp radishes if you like.

4 SERVINGS

Chicken

EASY CHICKEN BAKE

3 boneless chicken breasts or cutlets, weighing about 10 ozs. each
1 teaspoon paprika
¼ teaspoon salt
¼ teaspoon pepper
1 package (8 ozs.) medium noodles
1 can (16 ozs.) cut green beans
1 jar (2 ozs.) sliced pimientos, drained and diced
2 cans (10¾ ozs. each) condensed cream of chicken soup
1 cup dry white wine
2 tablespoons grated Parmesan cheese

1. Rinse chicken and dry on paper toweling. Pull off skin; cut each breast in half.
2. Combine paprika, salt, and pepper in a cup; rub into both sides of chicken.
3. Place uncooked noodles in a layer in a baking dish, 13x9x2 inches.
4. Drain liquid from beans into a cup; layer beans and pimientos over noodles; place chicken in a single layer on top.
5. Preheat oven to 375°.
6. Combine soup, wine, and ½ cup of the liquid from beans in a medium saucepan; heat, stirring several times, to boiling. Pour around chicken into dish; cover.
7. Bake 1 hour; uncover. Sprinkle Parmesan cheese on top. Bake 10 minutes longer, or until chicken and noodles are tender. 6 SERVINGS

Fried Chicken

HINTS FOR FRIED CHICKEN

Generally the pieces of chicken are dipped in liquid before coating with flour or other dry ingredients.

Materials for dipping: Beaten egg with water, milk, orange juice, lemon juice, or herbs; undiluted evaporated milk; buttermilk; a marinade.

Materials for coating: Seasoned flour with herbs such as tarragon, thyme, sage, oregano, or basil; instant potato flakes; crushed corn flakes or other dry cereals; finely crushed pretzels or herb stuffing mix; pancake or waffle mix or cornbread mix.

Methods of frying:

Pan frying—Heat in a heavy skillet over medium heat enough fat or cooking oil to cover bottom to a depth of ½ inch. Put meatiest pieces of chicken skin side down in skillet. Add less meaty pieces as first ones brown. Turn with tongs or two spoons to brown all sides. When evenly browned, reduce heat, add 1 to 2 tablespoons water, and cover skillet. Cook slowly 25 to 40 minutes, or until thickest pieces are tender when pierced with a fork. Uncover skillet last 10 minutes of cooking to crisp the crust.

Deep frying—Heat fat for deep frying to 350°F. Deep fry only as many pieces of chicken at one time as will lie uncrowded one layer deep in the hot fat. Deep fry chicken 10 to 13 minutes, or until tender and golden brown. (Chicken livers require only about 1 minute frying time.) Turn pieces with tongs several times. Drain over fat a few seconds; remove to absorbent paper to drain thoroughly. Be sure fat is heated to 350°F before frying each layer of chicken.

EMPRESS CHICKEN

½ cup butter or margarine
1 clove garlic, crushed
1 broiler-fryer, 2½ lbs., cut up
½ cup herb-seasoned stuffing mix, rolled fine
1 teaspoon salt
½ teaspoon black pepper
½ teaspoon paprika
1 tablespoon snipped parsley

1. Put butter and garlic into a large electric skillet and heat to 360°F.
2. Coat chicken pieces with a mixture of the stuffing mix, salt, pepper and paprika. Put chicken pieces into the skillet; brown evenly on all sides.
3. Reduce heat to 260°F and allow chicken to cook, uncovered, until tender, about 30 minutes, turning occasionally. Sprinkle with parsley and serve with *Cherry-Filled Peaches*.

4 SERVINGS

SWISS-CAPPED GLAZED CHICKEN

2 broiler-fryers, 2½ to 3 lbs. each, cut up
½ cup all-purpose flour
⅔ cup orange juice
2 tablespoons lemon juice

2 teaspoons salt
¼ teaspoon pepper
¼ to ½ cup butter or margarine
1½ cups currant jelly
1 cup finely shredded Swiss cheese
½ cup toasted slivered blanched almonds
½ teaspoon paprika

1. Coat chicken pieces with a mixture of the flour, salt, and pepper.
2. Heat butter in a large skillet. Add chicken pieces, skin side down, and brown evenly.
3. Meanwhile, beat together the jelly and orange and lemon juices.
4. Pour jelly mixture over browned chicken pieces. Cover skillet and simmer about 45 minutes, or until chicken is tender. Spoon glaze over chicken occasionally during cooking.
5. Top evenly with cheese, almonds, and paprika. Place under broiler 4 inches from source of heat until cheese is melted, about 1 minute. Serve immediately. ABOUT 8 SERVINGS

GOOD FORTUNE CHICKEN WITH PINEAPPLE PIQUANT

1 egg, fork beaten
⅓ cup water
1 tablespoon milk
¼ cup flour
1 tablespoon cornstarch
1 tablespoon cornmeal
⅛ teaspoon baking powder
12 small chicken legs
Fat for deep frying heated to 350°F
½ cup green pepper chunks
½ cup onion chunks
1 tablespoon cooking oil
1 can (about 15 oz.) pineapple chunks (reserve syrup)
½ cup cider vinegar
½ cup packed brown sugar
2 tablespoons soy sauce
¼ cup water
1 tablespoon cornstarch

1. Beat the egg, water, and milk with a mixture of flour, cornstarch, cornmeal, and baking powder in a bowl until smooth. Dip each chicken leg into the batter and drain over bowl a few seconds.
2. Fry pieces in hot fat 15 minutes, or until chicken is crisp brown and tender. Remove with slotted spoon and drain over fat; place on absorbent paper.
3. Meanwhile, cook green pepper and onion in the hot cooking oil in a large skillet until crisp-tender, stirring occasionally. Push vegetables to one side of skillet.
4. Pour in reserved pineapple syrup; add vinegar, brown sugar, soy sauce, and a mixture of water and cornstarch. Stir until blended. Mix in pineapple.

Bring rapidly to boiling, stirring constantly; cook 3 minutes.
5. Serve chicken legs with sauce as an appetizer or main dish. If desired, add *1 tablespoon sesame seed* to sauce, or sprinkle over chicken when served. 4 TO 6 SERVINGS

MANCHA MANTELES

Mexicans have given this incomparable creation its strangely apt name which translates as Tablecloth Stainer!

3 tablespoons butter
3 tablespoons olive oil
1 lb. lean boneless pork, cut in 1-in. pieces
2 broiler-fryers, 2½ to 3 lbs. each, cut up, seasoned, and floured*
1 large onion, sliced
1 green pepper, sliced
1 can (6 oz.) tomato paste
¼ cup unblanched almonds, toasted
1 tablespoon sesame seed, toasted
¼ cup sugar
1½ teaspoons salt
1 tablespoon chili powder
1 teaspoon ground cinnamon
3 whole cloves
1 bay leaf
2 cups cubed raw sweet potato
1 cup fresh pineapple pieces
1 cup diced tart apple

1. Heat half the butter and half the olive oil in a large skillet. Add pork and brown well; remove to a large saucepot. Set aside.
2. Brown chicken evenly in skillet adding the remaining butter and olive oil as needed. Transfer chicken to the saucepot.
3. Add onion and green pepper to drippings in skillet and cook about 5 minutes, stirring occasionally. Remove from heat and spoon into an electric blender container. Add tomato paste, almonds, and sesame seed; blend until smooth.
4. Return mixture to skillet; stir in *4 cups hot water* and sugar, salt, chili powder, cinnamon, cloves, and bay leaf. Bring to boiling; simmer, uncovered, about 15 minutes.
5. Pour the sauce over chicken and pork in saucepot. Bring to boiling and simmer, covered, about 30 minutes. Add the sweet potato and cook 15 minutes longer. Stir in the pineapple and apple; heat thoroughly.
6. Serve in soup plates. 8 TO 10 SERVINGS
*If available, use a 4- to 5-pound chicken and adjust the cooking time accordingly.

Chicken

CHICKEN AMANDE

1 broiler-fryer, about 3 lbs., cut up
3 tablespoons shortening
1 clove garlic, minced
¼ cup chopped onion
2 tablespoons flour
2 tablespoons tomato paste
1½ cups chicken broth (dissolve 2 chicken bouillon cubes in 1½ cups boiling water)
1 teaspoon seasoned salt
½ teaspoon black pepper
½ teaspoon crushed tarragon
½ cup toasted slivered blanched almonds
¾ cup dairy sour cream
2 tablespoons shredded Parmesan cheese

1. Brown chicken on all sides in hot shortening in a large skillet; remove pieces as they brown.
2. Add garlic and onion to skillet and cook, stirring occasionally.
3. Stir in flour and tomato paste; pour in chicken broth. Cook slowly, stirring constantly, until mixture boils. Return chicken to skillet. Sprinkle with a mixture of seasoned salt, pepper, and tarragon; top with ¼ cup of the almonds. Cover and cook over low heat 45 to 60 minutes, or until tender. Remove chicken pieces to a hot serving dish.
4. Add sour cream gradually to the sauce, stirring constantly. Heat thoroughly (do not boil). Pour over chicken. Sprinkle with the Parmesan cheese and remaining almonds.   ABOUT 6 SERVINGS

CHICKEN CACCIATORE

Cacciatore, meaning "hunter" in Italian, indicates that the food, usually chicken, is prepared in the "hunter's style," that is, simmering the fowl in a well-seasoned tomato and wine sauce.

¼ cup cooking oil
1 broiler-fryer, 2½ lbs., cut up
2 onions, sliced
2 cloves garlic, minced
3 tomatoes, quartered
2 green peppers, sliced
1 small bay leaf
1 teaspoon salt
¼ teaspoon pepper
½ teaspoon celery seed
1 teaspoon crushed oregano or basil
1 can (8 oz.) tomato sauce
¼ cup sauterne
8 oz. spaghetti, cooked according to pkg. directions

1. Heat oil in a large heavy skillet; add chicken and brown on all sides. Remove from skillet.
2. Add onion and garlic to oil remaining in skillet and cook until onion is tender but not brown; stir occasionally.
3. Return chicken to skillet and add the tomatoes, green pepper, and bay leaf.
4. Mix the salt, pepper, celery seed, and oregano and blend with tomato sauce; pour over all.
5. Cover and cook over low heat 45 minutes. Blend in wine and cook, uncovered, 20 minutes longer. Discard bay leaf.
6. Put the cooked spaghetti onto a hot serving platter and top with the chicken and sauce.
   ABOUT 6 SERVINGS

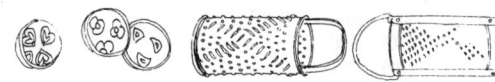

ANTOINE'S CHICKEN CREOLE

Crisply fried chicken served in a wonderfully flavored creole sauce is a popular item at Antoine's in New Orleans, Louisiana. For elegance, each portion of chicken may be placed on a ripe avocado half and the sauce poured over all.

1 broiler-fryer, 2½ to 3 lbs., cut up
¼ cup olive oil
1 can (16 oz.) tomatoes
2 tablespoons butter
1 teaspoon salt
⅛ teaspoon pepper
⅛ teaspoon cayenne pepper
1 sprig thyme
1 bay leaf
1 tablespoon minced parsley
3 cloves garlic, minced
1 tablespoon butter
1 tablespoon flour
6 chopped shallots (or ½ cup minced onion)
5 tablespoons chopped green pepper
½ cup white wine

1. Wipe chicken pieces with a damp cloth. Sauté in olive oil, turning to brown all sides.
2. Combine tomatoes and 2 tablespoons butter in a saucepan and simmer 10 minutes, stirring occasionally. Add salt and peppers. Cook 10 minutes. Add thyme, parsley, bay leaf, and garlic. Cook 15 minutes, or until sauce is thick.
3. Melt 1 tablespoon butter in a heavy saucepot or deep skillet; blend in flour and cook until browned. Add shallots and green pepper; brown slightly. Add chicken and wine; cover and simmer 45 minutes, or until chicken is tender.   4 TO 6 SERVINGS

CHICKEN FRICASSEE

1 stewing chicken, 4 to 5 lbs., cut up	1 bay leaf
	2 teaspoons salt
1 large onion, quartered	3 peppercorns
6 stalks celery with leaves, cut in pieces	¼ cup flour
	1 cup cream
½ bunch parsley	2 teaspoons lemon juice

1. Put chicken, gizzard, heart, and neck into a kettle. Refrigerate liver. (If desired, brown chicken pieces in a skillet with hot fat; pieces may be coated with seasoned flour before frying.)
2. Add hot water to kettle to barely cover; add onion, celery, parsley, bay leaf, salt, and peppercorns. Bring water to boiling; remove foam.
3. Cover kettle tightly and simmer 2 to 3 hours, or until thickest pieces of chicken are tender when pierced with a fork. Add liver last 15 minutes of cooking.
4. Remove chicken and giblets from broth. Strain broth and cool slightly; skim off fat.
5. Heat 4 tablespoons of chicken fat in the kettle; blend in flour and heat until bubbly, stirring constantly.
6. Continue stirring and gradually add 2 cups of the chicken broth and the cream. Bring to boiling; cook and stir 1 to 2 minutes. Mix in the lemon juice and chicken pieces; heat thoroughly.
7. Serve chicken and gravy in a warm serving dish and garnish with *parsley*. ABOUT 6 SERVINGS

NOTE: For additional flavor, add *1½ teaspoons monosodium glutamate* and *1 chicken bouillon cube* to cooking liquid.

CHICKEN AND DUMPLINGS: Follow recipe for Chicken Fricassee. For the last 12 minutes of cooking, add liver and *Cornmeal Dumplings, below*, to kettle. Cover tightly and continue cooking over medium heat 12 minutes without removing cover. Remove dumplings and chicken to a warm serving dish; keep warm. Prepare gravy and spoon over chicken and dumplings. ABOUT 6 SERVINGS

CORNMEAL DUMPLINGS

1 cup all-purpose flour	3 tablespoons shortening
3 teaspoons baking powder	
	1 egg, well beaten
½ teaspoon salt	¾ cup milk
1 cup cornmeal	

1. Sift the flour, baking powder, and salt together into a bowl. Stir in cornmeal. Cut in shortening with pastry blender until pieces are the size of peas. Add a blend of egg and milk; with a fork, stir until just blended.
2. Drop batter by tablespoonfuls onto hot chicken mixture and proceed as directed.

LE COQ AU VIN

This version of the well-known chicken and wine dish is a specialty of La Cremaillere, Banksville, New York.

2 broiler-fryers, 2 lbs. each	8 small white onions
	1 slice salt pork, diced
2 tablespoons flour	2 cups red wine
¼ cup butter	1 cup brown gravy
6 fresh mushrooms	Bouquet garni, *page 9*

1. Separate legs and breasts of chickens. Season with *salt* and *pepper* to taste and roll in flour.
2. Heat the butter in a large saucepan, add the chicken, mushrooms, onions, and salt pork. Cover and cook slowly for 15 minutes.
3. Drain all the fat from saucepan, add the wine, gravy, and bouquet garni; cook 15 minutes longer. Season to taste and serve. 4 SERVINGS

OLD-FASHIONED CHICKEN PIE

1 stewing chicken, 4 to 5 lbs., cut up	4 carrots, scraped and sliced
1 small onion	3 stalks celery, cut in pieces
2 pieces (3 in. each) celery with leaves	
	2 small onions
3 sprigs parsley	¼ to ½ teaspoon salt
2 teaspoons salt	Biscuit dough (made from 1½ cups flour, or use a mix), rolled out
2 or 3 peppercorns	
1 small bay leaf	
4 medium-sized potatoes, pared and quartered	

1. Put chicken pieces into a 4-quart kettle. Add *1 quart hot water*, 1 onion, celery, parsley, 2 teaspoons salt, peppercorns, and bay leaf. Cover; bring to boiling; remove foam. Cover tightly and simmer 2 to 3 hours, or until thickest pieces are fork-tender.
2. Remove chicken from broth and cool slightly; remove meat from bones. Cut meat in 1-inch pieces. Set aside. Strain and cool broth; remove fat. Reserve broth.
3. Bring reserved chicken broth to boiling. Add

the vegetables and salt. Cook, covered, about 20 minutes, or until tender. Remove vegetables with slotted spoon and place in a 2-quart deep casserole along with the chicken pieces.

4. To prepare gravy, combine ½ *cup water* and ¼ *cup flour* in a jar. Cover and shake until blended. Stirring constantly, add gradually to boiling broth; cook and stir 3 to 5 minutes.

5. Pour gravy into casserole. (There should be enough gravy to "float" chicken and vegetable pieces without mixture being too liquid.) Top with cutout biscuits placed so they just touch.

6. Bake at 425°F 15 to 20 minutes, or until biscuits are golden brown.   6 TO 8 SERVINGS

AVOCADO-CHICKEN CASSEROLE

1 small ripe avocado	1 cup shredded sharp Cheddar cheese
1 tablespoon lemon juice	
¼ cup butter or margarine	1 cup wide noodles, cooked and drained
5 tablespoons flour	2 chicken breasts, cooked, skinned, boned, and sliced (white meat of roast turkey or capon may be used)
½ teaspoon salt	
⅛ teaspoon white pepper	
1½ cups cream	
¾ cup milk	

1. Peel avocado; cut into slices ¼ to ½ inch thick. Put slices into a bowl and drizzle with lemon juice; turn slices gently a few times.

2. Heat the butter in a saucepan. Blend in flour, salt, and pepper; heat until bubbly. Gradually add cream and milk, stirring constantly. Bring to boiling; cook and stir 1 to 2 minutes.

3. Remove from heat. Add the cheese all at one time and stir until cheese is melted; remove 1 cup of the sauce and set aside. Mix the cooked noodles into remaining sauce.

4. Arrange the chicken slices on the bottom of a greased 1-quart shallow baking dish. Spoon the sauced noodles over chicken slices, arrange avocado slices on top, and carefully spoon the reserved sauce over avocado. Sprinkle lightly with *paprika*.

5. Heat in a 350°F oven about 25 minutes, or until thoroughly heated and top is delicately browned.
    4 SERVINGS

TANGERINE CHICKEN

1 broiler-fryer, weighing about 3 lbs., quartered	1½ teaspoons salt
	¾ teaspoon ground ginger
2 tablespoons butter or margarine	2 cups reconstituted frozen tangerine juice
2 tablespoons salad oil	3 cups hot cooked rice
4 tablespoons all-purpose flour	2 tablespoons chopped slivered almonds
2 tablespoons sugar	

1. Rinse chicken and dry on paper toweling. Brown pieces slowly in butter and salad oil in a large skillet; place in a single layer in a shallow baking dish. Pour off all drippings, then measure 2 tablespoons and return to skillet.

2. Preheat oven to 350°F.

3. Stir flour, sugar, salt, and ginger into drippings; cook, stirring constantly, until bubbly. Stir in tangerine juice; continue cooking and stirring until sauce thickens and boils 1 minute; pour over chicken; cover.

4. Bake 60 minutes, or until chicken is tender.

5. Toss hot rice with almonds; spoon onto a large serving platter. Arrange chicken on top. Pass sauce separately to spoon over all.   4 SERVINGS

CHICKEN-CRAB MEAT CASSEROLE ROSEMARY

A rich combination of chicken, seafood, and avocado—luncheon fare for sophisticated tastes.

½ cup butter	2 cans (6½ oz. each) crab meat, drained and flaked (bony tissue removed)
2 tablespoons finely chopped onion	
7 tablespoons flour	
¾ teaspoon salt	1½ cups avocado chunks
¾ teaspoon paprika	
1 teaspoon rosemary, crushed	Lemon juice
	1 cup coarse fresh bread crumbs, browned in 2 tablespoons butter
2 cups chicken broth	
2 cups dairy sour cream	
3 cups cooked chicken pieces	

1. Heat the butter and onion in a saucepan until onion is golden. Blend in a mixture of flour, salt, paprika, and rosemary. Heat until bubbly. Remove from heat.

2. Gradually add the chicken broth, stirring constantly. Bring to boiling, stirring constantly, and boil 1 to 2 minutes. Remove from heat and blend in

the sour cream in small amounts, then the chicken and crab meat.
3. Drizzle avocado with lemon juice to prevent discoloration. Blend into the mixture. Turn into a 2-quart baking dish. Top evenly with the browned bread crumbs.
4. Heat in a 350°F oven about 30 minutes. Remove from oven and garnish one corner of the dish with a small bunch of *watercress*.

8 TO 10 SERVINGS

TURKEY

ROAST TURKEY

1 ready-to-cook turkey   Melted fat

1. Rinse bird with cold water. Drain and pat dry with absorbent paper or soft cloth.
2. Prepare cooked giblets and broth for gravy (see instructions).
3. Prepare favorite stuffing.
4. Rub body and neck cavities with *salt*. Fill lightly with stuffing. (Extra stuffing may be put into a greased covered baking dish or wrapped in aluminum foil and baked with turkey the last hour of roasting time.)
5. Fasten neck skin to back with skewer and bring wing tips onto back. Push drumsticks under band of skin at tail, or tie with cord. Set, breast up, on rack in shallow roasting pan. Brush with melted fat.
6. If meat thermometer is used, place it in center of inside thigh muscle or thickest part of breast meat. Be sure that tip does not touch bone. If desired, cover top and sides of turkey with cheesecloth moistened with melted fat. Keep cloth moist during roasting by brushing occasionally with fat from the bottom of pan.
7. Roast, uncovered, at 325°F until turkey tests done (the thickest part of the drumstick feels soft when pressed with fingers and meat thermometer registers 180°F to 185°F).
8. When turkey is two thirds done, cut band of skin or cord at drumsticks. Roast until done. For easier carving, let turkey stand 20 to 30 minutes, keeping it warm. Meanwhile, if desired, prepare gravy from drippings.
9. Remove cord and skewers from turkey and place on heated platter. Garnish platter and, if desired, put paper frills on drumsticks.
NOTE: If desired, turkey may be roasted in heavy-duty aluminum foil. Brush bird thoroughly with melted fat; wrap securely in foil; close with a drugstore or lock fold to prevent leakage of drippings. Place, breast up, in roasting pan (omit rack). Roast a 10- to 12-pound turkey at 450°F about 3 hours. About 20 minutes before end of roasting time, remove from oven. Quickly unfold foil to edge of pan. Insert meat thermometer. Return uncovered bird to oven and complete cooking. (Turkey will brown sufficiently in this time.)

FRIED TURKEY

2 roaster-fryer turkeys,   Seasoned flour
   4 to 5 lbs. each, cut   Shortening
   in serving-sized   1 to 2 tablespoons water
   pieces

1. Coat turkey pieces well with seasoned flour. Put, skin side down, in a large skillet of heated shortening (about ½ inch deep). Cook, turning to brown evenly on all sides.
2. Reduce heat, add water, and cover skillet tightly. Cook slowly 50 to 60 minutes, or until turkey is tender. Cook uncovered last 10 minutes to crisp skin.

12 SERVINGS

TURKEY KABOBS

1½ lbs. boned cooked   ¼ cup honey
   turkey, cut in chunks   ¼ cup cooking oil
1 can (about 20 oz.)   1 teaspoon dry mustard
   pineapple chunks,   2 tablespoons finely
   drained (reserve ¼   chopped green onion
   cup syrup)   Cherry tomatoes
½ cup soy sauce   2 cans (5 oz. each)
½ cup ketchup   whole water chestnuts
⅓ cup white wine vinegar

1. Marinate the turkey chunks overnight in a mixture of the reserved pineapple syrup, soy sauce, ketchup, vinegar, honey, oil, dry mustard, and on-

ion; turn chunks occasionally. Drain and reserve marinade.
2. Thread turkey, pineapple, tomatoes (if large, cut in half), and water chestnuts onto ten 8-inch skewers. Brush generously with marinade.
3. Broil about 2 inches from source of heat 3 to 5 minutes or until lightly browned, turning and brushing frequently with the marinade.   10 KABOBS

TURKEY MOLE POBLANO

½ cup cooking oil	2 tablespoons seedless raisins
2 cloves garlic, minced	
2 tablespoons puréed fresh small red chiles (seeds and stems removed before forcing through a food mill)	½ cup fine bread crumbs
	1 tablespoon chili powder
	1 teaspoon salt
	¼ teaspoon pepper
½ cup almonds	¼ teaspoon ground coriander
2 tablespoons peanuts	
2 tablespoons sesame seed	⅛ teaspoon ground cloves
1 cup drained canned tomatoes	Few grains ground ginger
1 cup chicken broth	1 piece (3 in.) stick cinnamon
½ oz. (½ sq.) unsweetened chocolate, melted	Turkey slices

1. Heat oil and garlic together in a heavy skillet, then add chile pulp.
2. Meanwhile, put nuts and sesame seed into an electric blender container. Chop finely.
3. Add remaining ingredients except stick cinnamon and turkey to blender container and blend to a smooth paste. Stir into the oil in skillet and add the stick cinnamon; simmer, stirring frequently, until thickened, about 15 minutes.
4. Pour mole over cooked sliced turkey in a shallow baking dish. Cover; heat in a 350°F oven 20 minutes.   SAUCE FOR 6 TO 8 SERVINGS

CARIBBEAN TURKEY

4 small turkey drumsticks, weighing about 2 lbs.	1 clove of garlic, chopped
	2 teaspoons curry powder
¼ cup all-purpose flour	1 can (16 ozs.) tomatoes
1½ teaspoons salt	¼ cup currants
¼ teaspoon pepper	1 tablespoon cornstarch
¼ cup salad oil	3 cups hot cooked rice
1 large onion, chopped (1 cup)	1 medium-sized green pepper, quartered, cored, and chopped

1. Rinse drumsticks and pat dry with paper toweling. Shake in mixture of flour, ½ teaspoon of the salt, and pepper in a transparent bag. Brown slowly in salad oil in a large skillet; place in a baking dish, 13x9x2 inches.
2. Preheat oven to 375°F.
3. Stir onion, green pepper, garlic, and curry powder into drippings; sauté until onion and pepper are soft. Stir in remaining 1 teaspoon salt, tomatoes, and currants; heat to boiling. Pour over turkey; cover.
4. Bake 1¾ hours, or until turkey is tender; remove from dish; keep hot.
5. Pour sauce into a small saucepan; skim off any fat; reheat sauce to boiling.
6. Blend cornstarch with a little water in a cup until smooth; stir into boiling sauce. Cook, stirring constantly, until sauce thickens and boils 3 minutes.
7. Spoon rice onto a large serving platter; arrange drumsticks on top. Spoon part of the sauce over turkey, then serve remainder separately.
   4 SERVINGS

TARRAGON TURKEY ROLLS

2 cups finely diced cooked turkey	2 cups biscuit mix
	½ cup water
½ cup diced celery	1 tablespoon instant minced onion
¼ cup chopped green onions	
	1 tablespoon butter or margarine
⅓ cup mayonnaise or salad dressing	1 can (10¾ ozs.) condensed cream of chicken soup
¼ teaspoon dried tarragon, crushed	
¼ teaspoon salt	½ cup milk
1 tablespoon lemon juice	

1. Preheat oven to 375°F.
2. Combine turkey, celery, and green onions in a medium bowl. Blend mayonnaise, tarragon, salt, and lemon juice in a cup; fold into turkey mixture.
3. Combine biscuit mix and water in a medium bowl; stir lightly with a fork until dough holds together. Turn out onto a lightly floured cloth; knead ½ minute. Roll out to a square, 12x12 inches; cut in half lengthwise and in thirds crosswise to make 6 rectangles.
4. Spread about ⅓ cup of the turkey mixture over

each rectangle; starting at a short end, roll up, jelly-roll fashion; pinch edges to seal. Place rolls, seam side down, on a greased large cookie sheet; cut two or three slits in top of each.
5. Bake 30 minutes, or until golden.
6. While rolls bake, sauté instant onion lightly in butter in a small saucepan; stir in soup and milk. Heat slowly to boiling. Serve over turkey rolls.   6 SERVINGS

TURKEY DIVAN

1 package (10 ozs.) frozen broccoli spears
2 large carrots, pared and cut in sticks
8 small slices cooked turkey
1 envelope instant chicken broth
1¼ cups milk
2 tablespoons dry sherry
½ cup grated Parmesan cheese
¼ cup butter or margarine
¼ cup all-purpose flour
½ cup whipping cream, whipped

1. Cook broccoli as label directs; drain. Cook carrot sticks in boiling water in a medium saucepan 10 minutes, or until tender; drain. Place vegetables in 4 individual broilerproof baking dishes; arrange turkey slices on top.
2. Preheat broiler.
3. Melt butter in a medium saucepan; stir in flour and chicken broth. Cook, stirring constantly, until bubbly. Stir in milk; continue cooking and stirring until mixture thickens and boils 1 minute; remove from heat. Stir in sherry and ¼ cup of the cheese; lightly fold in whipped cream. Pour over layers in baking dishes; sprinkle remaining ¼ cup cheese on top.
4. Broil, 4 to 6 inches from heat, 2 to 3 minutes, or until tops brown lightly.   4 SERVINGS

DUCKLING

ROAST DUCKLING À L'ORANGE

2 ready-to-cook ducklings, 4 lbs. each
1 to 2 teaspoons salt
Apricot-Rice Stuffing, page 150
1 cup orange juice
2 tablespoons butter or margarine
Orange Gravy, *below*

1. Rinse ducklings and pat dry with absorbent paper. Rub cavities of ducklings with salt.
2. Prepare Apricot-Rice Stuffing and set aside.
3. Heat orange juice and butter together over low heat until butter is melted. Remove from heat and, using a pastry brush, brush cavities with the mixture.
4. Lightly fill body and neck cavities with the stuffing; do not pack. To close body cavities, sew, or skewer and lace with cord; fasten neck skin to backs and wings to bodies with skewers. Place ducklings, breast up, on rack in roasting pan. Brush with juice mixture.
5. Roast, uncovered, at 325°F 2½ to 3 hours. To test doneness, move leg gently by grasping end bone; drumstick-thigh joint should move easily. Brush frequently with orange juice mixture; pour off and reserve drippings as they accumulate.
6. Place ducklings on a heated platter; remove skewers and cord. Garnish with *broiled orange slices* and *parsley*; serve with Orange Gravy.
   6 TO 8 SERVINGS

ORANGE GRAVY: Leaving brown residue in roasting pan, pour drippings and fat into a bowl. Allow fat to rise to surface; skim off fat and reserve 3 tablespoons; put reserved fat into roasting pan. Blend in *3 tablespoons flour*, *¼ teaspoon salt*, and *⅛ teaspoon black pepper*. Stirring constantly, heat until mixture bubbles. Remove from heat. Continue to stir while slowly adding *2 cups reserved drippings* plus orange juice. Return to heat and cook rapidly, stirring constantly, until gravy thickens. Cook 1 to 2 minutes longer. While stirring, scrape bottom and sides of pan to blend in brown residue. Blend in *⅓ cup orange marmalade*. Remove from heat; pour into gravy boat and serve hot.

DUCK WITH OLIVES
(Canard aux Olives)

This recipe is from the Hotel Aiglon, Menton, France.

1 ready-to-cook duckling, 4 lbs.
⅓ cup olive oil
1 cup carrot slices
1 cup coarsely chopped onion
½ teaspoon salt
⅛ teaspoon pepper
¼ teaspoon rosemary
2 small stalks celery
2 to 3 sprigs parsley
1 bay leaf
⅓ cup cognac
2 tablespoons tomato paste
2 cups chicken broth
⅓ cup white wine
16 whole pitted green olives

1. Rinse duckling and cut into quarters. Cut away and discard excess fat.
2. Brown duck in olive oil in a large heavy skillet. Add the carrots, onion, salt, pepper, and rosemary. Tie the celery, parsley, and bay leaf together and add to skillet. Brown the vegetables. Pour off excess fat. Add cognac and ignite.
3. When flaming stops, add a blend of the tomato paste, broth, and wine to skillet.
4. Cover and roast at 350°F about 1½ hours, or until duck is tender.
5. Place duck pieces on heated platter.
6. Strain the sauce into a saucepan; add the olives. Heat until very hot. Immediately pour over the duck. Serve immediately. 4 SERVINGS

GOOSE

ROAST GOOSE

1 ready-to-cook goose, 8 to 10 lbs.
1 tablespoon salt
¼ teaspoon black pepper
1 lb. cooking apples, pared and quartered
¾ lb. prunes (soaked in warm water, drained, and pitted)
1 tablespoon sugar

1. Rinse goose and remove any large layers of fat from the body cavity. Pat dry with absorbent paper. Rub body and neck cavities with a mixture of the salt and pepper.
2. Mix apples, prunes, and sugar together; lightly spoon mixture into cavities. To close body cavity, sew, or skewer and lace with a cord. Fasten neck skin to back with skewer. Loop cord around legs, tighten slightly, and tie around a skewer inserted on the back above tail. Rub skin of goose with a little *salt*.
3. Place goose, breast down, on a rack in a shallow roasting pan.
4. Roast, uncovered, at 325°F 2½ hours, removing fat from pan several times during this period. Turn goose, breast up, and roast 45 to 60 minutes longer, or until goose tests done. To test for doneness, move leg gently by grasping end of bone. When done, drumstick-thigh joint moves easily or twists out.
5. Transfer goose to a carving board or heated serving platter while preparing Gravy, *below*. Garnish as desired. ABOUT 8 SERVINGS

GRAVY: Pour off all but ¼ cup of drippings from roasting pan. Add about *2 cups hot water*; bring to boiling, stirring to loosen browned residue. Stir in a smooth mixture of *½ cup cold water* and *¼ cup flour*. Bring to boiling and boil 1 to 2 minutes, stirring constantly. Season to taste. If desired, add *2 tablespoons currant jelly* and *cooked giblets*.

ROCK CORNISH GAME HENS

GAME HENS WITH SPICY STUFFING

3½ cups slightly dry bread cubes
½ cup chopped, drained sweet mixed pickles
½ cup chopped celery
¼ cup butter or margarine
½ cup diced dried figs
1 egg, slightly beaten
¼ teaspoon salt
⅛ teaspoon poultry seasoning
4 frozen Rock Cornish game hens (1 lb. each), thawed
2 tablespoons butter or margarine, melted

1. Toss together lightly in a bowl the bread cubes, pickles, figs, egg, salt, and poultry seasoning.
2. Sauté celery in ¼ cup butter 1 minute. Toss with bread mixture. Spoon into cavities of hens; truss and arrange securely on a spit.
3. Roast hens on rotisserie about 1 hour, or until well browned and tender, brushing occasionally with melted butter.   4 SERVINGS

LIME-GLAZED GAME HENS

½ cup butter or margarine, melted
2 tablespoons brown sugar
3 to 4 tablespoons lime juice
2 teaspoons soy sauce
4 frozen Rock Cornish game hens, 1 to 1¼ lbs. each, thawed
2 teaspoons salt

1. Blend butter, brown sugar, lime juice, and soy sauce; set aside.
2. Clean, rinse, and pat hens dry with absorbent paper. Rub cavities with salt and brush with some of the butter mixture.
3. To close cavities fasten with skewers. Skewer neck skin to backs and wings to bodies. Place hens, breast up, in a shallow roasting pan. Brush hens with butter mixture.
4. Roast, uncovered, following package directions for time and temperature. While roasting, baste hens with any remaining butter mixture. Roast until hens test done (drumstick-thigh joints move easily). Arrange hens on a warm serving platter.   4 SERVINGS

ROAST ROCK CORNISH GAME HENS

Wild Rice Stuffing, page 150
8 Rock Cornish game hens, about 1 lb. each
4 teaspoons salt
½ cup unsalted butter, melted

1. Prepare stuffing and set aside.
2. Clean, rinse, and pat game hens dry with absorbent paper. Rub cavities of the hens with the salt. Lightly fill body cavities with the stuffing. To close body cavities, sew or skewer and lace with cord. Fasten neck skin to backs and wings to bodies with skewers.
3. Place game hens, breast up, on rack in roasting pan. Brush each hen with butter (about 1 tablespoon).
4. Roast, uncovered, at 350°F; frequently baste hens during roasting period with drippings from roasting pan. Roast 1 to 1½ hours, or until hens test done. To test for doneness, move leg gently by grasping end bone; drumstick-thigh joint moves easily when hens are done. Remove skewers, if used.
5. Transfer hens to a heated serving platter and garnish with sprigs of *watercress*, or as desired.   8 SERVINGS

ROAST SQUAB: Follow directions for Roast Rock Cornish Game Hens. Substitute *squab* weighing ¾ to 1 pound each (ready-to-cook weight).

STUFFINGS FOR POULTRY

APPLE STUFFING

2 medium-sized apples, pared and diced (about 2 cups, diced)
⅓ cup chopped celery with leaves
⅓ cup chopped onion
8 cups soft bread cubes
¾ cup melted butter
2 teaspoons salt
¼ teaspoon pepper
1 teaspoon marjoram
¾ cup apple cider

1. Combine apple, celery, and onion with bread cubes in a large bowl. Toss with butter, salt, pepper, and marjoram.
2. Pour cider over bread mixture and toss until thoroughly mixed. Spoon the stuffing lightly into neck and body cavities of bird (do not pack).
   STUFFING FOR THREE 4-POUND DUCKLINGS

CHESTNUT STUFFING

¼ cup butter
1 small onion, chopped
½ cup chopped celery
1 cup soft bread crumbs
1 tablespoon chopped parsley
1 teaspoon salt
⅛ teaspoon pepper
2 lbs. chestnuts, cooked* and cut in pieces
½ cup cream

1. Heat butter in a skillet; add onion and celery; cook until onion is transparent and celery tender.
2. Remove skillet from heat. Add bread crumbs, parsley, salt, and pepper; mix well.
3. Put half of the chestnuts through a ricer or food mill; coarsely chop remaining ones.
4. Combine the chestnuts with bread mixture;

Stuffings for Poultry

drizzle cream over stuffing and toss lightly.
5. Lightly spoon stuffing into neck and body cavities of bird (do not pack). ABOUT 3⅓ CUPS STUFFING
*Roast chestnuts as directed on *page 12*. Put shelled chestnuts into boiling *salted water* to cover and boil 20 minutes, or until tender. Cool.

CORN-AND-ONION STUFFING

1 can (12 ozs.) whole-kernel corn
Turkey or chicken broth
6 cups herb-seasoned stuffing mix (about 1½ packages)
1¼ teaspoons salt
¼ teaspoon dried basil, crushed
3 cups chopped green onions
1 cup chopped celery
6 tablespoons butter or margarine

1. Drain liquid from corn into a 2-cup measure; add enough turkey or chicken broth to measure 1½ cups.
2. Combine corn, stuffing mix, salt, and basil in a large bowl.
3. Sauté green onions and celery in butter until soft in a large skillet. Stir in the 1½ cups corn liquid; heat to boiling. Pour over stuffing mixture; toss until evenly moist.
ABOUT 9 CUPS OR ENOUGH TO STUFF A 12-LB. TURKEY

OLD-FASHIONED CORNBREAD STUFFING

1 cup dark or golden seedless raisins
1½ cups thinly sliced celery
8 cups soft white-bread crumbs
6 cups cornbread crumbs
1 cup coarsely chopped salted toasted almonds
½ cup chopped parsley
1 teaspoon poultry seasoning
1 teaspoon ground nutmeg
1 teaspoon salt
½ teaspoon pepper
⅔ cup giblet broth
½ cup instant minced onion
¾ cup butter or margarine, melted
2 eggs, beaten

1. Combine raisins, celery, crumbs, almonds, and parsley. Sprinkle with a mixture of the poultry seasoning, nutmeg, salt, and pepper.
2. Add broth and onion to butter; add butter mixture and eggs to crumb mixture, mixing lightly.
3. Spoon mixture lightly into turkey; or shape into stuffing balls, place on greased baking sheet, and bake at 350°F 20 minutes, or until lightly browned.
STUFFING FOR A 15-POUND TURKEY OR 20 BALLS

HERBED STUFFING

Cooked Giblets and Broth
4 qts. ½-in. bread cubes
1 cup snipped parsley
2 to 2½ teaspoons salt
2 teaspoons thyme
2 teaspoons rosemary, crushed
2 teaspoons marjoram
1 teaspoon ground sage
1 cup butter or margarine
1 cup coarsely chopped onion
1 cup coarsely chopped celery with leaves

1. Prepare Cooked Giblets and Broth. Set aside 1 cup chopped cooked giblets and the broth.
2. In a large bowl, toss bread cubes with the reserved chopped giblets, parsley, and a mixture of salt, thyme, rosemary, marjoram, and sage.
3. Melt butter in a skillet; add chopped onion and celery. Cook over medium heat about 5 minutes, stirring occasionally. Toss with the bread mixture.
4. Add 1 to 2 cups broth (depending upon how moist a stuffing is desired), mixing lightly until ingredients are thoroughly blended. Lightly fill body and neck cavities of turkey (do not pack).
STUFFING FOR A 14- TO 15-POUND TURKEY

WILD RICE STUFFING

1 cup wild rice, cooked, *page 11*
½ lb. fresh mushrooms, sliced
2 tablespoons chopped onion
½ cup butter or margarine
½ teaspoon crushed sage leaves (optional)
Dash thyme (optional)

1. While wild rice is cooking, lightly brown the mushrooms with onion in ¼ cup heated butter in a skillet. Toss gently with the wild rice and herbs.
2. Add remaining ¼ cup butter, melted, and continue tossing until thoroughly mixed. Add *salt* and *pepper* to taste. ABOUT 4 CUPS STUFFING

APRICOT-RICE STUFFING

¼ cup orange juice
¼ cup butter or margarine, melted
½ teaspoon salt
¼ teaspoon pepper
⅛ teaspoon thyme
⅛ teaspoon ground nutmeg
⅛ teaspoon ground cloves
3½ cups cooked rice
1 cup finely chopped dried apricots
¼ cup finely chopped onion
¼ cup finely chopped celery
2 tablespoons finely chopped parsley

Combine all ingredients in a large bowl. Toss lightly until thoroughly mixed. ABOUT 5 CUPS STUFFING

Chapter 7
FISH & SHELLFISH

Fish and shellfish have always been highly prized as delicious food by those who have had access to fresh supplies. Refrigerated shipping facilities now make supplies available to everyone.

Fish are especially valuable for their excellent sources of highly digestible protein and for their fine mineral and vitamin content. Fat fish, such as salmon and mackerel, are rich in both vitamins A and D.

Research has determined that the fish flesh of all species is approximately equal in nutritional properties. The homemaker can, therefore, determine her choice by flavor, texture, and color.

FISH

AVAILABILITY

Fresh fish are best prepared as soon as possible after being caught. When fresh, they have red gills, bright eyes, and bright-colored scales adhering tightly. The flesh is firm and elastic, and practically free from odor. Fresh fish should be packed in ice until purchased; at home, wrap in foil or moisture-vaporproof material and store in the refrigerator.

Frozen fish is available the year around in market forms such as steaks, fillets, and sticks. It should be solidly frozen and *never refrozen after thawing.*

Salted fish are prepared either by "dry-salting" or by pickling in a brine. Firm, coarse-fleshed fish such as cod, hake, and haddock are dry-salted by packing in dry salt after cleaning. Fat and oily fish are "salted" in brine, then are frequently smoked. Finnan Haddie is prepared in this way.

Smoked fish is a delicacy; salmon, whitefish, and haddock are popular varieties. It is usually eaten without further cooking.

Canned fish is easy to store and convenient to serve. Sardines, tuna, cod, salmon, mackerel, and kippered herring are some of the varieties.

STORAGE

To store fresh fish, wrap the whole fish or fillets or steaks in moisture-vaporproof material or in waxed paper. Use fish the same day as purchased, if possible. Place in freezer if fish is not to be used in one or two days.

BAKED FISH WITH SHRIMP STUFFING

1 dressed whitefish, bass, or lake trout, 2 to 3 lbs.
1 cup chopped cooked shrimp
1 cup chopped fresh mushrooms
1 cup soft bread crumbs
½ cup chopped celery
¼ cup chopped onion
2 tablespoons chopped parsley
¾ teaspoon salt
Few grains pepper
½ teaspoon thyme
¼ cup melted butter or margarine
2 to 3 tablespoons apple cider
2 tablespoons melted butter or margarine

1. Rinse fish under cold water; drain well and pat dry with absorbent paper. Sprinkle fish cavity generously with *salt.*

2. Combine in a bowl the shrimp, mushrooms, bread crumbs, celery, onion, parsley, salt, pepper, and thyme. Gradually pour ¼ cup melted butter over bread mixture, tossing lightly.
3. Lightly pile stuffing into fish. Fasten with skewers and lace with cord. Place fish in a greased shallow baking pan and brush with a mixture of the cider and 2 tablespoons melted butter.
4. Bake at 375°F, brushing occasionally with cider mixture, 25 to 30 minutes, or until fish flakes easily when pierced with a fork. If desired, place fish under broiler 3 to 5 minutes.
5. Transfer to a heated platter and remove skewers and cord. Garnish platter with sprigs of *parsley*. Serve with *scalloped potatoes* and *buttered French-style green beans*. 4 TO 6 SERVINGS

FLOUNDER STUFFED WITH CRAB MEAT
This truly memorable baked fish dish is served at the Ben Gross Restaurant, Irwin, Pennsylvania.

1 lb. lump crab meat, bony membrane removed
1 slice white bread, crusts trimmed and bread cut in ¼-in. cubes
3 tablespoons lemon juice
1 tablespoon dry sherry
¾ teaspoon Worcestershire sauce
¼ teaspoon Tabasco
¾ teaspoon salt
¾ teaspoon dry mustard
⅛ teaspoon seasoned salt
1 cup Medium White Sauce, *page 196*
1 egg yolk
Butter
4 fresh flounder fillets (about 2 lbs.) with pockets cut in sides

1. Combine the crab meat (do not break up lumps) with bread cubes, lemon juice, sherry, Worcestershire sauce, Tabasco, salt, dry mustard, and seasoned salt. Mix gently; add a mixture of the white sauce and egg yolk. Continue tossing lightly.
2. Butter flounder and fill pockets with the crab meat stuffing. Put into a shallow baking dish. Sprinkle generously with *paprika*.
3. Bake at 350°F 10 to 12 minutes and brown under broiler before serving. 4 SERVINGS

BAKED RESTIGOUCHE SALMON BREVAL
The chef de cuisine of the Royal York Hotel, Toronto, Canada, contributed this recipe. Restigouche salmon, noted for its fine texture and delicate flavor, comes from the wide, scenic Restigouche River in the province of New Brunswick, Canada. It normally commands a high price due to a short fishing season and a limited supply. If this salmon is not available, substitute any salmon steaks.

4 Restigouche salmon steaks, 8 oz. each
1 cup sliced fresh mushrooms
4 green onions, finely chopped
2 tomatoes, peeled and finely diced
1 tablespoon lemon juice
1 cup dry white wine
¾ cup fish stock or water
3 tablespoons butter
2 tablespoons flour
1 egg yolk, beaten
⅓ cup heavy cream, whipped
1 tablespoon chopped parsley

1. Place fish in a buttered shallow baking dish; sprinkle with *salt* and *pepper*.
2. Combine the mushrooms, green onions, tomatoes, and lemon juice and spoon over the steaks.
3. Bring wine and stock to boiling and pour over steaks. Cover with buttered brown paper.
4. Bake at 350°F about 20 minutes. Remove salmon to heat-resistant platter; trim off skin and remove center bones.
5. Pour liquid into a saucepan, set over low heat and reduce liquid by one third. Blend butter and flour, add to liquid and cook, stirring until smooth and thickened.
6. Stir a little sauce into beaten egg yolk and blend into hot mixture; cook about 1 minute. Fold in whipped cream and parsley. Remove from heat immediately and taste for seasoning, adding *salt* and *cayenne pepper* as needed. Pour sauce over fish.
7. Place under broiler 2 to 3 minutes to glaze to a golden color. 4 SERVINGS

FISH FILLETS VIENNESE

2 lbs. fresh or thawed frozen sole fillets
1 teaspoon salt
4 teaspoons lemon juice
1½ cups dairy sour cream
6 slices bacon, diced, panbroiled, and drained
¾ cup diced cucumber
1 tablespoon capers

* Harvest Pork (page 97)

1 tablespoon prepared English mustard	¼ cup shredded Parmesan cheese
1 tablespoon flour	

1. Sprinkle fish evenly with salt. Arrange one third of the fish fillets in a buttered 2-quart shallow casserole. Sprinkle evenly with the lemon juice.
2. Combine sour cream, mustard, and *few grains salt*, and blend in the flour.
3. Cover fish fillets with one third of sour cream mixture. Top with one third of bacon, one fourth cup of cucumber, and 1 teaspoon capers; repeat twice. Top with cheese.
4. Bake at 375°F about 25 minutes.

6 TO 8 SERVINGS

RED SNAPPER WITH OYSTER STUFFING

1 whole red snapper, weighing about 4½ lbs., dressed	1 can (8 ozs.) oysters ½ cup light cream 2 tablespoons chopped parsley
1 medium onion, chopped (½ cup)	Salt
½ cup chopped celery	4 cups coarsely crushed unsalted soda crackers
6 tablespoons butter or margarine	

1. Wash snapper inside and out; pat dry with paper toweling.
2. Sauté onion and celery in 4 tablespoons of the butter until soft in a medium skillet.
3. Drain liquid from oysters into a small bowl; stir in cream; stir into onion mixture with parsley and ½ teaspoon salt. Drizzle over crackers in a large bowl; add oysters; toss lightly until evenly moistened.
4. Preheat oven to 350°F.
5. Sprinkle snapper lightly inside and out with salt; stuff oyster mixture into cavity; close opening with wooden picks. Place in a greased large shallow baking pan.
6. Melt remaining 2 tablespoons butter in a small skillet; brush part over snapper.
7. Bake, brushing once or twice more with remaining melted butter, 45 minutes, or until fish flakes easily when tested with a fork.
8. Lift snapper onto a large serving platter. Garnish top with thin slices of lemon and edge with parsley if you like.

6 SERVINGS

NOTE: If you have any stuffing leftover, spoon it into a casserole, cover, and bake in the same oven with fish for 35 minutes.

Sauce-Crowned Meat Ring (page 121)

Some fish markets will also be happy to bone the fish for you if you like, or you can do it yourself this way: make a cut along each inside edge of the backbone, snipping through rib bones with poultry shears just deep enough to loosen the bone. (Be careful not to cut through the meat on the back.) Next cut through the backbone at each end, then carefully pull out the backbone, scraping meat away from the bone with a knife as you go.

POMPANO FLORENTINE

Mornay Sauce, *page 197*	2 tablespoons lemon juice
1 pkg. (10 oz.) frozen chopped spinach	1 teaspoon salt
4 pompano fillets, 6 oz. each	⅛ teaspoon black pepper
¼ cup butter or margarine, melted	

1. Prepare Mornay Sauce; set aside. Cook spinach according to package directions.
2. Meanwhile, place pompano fillets, skin side down, on a greased broiler rack. Brush with one half of a mixture of the butter and lemon juice. Broil 2 inches from source of heat about 8 minutes, or until fish flakes easily. During broiling, brush fillets with remaining butter mixture.
3. When spinach is tender, drain thoroughly. Combine with 1 cup of the Mornay Sauce; keep hot.
4. When fillets are done, sprinkle with a mixture of salt and pepper. Spoon about ¾ cup Mornay Sauce over fillets. Broil 2 to 3 minutes, or just until sauce is lightly browned.
5. Arrange spinach mixture in four servings on a heated serving platter. Carefully place fillets over the spinach. Pour remaining Mornay Sauce around fillets. Garnish platter with *parsley sprigs* and *lemon wedges*.

4 SERVINGS

BROILED TROUT

Purchase one 8- to 10-ounce *trout* for each serving; if desired, remove head and fins. Rinse trout quickly under cold running water and dry thoroughly. Brush cavity of fish with tart *French dressing* and sprinkle generously with *instant minced onion* and *salt*. Brush trout generously with French dressing and arrange in a greased large shallow baking pan or on a broiler rack.

Fish

Broil trout about 3 inches from source of heat 5 to 8 minutes on each side, or until fish flakes easily; brush with dressing during broiling. Remove trout to heated platter.

FLOUNDER DINNER AU GRATIN

2 packages (10 ozs. each) frozen cut asparagus	½ teaspoon salt
	Dash of pepper
4 flounder fillets, weighing about 1 lb.	1 cup shredded sharp Cheddar cheese (4 ozs.)
2 tablespoons butter or margarine	⅓ cup evaporated milk
	½ teaspoon dry mustard
1 tablespoon lime juice	

1. Preheat broiler.
2. Cook asparagus as label directs; drain well. Spoon into a broilerproof baking dish to make a layer. (Or spoon into 4 individual baking dishes.)
3. Grease rack on broiler pan; place flounder in a single layer on rack.
4. Melt butter in a small saucepan; stir in lime juice. Brush generously over flounder; sprinkle salt and pepper over top.
5. Broil, 6 inches from heat, 5 minutes; brush remaining butter mixture over top.
6. Broil 2 minutes longer, or until flounder flakes easily when tested with a fork. Arrange over asparagus in dish.
7. While flounder cooks, combine cheese, evaporated milk, and mustard in a small saucepan; heat very slowly, stirring constantly, until cheese melts and is smooth; spoon in a ribbon over flounder.
8. Broil, 6 inches from heat, 4 minutes, or until sauce bubbles up and browns lightly. Garnish with lime slices if you like.   4 SERVINGS

FISH FILLETS MORNAY

2 lbs. fresh or frozen fish fillets, thawed	⅛ teaspoon pepper
	Butter or margarine
½ cup yellow cornmeal	Toasted blanched almonds
1½ teaspoons salt	
	Mornay Sauce, *page 197*

1. Cut the fillets into serving-sized pieces. Coat with a mixture of cornmeal, salt, and pepper.
2. Fry in hot butter in a skillet until crisp and browned on both sides.
3. Serve fish, topped with almonds, on heated platter; surround with the sauce. ABOUT 6 SERVINGS

HALIBUT PARMESAN

6 fresh or frozen halibut steaks, weighing about 2 lbs.	1 tablespoon minced onion
	1 tablespoon lemon juice
	½ teaspoon salt
1 cup (8 oz. carton) dairy sour cream	Paprika
¼ cup grated Parmesan cheese	

1. Preheat oven to 375°F.
2. Place steaks in a single layer in a greased shallow baking dish.
3. Mix sour cream, cheese, onion, lemon juice, and salt in a small bowl; spread over steaks; sprinkle paprika generously on top.
4. Bake 25 minutes, or until halibut flakes easily when tested with a fork. Place on a large serving platter. Garnish with clusters of watercress if you like.   6 SERVINGS

CODFISH CAKES

1 lb. salt codfish	2 eggs, beaten
4 to 6 medium-sized potatoes (about 2 lbs.)	½ teaspoon paprika
	⅛ teaspoon pepper
2 tablespoons butter or margarine	Fat for deep frying heated to 365°F

1. Cover codfish with cold water to freshen. Let stand in the cold water at least 4 hours; change water 3 or 4 times during that period. (Or follow directions on package.) Drain fish and remove any pieces of bone. Flake and set aside.
2. Wash, pare, and cut potatoes into pieces. Combine fish and potatoes in a saucepan. Cook covered, in boiling water to cover, about 20 minutes, or until potatoes are tender.
3. Thoroughly drain and mash potatoes and fish. Whip in the butter and a mixture of the eggs, paprika, and pepper until mixture is fluffy.
4. Deep fry by dropping spoonfuls of the mixture into the hot fat. Drop only as many at one time as will float uncrowded one layer deep. Turn cakes as they brown, cooking each 2 to 5 minutes or until golden brown. Drain on absorbent paper.
5. Serve with a *tomato sauce* or *cream sauce*.
                6 SERVINGS

FRIED SMELTS

2 doz. smelts	Fine bread crumbs
1 egg, beaten	Fat for deep frying
1 tablespoon water	heated to 360°F

1. Clean the smelts, leaving on the heads and tails; rinse and pat dry.
2. Sprinkle with *salt* and *pepper*; shake in a bag with *flour*; dip in a mixture of the egg and water; roll in crumbs. Let stand about 15 minutes.
3. Fry smelts without crowding in heated fat 3 to 4 minutes. Drain on absorbent paper.
4. Garnish with *parsley*; serve with *tartar sauce*.

4 SERVINGS

SCALLOPED HADDOCK EN COQUILLES

1 medium onion, peeled and sliced	2 tablespoons all-purpose flour
2 lemon slices	1½ teaspoons dry mustard
3 sprigs of parsley	Few drops red-pepper seasoning
1 bay leaf	
1½ teaspoons salt	2 cups milk
3 cups water	1 tablespoon lemon juice
1 lb. haddock	1 cup fresh bread crumbs (2 slices)
2 tablespoons butter or margarine	3 hard-cooked eggs

1. Combine onion, lemon slices, parsley, bay leaf, ½ teaspoon of the salt, and water in a large skillet; heat to boiling. Add haddock; cover. Poach 5 minutes, or until fish flakes easily when tested with a fork; drain; cool. Break fish into large flakes, removing any bones.
2. Preheat oven to 350°F.
3. Melt butter in a large saucepan; stir in flour, mustard, red-pepper seasoning, and remaining 1 teaspoon salt; cook, stirring constantly, until bubbly.
4. Stir in milk; continue cooking and stirring until sauce thickens and boils 1 minute; remove from heat. Stir in lemon juice, haddock, and ½ cup of the bread crumbs.
5. Chop 1½ eggs; fold into fish mixture; spoon into 4 large scallop shells. Sprinkle remaining ½ cup bread crumbs on top. For easy handling, set shells in a large shallow pan.
6. Bake 20 minutes, or until bubbly and topping is golden.
7. Slice remaining 1½ eggs; arrange over shells as a garnish.

4 SERVINGS

CORNMEAL-CRUSTED MOUNTAIN TROUT

Pour *peanut oil*, to a depth of ½ inch, into a skillet and heat oil to 350°F. Meanwhile, rinse and dry *trout* (do not scale); allow 1 trout per person. Coat trout with a mixture of *cornmeal* and *salt* and *pepper* to taste. Place in hot oil (do not crowd) and cook until golden on both sides, turning only once.

POACHED SALMON AROMATIC

Salmon poached in a well-seasoned court bouillon was one of the reasons for Anthony Dardanelli's fine reputation as a gourmet chef in one of Philadelphia, Pennsylvania's hotel dining rooms.

2 qts. water	2 whole cloves
1 teaspoon salt	¼ stick cinnamon
1 cup cider vinegar	¼ teaspoon oregano
½ medium-sized onion	¼ teaspoon thyme
½ carrot, cut in pieces	¼ teaspoon rosemary
½ stalk celery, cut in pieces	¼ teaspoon basil
1 large clove garlic	⅛ teaspoon nutmeg
2 bay leaves	6 salmon steaks

1. Combine in a large kettle the water, salt, vinegar, vegetables, and spices and herbs (tied in a square of cheesecloth). Bring to boiling; cook 10 minutes.
2. Tie salmon in cheesecloth and place in boiling bouillon. Allow to simmer about 12 minutes.
3. Remove salmon from bouillon and serve with *lemon wedges* and *Hollandaise Sauce, page 197*.

6 SERVINGS

CRAB-STUFFED SOLE

1 package (6 ozs.) frozen Alaska king crab meat	3 tablespoons butter or margarine
1½ cups fresh bread crumbs (3 slices)	2 tablespoons lemon juice
1 egg, beaten	1 package (1 oz.) white wine sauce mix
½ teaspoon salt	Milk
6 fillets of sole, weighing about 1½ lbs.	Water
	⅛ teaspoon dried tarragon, crushed

1. Thaw crab meat and drain well; flake in a medium bowl. Stir in bread crumbs, egg, and salt until well blended.
2. Preheat oven to 375°F.

Fish

3. Lay fillets flat on waxed paper. Spread crab mixture over each; roll up, jelly-roll fashion; fasten with wooden picks. Place rolls, seam side down, in a shallow baking dish. Dot 2 tablespoons of the butter over top, then sprinkle lemon juice over all; cover.
4. Bake 20 minutes, or until fish flakes easily when tested with a fork.
5. While rolls cook, prepare sauce mix with milk, water, and remaining 1 tablespoon butter in a small saucepan; stir in tarragon.
6. Place rolls around edge on a large serving platter. Pour sauce into a small bowl; place in center. Or serve rolls on a bed of buttered carrots and lima beans; spoon some of the sauce over rolls, then serve remainder separately. 6 SERVINGS

SAVORY SALMON KABOBS

1 can (16 oz.) salmon, drained and flaked	¼ cup finely chopped onion
1 egg, slightly beaten	¼ teaspoon Worcestershire sauce
1 cup shredded Cheddar cheese	⅛ teaspoon Tabasco
½ cup fine dry bread crumbs	¼ cup butter

1. Combine in a bowl all ingredients except the butter. Divide mixture into 6 portions and press firmly around wooden skewers into oblong shapes.
2. Melt butter over medium heat in a large heavy skillet. Add kabobs and brown evenly, turning frequently. Serve with *Tangy Cheese-Broccoli Sauce, below*. 6 SERVINGS

TANGY CHEESE-BROCCOLI SAUCE

2 tablespoons butter	1 tablespoon lemon juice
2 tablespoons flour	1 teaspoon Worcestershire sauce
½ teaspoon salt	
1 can (14½ oz.) evaporated milk	1 pkg. (10 oz.) frozen chopped broccoli, cooked and drained
1 cup shredded Cheddar cheese	

1. Melt butter in a heavy saucepan over medium heat. Blend in a mixture of the flour and salt; cook until bubbly. Remove from heat and add evaporated milk gradually, stirring constantly. Return to heat; cook and stir until sauce comes to boiling and is thickened and smooth. Cook 1 to 2 minutes.
2. Reduce heat to low and stir in the cheese, lemon juice, Worcestershire sauce, and cooked broccoli; heat only until cheese is melted.
3. Serve immediately over salmon kabobs.
ABOUT 3½ CUPS SAUCE

GOLDEN TUNA FLORENTINE

2 packages (10 ozs. each) spinach	¼ teaspoon dry mustard
7 tablespoons butter or margarine	2 cups milk
	1 cup shredded sharp Cheddar cheese (4 ozs.)
1 cup fresh bread crumbs (2 slices)	2 cans (about 7 ozs. each) tuna, drained and broken into chunks
4 tablespoons all-purpose flour	2 medium tomatoes, sliced thin
Salt	
¼ teaspoon pepper	

1. Wash spinach thoroughly; dry well with paper toweling; chop coarsely.
2. Melt butter in a medium saucepan; measure out 2 tablespoons and toss with bread crumbs in a small bowl. Measure 1 tablespoon into a cup and set aside.
3. Stir flour, ½ teaspoon salt, pepper, and mustard into rest of butter in saucepan; cook, stirring constantly, until bubbly. Stir in milk; continue cooking and stirring until sauce thickens and boils 1 minute; stir in cheese until melted.
4. Preheat oven to 350°F.
5. Place tuna in a 2-quart shallow baking dish to make a layer; spoon half of the cheese sauce over top.
6. Stir rest of sauce into spinach in a medium bowl; spread in an even layer over tuna; sprinkle buttered bread crumbs on top.
7. Bake 25 minutes, or until bubbly. Arrange tomato slices, overlapping, around edge in dish; brush remaining 1 tablespoon melted butter over slices; sprinkle lightly with salt.
8. Bake 10 minutes longer, or just until tomatoes are hot. 6 SERVINGS

SKILLET TUNA SUPREME

Serve your family this quick-as-a-wink entrée with a flourish — it's mighty fine eating.

⅔ cup chopped onion	2 to 3 tablespoons brown sugar
1 green pepper, cut in slivers	1 teaspoon grated lemon peel
2 tablespoons cooking or salad oil	

1 can (10¾ oz.) condensed tomato soup	3 tablespoons lemon juice
2 teaspoons soy sauce	2 cans (6½ or 7 oz. each) tuna, drained

1. Cook onion and green pepper until almost tender in hot oil in a large skillet; stir occasionally.
2. Mix in the tomato soup, soy sauce, brown sugar, and lemon peel and juice. Bring to boiling; simmer 5 minutes.
3. Mix in the tuna, separating it into small pieces. Heat thoroughly.
4. Serve with fluffy hot *cooked rice*. Garnish with *toasted sesame seed* and *chow mein noodles*.

ABOUT 6 SERVINGS

DEVILED SALMON

2 cans (8 ozs. each) salmon	1 teaspoon salt
1 cup thinly sliced celery	3 cups milk
4 tablespoons butter or margarine	Few drops red-pepper seasoning
¼ cup all-purpose flour	1 tablespoon lemon juice
2 tablespoons prepared hot mustard	3 hard-cooked eggs, diced
	1½ cups coarsely crushed saltines

1. Drain liquid from salmon; remove bones and skin; break salmon into chunks.
2. Preheat oven to 350°F.
3. Sauté celery in butter until soft in a medium saucepan; stir in flour; cook, stirring constantly, until bubbly. Stir in mustard, salt, milk, and red-pepper seasoning; continue cooking and stirring until mixture thickens and boils 1 minute; remove from heat. Stir in lemon juice; fold in salmon and eggs.
4. Spoon about one third into a 1½-quart baking dish; top with one third of the cracker crumbs. Repeat layers.
5. Bake 45 minutes, or until bubbly. Garnish with hard-cooked egg quarters and parsley if you like.

6 SERVINGS

YANKEE DOODLE TUNA BAKE

2 cans (10¾ ozs. each) condensed cream of celery soup	1 package (8 ozs.) process American cheese, shredded
2 cups milk	3 hard-cooked eggs, sliced
1 package (8 ozs.) spaghetti, broken into 2-inch lengths	1 can (4 ozs.) sliced pimientos, drained and diced

2 cans (about 7 ozs. each) tuna, drained and broken into chunks	1 medium onion, chopped (½ cup)
	⅓ cup grated Romano cheese

1. Preheat oven to 375°F.
2. Blend soup and milk in a large bowl; stir in spaghetti, tuna, shredded cheese, eggs, pimientos, and onion; mix well. Spoon into a 3-quart baking dish; cover tightly.
3. Bake 1 hour and 15 minutes; uncover. Sprinkle Romano cheese on top.
4. Bake 10 minutes longer, or until cheese browns lightly.

8 SERVINGS

FISH STICK SPECIAL

1 pkg. (10 oz.) frozen fish sticks	2 tablespoons chopped onion
¼ cup chopped toasted almonds	¼ cup milk
1 cup shredded Cheddar cheese	½ cup chopped sweet mixed pickles
	2 tablespoons buttered dry bread crumbs

1. Arrange fish sticks in a shallow baking dish.
2. Mix the remaining ingredients except bread crumbs and spoon over fish. Top with crumbs.
3. Heat in a 425°F oven 15 to 20 minutes.

ABOUT 4 SERVINGS

TUNA EMPANADAS

1 can (about 7 ozs.) tuna	¼ cup mayonnaise or salad dressing
1 hard-cooked egg, chopped	1 package refrigerated flaky biscuits
1 small onion, chopped (¼ cup)	1 small can evaporated milk (⅔ cup)
2 tablespoons chopped parsley	⅓ cup water
½ teaspoon salt	4 slices process American cheese, cut up
Few drops red-pepper seasoning	½ teaspoon Worcestershire sauce

1. Preheat oven to 400°F.
2. Drain liquid from tuna; flake tuna in a medium bowl. Stir in egg, onion, parsley, salt, red-pepper seasoning, and mayonnaise until blended.
3. Separate biscuits; roll each to a 5-inch round on a lightly floured cloth; spoon a scant 2 tablespoons of the tuna mixture onto half of each. Moisten one edge

of each round and fold dough over to cover filling completely; press edges with a fork to seal. Cut several slits in top of each to let steam escape; place on a cookie sheet.
4. Bake 15 minutes, or until golden.
5. While turnovers bake, combine evaporated milk, water, cheese, and Worcestershire sauce in a small saucepan; heat slowly, stirring constantly, until cheese melts and sauce is smooth and hot.
6. Place turnovers on serving plates; spoon cheese sauce over top. 4 TO 6 SERVINGS

PALOS VERDES STEW

1 medium onion, chopped (½ cup)
2 tablespoons salad oil
1 can (10¾ ozs.) condensed tomato soup
1 can (8 ozs.) green peas
1 can (12 ozs.) Mexican-style corn
1 can (about 7 ozs.) tuna, drained and broken into chunks
¼ teaspoon dried basil, crushed
¼ teaspoon salt
1 cup packaged precooked rice

1. Sauté onion in salad oil until soft in a medium saucepan. Stir in tomato soup, peas and liquid, corn and liquid, tuna, basil, and salt. Heat to boiling; simmer 10 minutes.
2. Prepare rice as label directs; spoon onto serving plates; spoon tuna mixture on top. 4 SERVINGS

CREOLE COD

2 packages (16 ozs. each) frozen cod, partly thawed
1 large green pepper, quartered, seeded, and diced (1 cup)
4 tablespoons butter or margarine
1 can (8 ozs.) tomato sauce
1 teaspoon dried thyme, crushed
1 medium onion, chopped (½ cup)
½ cup thinly sliced celery
1 teaspoon salt
⅛ teaspoon pepper

1. Preheat oven to 350°F.
2. Cut cod into 6 serving-sized blocks; place in a single layer in a 12x8x2-inch baking dish.
3. Sauté green pepper, onion, and celery in butter until soft in a large skillet; stir in tomato sauce, thyme, salt, and pepper; heat, stirring several times, to boiling. Spoon over fish; cover.
4. Bake 45 minutes, or until fish flakes easily when tested with a fork. Serve from baking dish with small whole white potatoes and thin cucumber slices if you like. 6 SERVINGS

FISH AND CHIPS

1 package (9 ozs.) frozen fish sticks
1 package (9 ozs.) frozen French fried potatoes
½ cup mayonnaise or salad dressing
1 teaspoon prepared mustard
1 tablespoon catsup
1 tablespoon cider vinegar
2 small sweet pickles, minced

1. Preheat oven to 425°F.
2. Place fish sticks and frozen potatoes in separate shallow baking pans; heat in oven as labels direct.
3. While fish heats, mix mayonnaise, mustard, catsup, vinegar, and pickles in a small bowl; place in center of a large serving plate. Arrange fish sticks and potatoes around edge. To serve, let everyone pick up fish and potatoes in his fingers and dip into sauce.
4 SERVINGS

SHELLFISH

Clams

There are two general types of clams, the soft clams and the hard or quahog clams. The latter group is divided into three classes: the littlenecks, small in size; the cherrystones, medium-sized; and the large chowder clams. The littleneck and cherrystone clams may be used raw.

When purchased, the shells should be tightly closed or should close at a touch. They may be opened with a knife or be steamed open.

PAELLA

1 cup olive or other cooking oil
1 broiler-fryer chicken, 2 lbs., cut up
½ cup diced boiled ham or smoky sausage
1 tablespoon minced onion
2 cloves garlic, minced
2 ripe tomatoes, peeled and coarsely chopped
1½ teaspoons salt
1½ lbs. fresh shrimp, shelled and deveined
12 small clams in shells, scrubbed
2 cups uncooked long grain white rice
4 cups hot water
1 cup fresh or frozen green peas
¼ cup coarsely chopped parsley
Few shreds saffron
1 rock lobster tail, cooked and meat cut in pieces, or 1 pkg. frozen crab meat, thawed and drained
1 can or jar (7 oz.) whole pimientos

1. Heat oil in paellera or large skillet; cook chicken and ham about 10 minutes, turning chicken to brown on all sides. Add onion and garlic and cook 2 minutes. Add tomatoes, salt, shrimp, and clams; cover and cook 5 to 10 minutes, or until clam shells open. Remove clams and keep warm.
2. Stir in rice, water, peas, parsley, and saffron. Cover and cook, stirring occasionally, 25 minutes, or until rice is just tender. Mix in the lobster, half of the pimiento, and the reserved clams in shells; heat until very hot. Serve garnished with remaining pimiento.   8 TO 10 SERVINGS

CLAM PIE

3 tablespoons butter or margarine
½ cup chopped onion
2 tablespoons flour
½ teaspoon salt
3 cans (7½ oz. each) minced clams, drained (reserve ½ cup liquid)
½ cup milk
1 can (16 oz.) whole cooked potatoes, drained and diced
2 tablespoons snipped parsley
Pastry for a 1-crust 8-in. pie

1. Heat butter in a large skillet; add the onion and cook until transparent.
2. Blend in flour, salt, and a *few grains pepper*. Heat until bubbly. Add the reserved clam liquid and the milk gradually, stirring constantly. Bring to boiling; cook and stir 1 to 2 minutes.
3. Remove from heat. Mix in potatoes, clams, and parsley. Turn into an 8-inch pie pan.
4. Prepare pastry and roll out to fit over clam mixture. Cut a simple design near center of pastry to allow steam to escape during baking. Place pastry on clam mixture and flute edge.
5. Bake at 450°F about 20 minutes, or until pastry is lightly browned.   4 TO 6 SERVINGS

Crabs & Crab Meat

Crabs are generally divided into two classes, the hard-shelled crab and the soft-shelled crab. The latter is not a different variety, but merely a crab caught after it has shed its shell and before it has developed a new one. Crabs when purchased alive should be vigorous and lively. The cooked crab meat may be purchased iced or frozen (it is very perishable) or in cans. Soft-shelled crabs are usually fried or broiled, while the hard-shelled crabs are boiled and the meat removed for use in various dishes.

CRAB MEAT À LA SARDI
From Sardi's in New York City.

1½ cups cooked crab meat (bony tissue removed)
¼ cup sherry, warmed
12 asparagus spears, cooked just tender
1 cup Sardi Sauce, *below*
2 tablespoons grated Parmesan cheese

1. Sprinkle crab meat with sherry; set aside for 10 minutes.
2. Turn crab-sherry mixture into a heated shallow baking dish; arrange asparagus spears on the top, cover with Sardi Sauce, and sprinkle with cheese.
3. Place under broiler until cheese is lightly browned, and serve piping hot.   2 SERVINGS

SARDI SAUCE

½ cup sherry
¼ cup light cream
1¾ cups Sauce Velouté, *page 160*
½ cup Hollandaise Sauce, *page 197*
½ cup whipped cream

1. Reduce sherry by cooking it rapidly 3 minutes; heat light cream.
2. Add reduced sherry and heated cream to Sauce Velouté; let cool.
3. Fold in Hollandaise Sauce and whipped cream.   ABOUT 3 CUPS SAUCE

Shellfish

SAUCE VELOUTÉ (Sardi's): Make a white roux by melting ½ *cup butter* and blending with about ½ *cup all-purpose flour.* Cook and stir until bubbly but do not allow it to color. Add about *5 cups white veal broth,* a little at a time, stirring constantly with a whisk. Bring to boiling and continue cooking slowly for 30 minutes without stirring. Season the sauce very lightly since it is the basis for a number of white sauces. As soon as it is done remove all fat and strain into a bowl through a pointed sieve. While it cools stir from time to time to prevent a skin from forming. It will keep well for several days in the refrigerator. Store in freezer if kept for a longer period.

CRAB MEAT AU GRATIN
A delicately rich dish—excellent with broccoli or asparagus accented with browned butter sauce.

½ cup butter	2 tablespoons grated
⅔ cup all-purpose flour	onion
2 teaspoons salt	⅓ cup slivered blanched
2⅔ cups milk	almonds, toasted
2 cans (6½ oz. each) crab meat, drained and separated in pieces	4 hard-cooked eggs, chopped
	1 cup shredded sharp Cheddar cheese
4 cups chopped celery	1 tablespoon butter
½ cup chopped green pepper	2½ cups small bread cubes
2 pimientos, drained and chopped	

1. Heat ½ cup butter in a saucepan. Add a mixture of the flour and salt; blend well. Heat until bubbly, stirring constantly. Gradually add milk, stirring until blended. Bring to boiling; cook and stir 1 to 2 minutes.
2. Mix crab meat, celery, green pepper, pimiento, onion, almonds, and eggs into sauce. Turn into a 2-quart shallow casserole. Sprinkle with cheese.
3. Heat 1 tablespoon butter in a skillet. Add bread cubes and toss until coated. Spoon cubes over casserole.
4. Heat in a 350°F oven 35 minutes. If desired, garnish with slices of *hard-cooked eggs.*

8 TO 10 SERVINGS

CRAB SOUFFLE

1 can (6½ ozs.) crab meat	½ teaspoon salt
	1½ cups milk
1 tablespoon grated onion	6 eggs, separated
4 tablespoons butter or margarine	Swiss Cheese Sauce
4 tablespoons all-purpose flour	

1. Drain liquid from crab meat; flake meat fine.
2. Sauté onion in butter in a medium saucepan until soft; stir in flour and salt. Cook, stirring constantly, until bubbly. Stir in milk; continue cooking and stirring until sauce thickens and boils 1 minute; cool while beating eggs.
3. Preheat oven to 350°F.
4. Beat egg whites in a medium bowl until they stand in soft peaks. Beat egg yolks in a large bowl until thick and creamy; slowly beat in cooled sauce and crab; fold in beaten egg whites. Pour into a 2½-quart soufflé dish; gently run a spatula through mixture 1 inch in from edge of dish.
5. Bake 50 minutes, or until puffed and firm in center. Serve at once with Swiss Cheese Sauce. 6 SERVINGS

CRAB RAVIGOTE
A recipe from Brennan's Restaurant in New Orleans.

2 tablespoons butter	⅓ cup coarsely chopped pimiento
2 tablespoons flour	1 tablespoon capers
½ teaspoon salt	1 teaspoon tarragon vinegar
Few grains cayenne pepper	
1 cup milk	1 cup lump crab meat
⅓ cup chopped cooked green pepper	⅓ cup Hollandaise Sauce, *page 197*

1. Heat butter in a saucepan; blend in flour, salt, and cayenne pepper and heat until bubbly. Gradually add milk, stirring constantly. Cook and stir until boiling; cook 1 minute.
2. Stir in remaining ingredients and heat thoroughly.
3. Serve in 8-ounce individual casseroles or on *rusks.* 2 SERVINGS

CRAB DIVAN

1 package (10 ozs.) frozen broccoli spears	1 tablespoon minced onion
1 can (7 ozs.) crab meat	½ teaspoon salt

Shellfish

2 hard-cooked eggs, diced
1 tablespoon butter or margarine
1 tablespoon all-purpose flour
1 cup milk
2 egg whites
¼ cup mayonnaise or salad dressing
2 tablespoons lemon juice

1. Cook broccoli as label directs; drain well; place in 4 large scallop shells. For easy handling, set shells in a large shallow pan.
2. Drain liquid from crab. Break meat into small chunks in a medium bowl; add diced eggs.
3. Preheat oven to 350°F.
4. Melt butter in a small saucepan; stir in flour, onion, and salt; cook, stirring constantly, until blended. Stir in milk; continue cooking and stirring until mixture thickens and boils 1 minute. Fold into crab-meat mixture; spoon evenly over broccoli.
5. Beat egg whites in a small bowl until they form firm peaks; fold in mayonnaise and lemon juice. Spoon over crab mixture.
6. Bake 30 minutes, or until topping is puffed and golden. 4 SERVINGS

BOOKY BAKED CRAB

This recipe is from Bookbinder's Sea Food House, Philadelphia, Pennsylvania.

½ cup butter
¾ cup all-purpose flour
1 cup milk
3 egg yolks, beaten
Few grains salt
Few grains pepper
Pinch dry mustard
1 teaspoon Worcestershire sauce
3 lbs. large lump crab meat

1. Melt butter in a saucepan; stir in flour to make a paste. Remove from heat and stir in the milk.
2. Cook and stir until very thick and smooth. Blend a little sauce into egg yolks and return to sauce; mix well. Mix in the salt, pepper, dry mustard, Worcestershire sauce, and the crab meat.
3. Form into 6 patties and place in a shallow baking dish.
4. Bake at 350°F 15 to 20 minutes. 6 SERVINGS

CRAB STRATA

1 can (6½ ozs.) crab meat, drained
3 cups half-inch cubes French bread
3 tablespoons melted butter or margarine
4 eggs
3 cups milk
2 cups shredded sharp Cheddar cheese (8 ozs.)
3 tablespoons all-purpose flour
1 teaspoon salt
2 teaspoons prepared horseradish mustard

1. Flake crab meat.
2. Place one third of the bread cubes in a 2-quart deep baking dish; top with one third each of the crab meat and cheese. Sprinkle 1 tablespoon of the flour over cheese, then drizzle 1 tablespoon of the butter on top. Repeat layers.
3. Beat eggs in a medium bowl; stir in milk, salt, and mustard; pour over layers in baking dish; cover. Chill overnight.
4. Preheat oven to 350°F.
5. Bake casserole, uncovered, 1 hour and 10 minutes, or until puffed and golden. Let stand 10 minutes before serving. 6 SERVINGS

Lobsters & Lobster Meat

Lobster is the aristocrat of shellfish. It is one of those seasonal luxuries that modern air transport and the frozen food industry have made available any season. Those that come from along New England's cold coastal waters are the choicest of seafood because they have the largest claws which contain more meat than most.

LOBSTER TAILS, THERMIDOR

2 (1½ lbs. each) frozen rock lobster tails
2 tablespoons butter
2 tablespoons flour
½ teaspoon salt
1 teaspoon paprika
⅛ teaspoon Tabasco
1 teaspoon prepared mustard
1½ cups cream
2 cups (½ lb.) shredded Cheddar cheese
1 teaspoon Worcestershire sauce
¼ cup butter
¼ cup chopped green pepper
½ lb. fresh mushrooms, sliced lengthwise

1. Drop frozen lobster tails into boiling *salted* water. Bring to boiling; simmer 25 to 30 minutes.
2. Meanwhile, heat the 2 tablespoons butter in a large saucepan. Stir in the flour, salt, and paprika and cook until mixture bubbles; blend in Tabasco and mustard. Add cream gradually, stirring until well blended. Bring rapidly to boiling and boil 1 to 2 minutes, stirring constantly. Remove from heat. Add cheese and Worcestershire sauce; stir until

Oysters

Oysters in the shell are sold by the dozen. They must be alive with shells tightly closed; when dead, the shells open automatically and shellfish are no longer edible.

Shucked oysters are graded as to size and are sold by the pint, quart, or gallon. They should be plump with no sunken areas or evidence of shrinkage. The liquor should be clear, fresh, and sweet smelling. The dealer should have them well iced.

Shucked oysters may be purchased in cans or frozen. Fresh shucked oysters packed in cans and labeled "Perishable, Keep Refrigerated" must be refrigerated in the home. Frozen oysters should not be thawed until ready to use and never refrozen.

How to open oysters — Wash oyster shells thoroughly and rinse in cold water but do not soak. Insert a strong thin knife between shells near the thick end and run it around back of shell until muscle holding shells is cut. Discard flat shell, save liquor from oysters, and remove any small pieces of shell from oysters. Serve oysters on the deep half of the shell.

(continued from previous page)

cheese is melted. Cover; set aside and keep warm.

3. Remove cooked lobster tails and place under running cold water for 1 minute, or until cool enough to handle. With scissors, cut along each edge of bony membrane on the underside of each shell; remove and discard the membrane.

4. Gently remove meat from shells, cut into ½-inch pieces, and add to sauce. Reserve shells.

5. Heat the ¼ cup butter in a skillet; add green pepper and mushrooms and cook about 5 minutes, or until mushrooms are lightly browned, stirring occasionally. Blend green pepper-mushroom mixture into the cheese sauce.

6. Fill lobster shells with mixture and top with a mixture of *2 tablespoons cracker crumbs, ¼ cup shredded Parmesan cheese,* and *2 tablespoons melted butter.*

7. Set under broiler 4 inches from source of heat 2 to 3 minutes, or until sauce is bubbly and top is lightly browned. Garnish base of each tail with *watercress* and serve immediately.   6 SERVINGS

SHRIMP AND LOBSTER STEW
(El Pescador Caribe Hilton)

A recipe from the Hilton Hotel, San Juan, Puerto Rico.

1. For each serving allow *6 fresh shrimp* and *3 medallions (rounds) raw lobster meat.* Melt *2 ounces lard or other fat* in a copper skillet and sauté shrimp and lobster meat with *1 shallot, 1 tablespoon diced peeled tomato, 1 teaspoon chopped onion, 1 teaspoon chopped green pepper,* and *½ teaspoon chopped parsley.* Stir the mixture and add *2 ounces dry sherry.*

2. In another pan, sauté *3 diced fresh mushrooms* in *1 tablespoon butter* 3 minutes. Add *3 tablespoons cooked rice* and *½ cup cooked green peas;* sauté 5 minutes. Add the shrimp and lobster mixture, blending well. Correct the seasoning with *salt* and *pepper* and cook 5 minutes longer.

3. Deglaze the copper skillet with *1 ounce brandy;* flame the spirit and add *3 tablespoons beef stock* and *juice of ½ lemon.* Pour the sauce over the seafood mixture and serve in a soup plate.

OYSTERS PIQUANTE IN THE HALF SHELL
Serve as an appetizer or the fish course of a dinner.

1 qt. (about 36) large oysters	1 teaspoon lemon juice
1 cup mayonnaise	3 to 4 drops Tabasco
2 tablespoons chili sauce	¼ teaspoon salt
1 tablespoon butter or margarine, melted	Few grains pepper
1½ teaspoons prepared mustard	⅛ teaspoon paprika
	1 cup buttered soft bread crumbs

1. Set out 12 small shell-shaped ramekins. (If oysters are purchased in shells, use deep half of each shell.)

2. Drain oysters; discard liquor; place 3 oysters in each ramekin or shell.

3. Blend the mayonnaise, chili sauce, butter, mustard, lemon juice, Tabasco, and a mixture of salt, pepper, and paprika. Spoon mayonnaise mixture over oysters. Top with the buttered crumbs.

4. Broil about 3 inches from source of heat 5 minutes, or until oysters begin to curl at edges and crumbs are golden brown.   12 SERVINGS

SCALLOPED OYSTERS

1 qt. oysters	Cream or milk
3 cups cracker crumbs (about 48 saltines, crushed)	1 teaspoon salt
	⅛ teaspoon pepper
	⅓ cup finely chopped onion
2 to 4 tablespoons butter or margarine, melted	½ cup butter or margarine

1. Drain oysters, reserving liquor in a 2-cup measuring cup. Pick over oysters and remove any shell particles. Set aside.
2. Lightly toss 1 cup of the cracker crumbs with melted butter; set aside.
3. Add enough cream or milk to reserved oyster liquor to make 2 cups. Stir in the salt and pepper.
4. Line a greased 2-quart shallow casserole with 1 cup of the unbuttered crumbs. Spoon half of the oysters over crumbs. Pour 1 cup of liquid over all. Sprinkle with half of the onion and dot with half of the butter. Repeat. Top with the buttered crumbs.
5. Bake at 350°F 20 to 25 minutes, or until thoroughly heated.   6 TO 8 SERVINGS

Scallops

Scallops are derived from a variety of shellfish of which the only part considered edible is the eye muscle which opens the shell. This muscle is cut out and the remainder discarded. There are two types, the tiny *bay scallop* and the larger *sea scallop*. Scallops should be cream colored rather than white and are sold by the pound. They are also available frozen and should have a sweetish odor.

SCALLOPS EN BROCHETTE WITH ONION RISOTTO

1 lb. fresh sea scallops	3 green onions, trimmed and sliced thin
16 cherry tomatoes, stemmed	
	1 envelope instant chicken broth
6 tablespoons butter or margarine	
	1 cup water
½ teaspoon dried basil, crushed	1 cup packaged precooked rice
¼ teaspoon salt	

1. Preheat oven to 350°.
2. Rinse scallops under running cold water; drain.
3. Thread scallops and cherry tomatoes onto 4 long skewers, dividing evenly; place in a large shallow baking pan.
4. Melt 4 tablespoons of the butter in a small saucepan; stir in basil and salt; brush part over scallops.
5. Bake 10 minutes; turn and brush all over again with butter mixture. Bake 20 minutes longer, or until scallops are tender when tested with a fork.
6. While scallops cook, sauté green onions lightly in remaining 2 tablespoons butter in a small saucepan; stir in chicken broth and water. Heat to boiling; stir in rice; cover; turn off heat. Let stand 5 minutes, or until liquid is absorbed and rice is tender.
7. Spoon rice mixture onto a large serving platter; arrange skewers on top.   4 SERVINGS

SCALLOPS GOURMET IN PATTY SHELLS

2 lbs. frozen scallops, thawed and rinsed (under running cold water)	2 tablespoons flour
	¼ cup butter or margarine
	½ lb. fresh mushrooms, sliced lengthwise
1 cup boiling water	3 medium-sized tomatoes, cut in pieces
¼ cup lemon juice	
1 medium-sized onion, sliced	½ lb. sliced bacon, cut into ½-in. crosswise strips and fried until golden brown
2 large parsley sprigs	
1 bay leaf	
1 teaspoon salt	
2 tablespoons butter or margarine	6 puff paste patty shells, heated
1 large clove garlic, minced	

1. Cut scallops in half, then cut into thin crosswise slices. Combine with the boiling water, lemon juice, onion, parsley, bay leaf, and salt in a large saucepan; simmer, uncovered, for 3 minutes. Drain, reserving 1 cup liquid, and set aside.
2. Heat 2 tablespoons butter with the garlic in the saucepan; blend in the flour and cook until mixture bubbles. Remove from heat. Add the 1 cup reserved scallop liquid gradually, blending well. Bring rapidly to boiling and boil 1 to 2 minutes, stirring constantly. Set aside and keep warm.
3. Heat the ¼ cup butter in a skillet; add mushrooms and cook about 5 minutes, or until lightly browned, stirring occasionally.
4. Blend the mushrooms, tomatoes, and scallops into the sauce and heat thoroughly. Stir in the bacon; spoon mixture into patty shells; replace pastry lids. Reserve remaining mixture for sauce.
5. Thread colored picks with a *carrot curl*, small *gherkin*, cut in half lengthwise, and a *bacon curl*; insert securely in rim of patty shell.
6. Serve immediately with the hot sauce in a gravy boat.   6 SERVINGS

Shellfish

COQUILLES SAINT-JACQUES

⅓ cup dry white wine	2 tablespoons all-purpose flour
1 cup water	½ teaspoon salt
½ teaspoon garlic salt	¼ teaspoon pepper
1 lb. fresh or frozen sea scallops	¼ cup light cream
	2 egg yolks
1 can (3 or 4 ozs.) chopped mushrooms	1 cup fresh white bread crumbs (2 slices)
1 small onion, chopped (¼ cup)	2 tablespoons grated Parmesan cheese
4 tablespoons butter or margarine	2 tablespoons chopped parsley

1. Combine wine, water, and garlic salt in a large skillet; heat to boiling.
2. Quarter scallops. (No need to thaw first.) Place in boiling liquid; cover. Simmer 5 to 7 minutes, or until tender. Lift from liquid with a slotted spoon and place in a small bowl. Cook down liquid rapidly until it measures ¾ cup. Drain liquid from mushrooms and add to cup.
3. Sauté onion in 2 tablespoons of the butter until soft in same skillet; stir in flour, salt, and pepper; cook, stirring constantly, until bubbly. Stir in the mushroom-scallop liquid and cream. Continue cooking and stirring until mixture thickens and boils 1 minute.
4. Beat egg yolks slightly in a small bowl. Slowly stir in about ½ cup of the hot mixture, then stir back into rest of mixture in skillet; cook 1 minute longer. Stir in mushrooms and scallops. Spoon evenly into 4 large scallop shells. For easy handling, place shells in a large shallow pan.
5. Preheat broiler.
6. Melt remaining 2 tablespoons butter in a small saucepan; add bread crumbs; toss lightly. Sprinkle over scallop mixture; sprinkle cheese on top.
7. Broil, 4 inches from heat, 3 to 4 minutes, or until topping is toasted. Sprinkle parsley over each serving.

4 SERVINGS

Shrimp

Fresh shrimp with heads removed are sold by the pound either fresh or frozen. Shrimp are graded according to the number per pound—jumbo (under 25); large (25 to 30); medium (30 to 42); and small (42 and over). *Cooked shrimp* with shells removed are also sold by the pound; the meat is pink. *Canned shrimp* are available in several sizes of cans and may be used in place of cooked shrimp.

COOKED SHRIMP

1 lb. fresh shrimp with shells	3 tablespoons lemon juice
2 cups water	1 tablespoon salt

1. Wash the shrimp in cold water. Drop shrimp into a boiling mixture of remaining ingredients. Cover tightly. Simmer 5 minutes, or only until shrimp are pink in color. (Avoid overcooking as it toughens shrimp.) Drain and cover with cold water to chill. Drain shrimp again.
2. Remove tiny legs from shrimp; peel off shells. Cut a slit along back (curved surface) of each shrimp just deep enough to expose the black vein. With knife point remove vein in one piece. Rinse quickly in running cold water. Drain on absorbent paper. Store in refrigerator until ready to use.

½ TO ¾ POUND COOKED SHRIMP

SHRIMP ERNIE

Named for the owner, Ernest Coker, these shrimp are served at Ye Old College Inn, Houston, Texas, as an hors d'oeuvre or an entrée.

2 lbs. fresh shrimp, peeled and deveined	¼ cup ketchup
	1 teaspoon paprika
2 cups cooking or salad oil	1 small clove garlic, minced
1 tablespoon salt	

1. Marinate shrimp overnight in refrigerator in a mixture of remaining ingredients.
2. When ready to broil, put shrimp on sides in a large shallow pan, pour some marinade over them and broil slowly until lightly browned on both sides, allowing 7 to 8 minutes for each side and brushing occasionally with marinade.
3. Serve shrimp on frilled wooden picks from a heated platter.

6 TO 8 SERVINGS

SHRIMP LOUIS BAKE

1½ cups uncooked regular rice	1¼ teaspoons dry mustard
1 bag (16 ozs.) frozen shrimp	3 cups milk
	½ cup mayonnaise or salad dressing
8 tablespoons butter or margarine	½ cup chili sauce
1 cup fresh bread crumbs (2 slices)	¼ cup chopped green onions
6 tablespoons all-purpose flour	1 package (10 ozs.) frozen green peas
1¼ teaspoons salt	Parsley

1. Cook rice as label directs; spoon into a 2½-quart baking dish.
2. Cook shrimp as label directs; drain.
3. Preheat oven to 350°F.
4. Melt 7 tablespoons of the butter in a medium saucepan; measure out 1 tablespoon and toss with bread crumbs in a small bowl.
5. Stir flour, salt, and mustard into remaining melted butter in pan; cook, stirring constantly, until bubbly. Stir in milk; continue cooking and stirring until sauce thickens and boils 1 minute; remove from heat. Stir in mayonnaise and chili sauce until mixture is smooth and blended. Stir in green onions; pour over rice.
6. Set aside 2 or 3 shrimp for garnish, then add rest to rice mixture; stir lightly until blended. Sprinkle buttered bread crumbs evenly over top.
7. Bake 45 minutes, or until bubbly and topping is toasted.
8. While casserole bakes, cook peas as label directs; drain. Season with remaining 1 tablespoon butter. Spoon around edge in baking dish. Garnish with saved shrimp and parsley.   8 SERVINGS

SHRIMP JAMBALAYA

3 tablespoons butter or margarine
½ cup chopped onion
½ cup chopped green onion
½ cup chopped green pepper
½ cup chopped celery
¼ lb. diced cooked ham
2 cloves garlic, minced
2 cups chicken broth
3 large tomatoes, coarsely chopped
¼ cup chopped parsley
½ teaspoon salt
⅛ teaspoon pepper
¼ teaspoon thyme
⅛ teaspoon cayenne pepper
1 bay leaf
1 cup uncooked rice
3 cans (4½ oz. each) shrimp, rinsed under running cold water
¼ cup coarsely chopped green pepper

1. Heat butter in a large heavy skillet over low heat. Stir in onion, green onion, green pepper, celery, ham, and garlic. Cook over medium heat about 5 minutes, or until onion is tender, stirring occasionally.
2. Stir in chicken broth, tomatoes, parsley, salt, pepper, thyme, cayenne pepper, and bay leaf; cover and bring to boiling.
3. Add rice gradually, stirring with a fork. Simmer, covered, 20 minutes, or until rice is tender.
4. Mix in shrimp and remaining green pepper. Simmer, uncovered, about 5 minutes longer.
   6 to 8 SERVINGS

INDIENNE SHRIMP

1 bag (16 ozs.) frozen shrimp
5 tablespoons butter or margarine
2 teaspoons curry powder
5 tablespoons all-purpose flour
Dash of pepper
2½ cups chicken broth (from two 13¾-oz. cans)
1 jar (4 ozs.) baby-food apricots
4 small green-tipped bananas
3 cups hot cooked rice

1. Cook shrimp as label directs; drain. Set aside.
2. Melt butter in a large skillet; stir in curry powder; cook 1 minute. Stir in flour and pepper; cook, stirring constantly, until bubbly. Stir in chicken broth; continue cooking and stirring until sauce thickens and boils 1 minute; stir in baby apricots. Taste and add salt, if needed.
3. Preheat oven to 375°F.
4. Peel bananas; cut diagonally into ¾-inch slices; place in a pie plate. Spoon about 1 cup of the curry sauce over top.
5. Bake 5 minutes; remove from oven; keep hot.
6. Stir shrimp into rest of sauce; heat slowly to boiling.
7. Spoon rice around edge of a large deep serving platter; spoon shrimp mixture into center; spoon banana mixture around shrimp.   6 SERVINGS

CURRIED PRAWNS

The El Prado in the Clift Hotel, San Francisco, serves this delightful curried shrimp.

1 lb. large Louisiana prawns, peeled and deveined
2 tablespoons butter
1 tablespoon chopped scallions
1 tablespoon flour
1 teaspoon curry powder
¼ cup sauterne
2 cups cream

1. Sauté prawns in heated butter in skillet 2 to 3 minutes; add scallions and sauté 3 to 4 minutes longer. Sprinkle with a mixture of flour and curry powder. Cook and stir about 3 minutes.
2. Stir in the wine and cream and simmer mixture 10 minutes, stirring occasionally. Transfer prawns to a chafing dish using a slotted spoon.
3. Continue cooking the sauce over low heat to desired consistency. Correct the seasoning and pour over the prawns. Serve with *hot rice*.
   2 SERVINGS

SHRIMP À LA KING

A luncheon dish that has remained a favorite at Antoine's in New Orleans for almost a century.

2 cups white wine	2 tablespoons flour
2 minced shallots, or ¼ cup minced onion	2 tablespoons butter
	Juice of ¼ lemon (about 2 teaspoons)
1 cup oyster liquid, fish stock, or chicken broth	½ cup light cream
	2 egg yolks, well beaten
1½ lbs. fresh shrimp, peeled and deveined	Toast points

1. Combine wine, shallots, and oyster liquid in a saucepan; bring to boiling and add shrimp. Simmer 15 minutes. Drain and reserve ¾ cup stock. **Cook shrimp as label directs; drain.**
2. Meanwhile, stir flour into melted butter in a saucepan, making a roux. Blend in reserved stock; cook and stir until mixture thickens. Add shrimp and cook over low heat. Stir in lemon juice.
3. Add cream to beaten yolks. Mix well and add hot shrimp mixture, stirring constantly. Serve on toast points and garnish with *parsley*.

4 TO 6 SERVINGS

SHRIMP À LA CREOLE

After sampling food the world over, actor Robert Taylor once concluded that this easily prepared shrimp dish was one of his favorites.

½ cup chopped onion	½ cup chopped celery
1 large clove garlic, crushed	1½ to 2 teaspoons salt
	¼ teaspoon thyme
2 tablespoons butter or margarine	Cayenne pepper
	2 bay leaves
1 tablespoon flour	2 lbs. fresh shrimp, peeled and deveined
6 large ripe tomatoes, peeled and chopped (about 5 cups)	

1. Lightly brown onion and garlic in heated butter in a large heavy skillet, stirring occasionally. Blend flour into mixture. Stir in tomatoes, celery, salt, thyme, cayenne pepper to taste, and bay leaves. Simmer about 10 minutes, stirring occasionally.
2. Add shrimp, cover skillet and cook over low heat 10 minutes.
3. Serve immediately over *hot rice*.

6 SERVINGS

SCAMPI FLAMINGO

A recipe from the Danieli Royal Excelsior in Venice, Italy.

½ cup butter	3 tablespoons cognac
1 cup chopped celery	2 cups light cream
¼ cup chopped carrot	⅓ cup sherry
¼ cup chopped onion	¼ cup Sauce, *below*
¼ teaspoon thyme	½ cup butter
2 lbs. fresh shrimp with shells	½ teaspoon lemon juice

1. Heat ½ cup butter in a large skillet. Sauté vegetables with thyme until lightly browned. Add shrimp and brown carefully.
2. Add cognac and flame it. Add cream, sherry, and Sauce; cook 15 minutes.
3. Remove shrimp; shell and devein them; keep warm.
4. Add ½ cup butter and the lemon juice to sauce; cook about 5 minutes. Strain through a fine sieve and pour over the shrimp.
5. Serve sauce and shrimp separately with *rice*.

ABOUT 4 SERVINGS

SAUCE: Follow recipe for *Béchamel Sauce, page 196.* Use *½ cup broth* and *½ cup cream* for the liquid. Stir in *½ teaspoon ground nutmeg* after sauce thickens.

Chapter 8
VEGETABLES

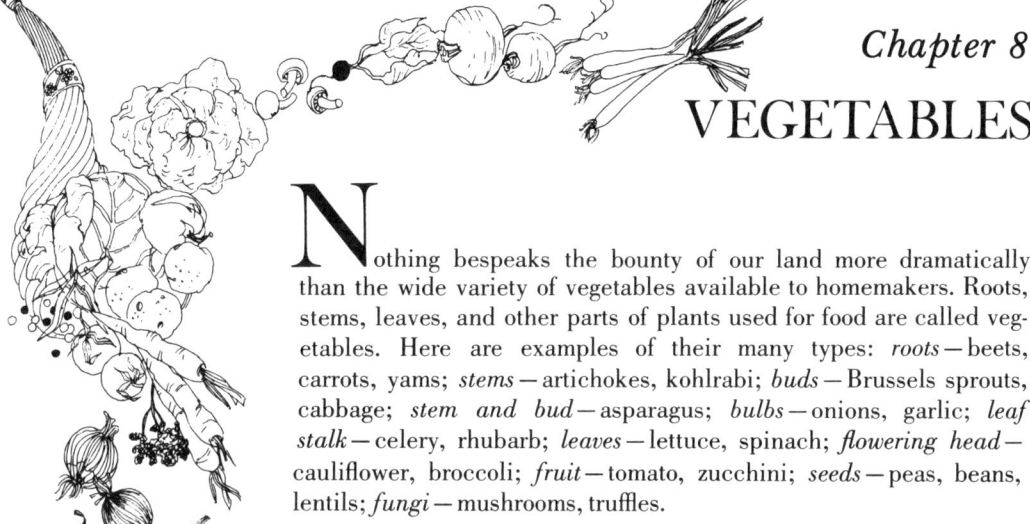

Nothing bespeaks the bounty of our land more dramatically than the wide variety of vegetables available to homemakers. Roots, stems, leaves, and other parts of plants used for food are called vegetables. Here are examples of their many types: *roots*—beets, carrots, yams; *stems*—artichokes, kohlrabi; *buds*—Brussels sprouts, cabbage; *stem and bud*—asparagus; *bulbs*—onions, garlic; *leaf stalk*—celery, rhubarb; *leaves*—lettuce, spinach; *flowering head*—cauliflower, broccoli; *fruit*—tomato, zucchini; *seeds*—peas, beans, lentils; *fungi*—mushrooms, truffles.

SELECTION

Choose vegetables, whether fresh, frozen, or canned, according to the intended use. For example, appearance is of prime importance when selecting vegetables for a vegetable plate, while of lesser importance for soup.

Fresh vegetables should be firm and blemish-free. Buy from a reliable market where good methods of handling vegetables are practiced and where there is a quick turnover of the more perishable items.

Vegetables at the peak of their season are usually more flavorful and lower priced than when they are out of season.

When selecting vegetables at the market, refrain from pinching, squeezing, or unnecessary touching. Handle gently to prevent bruising.

STORAGE

Fresh vegetables—Store less perishable vegetables, such as cabbage, potatoes, dry onions, winter squash, and rutabagas, in a cool, dry, well-ventilated place without beforehand washing. Keep onions separate from other vegetables. Store potatoes in a dark place and not directly on the floor.

Wash other vegetables, such as radishes, lettuce, and other leaf vegetables before storing; drain thoroughly and gently pat dry with a soft clean towel or absorbent paper. Rinse head lettuce under running water, drain, and shake off excess water thoroughly. For long storage do not remove core until lettuce is used. Place vegetables in refrigerator in vegetable drawers or plastic bags, or wrap tightly in waxed paper or moisture-vaporproof material to prevent vegetables from wilting unless refrigerator maintains a high humidity. Do not soak vegetables for any length of time when washing them. If they are wilted, put them in icy water for only a few minutes. Shake off all moisture left from washing, drain thoroughly, and gently pat dry.

Store peas and lima beans in the pod to keep fresh. Pods may be washed before storage; quickly rinse peas and lima beans after shelling.

Frozen vegetables—Store in home freezer or in freezing compartment of refrigerator until ready to use. If package starts to thaw, use at once.

Canned vegetables—Store in a cool, dry place away from heat-producing objects. Rust on a can and dents in a can do not indicate spoilage unless there is evidence of leakage.

PREPARATION

Wash vegetables before cooking, even though they look clean. A vegetable brush is almost a necessity. Leave edible peel on vegetables or use a vegetable parer or sharp knife to keep parings as thin as possible. Many minerals and vitamins are located just

Vegetables

under the peel, so cook scrubbed vegetables with skins on whenever possible. Peel after cooking them if desired.

Sometimes vegetables, particularly those of the bud and head groups (broccoli, cauliflower, artichokes, etc.), are immersed for a short time in icy cold salted water. This freshens the fiber and drives out any insects that have taken refuge in the crevices.

To clean leaf vegetables such as spinach, cut off and discard tough stems, roots, and bruised leaves. Rinse by lifting up and down several times in a large amount of water, changing water frequently. Do this until the water is clear and always lift the leaves out of the water rather than pouring off the rinsing water. This permits any sand to sink to the bottom.

To clean asparagus trim off the hard portion and the scales of stalks up to the heads. The French method for preparing it for cooking is to remove the outer flesh of the stalks or spears, especially around the tough lower portions. It is done with a sharp knife, shaving off the skin. Asparagus which has been "pared" in this manner requires less cooking time to tenderize it and almost the whole spear is edible except for the tough lower portion.

Cooking to Retain Food Values

Many vegetables can be and are eaten uncooked with all their values intact. But many more need to be cooked before they can be served. To prepare taste-tempting vegetables and to retain their abundant minerals and vitamins, use a cooking method which results in the least possible loss of these values.

Baking—Dry-bake in their skins such vegetables as whole potatoes, sweet potatoes, squash, onions, and tomatoes. Bake them in a hot oven until tender when pierced with a fork. Remove the skins when vegetables are baked in casseroles or in a roasting pan around a meat roast.

Au gratin and scalloping are other forms of baking especially good when fresh vegetables are used. In the latter method, layers of vegetable are alternated in a baking dish or ring mold with white sauce, cream or milk, and seasonings. For au gratin vegetables a covering of buttered crumbs or buttered crumbs with shredded cheese is added.

Boiling—This is the method probably used most by homemakers. To insure the best flavor, color, and food value in vegetables cook them only until they are tender. To shorten the cooking time, cut, slice, dice, or coarsely shred vegetables. The less water used in covering them the more nutrients are retained in the cooked vegetable. For young tender vegetables, ½ to 1 cup water is usually enough to cook enough vegetables for six servings. Mature root vegetables must be cooked a longer time and require enough water to cover them.

Most of the minerals occurring in vegetables are easily dissolved in water and the loss of vitamins during boiling takes place in several ways. They may be destroyed by overheating, by prolonged exposure to the air, and by dissolving in the cooking water. If this liquid is drained off the cooked vegetables and discarded, the principal food values gained by the intelligent buying of vegetables have been lost. Avoid this loss by using the least amount of water needed to keep the vegetable from scorching. By the time the vegetable is tender most of the cooking water will be evaporated. Liquid from vegetables may be used in soups, sauces, or gravies.

A desirable boiled vegetable is free from excess water, retains its original color, and is well seasoned. Pieces are uniform in size and attractive.

To cook leaf vegetables and greens, such as spinach, chard, and dandelion, use only the water that clings to the leaves after the final washing. Put the greens into a saucepan, add the salt in layers throughout. Cover tightly and cook quickly until steam escapes from pan, then reduce heat and cook slowly so that leaves do not stick to the pan.

To cook asparagus, after washing and trimming tie stalks in bundles and stand upright in a small, very deep pan or kettle (a deep coffee pot is convenient). Add boiling water to a depth of at least 2 inches, cover loosely, and cook until asparagus is just tender. Or, put asparagus into a skillet with boiling salted water to a depth of 1 inch. Cook, uncovered, 5 minutes; cover and cook until just tender.

To cook broccoli, after washing split the stalks which are over ½ inch thick through center lengthwise. Tie stalks in a bundle and stand upright in a deep pan. Add boiling water up to the flowerets. Cover pan loosely and cook until just tender.

To cook strong-flavored vegetables (cauliflower, mature cabbage, and Brussels sprouts), cover loosely and cook in a large amount of water. To restore color of red cabbage, add a small amount of vinegar at the end of the cooking period.

To heat canned vegetables, bring to boiling the liquid drained from the vegetable and boil until reduced to one half. Return vegetable to liquid and heat quickly. Do not boil.

To heat home-canned vegetables, boil 10 minutes (not required for tomatoes and sauerkraut).

To cook dried (dehydrated) vegetables, soak, then cook as directed for specific recipe. Dried beans should be soaked before cooking. *For quick method*, put beans and measured amount of water into a saucepan. Bring to boiling and boil rapidly 2 minutes. Cover tightly, remove from heat, and set aside 1 hour. Cook, using the soaking water. *For overnight method*, put beans and measured amount of water into a saucepan. Cover and let stand overnight. Cook, using the soaking water.

To cook frozen vegetables, follow directions on package. Do not thaw before cooking (thaw corn on the cob and partially thaw spinach). Break apart frozen block with a fork during cooking. Use as little boiling salted water as possible.

Broiling — Follow directions with specific recipes.

Frying and Deep-Frying — Follow directions with specific recipes.

Panning — Finely shred or slice vegetables. Cook slowly until just tender in a small amount of fat, in a covered, heavy pan. Occasionally move pieces with a spoon to prevent sticking and burning.

Steaming — Cooking in a pressure saucepan is a form of steaming. Follow directions given with saucepan as overcooking may occur in seconds.

NOTE: Some saucepans having tight-fitting covers may lend themselves to steaming vegetables in as little as 1 teaspoon water, no water, or in a small amount of butter, margarine, or shortening.

HELPFUL HINTS ABOUT VEGETABLES

- To freshen fresh asparagus, stand the stalks upright in icy cold water.
- To remove the skins from carrots easily, cover them with boiling water and let stand for a few minutes until the skin loosens.
- To keep cauliflower white while cooking, use half milk and half water; cook, uncovered, until just tender.
- To make celery curls, cut stalks (about 3 inches long) lengthwise into thin strips to within 1 inch of end. Place in cold water until strips begin to curl.
- To make celery very crisp, let stand in icy cold water to which 1 teaspoon sugar per quart of water has been added.
- To garnish lettuce leaves sprinkle some paprika on waxed paper and dip edges of leaves into it.
- To keep onions from affecting eyes, peel them under running water.
- To prevent odor while cooking onions and cabbage, add 1 tablespoon lemon juice or a wedge of lemon to the cooking water.
- To extract juice from onion, cut a slice from the root end and scrape juice from center outward, using edge of a teaspoon.
- To finely cut onion, peel, cut off a slice, then cut exposed surface into $\frac{1}{8}$-inch squares as deep as is needed. Then slice across thinly.
- To keep fresh parsley, mint, and watercress fresh and crisp, wash thoroughly, shake off excess water, and place uncrowded in a glass jar; cover and refrigerate.
- To freshen withered parsnips, carrots, potatoes, cabbage, lettuce, etc., let stand in icy cold salted water.
- To keep leftover pimientos from spoiling, put into a small jar, pour enough cooking or salad oil over top to cover, and place, tightly covered, in refrigerator.
- To keep potato skins soft and tender enough to eat, grease them before baking.
- To prevent sweet potatoes and apples from discoloring after paring, place them in salted water at once.
- To remove skin from a tomato quickly, place fork through stem end and plunge tomato into boiling water for a few seconds, then into cold water. Or hold tomato over direct heat for a few seconds; remove from heat and break the skin at blossom end; peel skin back.
- To restore sweetness to overmature vegetables, add a little sugar to cooking water.

VEGETABLES A TO Z

A Artichokes • Asparagus

ARTICHOKES VÉRONIQUE

A creamy sauce rich with lobster meat, Gruyère cheese, and grapes provides the flavor accent for cooked artichokes in this glamorous entrée.

6 large artichokes, cooked (see How to Cook Artichokes, page 170

⅛ teaspoon dry mustard
⅛ teaspoon ground nutmeg
2½ cups milk
1 cup heavy cream

Artichokes

½ cup butter or
  margarine
¼ cup finely chopped
  onion
⅓ cup flour
1½ teaspoons salt
⅛ teaspoon pepper
1 teaspoon mono-
  sodium glutamate

1 egg, slightly beaten
4 oz. process Gruyère
  cheese, cut in pieces
2 cups diced cooked
  South African rock
  lobster tail meat
  (reserve shells)
½ cup small grapes

1. While artichokes are cooking, heat butter in the top of a large double boiler. Add onion and cook over medium heat about 3 minutes. Stir in a mixture of the flour, salt, pepper, monosodium glutamate, dry mustard, and nutmeg. Heat until bubbly. Gradually add the milk and cream stirring constantly until smooth. Bring to boiling; boil 1 to 2 minutes, stirring to keep mixture cooking evenly.
2. Mix a small amount of the hot mixture with the egg and stir into the hot white sauce. Cook over boiling water 3 to 5 minutes, stirring occasionally.
3. Add the cheese and stir until cheese is melted. Stir in lobster meat and grapes; heat thoroughly.
4. Transfer artichokes to a heated platter. Fill with the sauce.
5. Garnish platter with lobster shells, *lemon wedges*, and clusters of *grapes*.   6 SERVINGS

HOW TO COOK ARTICHOKES

4 medium-sized
  artichokes
1 clove garlic, split

1 lemon slice
2 tablespoons olive oil
1 teaspoon salt

1. Remove about 1 inch from tops of artichokes by cutting straight across with a sharp knife. Cut off stems about 1 inch from base; remove and discard lower outside leaves. With scissors, clip off tips of remaining leaves. If desired, soak the artichokes 20 to 30 minutes in cold *salted water*; rinse and drain.
2. Set the artichokes right side up in 1-inch boiling water in a saucepot. Add garlic, lemon slice, oil, and salt. Cook covered about 45 minutes, or until stem can be easily pierced with a fork.
3. Drain artichokes and cut off stems at base; spread each artichoke open and pull out center leaves. Using a spoon, remove and discard the "choke" or fuzzy part. (Center opening should hold about ⅓ cup filling.) Proceed as directed in recipe.
   4 COOKED ARTICHOKES

ARTICHOKES IN MUSHROOM CREAM
Artichoke hearts in a creamy mushroom sauce served in crisp patty shells makes a distinctive dish.

2 pkgs. (9 oz. each)
  frozen artichoke
  hearts
¼ cup butter
4 oz. fresh mushrooms,
  coarsely chopped
2 tablespoons finely
  chopped onion
2½ tablespoons flour
¼ teaspoon salt
⅛ teaspoon white
  pepper

⅛ teaspoon ground
  nutmeg
¾ cup chicken broth
  (dissolve 1 chicken
  bouillon cube in ¾
  cup boiling water)
¾ cup cream
2 egg yolks, slightly
  beaten
2 tablespoons snipped
  parsley
½ teaspoon capers
8 patty shells

1. Cook artichoke hearts according to package directions, substituting *seasoned salt* for salt. Drain and set aside.
2. Meanwhile, heat butter in a double-boiler top; add mushrooms and onion and cook, stirring occasionally, until mushrooms are lightly browned.
3. Blend in a mixture of the flour, salt, pepper, and nutmeg. Heat until bubbly. Remove from heat and add broth and cream gradually, stirring constantly; bring sauce to boiling and cook 1 to 2 minutes, stirring constantly.
4. Remove from heat and vigorously stir about 3 tablespoons of the mixture into egg yolks. Immediately return to double boiler. Cook over boiling water 3 to 5 minutes, stirring slowly so mixture cooks evenly.
5. Mix in artichoke hearts, parsley, and capers. Heat thoroughly.
6. Spoon mixture into warm patty shells. Replace patty shell tops or garnish with a tiny fancy shape cut from a crimson *cinnamon apple* or a *grenadine pear*.   8 SERVINGS

ARTICHOKES MILANESE

3 cups fresh bread
  crumbs (6 slices)
1 small onion, minced
  (¼ cup)
½ cup minced pepperoni
  sausage
½ cup chopped parsley
½ teaspoon garlic salt

⅛ teaspoon pepper
⅓ cup grated Romano
  cheese
6 large artichokes
6 tablespoons salad oil
Melted butter or
  margarine

1. Mix bread crumbs, onion, pepperoni, parsley, garlic salt, pepper, and cheese in a medium bowl.
2. Cut stems from artichokes to even the base. Slice about an inch from tops with a sharp knife; snip off any spiny tips. Carefully spread tops open; pull out any yellowed leaves from center, then scoop out fuzzy chokes. Wash artichokes; dry.
3. Spoon stuffing mixture into hollows in artichokes; stand them in a large saucepan; drizzle salad oil over each.
4. Pour boiling water into saucepan to a 2-inch depth; heat to boiling again; cover. Cook 40 minutes, or until a leaf pulls easily from the base. Lift artichokes from liquid with a slotted spoon; drain.
5. Place on serving plates; add individual bowls of melted butter to use as a dip. **6 SERVINGS**

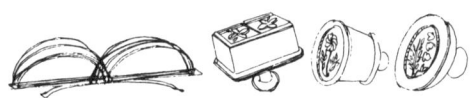

ASPARAGUS SUPREME

2 tablespoons minced onion	1 cup undiluted evaporated milk
2 tablespoons butter or margarine	3 pkgs. (10 oz. each) frozen asparagus pieces, cooked and drained
1 tablespoon flour	
½ teaspoon salt	
½ teaspoon paprika	4 oz. process sharp Cheddar cheese, shredded
¼ teaspoon dry mustard	
½ teaspoon Worcestershire sauce	2 tablespoons fine dry bread crumbs

1. Cook onion in hot butter in a saucepan until onion is soft, but not browned. Blend in flour, salt, paprika, dry mustard, and Worcestershire sauce. Heat until bubbly.
2. Remove from heat. Add the evaporated milk gradually, stirring constantly. Bring to boiling; cook 1 to 2 minutes.
3. Turn asparagus into a 1-quart shallow baking dish. Pour sauce over asparagus and mix lightly with a fork. Sprinkle the cheese and bread crumbs over top.
4. Set under broiler with top of mixture 2 to 3 inches from source of heat and broil 3 to 5 minutes, or until crumbs are lightly browned and cheese is melted. **ABOUT 8 SERVINGS**

ASPARAGUS SEVILLE

1½ lbs. fresh asparagus	½ cup orange juice
Salt	1 tablespoon lemon juice
1 package (8 ozs.) cream cheese	1 teaspoon sugar
1 teaspoon grated orange rind	

1. Break tough woody ends from asparagus; wash spears. Remove scales with a small sharp knife; wash stalks again.
2. Tie stalks in serving-sized bundles; stand upright in a deep saucepan. Pour in boiling water to a 1-inch depth; salt lightly; cover.
3. Cook 15 minutes, or just until crisp-tender; drain. Keep warm.
4. Blend cream cheese, orange rind, orange and lemon juices, sugar, and ¼ teaspoon salt in a small saucepan; heat slowly, stirring constantly, until sauce is smooth and hot.
5. Place asparagus on a large serving platter; cut away strings. Spoon sauce in a ribbon on top.
6 SERVINGS

B Beans • Beets • Broccoli • Brussels Sprouts

MEXICAN BEANS
(Frijoles)

This popular Mexican dish is usually made of seasoned red kidney beans, or cow peas, cooked, fried, and mashed. The mixture is then refried as needed.

1 lb. dried pinto beans	1 teaspoon salt
6 cups water	½ cup lard*

1. Wash beans; put into saucepan with water, bring to boiling and boil rapidly 2 minutes. Remove from heat and cover tightly 1 hour.
2. Add salt, bring to boiling and simmer 1 to 2 hours or until beans are tender. Drain and reserve liquid.
3. Heat the lard in a large heavy skillet and add some of the drained beans. Mash them well; add a small amount of the liquid and blend. Continue adding remainder of beans and liquid alternately, mashing and blending after each addition. Continue cooking over low heat 15 to 20 minutes, or until very thick, stirring frequently. **8 TO 10 SERVINGS**

*¼ cup bacon drippings may be substituted.

MEXICAN REFRIED BEANS (Frijoles Refritos): Follow recipe for Frijoles. To refry, heat with additional lard in skillet, stirring until beans are thoroughly heated and fat is completely absorbed.

Beans

BUCKAROO BEANS

Beans are cooked leisurely, absorbing full flavor from the rich brown sauce formed during cooking.

1 lb. dried pinto or red beans	1 can (16 oz.) whole tomatoes
6 cups water	½ cup coarsely chopped green pepper
2 medium-sized onions, thinly sliced	2 tablespoons brown sugar
2 large cloves garlic, thinly sliced	2 teaspoons chili powder
1 small bay leaf	½ teaspoon dry mustard
1 teaspoon salt	¼ teaspoon crushed oregano or cumin
½ lb. salt pork, slab bacon, or smoked ham	

1. Wash beans, drain, and place in heavy kettle or saucepot with the water; bring rapidly to boiling. Boil 2 minutes and remove from heat. Set aside covered 1 hour. (If desired, pour the water over the washed beans in kettle, cover and let stand overnight. Do not drain.)
2. Stir in the onion, garlic, bay leaf, and salt. (If salt pork is used add salt later.)
3. Wash salt pork thoroughly. Slice through pork or bacon twice each way not quite to the rind. Cut ham into ½-inch cubes, if used. Add meat to beans and bring rapidly to boiling. (To prevent foam from forming, add *1 tablespoon butter or margarine.*) Cover tightly and cook slowly about 1½ hours.
4. Stir in tomatoes, green pepper, and a mixture of the remaining ingredients. Bring rapidly to boiling and reduce heat. Season to taste with *salt* and simmer, covered, 6 hours or longer; remove cover the last hour of cooking, if desired. If necessary, gently stir beans occasionally to avoid sticking on bottom of kettle. There should be just enough liquid remaining on beans to resemble a medium-thick sauce.
5. Serve piping hot in soup plates.

ABOUT 6 SERVINGS

FRENCH-STYLE GREEN BEANS WITH WATER CHESTNUTS

1 can (5 oz.) water chestnuts, drained, and sliced, then slivered	½ teaspoon salt
	Few grains pepper
	2 tablespoons lemon juice
3 tablespoons chopped onion	1 teaspoon soy sauce
¼ cup butter or margarine	1 lb. fresh green beans, Frenched, cooked, and drained

1. Brown water chestnuts and onion in hot butter in a large skillet. Stir in a mixture of salt, pepper, lemon juice, and soy sauce. Heat thoroughly.
2. Toss sauce with hot beans. ABOUT 6 SERVINGS

CREAMY GREEN BEAN CASSEROLE

1 can (5 oz.) water chestnuts, drained and sliced	½ teaspoon salt
	Few grains pepper
1 can (16 oz.) bean sprouts, drained	2 pkgs. (10 oz. each) frozen cut green beans, cooked and drained
1 can (4 oz.) mushrooms, drained	
1 can (10½ oz.) condensed cream of mushroom soup	1 can (3½ oz.) French-fried onion rings

1. Combine in a large bowl the water chestnuts, bean sprouts, mushrooms, and a mixture of soup, salt, and pepper.
2. Add beans and toss lightly. Turn into a 2-quart casserole. Top with onion rings.
3. Set in a 325°F oven about 25 minutes, or until thoroughly heated. ABOUT 8 SERVINGS

GREEN BEANS GRUYÈRE

1½ lbs. green beans, tipped and cut in 1-inch lengths	½ cup milk
	Few drops red-pepper seasoning
1 package (6 ozs.) process Gruyere cheese	Paprika

1. Cook beans, covered, in boiling salted water in a large saucepan 20 minutes, or until crisp-tender; drain; return to pan.
2. Cut cheese in small pieces; combine with milk in a small saucepan. Heat very slowly, stirring constantly, until cheese melts completely and sauce is smooth. Stir in red-pepper seasoning. Pour over beans; heat just until hot.
3. Spoon into a large serving bowl; sprinkle paprika over top. 6 SERVINGS

GREEN BEANS WITH GARLIC

2 cloves garlic, minced
1 cup chopped celery
¼ cup butter or margarine
2 pkgs. (9 oz. each) frozen French-style green beans

1. Cook garlic and celery until just tender in hot butter in a large heavy skillet.
2. Add beans; cover and cook (break frozen blocks apart with a fork as they thaw) about 5 minutes, or until beans are just tender.
3. Sprinkle hot beans with *seasoned salt*, turn into a heated serving bowl and top generously with buttered-browned sliced almonds.

ABOUT 8 SERVINGS

CRUNCHY WAX BEANS

2 cans (16 oz. each) wax beans
½ cup butter or margarine
2 teaspoons grated onion
1 teaspoon lime juice
1 cup corn flakes, coarsely crumbled
2 teaspoons snipped parsley

1. Heat beans with liquid in a saucepan; drain.
2. Meanwhile, heat butter and onion over low heat until butter is browned. Stir in lime juice and corn flakes; toss with hot beans and parsley.

ABOUT 8 SERVINGS

LIMA BEANS AU GRATIN

1 cup dry bread crumbs
2 tablespoons butter or margarine
1 tablespoon chopped parsley
½ teaspoon rosemary
½ teaspoon oregano
6 slices bacon, diced and panbroiled
¼ cup butter or margarine
½ clove garlic, minced
2 tablespoons flour
1½ teaspoons salt
1½ teaspoons dry mustard
2 cups milk
1½ tablespoons instant minced onion
6 oz. sharp Cheddar cheese, shredded
1 pimiento, chopped and well drained
5 cups cooked dried large lima beans (about 2 cups, uncooked)

1. Lightly brown the bread crumbs in 2 tablespoons hot butter in a skillet. Remove from heat and mix in parsley, rosemary, oregano, and bacon.
2. Heat the ¼ cup butter with garlic; blend in flour, salt, and dry mustard. Heat until bubbly.
3. Add milk gradually, stirring constantly. Add onion and bring to boiling, stirring constantly until sauce thickens; cook 1 to 2 minutes.
4. Remove from heat; add cheese and stir until melted. Mix in pimiento. Turn lima beans into a 2½-quart casserole. Add cheese sauce and mix with beans. Top with crumbs.
5. Bake at 350°F 30 to 35 minutes.

8 SERVINGS

SUNSHINE SUCCOTASH

4 tablespoons butter or margarine
½ cup water
1 package (10 ozs.) frozen small lima beans
1 package (10 ozs.) frozen whole-kernel corn
3 small zucchini, trimmed and cut in 1½-inch long sticks
3 tablespoons lemon juice

1. Combine butter and water in a large skillet; heat to boiling. Stir in limas; heat to boiling again; cover. Cook 5 minutes.
2. Stir in corn and zucchini; heat to boiling again; cover. Cook 4 to 5 minutes, or just until vegetables are crisp-tender. Stir in lemon juice.
3. Spoon into a serving bowl. Garnish with several thin slices of lemon if you like.

8 SERVINGS

LIMA BEAN BAKE

2 pkgs. (10 oz. each) frozen lima beans
2 tablespoons instant minced onion
½ lb. frankfurters
½ cup ketchup
⅓ cup molasses
3 gingersnaps, crushed
2 tablespoons dark brown sugar
1 tablespoon dry mustard
½ teaspoon salt
½ teaspoon paprika
1½ teaspoons Worcestershire sauce

1. Cook lima beans with onion; drain.
2. Cut frankfurters into halves lengthwise; cut each in half crosswise. Set aside.
3. Mix hot beans with remaining ingredients.
4. Spoon half of bean mixture into a 1½-quart casserole. Arrange half of frankfurters spoke-fashion over beans. Repeat layering.
5. Heat in a 375°F oven about 15 minutes, or until thoroughly heated.

ABOUT 6 SERVINGS

BEETS IN ORANGE SAUCE
A recipe from Brae Loch Inn, Cazenovia, New York.

- 8 to 10 cooked beets, sliced
- 1 small onion, grated
- 3 tablespoons sugar
- 1 tablespoon cider vinegar
- 1 tablespoon butter, melted
- 4 teaspoons grated orange peel
- ½ cup orange juice
- Salt to taste

Mix all ingredients in a saucepan. Cover tightly and simmer 15 minutes.   4 TO 6 SERVINGS

BEETS À LA RUSSE

- 2 tablespoons butter
- 1 tablespoon flour
- 2 tablespoons sugar
- 2 tablespoons cider vinegar
- 1 can or jar (16 oz.) small whole beets, drained and shredded
- ½ cup dairy sour cream

Heat butter in a saucepan. Blend in flour and heat until bubbly. Stir in sugar, vinegar, and beets. Heat thoroughly. Blend in sour cream and heat thoroughly (do not boil).   6 SERVINGS

BROCCOLI WITH HORSERADISH CREAM

- ½ teaspoon prepared horseradish
- ½ teaspoon prepared mustard
- ⅛ teaspoon salt
- ¾ cup dairy sour cream
- 2 lbs. broccoli, cooked and drained

Blend horseradish, mustard, salt, and sour cream in a small saucepan. Heat just until hot. Pour over hot broccoli.   ABOUT 4 SERVINGS

BROCCOLI WITH MUSTARD CREAM

- 1 bunch broccoli weighing about 1½ lbs.
- Salt
- ¼ cup butter or margarine
- ½ cup mayonnaise or salad dressing
- 1 tablespoon prepared mustard

1. Wash broccoli; trim leaves and tough ends. Cut stalks and flowerets into 3-inch lengths; for even cooking, pare thick stalks and split lengthwise.
2. Put stalks in the bottom and flowerets on top in a large saucepan. Pour in boiling water to a 1-inch depth; salt lightly; cover. Cook 12 minutes, or just until crisp-tender; drain. Place on a large serving platter; keep warm.
3. Melt butter in a small saucepan; remove from heat. Beat in mayonnaise, mustard, and a dash of salt until smooth; heat very slowly until hot. (Do not let mixture boil.)
4. Spoon sauce over broccoli. Garnish platter with lemon wedges if you like.   6 SERVINGS

BROCCOLI RING

- 3 tablespoons flour
- ½ teaspoon salt
- Few grains black pepper
- 3 tablespoons butter or margarine
- 1 cup milk
- 1 cup mayonnaise
- 6 eggs, beaten
- 2 tablespoons grated onion
- 2 cups chopped cooked broccoli

1. Blend flour, salt, and pepper into hot butter in a saucepan. Heat until bubbly.
2. Remove from heat. Add milk gradually, blending thoroughly. Bring to boiling; stir and cook 1 to 2 minutes.
3. Blend mayonnaise into sauce. Add mixture slowly to beaten eggs, stirring well. Lightly mix in grated onion and cooked broccoli.
4. Pour mixture into a greased 1½-quart ring mold. Set mold in a pan in a 300°F oven. Add boiling water to pan to a depth of 1 inch. Bake about 35 minutes, or until custard tests done.
5. Unmold onto warm serving plate. Serve with *creamed chicken* garnished with strips of *pimiento* and *mushrooms* lightly browned in *butter*.
   ABOUT 6 SERVINGS

BRUSSELS SPROUTS WITH CHESTNUTS

- ½ lb. Brussels sprouts
- 1 beef bouillon cube
- ½ lb. chestnuts
- ½ teaspoon salt
- Few grains pepper
- Few grains ground nutmeg
- Butter or margarine
- ¼ cup buttered bread crumbs

1. Cook Brussels sprouts; drain, reserving ½ cup liquid. Dissolve bouillon cube in liquid; set aside.
2. Rinse chestnuts, make a slit on two sides of each shell and put into a saucepan; cover with boiling water and boil about 20 minutes.
3. Remove shells and skins; return nuts to saucepan and cover with boiling salted water. Cover and simmer 8 to 20 minutes or until chestnuts are tender; drain.
4. Mix chestnuts with Brussels sprouts. Turn one half of mixture into a buttered 1-quart casserole.

Sprinkle with half of a mixture of salt, pepper, and nutmeg. Dot generously with butter. Repeat procedure. Pour beef broth over all. Sprinkle with buttered crumbs.

5. Heat in a 350°F oven 15 to 20 minutes, or until crumbs are lightly browned. 4 SERVINGS

BEST-EVER BRUSSELS SPROUTS

1 lb. Brussels sprouts, shredded	¼ cup heavy cream
½ cup butter or margarine	¾ teaspoon salt
	¾ teaspoon sugar
	Few grains pepper

1. Add shredded Brussels sprouts to hot butter in a saucepan. Cook, stirring constantly, about 5 minutes, or until just tender.
2. Add a mixture of remaining ingredients. Cook 2 to 3 minutes, or until thoroughly heated; stir constantly. 4 TO 6 SERVINGS

C   Cabbage · Carrots · Cauliflower · Celery & Celery Root · Corn

NEW CABBAGE IN ORANGE SAUCE

2 tablespoons butter or margarine	¼ teaspoon salt
2 tablespoons sugar	¼ teaspoon pepper
1½ tablespoons lemon juice	3 cups (about ½ lb.) coarsely shredded new cabbage
1 teaspoon grated onion	1 orange, thinly sliced and quartered
½ teaspoon monosodium glutamate	½ cup orange juice

1. Melt butter in a skillet. Add sugar, lemon juice, onion, monosodium glutamate, salt, pepper, cabbage, and orange pieces. Stir to mix thoroughly. Pour in orange juice.
2. Simmer, stirring occasionally, until cabbage is just tender, about 3 minutes. Serve at once in individual sauce dishes. ABOUT 6 SERVINGS

BAVARIAN CABBAGE

1 large onion, chopped (1 cup)	2 tablespoons brown sugar
2 tablespoons butter or margarine	8 cups finely shredded red cabbage (about 2 lbs.)
2 large tart apples, pared, quartered, cored, and diced	⅓ cup cider vinegar
	½ cup water
	1½ teaspoons salt
	¼ cup currant jelly

1. Trim cabbage and shred fine, discarding core. (There should be about 8 cups.)
2. Sauté onion in butter in a large skillet until soft; stir in apples and brown sugar; sauté 2 minutes.
3. Add cabbage; toss lightly to mix with drippings, then stir in vinegar; heat to boiling. Stir in water; cover.
4. Simmer 45 minutes, or until cabbage is tender. Stir in salt and jelly; cover again; reheat to boiling. Spoon into a serving bowl. Garnish with thin apple slices if you like. 6 SERVINGS

RED CABBAGE, DANISH STYLE

1 large head red cabbage	½ teaspoon salt
⅓ cup butter	⅔ cup red currant syrup, or melted red currant jelly
6 tablespoons cider vinegar	2 large cooking apples, pared, cored, and sliced
6 tablespoons water	
1 teaspoon sugar	

1. Cut cabbage into quarters, cut out core, and remove tough outer leaves. Shred coarsely.
2. Add cabbage to hot butter in a large heavy skillet; cook about 5 minutes to soften, turning frequently with a spoon.
3. Stir in a mixture of vinegar, water, sugar, and salt, then the syrup and apples. Cover; simmer about 1½ hours, stirring occasionally.
  ABOUT 8 SERVINGS

BELGIAN CARROTS PHANTASIE

This recipe, created by Executive Chef Enrico Wintrich, is featured in the 71 Club atop Chicago's Executive House.

2 tablespoons butter	1 pound Belgian carrots, cooked and puréed
2 tablespoons sugar	
¼ teaspoon salt	

1 tablespoon honey
4 oz. dried figs, snipped
½ bunch green onions, finely chopped

1. Put butter, sugar, salt, and honey into a saucepan. Set over heat about 2 minutes, or until butter is melted. Stir in the figs and simmer, covered, about 4 minutes.
2. Mix in carrots and heat thoroughly. Top with the green onions before serving.   6 SERVINGS

HERBED CARROTS WITH GRAPES

1½ lbs. carrots
½ teaspoon salt
1 teaspoon basil
½ cup butter or margarine
1 small clove garlic, minced
½ teaspoon thyme
¼ teaspoon celery salt
1 cup seedless grapes
1 tablespoon lemon juice
⅛ teaspoon salt
Few grains pepper

1. Wash and pare carrots; cut into 3x¼-inch strips. Put into a saucepan; add the ½ teaspoon salt, basil, and enough boiling water to almost cover. Cook covered 12 to 15 minutes, or until carrots are crisp-tender.
2. Meanwhile, melt butter and add garlic, thyme, and celery salt. Set aside.
3. When carrots are cooked, remove from heat immediately. Add grapes and let stand covered 1 to 2 minutes; drain off liquid.
4. Stir lemon juice into garlic butter and pour over hot carrots. Season with salt and pepper; toss mixture gently.   6 TO 8 SERVINGS

ORANGE-BUTTER CARROTS

1 bag (16 ozs.) carrots
1 teaspoon sugar
½ teaspoon salt
2 teaspoons grated orange rind
2 tablespoons orange juice
¼ cup butter or margarine

1. Preheat oven to 350°F.
2. Place shredded carrots in a 1-quart baking dish. Sprinkle sugar, salt, and orange rind over top; drizzle orange juice over all; dot evenly with butter; cover tightly.
3. Bake 30 minutes; stir lightly. Bake 30 minutes longer, or until carrots are tender.   4 SERVINGS

SPICED CARROTS

1 lb. small carrots, scraped
⅓ cup thawed frozen orange juice concentrate
⅓ cup hot water
1 thin slice lemon
1 teaspoon grated onion
2 teaspoons brown sugar
½ teaspoon salt
Few grains white pepper
1 piece (1 in.) stick cinnamon
2 whole cloves
2 whole allspice
Several blades whole mace
2 tablespoons butter or margarine

1. Put carrots into a large heavy skillet or saucepan. Mix the orange juice concentrate, water, and remaining ingredients; pour over carrots.
2. Cover tightly and bring to boiling. Reduce heat and simmer until carrots are tender, about 20 minutes. Remove spices before serving.
    ABOUT 6 SERVINGS

CAULIFLOWER SUPREME

½ lb. fresh mushrooms, sliced
½ cup butter
½ cup all-purpose flour
1 teaspoon salt
2 cups milk
2 pkgs. (10 oz. each) frozen cauliflower, cooked and drained
6 slices pasteurized process pimiento cheese
Paprika

1. Cook mushrooms in hot butter in a skillet until lightly browned. Remove mushrooms with slotted spoon and set aside.
2. Blend flour and salt into butter in skillet. Heat until bubbly. Add milk gradually, stirring constantly. Continue stirring and bring rapidly to boiling; cook 1 to 2 minutes. Stir in mushrooms.
3. Arrange half of cauliflower over bottom of lightly greased 1½-quart casserole. Cover with half of the sauce and 3 slices of cheese. Repeat layering. Sprinkle top with paprika.
4. Heat in a 350°F oven about 15 minutes, or until cheese is melted and mixture is bubbly.
    6 TO 8 SERVINGS

CELERY AND ALMONDS AU GRATIN

A recipe from Latham's on Cape Cod, Brewster, Massachusetts.

4 cups 1-in. celery pieces
½ cup coarsely chopped blanched almonds
3 tablespoons flour
¼ teaspoon salt
Few grains pepper
3 tablespoons butter
1½ cups chicken broth
½ cup cream
1 cup shredded sharp Cheddar cheese
Buttered coarse dry bread crumbs

1. Cook celery, covered, in a small amount of boiling water until crisp-tender; drain.
2. Mix celery and almonds in a 1½-quart casserole and set aside.
3. Blend a mixture of flour, salt, and pepper into hot butter and cook until bubbly. Gradually add chicken broth and cream, stirring constantly. Bring to boiling; stir and cook 1 to 2 minutes.
4. Pour over celery and almonds in casserole. Sprinkle with cheese and cover with bread crumbs.
5. Bake at 350°F 15 minutes, or until sauce is bubbly and crumbs are golden brown.

ABOUT 6 SERVINGS

TARRAGON CELERY

1 medium-sized bunch of celery
2 tablespoons butter or margarine
1 envelope instant chicken broth
½ teaspoon dried tarragon, crushed
½ teaspoon salt
Dash of pepper
¼ cup water

1. Trim celery and separate stalks. Cut into 1-inch lengths; for even cooking, split any large pieces lengthwise. (Celery should measure about 6 cups.)
2. Melt butter in a large skillet; stir in chicken broth, tarragon, salt, pepper, and water; heat to boiling. Stir in celery; cover. Steam 10 minutes, or until celery is crisp-tender. Spoon into a serving bowl.   6 SERVINGS

CELERY ROOT WITH MUSHROOMS AND CAPERS

2 cups cubed cooked celery root*
¼ cup fine dry bread crumbs
¼ cup butter
1 cup sliced fresh mushrooms
2 tablespoons butter
2 tablespoons capers

1. Coat celery root with bread crumbs.
2. Add celery root cubes to the ¼ cup hot butter in a skillet and turn frequently to brown all sides.
3. Cook mushrooms until tender in 2 tablespoons butter in a skillet.
4. Lightly mix mushrooms and capers with browned celery cubes.   ABOUT 6 SERVINGS

To prepare and cook celery root— Wash, cut off ends, and pare one 1½-pound celery root. Cut into crosswise slices ½-inch thick. Put into a saucepan with *1 lemon*, sliced. Pour in enough *boiling water* to cover celery root. Cover, bring to boiling and cook 5 to 10 minutes, or until tender. Drain.

CORN PUDDING

2¾ cups milk
6 or 7 fresh ears of corn
4 eggs, slightly beaten
1 tablespoon butter
1 teaspoon sugar
1 teaspoon salt
¼ teaspoon pepper
½ teaspoon monosodium glutamate
2 tablespoons finely cut pimiento
2 tablespoons finely chopped green pepper
2 tablespoons grated onion

1. Scald milk in the top of a double boiler over boiling water.
2. Meanwhile, cut corn kernels from cobs. Using a blender if desired, finely chop enough kernels to yield 2 cups. Put into a large saucepan with 1 cup of the scalded milk. Cover and simmer over low heat for 10 minutes, stirring occasionally.
3. Add a small amount of the scalded milk from double boiler to eggs, stirring vigorously. Add to remaining scalded milk and blend. Mix in butter and a blend of the sugar, salt, monosodium glutamate, and pepper.
4. Stir pimiento, green pepper, and onion into the corn. Adding gradually, stir in the hot milk mixture and pour into a greased 1½-quart shallow baking dish.
5. Place filled baking dish in a pan set on oven rack. Pour in boiling water to a depth of 1-inch.
6. Bake at 325°F 55 to 60 minutes, or until a knife comes out clean when inserted halfway between center and edge of baking dish.   6 TO 8 SERVINGS

Eggplant

CORN WITH MUSHROOMS

¼ cup thinly sliced green onion	1 can (12 oz.) whole kernel corn, drained
⅔ cup coarsely chopped mushrooms	½ cup cream
	½ teaspoon salt
2 tablespoons butter or margarine	⅛ teaspoon pepper
	2 tablespoons snipped parsley

1. Cook onion and mushrooms in hot butter in skillet 5 minutes.
2. Add corn and stir mixture gently while heating thoroughly.
3. Add cream, salt, pepper, and parsley. Keep over very low heat until ready to serve.

4 TO 6 SERVINGS

SCALLOPED CORN

This recipe was contributed by Mrs. Hubert Humphrey, wife of the former Vice President.

1 egg	Butter
1 cup cream-style corn	⅓ cup half and half
1 cup canned whole kernel corn (including 3 tablespoons liquid)	24 to 30 soda crackers, crushed (reserve enough for topping)

1. Beat egg in a bowl with a fork until frothy. Blend in *salt* and *pepper* to taste and the corn. Add chunks of butter (about 2 tablespoons), half and half, and cracker crumbs; mix well.
2. Turn into a buttered 1-quart casserole. Top with reserved crumbs and dot generously with *butter*. Bake at 350°F 30 minutes.

6 SERVINGS

E Eggplant

EGGPLANT AMANDINE

1 medium-sized eggplant, sliced, pared and cut in small cubes	1 small onion, finely chopped
	¼ cup finely snipped parsley
¾ cup slivered blanched almonds	¾ cup cracker crumbs
	2 eggs, slightly beaten
¼ cup butter or margarine	2 tablespoons milk
	1 cup thinly sliced Cheddar cheese

1. Cook eggplant in ½ *cup boiling salted water* until just tender. Drain thoroughly. Mash with a fork and beat until fluffy.
2. Lightly brown the almonds in 1 tablespoon butter in a skillet. Remove and keep warm.
3. Brown onion lightly in butter in skillet. Mix onion and parsley with eggplant.
4. Heat 3 tablespoons butter in the skillet. Add cracker crumbs and toss to coat crumbs. Blend crumbs and ½ cup almonds with eggplant mixture. Blend in a mixture of eggs and milk.
5. Turn into a greased 1-quart baking dish. Top with cheese and remaining almonds.
6. Bake at 350°F 30 minutes. Remove from oven. Sprinkle with *paprika* and garnish with *snipped parsley*. Return to oven and heat 10 minutes.

ABOUT 8 SERVINGS

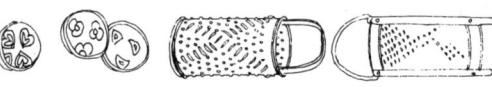

BRINGAL BERTIE GREEN

An eggplant-banana dish from The Astor Club, Berkeley Square, Mayfair, London, England.

1 large eggplant	1 clove garlic, minced
¼ cup olive oil	¼ teaspoon salt
¼ cup finely chopped onion	1 banana with brown-flecked peel
2 tablespoons butter	2 tablespoons grated Parmesan cheese
2 medium tomatoes, peeled and chopped	

1. Cut eggplant lengthwise into halves; score the cut surfaces with a knife. Add eggplant to hot olive oil in a large heavy skillet and cook about 15 minutes on each side, or until tender.
2. Carefully scoop out eggplant, reserving shells. Chop eggplant finely; set aside.
3. Cook onion in hot butter until tender. Mix in tomato, garlic, salt, and eggplant; cook about 10 minutes.
4. Spoon mixture into the eggplant shells.
5. Peel and slice banana lengthwise. Place a banana half on top of each filled shell and sprinkle with cheese.
6. Broil 4 inches from source of heat until cheese is melted, about 5 minutes.
7. Serve with *hollandaise sauce*.

4 SERVINGS

PARMESAN-EGGPLANT SLIMS

In this recipe sliced eggplant is coated with a mixture of crumbs, Parmesan cheese, and Italian salad dressing mix. Crisply fried in olive oil these slices are irresistible.

32 round scalloped crackers, finely crushed (1⅓ cups)	½ cup olive oil
	1 clove garlic, cut in half
2 tablespoons shredded Parmesan cheese	1 medium-sized eggplant, cut crosswise in ¼-in. slices
2 teaspoons Italian salad dressing mix	1 egg, slightly beaten

1. Blend crumbs, cheese, and salad dressing mix.
2. In a large skillet, heat olive oil and garlic over low heat about 10 minutes; remove garlic.
3. Dip eggplant into crumb mixture, then into egg and again into crumbs. Pour off and reserve all but a few tablespoons of oil. Add enough slices to lie flat in skillet; fry about 3 minutes on each side, or until browned. Repeat with remaining slices, adding oil as needed.
4. To serve, overlap two rows of eggplant slices on a heated platter; garnish with *parsley*. If desired, mound *Crunchy Wax Beans, page 173*, on each side of eggplant.   ABOUT 8 SERVINGS

RATATOUILLE WITH SPANISH OLIVES

Ratatouille, a vegetable stew typical of the Provence countryside in France, is sometimes served as a cold hors d'oeuvre.

1 medium-sized eggplant, pared and cut in 3x½-in. slices	2 cloves garlic, minced
	3 tomatoes, peeled and cut in strips
2 zucchini, cut in ¼-in slices	1 cup sliced pimiento-stuffed olives
1 teaspoon salt	¼ cup chopped parsley
½ cup olive oil	1 teaspoon salt
2 onions, thinly sliced	¼ teaspoon pepper
2 green peppers, thinly sliced	

1. Toss eggplant and zucchini with 1 teaspoon salt and let stand 30 minutes. Drain and then dry on absorbent paper.
2. Heat ¼ cup of the oil in a large skillet and lightly brown eggplant strips and then zucchini slices. Remove with slotted spoon and set aside.
3. Heat remaining ¼ cup oil in the skillet; cook onion and green pepper until tender. Stir in garlic. Put tomato strips on top; cover and cook 5 minutes. Gently stir in eggplant, zucchini, olives, parsley, 1 teaspoon salt, and the pepper.
4. Simmer, covered, 20 minutes. Uncover and cook 5 minutes; baste with juices from bottom of pan. Serve hot or cold.   6 TO 8 SERVINGS

G Green Peppers

STUFFED PEPPERS

4 large green peppers	¼ teaspoon dry mustard
½ cup butter or margarine	¼ teaspoon garlic salt
	⅛ teaspoon pepper
2 cups diced ham	1½ cups tomato juice
1 cup cooked rice	¼ lb. Cheddar cheese, cut in 8 slices
2 tablespoons minced onion	

1. Cut green peppers into halves lengthwise; remove and discard white fiber and seeds. Drop pepper halves into boiling *salted water*; simmer 5 minutes. Remove and invert to drain.
2. Heat butter in a saucepan. Add ham and toss lightly with a fork. Mix in rice, onion, dry mustard, garlic salt, and pepper.
3. Pour tomato juice into a 2-quart shallow baking dish.
4. Spoon filling into pepper halves, heaping slightly. Place a slice of cheese on top of each filled pepper and set peppers in dish.
5. Bake at 350°F about 20 minutes. Increase temperature to 400°F and bake 10 minutes, or until cheese is lightly browned.
6. Spoon tomato juice over peppers before serving.   4 SERVINGS

M Mushrooms

GALLATIN'S MUSHROOMS À LA CRÈME GEORGE

A specialty of Gallatin's, Monterey, California.

½ lb. fresh mushrooms (stems chopped)	½ cup dairy sour cream
	¼ teaspoon monosodium glutamate
1 teaspoon butter	
1 teaspoon dry sherry or Madeira	

Noodles

1. Sauté mushrooms in butter in a small pan 2 minutes. Add sherry and cook 1 minute.
2. Add sour cream, monosodium glutamate, and *salt* and *pepper* to taste; heat thoroughly (do not boil).
3. Serve on *toast points*. 2 SERVINGS

FRESH MUSHROOM SOUS CLOCHE

These wine flavored mushrooms baked under glass bells are served at Antoine's, New Orleans.

1 cup water	1 tablespoon flour
½ cup white wine	Juice of ½ lemon
3 tablespoons butter	1 egg yolk
1 lb. fresh mushrooms, cleaned	¼ cup light cream
	Toast

1. Combine water, wine, and 1 tablespoon of the butter; add to the mushrooms in a saucepan. Bring to boiling; cover and let simmer 10 minutes. Drain, reserving broth.
2. Heat 2 tablespoons butter and blend in flour. Gradually add reserved broth, stirring constantly. Bring to boiling; stir and cook 1 to 2 minutes.
3. Thinly slice the mushrooms; mix into sauce with lemon juice. Cook 5 minutes.
4. Beat the egg yolk with cream. Gradually add mushroom mixture and mix well. Pour into heated glass bell, seal bottom of bell with round piece of toast cut to fit. Turn bell over into porcelain shirred-egg dish. Serve immediately. (The bell is removed at the table.) Or serve mushrooms on toast, omitting the bell. 4 SERVINGS

N Noodles

GROUND BEEF-NOODLE SCALLOP

2 to 3 tablespoons shortening	¼ teaspoon pepper
2 cups chopped onion	¼ cup soy sauce
2 lbs. ground beef	1 teaspoon Worcestershire sauce
1 can (4 oz.) sliced mushrooms, drained	8 oz. fine noodles, cooked and drained
1 can (10½ oz.) condensed cream of chicken soup	8 oz. sharp Cheddar cheese, shredded
1¼ cups milk	1 can (5 oz.) chow mein noodles
2 teaspoons salt	¼ lb. salted mixed nuts

1. Heat shortening in a large skillet. Add the onion and cook about 5 minutes, turning occasionally with a spoon. Add the meat and separate into pieces. Cook until meat is browned and onion is tender.
2. Combine mushrooms and soup. Add the milk gradually, stirring until smooth. Blend in the salt, pepper, soy sauce, and Worcestershire sauce. Stir into meat mixture in skillet and cook until heated thoroughly.
3. Turn cooked noodles into a 3-quart shallow baking dish. Spread the meat-soup mixture over the noodles. Top with the shredded cheese.
4. Heat in a 350°F oven 15 minutes. Remove from oven and distribute chow mein noodles and nuts over surface. Return to oven and heat 10 minutes. ABOUT 10 SERVINGS

GERMAN NOODLE RING

1 cup medium noodles, cooked and drained	3 tablespoons butter or margarine
3 tablespoons flour	1½ cups milk
½ teaspoon salt	6 oz. Swiss cheese, cut in pieces
½ teaspoon paprika	2 eggs, well beaten

1. Spoon noodles into a buttered 1½-quart ring mold.
2. Blend flour, salt, and paprika into hot butter in a saucepan. Heat until bubbly. Remove from heat. Add milk gradually, stirring constantly. Bring to boiling; cook 1 to 2 minutes.
3. Remove from heat and add cheese all at one time; stir rapidly until cheese is melted. Reserve half of sauce to use later.
4. Add beaten eggs gradually to remaining sauce, blending well. Pour over noodles in mold.
5. Set mold in a pan in a 350°F oven. Pour hot water into pan to a depth of 1 inch. Bake about 40 minutes, or until mixture is set.
6. Unmold onto a large platter and pour remaining cheese sauce over mold. ABOUT 8 SERVINGS

TAGLIARINI

3 tablespoons olive oil	1 can (12 oz.) whole kernel corn with liquid
1 lb. ground beef	
1½ teaspoons salt	

Onions

⅛ teaspoon pepper
Few grains cayenne pepper
1 medium-sized onion, chopped
1 clove garlic, minced
1 medium-sized green pepper, chopped
1 can (28 oz.) Italian-style tomatoes
1 can (7 oz.) pitted ripe olives, drained
½ cup olive liquid
4 oz. (about 1½ cups) medium noodles, uncooked
¼ lb. sharp Cheddar cheese, shredded

1. Heat olive oil in a large skillet. Brown meat in skillet. Add salt and peppers, onion, garlic, and green pepper; cook, stirring frequently, until onion is soft.
2. Add remaining ingredients except cheese; stir to blend well. Cover closely and cook over low heat about 35 minutes, or until noodles are tender; stir occasionally.
3. Before serving, blend in cheese and heat only until cheese is melted.   8 TO 10 SERVINGS

CRÊPES FARCIE
A recipe from Au Petit Jean Restaurant in Beverly Hills, California.

½ lb. spinach, cooked, drained, and forced through food chopper
2 egg yolks, slightly beaten
¼ teaspoon salt
Few grains pepper
1 cup all-purpose flour
2 tablespoons butter
½ cup onion, finely chopped
½ cup finely chopped fresh mushrooms
1 truffle, finely chopped
1½ cups finely chopped cooked chicken breast
1 cup milk
1 tablespoon sherry
2 tablespoons grated Parmesan cheese
Béchamel Sauce, page 196

1. Mix spinach with egg yolks, salt, and pepper. Add flour and mix until blended.
2. On a lightly floured surface, roll out dough 1/16 inch thick. Cut into 4-inch squares.
3. Add squares one at a time to boiling *salted water* and cook about 2 minutes, or until tender. Remove with a slotted spoon; cool separately.
4. Heat butter in a skillet. Add onion, mushrooms, truffle, and chicken; cook about 10 minutes, stirring occasionally. Gradually add milk, stirring constantly. Mix in sherry and cheese. Set aside.
5. Spoon filling along center of each pasta square and roll to form a tube. Arrange rolls in a shallow baking pan and pour Béchamel Sauce, thinned with a little *sherry* over all. Sprinkle with *grated Parmesan cheese.*
6. Set in a 350°F oven until thoroughly heated.
   4 SERVINGS

FETTUCCINE ALFREDO
Butter-tossed green noodles flavored with herb and garlic is an unforgettable experience when dining at Alfredo's in Rome, Italy.

1 lb. green noodles
2 tablespoons olive oil
1 teaspoon chopped fresh basil
1 clove garlic, minced

1. Cook noodles in boiling *salted water* until just tender; drain.
2. In a chafing dish, heat olive oil, basil, and garlic. Toss the noodles in hot oil with a fork until they are very hot.
3. Sprinkle generously with *grated Parmesan cheese,* adding a generous piece of *butter,* and toss again a moment before serving.   ABOUT 8 SERVINGS

FETTUCCINE AL BURRO ALFREDO: Cook *egg noodles* in boiling *salted water* until barely tender, *al dente;* drain thoroughly. Bring quickly to the table in a heated serving bowl and rapidly toss and twirl with a generous amount of *fresh unsalted butter* and *finely grated Parmesan or Romano cheese* so that the butter and cheese melt so quickly that the fettuccine can be served piping hot.

O Onions

GLAZED ONIONS

2 tablespoons brown sugar
¼ cup butter
8 small onions (about 1 lb.), peeled, cooked and dried

Blend brown sugar into hot butter in a skillet and stir until sugar is dissolved. Add cooked onions to skillet and turn several times to glaze evenly.
   4 SERVINGS

ONION CASSEROLE

½ cup milk
¼ cup butter
¼ teaspoon salt
⅛ teaspoon pepper
1½ lbs. onions, peeled and thickly sliced
2 egg yolks, fork beaten
½ cup dairy sour cream
1 cup finely shredded sharp Cheddar cheese
⅓ cup dry bread crumbs

1. Heat milk, butter, salt, and pepper in a saucepan. Add onion and cook covered until tender, about 15 minutes.
2. Turn onion mixture into a 1-quart casserole and pour a mixture of egg yolks, sour cream, and cheese over onions. Top with bread crumbs.
3. Heat in a 350°F oven 10 to 12 minutes.

ABOUT 6 SERVINGS

ONIONS SUPERB

Whole cloves
2 lbs. (about 20) small onions, peeled, cooked, and drained
2 tablespoons sugar
7 tablespoons butter or margarine
2 tablespoons flour
1½ teaspoons seasoned salt
Few grains pepper
¾ cup cream
¾ cup chicken broth
¾ cup bread crumbs

1. Insert a clove in each cooked onion.
2. Add sugar to 3 tablespoons hot butter in a skillet and stir until blended. Add a few onions at a time and cook until lightly browned, turning to glaze evenly. Remove onions with a slotted spoon to a shallow baking dish. Set aside.
3. Blend a mixture of flour, seasoned salt, and pepper into 2 tablespoons hot butter in a saucepan. Heat until bubbly. Stir in cream and chicken broth and bring to boiling; cook and stir 1 to 2 minutes. Pour sauce over onions in baking dish.
4. Lightly brown bread crumbs in 2 tablespoons hot butter. Sprinkle over creamed onions.
5. Heat in a 350°F oven 30 minutes.

4 TO 6 SERVINGS

LACY FRENCH-FRIED ONION RINGS

The popularity rating of these sweet, redolent onion rings will be great, so be sure to deep-fry plenty. They freeze well and can be oven-heated later for another occasion.

1 cup all-purpose flour
1 teaspoon baking powder
1 tablespoon cooking or salad oil
4 sweet Spanish onions
¼ teaspoon salt
1 egg, well beaten
1 cup milk
Fat for deep frying heated to 375°F

1. Blend the flour, baking powder, and salt; set aside.
2. Combine the egg, milk, and oil in a bowl and beat until thoroughly blended. Beat in the dry ingredients until batter is smooth. Cover and set aside while preparing onions.
3. Cut off root ends of onions; slip off the loose skins. Slice onions ¼ inch thick and separate into rings.
4. Using a long-handled two-tined fork, immerse a few onion rings at a time into the batter, lift out and drain over bowl a few seconds before dropping into heated fat. Turn only once as they brown. Do not crowd the rings.
5. When rings are golden brown on both sides, lift out and drain on absorbent paper-lined baking sheet. Serve hot with *salt* or *garlic salt*.

ABOUT 6 SERVINGS

LACY CORNMEAL FRIED ONION RINGS: Follow recipe for Lacy French-Fried Onion Rings. Reduce flour to ⅔ cup and blend in ½ *cup yellow cornmeal.*
To freeze french-fried onions—leaving the crisp, tender rings on the absorbent paper-lined baking sheet on which they were drained, place in freezer and freeze quickly. Then carefully remove rings to moisture-vaporproof containers with layers of absorbent paper between layers of onions. The rings may overlap some, but do not have layers too deep. Cover container tightly, label, and freeze.
To reheat frozen french-fried onions—Removing the desired number of onion rings, arrange them (unthawed) in a single layer on a baking sheet. Heat in a 375°F oven several minutes, or only until the rings are crisp and as hot as when they came from the fat.

P Peas • Potatoes

PEAS AND ONIONS WITH LEMON BUTTER

2 pkgs. (10 oz. each) frozen green peas
2 teaspoons sugar
1 jar (16 oz.) whole white onions, drained
¼ cup butter
1 tablespoon brown sugar
½ teaspoon salt
¼ teaspoon pepper
1 tablespoon lemon juice

1. Cook peas, adding sugar to water; drain.
2. Chop enough onions to yield ½ cup; set remaining onions aside.
3. Lightly brown chopped onions in hot butter in a saucepan. Blend in a mixture of brown sugar, salt, and pepper, then lemon juice and *¼ cup water*; heat thoroughly.
4. Toss hot peas and whole onions with lemon butter.   ABOUT 10 SERVINGS

FRENCH PEAS
Fresh peas cooked in the French manner . . . with lettuce . . . is a gastronomical experience.

3 lbs. fresh green peas	1 teaspoon monosodium glutamate
1 small head lettuce	¼ teaspoon pepper
4 scallions or green onions	3 tablespoons butter, melted
3 tablespoons butter, cut in pieces	2 tablespoons finely chopped parsley
2 teaspoons sugar	2 tablespoons chopped chives
1½ teaspoons salt	

1. Shell peas, reserving one third of tenderest pods. Put reserved pods on a square of cheesecloth and tie corners securely together, forming a bag.
2. Cut out core of head lettuce. Tear solid portion of head into pieces. Put about half of lettuce pieces into a large saucepan; set remaining pieces aside.
3. Trim green tops of scallions to a length of 2 to 3 inches. Chop and add to saucepan with reserved peas, pea pods, 3 tablespoons butter, sugar, salt, monosodium glutamate, and pepper. Cover with remaining lettuce pieces. Cover and cook until peas are tender, 15 to 20 minutes. Remove from heat. Discard pea pods.
4. Add the remaining ingredients to saucepan. Toss lightly to mix thoroughly.   ABOUT 6 SERVINGS

HERBED PEAS AND CELERY

½ cup thinly sliced celery	½ teaspoon sugar
1 tablespoon thinly sliced green onion	½ teaspoon salt
	Few grains pepper
¼ cup butter or margarine	¼ teaspoon ground nutmeg
1 pkg. (10 oz.) frozen green peas	¼ teaspoon chervil
	1 teaspoon lime juice

1. Partially cook celery and onion in hot butter in a saucepan. Add peas and a mixture of sugar, salt, pepper, nutmeg, and chervil.
2. Cover and cook until peas are tender, 5 to 7 minutes. Stir in lime juice.   ABOUT 4 SERVINGS

BAKED POTATOES

Wash and scrub *potatoes*; dry with absorbent paper. If desired, rub with *fat* for softer skins. Prick with a fork. Set potatoes on oven rack or baking sheet and bake at 400°F 45 to 60 minutes, or until potatoes are soft when pressed with fingers (protected from heat by paper napkin). Remove from oven. To make potatoes mealier, gently roll back and forth on a flat surface.

STUFFED POTATOES

6 medium-sized baking potatoes, baked	2 tablespoons milk
	2 tablespoons butter or margarine
½ cup coarsely chopped onion	2 teaspoons salt
½ cup coarsely chopped green pepper	¼ teaspoon white pepper
3 tablespoons butter or margarine	1 teaspoon paprika
1 medium-sized tomato, chopped	¼ teaspoon crushed rosemary leaves

1. While potatoes are baking, cook onion and green pepper in 3 tablespoons hot butter in a skillet. Add tomato and cook 1 minute.
2. Cut a thin lengthwise slice from each baked potato. With a spoon, scoop out each potato without breaking skin. Thoroughly mash or rice scooped-out potato. Whip in milk with remaining ingredients until potatoes are fluffy. Blend in vegetable mixture.
3. Pile mixture lightly into potato shells. Arrange on baking sheet. Sprinkle with *paprika*.
4. Bake at 400°F 20 minutes, or until thoroughly heated and lightly browned.   6 SERVINGS

FRANCONIA POTATOES
(Oven-Browned)

Pare *potatoes* (cut very large potatoes into halves lengthwise). Cook in boiling *salted water* 10 to 15 minutes; drain. Arrange potatoes in shallow baking pan around a roast 40 to 50 minutes before end of roasting time. Turn potatoes often during baking, basting with drippings in roasting pan. When tender remove from pan and serve with roast.

SAUSAGE-STUFFED POTATOES

4 baking potatoes	1 teaspoon sugar
1 small onion, chopped (¼ cup)	1 teaspoon salt
	2 tablespoons vinegar
3 tablespoons salad oil	2 tablespoons chopped parsley
1 can (5 ozs.) Vienna sausages, drained and sliced	

1. Preheat oven to 425°F.
2. Scrub potatoes; place in a shallow pan.
3. Bake 1 hour, or until tender. Remove from oven and cool until easy to handle. Cut a thin slice from the top of each potato; scoop out insides in large chunks; dice, if needed. Set shells aside.
4. Sauté onion in salad oil in a skillet until soft; stir in sausages; brown lightly.
5. Stir in sugar, salt, vinegar, and diced potatoes; heat,stirring gently several times, 5 minutes, or until potatoes are hot and dressing is absorbed. Pile back into shells; sprinkle parsley over tops. 4 SERVINGS

SCALLOPED POTATOES

6 medium-sized potatoes, pared and thinly sliced	1½ teaspoons salt
	⅛ teaspoon pepper
	3 tablespoons butter or margarine
⅓ cup chopped onion	
3 tablespoons flour	2½ cups milk, scalded

1. Put a third of the potato slices into a greased 2-quart casserole. Sprinkle with about a third of onion and a third of blended flour, salt, and pepper. Dot with 1 tablespoon of butter. Repeat layering twice, ending with butter. Pour the hot milk over potatoes. Cover casserole.
2. Bake at 350°F 30 minutes. Remove cover; bake 60 to 70 minutes, or until potatoes are tender. Remove from oven. Let stand about 5 minutes before serving. ABOUT 6 SERVINGS

AU GRATIN POTATOES: Follow recipe for Scalloped Potatoes. After potatoes have baked for 30 minutes and cover has been removed, top with a layer of either buttered *bread crumbs*, shredded *Cheddar or Parmesan cheese*, or a blend of crumbs and cheese. Bake, uncovered, 60 to 70 minutes.

POTATOES ANNA

6 to 8 medium-sized potatoes, pared, and thinly sliced	½ cup butter or margarine

1. Dry potato slices thoroughly with absorbent paper. Arrange even layers of potatoes in a buttered 2-quart baking dish; overlap slices about ¼ inch. Sprinkle each layer with a mixture of *salt* and *pepper* and dot with some of the butter.
2. Bake at 425°F 40 to 60 minutes, or until potatoes are tender and golden brown.
3. To remove from dish for serving, run a spatula around edge to loosen. Invert onto warm serving plate. 6 TO 8 SERVINGS

SUGAR-BROWNED POTATOES

This Danish specialty is almost as popular in Denmark as their famous pastries.

2 to 3 lbs. small potatoes	6 tablespoons sugar
	3 tablespoons butter

1. Cook potatoes until almost tender. Drain and peel. Rinse with cold water; dry with absorbent paper.
2. Heat sugar in a heavy light-colored skillet. With back of a wooden spoon, gently keep sugar moving toward center of skillet until it is melted. Heat until syrup is a light golden brown.
3. Stir in butter and heat until butter and sugar are thoroughly blended.
4. Add potatoes and turn them gently to coat; remove from heat and before serving turn them until coated. ABOUT 8 SERVINGS

CHIPPED BEEF AND POTATO BOATS

6 tablespoons butter or margarine	2½ cups milk
	¼ cup mayonnaise or salad dressing
4 tablespoons all-purpose flour	
	1 jar (5 ozs.) dried beef, shredded
1 envelope instant chicken broth	
	4 hot baked potatoes

1. Melt 4 tablespoons of the butter in a medium saucepan; stir in flour and chicken broth. Cook, stirring constantly, until bubbly. Stir in 2 cups of the milk; continue cooking and stirring until sauce thickens and boils 1 minute; remove from heat. Stir in mayonnaise and dried beef.
2. Cut each potato in half lengthwise; scoop out centers into a large bowl, being careful not to break shells; place each two shells on a serving plate.
3. Add remaining 2 tablespoons butter and ½ cup milk to potatoes; beat until light and fluffy.

4. Spoon potatoes into one shell on each plate and dried-beef mixture into the other. Serve hot.

4 SERVINGS

SUPERB HASH-BROWN POTATO PATTIES

1 tablespoon flour	3 tablespoons evaporated milk
½ teaspoon salt	1 teaspoon onion juice
½ teaspoon paprika	1 egg, beaten until thick and piled softly
3 oz. cream cheese, softened	
6 tablespoons shredded extra-sharp Cheddar cheese	1 carton (12 oz.) frozen shredded hash brown potatoes, partially thawed and carefully separated
1 tablespoon snipped parsley	

1. Blend a mixture of the flour, salt, and paprika with the cream cheese in a mixing bowl. Mix in the shredded cheese and parsley. Gradually add the evaporated milk and onion juice and stir until well blended. Gently blend in the well-beaten egg; then potatoes.
2. Heat *butter or margarine* in a heavy skillet over medium heat. Spoon about ¼ cup of mixture for each patty into hot skillet and cook until golden browned and crisp on one side. Turn patties and brown other side. Drain on absorbent paper. Serve on heated platter.

8 TO 10 PATTIES

NOTE: For large pancakes, use about ¾ cup of mixture.

O'BRIEN POTATOES

6 or 7 medium potatoes, cooked and peeled	2 tablespoons minced pimiento
3 to 4 tablespoons fat	⅓ cup milk
¼ cup chopped onion	1 teaspoon salt
¼ cup minced green pepper	¼ teaspoon pepper
	¼ teaspoon paprika

1. Dice or coarsely chop the potatoes; set aside.
2. Heat the fat in a large skillet. Mix in the onion, green pepper, pimiento, and potatoes. Add the milk and sprinkle with a blend of seasonings; cook, stirring frequently, until potatoes are lightly browned.
3. Turn into a heated serving dish and garnish with *parsley sprigs*.

6 SERVINGS

FRENCH-FRIED POTATOES

About 20 minutes before frying the potatoes, fill a deep saucepan two-thirds full with *vegetable shortening, all-purpose shortening, lard,* or *cooking oil* for deep frying and heat to 300°F. Meanwhile, wash and pare *6 medium-sized (about 2 pounds) potatoes.* Use a knife or fancy cutter to cut potatoes. Trim off sides and ends to form large blocks. Cut lengthwise into about ¾-inch slices; stack evenly. Cut lengthwise into sticks about ¾ inch wide. Pat dry with absorbent paper. Fry about 1 cup at a time in hot fat until potatoes are transparent but not browned. Remove from fat and drain on absorbent paper. Just before serving, heat fat to 360°F. Return potatoes to fat, frying 1 cup at a time. Fry until crisp and golden brown. Drain on absorbent paper. Sprinkle with *salt.* Serve immediately or keep warm in oven.

ABOUT 6 SERVINGS

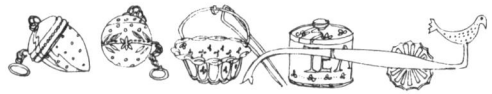

POTATOES ROESTI

1 large potato, pared	¼ teaspoon salt
⅓ cup butter or margarine	

1. Cut potato lengthwise into ⅛-inch slices. Cut each slice into lengthwise strips ⅛ inch thick. Pat potato strips dry with absorbent paper.
2. Melt butter in a 6-inch skillet. Pour off and reserve all but 1 tablespoon.
3. Arrange strips crisscross-fashion to a 1½-inch depth in hot skillet. Pour remaining melted butter over strips. Sprinkle with salt.
4. Heat rapidly until butter sizzles. Reduce heat to medium and cook about 15 minutes, or until underside is browned.
5. Drain off butter and reserve. Using wide spatula, turn carefully, keeping potato cake intact. Return about one half of butter to skillet; reserve remaining butter to use if frying additional potatoes. Cook 8 to 10 minutes longer over medium heat or until potatoes are browned on second side (butter should be sizzling).
6. Drain off butter and remove potatoes from skillet.

1 SERVING

SKILLET POTATOES AU GRATIN

4 large potatoes, pared and sliced
½ cup finely chopped onion
1 teaspoon salt
¼ teaspoon black pepper
1 cup water
½ cup cream
¼ cup butter or margarine, melted
½ cup shredded sharp Cheddar cheese
½ cup bread crumbs
2 tablespoons butter or margarine
3 slices bacon, diced and pan broiled

1. Put sliced potatoes, onion, salt, pepper, and water into a heavy skillet; cover and bring to boiling. Cook about 10 minutes, or until potatoes are just tender.
2. Add cream, melted butter, and cheese to skillet and mix lightly. Cook uncovered over low heat about 10 minutes, or until thoroughly heated.
3. Meanwhile, lightly brown bread crumbs in 2 tablespoons butter in a small skillet.
4. Transfer potatoes to warm serving dish and top with crumbs and bacon.   6 SERVINGS

DUTCH STEWED POTATOES

1 onion, sliced
1 tablespoon butter or other shortening
2 cups diced raw potatoes
1 teaspoon salt
Few grains pepper
1 teaspoon minced parsley
¾ cup boiling water
1 tablespoon water
2 teaspoons flour

1. Cook onion 5 minutes in hot butter in a large skillet. Add potatoes and a mixture of salt, pepper, and parsley. Pour in boiling water and cook covered until tender, about 20 minutes.
2. Blend water and flour. Stir into mixture in skillet, bring to boiling and cook 1 to 2 minutes.
   4 SERVINGS

R   Rutabagas • Rice

WHIPPED RUTABAGAS

Scrub *rutabagas*; pare and cut into pieces. Cook, covered, in boiling *salted water* until tender, about 25 minutes. Drain; season and beat in the desired amount of *butter or margarine* and *hot milk or cream*, whipping until fluffy. If desired, beat in an equal amount or less of *seasoned whipped potatoes*.

RUTABAGA SOUFFLÉ

1 cup mashed cooked rutabaga
½ cup hot instant mashed potatoes (prepared according to pkg. directions)
1 cup milk
2 tablespoons cornstarch
½ teaspoon salt
⅛ teaspoon pepper
1 tablespoon brown sugar
⅛ to ¼ teaspoon ground mace
3 eggs, separated
2 tablespoons fine dry bread crumbs
1 tablespoon butter or margarine, melted
2 tablespoons shredded Parmesan cheese

1. Beat the mashed rutabaga and potatoes together; set aside.
2. Blend the milk with cornstarch in a saucepan. Bring to boiling over low heat; stir and cook about 3 minutes. Stir in the salt, pepper, brown sugar, and mace.
3. Add the hot mixture gradually to slightly beaten egg yolks, stirring constantly. Beat into mashed vegetables, blending thoroughly.
4. Beat egg whites until stiff, not dry, peaks are formed. Fold into rutabaga mixture. Turn into a 1½-quart casserole.
5. Toss bread crumbs with butter and cheese. Spoon over top of soufflé.
6. Bake at 325°F about 50 minutes, or until a silver knife comes out clean when inserted halfway between center and edge of casserole. Serve immediately.   ABOUT 6 SERVINGS

FRIED RICE

¾ cup uncooked rice
2 tablespoons very finely chopped fresh mushrooms
2 tablespoons butter
¼ to ½ teaspoon grated onion
2½ cups chicken broth (dissolve 3 chicken bouillon cubes in 2½ cups boiling water)
1 tablespoon finely chopped carrot
1 tablespoon finely chopped green pepper

1. Add rice, mushrooms, and onion to hot butter in a large heavy skillet; cook until golden brown.
2. Stir broth into rice mixture. Cover and cook over low heat 30 minutes, or until rice is tender.
3. Add carrot and green pepper and toss lightly.
   ABOUT 8 SERVINGS

SPANISH RICE CASSEROLE

Polly Bergen serves this as a main dish at family dinners or at a big buffet. The amount of seasonings depends on whether you like food hot or mild.

3 tablespoons olive oil	1 dash Tabasco (optional)
2 large onions, finely chopped	2 teaspoons salt
2 green peppers, finely chopped	Pepper to taste
1 clove garlic, minced	1½ teaspoons chili powder
2 lbs. ground round steak or chuck	Few grains cayenne pepper
2 cans (28 oz. each) Italian-style tomatoes	2 bay leaves
	2 or 3 whole cloves
1 can (6 oz.) tomato paste	1 to 2 cups uncooked long grain rice, cooked
1 tablespoon wine vinegar	Grated Parmesan cheese
1 tablespoon Worcestershire sauce (optional)	

1. Heat olive oil in a large skillet or Dutch oven. Add onion, green pepper, and garlic; cook over medium heat until tender and lightly browned. Remove vegetables with a slotted spoon; set aside.
2. Add ground meat to oil remaining in skillet. Cook over medium heat until lightly browned, stirring occasionally.
3. Add reserved cooked vegetables, tomatoes (including liquid), tomato paste, vinegar, Worcestershire sauce, Tabasco, salt, pepper, chili powder, cayenne pepper, bay leaves, and cloves; stir thoroughly to blend well.
4. Cover skillet and simmer "as long as you want to;" stir occasionally to prevent sticking.
5. Combine desired amounts of rice and sauce; mix until each rice kernel is coated with sauce. Turn into a large casserole. Sprinkle with Parmesan cheese.
6. Cover and set in a 300°F oven just until heated through, 30 to 45 minutes. 8 TO 10 SERVINGS

NOTE: Polly says the sauce improves with cooking—even as long as all day—and is good for spaghetti or, with addition of kidney beans, for chili. She makes up a large amount and freezes part of it.

RICE PILAF

A recipe from The Imperial House, Chicago, Illinois.

6 tablespoons olive oil	4 cups well-seasoned chicken broth
¼ cup finely chopped onion	1½ teaspoons salt
2 cups uncooked long grain rice	½ cup shredded Cheddar cheese

1. Heat oil in a large heavy skillet having a heat-resistant handle. Add onion and rice; cook over low heat 3 minutes, or until rice is golden.

GREEN RICE

1½ cups packaged precooked rice	⅓ cup finely snipped parsley
½ cup shredded sharp Cheddar cheese	⅓ cup finely chopped green onion with tops
¼ cup butter or margarine	2 eggs, well beaten
⅓ cup finely chopped spinach	1½ cups milk, scalded

1. Cook rice according to package directions substituting chicken broth for water and omitting salt. (To prepare chicken broth, dissolve 1 chicken bouillon cube in the boiling water.)
2. Stir cheese and butter into hot cooked rice. Add spinach, parsley, and green onion; mix well. Add beaten eggs and milk; blend lightly but thoroughly. Turn into heat-resistant individual molds or custard cups or a 2-quart shallow baking dish.
3. Bake at 350°F about 30 minutes, or until set.
4. If rice is baked in molds, unmold and garnish with sprigs of *watercress* inserted into top of each mold. If baked in a dish, garnish one corner of baking dish with strips of *green pepper* forming petals of a flower and *sieved hard-cooked egg yolk* for center of flower. 6 TO 8 SERVINGS

RICE AND CHICKEN AMANDINE

¼ cup chopped onion	2 tablespoons chopped pimiento
½ clove garlic, minced	2 tablespoons chopped parsley
¼ cup butter	
⅓ cup flour	
2 cups chicken broth	¼ teaspoon ground nutmeg
1 cup cream	¼ teaspoon thyme
2½ cups cooked chicken pieces	¼ teaspoon marjoram

3 cups cooked rice
½ cup toasted slivered blanched almonds
1 teaspoon salt
⅛ teaspoon pepper

1. Add onion and garlic to hot butter in a large heavy skillet; cook until onion is soft. Blend in flour and heat until bubbly. Remove from heat.
2. Add chicken broth gradually, stirring constantly. Bring to boiling; cook 1 to 2 minutes. Stir in cream; heat thoroughly (do not boil). Add remaining ingredients and mix well. Turn into a greased 2-quart casserole.
3. Set in a 375°F oven for about 25 minutes, or until mixture is thoroughly heated.

ABOUT 6 SERVINGS

WILD RICE WITH MUSHROOMS

½ lb. fresh mushrooms, sliced
2 tablespoons finely chopped onion
¼ cup butter or margarine
1 cup wild rice, cooked, *page 11*, and drained
⅓ cup melted butter or margarine

1. Cook mushrooms and onion in ¼ cup butter in a skillet until mushrooms are lightly browned.
2. Combine mushrooms, wild rice, and melted butter; toss gently until mushrooms and butter are evenly distributed throughout rice. 8 SERVINGS

S Sauerkraut • Spaghetti • Spinach • Squash • Sweet Potatoes and Yams

KRAUT WITH APPLES
(Kraut mit Äpfeln)
Serve this adaptation of a German cooked sauerkraut speciality as an accompaniment to pork.

4 cups drained sauerkraut
2 apples, thinly sliced
½ cup apple cider
1 tablespoon light brown sugar
2 tablespoons butter or margarine

Mix all ingredients. Cover and simmer 5 minutes, or until apples are tender. Garnish with *apple wedges* and *parsley*. ABOUT 8 SERVINGS

SAUERKRAUT WITH CARAWAY
An old Pennsylvania Dutch recipe.

½ cup chopped onion
2 tablespoons butter or margarine
2 cans (16 oz. each) sauerkraut
1 potato, pared and grated (about ¾ cup)
1 teaspoon caraway seed
Boiling water (about 2 cups)

1. Add onion to hot butter in a heavy saucepan and cook until onion is golden. Stir in sauerkraut and cook 8 minutes.
2. Mix in potato and caraway seed. Pour in boiling water to cover.
3. Cook, uncovered, over low heat about 30 minutes. Cover and continue cooking 30 minutes. If desired, *1 or 2 tablespoons brown sugar* may be blended into mixture during the last 5 minutes.

6 TO 8 SERVINGS

SPAGHETTI SUPREME

2 tablespoons chopped parsley
1 teaspoon basil
3 cloves garlic, minced
3 tablespoons olive oil
2 teaspoons French mustard
1 teaspoon anchovy paste
⅛ teaspoon salt
⅛ teaspoon freshly ground black pepper
¼ cup water
7 oz. spaghetti, cooked and drained
½ cup shredded Parmesan cheese
½ cup heavy cream

1. Add parsley, basil, and garlic to hot olive oil in a skillet and cook about 3 minutes.
2. Stir in mustard, anchovy paste, salt, pepper, and water; cook about 5 minutes.
3. Meanwhile, alternate layers of hot spaghetti and Parmesan cheese on a warm platter.
4. Stir cream into the sauce, heat thoroughly (do not boil), and pour over the spaghetti. Serve hot.

ABOUT 4 SERVINGS

SPAGHETTI WITH TUNA-TOMATO SAUCE

1 cup finely chopped onion
1 clove garlic, minced
¼ cup butter or margarine
1 can (28 oz.) tomatoes
½ teaspoon monosodium glutamate
⅛ teaspoon pepper
½ teaspoon sugar
½ teaspoon basil
½ teaspoon oregano

1 can (8 oz.) tomato sauce
½ cup shredded Parmesan cheese
¼ cup minced parsley
1 teaspoon salt
1 can (9¼ oz.) chunk-style tuna, drained and flaked
7 or 8 oz. spaghetti, cooked and drained
2 tablespoons butter or margarine

1. Cook onion and garlic about 5 minutes in ¼ cup hot butter in a large saucepan or skillet. Stir in tomatoes, tomato sauce, cheese, parsley, and seasonings. Bring to boiling, stirring occasionally; simmer about 20 minutes. Add tuna and simmer about 15 minutes, stirring frequently.
2. Toss spaghetti with 2 tablespoons butter until melted. Serve hot sauce over spaghetti.

ABOUT 6 SERVINGS

TURKEY PARMAZZINI

This dish may not be authentically Italian — but certainly worthy of the tradition.

2 tablespoons butter or margarine
1¼ cups sliced fresh mushrooms
¼ cup butter or margarine
¼ cup flour
¼ teaspoon salt
2 cups milk
1¼ cups cream
2 teaspoons paprika
2 egg yolks, slightly beaten
4 cups julienne of cooked turkey
⅔ cup julienne of cooked ham
2 cups shredded Parmesan cheese
2 tablespoons butter or margarine
8 oz. long spaghetti, cooked and drained
1 tablespoon butter or margarine, melted

1. Heat 2 tablespoons butter in a skillet; add the mushrooms and cook over medium heat until mushrooms are lightly browned and tender.
2. Heat ¼ cup butter in a large heavy saucepan. Blend in flour and salt; heat until mixture bubbles. Gradually add milk, stirring constantly. Bring to boiling; stir and cook 1 to 2 minutes.
3. Blend in the cream and paprika; heat thoroughly over medium heat.
4. Vigorously stir about 3 tablespoons hot sauce into egg yolks; immediately blend into mixture in saucepan. Stir and cook about 2 minutes.
5. Blend in the turkey, ham, cooked mushrooms, and ½ cup Parmesan cheese; heat thoroughly.
6. Add 2 tablespoons butter to hot cooked spaghetti and toss until butter is melted. Add 1 cup Parmesan cheese to the spaghetti and toss to mix.
7. Turn spaghetti into a 2½-quart casserole and pull up around edge of casserole. Spoon sauce into center, sprinkle remaining Parmesan cheese over sauce, and drizzle the melted butter evenly over all. Sprinkle with *paprika*.
8. Heat in a 350°F oven about 15 minutes.

6 TO 8 SERVINGS

LASAGNE

Tomato Meat Sauce, *page 190*
1 lb. lasagne noodles, cooked, drained and rinsed
2 lbs. ricotta cheese
1 lb. mozzarella or scamorze cheese, shredded
1 cup shredded Parmesan cheese

1. Prepare Tomato Sauce.
2. Spread about 1 cup Tomato Sauce in a buttered 13x9x2-inch baking dish. Using a fourth of each, add a layer of noodles and then one of tomato sauce. Using a third of each, top evenly with 3 cheeses. Repeat layering and end with sauce.
3. Heat in a 375°F oven about 30 minutes, or until bubbly. Allow to stand 10 to 15 minutes to set layers before serving. Cut into squares.

12 TO 15 SERVINGS

SHRIMP LASAGNA

1 package (8 ozs.) lasagna noodles
1 tablespoon salad oil
1 package (16 ozs.) frozen uncooked shrimp
2 cans (10¾ ozs. each) condensed cream of shrimp soup
1 package (8 ozs.) cream cheese, softened
1 egg
1 carton (16 ozs.) cream-style cottage cheese
1 large onion, chopped (1 cup)
1 teaspoon dillweed
1 teaspoon salt
¼ teaspoon pepper
3 medium fresh tomatoes, sliced
1 cup shredded Edam cheese (4 ozs.)

1. Cook noodles with salad oil in a kettle of boiling water as label directs; drain; return to kettle. Cover with cold water to keep noodles from sticking together.
2. Cook shrimp as label directs; drain. Combine with soup in a medium bowl.
3. Beat cream cheese and egg until fluffy in a medium bowl; stir in cottage cheese, onion, dillweed, salt, and pepper.
4. Preheat oven to 350°F.

5. Lift noodles, one at a time, from water and drain well; place 4 in the bottom of a greased baking dish, 13x9x2 inches to cover.
6. Spread half of the cheese mixture over noodles, cover with another layer of noodles, all of the shrimp sauce, rest of noodles, and rest of cheese mixture. Arrange tomato slices in rows on top; sprinkle each very lightly with salt if you like. Sprinkle shredded cheese evenly over tomatoes.
7. Bake 1 hour, or until bubbly and cheese melts and browns lightly. Let stand 15 minutes; cut into blocks.

8 SERVINGS

LINGUINE WITH MARINARA SAUCE
Long, thin, flat Italian noodles are called linguine, that being the Italian word for tongue.

2 medium-sized cloves garlic, sliced	⅛ teaspoon pepper
½ cup olive oil	1 teaspoon oregano
1 can (28 oz.) tomatoes, sieved	¼ teaspoon chopped parsley
1¼ teaspoons salt	8 oz. linguine, cooked and drained

1. Brown garlic in hot olive oil in a large deep skillet. Add gradually, stirring constantly, a mixture of the tomatoes, salt, pepper, oregano, and parsley. Cook rapidly uncovered about 15 minutes, or until sauce is thickened; stir occasionally. If sauce becomes too thick, stir in ¼ to ½ cup water.
2. Serve sauce hot with the linguine.

ABOUT 6 SERVINGS

TOMATO MEAT SAUCE

¼ cup olive oil	1 tablespoon salt
½ cup chopped onion	1 bay leaf
½ lb. beef chuck	1 can (6 oz.) tomato paste
½ lb. pork shoulder	
7 cups canned tomatoes with liquid, sieved	

1. Heat the olive oil in a saucepot. Add onion and cook until lightly browned. Put the meat into saucepot and brown on all sides. Stir in tomatoes and salt. Add bay leaf. Cover; simmer about 2½ hours.
2. Mix tomato paste into sauce. Simmer, uncovered, stirring occasionally, about 2 hours, or until thickened. If sauce becomes too thick, add ½ *cup water.*
3. Remove meat and bay leaf from sauce. Serve sauce over *cooked spaghetti.* ABOUT 4 CUPS SAUCE

ITALIAN SPAGHETTI SAUCE
A sauce well worth the time spent in preparation.

½ cup olive oil	1 teaspoon sugar
1½ cups finely chopped onion	½ teaspoon celery salt
4 cloves garlic, finely chopped	½ teaspoon crushed red pepper
1 lb. ground beef	Dash chili powder
½ lb. ground veal	Dash ground cinnamon
½ lb. sweet Italian sausage, cut in small pieces	Dash fennel seed
	Dash oregano
	3 bay leaves
1 (28 oz.) can Italian-style tomatoes	4 whole allspice, crushed
2 cans (6 oz. each) tomato paste	1 green pepper, chopped (about ¾ cup)
1 can (10¾ oz.) condensed tomato soup	½ lb. fresh mushrooms, sliced lengthwise
1 cup water	½ cup chopped pimiento-stuffed olives
1½ cups dry red wine	
1½ teaspoons Worcestershire sauce	1 jar (4 oz.) pimientos, drained and chopped
1 teaspoon salt	

1. Heat the olive oil in a large skillet. Add the onion and garlic and cook until onion is tender, about 5 minutes. Add the beef, veal, and sausage. Brown well, stirring occasionally.
2. Combine in a large heavy saucepan or saucepot the remaining ingredients except mushrooms, olives, and pimientos. Stir in the meat and onion.
3. Simmer, uncovered, at least 4 hours, stirring occasionally. If necessary, add a little hot water as sauce thickens during cooking. Remove bay leaves.
4. About 30 minutes before sauce is done, stir in mushrooms, olives and pimientos.
5. Serve sauce over *cooked spaghetti* and top with *grated Romano cheese.* ABOUT 4½ PINTS SAUCE

SEAFOOD SPAGHETTI SAUCE
The San Francisco, Paris, France, serves Spaghetti aux Fruits de Mer, which is similar to this recipe.

1 lb. cooked shrimp, peeled and deveined	6 large ripe tomatoes, peeled and chopped
1 lb. cooked lobster meat, cut in pieces	2 teaspoons tarragon, crushed
1 env. Italian salad dressing mix, prepared according to directions	¼ teaspoon ground saffron
	¾ teaspoon salt
	¼ teaspoon pepper

½ cup olive oil
2½ cups chopped onion
2 tablespoons snipped parsley

1. Marinate the shrimp and lobster meat in the prepared dressing for 1½ hours; drain thoroughly.
2. Meanwhile, heat the olive oil in a large saucepan. Add the onion and cook until tender.
3. Stir in the tomatoes, tarragon, saffron, salt, and pepper; simmer, covered, 30 minutes, stirring occasionally.
4. Stir the drained marinated seafood into the tomato sauce and heat thoroughly. Stir in the parsley and serve over *cooked spaghetti*.

ABOUT 3½ PINTS SAUCE

CREAMED SPINACH WITH ALMONDS

1 tablespoon flour
¾ teaspoon salt
⅛ teaspoon ground nutmeg
1 tablespoon butter or margarine
1 cup cream
2 tablespoons toasted almond halves
1 pkg. (10 oz.) frozen spinach, cooked and drained

1. Blend flour, salt, and nutmeg into hot butter in a saucepan. Heat until bubbly. Gradually add cream, stirring constantly. Bring to boiling; stir and cook 1 to 2 minutes.
2. Add almonds and spinach to sauce; mix lightly to blend. Serve garnished with *tomato wedges*.

ABOUT 4 SERVINGS

SPINACH CHEESE TART

Cheese Pastry for 1-Crust Pie, *page 253*
3 cups coarsely chopped cooked spinach (about 2¼ lbs. raw)
½ cup shredded Parmesan cheese
½ cup minced onion
¼ cup heavy cream
¼ cup butter or margarine, melted
½ cup cracker crumbs
2 tablespoons butter or margarine, melted

1. Prepare pastry shell; partially bake only about 8 minutes, or until slightly browned. Remove pastry shell from oven to a wire rack and reduce oven temperature to 375°F.
2. Meanwhile, combine spinach, cheese, onion, cream, and ¼ cup butter; mix thoroughly. Turn spinach mixture into partially baked pastry shell. Sprinkle with a mixture of crumbs and remaining butter.
3. Return tart to oven and bake about 15 minutes, or until pastry and crumbs are golden brown and spinach mixture is heated through.

ONE 9-INCH TART

HI-STYLE SPINACH

2 pkgs. (10 oz. each) frozen chopped spinach
¼ cup water
3 slices white bread, (crusts removed), cut in ½-in. cubes
⅓ cup butter or margarine
1½ teaspoons Worcestershire sauce
1 teaspoon grated onion
½ clove garlic, minced
½ teaspoon seasoned salt
3 tablespoons butter or margarine, melted
1 cup coarse fresh bread crumbs
⅓ cup shredded Parmesan cheese

1. Heat spinach with water only until thawed. Remove from heat (do not drain) and mix in the bread cubes, ⅓ cup butter, Worcestershire sauce, onion, garlic, and seasoned salt. Bring to boiling, reduce heat and simmer 10 minutes.
2. Turn mixture into an 8-inch square pan.
3. Toss 3 tablespoons butter into crumbs and cheese; sprinkle over top.
4. Heat in a 400°F oven 10 to 12 minutes, or until crumbs are golden brown.

6 TO 8 SERVINGS

CORN-FILLED ACORN SQUASH

3 small acorn squash, washed, halved, and seedy centers removed
½ cup chopped green pepper
1 clove garlic, minced
3 tablespoons butter or margarine
2 cups canned whole kernel corn, drained
¼ teaspoon salt
½ teaspoon monosodium glutamate
¼ teaspoon black pepper
1 teaspoon basil, crushed
1 cup soft fine bread crumbs
3 tablespoons butter or margarine, melted
3 tablespoons sesame seed, toasted
3 tablespoons shredded Parmesan cheese
2 tablespoons snipped parsley

1. Place squash halves, cut side down, in a shallow baking pan; pour in boiling water to a depth of ¼ inch. Bake at 400°F about 35 minutes, or until squash is almost tender.

Sweet Potatoes and Yams

2. Meanwhile, cook green pepper and garlic in 3 tablespoons hot butter in a skillet about 5 minutes, stirring occasionally. Remove from heat. Add corn and a mixture of salt, monosodium glutamate, pepper, and basil. Toss to mix; set aside.
3. Toss bread crumbs with remaining ingredients; set aside.
4. When squash is almost tender, remove from oven. Turn right side up. Butter each cavity generously and season with *salt* and *pepper*. Spoon the corn mixture into cavities. Sprinkle crumbs evenly over top.
5. Return to oven and continue baking until squash is tender and crumbs are browned, about 20 minutes. 6 SERVINGS

BAKED ACORN SQUASH: Follow step 1 of Corn-Filled Acorn Squash. Turn halves cavity side up and sprinkle with *salt, pepper,* and *brown sugar;* dot generously with *butter* or *margarine.* Return to oven and bake until tender.

DIXIE SQUASH

2 medium-sized acorn squashes, halved lengthwise
1 tablespoon butter or margarine, melted
1 teaspoon salt
2/3 cup uncooked regular rice
1/4 cup thinly sliced green onions
8 slices bacon, cooked and crumbled
1/2 cup dairy sour cream
1 teaspoon prepared hot spicy mustard

1. Preheat oven to 400°F.
2. Scoop out seeds from squash halves. Brush melted butter over hollows; season with 1/2 teaspoon of the salt. Place, cut sides down, in a greased shallow baking pan.
3. Bake 45 minutes, or until tender; turn halves right side up in pan.
4. While squashes bake, cook rice as label directs; remove from heat; stir in onions and bacon. Blend sour cream, mustard, and remaining 1/2 teaspoon salt in a cup; fold into rice mixture. Spoon into hollows in squashes.
5. Bake 15 minutes, or until hot. 4 SERVINGS

ACORN SQUASH STUFFED WITH HAM AND APPLE

3 medium-sized acorn squash, washed, halved, and seedy centers removed
1 cup diced tart cooking apples
2 cups diced ham
1 teaspoon dry mustard
1/4 teaspoon pepper
2 tablespoons butter, melted
2 teaspoons chopped onion

1. Bake squash, following step 1 of *Corn-Filled Acorn Squash, page 191.* Invert squash halves and sprinkle lightly with *salt.*
2. Combine remaining ingredients and spoon into squash cavities.
3. Return to oven and bake 20 minutes, or until apples are tender. 6 SERVINGS

SPICY WHIPPED SWEET POTATOES

6 medium-sized (about 2 lbs.) sweet potatoes, cooked, peeled, and mashed
1/4 cup butter or margarine
1/3 to 1/2 cup hot milk
1/4 cup firmly packed light brown sugar
1/2 teaspoon ground nutmeg
1/4 teaspoon ground cinnamon
1/4 teaspoon ground ginger
1/2 teaspoon salt
1/8 teaspoon pepper

Whip potatoes with remaining ingredients until fluffy. ABOUT 6 SERVINGS

SWEET POTATO PUDDING

Executive Chef Monsieur Robert Machax of the Executive House's Aruba Caribbean Hotel-Casino, Netherlands Antilles, adapted this recipe for American homemaker portions.

2 eggs
2 cups pared and grated raw sweet potatoes
1 cup sugar
1/2 teaspoon ground cinnamon
1 cup rich milk
1/4 cup melted butter
1/2 teaspoon grated lemon peel
2 teaspoons lemon juice

1. Beat eggs in a bowl until light. Mix in the potatoes. Beat in sugar, cinnamon, and a *dash ground nutmeg.* Stir in remaining ingredients in order. Turn into a buttered 1 1/2-quart baking dish.
2. Bake at 350°F about 30 minutes; stir pudding with a spoon, blending sides with center. Continue to bake 15 minutes. 6 TO 8 SERVINGS

YAMS AND BROCCOLI WITH PROVOLONE SAUCE

1 can (8 oz.) small onions
¼ teaspoon seasoned salt
1 pkg. (10 oz.) frozen broccoli spears
½ cup well-seasoned chicken broth
2 tablespoons butter or margarine, browned
⅓ cup maple-blended syrup, heated
4 medium-sized yams, cooked, peeled, and quartered
Provolone Sauce, page 197

1. Heat onions in their liquid with the seasoned salt; drain and keep warm.
2. Cook broccoli in the broth until just tender.
3. Drain broccoli and drizzle with browned butter. Pour the syrup over the hot yams. Arrange broccoli, yams, and onions in a heated 2-quart shallow baking dish.
4. Pour all but several tablespoonfuls of the hot Provolone Sauce over vegetables. Fold *2 or 3 tablespoons whipped cream* into remaining sauce and spoon over top. Set under broiler about 4 inches from source of heat until browned on top.

ABOUT 6 SERVINGS

T Tomatoes

FRIED TOMATOES

4 firm ripe or green tomatoes
½ cup cornmeal
1 teaspoon salt
⅛ teaspoon pepper
¼ cup butter or margarine

1. Cut out stem ends of tomatoes and slice ½ inch thick.
2. Mix cornmeal, salt, and pepper in a shallow dish. Coat both sides of tomato slices with the mixture.
3. Heat butter in a skillet. Add as many tomato slices at one time as will lie flat in skillet. Lightly brown both sides, turning once; cook only until tender. Add butter as needed. ABOUT 4 SERVINGS

CREAMED TOMATOES: Follow recipe for Fried Tomatoes. Add *½ teaspoon sugar* to cornmeal mixture. When tomatoes are lightly browned, stir to break up; cook 5 minutes. Just before serving, stir in *2 tablespoons cream.*

BAKED TOMATO HALVES WITH DANISH BLUE CHEESE

4 medium-sized firm ripe tomatoes, cut in halves
¼ teaspoon salt
⅛ teaspoon sugar
¼ teaspoon pepper
2 slices pumpernickel, crumbled
4 teaspoons melted butter
2 oz. Danish blue cheese, crumbled

1. Put the tomato halves, cut side up, in a buttered shallow baking dish. Sprinkle with a mixture of salt, sugar, and pepper.
2. Toss bread crumbs with melted butter. Mix in cheese. Spoon an equal amount onto each tomato half.
3. Bake at 350°F 15 minutes. Garnish with *watercress or parsley.* 8 TOMATO HALVES

BAKED TOMATOES, GENOA STYLE
(Pomodori Genovese)

4 firm ripe tomatoes, cut in halves and seeded
¼ cup olive oil
2 cloves garlic, minced
1½ teaspoons salt
½ teaspoon pepper
1½ teaspoons marjoram, crushed
¼ cup finely snipped parsley
½ cup shredded Parmesan cheese

1. Put tomato halves, cut side up, in a shallow baking dish. Sprinkle lightly with *sugar.*
2. Mix the olive oil, garlic, salt, pepper, and marjoram. Spoon an equal amount onto each tomato half. Sprinkle with parsley and cheese.
3. Bake at 350°F about 20 minutes, or until lightly browned. 4 SERVINGS

SCALLOPED TOMATOES

1 cup chopped onion
1 can (29 oz.) tomatoes, drained and cut in pieces
⅓ cup cheese cracker crumbs
1 tablespoon parsley flakes
1½ teaspoons sugar
1 teaspoon seasoned salt
1 cup dairy sour cream
3 slices crisp toast, cut in ¼-to ½-in. cubes
2 tablespoons butter
Parsley flakes

1. Mix the onion, tomatoes, crumbs, parsley

flakes, sugar, and salt in a greased 1¼-quart shallow baking dish. Spoon sour cream evenly over top.
2. Add toast cubes to hot butter in a skillet and toss until all sides are coated.
3. Spoon toast cubes over sour cream; sprinkle with parsley flakes.
4. Heat thoroughly in a 325°F oven about 20 minutes. Serve in sauce dishes.   ABOUT 6 SERVINGS

BAKED HASH-STUFFED TOMATOES

4 large firm ripe tomatoes	2 teaspoons prepared hot spicy mustard
1 can (15½ ozs.) corned-beef hash	½ teaspoon dried oregano, crushed
1 egg	
1 cup corn-bread stuffing mix	¼ cup shredded mozzarella cheese

1. Preheat oven to 350°F.
2. Cut a thin slice from the top of each tomato; scoop out insides into a bowl, then drain pulp and chop. Turn tomato shells upside down on paper toweling to drain.
3. Combine corned-beef hash, egg, stuffing mix, mustard, oregano, and chopped tomato pulp in a medium bowl; mix well. Pile into tomato shells. Place tomatoes in a shallow baking pan; sprinkle cheese over stuffing. (If you have any stuffing leftover, bake in a small casserole, uncovered, alongside tomatoes.)
4. Bake tomatoes 20 minutes, or until stuffing is hot and cheese melts and browns lightly.   4 SERVINGS

Z Zucchini

SEASONED ZUCCHINI

Wash desired amount of *zucchini*, trim off ends, and cut into thin slices. Heat a small amount of *butter*, *margarine*, *or olive oil* in a skillet. Add zucchini slices and cook quickly until tender. Season as desired.

ZUCCHINI PROVENÇALE

8 to 10 small (2½ lbs.) zucchini	2 cans (6 oz. each) tomato paste
⅔ cup coarsely chopped onion	1 clove garlic, minced
	1 teaspoon salt
¼ lb. fresh mushrooms, sliced lengthwise	½ teaspoon monosodium glutamate
3 tablespoons olive oil	⅛ teaspoon pepper
⅔ cup shredded Parmesan cheese	

1. Wash, trim off ends, and cut zucchini crosswise into ⅛-inch slices.
2. In a covered saucepan, cook zucchini, onion, and mushrooms in hot oil 10 to 15 minutes, or until zucchini is just tender; stir occasionally.
3. Remove from heat and, with a fork, mix in about half of the cheese. Blend in a mixture of the tomato paste and remaining ingredients. Turn into a 2-quart casserole and sprinkle with remaining cheese.
4. Heat in a 350°F oven 20 to 30 minutes, or until very hot.   8 SERVINGS

STUFFED ZUCCHINI

4 zucchini (each about 4½ in. long), scrubbed and cut in halves lengthwise	2 tablespoons minced parsley
	½ teaspoon lemon juice
	½ teaspoon salt
½ cup chopped onion	Few grains pepper
1 tablespoon olive oil	1 egg yolk, beaten
3 tablespoons fine dry bread crumbs	Fat for deep frying heated to 365°F
2 cloves garlic, minced	

1. Hollow centers of zucchini by scooping out some of pulp; reserve. Drop shells into boiling *salted water;* cook until just tender, about 4 minutes. Drain. Chop reserved pulp; set aside.
2. Cook onion about 5 minutes in hot oil in a skillet. Remove from heat.
3. **Add crumbs, garlic,** parsley, lemon juice, salt, pepper, and egg yolk to onion along with chopped pulp; blend thoroughly.
4. Fill zucchini shells with mixture. Dip in a mixture of *1 egg yolk* beaten with *1 tablespoon olive oil*. Coat evenly with *fine dry bread crumbs*.
5. Fry zucchini in heated fat about 1 minute, **or** until lightly browned. Fry only as many stuffed shells at one time as will float uncrowded one layer deep in fat. Remove with slotted spoon and drain on absorbent paper.   8 SERVINGS

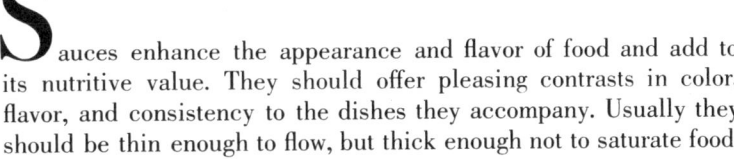

Chapter 9
SAUCES & GRAVIES

Sauces enhance the appearance and flavor of food and add to its nutritive value. They should offer pleasing contrasts in color, flavor, and consistency to the dishes they accompany. Usually they should be thin enough to flow, but thick enough not to saturate food.

Basic sauces for meat, poultry, fish, and vegetables are few in number, but their variations are almost limitless. Wherever spices, herbs, seasonings, and a few basic ingredients are available, the art of sauce making is open to amateur and professional alike.

White Sauce—Foremost among basic sauces is white sauce. This is the indispensable base for innumerable sauces and is frequently used in other food preparation as well—in cream soups, casserole dishes, croquettes, and soufflés. Four main groups are made from the basic sauce by varying the type of liquid used or by browning the flour.

White sauce, as the name implies, is made with milk or cream. Spices, seasonings, and condiments add their piquant flavor to many variations of white sauce. A second group is created by the substitution of meat or vegetable stock or water for milk, an example being *gravy*. To a third group belong the brown sauces which result when the flour used for thickening white sauce is browned before adding the liquid. Some gravies are also included in this group. A fourth group results from the substitution of tomato juice or purée for milk.

A white sauce provides the base for a group of French sauces often used to enhance meat, poultry, fish, or vegetable dishes. Included are:

Béchamel sauce—a white sauce with chicken stock and cream used for the liquid and often seasoned with onion.

Bercy sauce—a white sauce using fish stock for the liquid and cooking chopped shallots in the butter before adding the flour. There are variations of this sauce, some of which use wine for the liquid.

Mornay sauce—a white sauce to which cheese (Parmesan or Gruyère) and egg yolks have been added and using cream and chicken or veal stock for the liquid.

Velouté sauce—a white sauce using chicken or veal stock for the liquid and sometimes seasoned with ground nutmeg. Velouté sauce, when served with fish, may call for fish stock instead of chicken or veal.

One may find a variety of interpretations of these sauces in cookbooks and as they are prepared by famous chefs.

Hollandaise Sauce—Another well-known sauce used as a base for others. It is a rich sauce made with egg yolks, seasonings, lemon juice, and butter.

Béarnaise sauce—a Hollandaise based sauce with herbs such as tarragon, chervil, and parsley added to it. Some versions of Béarnaise sauce have wine as an ingredient.

BROWN ROUX
Used for thickening brown sauces, this paste may be made in advance and stored in refrigerator until needed.

Melt *1 cup butter or other fat* in a heavy skillet; blend in *1 cup all-purpose flour* to form a smooth paste. Stir and cook over low heat until mixture is light brown and roux is thoroughly cooked.

ABOUT 1 CUP

SAUCES

MEDIUM WHITE SAUCE
(Cream Sauce)

2 tablespoons butter or margarine
2 tablespoons flour
½ teaspoon salt
⅛ teaspoon pepper
1 cup milk (use light cream for richer sauce)

1. Heat butter in a saucepan. Blend in flour, salt, and pepper; heat and stir until bubbly.
2. Gradually add the milk, stirring until smooth. Bring to boiling; cook and stir 1 to 2 minutes longer.   ABOUT 1 CUP

THICK WHITE SAUCE: Follow recipe for Medium White Sauce. Use *3 to 4 tablespoons flour* and *3 to 4 tablespoons butter.* Use in preparation of soufflés and croquettes.

THIN WHITE SAUCE: Follow recipe for Medium White Sauce. Use *1 tablespoon flour* and *1 tablespoon butter.* Use as a base for cream soups.

BÉCHAMEL SAUCE

This sauce is named for its originator, Louis de Béchamel, Lord Steward of the Household in the Court of King Louis XIV.

Follow recipe for Medium White Sauce. Substitute *½ cup chicken broth* for *½ cup milk.* Stir in *1 tablespoon minced onion.* Serve hot on vegetables, fish, hard-cooked eggs, or poultry.

NORMANDY SAUCE

The flavor of almost any vegetable may be enhanced with this sauce. Use it freely with these — celery, carrots, cauliflower, asparagus, green peas, or salsify — all typical of Normandy, France.

Follow recipe for Medium White Sauce using 1½ times the recipe. Substitute *½ cup light cream* and *1 cup cider* for milk. Blend in *¼ teaspoon lemon juice* and *½ teaspoon ground nutmeg.*

BERCY SAUCE

A shallot sauce used as a topping for cooked fish before it is placed under broiler or in oven to brown.

Follow recipe for Medium White Sauce. Cook *1 tablespoon chopped shallots* in the butter before stirring in flour. Substitute *fish stock* for milk.

BROWN OR ESPAGNOLE SAUCE

This basic sauce is used as an ingredient in other sauces and may be stored about a week in the refrigerator or for a longer time in the freezer.

¼ cup chopped green onion
½ cup chopped celery
½ cup chopped carrot
2 tablespoons cooking oil
2 qts. water
3 beef bouillon cubes
3 chicken bouillon cubes
1 small bay leaf
Pinch ground thyme
Few grains freshly ground black pepper
2 tablespoons tomato sauce
½ cup water
¼ cup flour

1. Using a large saucepot, cook onion, celery, and carrot in hot oil until dark brown; do not burn. Add 2 quarts water, bouillon cubes, bay leaf, thyme, and pepper; bring to boiling and then simmer until stock is reduced by half.
2. Strain. Stir in tomato sauce; bring to boiling.
3. Vigorously shake the water and flour in a screwtop jar. Gradually add to boiling mixture, stirring constantly. Cook 1 to 2 minutes, then simmer about 30 minutes, stirring occasionally.   1 QUART

NOTE: If desired, thicken sauce with *4 tablespoons Brown Roux, page 195,* instead of the flour-water mixture. Add the roux after the tomato sauce. To avoid lumping, blend some of the hot liquid mixture into roux, stirring until smooth. Then stir into remaining liquid and bring to boiling. Simmer as directed.

BORDELAISE SAUCE

A tasty sauce containing red wine usually served over broiled meat, often beef.

4 shallots, finely chopped
2 to 3 tablespoons butter
1 cup red wine
1 cup Brown Sauce, above
Few drops lemon juice
1 teaspoon finely minced parsley

1. Sauté shallots in butter in a small saucepan. Add the wine and cook over low heat until reduced to one half.
2. Strain. Add Brown Sauce and continue heating. Add lemon juice and parsley.   ABOUT 1½ CUPS

MORNAY SAUCE

This French cheese sauce may be served over fish or vegetables, or as a topping for a casserole.

3 tablespoons flour	¾ cup light cream
3 tablespoons butter or margarine	2 egg yolks, fork beaten
¾ cup vegetable broth (dissolve 1 vegetable bouillon cube in ¾ cup boiling water)	½ cup shredded Parmesan cheese
	1 tablespoon butter or margarine

1. Blend the flour into 3 tablespoons hot butter in the top of a double boiler. Heat until bubbly. Stir in the broth and cream and bring to boiling; stir and cook 1 to 2 minutes longer.
2. Stir about ¼ cup of hot sauce into egg yolks. Immediately return to mixture in double boiler. Cook over boiling water about 5 minutes stirring occasionally.
3. Remove from heat and add cheese and remaining butter, stirring until cheese is melted.

ABOUT 1½ CUPS

NOTE: If desired, *1½ ounces Gruyère cheese*, cut in small pieces, may be substituted for Parmesan cheese.

HOT RAVIGOTE SAUCE

A French sauce made with veal or chicken stock flavored with herbs and white wine. It is served on hot or cold meat, fish, seafood, and vegetables.

½ cup white wine	1 teaspoon minced chervil
¼ cup vinegar	
5 tablespoons butter	1 teaspoon minced tarragon
¼ cup flour	
2 cups seasoned veal or chicken broth	1 teaspoon chopped chives
1 shallot, minced	

1. Cook wine and vinegar in a saucepan over low heat until reduced to one half.
2. Heat 3 tablespoons butter and blend in the flour. Stir in broth and cook until thickened, stirring constantly.
3. Add to wine and simmer 5 minutes. Add remaining butter and mix well. Stir in shallot and remaining ingredients. Season to taste with *salt* and *pepper*.

ABOUT 2½ CUPS

HOLLANDAISE SAUCE

This rich sauce is used to enhance many foods . . . cooked green vegetables, chicken and turkey, egg dishes, and others.

2 egg yolks	2 tablespoons lemon juice or tarragon vinegar
2 tablespoons cream	
¼ teaspoon salt	
Few grains cayenne pepper	½ cup butter

1. In the top of a double boiler, beat egg yolks, cream, salt, and cayenne pepper until thick with a whisk beater. Set over hot (not boiling) water. (Bottom of double-boiler top should not touch water.)
2. Add the lemon juice gradually, while beating constantly. Cook, beating constantly with the whisk beater, until sauce is the consistency of thick cream. Remove double boiler from heat, leaving top in place.
3. Beating constantly, add the butter, ½ teaspoon at a time. Beat with whisk beater until butter is melted and thoroughly blended in.

ABOUT 1 CUP

NOTE: If necessary, the sauce may be kept hot 15 to 30 minutes over hot water. Keep covered and stir sauce occasionally.

BÉARNAISE SAUCE: Follow recipe for Hollandaise Sauce. Add 1 peppercorn, crushed, with the salt. Blend in, after the butter, *3 tablespoons finely chopped fresh herbs* such as tarragon, chervil, shallots (or green onion or chives), and parsley.

PROVOLONE SAUCE

1½ tablespoons flour	1½ cups milk
¼ teaspoon celery seed	1½ cups (about 6 oz.) shredded provolone cheese
⅛ teaspoon pepper	
1½ tablespoons butter or margarine	

1. Stir a mixture of the flour, celery seed, and pepper into hot butter in a heavy saucepan. Cook until bubbly.
2. Add milk gradually, stirring constantly. Bring rapidly to boiling; stir and cook 2 minutes. Remove from heat and stir in the cheese until melted. Use immediately.

1½ CUPS SAUCE

Sauces

ENGLISH MUSTARD SAUCE

A sauce that is especially compatible with hot corned beef.

1 tablespoon flour
1 teaspoon dry mustard
⅛ teaspoon salt
⅛ teaspoon pepper
½ cup water
1 tablespoon cider vinegar
1 tablespoon butter
1 tablespoon prepared mustard

1. Combine the flour, dry mustard, salt, and pepper in a heavy saucepan. Gradually add the water and vinegar; cook, stirring, until boiling; cook 1 to 2 minutes longer.
2. Remove from heat; stir in butter and mustard. Serve hot.

ABOUT ½ CUP

DILLED MUSHROOM SAUCE

¼ cup chopped onion
¼ cup chopped fresh mushrooms
2 tablespoons butter or margarine
2 tablespoons flour
¼ teaspoon salt
Few grains pepper
¼ teaspoon dill weed, crushed
1 cup milk
1 teaspoon grated lemon peel

1. Cook onion and mushrooms in hot butter in a heavy saucepan over medium heat about 5 minutes. Blend in a mixture of flour, salt, pepper, and dill weed. Cook, stirring constantly, until bubbly.
2. Remove from heat and gradually add milk, continuing to stir. Add lemon peel. Bring rapidly to boiling and boil 1 to 2 minutes, stirring constantly. Serve hot.

ABOUT 1 CUP

QUICK TOMATO SAUCE

2 tablespoons butter or margarine
¼ cup coarsely chopped celery
¼ cup coarsely chopped green pepper
2 tablespoons finely chopped onion
1 can (10¾ oz.) condensed tomato soup
⅓ cup water
2 tablespoons lemon juice
1 tablespoon Worcestershire sauce
2 tablespoons brown sugar
1 teaspoon dry mustard
½ teaspoon salt
Few grains pepper

1. Heat the butter in a skillet. Add the vegetables and cook, stirring frequently, until celery and green pepper are tender.
2. Gradually add a mixture of soup, water, lemon juice, and Worcestershire sauce, stirring constantly. Mix in a blend of the remaining ingredients. Simmer, uncovered, about 5 minutes.

ABOUT 2 CUPS

SALSA ITALIANA

A special sauce to complement many main dishes.

1 cup chopped onion
¼ cup olive oil or cooking oil
1 clove garlic, minced
¼ cup grated carrot
1 tablespoon finely snipped parsley
¼ teaspoon basil, crushed
⅛ teaspoon thyme, crushed
2 cans (8 oz. each) tomato sauce
½ cup beef broth (dissolve ½ beef bouillon cube in ½ cup boiling water)

1. Add onion to hot oil in saucepan and cook until tender. Stir in the garlic, carrot, and parsley; cook about 3 minutes, stirring frequently.
2. Blend in remaining ingredients. Simmer gently until flavors are blended, about 10 minutes.

ABOUT 3 CUPS

ORANGE BARBECUE SAUCE

¼ cup packed brown sugar
½ teaspoon dry mustard
⅛ teaspoon ground cloves
½ teaspoon Worcestershire sauce
⅓ cup chopped onion
1½ teaspoons grated orange peel
⅓ cup orange juice
¾ cup ketchup
1½ cups water

Mix all ingredients in a heavy saucepan; bring to boiling, stirring until sugar is dissolved. Reduce heat; simmer, uncovered, about 30 minutes, stirring occasionally.

ABOUT 2¼ CUPS

SAUCE ORIENTAL

1½ tablespoons cornstarch
1 can (11 oz.) mandarin oranges, drained (reserve syrup)
½ cup maple syrup
2 tablespoons lemon juice
2 tablespoons dark seedless raisins
1 tablespoon butter or margarine

1. Combine cornstarch, reserved orange syrup, maple syrup, and lemon juice in a saucepan; stir until smooth. Add raisins. Bring to boiling over medium heat, stirring constantly; boil 3 minutes.
2. Stir in butter and oranges; simmer 2 minutes.
3. Serve hot with *roast duckling*. ABOUT 1⅔ CUPS

TERIYAKI SAUCE
A sauce complementary to shellfish, especially crab meat.

½ cup pineapple juice
¼ cup brown sugar
2 tablespoons soy sauce
1 tablespoon salad oil
¾ teaspoon ground ginger
¼ teaspoon salt
1 clove garlic, minced

Combine all ingredients in small saucepan. Heat to blend flavors. ABOUT ⅔ CUP

TANGY PLUM SAUCE FOR POULTRY

1 can or jar (17 oz.) purple plums, drained (reserve ¼ cup syrup)
½ cup frozen orange juice concentrate, thawed
½ teaspoon Worcestershire sauce

1. Pit plums, and force through a sieve or food mill into a bowl. Blend in reserved syrup, orange juice, and Worcestershire sauce.
2. During final hour of roasting, brush *turkey* (or other poultry) with the sauce at 15-minute intervals. If desired, blend remaining sauce into gravy. ABOUT 1½ CUPS

TARRAGON BUTTER

¼ cup butter, melted
2 tablespoons lemon juice
1 teaspoon minced onion
¼ teaspoon salt
½ teaspoon crushed tarragon

Combine melted butter with remaining ingredients. Serve hot over fish or shellfish.
ABOUT 6 TABLESPOONS

TARTAR SAUCE
A favorite for hot or cold fish and shellfish.

1 to 2 teaspoons minced onion
1½ to 2 tablespoons chopped sweet pickle, drained
1 to 2 tablespoons chopped green olives, drained
¾ cup mayonnaise

Combine all ingredients. Store in covered jar in refrigerator. ABOUT 1 CUP

ROSEMARY PLUM SAUCE
This versatile sauce is a perfect complement for meat and poultry. Blended with only a small amount of the Rosemary Brew, it is also delightful over waffles, pancakes, and fritters.

1 jar or can (17 oz.) purple plums, drained (reserve syrup)
½ cup dark corn syrup
Rosemary Brew, *below*
3 to 4 tablespoons butter or margarine

1. Pit plums and purée pulp in an electric blender.
2. Mix purée with corn syrup, Rosemary Brew, and butter in a saucepan.
3. Heat thoroughly, stirring occasionally.
ABOUT 2¾ CUPS

ROSEMARY BREW: In a small saucepan, bring 1 cup reserved plum syrup to boiling. Mix in *2 tablespoons rosemary leaves* and simmer. Remove from heat, cover, and let stand about 10 minutes. Strain through a fine sieve.

SOUR CREAM SAUCE

1 cup dairy sour cream
1 tablespoon sugar
Salt to taste
Dash cayenne pepper
½ teaspoon dry mustard
1 to 2 tablespoons vinegar

Combine all ingredients, mix thoroughly, and chill. Serve with *cold fish, poultry,* and *meats.* 1 CUP

MAYONNAISE-SOUR CREAM SAUCE: Follow recipe for Sour Cream Sauce. Add *1 to 2 teaspoons grated lemon peel.* Substitute *½ cup mayonnaise* for ½ cup dairy sour cream.

CUCUMBER SAUCE: Follow recipe for Sour Cream Sauce. Add *1 cup chopped pared cucumber.* Omit the mustard and add *2 tablespoons prepared horseradish.*

GRAVIES

BROWN GRAVY

Remove roasted meat or poultry from roasting pan. Leaving brown residue in the pan, pour the drippings into a bowl. Allow the fat to rise to surface; skim off fat and reserve. (Remaining drippings in bowl are meat juices which should be used as part of the liquid in the gravy.)

Method I:

3 tablespoons fat	2 cups liquid, warm or
3 tablespoons flour	cool (water; drippings;
½ teaspoon salt	meat, chicken, or
⅛ teaspoon pepper	vegetable broth; or milk)

1. Add the fat to roasting pan (with brown residue); stir in the flour and seasonings until smooth. Heat until bubbly. Brown slightly if desired.
2. Stir in the liquid and cook until sauce thickens; continue stirring and cooking 2 or 3 minutes longer, scraping bottom and sides of roasting pan to blend in the brown residue. ABOUT 2 CUPS GRAVY

Method II:

2 cups chicken or meat broth (fat skimmed)	¼ cup flour
½ cup cold broth or water	½ teaspoon salt
	⅛ teaspoon pepper

1. Bring the broth to boiling in a saucepan. Drippings from roasted meat or poultry may be substituted for part of the broth. If necessary, add milk or water to drippings to make 2 cups liquid.
2. Measure broth and flour into a screw-top glass jar or shaker. Cover jar and shake until flour and broth are blended. Stirring boiling broth constantly, add flour mixture, a small amount at a time and bring to boiling after each addition. Cook and stir, adding only enough flour mixture until gravy is desired consistency. Add seasonings to taste. When gravy is thickened, cook 2 or 3 minutes longer. ABOUT 2½ CUPS GRAVY

GIBLET GRAVY: Follow either method adding chopped *giblets* the last several minutes of cooking.

RED EYE GRAVY

Tennessee Ernie Ford says his Red Eye Gravy—which he also calls Poor Man's Au Jus—can only be made from country cured Tennessee ham, no other kind will work. He insists that the real country hams are a deep red color, which gives the gravy it's name. This ham can only be fried—not baked.

Fry thick slices of *Tennessee ham*. Remove meat from the skillet, skim off the excess fat that rises to the surface. Add *4 tablespoons cold coffee*. That's it! Serve over *grits* and *hot biscuits*.

GINGERSNAP GRAVY

1. Drain *drippings* and *fat* from roasting pan. Allow fat to rise to surface and skim it off; reserve 3 tablespoons. Heat the fat and drippings (about ¾ cup) in a saucepan; blend in *6 finely crushed gingersnaps*; heat until mixture bubbles.
2. Remove from heat and gradually add *1 cup water*, blending well. Bring to boiling and boil 1 to 2 minutes, stirring constantly. Season with *salt* and *pepper* as desired. ABOUT 1½ CUPS GRAVY

GINGER GRAVY: Follow recipe for Gingersnap Gravy. Substitute a mixture of *3 tablespoons flour, ½ teaspoon monosodium glutamate, ¼ teaspoon salt, ⅛ teaspoon black pepper*, and *½ teaspoon ground ginger* for the gingersnaps.

TURKEY OR CHICKEN GRAVY

6 tablespoons flour	4 cups liquid (reserved
½ teaspoon salt	giblet broth and
¼ teaspoon pepper	turkey drippings, or chicken broth)

1. Remove roasted turkey from roasting pan. Leaving brown residue in pan, pour drippings into a bowl. Allow fat to rise to surface; skim off and reserve fat. Reserve remaining drippings for part of gravy liquid.
2. Measure 6 tablespoons reserved fat into roasting pan and blend in flour, salt, and pepper until smooth. Stirring constantly, heat until mixture bubbles. Brown slightly, if desired. Remove from heat and slowly blend in the liquid.
3. Return to heat and cook rapidly, stirring constantly, until gravy thickens. Cook 1 to 2 minutes longer. While stirring, scrape bottom and sides of pan to blend in brown residue. ABOUT 4 CUPS GRAVY

Chapter 10
SALADS & SALAD DRESSINGS

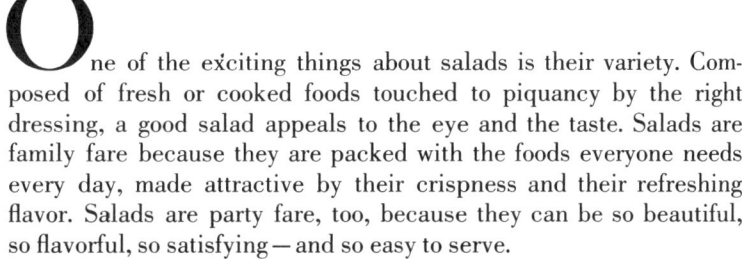

One of the exciting things about salads is their variety. Composed of fresh or cooked foods touched to piquancy by the right dressing, a good salad appeals to the eye and the taste. Salads are family fare because they are packed with the foods everyone needs every day, made attractive by their crispness and their refreshing flavor. Salads are party fare, too, because they can be so beautiful, so flavorful, so satisfying — and so easy to serve.

Salads come in many forms: they may be appetizers, garnitures, accompaniments, main dishes, desserts, or a whole meal; they may be made individually, or may be big enough to serve the whole party; and they may be crisp and cool, molded, frozen, or even hot. With all this variety, don't let yourself or your family get into a salad rut!

SALAD POINTERS

A salad is only as good as its makings so select the ingredients with care. Greens should be fresh, crisp, and dry, vegetables garden fresh, and fruits firm, fully ripe, and free from blemish. When using canned products, choose those of good quality and appearance.

Chill all salad ingredients, bowls, and plates thoroughly. With the exception of a few hot salads, coldness is essential to the appeal of all salads.

Trim and rinse greens under running cold water, handling them carefully to avoid bruising. Shake off the excess moisture and then gently pat dry before putting them into a plastic bag or the vegetable drawer and into your refrigerator. Wet greens not only make watery salads, they present a surface to which an oil dressing cannot cling.

Greens should always be broken or torn, never cut (except in the case of head lettuce which is to be served in wedges or quarters).

Tomatoes may be peeled or not, as your family prefers, for use in salads. Unpeeled tomato shells or tomato cups are sturdier and keep their shape better; peeled ones are easier to cut with a fork.

Tomato wedges or chunks should be added to tossed salads just before serving, as their juice tends to make the dressing watery.

Fruits that tend to discolor after peeling or paring (such as avocados, bananas, apples, fresh peaches and pears) should be brushed with pineapple or citrus fruit juice unless they are to be tossed immediately with an acid fruit or salad dressing.

Final assembling of ingredients for a salad of fresh fruits, vegetables, or greens should be done *just* before serving. Many main-dish salads, potato and macaroni salads, and cooked-vegetable salads improve in flavor when the mixture is prepared an hour or so ahead of serving time and allowed to stand in the refrigerator to chill and blend the individual flavors. But even these mixtures should be combined with their green garnishes at the last moment.

Avoid unnecessary handling of salad materials. Salads should always have that fresh-from-the-refrigerator look which is so appealing to the eye and tempting to the taste. Arrange fruits or vegetables on the salad plate if the salad requires it, but don't *rearrange* them.

GREEN & VEGETABLE SALADS

SALAD GREEN VARIETIES & PREPARATION

The many varieties of greens star in the tossed salad and form the background of other salads. Select greens that are fresh and crisp and blemish-free. In general, rinse them before storing, drain thoroughly, and gently pat dry with a soft, clean cloth or absorbent paper. Put into the refrigerator in the vegetable drawer or a plastic bag, or wrap tightly in aluminum foil or other moisture-vaporproof material to prevent wilting. Avoid soaking greens when rinsing them. If necessary, crisp them by placing in ice and water for a short time. Before using, remove all moisture left from rinsing and crisping.

ASPARAGUS VINAIGRETTE
In this version of the ever-appealing asparagus served in the French manner, flavor perfection is easily achieved using a salad dressing mix in preparing the "vinaigrette."

1 env. herb-flavored oil-and-vinegar salad dressing mix	1 tablespoon finely chopped chives
Tarragon-flavored white wine vinegar	2 teaspoons capers
Water	1 hard-cooked egg, finely chopped
Salad oil	Cooked asparagus spears, chilled
2 tablespoons chopped parsley	

1. Prepare salad dressing mix as directed on package, using vinegar, water, and salad oil.
2. Using 1 cup of the dressing, mix well with parsley, chives, capers and egg. Chill thoroughly.
3. To serve, arrange chilled asparagus in six bundles on a chilled serving plate lined with *Boston lettuce*. Garnish each bundle with a *pimiento strip*. Complete platter with *cucumber slices* and *radish roses*. Mix dressing well before spooning over asparagus. 6 SERVINGS

COLIFLOR ACAPULCO
Mexico has contributed this flamboyant salad.

1 large head cauliflower	Lettuce
Marinade, *below*	1 jar (16 oz.) sliced pickled beets, drained and chilled
1 can (15 oz.) garbanzos, drained	1 large cucumber, thinly sliced and chilled
1 cup pimiento-stuffed olives	Radish roses
Pimientos, drained and cut lengthwise in strips	Guacamole, *page 19*

1. Cook the cauliflower in boiling *salted water* about 10 minutes, or just until tender; drain. Place cauliflower, head down, in a deep bowl and pour the marinade over it. Chill several hours or overnight; occasionally spoon marinade over all.
2. Shortly before serving, thread garbanzos, pimiento-stuffed olives, and pimiento strips onto wooden picks for decorative kabobs. Set aside while arranging salad.
3. Drain the cauliflower. Line a chilled serving plate with crisp lettuce and place cauliflower, head up, in the center. Arrange the pickled beet and cucumber slices around the base, tucking in *parsley sprigs* and the radish roses.
4. Spoon and spread Guacamole over the cauliflower. Decorate with *cashew nuts* and the kabobs. Serve cold. 6 TO 8 SERVINGS

MARINADE: Combine *1½ cups salad oil*, *½ cup lemon juice*, *1½ teaspoons salt*, and *1 teaspoon chili powder*. Shake the marinade well before pouring it over the cauliflower.

CUCUMBER SALAD BOWL

1 envelope onion salad dressing mix	1 medium cucumber
Vinegar	1 can (11 ozs.) mandarin orange segments, drained
Water	
Salad oil	1 large head romaine, broken into bite-sized pieces

1. Combine salad dressing mix, vinegar, water, and salad oil in a jar as label directs; chill.
2. Draw a fork lengthwise through rind of cucumber

to make a ridged design; slice cucumber in thin rounds.
3. Place romaine in a large salad bowl. (There should be 8 cups.) Tuck cucumber slices and orange segments into bowl around romaine. Drizzle ½ cup of the salad dressing over top; toss until evenly mixed. (Chill remaining salad dressing to use another day.)

6 SERVINGS

CRUNCHY PEANUT COLE SLAW

3 cups finely chopped green cabbage
1 cup finely chopped red cabbage
1 cup finely chopped celery
1 cup coarsely chopped cauliflower
1 cup dairy sour cream
1 cup mayonnaise
1 tablespoon sugar
1 teaspoon salt
1 tablespoon tarragon vinegar
½ cup finely chopped cucumber
¼ cup finely chopped green onion
¼ cup finely chopped green pepper
1 tablespoon butter or margarine
½ cup coarsely chopped salted peanuts
2 tablespoons shredded Parmesan cheese

1. Toss the green and red cabbage, celery, and cauliflower together and chill.
2. Combine the sour cream, mayonnaise, sugar, salt, vinegar, cucumber, green onion, and green pepper for the salad dressing and chill thoroughly.
3. Melt butter in a small skillet; add peanuts and heat several minutes until lightly browned. Remove from heat and immediately stir in the Parmesan cheese. Set aside.
4. Just before serving, toss chilled vegetables with the dressing and top with the peanut mixture.

8 SERVINGS

TOMATO-CREAM SLAW

1 cup dairy sour cream
¼ cup mayonnaise
½ cup tomato sauce
2 tablespoons cider vinegar
2 tablespoons sugar
1 teaspoon celery seed
1 small head cabbage, coarsely shredded

1. Combine in a bowl the sour cream, mayonnaise, tomato sauce, vinegar, sugar, and celery seed. Refrigerate at least 1 hour for flavors to blend and dressing to chill.
2. Put shredded cabbage into a bowl and chill.
3. Just before serving, pour the dressing over the cabbage and toss lightly to mix.   ABOUT 6 SERVINGS

PIQUANT CUCUMBER SLICES

2 tablespoons sugar
1 teaspoon salt
⅛ teaspoon white pepper
1 teaspoon celery seed
¼ cup cider vinegar
1 tablespoon lemon juice
1 cucumber, rinsed (do not pare)
¼ cup coarsely chopped onion
2 tablespoons chopped parsley

1. Combine the sugar, salt, white pepper, celery seed, vinegar, and lemon juice in a bowl; blend thoroughly.
2. Score cucumber by drawing tines of a fork lengthwise over entire surface. Cut into ⅛-inch slices.
3. Add cucumber to vinegar mixture with onion and parsley; toss to coat evenly.
4. Chill thoroughly, turning several times.

ABOUT 4 SERVINGS

GAZPACHO SALAD BOWL

1 envelope old-fashioned French salad dressing mix
2 tablespoons water
⅔ cup salad oil
⅔ cup tomato juice
¼ cup vinegar
1 small head iceberg lettuce
1 small avocado
Lemon juice
1 small cucumber, scored and sliced
1 small red onion, peeled, sliced, and separated into rings
1 large carrot, pared and shredded
2 hard-cooked eggs, sliced
1 cup packaged cheese croutons

1. Combine dressing mix and water in a jar with a tight lid; shake well. Add salad oil, tomato juice, and vinegar; shake well again; chill.
2. Just before serving, break lettuce into bite-sized pieces and place in a large salad bowl.
3. Peel avocado; cut in half and pit; slice halves crosswise. Dip slices in lemon juice in a pie plate to prevent darkening.
4. Arrange avocado, cucumber slices, onion rings, carrot, and eggs in sections, spoke fashion, on top of lettuce; pile croutons in center.
5. Drizzle ¾ cup of the tomato dressing over top; toss lightly to mix. (Chill remaining dressing to use another day.)

8 SERVINGS

Green & Vegetable Salads

WILTED LETTUCE

Visitors to Pennsylvania Dutch country are likely to be treated to this old-fashioned lettuce dish. Fresh tender leaf lettuce of early summer is often used.

1 large head lettuce	2 tablespoons heavy
6 slices bacon, diced	cream
½ cup water	1 tablespoon sugar
¼ cup cider vinegar	¼ teaspoon salt

1. Tear lettuce into pieces into a bowl; set aside.
2. Fry bacon until crisp in a skillet; reserve ¼ cup drippings. Drain bacon on absorbent paper; set aside.
3. Stir the remaining ingredients into drippings in skillet. Heat mixture just to boiling, stirring constantly.
4. Immediately pour vinegar mixture over the lettuce and toss lightly to coat thoroughly. Top with the bacon.   ABOUT 8 SERVINGS

BLUE RIBBON POTATO-ONION SALAD

2 lbs. potatoes, cooked and peeled	3 hard-cooked eggs, chopped
2½ tablespoons cider vinegar	1 cup diced celery Onion Sour Cream
1 tablespoon salad oil	Dressing, *below*
1½ teaspoons salt	

1. Cut potatoes into ½ inch cubes and put into a bowl. Toss with a mixture of vinegar, oil, and salt. Add eggs, celery, and dressing; toss until mixed. Cover and chill thoroughly.
2. Turn salad into a chilled salad bowl.
    10 TO 12 SERVINGS

ONION-SOUR CREAM DRESSING: Combine *1¾ cups dairy sour cream, ½ teaspoon sugar, few grains pepper, 2 tablespoons cider vinegar, 1½ teaspoons prepared mustard, ½ cup grated onion* (or blender puréed), and *½ cup sliced ripe olives*. Chill until ready to use.   ABOUT 2½ CUPS DRESSING

GARDEN POTATO SALAD

2 cans (16 oz. each) potato salad	1 medium-sized cucumber, rinsed, pared, and diced
⅔ cup thinly sliced radishes (about 8 radishes)	6 green onions, cut in ½-inch pieces

Turn potato salad into a bowl. Add the radishes, cucumber, and onion; lightly toss together. Chill thoroughly. Before serving, toss lightly.
    ABOUT 8 SERVINGS

LEMON-GINGER CARROTS

1 bag (20 oz.) frozen small whole carrots	2 tablespoons chopped parsley
¼ cup salad oil	1 teaspoon sugar
2 tablespoons lemon juice	½ teaspoon salt
1 tablespoon minced onion	½ teaspoon ground ginger
	Romaine

1. Cook carrots as label directs; drain. Place in a medium bowl.
2. While carrots cook, combine salad oil, lemon juice, onion, parsley, sugar, salt, and ginger in a jar with a tight lid; shake well to mix. Pour over warm carrots; stir lightly to coat; cover. Chill several hours to season.
3. When ready to serve, line a medium salad bowl with romaine; spoon carrot mixture into center. Garnish with several small white onion rings if you like.   6 SERVINGS

SPINACH-BEET SALAD

Wash, discard bruised leaves, drain, dry, and tear enough *spinach* into pieces to yield about 2 quarts. Turn into a salad bowl; cover and chill. Meanwhile, pour *French dressing* over *2 cups julienne beets*; chill. When ready to serve, add marinated beets and *Herb Croutons, below*, to spinach in bowl; gently turn and toss until greens are evenly coated with dressing. Garnish with *hard-cooked egg slices*. Serve immediately.
    6 TO 8 SERVINGS

HERB CROUTONS: Trim crusts from *2 slices toasted white bread* and cut into ¼- to ½-inch cubes. Heat *2 tablespoons butter or margarine* in a small skillet over low heat. Add *¼ teaspoon thyme*, crushed, *¼ teaspoon marjoram*, crushed, and bread cubes. Turn and toss cubes until all sides are coated and croutons are browned.
    ABOUT ⅔ CUP

SALADE PROVENÇALE

2 green peppers, cut in strips	½ Bermuda onion, peeled and sliced
¼ cup oil (part salad oil and part olive oil)	4 oz. fresh mushrooms, cleaned and sliced lengthwise
3 firm ripe tomatoes, washed and cut in pieces	12 whole pitted ripe olives

1. Fry the green pepper strips in the oil until partially tender.
2. Remove strips to a bowl. Add the tomatoes, onion, mushrooms, and olives; toss.
3. Shake well in a covered jar, *4 parts oil* (half salad oil and half olive oil, including the oil from frying), *1 part white wine vinegar, salt* and *pepper* to taste, and *1 cut clove garlic.* Remove garlic before pouring dressing over salad; toss gently until well coated. Marinate at room temperature about 1 hour, turning occasionally. Chill.
4. Sprinkle generously with *freshly ground black pepper.*

ABOUT 6 SERVINGS

FRUIT SALADS

HELPFUL HINTS ABOUT FRUITS
- To obtain maximum juice from lemons and limes, firmly roll the fruit on a hard surface before extracting juice.
- To extract juice from a lemon when only a small amount is needed, puncture fruit with a fork and gently squeeze out desired amount of juice.
- To keep juice in fruit which has been cut, cover exposed part with waxed paper and place fruit, cut side down, on a dish, or fit cut side with a transparent bowl cover.
- To remove pits from cherries, insert a new pen point into penholder, pointed end in, and remove pits with the rounded end of pen point.

WALDORF SALAD
An always-popular salad said to have been created by a chef at the Waldorf in New York.

2 medium-sized red apples, rinsed, cored, and diced (about 2 cups)	½ cup coarsely chopped walnuts
1 cup diced celery	¼ cup mayonnaise
	4 crisp cup-shaped lettuce leaves

1. Combine the apples, celery, and walnuts in a bowl; add mayonnaise and toss to mix thoroughly. Chill in refrigerator.
2. To serve, place lettuce leaves on individual salad plates, and spoon a portion of the salad mixture into each.

4 SERVINGS

NOTE: If desired, add about ⅓ cup *golden raisins* and/or ⅓ cup *seeded, halved Tokay grapes* to salad mixture. Increase mayonnaise to ½ cup. Or, omit celery and raisins and add about ⅓ cup *cut-up dates* and ⅓ cup *miniature marshmallows* to the salad. Use ½ cup mayonnaise and combine with about ½ cup *whipped cream,* if desired.

STRAWBERRY-PINEAPPLE CROWN

1 package (3 ozs.) strawberry-flavored gelatin	1 tablespoon lemon juice
1 cup boiling water	1 package (8 ozs.) cream cheese, softened
¾ cup cold water	1 container (4½ ozs.) frozen whipped topping, thawed
1 can (20 ozs.) pineapple chunks in juice	1 pint (2 cups) strawberries, washed, hulled, and sliced
1 package (3 ozs.) lemon-flavored gelatin	Boston lettuce

1. Dissolve strawberry gelatin in boiling water in a medium bowl; stir in cold water. Chill 20 minutes, or until mixture is syrupy-thick.
2. While gelatin chills, drain juice from pineapple into a 1-cup measure; add water to make 1 cup. Heat to boiling in a small saucepan; remove from heat. Stir in lemon gelatin until dissolved, then lemon juice; cool slightly.
3. Beat lemon gelatin mixture into cream cheese in a medium bowl until smooth; fold in whipped topping and pineapple. Chill until mixture starts to thicken.
4. Stir strawberries into thickened strawberry gelatin; spoon into a 2-quart mold. Place mold in a shallow pan of ice and water to speed setting. Chill strawberry layer until sticky-firm. Carefully spoon pineapple mixture on top; remove from water. Chill in refrigerator overnight until firm.
5. When ready to serve, loosen salad around edge with a knife; dip mold in and out of warm water; invert onto a serving plate; lift off mold. Garnish plate with small lettuce leaves and whole strawberries if you like.

10 SERVINGS

CHEF'S FRUIT SALAD

1 qt. shredded salad greens
6 cups mixed fruit
Celery Seed Cream Salad Dressing, *page 215*
1½ cups Swiss cheese strips
1½ cups cooked ham or turkey strips
Cinnamon-Buttered Raisins, *below*

Line a salad bowl with crisp *salad greens*. Add shredded greens. Arrange fruit in bowl. Spoon some of the desired dressing over all. Top with cheese and ham strips alternately with Cinnamon-Buttered Raisins. Serve with remaining dressing.

ABOUT 6 SERVINGS

CINNAMON-BUTTERED RAISINS: Mix *1 tablespoon butter or margarine,* melted, *¼ cup dark raisins, ½ cup golden raisins,* and *½ teaspoon ground cinnamon* in a skillet. Set over low heat and stir 5 minutes. Cool.

ABOUT 1 CUP RAISINS

MOLDED SALADS

GELATIN TECHNIQUES

Dissolve unflavored gelatin. Modern high quality unflavored gelatin softens almost instantly in cold water or other cold liquid so "soaking" is no longer necessary. Generally, ½ cup cold liquid is used to soften each envelope of gelatin. To completely dissolve gelatin, stir in a saucepan over low heat.

Whenever a recipe calls for more than 1 tablespoon of sugar, the gelatin may be combined with the sugar (omitting softening in cold water) and the mixture slowly heated in fruit juice, milk, cream, or whatever liquid is used in the recipe, heating only until gelatin and sugar are dissolved.

Chill gelatin mixtures either by setting the bowl in the refrigerator or by putting it in a pan containing ice and water. If placed in refrigerator, stir occasionally; if placed over ice and water (a quicker method), stir frequently. If the gelatin mixture is clear, chill until slightly thicker than the consistency of thick, unbeaten egg white before adding any solid ingredients. If the mixture contains ingredients which thicken it or make it opaque, chill until it begins to gel (becomes slightly thicker); mix in solid ingredients only after mixture begins to gel.

Prevent separation of layered molds by chilling gelatin mixtures until set but not firm (sticky to the touch and not smooth on surface); layers should be of almost the same consistency when turning one mixture onto another so that they will be fused when unmolded.

Unmold gelatin from a plain ring mold by carefully running a pointed knife around inside of mold to loosen. Loosen a fancy mold by running the knife almost to bottom of mold in several places. If gelatin mold does not loosen readily, dip it into warm (not hot) water for only about 10 seconds. Invert mold onto a chilled serving plate which has been rinsed with cold water (so mold may be centered).

Beat heavy (whipping) cream to a medium consistency (piles softly) when it is to be blended with a gelatin mixture.

AVOCADO MOUSSE

There's an appealing blend of flavors in this rich gelatin mold, a prestigious addition to a spring luncheon menu.

1 env. unflavored gelatin
1 cup water
3 cups mashed ripe avocado (about 4 medium-sized)
2 tablespoons grated onion
1 teaspoon salt
1 teaspoon grated lemon peel
1 teaspoon prepared horseradish
½ cup mayonnaise
2 tablespoons lemon juice
½ cup chilled heavy cream, whipped

1. Sprinkle gelatin over ½ cup of the water in a saucepan to soften. Stir over low heat until gelatin is dissolved. Remove from heat and stir in the remaining ½ cup water. Set the gelatin aside to cool.
2. Meanwhile, blend remaining ingredients except cream in a large bowl. Stir cooled gelatin into

the avocado mixture. Chill until mixture is slightly thickened.
3. Fold in the whipped cream and turn into a 1½-quart ring mold. Chill until firm.
4. When ready to serve, unmold onto a chilled serving plate. Fill center of ring with large sprigs of *watercress*. ABOUT 12 SERVINGS

CHERRY-COTTAGE CHEESE SALAD MOLD
A delicious combination of cherries, pineapple, cottage cheese, olives, and nuts with compatible seasonings in a decorative mold.

1 cup boiling water	1 can (13-oz.) crushed
1 pkg. (3 oz.) cherry-flavored gelatin	pineapple, drained (reserve ½ cup syrup)
1 can (17 oz.) pitted dark sweet cherries in heavy syrup, drained (reserve 1 cup syrup)	1½ cups creamed cottage cheese, sieved
	¼ cup chopped pecans
	1 teaspoon sugar
½ cup chopped pecans	½ teaspoon celery salt
¼ cup finely chopped pitted green olives	½ teaspoon celery seed
	1 teaspoon grated onion
1 cup boiling water	½ teaspoon grated lemon peel
1 pkg. (3 oz.) lemon-flavored gelatin	

1. Pour 1 cup boiling water over cherry-flavored gelatin in a medium-sized bowl and stir until dissolved. Mix in the reserved cherry syrup (add water to make 1 cup if necessary). Chill until slightly thicker than thick, unbeaten egg white.
2. Meanwhile, halve cherries. Fold cherries, the ½ cup chopped pecans, and olives into thickened gelatin. Spoon into a 7-cup heart-shaped or other fancy mold. Chill until just set, but not firm.
3. Meanwhile, pour 1 cup boiling water over lemon-flavored gelatin in a medium-sized bowl and stir until dissolved. Mix in the reserved pineapple syrup. Chill until slightly thicker than thick, unbeaten egg white.
4. Blend pineapple, cottage cheese, and remaining ingredients and stir into thickened gelatin until thoroughly mixed. Spoon over cherry layer; chill until firm, at least 3 hours.
5. Unmold onto chilled serving plate; garnish with *lettuce*. Pipe *dairy sour cream* around the outer top edge of mold. 8 TO 10 SERVINGS

CRANBERRY SALAD
Perky with horseradish, this relish-type salad is a perfect foil for roast turkey.

2 cups fresh cranberries	2 tablespoons prepared horseradish
1 large red apple, pared, quartered, and cored	¼ teaspoon salt
	4 teaspoons unflavored gelatin
1 lemon, peeled, quartered, and seeds removed	½ cup cold water
	¼ cup chilled heavy cream, whipped
1 cup orange marmalade	

1. Put cranberries, apple, and lemon through coarse blade of food chopper. Add marmalade, horseradish, and salt; blend thoroughly.
2. Sprinkle gelatin over cold water to soften. Stir over low heat until gelatin is dissolved. Blend in the fruit mixture. Chill until just set, but not firm.
3. Fold whipped cream into gelatin mixture and turn into a 1-quart fancy mold. Chill until firm.
4. Unmold onto a serving platter and garnish with sprigs of *watercress*. 6 TO 8 SERVINGS

GRAPEFRUIT-LIME MOLD

½ cup sugar	2 env. unflavored gelatin
1 cup fresh grapefruit sections (cut in pieces if very large)	1 can (8¾ oz.) crushed pineapple, drained (reserve syrup)
½ cup fresh lime juice	¼ cup quartered maraschino cherries, well drained
1 pt. lime sherbet, softened	

1. Sprinkle ¼ cup sugar over grapefruit.
2. Add lime juice to sherbet; as sherbet melts, stir occasionally to blend.
3. Combine remaining sugar and gelatin in a saucepan. Add enough water to pineapple syrup to make 2 cups liquid. Mix 1 cup of the liquid into the gelatin mixture. Stir over low heat until gelatin is dissolved. Remove from heat; add remaining liquid and the sherbet. If necessary, beat with hand rotary or electric beater until well mixed.
4. Chill until mixture is the consistency of thick, unbeaten egg white, stirring occasionally.
5. Fold in grapefruit (including syrup), pineapple, and cherries. Turn into a 5-cup star-shaped mold. Chill until firm.
6. Unmold onto serving plate. 6 TO 8 SERVINGS

Molded Salads

ORANGE-CROWNED CHEESE SALAD

1 cup boiling water
1 pkg. (3 oz.) lemon-flavored gelatin
1 can (6 oz.) frozen orange juice concentrate, thawed
3 tablespoons cold water
16 large orange sections (about 2 large oranges)
1½ cups creamed cottage cheese, sieved
½ teaspoon salt
1 pt. ripe strawberries, rinsed
1 medium-sized ripe avocado, sieved

1. Pour boiling water over gelatin in a bowl and stir until gelatin is dissolved. Mix in the orange juice concentrate and cold water. Chill until slightly thicker than thick, unbeaten egg white.
2. Arrange orange sections in bottom of a 1½-quart fancy tubed mold.
3. Divide gelatin mixture into halves. Blend cottage cheese and salt into one half. Set other half aside. Turn cottage cheese mixture into mold. Chill until almost set, but not firm.
4. Meanwhile, hull ¾ cup of the strawberries and cut them into halves; reserve whole berries for garnish. Arrange berry halves on gelatin mixture in mold with rounded sides against mold.
5. Blend sieved avocado into other half of slightly thickened gelatin. Turn avocado mixture into mold over first layer. Chill until firm.
6. Unmold onto chilled serving plate and garnish with reserved whole strawberries.   6 TO 8 SERVINGS

MOLDED FRUIT COMPOTE SALAD

This beautiful salad is given distinction by an unusual and easily made dressing.

1 cup apricot nectar
1 pkg. (3 oz.) orange-flavored gelatin
¾ cup orange juice
¼ cup lemon juice
1 can (30 oz.) fruits for salad, drained and cut in pieces
Curry Mayonnaise Dressing, *below*

1. Heat apricot nectar to boiling. Pour over gelatin in a bowl and stir until gelatin is dissolved. Mix in orange and lemon juices.
2. Chill until gelatin is slightly thicker than thick, unbeaten egg white.
3. Stir in the fruit. Turn into 6 individual molds. Chill until firm.
4. Unmold onto a chilled serving plate. Garnish with crisp *lettuce* or *curly endive*. Serve with Curry-Mayonnaise Dressing.   6 SERVINGS

CURRY-MAYONNAISE DRESSING

1 cup mayonnaise
2 tablespoons confectioners' sugar
1 teaspoon curry powder
1 teaspoon lemon juice
Few grains salt
¼ cup heavy cream, whipped

Blend the mayonnaise with the confectioners' sugar, curry powder, lemon juice, and salt. Fold in the whipped cream. Refrigerate until ready to use.
ABOUT 1½ CUPS DRESSING

SPARKLING FRESH PEACH MOLD

2 env. unflavored gelatin
¼ cup sugar
¾ cup water
3 cups white grape juice
¼ cup lemon juice
4 medium-sized ripe peaches, peeled and sliced
1½ cups red raspberries or blueberries

1. Blend gelatin and sugar in a saucepan. Mix in water; stir over low heat until gelatin and sugar are dissolved.
2. Remove from heat and stir in the grape juice and lemon juice. Chill until mixture is the consistency of thick, unbeaten egg white.
3. Arrange half of the sliced peaches and raspberries in a 1½-quart ring mold. Spoon half of the chilled gelatin over fruit. Arrange the remaining fruit in the mold and spoon remaining gelatin over fruit. Chill until firm.
4. Unmold onto a chilled serving plate.
ABOUT 8 SERVINGS

PARTY-PERFECT SALAD MOLDS

2 pkgs. (12 oz. each) frozen sliced peaches, thawed
2 pkgs. (3 oz. each) orange-flavored gelatin
2 cups ginger ale
½ cup lemon juice
½ cup maraschino cherries, quartered
¼ cup chopped celery
¼ cup chopped green pepper

1. Drain and set peaches aside, reserving syrup. Add enough water to syrup to make 1½ cups; bring to boiling.
2. Add boiling liquid to gelatin in a bowl and stir until gelatin is dissolved. Mix in ginger ale and lemon juice.
3. Chill until slightly thicker than thick, unbeaten egg white.

4. Blend in peaches and remaining ingredients. Spoon into twelve ½-cup individual molds. Chill until firm.
5. Unmold onto chilled salad plates.   12 SERVINGS

PEACH MELBA MOLD

1 can (29 ozs.) cling peach slices
1 package (3 ozs.) raspberry-flavored gelatin
1 package (3 ozs.) lemon-flavored gelatin
1 cup boiling water
1 can (6 ozs.) pineapple juice
½ cup mayonnaise or salad dressing
Leaf lettuce

1. Drain syrup from peaches into a 2-cup measure; add water to make 2 cups. Dice peaches and set aside.
2. Heat syrup to boiling in a small saucepan; remove from heat; stir in raspberry gelatin until dissolved. Pour into a 1¾-quart mold. Chill just until mixture is sticky-firm to the touch.
3. While raspberry mixture chills, dissolve lemon gelatin in boiling water in a medium bowl; stir in pineapple juice, then beat in mayonnaise. Chill until mixture starts to thicken; fold in peaches. Spoon over sticky-firm raspberry layer in mold. Chill in refrigerator overnight until firm.
4. When ready to serve, loosen salad around edge with a knife; dip mold in and out of warm water; invert on a large serving plate; lift off mold. Circle plate with lettuce. Garnish with additional peach slices and raspberries if you like.   6 TO 8 SERVINGS

COCONUT-CREAM SALAD

1 cup boiling water
1 pkg. (3 oz.) lime-flavored gelatin
¼ cup sugar
1 can (8¾ oz.) crushed pineapple, drained (reserve syrup)
1¼ cups (about 3½ oz.) flaked coconut
1 cup chilled heavy cream, whipped

1. Pour boiling water over gelatin and sugar in a bowl. Stir until gelatin is dissolved.
2. Add enough water to the pineapple syrup to measure ½ cup liquid. Mix into gelatin. Chill until mixture is slightly thickened.
3. Stir in the pineapple and coconut. Fold in the whipped cream. Turn into a 5-cup mold and chill until firm.
4. Unmold onto a chilled serving plate. Garnish with pieces of *maraschino cherries*.
ABOUT 8 SERVINGS

SPICED PEACH CROWN

1 can (16 ozs.) cling peach slices
1 3-inch piece stick cinnamon
1 teaspoon whole cloves
⅓ cup white vinegar
Water
2 packages (3 ozs. each) orange-flavored gelatin
1 cup (8 oz. carton) dairy sour cream
¼ cup mayonnaise or salad dressing
1 teaspoon sugar
1 teaspoon grated orange rind
Chicory or curly endive
1 can (8 ozs.) jellied cranberry sauce

1. Drain syrup from peaches into a small saucepan; add cinnamon, cloves, and vinegar to syrup.
2. Heat to boiling; simmer 10 minutes. Strain into a 2-cup measure; add water to make 2 cups. Return to saucepan; reheat to boiling. Stir into gelatin in a small bowl until gelatin dissolves, then stir in 1 cup cold water.
3. Arrange enough of the peach slices in the bottom of a 1-quart mold to make a pretty pattern; pour in ½ cup of the gelatin mixture. Place mold in a pan of ice and water to speed setting. Let stand just until gelatin is sticky-firm.
4. Dice any remaining peach slices; stir into remaining orange gelatin; spoon over layer in mold. Chill in refrigerator several hours, or until firm.
5. Combine sour cream, mayonnaise, sugar, and orange rind in a small bowl; chill.
6. Just before serving, loosen salad around edge with a knife; dip mold in and out of warm water. Invert onto a serving plate; lift off mold. Frame with chicory or curly endive.
7. Slice cranberry sauce; cut each slice in half; overlap around base of mold. Serve with sour-cream dressing.   6 SERVINGS

RHUBARB-STRAWBERRY MOLD

1 lb. rhubarb
¾ cup sugar
¼ cup water
1 pkg. (3 oz.) strawberry-flavored gelatin
1 cup cold water
1 cup sliced sweetened fresh strawberries, or 1 pkg. (10 oz.) frozen strawberries, thawed

1. Wash rhubarb; cut off stem ends and leaves;

peel stalks only if skin is tough. Cut into 1-inch pieces (about 3 cups, cut) and put into a saucepan with the sugar and ¼ cup water. Set over low heat and stir until sugar is dissolved. Cover and cook slowly about 15 minutes, or until rhubarb is tender.
2. Drain rhubarb, reserving the hot syrup. Set rhubarb aside to cool.
3. Add enough boiling water to syrup to make 1 cup liquid. Pour over gelatin in a bowl and stir until gelatin is dissolved. Blend in the cold water. Chill until gelatin is slightly thickened.
4. Blend in the cooked rhubarb and strawberries. Turn into a 1-quart mold. Chill until firm.
5. Unmold onto chilled serving plate and, if desired, garnish with *whole strawberries* sprinkled with *confectioners' sugar*. 6 TO 8 SERVINGS

EXQUISITE CUCUMBER MOLD

4 to 5 medium-sized cucumbers
2 env. unflavored gelatin
½ cup cold water
1½ cups mayonnaise
2½ tablespoons prepared horseradish
2 tablespoons grated onion
10 to 15 drops green food coloring
1 teaspoon salt
¼ teaspoon white pepper
1 cup chilled heavy cream, whipped

1. Rinse cucumbers, pare, cut lengthwise into halves, and discard seeds. Cut cucumbers into pieces. Finely grind enough cucumbers in an electric blender to make 3 cups pulp. Set aside.
2. Sprinkle gelatin evenly over cold water in a small saucepan; stir over low heat until completely dissolved. Set aside.
3. Measure mayonnaise into a large bowl and mix in cucumber pulp, horseradish, onion, food coloring, and a blend of salt and white pepper. Add the dissolved gelatin gradually, stirring constantly until thoroughly blended.
4. Chill until mixture is slightly thickened. Fold in whipped cream and turn into a 2-quart fancy mold. Chill until firm, about 6 hours.
5. Unmold onto a chilled serving plate.
  8 TO 10 SERVINGS

POTATO SALAD MOLD

1 env. unflavored gelatin
¾ cup chicken broth, cooled (dissolve 2 chicken bouillon cubes in ¾ cup boiling water)
2 jars (16 oz. each) mayonnaise-style potato salad
½ cup sliced celery
¼ cup sliced green onions
1 teaspoon garlic salt
1 cup dairy sour cream

1. Sprinkle gelatin over broth in a saucepan to soften. Stir over low heat until gelatin is dissolved. Chill until mixture is slightly thickened.
2. Blend in remaining ingredients. Turn into a 5½-cup ring mold. Chill until firm.
3. Unmold onto a chilled serving plate.
  ABOUT 8 SERVINGS

DANISH POTATO SALAD PLATTER

1 bag (16 ozs.) frozen hashed brown potatoes
½ cup water
1½ teaspoons seasoned salt
1 medium onion, chopped (½ cup)
1 small green pepper, quartered, seeded, and cut in thin strips
½ medium red pepper, seeded and diced (½ cup)
4 hard-cooked eggs
1 package (8 ozs.) cream cheese, softened
½ cup bottled chunky blue cheese salad dressing
1 tablespoon milk
Few drops red-pepper seasoning
1 bunch fresh broccoli, weighing about 1½ lbs.
2 tablespoons bottled thin French dressing
Boston lettuce
2 medium tomatoes, sliced thin

1. Combine frozen potatoes, water, and ½ teaspoon of the salt in a large skillet; heat to boiling; cover. Simmer 5 minutes, or until potatoes are tender and liquid is absorbed. Combine potatoes with onion and green and red peppers in a large bowl.
2. Dice three of the eggs and remaining white; add to potato mixture. Set remaining yolk aside for garnish.
3. Combine cream cheese, blue cheese dressing, milk, red-pepper seasoning, and remaining 1 teaspoon salt in a small bowl; beat until smooth. Fold into potato mixture; cover. Chill several hours to season.
4. Wash broccoli; trim leaves and tough ends. Cut **stalks and flowerets into 3-inch lengths; for even** cooking, pare thick stalks and split lengthwise.

5. Place stalks on bottom and flowerets on top in a large skillet. Pour in boiling water to a 1-inch depth; cover. Cook 12 minutes, or just until crisp-tender; drain well; place in a shallow dish. Drizzle French dressing over top; cover. Chill at least an hour to season.
6. When ready to serve, spoon potato salad into the center of a large, lettuce-lined platter or tray; press remaining egg yolk through a sieve on top. Arrange broccoli at ends of platter, overlap tomato slices along sides. 6 SERVINGS

TONGUE-VEGETABLE SALAD MOLD

- 1 smoked tongue (2½ to 3 lbs.)
- ½ cup cold water
- 1 env. unflavored gelatin
- 1½ cups vegetable broth (dissolve 2 vegetable bouillon cubes in 1½ cups boiling water)
- 2 hard-cooked eggs, chilled and cut crosswise into 10 uniform slices
- 2 env. unflavored gelatin
- 2 beef bouillon cubes
- ½ cup lemon juice
- 2 teaspoons grated onion
- 3 tablespoons sugar
- ½ teaspoon Worcestershire sauce
- ¼ cup prepared horseradish
- ⅓ cup chopped sweet pickle
- 1 cup finely diced celery
- ½ cup finely diced green pepper

1. Cook tongue according to package directions; chill thoroughly; reserve 3 cups tongue stock. Cut about 9 thin, uniform center slices of tongue; prepare 1½ cups finely diced tongue.
2. Prepare all remaining ingredients for both layers of the salad before starting mold.
3. Lightly oil a 2-quart ring mold with salad oil (not olive oil); set aside to drain.
4. For aspic layer, sprinkle 1 envelope gelatin evenly over ½ cup cold water to soften. Place over hot water to dissolve.
5. Stir dissolved gelatin into hot vegetable broth and blend thoroughly. Pour 1 cup of the mixture into bottom of mold; place mold and remaining gelatin mixture in refrigerator to chill until slightly thickened.
6. Arrange egg slices over chilled gelatin mixture in mold; spoon remaining gelatin mixture over eggs; chill until just set, but not firm.
7. For tongue-vegetable layer, sprinkle 2 envelopes gelatin evenly over 1 cup cold tongue stock to soften.
8. Heat remaining 2 cups of tongue stock until very hot; add beef bouillon cubes and stir until blended; pour over softened gelatin and stir until gelatin is dissolved. Stir in the lemon juice, onion, sugar, Worcestershire sauce, and horseradish.
9. Chill over ice and water, stirring frequently, until mixture is slightly thickened. Blend in the tongue, pickle, celery, and green pepper.
10. To complete mold, arrange the slices of tongue, rounded end down, against the sides of the mold. Spoon vegetable-gelatin mixture into mold; be sure slices of tongue remain in place. (Both layers should be of the same consistency when combined.) Chill until firm.
11. Unmold onto a chilled serving plate.
ABOUT 10 SERVINGS

HAM MOUSSE

- 2 env. unflavored gelatin
- 1 cup cold water
- 1 tablespoon prepared mustard
- Few grains cayenne pepper
- 4 cups finely chopped cooked ham
- 2 tablespoons chopped pimiento
- 2 tablespoons chopped sweet pickle
- 1 cup chilled heavy cream, whipped

1. Soften gelatin in cold water in a saucepan. Dissolve completely over low heat.
2. Remove from heat. Stir in the mustard and cayenne pepper; cool. Chill until mixture is slightly thickened.
3. Blend in the ham, pimiento, and pickle. Fold in whipped cream.
4. Turn into a 1½-quart mold. Chill until firm.
5. When ready to serve, unmold onto a chilled serving plate. Garnish top of mold with *pimiento strips*. Spoon *Spicy Gelatin Cubes, below,* around mold. ABOUT 8 SERVINGS

SPICY GELATIN CUBES: Measure *1⅔ cups spiced peach syrup.* Heat 1 cup of syrup until boiling; pour over *1 package (3 ounces) cherry-flavored gelatin* and stir until gelatin is dissolved. Stir in remaining syrup, *⅓ cup water,* and *¼ teaspoon almond extract.* Pour into an 8-inch square pan and chill until firm. When ready to serve, cut gelatin into ½-inch cubes. Spoon cubes around Ham Mousse.

CRAB MEAT SALAD

Cooked Pineapple Salad Dressing, *below*
2 cups boiling water
2 pkgs. (3 oz. each) lemon-flavored gelatin
½ teaspoon salt
1 cup cold water
3 tablespoons cider vinegar
¼ cup large-curd creamed cottage cheese, sieved
½ cup coarsely chopped salted almonds
½ cup finely chopped celery
¼ cup finely chopped green pepper
1 tablespoon grated onion
2 teaspoons chopped pimiento
¾ lb. fresh crab meat, separated in pieces (bony tissue removed)
½ cup chilled heavy cream, whipped
Fresh pineapple, thinly sliced pieces

1. Prepare salad dressing; chill thoroughly.
2. Pour boiling water over gelatin and salt in a bowl; stir until gelatin is dissolved. Blend in the cold water and vinegar. Chill until mixture is slightly thickened.
3. Thoroughly mix cottage cheese, almonds, celery, green pepper, onion, and pimiento with ½ cup of the salad dressing. Gently blend in crab meat.
4. Stir the crab meat mixture into slightly thickened gelatin. Turn into a 2-quart fancy mold and chill until firm.
5. Fold the whipped cream into the remaining salad dressing. Chill until ready to serve.
6. Unmold salad onto chilled serving plate and surround mold with the chilled sliced pineapple. Serve with the salad dressing.   ABOUT 8 SERVINGS

COOKED PINEAPPLE SALAD DRESSING

½ cup butter or margarine
2 tablespoons flour
2 tablespoons sugar
Few grains salt
1 cup unsweetened pineapple juice
1 egg, slightly beaten
2 tablespoons lemon juice

1. Melt the butter in a heavy saucepan. Blend in flour, sugar, and salt; heat until mixture bubbles.
2. Add pineapple juice gradually, stirring constantly. Bring to boiling; stir and cook 3 minutes.
3. Stir about 3 tablespoons of the hot mixture into the beaten egg. Immediately blend into the mixture in saucepan and cook 3 minutes, stirring constantly.
4. Remove from heat and stir in lemon juice. Cool; chill. Store in a covered jar.

ABOUT 1½ CUPS DRESSING

MOLDED LOBSTER ELEGANCE

2½ env. unflavored gelatin
1 cup cold water
3 egg yolks
1 cup strong chicken broth, cooled (dissolve 2 chicken bouillon cubes in 1 cup boiling water)
1¼ teaspoons salt
¼ teaspoon pepper
2 teaspoons grated onion
1 teaspoon prepared mustard
1 teaspoon prepared horseradish
3 cups cooked lobster meat
3 tablespoons lemon juice
1½ cups chilled heavy cream, whipped
¼ cup finely chopped toasted almonds
¼ cup finely chopped celery
¼ cup finely chopped pimiento-stuffed olives

1. Soften the gelatin in the cold water in a small bowl. Set aside.
2. Meanwhile, beat the egg yolks in the top of a double boiler. Add the broth gradually, stirring constantly. Mix in the salt and pepper. Stirring constantly, cook over simmering water until smooth and slightly thickened, 5 to 8 minutes.
3. Remove from simmering water, immediately add the softened gelatin, and stir until gelatin is dissolved. Stir in the grated onion, mustard, and horseradish. Cool; chill until mixture is slightly thickened.
4. Cut the lobster meat into small pieces and put into a large bowl. Drizzle lemon juice evenly over lobster.
5. Fold whipped cream into the slightly thickened gelatin mixture. Mix almonds, celery, and olives with the lobster. Pour the whipped cream mixture over lobster and fold together. Turn mixture into a 1½-quart mold. Chill until firm, 4 to 5 hours or overnight.
6. Unmold onto a chilled serving plate. Garnish with *watercress*.   10 TO 12 SERVINGS

SUPER TUNA RING

8 oz. cream cheese
1 can (10¾ oz.) condensed tomato soup
2 env. unflavored gelatin
1 cup cold water
1 cup mayonnaise
¼ teaspoon marjoram, crushed
4 teaspoons Worcestershire sauce
1½ cups chopped celery
¼ cup chopped green onion

¼ teaspoon salt	2 cans (6½ or 7 oz.
⅛ teaspoon pepper	each) tuna, drained and flaked

1. Melt the cream cheese in the top of a double boiler over boiling water, stirring occasionally. Blend in the tomato soup until smooth. Remove from heat.
2. Soften gelatin in water in a small saucepan. Set over low heat and stir until gelatin is dissolved. Blend into cheese-tomato mixture. Stir in mayonnaise, salt, pepper, marjoram, and Worcestershire sauce until blended. Cover and chill until mixture is slightly thickened.
3. Mix the celery, onion, and tuna into chilled gelatin until well blended. Turn into a 1½-quart ring mold. Chill until firm, at least 8 hours or overnight.
4. Unmold onto a chilled serving plate. Fill center and garnish edge with *watercress*.   12 SERVINGS

SENATE SALAD BOWL WITH SHRIMP-TOMATO ASPIC
A variation of the Senate Salad served in the United States Senate dining room.

1½ cups tomato juice	1 pkg. (9 oz.) frozen artichoke hearts
1 pkg. (3 oz.) lemon-flavored gelatin	Curly endive, lettuce, spinach, watercress
1 teaspoon salt	1 can frozen grapefruit sections, thawed and drained
Few grains cayenne pepper	
1½ teaspoons grated onion	½ cup sliced ripe olives
1½ teaspoons prepared horseradish	½ cup crumbled blue cheese
¾ lb. cooked shrimp, peeled and deveined	

1. Heat 1 cup of the tomato juice until very hot. Pour over gelatin in a bowl and stir until gelatin is dissolved. Stir in remaining tomato juice with salt, cayenne pepper, onion, and horseradish.
2. Pour mixture into an 8x4x2-inch loaf pan. Chill until mixture is slightly thickened.
3. Arrange 12 of the shrimp in 2 even rows in the gelatin mixture, with shrimp extending partly above surface. (Chill remaining shrimp for use in salad bowl.) Chill until firm, about 1½ hours.
4. Meanwhile, cook artichoke hearts according to package directions; cool; chill thoroughly.
5. Tear greens into pieces to yield about 2 cups of each. Mix in a large salad bowl; chill.
6. Just before serving, toss drained grapefruit sections, reserved shrimp, artichoke hearts, and ripe olives with greens; top with blue cheese.
7. Cut aspic into 12 squares with shrimp in the center of each. Arrange aspic squares on salad. Serve with *French dressing*.   6 SERVINGS

VEGETABLE ASPIC

1 pkg. (10 oz.) frozen mixed vegetables	2 tablespoons lemon juice
½ teaspoon monosodium glutamate	1 tablespoon prepared horseradish
4 teaspoons unflavored gelatin	1 teaspoon grated onion
¾ cup cold water	½ teaspoon celery seed
1½ cups vegetable broth (dissolve 2 vegetable bouillon cubes in 1½ cups boiling water)	½ teaspoon salt
	⅛ teaspoon pepper
	½ cup finely shredded cabbage
	2 tablespoons finely snipped parsley

1. Cook mixed vegetables according to package directions, adding monosodium glutamate with the salt; drain and chill the vegetables.
2. Soften gelatin in cold water in a saucepan. Stir over low heat until gelatin is dissolved. Blend in the broth, lemon juice, horseradish, onion, celery seed, salt, and pepper.
3. Chill until gelatin is the consistency of thick, unbeaten egg white. Stir in the chilled cooked vegetables, cabbage, and parsley. Turn into a 1-quart mold. Chill until firm.
4. Unmold onto chilled serving plate.
   ABOUT 6 SERVINGS

DANISH BLUE CHEESE MOUSSE
An elegant salad or appetizer party mold.

1 env. unflavored gelatin	2 egg whites, beaten to stiff, not dry, peaks
½ cup cold water	
½ cup toasted chopped almonds	1 cup chilled heavy cream, whipped to soft peaks
¼ lb. Samsoe cheese, grated	½ teaspoon salt
¼ lb. Danish blue cheese	⅛ teaspoon white pepper
	¼ teaspoon dry mustard

Main-Dish Salads

1. Soften gelatin in cold water in a saucepan; stir over low heat until gelatin is dissolved.
2. Using a fork, gently mix almonds and Samsoe cheese in a large bowl. Using fork, break off small pieces of the blue cheese. Gently and quickly, using fingertips, crumble pieces into the bowl with the Samsoe cheese and almonds. Toss lightly with fork just until mixed.
3. Fold beaten egg whites and whipped cream together and then fold into cheese. Mix in gelatin and a blend of salt, pepper, and dry mustard. Turn into a loaf pan. Chill until firm, about 4 hours.
4. Unmold. Garnish top with a row of *lettuce-heart leaves*; put a *maraschino cherry* in each.

12 SERVINGS

DEVILED EGG SALAD

6 eggs
1 env. unflavored gelatin
¼ cup cold water
¼ cup ketchup
2 tablespoons cider vinegar
3 oz. cream cheese
½ cup mayonnaise
1 teaspoon grated onion
1 teaspoon salt
3 drops Tabasco
¼ cup chopped green pepper
¼ cup chopped celery
2 tablespoons finely chopped pimiento
1 tablespoon finely chopped parsley

1. Hard-cook, chop, and chill the eggs.
2. Soften gelatin in cold water in a saucepan; dissolve over low heat. Stir in the ketchup and vinegar.
3. Beat together cream cheese, mayonnaise, onion, salt, and Tabasco until fluffy. Gradually add gelatin mixture, blending well. Mix in the eggs and remaining ingredients. Turn into six ½-cup molds. Chill until firm.
4. Unmold onto *lettuce*.

6 SERVINGS

CAPE COD TURKEY SALAD

1 frozen boneless turkey roast, weighing 2 lbs.
1½ cups diagonally sliced celery
1 can (8 ozs.) jellied cranberry sauce
½ medium-sized firm ripe honeydew melon
½ cup whipping cream
¼ cup dairy sour cream
1 tablespoon lime juice
2 teaspoons finely chopped crystallized ginger
1 head Boston lettuce
2 tablespoons coarsely broken pecans

1. Roast turkey as label directs; remove from foil pan; chill. Cut meat into cubes. (There should be 3 cups.) Combine with celery in a large bowl.
2. Open cranberry can at both ends and push out sauce; cut into 6 slices, then cut into small cubes; place in a small bowl and chill.
3. Pare honeydew; scoop out seeds. Cut melon in half lengthwise, then cut crosswise into thin slices; cover and chill.
4. Just before serving, combine whipping cream and sour cream in a small bowl; beat until mixture forms soft peaks. Fold in lime juice and ginger; fold about three fourths into turkey mixture.
5. Line a large salad bowl with lettuce; break remainder into bite-sized pieces and place in bowl. Spoon turkey mixture on top. Overlap honeydew slices around edge in bowl; spoon cranberry cubes in a ring next to melon.
6. Spoon remaining dressing on top of turkey mixture; sprinkle pecans over dressing.

6 SERVINGS

MAIN-DISH SALADS

ALL-SEASONS MACARONI SALAD

1 cup dairy sour cream
½ cup Italian salad dressing
½ teaspoon salt
¼ teaspoon seasoned salt
Few grains pepper
½ lb. bacon, panbroiled and crumbled
2 hard-cooked eggs, chopped
¼ cup chopped pimiento
1 large tomato, diced
2 cups (8 oz.) elbow macaroni, cooked and drained
1½ cups diced cooked chicken
2 tablespoons lemon juice
1 avocado, peeled and sliced
Curly endive

1. Mix together in a bowl the sour cream, salad dressing, salts, and pepper; add macaroni and chicken and mix well. Chill thoroughly.

2. Add bacon, eggs, pimiento, and tomato to macaroni; toss lightly. Turn into salad bowl.
3. Sprinkle lemon juice over avocado slices. Garnish salad with avocado and endive. Additional bacon, chicken, eggs, pimiento, and tomato may be used to garnish, if desired.   6 SERVINGS

ANTIPASTO TOSS

2 lbs. fresh lima beans, shelled (2 cups)
⅔ cup bottled Italian salad dressing
1 large head iceberg lettuce
1 large red pepper, quartered, seeded, and cut into strips
1 small red onion, peeled, sliced, and separated into rings
1 package (8 ozs.) sliced provolone cheese, cut in strips
1 package (6 ozs.) sliced salami, cut in strips
½ cup small pimiento-stuffed olives

1. Cook lima beans, covered, in boiling salted water in a medium saucepan 15 minutes, or until crisp-tender; drain. Place in a medium bowl; stir in 3 tablespoons of the Italian dressing; chill.
2. When ready to serve, break lettuce into bite-sized pieces; place on a large deep platter. Arrange limas, pepper strips, onion rings, cheese, salami, and olives in rows on top. Drizzle remaining salad dressing over all.
   6 TO 8 SERVINGS

PARTY CHICKEN SALAD

Celery Seed-Cream Dressing, *below*
3 cups cooked chicken cubes (use white meat)
1½ cups chopped celery
1 cup halved seedless grapes
¼ cup finely cut coconut
⅓ cup chopped toasted blanched almonds

1. Prepare Celery Seed-Cream Dressing.
2. Lightly toss chicken and remaining ingredients. Using just enough to coat evenly, add the dressing and toss gently. Garnish with *parsley*.
   ABOUT 6 SERVINGS

CELERY SEED-CREAM DRESSING

¼ cup sugar
1 tablespoon flour
½ teaspoon dry mustard
½ teaspoon salt
⅛ teaspoon pepper
2 tablespoons butter or margarine
2 teaspoons confectioners' sugar
½ teaspoon dry mustard
1¼ cups lemon-lime carbonated beverage (room temperature)
4 egg yolks, slightly beaten
½ cup chilled heavy cream, whipped
2 teaspoons celery seed

1. Combine sugar, flour, ½ teaspoon dry mustard, salt, and pepper together in top of a double boiler. Add 1 cup of the carbonated beverage gradually, blending well.
2. Cook and stir until mixture comes to boiling; cook 1 to 2 minutes. Stir in remaining ¼ cup carbonated beverage.
3. Vigorously stir about 3 tablespoons of the hot mixture into the beaten egg yolks; immediately blend into mixture in top of double boiler. Set over simmering water and cook 3 to 5 minutes, stirring occasionally.
4. Remove from heat and stir in the butter. Cool; chill thoroughly.
5. Before serving, with a final few strokes, blend a mixture of confectioners' sugar and ½ teaspoon dry mustard into whipped cream. Blend whipped cream and celery seed into salad dressing.
   ABOUT 2¼ CUPS DRESSING

SALDE SICILIANO

This salad, a combination of novel ingredients, was served as a "meal in itself" for luncheon, or as the appetizer-salad course before the entrée at dinner in the Salon Reál dining room of the Executive House's Condado Beach Hotel in San Juan, Puerto Rico. It is a creation of Executive Chef Robert Halberg.

1 whole clove garlic
4 anchovy fillets
Juice of 1 lemon
6 tablespoons Burgundy
¾ cup olive oil
Oregano leaves (¼ oz. or 2½ tablespoons)
Peppercorns, crushed (⅛ oz. or ¾ teaspoon)
2 cloves garlic, minced
1 pimiento, diced
3 tomatoes, diced
1 cup cooked green beans
1 cup diced hearts of artichoke
1 cup diced hearts of palm
1 head romaine lettuce, torn in pieces
1 head iceberg lettuce, torn in chunks
2 slices bread, toasted and cut in cubes
¼ lb. Gorgonzola cheese, crumbled

1. Rub a large wooden salad bowl with the whole clove of garlic. Add anchovy fillets. Rub bowl again with the garlic and anchovies; mash together form-

ing a paste. Blend in, stirring vigorously, the lemon juice, Burgundy, olive oil, oregano, and pepper. (If necessary, correct seasonings to taste.)
2. Blend in minced garlic, diced pimiento, and tomatoes. Add green beans, hearts of artichoke and palm, romaine, and iceberg lettuce. Toss lightly.
3. Add croutons and cheese. Again, toss lightly. Serve on chilled salad plates immediately.

4 TO 8 SERVINGS

NIÇOISE BUFFET PLATTER

1 lb. green beans, tipped
2 medium potatoes, pared and cubed
1 envelope old-fashioned French salad dressing mix
Water
Vinegar
Salad oil
2 medium tomatoes, each cut into 6 wedges
1 medium head iceberg lettuce, broken into bite-sized pieces
2 cans (about 7 ozs. each) tuna, drained and broken into chunks
2 hard-cooked eggs, sliced
1 cup pitted ripe olives
1 can (2 ozs.) rolled anchovy fillets, drained

1. Cook green beans, covered, in boiling salted water in a medium saucepan 25 minutes, or until crisp-tender; drain. Place in a pie plate.
2. Cook potatoes, covered, in boiling salted water in a small saucepan 12 minutes, or until tender; drain. Place in a second pie plate.
3. Prepare salad dressing mix with water, vinegar, **and salad oil as label directs; drizzle 2 tablespoons** over each vegetable; toss lightly to mix; cover. Chill several hours to season.
4. Just before serving, place lettuce on a large platter. Pile tuna in center. Arrange green beans on platter to divide into 4 sections; place potatoes, tomatoes, eggs, and olives in between. Garnish tuna with anchovies. Pass remaining salad dressing to spoon over all.

6 SERVINGS

CRAB LOUIS

A well-known salad which back in 1904 the metropolitan tenor, Enrico Caruso, was reputed to have repeatedly ordered at the Seattle's Olympic Club until the supply was exhausted.

1 cup mayonnaise
¼ cup chili sauce
1 tablespoon lemon juice
¼ cup finely chopped onion
¼ cup finely chopped green pepper
1 teaspoon Worcestershire sauce
1 teaspoon prepared horseradish
¼ teaspoon salt
2 tablespoons chopped green olives
Shredded lettuce
Crab meat (about 3 cups)

1. Blend all ingredients, except lettuce and crab meat.
2. Prepare desired amount of lettuce and put on chilled salad plates. Arrange crab meat on lettuce and spoon a generous amount of dressing over each serving. Garnish with *ripe olives*, wedges of *hard-cooked egg, tomato,* and *lemon.*

ABOUT 8 SERVINGS

GALA LOBSTER SALAD

1 cup mayonnaise
½ cup chili sauce
¼ cup orange juice
2 tablespoons lemon juice
1 tablespoon chopped parsley
1 tablespoon chopped hard-cooked egg
2 tomatoes, peeled and diced
¼ small cucumber, scored, sliced, and cut in wedges
1 ripe banana, peeled and diced
1 small apple, pared and diced
3 tablespoons capers
2½ cups chilled lobster meat, separated in pieces

1. Blend mayonnaise, chili sauce, orange and lemon juices, parsley, and egg; chill.
2. Combine remaining ingredients. Lightly toss with enough chilled dressing to coat evenly.
3. Mound individual servings on chilled plates lined with *salad greens.*

8 SERVINGS

SEAFOOD SALAD SUPREME
Seafood is dressed up with extra gourmet touches in this salad . . . truly superb cuisine.

1 can (6½ oz.) crab meat, drained and separated
1 can (7 oz.) shrimp, drained and cut in pieces
1 can (6 oz.) lobster, drained and cut in pieces
1 can (6½ or 7 oz.) tuna, drained and separated in small pieces
¼ cup sliced green onions
1 medium-sized ripe avocado, chilled
3 tablespoons lemon juice
3 hard-cooked eggs, finely diced
2 medium-sized ripe tomatoes, chilled and diced

Honey-Glazed Filbert Roast Chicken (page 135)

2 quarts (1 head) shredded lettuce
1 cup diced celery
½ cup chopped walnuts
⅓ cup sliced radishes
1 cup mayonnaise
¼ cup cream
1 teaspoon salt
¼ teaspoon pepper

1. Combine seafood in a bowl, cover and refrigerate.
2. Put into a large salad bowl the lettuce, celery, walnuts, radishes, and green onions. Chill 1 hour.
3. When ready to serve, dice the avocado. Drizzle with lemon juice and toss lightly. Add avocado to salad bowl along with seafood, eggs, and tomatoes.
4. Combine the mayonnaise, cream, salt, and pepper. Pour over salad ingredients and toss lightly.
5. Serve in crisp *lettuce cups*.   8 TO 10 SERVINGS

  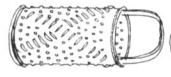 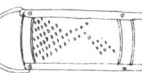

SHRIMP AND AVOCADO SALAD

1 cup wine vinegar
⅓ cup water
½ cup lemon juice
1 cup salad oil
¼ cup chopped parsley
2 cloves garlic, minced
1 tablespoon salt
¼ teaspoon freshly ground black pepper
1 tablespoon sugar
1 teaspoon dry mustard
1 teaspoon thyme, crushed
1 teaspoon oregano, crushed
2 lbs. large cooked shrimp, peeled, and deveined
3 small onions, sliced
⅓ cup chopped green pepper
2 ripe avocados, peeled and sliced

1. For marinade, combine vinegar, water, lemon juice, oil, parsley, and garlic in a bowl or a screw-top jar. Add a mixture of salt, pepper, sugar, dry mustard, thyme, and oregano; blend thoroughly.
2. Put shrimp, onions, and green pepper into a large shallow dish. Pour marinade over all, cover, and refrigerate 8 hours or overnight.
3. About 1 hour before serving, put avocado slices into a bowl. Pour enough marinade from shrimp over the avocado to cover completely.
4. To serve, remove avocado slices and shrimp from marinade and arrange on crisp *lettuce* in a large serving bowl.   ABOUT 8 SERVINGS

* *Ham Jubilee and Succotash (page 106)*

SALADE NIÇOISE

A salad served in restaurants in Nice, France, probably inspired the many variations which bear this name appearing on European menus.

Salad Dressing, *below*
3 medium-sized cooked potatoes, sliced
1 pkg. (9 oz.) frozen green beans, cooked
1 clove garlic, cut in half
1 small head Boston lettuce
2 cans (6½ or 7 oz. each) tuna, drained
1 mild onion, quartered and thinly sliced
2 ripe tomatoes, cut in wedges
2 hard-cooked eggs, quartered
1 can (2 oz.) rolled anchovy fillets, drained
¾ cup pitted ripe olives
1 tablespoon capers

1. Pour enough salad dressing over warm potato slices and cooked beans (in separate bowls) to coat vegetables.
2. Before serving, rub the inside of a large shallow salad bowl with the cut surface of the garlic. Line the bowl or a large serving platter with the lettuce.
3. Unmold the tuna in center of bowl and separate into chunks.
4. Arrange separate mounds of the potatoes, green beans, onion, tomatoes, and hard-cooked eggs in colorful groupings around the tuna. Garnish with anchovies, olives, and capers.
5. Pour dressing over all before serving.
   6 TO 8 SERVINGS

SALAD DRESSING: Combine in a jar or bottle *½ cup olive oil or salad oil, 2 tablespoons red wine vinegar,* a mixture of *1 teaspoon salt, ½ teaspoon pepper,* and *1 teaspoon dry mustard, 1 tablespoon finely chopped chives,* and *1 tablespoon finely chopped parsley.* Shake vigorously to blend well before pouring over salad.   ABOUT ⅔ CUP

HAM MOUSSE VERONIQUE

2 envelopes unflavored gelatin
¼ cup sugar
⅛ teaspoon salt
1½ cups water
¼ cup lime juice
Green and yellow food colorings
1 canned ham, weighing 1 lb.
1 can (8 ozs.) water chestnuts, drained and chopped
¼ cup chopped dill pickle
1 can (13¾ ozs.) chicken broth
½ cup seedless green grapes
¾ cup mayonnaise or salad dressing
2 teaspoons prepared mustard
Chicory or curly endive
¼ small cucumber, scored and sliced thin

1. Mix 1 envelope of the gelatin with sugar and salt in a small saucepan; stir in ½ cup of the water. Heat, stirring constantly, until gelatin dissolves; remove from heat. Stir in remaining water and lime juice, then drop green food coloring and 2 drops yellow to tint lime color. Set aside.
2. Scrape gelatin coating from ham; put meat through a food grinder, using a fine blade. Combine with water chestnuts and chopped pickle in a medium bowl.
3. Sprinkle remaining 1 envelope gelatin over 1 cup of the chicken broth in a small saucepan; heat, stirring constantly, until gelatin dissolves; remove from heat. Stir in remaining chicken broth. Chill in refrigerator 20 minutes, or until mixture starts to thicken.
4. Pour lime gelatin mixture into a 1¾-quart mold; set mold in a shallow pan of ice and water to speed setting. Let stand, stirring several times, until mixture starts to thicken; stir in grapes. Continue chilling just until sticky-firm to the touch.
5. Beat mayonnaise and mustard into thickened chicken-broth mixture; fold in ham mixture. Carefully spoon over sticky-firm layer in mold; remove from ice and water. Chill in refrigerator overnight, until firm.
6. When ready to serve, loosen salad around edge with a knife. Dip mold in and out of warm water; invert on a large serving plate. Frame with sprigs of chicory and cucumber slices cut in half. 6 SERVINGS

CURRIED CHICKEN SALAD

1 broiler-fryer, weighing about 3 lbs.
¼ teaspoon lemon-pepper
2 egg whites
1 small onion, peeled and quartered
Few celery tops
1½ teaspoons salt
2 cups water
1 envelope unflavored gelatin
¾ teaspoon curry powder
1 cup whipping cream
1 cup mayonnaise or salad dressing
1 can (8 ozs.) water chestnuts, drained and diced
Romaine
2 hard-cooked eggs, sliced

1. Combine chicken, onion, celery tops, 1 teaspoon of the salt, and water in a kettle. Heat to boiling; cover. Simmer 45 minutes, or until chicken is tender. Remove from broth and cool until easy to handle, then take meat from bones and dice. (There should be 2½ cups.) Strain broth into a small bowl; cool.
2. Measure 1 cup of the broth into a small saucepan; sprinkle gelatin over top to soften. Heat, stirring constantly, until gelatin dissolves; remove from heat. Stir in curry powder, lemon-pepper, and remaining ½ teaspoon salt. Chill 20 minutes, or until mixture is syrupy-thick.
3. While gelatin mixture chills, beat egg whites until they stand in soft peaks in a small bowl; beat cream until stiff in a medium bowl.
4. Beat mayonnaise into thickened gelatin mixture; stir in diced chicken and water chestnuts; fold in beaten egg whites and whipped cream. Spoon into a 1¾-quart mold. Chill in refrigerator overnight until firm.
5. When ready to serve, loosen salad around edge with a knife; dip mold in and out of warm water; invert onto a large serving plate; lift off mold. Circle salad with small romaine leaves and egg and cucumber slices if you like. 8 SERVINGS

SALAD DRESSINGS

A salad is complemented by the dressing, so suit it to the salad. Dressings should coat the greens, not drown them; they should accompany the salad, not hide it. Endless variations are possible using the basic French, mayonnaise, and cooked dressings. Others are the sweet or sour cream, cream or cottage cheese and yogurt dressings, and the bacon-vinegar type for wilted greens.

Mayonnaise has caused many a tear when it has broken or separated, probably because the oil was added too rapidly at the beginning or ingredients (egg yolk and oil) were not of the same temperature when combined. If separation occurs, it is possible to begin again and obtain a perfect *emulsion* of salad oil and egg yolk as follows: Combine 1 egg yolk, 1 tablespoon cold water, and a small amount of vinegar in a small mixer bowl or an electric blender container. Mix well and add the separated mayonnaise, a small amount at a time, beating constantly until an emulsion has re-formed.

FRENCH DRESSING

¼ cup lemon juice or cider vinegar	¼ teaspoon dry mustard
1 tablespoon sugar	¼ teaspoon pepper
¾ teaspoon salt	¾ cup salad oil or olive oil
¼ teaspoon paprika	

Combine all ingredients in a screw-top jar; shake well. Chill. Shake before using. ABOUT 1 CUP

CREAMY FRENCH DRESSING: Follow recipe for French Dressing. Blend ¼ *cup dairy sour cream* with the dressing.

CURRIED FRENCH DRESSING: Follow recipe for French Dressing. Mix ¼ *teaspoon curry powder* with seasonings.

LORENZO FRENCH DRESSING: Follow recipe for French Dressing. Add ¼ *cup finely chopped watercress* and *2 tablespoons chili sauce* to the dressing; shake well.

HONEY FRENCH DRESSING: Follow recipe for French Dressing, using lemon juice. Add ½ *cup honey* and ¼ *teaspoon grated lemon peel* to dressing and shake well. For added flavor, add ½ *teaspoon celery seed* and shake well.

HONEY-LIME FRENCH DRESSING: Follow recipe for French Dressing. Substitute ¼ *cup lime juice* for the lemon juice. Add ½ *cup honey* and ¼ *teaspoon grated lime peel* to dressing; shake well.

TANGY FRENCH DRESSING: Follow recipe for French Dressing. Add *3 to 4 tablespoons prepared horseradish* to the dressing and shake well.

TOMATO SOUP FRENCH DRESSING: Follow recipe for French Dressing. ADD ⅔ *cup condensed tomato soup, 1 tablespoon chopped onion,* and ½ *teaspoon marjoram* to the dressing; shake well.

GOURMET SALAD DRESSING

⅓ cup olive oil	½ teaspoon dry mustard
2 tablespoons red wine vinegar	⅛ teaspoon basil, crushed
3 tablespoons dry red wine	⅛ teaspoon tarragon, crushed
1½ teaspoons sugar	½ teaspoon Worcestershire sauce
1 teaspoon salt	
½ teaspoon freshly ground black pepper	

1. Combine oil, vinegar, wine, a mixture of sugar, salt, pepper, dry mustard, basil, and tarragon, and the Worcestershire sauce in a screw-top jar. Shake well to blend; chill thoroughly.

2. Just before serving, shake dressing vigorously and pour over *salad greens* and *artichoke hearts*; toss lightly. ABOUT ⅔ CUP

ORANGE SALAD DRESSING

¼ cup sugar	2 tablespoons tarragon vinegar
1 teaspoon salt	½ teaspoon grated onion
½ teaspoon dry mustard	¾ cup salad oil
¼ cup orange juice	
¼ cup light corn syrup	

1. Combine sugar, salt, and dry mustard in a small bowl. Add remaining ingredients except oil and beat with a hand rotary beater until blended.

2. Very gradually add the oil while beating constantly. Continue beating until mixture is of desired consistency. Chill. Stir before serving.
ABOUT 1½ CUPS

MAYONNAISE

2 egg yolks	Few grains cayenne pepper
1 tablespoon cider vinegar	½ teaspoon dry mustard
½ teaspoon salt	1 cup salad oil
¼ teaspoon sugar	1 tablespoon lemon juice
⅛ teaspoon white pepper	

1. Put the egg yolks, vinegar, salt, sugar, peppers, and dry mustard into a small bowl. Beat with a hand rotary beater until well blended. Add oil, 1 teaspoon at a time at first, beating vigorously after each addition. Gradually increase amounts added until one half of the oil has been used.

2. Alternately beat in small amounts of remaining oil and a few drops lemon juice. (If mayonnaise separates because oil has been added too rapidly, beat it slowly and thoroughly into 1 egg yolk, 1 tablespoon cold water, small quantity of vinegar, or a small portion of smooth mayonnaise.) Store in covered container in refrigerator. ABOUT 1½ CUPS

ELEGANT MAYONNAISE: Follow recipe for Mayonnaise. Into *1 cup chilled mayonnaise*, blend *1 teaspoon lemon juice, 1 teaspoon curry powder*, and *a few grains salt*. Beat ⅓ *cup chilled heavy cream* to soft peaks. With final few strokes, beat in *2 tablespoons confectioners' sugar*. Fold into mayonnaise.

Salad Dressings

THOUSAND ISLAND DRESSING: Follow recipe for Mayonnaise. Into ½ cup mayonnaise, mix *1 or 2 hard-cooked eggs*, sieved or finely chopped, *2 tablespoons chili sauce, 2 tablespoons finely chopped scallions* (with tops), *2 tablespoons chopped sweet pickle, 1 tablespoon chopped green olives,* and *½ teaspoon paprika.*

RUSSIAN DRESSING: Follow recipe for Mayonnaise. Into *½ cup mayonnaise,* blend *3 tablespoons chili sauce, 1 tablespoon minced onion,* and *½ teaspoon prepared horseradish.*

SOUR CREAM MAYONNAISE: Follow recipe for Mayonnaise. Into *½ cup mayonnaise,* blend *½ cup dairy sour cream, 2 teaspoons cider vinegar, 1 teaspoon sugar,* and *½ teaspoon dry mustard.*

GREEN GODDESS SALAD DRESSING

1 cup mayonnaise	3 tablespoons mashed anchovy fillets
½ cup dairy sour cream	1 tablespoon chopped chives
3 tablespoons tarragon vinegar	2 teaspoons chopped capers
1 tablespoon lemon juice	1 clove garlic, crushed
⅓ cup finely snipped parsley	⅛ teaspoon salt
3 tablespoons finely chopped onion	⅛ teaspoon pepper

1. Blend all ingredients thoroughly. Cover tightly and chill in refrigerator 3 to 4 hours.

2. To serve, add the dressing to crisp *salad greens* and gently turn and toss until greens are evenly coated. Serve immediately. ABOUT 2½ CUPS

ROQUEFORT CHEESE DRESSING

This quick-as-a-wink dressing for garden-fresh salad is a favorite at Idle Spurs (Steak House) in Barstow, California.

½ cup Roquefort cheese, crumbled or mashed	¼ teaspoon pepper
⅔ cup half and half	1 tablespoon paprika
1 teaspoon dry mustard	⅔ cup salad oil
½ teaspoon salt	2 tablespoons lemon juice

1. Blend cheese, cream, dry mustard, salt, pepper, and paprika together in an electric blender or beat in a bowl with a hand rotary beater.

2. Add oil, a tablespoon at a time, beating until thickened and smooth. Beat in lemon juice.

3. Store, covered, in refrigerator. ABOUT 2½ CUPS

CREAMY LEMON MAYONNAISE

1 cup mayonnaise	⅓ cup chilled heavy cream
3 tablespoons lemon juice	3 tablespoons confectioners' sugar
1 teaspoon grated lemon peel	

1. Combine mayonnaise and lemon juice and peel in a bowl; mix well.

2. Beat heavy cream until peaks are formed; beat in the confectioners' sugar with final few strokes. Fold into the lemon mayonnaise. ABOUT 1½ CUPS

PINEAPPLE SALAD DRESSING

A luncheon fruit salad plate will be enhanced with this fluffy, creamy, rich, delicately flavored dressing.

½ cup sugar	2 egg whites
1 tablespoon cornstarch	2 tablespoons sugar
⅛ teaspoon salt	2 tablespoons butter
1½ cups unsweetened pineapple juice	¾ cup chilled heavy cream, whipped to soft peaks
2 egg yolks, slightly beaten	

1. Blend the ½ cup of sugar, cornstarch, and salt in the top of a double boiler; stir in ½ cup of the pineapple juice. Over direct heat, bring mixture rapidly to boiling, stirring constantly; cook 2 to 3 minutes. Set over simmering water.

2. Vigorously stir about 3 tablespoons of the hot mixture into the egg yolks in a bowl and immediately blend into mixture in double boiler. Cook over simmering water 3 to 5 minutes. Stir slowly to keep mixture cooking evenly. Remove double boiler from heat.

3. Beat egg whites until frothy. Add the 2 tablespoons sugar gradually, beating well after each addition. Beat until glossy peaks are formed. Gently blend into the mixture in top of double boiler.

4. Heat the remaining 1 cup pineapple juice to lukewarm. Stirring constantly, gradually add to cooked pineapple-egg white mixture. Cook over simmering water until thick and smooth, stirring constantly, about 10 minutes. Add the butter and stir until melted.

5. Remove from heat and set aside to cool. Set in refrigerator to chill.

6. When pineapple mixture is chilled, gently fold into whipped cream. ABOUT 4 CUPS DRESSING

Chapter 11
CAKES & TORTES—FROSTINGS & FILLINGS

For many years the art of cakemaking remained unchanged. There were two basic types of cakes—the so-called "butter" cakes, and the cakes without butter or the sponge-type cakes. In recent years, however, quite different methods of mixing cakes have been developed, resulting in cakes of still other types. Standard methods of mixing and the more recent simplified methods are described here.

Butter-type (shortening) *Cakes*—These contain fat (butter, margarine, vegetable or all-purpose shortening, or lard) and a chemical leavening agent. They are prepared using the conventional "creaming" method which is probably the one most familiar to homemakers. Mixing is done manually or with an electric mixer. The shortening is creamed with the sugar and flavoring (or the flavoring is added with the liquid). Beaten eggs are then beaten into the creamed mixture and the dry and liquid ingredients added alternately, beginning and ending with dry ingredients. When using the electric mixer the unbeaten eggs may be added, one at a time, to the creamed mixture, beating thoroughly after each addition. Then, with the mixer at low speed, the dry ingredients and liquids are added alternately, beating only until the batter is smooth after each addition. At this point overbeating must be avoided as this reduces volume. Nuts, raisins, etc., are usually added last. Exceptions are recipes in which egg whites are beaten separately and gently folded into the batter.

One-Bowl Cakes (Quick Method)—For best results use vegetable or all-purpose shortening for these cakes. The method is to add the soft shortening to the sifted dry ingredients. Then add two thirds of the liquid to which the flavoring has been added. (When using all-purpose flour, add all the liquid at one time.) Beat mixture at medium speed of electric mixer for 2 minutes, scraping down the bowl, or beat by hand 2 minutes, 150 strokes per minute. Add remaining liquid and unbeaten eggs and beat 2 minutes longer, scraping down the bowl.

Cakes without Butter—This group includes angel food and sponge cakes. Well-beaten eggs are used as the leavening agent and the air beaten into them, along with the steam formed in the batter, causes the cake to rise. These cakes contain no fat or baking powder, except in an occasional recipe when a small amount of each is used. The old method of baking these cakes was to place them in a cold oven and bake them for an hour or longer at 300°F. Opinions vary today on the use of a preheated 325° or 350°F oven for a shorter period, or 375° or 400°F oven for an even shorter time.

Chiffon Cakes—These cakes contain cooking oil and baking powder. They have the lightness of a sponge cake and the richness of a "butter" cake.

Cake-Mix Cakes—The formulas and the mixing methods of these packaged mixes are almost foolproof (if directions on package are followed).

Tortes—These, as a class, are cake-like desserts, made light with eggs and often enriched with nuts. Bread crumbs, cracker or cookie crumbs, or grated nuts may take (wholly or in part) the place of flour. Tortes are coarser and more compact than cakes.

HELPFUL HINTS ABOUT CAKES

- Use fluted paper baking cups when preparing cupcakes. They save greasing of pans and eliminate sticking. They also make pan washing easy.
- Line cake pans with baking parchment or waxed paper for easy removal of cakes after baking. Grease pans (bottoms only) before lining with paper and grease the paper. Cut several pieces at one time to fit pans and keep on hand for future use. (Cut the circles for layer cake pans about ¼ inch smaller than size of pan.) After baked cakes are removed from pans, peel off paper immediately.
- For baking fruitcake, line the pan with heavy brown paper extending 1 inch above top of pan. When cake is baked, place on wire rack. When completely cooled, lift cake from pan and peel off paper.
- When baking an upside-down cake, line cake pan with aluminum foil, folding foil over the edges of pan. After cake is baked, let cool on rack about 5 minutes. Then place serving plate on top of cake, turn cake upside down and remove the pan. Carefully lift off the foil. Cake comes out of pan easily and pan is easy to clean.
- When making cakes (or cookies) which use shortening and call for flavoring extracts and/or ground spices, add them to the shortening before creaming with the sugar. The fat "carries" the extract and spice flavors through the batter.
- To make a lace-like decoration on a sponge or angel food cake or other unfrosted cake, place a sheer, lace paper doily on top of cake; sift confectioners' sugar over top; then carefully lift off doily.
- To make your own cinnamon sugar to be used for sprinkling over warm, not-to-be-frosted cakes and cupcakes, combine *½ cup fine granulated sugar* with *1 tablespoon ground cinnamon*. Keep the mixture on hand stored in a covered jar.
- If cooked white frosting has "sugared" somewhat, beat in a small amount of *lemon juice* until frosting is smooth.
- To make marshmallow flowers for cake decorating, use large white or colored *marshmallows*. With kitchen shears dipped in water, cut off strips about ⅛ inch thick. Place strips between 2 pieces of waxed paper and roll with rolling pin to make thin "petals." Arrange petals on frosted cake to simulate open flowers.

CONVENTIONAL CAKES

DELICATE WHITE CAKE

2¾ cups sifted cake flour
3 teaspoons baking powder
¾ teaspoon salt
1 cup vegetable shortening
1½ teaspoons vanilla extract
1½ cups sugar
1 cup milk
8 egg whites
½ cup sugar
Rich Coconut Fruit Filling, *below*

1. Sift flour, baking powder, and salt together.
2. Cream shortening with the extract and the 1½ cups sugar, beating until mixture is fluffy.
3. Beating only until smooth after each addition, alternately add flour mixture and milk.
4. In a large bowl, beat egg whites until frothy; beating constantly, add remaining sugar gradually and continue beating until stiff shiny peaks are formed. Fold into cake batter.
5. Turn batter into three 9-inch layer cake pans which have been lined on bottoms with waxed paper.
6. Bake at 350°F 20 to 25 minutes, or until cake tests done.
7. Cool in pans 10 minutes before removing to wire racks to cool thoroughly. Spread the filling between and on top of cake layers. Store overnight or about 8 hours in a cool place before serving.

ONE 9-INCH 3-LAYER CAKE

RICH COCONUT FRUIT FILLING

8 egg yolks, slightly beaten
1 cup sugar
½ cup butter (at room temperature)
⅓ cup bourbon
1⅓ cups flaked coconut
1 cup coarsely chopped pecans
¾ cup quartered candied cherries
¾ cup coarsely chopped seeded raisins

1. In a medium-sized saucepan combine the egg yolks, sugar, and butter. Cook over medium heat,

stirring constantly until sugar is dissolved and mixture is slightly thickened, 5 to 7 minutes.
2. Remove from heat and turn into a bowl. Cool slightly. Blend in the bourbon thoroughly.
3. Stir in the remaining ingredients. Cool thoroughly at room temperature before spreading on cooled cake layers. 3½ CUPS FILLING

NOTE: *2 tablespoons brandy flavoring* and *2 tablespoons water* may be substituted for the bourbon.

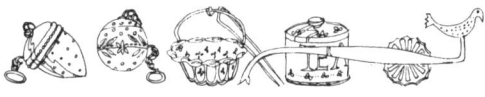

LINCOLN'S FAVORITE CAKE
Mary Todd, before her marriage to Abraham Lincoln, is said to have made this cake for him, and the verdict was— "the best in Kentucky."

3 cups sifted all-purpose flour	1 cup sugar
3 teaspoons baking powder	1 cup milk
	1¼ cups (about 7 oz.) toasted blanched almonds, finely chopped
¼ teaspoon salt	
1 cup butter	
1½ teaspoons vanilla extract	6 egg whites
	1 cup sugar
¼ teaspoon almond extract	Seafoam Frosting, (page 242)

1. Grease bottom only of a 10-inch tubed pan. Line with waxed paper cut to fit bottom; grease waxed paper. Set aside.
2. Sift the flour, baking powder, and salt together.
3. Cream butter with extracts. Add 1 cup sugar gradually, creaming until fluffy.
4. Beating only until smooth after each addition, alternately add dry ingredients in fourths and milk in thirds to the creamed mixture. Stir in the almonds.
5. Beat egg whites until frothy; add 1 cup sugar gradually, beating well. Continue beating until stiff peaks are formed. Gently fold meringue into batter just until blended. Turn batter into prepared pan and spread evenly.
6. Bake at 350°F about 1 hour, or until cake tests done.
7. Remove from oven and cool 15 minutes in pan on wire rack. Remove from pan; cool completely.
8. **Frost with Seafoam Frosting. Decorate with** finely cut *candied cherries.*
ONE 10-INCH TUBED CAKE

GOLD CAKE

2½ cups sifted cake flour	1½ teaspoons vanilla extract
4 teaspoons baking powder	1¼ cups sugar
	6 egg yolks (½ cup), well beaten
½ teaspoon salt	
⅔ cup butter or other shortening	⅔ cup milk

1. Sift flour, baking powder, and salt together.
2. Cream the butter with extract; gradually add the sugar, creaming well. Add the beaten egg yolks in thirds, beating thoroughly after each addition.
3. Beating until just blended after each addition, alternately add dry ingredients in thirds and liquid in halves to creamed mixture. Turn batter into a prepared 9-inch tubed pan.
4. Bake at 350°F about 55 minutes or until cake tests done.
5. Cool and remove from pans as directed for butter-type cakes. Sift *confectioners' sugar* over top.
ONE 9-INCH TUBED CAKE

ALMOND CAKE

2¼ cups sifted all-purpose flour	1 cup sugar
	3 eggs
2 teaspoons baking powder	1 can (12 oz.) almond cake and pastry filling (about 1¼ cups)
½ teaspoon salt	
1 cup butter	¼ cup milk
½ teaspoon vanilla extract	Almond Icing, *below*

1. Sift flour, baking powder, and salt together; set aside.
2. Cream the butter with extract. Add sugar gradually, beating vigorously. Add the eggs, one at a time, beating until light and fluffy after each addition. Mix in the almond filling.
3. Beating only until blended after each addition, alternately add dry ingredients in thirds and milk in halves to creamed mixture. Turn batter into a prepared 9-inch tubed pan.
4. Bake at 350°F 50 to 60 minutes, or until cake tests done.
5. Cool on wire rack as directed for butter-type cakes. Spoon Almond Icing over cake.
ONE 9-INCH TUBED CAKE

ALMOND ICING: Beat *¾ cup confectioners' sugar, 1 teaspoon soft butter, 1 teaspoon light corn syrup,*

⅛ teaspoon almond extract, and *1 tablespoon plus 1 teaspoon heavy cream* until smooth and of spreading consistency. ABOUT ⅓ CUP ICING

BANANA CAKE ROYALE

2 cups sifted all-purpose flour	⅔ cup vegetable shortening
3 teaspoons baking powder	2 teaspoons vanilla extract
½ teaspoon baking soda	⅔ cup sugar
1 teaspoon salt	3 egg yolks, well beaten
1 cup graham cracker crumbs (granular rather than fine)	3 egg whites
	½ cup sugar
	Filling and Topping:
1 teaspoon lemon juice	3 medium-sized ripe bananas
⅓ cup milk	Pineapple juice
1⅓ cups sieved ripe banana (3 to 4 bananas)	Sweetened Whipped Cream, *page 247*
	½ cup walnuts, chopped

1. Blend the flour, baking powder, baking soda, salt, and graham cracker crumbs; set aside.
2. Add lemon juice to milk and stir in the sieved banana; set aside.
3. Blend shortening and extract. Add the ⅔ cup sugar gradually, creaming until fluffy. Add the beaten egg yolks in halves, beating thoroughly after each addition.
4. Beating only until smooth after each addition, alternately add dry ingredients in fourths and banana-milk mixture in thirds to creamed mixture.
5. Beat egg whites until frothy. Add the ½ cup sugar gradually, continuing to beat until stiff peaks are formed. Gently fold meringue into batter just until blended. Turn batter into 3 prepared 8-inch layer cake pans.
6. Bake at 350°F 30 to 35 minutes, or until cake tests done.
7. Cool and remove from pans as directed for butter-type cakes. Cool completely.
8. For filling and topping, peel bananas and cut into slices; dip slices into pineapple juice. Place one cooled cake layer on serving plate and spread about one third of the Sweetened Whipped Cream over it. Arrange one third of the banana slices over the cream. Cover with the second layer and repeat procedure. Cover with third layer, spread remaining whipped cream over, and arrange remaining banana slices and chopped walnuts attractively on top. Serve immediately. ONE 8-INCH 3-LAYER CAKE

TURBAN CAKE
(Napfkuchen)

This cake of German origin is baked in a fluted mold. A semisweet chocolate glaze will add to its enhancement.

2¼ cups sifted all-purpose flour	½ cup sugar
2¼ teaspoons baking powder	4 egg yolks (⅓ cup), well beaten
½ cup butter	¾ cup milk
1 tablespoon grated lemon peel	4 egg whites (½ cup)
	½ cup sugar
1 teaspoon vanilla extract	Chocolate Glaze, *below*

1. Sift the flour and baking powder together; set aside.
2. Cream butter with lemon peel and extract. Add ½ cup sugar gradually, creaming until fluffy after each addition. Add the beaten egg yolks in thirds, beating well after each addition.
3. Beating only until smooth after each addition, alternately add dry ingredients in thirds and milk in halves to creamed mixture.
4. Beat the egg whites until frothy. Add ½ cup sugar gradually, beating well after each addition. Beat until stiff peaks are formed. Gently fold into batter. Turn into a greased 2-quart (8 inch) fluted tubed or turk's-head mold.
5. Bake at 350°F about 55 minutes, or until cake tests done.
6. Invert pan and let cake hang in pan 1 hour. Loosen from pan by running a small spatula carefully around tube and around edge of cake. Invert and remove pan. Spread warm Chocolate Glaze over the cake. Allow 2 to 3 hours for glaze to set. ONE 8-INCH CAKE

CHOCOLATE GLAZE: Melt *4 ounces semisweet chocolate pieces* over hot (not steaming) water. Remove from heat and stir until chocolate is melted. Blend in *¼ cup butter.*

BANANA JELLY SQUARES

2¼ cups sifted all-purpose flour	⅔ cup milk
	⅔ cup shortening
1½ cups granulated sugar	3 eggs
¾ teaspoon baking powder	1½ cups mashed ripe bananas (3 medium)
1 tablespoon lemon juice	1 jar (10 ozs.) strawberry jelly
1¼ teaspoons baking soda	
1 teaspoon salt	1 can (3½ ozs.) flaked coconut

1. Grease a baking pan, 13x9x2 inches; dust lightly with flour.
2. Preheat oven to 350°F.
3. Sift flour, sugar, baking soda, salt, and baking powder into a large bowl.
4. Stir lemon juice into milk in measuring cup; let stand several minutes. Add to flour mixture with shortening, eggs, and mashed bananas. Beat slowly with electric mixer until blended, then beat 3 minutes at high speed, scraping bowl several times. Pour into prepared pan, spreading top even.
5. Bake 35 minutes, or until golden and a wooden pick inserted into center comes out clean. Cool completely in pan on a wire rack.
6. Beat jelly with a fork or spoon in a small bowl until broken up; spread evenly over cake. Sprinkle coconut over jelly.
7. To serve, cut into squares.   12 SERVINGS

PRALINE CARROT CAKE

Caramel Syrup, *below*
Cooked Carrots, *below*
2½ cups sifted all-purpose flour
2 teaspoons baking powder
1 teaspoon salt
½ cup butter or margarine
1½ teaspoons vanilla extract
2 eggs, well beaten
2 cups pecans, coarsely chopped
Caramel Frosting

1. Prepare Caramel Syrup and Cooked Carrots; set aside.
2. Sift the flour, baking powder, and salt together.
3. Cream butter with extract; add the Caramel Syrup gradually, blending well. Add the eggs in thirds, beating thoroughly after each addition. Beat in the carrots.
4. Beating only until smooth after each addition, alternately add the dry ingredients in fourths and reserved 1 cup carrot syrup in thirds to creamed mixture. Mix in the pecans. Turn batter into a prepared 13x9x2-inch baking pan and spread evenly.
5. Bake at 350°F 45 to 50 minutes, or until cake tests done.
6. Set on a wire rack and cool completely in pan. Frost with Caramel Frosting.   ONE 13x9-INCH CAKE

CARAMEL SYRUP: Melt *1 cup sugar* in a heavy light-colored skillet (a black skillet makes it difficult to see the color of the syrup). With back of a wooden spoon, gently keep sugar moving toward center of skillet until sugar is completely melted and of a golden-brown color. Remove from heat. Being careful that steam does not burn hand, stir and gradually add *1 cup milk* a small amount at a time. Return to low heat and add *1 cup sugar* gradually, stirring constantly until completely dissolved. Remove from heat, blend in *1 tablespoon butter or margarine*, and cool to lukewarm.

COOKED CARROTS: Put *2 cups sliced carrots, 1 cup sugar,* and *1 cup boiling water* into a saucepan; stir until sugar is dissolved. Cover and simmer about 10 minutes, or until carrots are tender and syrup is clear. Drain carrots, reserving 1 cup syrup. Force carrots through a sieve or food mill. (If an electric mixer is to be used for mixing cake batter, do not sieve carrots.) Set aside to cool.

HONEY CAKE

2 cups sifted cake flour
1 teaspoon baking soda
¼ teaspoon salt
½ teaspoon ground cinnamon
½ teaspoon ground ginger
½ cup vegetable shortening
1 cup honey
1 egg
½ cup sour milk, *page 12*, or buttermilk
Fluffy Honey Frosting, *page 246*

1. Sift the flour, baking soda, salt, cinnamon, and ginger together and blend thoroughly; set aside.
2. Beat shortening and honey until light and thick. Add egg and beat thoroughly.
3. Beating only until blended after each addition, alternately add the dry ingredients in fourths and sour milk in thirds to creamed mixture. Turn batter into 2 prepared 8-inch layer cake pans and spread evenly to edges.
4. Bake at 375°F about 25 minutes, or until cake tests done.
5. Cool and remove from pans as directed for butter-type cakes. Fill cake layers and frost with Fluffy Honey Frosting.   ONE 8-INCH 2-LAYER CAKE

MAPLE SYRUP CAKE
One bite and it's easily understood why Vermonters are especially partial to this kind of cake.

2⅔ cups sifted cake flour	⅔ cup lightly packed light brown sugar
3 teaspoons baking powder	7 egg yolks, well beaten
¾ teaspoon salt	⅔ cup milk
¾ cup butter or margarine	⅔ cup maple syrup
	Maple Sugar Frosting
	½ cup chopped walnuts

1. Sift the flour, baking powder, and salt together; set aside.
2. Cream butter; gradually add brown sugar, creaming until fluffy. Add egg yolks in thirds, beating thoroughly after each addition.
3. Beating until smooth after each addition, alternately add the dry ingredients in fourths and a mixture of milk and maple syrup in thirds to the creamed mixture. Turn batter into 3 prepared 8-inch layer cake pans and spread evenly to edges.
4. Bake at 350°F 45 to 50 minutes, or until cake tests done.
5. Cool and remove from pans as directed for butter-type cakes. Fill and frost cake with Maple Sugar Frosting. Sprinkle walnuts around outside edge of top.   ONE 8-INCH 3-LAYER CAKE

MAPLE-BUTTERNUT CAKE: Follow recipe for Maple Syrup Cake. Blend in *½ cup coarsely chopped butternuts* just before turning batter into pans. Substitute butternuts for walnuts as topping.

ALMOND ROSETTE CAKES

1 package white cake mix	1 package (16 ozs.) confectioners' powdered sugar, sifted
1 package (3¾ ozs.) instant vanilla pudding mix	¼ cup light corn syrup
4 eggs	¼ teaspoon almond extract
¾ cup salad oil	Red food coloring
1 cup water	Gumdrop roses (directions follow)

1. Preheat oven to 350°F. Grease 12 muffin-pan cups and a baking pan, 9x9x2 inches.
2. Combine cake and pudding mixes in a large bowl. Add eggs, salad oil, and ¾ cup of the water all at once. Beat 5 minutes with electric mixer at medium speed. Spoon part of the batter into prepared muffin pans to fill each ⅔ full; spoon remaining batter into square pan.
3. Bake cupcakes 20 minutes and layer 30 minutes, or until tops spring back when lightly pressed with fingertip. Cool cakes in pans on wire racks 10 minutes. Loosen around edges with a knife; turn out onto racks; cool completely. (Wrap layer and set aside to frost for another dessert.)
4. Combine confectioners' sugar, corn syrup, remaining ¼ cup water, and almond extract in the top of a double boiler; tint pink with a few drops food coloring. Place over hot water; heat just until lukewarm; remove from heat, but leave over hot water to keep glaze thin as you work.
5. Place cupcakes, several at a time, upside down on a wire rack set over a bowl. Using a small measuring cup, pour frosting over cakes, turning each cake as you glaze it to make sure side is completely covered and smooth.
6. After all cakes have one coat, scrape frosting that drips into bowl back into pan; stir in 1 tablespoon water and reheat to lukewarm. Pour over cakes again to cover with a second coat. Let stand until glaze is firm.
7. When ready to serve, decorate each with a Gumdrop rose.   12 SMALL CAKES

GUMDROP ROSES—Sprinkle a cutting board generously with sugar. For each rose, roll out 2 large pink or red gumdrops to thin ovals about 2 inches long; cut each in half crosswise. Roll up one half tightly to form center of flower. Press remaining 3 halves, overlapping slightly, around center for petals. Press rose together tightly at base to hold in place.

ORANGE BLOSSOM CAKE

2½ cups sifted cake flour	2 teaspoons grated orange peel
2½ teaspoons baking powder	½ teaspoon grated lemon peel
½ teaspoon salt	1½ cups sugar
⅔ cup butter or margarine	3 eggs plus 2 yolks, well beaten
	1 cup orange juice

1. Sift the flour, baking powder, and salt together.
2. Cream the butter with orange and lemon peels. Add the sugar gradually, beating well. Add beaten eggs in thirds, beating well after each addition.
3. Beating until smooth after each addition, alter-

nately add dry ingredients in fourths and orange juice in thirds to creamed mixture. Turn batter into 2 prepared 9-inch layer cake pans and spread evenly to edges.
4. Bake at 350°F 25 to 30 minutes, or until cake tests done.
5. Cool and remove from pans as directed for butter-type cakes. Fill and frost layers with an *orange butter cream frosting*.

ONE 9-INCH 2-LAYER CAKE

SALTED PEANUT CAKE

1½ cups sifted all-purpose flour	1 cup sugar
½ teaspoon baking soda	1 egg
⅓ cup butter or margarine	¾ cup buttermilk
1 teaspoon vanilla extract	1 cup (about 5 oz.) salted peanuts, finely chopped

1. Sift flour and baking soda together; set aside.
2. Cream butter with extract. Gradually add sugar, creaming until fluffy. Add egg; beat thoroughly.
3. Beating only until smooth after each addition, alternately add dry ingredients in thirds and buttermilk in halves. Mix in peanuts. Turn batter into a greased 8x8x2-inch baking pan; spread evenly to edges.
4. Bake at 350°F about 50 minutes, or until cake tests done.
5. Cool completely in pan on wire rack. Sift *confectioners' sugar* evenly over top.

ONE 8-INCH SQUARE CAKE

UPSIDE-DOWN PEACH CAKE

¼ cup butter or margarine	1 egg
½ cup firmly packed light brown sugar	1 cup milk
	¼ cup chopped drained maraschino cherries
1 can (16 ozs.) cling peach slices, drained	1 package (2 ozs.) whipped topping mix
1 package cupcake mix	Vanilla

1. Preheat oven to 350°F.
2. Melt butter in a baking pan, 8x8x2 inches in oven as it heats; stir in brown sugar. Arrange peach slices in rows in sugar mixture.
3. Prepare cupcake mix with egg and ½ cup of the milk as label directs; fold in cherries. Spoon over peaches in pan.
4. Bake 45 minutes, or until top springs back when lightly touched with fingertip. Cool cake in pan on a wire rack 5 minutes; loosen around edges with a knife; invert cake onto a large serving plate. Let stand 5 minutes; lift off pan.
5. Prepare whipped topping mix with remaining ½ cup milk and vanilla as label directs. Cut cake into serving-size pieces; place on serving plates; serve warm with whipped topping.

8 SERVINGS

MARBLEIZED TUBED CAKE

½ cup sugar	1½ teaspoons vanilla extract
¾ teaspoon ground cinnamon	1 cup sugar
2 tablespoons cocoa	4 egg yolks, well beaten
3 cups sifted all-purpose flour	1 cup milk
3 teaspoons baking powder	4 egg whites
½ teaspoon salt	½ cup sugar
1 cup butter or margarine	2 tablespoons butter or margarine

1. Blend ½ cup sugar, cinnamon, and cocoa; set aside.
2. Sift the flour, baking powder, and salt together; set aside.
3. Cream the 1 cup butter with extract. Add the 1 cup sugar gradually, creaming until fluffy. Add beaten egg yolks in thirds, beating thoroughly after each addition.
4. Beating only until smooth after each addition, alternately add dry ingredients in fourths and milk in thirds to creamed mixture.
5. Beat egg whites until frothy; add the remaining ½ cup sugar gradually, beating well. Continue beating until stiff peaks are formed. Fold batter gently into beaten egg whites until just blended.
6. Gently turn one third of the batter into a greased and floured (bottom only) 10-inch tubed pan, spreading evenly. Sprinkle batter in pan with one third of the sugar mixture. Alternately layer remaining batter and sugar mixture, ending with sugar mixture on top. Cut through batter from center to outer edge at 1 to 2 inch intervals with a spatula to swirl sugar mixture through batter. Dot with remaining butter.

7. Bake at 375°F about 1 hour, or until cake tests done.
8. Remove from oven to wire rack and cool completely in pan. Sprinkle top lightly with *confectioners' sugar*.
ONE 10-INCH TUBED CAKE

SPICE CAKE WITH PRALINE FROSTING

3 cups sifted cake flour
1½ teaspoons baking powder
¾ teaspoon baking soda
¾ teaspoon salt
1½ teaspoons ground cinnamon
¾ teaspoon ground nutmeg
½ teaspoon ground allspice
½ teaspoon ground cloves

¾ cup butter
1 cup lightly packed light brown sugar
1 cup sugar
3 eggs, well beaten
1½ cups buttermilk
Praline Frosting:
2 egg whites
¼ teaspoon salt
1¾ cups lightly packed brown sugar
½ cup chopped pecans

1. Sift the flour, baking powder, baking soda, salt, and spices together and blend thoroughly; set aside.
2. Cream butter; gradually add the sugars, creaming until fluffy. Add the beaten eggs in thirds, beating thoroughly after each addition.
3. Beating only until blended after each addition, alternately add dry ingredients in fourths and buttermilk in thirds to creamed mixture. Turn batter into a greased (bottom only) 13x9x2-inch baking pan and spread evenly.
4. Bake at 350°F 55 to 60 minutes, or until cake tests done.
5. Set on wire rack while preparing frosting.
6. Beat the egg whites with salt until rounded peaks are formed. Gradually add the brown sugar, beating thoroughly. (If mixture becomes too thick to beat, blend in remaining sugar with a spoon.) Add the pecans and mix well.
7. Spread frosting over the partially cooled cake in pan. Return to oven and bake about 18 minutes, or until frosting is delicately browned.
8. Set on wire rack for 10 to 15 minutes to cool before cutting into squares. Serve warm.
ONE 13x9-INCH CAKE

APPLE BUTTER SPICE CAKE

Topping:
½ cup lightly packed light brown sugar
¾ cup chopped pecans
1 teaspoon ground cinnamon
½ teaspoon ground nutmeg
Batter:
2 cups sifted all-purpose flour
1 teaspoon baking powder

1 teaspoon baking soda
½ teaspoon salt
½ cup butter or margarine
1 teaspoon vanilla extract
1 cup sugar
2 eggs
¾ cup apple butter
½ cup whole bran cereal
1 cup dairy sour cream

1. Combine the ingredients for topping and set aside.
2. Sift the flour, baking powder, baking soda, and salt together; set aside.
3. Cream butter with extract; gradually add the sugar, beating until fluffy. Add the eggs, one at a time, beating thoroughly after each addition. Blend in the apple butter and cereal.
4. Beating only until smooth after each addition, alternately add dry ingredients in fourths and sour cream in thirds to creamed mixture. Turn half the batter into a greased (bottom only) 13x9x2-inch baking pan. Spread evenly to edges. Sprinkle half of the topping mixture over batter in pan. Spoon remaining batter into pan and spread evenly. Sprinkle with remaining topping.
5. Bake at 350°F about 30 minutes, or until cake tests done.
6. Cool cake completely in pan. Cut into squares and serve warm or cold. Top with *whipped cream*, if desired.
ONE 13x9-INCH CAKE

SOFT GINGERBREAD

Gingerbread was recorded in early colonial accounts and is still greatly appreciated in America.

3 cups sifted all-purpose flour
1 teaspoon baking soda
¼ teaspoon salt
2 teaspoons ground cinnamon
2 teaspoons ground ginger
1 teaspoon ground cloves

¼ teaspoon ground nutmeg
½ cup butter
1 cup sugar
2 eggs, well beaten
1 cup light molasses
¼ cup boiling water
1 cup sour milk, *page 12*

1. Sift the flour, baking soda, salt, and spices together and blend thoroughly; set aside.
2. Cream butter; gradually add sugar, creaming until fluffy. Add eggs in thirds, beating well after each addition. Add a mixture of molasses and boiling water gradually, mixing well.
3. Beating only until smooth after each addition, alternately add dry ingredients in fourths and sour milk in thirds to creamed mixture. Turn batter into a well greased (bottom only) 13x9x2-inch baking pan.
4. Bake at 350°F about 35 minutes, or until gingerbread tests done.
5. Cool in pan on wire rack.   ONE 13x9-INCH CAKE

OLD-FASHIONED MOLASSES CAKE

4⅓ cups sifted all-purpose flour	1½ teaspoons ground ginger
3 teaspoons baking powder	¾ teaspoon ground cloves
¾ teaspoon baking soda	¾ cup butter
1 teaspoon salt	¾ cup sugar
3 teaspoons ground cinnamon	1½ cups light molasses
	3 eggs, well beaten
	1½ cups hot water

1. Sift the flour, baking powder, baking soda, salt, and spices together and blend thoroughly.
2. Cream butter; gradually add sugar, creaming until fluffy. Add molasses gradually, mixing well. Blend in ½ cup of the dry ingredients. Add eggs in thirds, beating well after each addition.
3. Beating only until smooth after each addition, alternately add the remaining dry ingredients in fourths and hot water in thirds. Turn batter into a greased (bottom only) 13x9x2-inch baking pan and spread evenly to edges.
4. Bake at 350°F 50 minutes, or until cake tests done.
5. Cool cake completely in pan. Cut into squares and, if desired, serve with warm *applesauce*.
   ONE 13x9-INCH CAKE

PUMPKIN CAKE

2¼ cups sifted cake flour	½ cup butter or margarine
3 teaspoons baking powder	½ cup sugar
½ teaspoon baking soda	1 cup lightly packed dark brown sugar
½ teaspoon salt	2 eggs
1½ teaspoons ground cinnamon	¾ cup buttermilk
½ teaspoon ground allspice	¾ cup canned pumpkin
½ teaspoon ground ginger	½ cup finely snipped or chopped golden raisins

1. Sift the flour, baking powder, baking soda, salt, and spices together and blend thoroughly; set aside.
2. Cream butter; gradually add sugars, creaming until fluffy. Add eggs, one at a time, beating thoroughly after each addition.
3. Beating only until smooth after each addition, alternately add dry ingredients in fourths and a mixture of the buttermilk, pumpkin, and raisins in thirds to creamed mixture. Turn batter into 2 prepared 9-inch layer cake pans and spread evenly.
4. Bake at 350°F about 30 minutes, or until cake tests done.
5. Cool and remove from pans as directed for butter-type cakes.   TWO 9-INCH CAKE LAYERS

PUMPKIN MINIATURES: Follow recipe for Pumpkin Cake. Spoon batter into 1¾-inch muffin-pan wells lined with paper baking cups, half filling each. Bake at 375°F about 13 minutes, or until cupcakes test done. Remove from pans and cool on racks. Frost with *butter cream frosting*.
   6½ DOZEN CUPCAKES

OLD-FASHIONED CHOCOLATE CAKE
Said to have been a favorite of President William McKinley.

2 egg yolks, fork beaten	1½ teaspoons vanilla extract
6 oz. (6 sq.) unsweetened chocolate, melted	2 cups lightly packed brown sugar
½ cup hot water	1 cup sour milk, page 12
2 cups sifted cake flour	White Velvet Frosting, page 245
1 teaspoon baking soda	
½ teaspoon salt	
½ cup butter	

1. Stir egg yolks into melted chocolate. Gradually add the hot water, stirring constantly until smooth. Set aside to cool.
2. Sift flour, baking soda, and salt together; set aside.

3. Cream butter with extract; gradually add brown sugar, creaming thoroughly. Blend in chocolate mixture.
4. Beating only until blended after each addition, alternately add the dry ingredients in fourths and the sour milk in thirds to the creamed mixture. Turn into 2 prepared 8-inch layer cake pans and spread evenly to edges.
5. Bake at 350°F 30 minutes, or until cake tests done.
6. Cool and remove from pans as directed for butter-type cakes. Fill and frost.
ONE 8-INCH 2-LAYER CAKE

JERRY LEWIS' CHOCOLATE CAKE
Actor, producer, director Jerry Lewis is always on the go, but when wife Patti bakes his favorite cake, Jerry makes sure he has time to enjoy its chocolaty goodness.

2 cups sifted cake flour	2 oz. (2 sq.) unsweetened chocolate, melted and cooled
½ teaspoon salt	
½ cup butter or margarine	
1 teaspoon vanilla extract	1 cup sour milk, page 12
1½ cups sugar	1 teaspoon baking soda
2 eggs	1 tablespoon vinegar

1. Sift flour and salt together; set aside.
2. Cream butter with extract. Gradually add sugar, creaming until light and fluffy. Add eggs, one at a time, beating thoroughly after each addition. Blend in chocolate.
3. Beating only until smooth after each addition, alternately add dry ingredients in thirds and sour milk in halves to creamed mixture. Stir baking soda and vinegar together; immediately blend into batter. Turn into 2 prepared 9-inch layer cake pans and spread evenly to edges.
4. Bake at 375°F 25 minutes, or until cake tests done.
5. Cool and remove from pans as directed for butter-type cakes. Frost as desired.
TWO 9-INCH CAKE LAYERS

MRS. EISENHOWER'S DEVIL'S FOOD CAKE
A recipe from the wife of former President Dwight David Eisenhower.

⅔ cup cocoa	1 teaspoon vanilla extract
½ cup boiling water	
2½ cups sifted cake flour	2 cups sugar
	3 egg yolks
1¼ teaspoons baking powder	1 cup sour milk, page 12
1 teaspoon baking soda	3 egg whites, beaten to stiff, not dry, peaks
¼ teaspoon salt	
½ cup butter	Seven-Minute Frosting, page 242

1. Mix cocoa and water together; set aside to cool.
2. Sift flour, baking powder, baking soda, and salt together; set aside.
3. Cream butter with extract; gradually add sugar, creaming thoroughly. Add egg yolks, one at a time, beating thoroughly after each addition. Add cocoa mixture and beat until well blended.
4. Beating only until blended after each addition, alternately add dry ingredients in thirds and sour milk in halves to creamed mixture. Fold in beaten egg whites. Turn batter into 2 prepared 9-inch layer cake pans and spread evenly to edges.
5. Bake at 375°F 25 to 30 minutes, or until cake tests done.
6. Cool and remove from pans as directed for butter-type cakes. Fill and frost with Seven-Minute Frosting.
ONE 9-INCH 2-LAYER CAKE

WELLESLEY FUDGE CAKE
A favorite with the students of Wellesley, a school in the Massachusetts town of the same name.

4 oz. (4 sq.) unsweetened chocolate	½ cup butter or margarine
½ cup hot water	2 teaspoons vanilla extract
½ cup sugar	
2 cups sifted cake flour	1¼ cups sugar
1½ teaspoons baking powder	4 eggs, well beaten
	⅔ cup milk
½ teaspoon baking soda	Fudge Frosting
½ teaspoon salt	

1. Combine chocolate and water in a heavy saucepan. Place over very low heat, stirring constantly, until chocolate is melted. Add the ½ cup sugar and stir until dissolved. Set aside to cool.

2. Sift flour, baking powder, baking soda, and salt together; set aside.
3. Cream butter with extract; gradually add the 1¼ cups sugar, creaming until fluffy. Add eggs in thirds, beating thoroughly after each addition. Blend in chocolate mixture.
4. Beating only until smooth after each addition, alternately add dry ingredients in fourths and milk in thirds to creamed mixture. Turn batter into 2 prepared 8x8x2-inch baking pans and spread evenly to edges.
5. Bake at 350°F 25 to 30 minutes, or until cake tests done.
6. Cool and remove from pans as directed for butter-type cakes. Fill and frost with Fudge Frosting II. ONE 8-INCH SQUARE 2-LAYER CAKE

CHOCOLATE APPLESAUCE CAKE

3 cups sifted cake flour
¾ cup cocoa, sifted
2½ teaspoons baking powder
½ teaspoon baking soda
¾ teaspoon salt
1½ teaspoons ground cinnamon
¾ teaspoon ground nutmeg
½ teaspoon ground cloves
½ cup vegetable shortening
½ cup butter or margarine
1½ cups sugar
2 eggs, well beaten
1 cup thick sweetened applesauce
¾ cup sour milk, page 12 or buttermilk
¾ cup nuts, chopped

1. Sift flour, cocoa, baking powder, baking soda, salt, and spices together and blend; set aside.
2. Cream shortening and butter; gradually add sugar, creaming until fluffy. Add eggs in thirds, beating thoroughly after each addition.
3. Beating only until smooth after each addition, alternately add dry ingredients in fourths and a mixture of the applesauce and sour milk in thirds to the creamed mixture. Stir in the chopped nuts. Turn batter into an ungreased 10-inch tubed pan having a removable bottom.
4. Bake at 350°F about 1 hour, or until cake tests done.
5. Cool 15 minutes before removing from pan.

ONE 10-INCH TUBED CAKE

UPSIDE-DOWN LEMON CAKE
More pudding than cake and redolent with the fresh flavor of lemon, the whole family should give this dessert a high rating.

12 lemon slices (about 1½ lemons)
Sauce:
½ cup sugar
4 teaspoons cornstarch
⅛ teaspoon salt
¾ cup water
2 teaspoons grated lemon peel
2 tablespoons lemon juice
1½ tablespoons butter
1 drop yellow food coloring

Cake batter:
1½ cups sifted cake flour
2 teaspoons baking powder
½ teaspoon salt
¼ cup butter
1 teaspoon grated lemon peel
¾ cup sugar
1 egg
½ cup milk

1. Rinse, slice very thin, and remove seeds from enough lemons to yield 12 slices.
2. At four equal intervals around each slice, make cuts through peel almost to center. Arrange lemon slices on bottom of a greased (bottom only) 9x9x2-inch baking pan. (For a distinctive topping, slice about 3 lemons as indicated above, and overlap slices in rows to cover bottom of pan.)
3. For sauce, mix sugar, cornstarch, and salt together in a saucepan. Add water gradually, blending thoroughly.
4. Stirring constantly, bring mixture to boiling. Continue to stir and cook about 3 minutes.
5. Remove from heat and blend in lemon peel and juice, butter, and yellow food coloring.
6. Spoon about one half of the sauce into the pan to cover the lemon slices; reserve remaining sauce.
7. For cake batter, sift the flour, baking powder, and salt together; set aside.
8. Cream butter with lemon peel. Add sugar gradually, creaming until fluffy. Add egg, beating thoroughly.
9. Beating only until smooth after each addition, alternately add dry ingredients in thirds and milk in halves to creamed mixture. Turn batter into pan over lemon slices and spread evenly to edges.
10. Bake at 350°F about 40 minutes, or until cake tests done.
11. Remove from oven; let stand 2 to 3 minutes in pan on wire rack. Using a spatula, loosen cake from sides of pan and invert onto a serving plate. Allow pan to remain over cake 1 to 2 minutes. Remove

pan. Spoon remaining lemon sauce evenly over top of cake. Serve warm. 1 UPSIDE-DOWN CAKE

STRAWBERRY-LIME CREAM CAKE

1 cup graham-cracker crumbs
3 tablespoons butter or margarine, melted
2 envelopes unflavored gelatin
1¾ cups sugar
6 eggs, separated
1 cup water
1 teaspoon grated lime rind
½ cup lime juice
Green food coloring
1 cup whipping cream
1 pint strawberries
1 tablespoon cornstarch
Red food coloring

1. Blend cracker crumbs and melted butter in a small bowl; press evenly over bottom of an 8-inch springform pan.
2. Mix gelatin and 1 cup of the sugar in a small saucepan. Beat egg yolks in a small bowl; stir in ¾ cup of the water; stir into gelatin mixture. Cook slowly, stirring constantly, until gelatin dissolves and mixture coats spoon; remove from heat. Pour into a large bowl; stir in lime rind and juice and a few drops food coloring to tint bright green. Place bowl in a pan of ice and water to speed setting. Chill, stirring several times, until mixture starts to thicken.
3. While gelatin mixture chills, beat egg whites in a medium bowl until foamy; slowly beat in ½ cup of the remaining sugar until meringue stands in soft peaks. Beat cream in a medium bowl until stiff. Fold meringue, then whipped cream into thickened lime mixture until no streaks of white remain. Spoon into prepared pan. Chill several hours, or overnight, until firm.
4. Wash strawberries and hull; mash enough to measure ½ cup; pour into a small saucepan.
5. Dissolve cornstarch in remaining ¼ cup water; stir into saucepan with remaining ¼ cup sugar. Cook, stirring constantly, until mixture thickens and boils 1 minute; remove from heat. Stir in a few drops food coloring to tint deep pink; cool.
6. Loosen cake around edge of pan with a knife; release spring and carefully lift off side of pan. Place cake, on its metal base, on a large serving plate.
7. Cut remaining strawberries in half and arrange in a pretty pattern on top of cake. Spoon glaze over berries to coat, letting some drip down side of cake. Chill 20 minutes until glaze sets, or until serving time.
8. Slice cake into wedges. 10 TO 12 SERVINGS

PINEAPPLE UPSIDE-DOWN CAKE

Topping:
¼ cup butter or margarine
⅔ cup lightly packed brown sugar
5 canned pineapple slices (reserve ½ cup syrup)
5 maraschino cherries
Cake batter:
1½ cups sifted cake flour
2 teaspoons baking powder
½ teaspoon salt
½ cup butter or margarine
1 teaspoon vanilla extract
½ cup sugar
1 egg

1. For topping, heat the butter in an 8x8x2-inch baking pan (or in a 10-inch skillet with a heat-resistant handle); blend in the brown sugar and spread evenly. Arrange pineapple slices on top of the brown sugar mixture with a cherry in the center of each. Set aside.
2. For cake batter, sift the flour, baking powder, and salt together; set aside.
3. Cream the butter with extract. Add the sugar gradually, creaming until fluffy. Add egg and beat thoroughly.
4. Beating only until smooth after each addition, alternately add the dry ingredients in thirds and reserved pineapple syrup in halves to the creamed mixture. Turn batter over pineapple slices and spread evenly to edges of pan.
5. Bake at 350°F about 45 minutes (about 35 minutes for skillet), or until cake tests done.
6. Remove from oven; let stand 1 to 2 minutes in pan on wire rack. Using a spatula, loosen cake from sides of pan and invert onto a serving plate. Allow pan to remain over cake 1 to 2 minutes so syrup will drain onto cake. Remove from pan. Serve warm or cool. ONE UPSIDE-DOWN CAKE

CRANBERRY UPSIDE-DOWN CAKE: Follow recipe for Pineapple Upside-Down Cake. In topping, substitute *⅔ cup granulated sugar* for brown sugar. Blend *1 tablespoon grated orange peel* and *½ teaspoon vanilla extract* with sugar and butter in pan. Spread mixture evenly in pan. Omit pineapple and cherries; spoon a mixture of *2 cups cranberries*, washed and coarsely chopped, and *⅓ cup sugar* over mixture in pan. Proceed as directed for cake, substituting *½ cup milk* for pineapple syrup.

APRICOT UPSIDE-DOWN CAKE: Follow recipe for Pineapple Upside-Down Cake. Substitute the following topping: Simmer *½ pound dried apricots* in *2 cups water* until fruit is plump and tender. Cool and drain well. Thoroughly blend *3 tablespoons melted butter or margarine, ½ cup lightly packed brown sugar*, and *⅓ cup drained crushed pineapple*. Arrange apricots in lightly greased (bottom only) pan. Spoon pineapple mixture over apricots. Proceed as directed for cake, substituting *½ cup milk* for pineapple syrup.

PEACHY NUT UPSIDE-DOWN CAKE: Follow recipe for Apricot Upside-Down Cake. Substitute *½ pound dried peaches* for apricots. Put a *pecan half* in cavity of each peach and arrange nut side down in prepared pan.

MARASCHINO DATE-NUT CAKE

2 cups sifted all-purpose flour
2 teaspoons baking powder
¼ teaspoon salt
1 teaspoon ground allspice
1 teaspoon ground cinnamon
1½ cups drained maraschino cherries, sliced
1 cup (about 7 oz.) dates, cut in pieces
2 cups coarsely chopped pecans
¼ cup all-purpose flour
¾ cup butter or margarine
½ teaspoon vanilla extract
2 cups sugar
4 eggs
2 oz. (2 sq.) unsweetened chocolate, grated
1 cup cold unseasoned mashed potatoes
½ cup milk

1. Sift the flour, baking powder, salt, allspice, and cinnamon together and blend well; set aside.
2. Mix cherries, dates, pecans, and the ¼ cup flour; set aside.
3. Cream butter with extract. Add sugar gradually, creaming until fluffy. Add eggs, one at a time, beating thoroughly after each addition. Mix in the grated chocolate and cooled mashed potatoes.
4. Beating only until blended after each addition, alternately add dry ingredients in thirds and milk in halves to creamed mixture. Blend in fruit-nut mixture. Turn batter into a greased (bottom only) 13x9x2-inch baking pan and spread evenly to edges.
5. Bake at 300°F about 1½ hours, or until cake tests done.
6. Remove from oven to wire rack and cool cake completely in pan. ONE 13x9-INCH CAKE

CRUNCH-TOP RAISIN CAKE

⅓ cup lightly packed brown sugar
1 tablespoon flour
¼ teaspoon ground nutmeg
2 tablespoons butter or margarine
¼ cup blanched almonds, slivered
1½ cups sifted cake flour
2 teaspoons baking powder
½ teaspoon ground nutmeg
⅛ teaspoon salt
⅓ cup butter or margarine
2 teaspoons grated lemon peel
¾ cup sugar
1 egg
¼ cup water
3 tablespoons lemon juice
¾ cup dark seedless raisins, coarsely chopped

1. Blend the brown sugar, flour, and ¼ teaspoon nutmeg in a bowl. Using a pastry blender or two knives, cut in the 2 tablespoons butter until mixture is crumbly. Stir in the almonds; set aside.
2. Sift the cake flour, baking powder, ½ teaspoon nutmeg, and salt together; set aside.
3. Cream the ⅓ cup butter with lemon peel. Gradually add sugar, creaming until fluffy. Add egg and beat thoroughly.
4. Beating only until smooth after each addition, alternately add dry ingredients in thirds and a mixture of the water and lemon juice in halves to creamed mixture. Stir in the chopped raisins. Turn batter into a greased (bottom only) 8x8x2-inch baking pan and spread evenly to edges. Spoon almond mixture evenly over batter and press lightly.
5. Bake at 350°F 45 minutes, or until cake tests done.
6. Cool in pan on wire rack. Cut into squares and serve warm or cool. ONE 8-INCH SQUARE CAKE

POUND CAKE RING

2 cups sifted cake flour
1½ teaspoons baking powder
½ teaspoon salt
1 cup butter
1½ teaspoons vanilla extract
1¼ cups sugar
4 eggs, well beaten
½ cup milk
Citrus Glaze, *page 234*

1. Sift the flour, baking powder, and salt together; set aside.

2. Cream butter with extract. Gradually add sugar, creaming until fluffy. Add eggs in thirds, beating thoroughly after each addition.
3. Beating only until smooth after each addition, alternately add dry ingredients in thirds and milk in halves to creamed mixture. Turn batter into a greased (bottom only) 3-quart ring mold.
4. Bake at 325°F about 40 minutes, or until cake tests done.
5. Cool 10 minutes in pan on wire rack; remove and cool completely. Spoon hot Citrus Glaze over cake on serving plate.   1 RING-SHAPED CAKE

CITRUS GLAZE: Combine ½ cup light corn syrup, ½ cup sugar, ½ cup orange juice, and ¼ cup lemon juice in a saucepan. Stir over low heat until sugar is dissolved. Increase heat and boil 5 minutes.

OLD WILLIAMSBURG-STYLE FRUITCAKE

1 cup butter or margarine	8 oz. (1⅓ cups) diced candied pineapple
2⅓ cups sugar	8 oz. (1 cup) diced candied citron
4 egg yolks	
4 cups sifted all-purpose flour	2 cups flaked coconut, finely chopped
½ cup sherry	4 egg whites, beaten to stiff, not dry, peaks
1 lb. walnuts, chopped	
1 pkg. (15 oz.) golden raisins	Almond Paste, *below* Icing, *below*
8 oz. (1 cup) finely chopped candied red cherries	

1. Cream butter. Gradually add sugar, beating thoroughly after each addition. Add egg yolks, one at a time, beating until light and fluffy after each addition. Blend in 1 cup flour, then the sherry.
2. Mix the remaining flour, walnuts, the fruits, and coconut. Stir into mixture in bowl. Fold in beaten egg whites. Turn batter into a greased 10-inch tubed pan lined with greased brown paper or baking parchment. Spread evenly in pan.
3. Bake at 300°F 2¾ hours, or until cake tests done.
4. Cool completely on wire rack before removing the cake from the pan.
5. Brush cake with *sherry*. Wrap tightly in aluminum foil. Store in a cool place.
6. The day before the cake is to be served, brush top and sides of cake with a slightly beaten *egg white*. Place the round of Almond Paste on top of the cake and arrange pieces on sides; press edges to seal. Let dry at room temperature about 8 hours.
7. Reserving about 1 cup, spread Icing over sides and top of cake. Using a pastry bag and tube, decorate with reserved icing. Garnish with *flaked coconut* and *candied red and green cherries*. Let dry at room temperature about 4 hours.
          ONE 10-POUND DECORATED FRUITCAKE

ALMOND PASTE: Blend *1 pound (about 4 cups) ground blanched almonds, 1 pound confectioners' sugar, 3 egg whites, 1 tablespoon lemon juice, ½ teaspoon orange extract,* and *⅛ teaspoon almond extract.* Press into a ball. Roll out about one third of the ball into an 8-inch round on waxed paper dusted with *confectioners' sugar.* Roll remainder of ball into a 28x4-inch strip; cut into 4 pieces.

ICING: Add *3 cups confectioners' sugar* to *2 egg whites* and beat with electric mixer at high speed about 5 minutes. Blend in *2 tablespoons lemon juice.* Add *3 cups confectioners' sugar* gradually, beating the mixture well.

ONE-BOWL & QUICK CAKES

MERRIE COMPANIE CAKE
(One-Bowl Method)

2¾ cups sifted cake flour	¾ teaspoon orange extract
1¾ cups sugar	¾ teaspoon lemon extract
2 teaspoons baking powder	3 eggs
1¼ teaspoons salt	1 egg yolk
1 cup vegetable shortening	Fruit 'n' Nut White Mountain Frosting, *page 242*
¾ cup milk	

1. Sift the flour, sugar, baking powder, and salt into a large bowl. Add shortening, about ½ cup milk, and extracts. Beat 2 minutes with electric mixer at medium speed. Scrape down bowl.
2. Add remaining milk, eggs, and egg yolk and

beat 2 minutes. Turn batter into a prepared 9-inch tubed pan.
3. Bake at 375°F about 45 minutes, or until cake tests done.
4. Cool and remove from pan as directed for butter-type cakes. Frost with Fruit 'n' Nut White Mountain Frosting.   ONE 9-INCH TUBED CAKE

QUICK COCOA CAKE
(One-Bowl Method)

1⅓ cups sifted cake flour	2 eggs
1 cup sugar	¼ cup milk
½ cup cocoa	1½ teaspoons vanilla extract
1 teaspoon baking powder	½ cup milk
½ teaspoon baking soda	2 teaspoons cider vinegar
¼ teaspoon salt	Chocolate Butter Frosting, page 245
6 tablespoons vegetable shortening or all-purpose shortening	

1. Sift flour, sugar, cocoa, baking powder, baking soda, and salt together into a large bowl; blend to distribute cocoa. Add shortening.
2. Add a mixture of the eggs, ¼ cup milk, and extract to dry ingredients. Beat with electric mixer at medium speed for 2 minutes (or beat vigorously about 300 strokes). Scrape sides and bottom of bowl occasionally.
3. Add a mixture of ½ cup milk and the vinegar to batter. Beat at medium speed for 1 minute (or beat vigorously about 150 strokes). Turn batter into a greased 2-quart ring mold or an 8x8x2-inch baking pan.
4. Bake at 350°F about 30 minutes for cake ring and 35 minutes for square cake, or until cake tests done.
5. Remove from oven to wire rack and cool cake ring about 5 minutes before removing cake. If using a square pan, cool the cake completely in pan. Frost with **Chocolate Butter Frosting**.
   ONE CAKE MOLD OR 8-INCH SQUARE CAKE

CARAWAY CAKE

1½ cups sifted all-purpose flour	¼ cup lard
1 cup sugar	1 egg, beaten
2 teaspoons baking powder	¾ cup milk
¼ teaspoon salt	½ teaspoon vanilla extract
2 tablespoons caraway seed	2 tablespoons sugar

1. Sift the flour, 1 cup sugar, baking powder, and salt together into a bowl and mix in the caraway seed. Cut in lard with pastry blender or two knives until particles resemble rice kernels.
2. Add a mixture of egg, milk, and extract; mix until all ingredients are moistened. Turn batter into a prepared 11x7x1½-inch baking pan. Sprinkle the 2 tablespoons sugar over top.
3. Bake at 375°F 30 minutes, or until cake tests done.
4. Cool in pan on wire rack. Cut into squares.
   ONE 11x7-INCH CAKE

WHIPPED CREAM CAKE

1½ cups sifted cake flour	1½ teaspoons vanilla extract
1 cup sugar	¼ teaspoon lemon extract
2 teaspoons baking powder	1 cup chilled heavy cream, whipped to soft peaks
¼ teaspoon salt	
2 eggs	

1. Sift the flour, sugar, baking powder, and salt together; set aside.
2. Beat eggs and extracts in a large bowl until thick and piled softly. Gently fold in whipped cream. Sift about one fourth of the flour mixture at a time over the cream mixture, gently folding until just blended after each addition. Turn batter into 2 greased (bottoms only) 8-inch layer cake pans which have been lined on bottoms with waxed paper and greased again. Spread batter evenly to edges.
3. Bake at 350°F 30 minutes, or until cake tests done.
4. Cool and remove from pans as directed for butter-type cakes. Fill and frost as desired.
   TWO 8-INCH CAKE LAYERS

ANGEL FOOD & SPONGE CAKES

ANGEL FOOD CAKE

1 cup sifted cake flour
¾ cup sugar
1½ cups (about 12) egg whites
1 teaspoon cream of tartar
½ teaspoon salt
1 teaspoon vanilla extract
½ teaspoon almond extract
¾ cup sugar

1. Sift flour and ¾ cup sugar together four times; set aside.
2. Beat egg whites with cream of tartar, salt, and extracts until stiff, not dry, peaks are formed. Lightly fold in remaining sugar, 2 tablespoons at a time.
3. Gently folding until blended after each addition, sift about 4 tablespoons of the flour mixture at a time over meringue. Carefully slide batter into an ungreased 10-inch tubed pan, turning pan as batter is poured. Cut through batter with knife or spatula to break large air bubbles.
4. Bake at 350°F about 45 minutes, or until cake tests done.
5. Immediately invert pan and cool cake completely. Remove from pan as directed for sponge-type cakes. ONE 10-INCH TUBED CAKE

CHERRY-NUT ANGEL FOOD CAKE: Follow recipe for Angel Food Cake. Fold in *½ cup finely chopped nuts* and *¼ cup finely chopped, well-drained maraschino cherries* with last addition of flour mixture.

TOASTY-COCONUT ANGEL FOOD CAKE: Follow recipe for Angel Food Cake. Fold in *1 cup toasted flaked coconut* with last addition of flour mixture.

RAINBOW ANGEL FOOD CAKE: Follow recipe for Angel Food Cake. Divide batter equally among 3 bowls. Fold *2 drops red food coloring* into one portion, *2 drops yellow food coloring* and *¼ teaspoon lemon extract* into another, and *2 drops green food coloring* and *¼ teaspoon peppermint extract* into the third portion. Form 3 layers in pan.

MOCHA ANGEL DESSERT: Follow recipe for Angel Food Cake. Substitute four 9-inch layer cake pans for tubed pan. Lightly grease bottoms and line with waxed paper. Divide batter equally among the pans. Bake at 325°F 25 to 30 minutes, or until cake tests done. Meanwhile, prepare *Mocha-Mallow Whipped Cream, page 248.* Invert cake pans on wire racks; allow to cool completely. Remove layers from pans, peel off paper, and turn layers right side up. Place 1 cake layer on serving plate; spread about one fourth of Mocha-Mallow Whipped Cream over top. Cover with second layer; repeat procedure with remaining filling and layers. Chill. If desired, top with *chocolate curls.* ONE 9-INCH 4-LAYER CAKE

COCOA ANGEL FOOD CAKE

1 cup sifted cake flour
1 cup sugar
½ cup cocoa, sifted
1½ cups (about 12) egg whites
2 tablespoons cold water
1 teaspoon cream of tartar
¼ teaspoon salt
1 teaspoon vanilla extract
1 cup sugar

1. Sift the flour, 1 cup sugar, and cocoa together four times to distribute cocoa evenly; set aside.
2. Beat egg whites with water, cream of tartar, salt, and extract until stiff, not dry, peaks are formed. Lightly fold in the remaining sugar, 2 tablespoons at a time.
3. Gently folding until blended after each addition, sift about 4 tablespoons of dry ingredients at a time over meringue. Carefully slide batter into an ungreased 10-inch tubed pan. Cut through batter to remove any large air bubbles.
4. Bake at 350°F about 45 minutes, or until cake tests done.
5. Immediately invert pan and cool cake completely. Remove from pan as directed for sponge-type cakes. Sift *confectioners' sugar* over cake top. ONE 10-INCH TUBED CAKE

SPONGE CAKE

¾ cup (about 9) egg yolks
¾ cup sugar
1½ tablespoons grated lemon peel
1½ teaspoons vanilla extract
1½ cups sifted all-purpose flour
1¼ cups (about 9) egg whites
¾ teaspoon cream of tartar
½ teaspoon salt
¾ cup sugar

1. Beat egg yolks, ¾ cup sugar, lemon peel, and extract together until very thick.
2. Sift about one third of the flour at a time over egg yolk mixture, gently folding until just blended

after each addition. Set aside.
3. Beat the egg whites with cream of tartar and salt until frothy. Gradually add the remaining ¾ cup sugar, continuing to beat until stiff peaks are formed. Gently fold egg yolk mixture into meringue. Turn batter into an ungreased 10-inch tubed pan.
4. Bake at 325°F about 50 minutes, or until cake tests done.
5. Immediately invert pan and cool cake completely.
ONE 10-INCH TUBED CAKE

SUNSHINE CAKE

1½ cups sifted cake flour	1 teaspoon grated lemon peel
1 teaspoon baking powder	1½ cups sugar
½ teaspoon salt	⅓ cup cold water
½ cup (about 6) egg yolks	1 scant cup (about 6) egg whites
1 teaspoon lemon extract	1 teaspoon cream of tartar

1. Sift the flour, baking powder, and salt together; set aside.
2. Beat the egg yolks, extract, and lemon peel together. Gradually add the sugar, continuing to beat until mixture is very thick.
3. Beating just until blended after each addition, alternately add dry ingredients in thirds and water in halves to egg yolk mixture; set aside.
4. Beat egg whites with cream of tartar until stiff, not dry, peaks are formed. Fold egg yolk mixture into beaten egg whites until blended. Turn batter into ungreased 10-inch tubed pan.
5. Bake at 325°F about 1 hour, or until cake tests done.
6. Immediately invert pan and cool cake completely.
ONE 10-INCH TUBED CAKE

LEMON SUNSHINE CAKE SQUARES: Follow recipe for Sunshine Cake. Decrease cream of tartar to ½ teaspoon. If desired, blend *1 teaspoon rum extract* with the lemon. Turn batter into a 13x9x2-inch baking pan lined (bottom only) with waxed paper. Bake 35 to 40 minutes. Remove from oven to wire rack and cool 10 minutes in pan. Remove from pan immediately and peel off waxed paper; cool completely. Sprinkle lightly with *confectioners' sugar*, if desired. Cut into squares.

LEMON SUNSHINE LAYER CAKE: Follow recipe for batter of Lemon Sunshine Cake Squares. Divide batter equally into three 9-inch layer cake pans lined (bottom only) with waxed paper. Bake 15 to 18 minutes. Remove from oven to racks and cool 10 minutes. Remove from pans and peel off waxed paper; cool completely. For filling and frosting, blend fresh or frozen (thawed and well drained) *raspberries* with *Sweetened Whipped Cream, page 247*. Spread generously between cake layers. Frost top and sides of cake with additional Sweetened Whipped Cream and decorate with *raspberries*.
ONE 9-INCH 3-LAYER CAKE

BUTTER SPONGE CAKE
(Gâteau Génoise)

This moist, rich sponge cake of French origin is usually the basis for petits fours and other French pastries.

5 eggs (1 cup plus 1 tablespoon)	⅛ teaspoon almond extract
1 cup less 1 tablespoon sugar	1¼ cups sifted cake flour
¼ teaspoon vanilla extract	3 tablespoons butter, melted and cooled

1. Butter bottom of a 15x10x1-inch jelly roll pan; line with waxed paper and butter paper. Set aside.
2. Combine eggs and sugar in the top of a 3-quart double boiler. Set top over simmering water and beat constantly until mixture is thick and piles softly (about 10 minutes with electric mixer). Remove from heat; set top in cold water and continue beating until mixture is cooled, about 15 minutes. Blend in the extracts.
3. Sift one fourth of the flour at a time over egg mixture, gently folding just until blended after each addition.
4. Gradually add the melted butter, folding only until blended. Immediately turn batter into prepared pan and spread evenly.
5. Bake at 325°F about 25 minutes, or until cake tests done.
6. Loosen edges with a sharp knife and remove cake from pan. Carefully peel off paper and cool cake, top side up, on wire rack.
ONE 15x10-INCH CAKE

SMALL FANCY CAKES (Petits Fours): Follow recipe for Butter Sponge Cake. When cool, trim cake edges and cut cake into tiny diamonds, rounds, crescents, or ovals. Use shapes whole, or split and fill with sieved *raspberry or apricot jam*. Prepare *Glossy Vanilla Icing, page 246*. Arrange like shapes on cake racks over trays and in turn pour the icing over them, covering completely. Immediately affix icing flowers, or later pipe on decorations with decorating icing. For the first set of cakes use white icing. Return "spillover" to original pan. Add *yellow food coloring* for a pale yellow color and pour over second set of cakes. Return "spillover" and add either *green* (for chartreuse shade) or a drop of *red food coloring* for a rosy shade. If there is a fourth set, add *melted chocolate* and thin icing with a little hot water. As soon as icing is set a little, carefully slide a metal spatula under each cake and transfer it to a glassine petits fours case; push the case up around the sides of the little cake.

FRENCH PASTRY CAKES: Follow recipe for Butter Sponge Cake. Prepare a recipe of *Creamy Butter Frosting, page 245,* and one of *Chocolate Butter Frosting, page 245.* When cake is cool, trim edges and cut cake into 3x1¾-inch rectangles, squares, and rounds. Split each and fill with sieved *strawberry, apricot, or raspberry jam.* Frost the sides with Creamy Butter Frosting or Chocolate Butter Frosting, then roll in flaked *toasted almonds, ground pistachios* or *pecans* or *walnuts,* or *toasted coconut,* or enclose square cakes with sections of a chocolate bar. Frost the tops and decorate as desired with frosting swirls, *chocolate shot, candied cherries,* flaked *nuts, chocolate rolls,* piped *chocolate decorations.*

chill until completely cold.
6. Split cake crosswise into three even layers; place bottom layer on a large serving plate. Top with one quarter of the pudding mixture, second layer, and another quarter of pudding; place plain layer on top.
7. Beat cream in a medium bowl until stiff; fold into remaining pudding until no streaks of white remain. Spread over side and top of cake. Chill at least an hour, or until serving time.
8. Slice cake into wedges with a sharp knife.
10 TO 12 SERVINGS

SPONGE CAKE RING DESSERT

½ cup sifted cake flour	¼ teaspoon cream of tartar
⅛ teaspoon salt	3 tablespoons sugar
3 egg yolks	Fudge Glaze, *page 246*
¼ cup sugar	Luscious Butterscotch Sauce, *page 302*
2 tablespoons water	
1 teaspoon vanilla extract	
3 egg whites	

1. Sift flour and salt together; set aside.
2. Beat egg yolks, ¼ cup sugar, water, and extract together until very thick. Fold flour mixture into egg yolks until just blended. Set aside.
3. Beat egg whites with cream of tartar until frothy. Add the 3 tablespoons sugar gradually, continuing to beat until stiff peaks are formed.
4. Fold egg yolk mixture into meringue until blended. Turn batter into an ungreased 1½-quart ring mold.
5. Bake at 325°F about 30 minutes, or until cake tests done.
6. Immediately invert mold and cool cake completely.
7. When ready to serve, place the cooled cake ring on a serving plate. Brush Fudge Glaze over top of cake. Fill center of cake ring with scoops of *coffee or vanilla ice cream.* Drizzle Luscious Butterscotch Sauce over the ice cream. Pour remaining sauce into a pitcher and serve with the dessert. 6 TO 8 SERVINGS

DAFFODIL TORTE

2 tablespoons lemon juice	1 egg
Water	1 package (3¼ ozs.) lemon pudding and pie filling mix
Yellow food coloring	
1 package angel-cake mix	
1 teaspoon grated lemon rind	Granulated sugar
	1 cup whipping cream

1. Preheat oven to 375° F.
2. Measure lemon juice into a 2-cup measure; add water to make 1⅓ cups; stir in a few drops food coloring to tint deep yellow. Combine with egg-white mixture from cake mix package in a large bowl; beat as label directs.
3. Beat in flour mixture and lemon rind. Spoon into a 10-inch angel-cake pan.
4. Bake, cool, and remove from pan as label directs.
5. Beat egg in a medium saucepan; stir in water, pudding mix, and sugar and prepare as label directs;

CHIFFON CAKES

ORANGE CHIFFON CAKE

1 cup plus 2 tablespoons sifted cake flour
½ cup sugar
1½ teaspoons baking powder
½ teaspoon salt
¼ cup cooking oil
2 egg yolks
1 tablespoon grated orange peel
⅓ cup orange juice
½ cup (4 to 5) egg whites
¼ teaspoon cream of tartar
¼ cup sugar

1. Sift the flour, ½ cup sugar, baking powder, and salt together into a bowl. Make a well in center and add the oil, egg yolks, and orange peel and juice in order listed. Beat until smooth; set aside.
2. Beat the egg whites with cream of tartar until frothy. Gradually add the ¼ cup sugar, continuing to beat until stiff peaks are formed.
3. Slowly pour egg yolk mixture over entire surface of beaten egg white. Gently fold together until just blended. Turn batter into an ungreased 9x9x2-inch baking pan.
4. Bake at 350°F 30 to 35 minutes, or until cake tests done.
5. Immediately invert pan and cool cake completely before removing from pan.

ONE 9-INCH SQUARE CAKE

COCOA CHIFFON CAKE

½ cup cocoa
¾ cup boiling water
1¾ cups sifted cake flour
1 cup sugar
3 teaspoons baking powder
¾ teaspoon salt
½ cup cooking oil
7 egg yolks
2 teaspoons vanilla extract
1 cup (7 to 8) egg whites
½ teaspoon cream of tartar
¾ cup sugar

1. Mix cocoa and boiling water together until smooth; set aside to cool.
2. Sift the flour, sugar, baking powder, and salt together into a bowl. Make a well in the center of the dry ingredients; add oil, egg yolks, cooled cocoa mixture, and extract. Beat until smooth. Set aside.
3. Beat egg whites with cream of tartar until frothy. Gradually add ¾ cup sugar, continuing to beat until stiff peaks are formed.
4. Slowly pour egg yolk mixture over entire surface of meringue. Carefully fold together until just blended. Turn batter into an ungreased 10-inch tubed pan, turning pan as you pour in batter.
5. Bake at 325°F 55 minutes; increase temperature to 350°F and bake for 10 to 15 minutes, or until cake tests done.
6. Immediately invert pan and cool cake completely.

ONE 10-INCH TUBED CAKE

CUPCAKES & CAKELETS

CHOCOLATE CUPCAKES

½ cup milk
2 to 2½ oz. (2 to 2½ sq.) unsweetened chocolate
1 egg, slightly beaten
¼ cup sugar
1½ cups sifted cake flour
1¼ teaspoons baking powder
¼ teaspoon baking soda
⅛ teaspoon salt
½ cup butter or margarine
1 teaspoon vanilla extract
1 cup sugar
2 eggs, well beaten
½ cup dairy sour cream

1. Combine milk and chocolate in top of double boiler. Set over simmering water until milk is scalded and chocolate is melted. Stir until well blended.
2. Vigorously stir about 3 tablespoons of the hot milk mixture into the slightly beaten egg; immediately blend into mixture in double boiler. Cook 3 to 5 minutes, stirring constantly. Stir in the ¼ cup sugar.
3. Cook over simmering water about 5 minutes, stirring constantly. Remove from water and set aside to cool.
4. Sift flour, baking powder, baking soda, and salt

together; set aside.
5. Cream butter with extract. Add the 1 cup sugar gradually, creaming until fluffy after each addition.
6. Add beaten eggs in thirds, beating thoroughly after each addition. Blend in the cooled chocolate mixture.
7. Beating only until smooth after each addition, alternately add dry ingredients in thirds and sour cream in halves to creamed mixture. Line 2½-inch muffin-pan wells with paper baking cups or grease (bottoms only). Fill each well about one half full with batter.
8. Bake at 350°F 20 to 25 minutes, or until cakes test done.
9. Remove from pans. Cool.

ABOUT 2 DOZEN CUPCAKES

BANANA CUPCAKES

2 cups sifted cake flour	1 cup sugar
1 teaspoon baking soda	2 eggs
1 teaspoon salt	1 cup mashed ripe bananas (about 2 medium-sized bananas)
½ cup butter or margarine	
1 teaspoon vanilla extract	¼ cup dairy sour cream

1. Sift the flour, baking soda, and salt together.
2. Cream the butter with extract. Add the sugar gradually, beating thoroughly. Add the eggs, one at a time, beating until light and fluffy after each addition. Blend in banana.
3. Beating only until blended after each addition, alternately add dry ingredients in thirds and sour cream in halves to creamed mixture. Spoon batter into 2½-inch muffin-pan wells lined with paper baking cups or greased (bottoms only), filling each about two thirds full.
4. Bake at 350°F 25 to 28 minutes, or until cakes test done.
5. Remove from pans and cool. Cut a cone-shaped piece from top of each cupcake. Fill with *whipped dessert topping* or *sweetened whipped cream* and set tops in place.   18 CUPCAKES

PEANUT BUTTER CUPCAKES

2 cups sifted cake flour	½ cup peanut butter
2½ teaspoons baking powder	2 eggs
½ teaspoon salt	½ cup lightly packed brown sugar
⅓ cup shortening	¾ cup milk
1 teaspoon vanilla extract	Creamy Peanut Butter Frosting, *page 246*
1 cup lightly packed brown sugar	

1. Blend flour, baking powder, and salt; set aside.
2. Cream shortening and extract; gradually add the 1 cup brown sugar, creaming well. Beat in the peanut butter until thoroughly blended.
3. Beat eggs with remaining ½ cup brown sugar until thick. Add to creamed mixture and beat well.
4. Beating only until smooth after each addition, alternately add dry ingredients in fourths and milk in thirds to creamed mixture. Line 2½-inch muffin-pan wells with paper baking cups or grease (bottoms only). Fill each well about one half full with batter.
5. Bake at 350°F 25 to 30 minutes, or until cakes test done.
6. Remove from pans and cool. Frost.

ABOUT 2 DOZEN CUPCAKES

CHOCOLATE-COATED PARTY CAKES

These delicate cream filled cakes are similar to a German specialty called Mohrenköpfe.

4 egg yolks	1 cup sifted cake flour
⅓ cup sugar	1 cup sweetened whipped cream
1 teaspoon grated lemon peel	Fudge Glaze, *page 246*
4 egg whites	
⅓ cup sugar	

1. Beat egg yolks, ⅓ cup sugar, and lemon peel until very thick and lemon colored. Set aside.
2. Beat egg whites until frothy; add ⅓ cup sugar gradually, continuing to beat until stiff peaks are formed.
3. Fold egg yolk mixture into beaten whites until blended. Sprinkle about one fourth of the flour at a time over the egg mixture; fold together gently until just blended after each addition.
4. Turn batter into 12 greased (bottoms only) 2½x1¼-inch muffin-pan wells, filling each about two thirds full.
5. Bake at 325°F 18 minutes, or until delicately browned.
6. Cool slightly; run a spatula gently around sides of cakes; lift out and set on wire racks to cool.
7. Cut a thin slice from bottom of each cake and carefully hollow out the cake. Fill with sweetened

whipped cream and replace cake slice. Spoon Chocolate Glaze I over tops of cakes and allow glaze to set slightly before serving.

1 DOZEN SMALL CAKES

LADYFINGERS

3 egg whites (⅓ cup)
Few grains salt
⅓ cup sugar
2 egg yolks
¼ teaspoon orange extract
¼ teaspoon vanilla extract
⅓ cup all-purpose flour

1. Using an 18x12-inch baking pan, cut both brown and waxed paper to fit the bottom of pan.
2. Cut a ladyfinger pattern from paper or cardboard about 4½ inches long and ¾ inch wide. Trace the pattern on the brown paper in sets of six, forming 4 rows across. (There will be 24 patterns traced on paper with space between each pattern and between each row.)
3. Place brown paper in the pan and cover with the waxed paper. (This pattern will show through the waxed paper.)
4. Put egg whites and salt into a mixing bowl and beat until frothy; beat in the sugar gradually until stiff peaks are formed.
5. Beat egg yolks with extracts until very thick. Add to the meringue, folding gently until well blended. Sift the flour over all, a little at a time, folding gently after each addition.
6. Drop coupling into decorating bag; plug end with a cork and fill bag with batter. Pipe out dumbbell-shaped ladyfingers over the patterns.
7. Bake at 350°F 12 to 15 minutes, or until ladyfingers spring back when lightly touched.
8. Remove from oven and invert over a clean towel sprinkled with some *confectioners' sugar*. Discard the brown paper and immediately pull the waxed paper from ladyfinger halves. Put them together in pairs as soon as they are removed from paper. (After cooling, the halves will not adhere to each other.) Cool on wire racks and cover with a towel. Store in a covered container.

12 PAIRS LADYFINGERS

BLACK FOREST TORTE

1½ cups toasted filberts, grated*
6 tablespoons kirsch
6 egg whites
¼ cup flour
½ cup butter or margarine
1 cup sugar
6 egg yolks
4 oz. (4 sq.) semisweet chocolate, melted and cooled
Cherry Filling, *below*
3 cups chilled heavy cream
⅓ cup confectioners' sugar
Chocolate curls

1. Grease and lightly flour an 8-inch springform pan; set aside.
2. Blend grated filberts and flour; set aside.
3. Cream butter until softened. Beat in sugar gradually until mixture is light and fluffy. Add egg yolks, one at a time, beating thoroughly after each addition.
4. Blend in the chocolate and 2 tablespoons of the kirsch. Stir in nut-flour mixture until blended.
5. Beat egg whites until stiff, not dry, peaks are formed. Fold into batter and turn into the pan.
6. Bake at 375°F about 1 hour, or until torte tests done. (Torte should be about 1½ inches high and top may have a slight crack.)
7. Cool 10 minutes in pan on a wire rack; remove from pan and cool.
8. Using a long sharp knife, carefully cut torte into 3 layers. Place top layer inverted on a cake plate; spread with Cherry Filling.
9. Whip cream (1½ cups at a time) until soft peaks are formed, gradually adding half of the confectioners' sugar and 2 tablespoons of the kirsch to each portion.
10. Generously spread some of the whipped cream over the Cherry Filling. Cover with second layer and remaining Cherry Filling. Spread generously with more whipped cream and top with third torte layer. Frost entire torte with remaining whipped cream.
11. Decorate torte with reserved cherries and chocolate curls.

ONE 8-INCH TORTE

*To grate nuts, use a rotary-type grater with hand-operated crank.

CHERRY FILLING: Drain *1 jar (16 ounces) red maraschino cherries*, reserving ½ cup syrup. Set aside 13 cherries for decoration; slice remaining cherries. Set aside. Combine reserved syrup and *4 tablespoons kirsch*. In a saucepan, gradually blend syrup mixture into *1½ tablespoons cornstarch*. Mix in *1 tablespoon lemon juice*. Stir over medium heat until mixture boils ½ minute. Mix in sliced cherries and cool.

1⅓ CUPS FILLING

FROSTINGS & FILLINGS

A cake without frosting may be laden with virtues and be a fine creation. Yet somehow, cake seems to come into its glory only when it is decked in a sculptured or swirled coat of sweetness. Frostings may be plain or fancy, chocolate brown or pale as dawn, delicately laced with essence of fruits or flecked with fragments of nuts or candy. They may be prepared in many ways, but they are always designed for delight.

Sugar, in some form, is the main ingredient in cooked and uncooked frostings. As used in these recipes, *sugar* refers to granulated cane or beet sugar. Other forms of sugar and sweeteners used in frostings are confectioners' (powdered) sugar, brown sugar and granulated brown sugar, maple sugar and maple syrup, corn syrup, molasses, and honey. (See *page 5* for definitions.)

SEVEN-MINUTE FROSTING

1½ cups sugar
⅓ cup water
2 egg whites
1 tablespoon light corn syrup
⅛ teaspoon salt
1 teaspoon vanilla extract

1. Combine all ingredients except extract in the top of a double boiler; beat with hand rotary or electric beater until blended.
2. Place over boiling water; beat constantly until mixture will hold peaks.
3. Remove from water; add extract. Beat until cool and thick enough to spread.

ENOUGH TO FILL AND FROST ONE 9-INCH 2-LAYER CAKE

NOTE: Mixture may be tinted by gently stirring in one or more drops of *food coloring*.

CHOCOLATE SEVEN-MINUTE FROSTING: Melt *3 ounces (3 squares) unsweetened chocolate* and set aside to cool. Follow recipe for Seven-Minute Frosting; blend in chocolate when mixture holds peaks.

MARSHMALLOW FROSTING: Follow recipe for Seven-Minute Frosting. Add *16 marshmallows*, quartered, to hot frosting and beat until fluffy.

MOCHA SEVEN-MINUTE FROSTING: Follow recipe for Seven-Minute Frosting. Increase corn syrup to 2 tablespoons, omit extract, and add *2 tablespoons instant coffee* to sugar mixture. When frosting forms peaks, beat in *1 tablespoon maple extract*.

ORANGE SEVEN-MINUTE FROSTING: Follow recipe for Seven-Minute Frosting. Use only 2 tablespoons water and add *3 tablespoons orange juice*. Omit extract.

PEPPERMINT SEVEN-MINUTE FROSTING: Follow recipe for Seven-Minute Frosting. Omit vanilla extract; add ¼ teaspoon peppermint extract and several drops *red food coloring*.

PISTACHIO SEVEN-MINUTE FROSTING: Follow recipe for Seven-Minute Frosting. Substitute *½ to 1 teaspoon pistachio extract* for vanilla extract. Blend in *1 or 2 drops green food coloring*, if desired.

SEAFOAM FROSTING

1½ cups firmly packed dark brown sugar
2 egg whites
1 tablespoon light corn syrup
Dash of salt
¼ cup water
2 teaspoons vanilla

1. Combine brown sugar, unbeaten egg whites, corn syrup, salt, and water in the top of a double boiler; place over boiling water.
2. Cook, beating constantly with a rotary or electric beater, 7 minutes, or until frosting triples in volume and forms soft peaks; remove from heat. Beat in vanilla.

ENOUGH TO FILL AND FROST AN 8- OR 9-INCH DOUBLE-LAYER CAKE

FRUIT 'N' NUT WHITE MOUNTAIN FROSTING

½ cup sugar
2 tablespoons water
¼ cup light corn syrup
2 egg whites
½ teaspoon almond extract
½ cup (4-oz. jar) diced candied fruits
½ cup chopped walnuts

1. Mix sugar, water, and corn syrup in a small saucepan. Cover and bring to a rolling boil. Remove cover and set candy thermometer in place. Cook until thermometer registers 242°F, or syrup spins a 6- to 8-inch thread.
2. Meanwhile, beat egg whites until stiff, not dry, peaks are formed. Continue beating and pour hot

syrup slowly in a thin stream over the egg whites. Beat until of spreading consistency.

3. Blend in extract. With final few strokes fold in the fruits and walnuts.

ENOUGH TO FROST ONE 9-INCH TUBED CAKE OR TWO 8- OR 9-INCH CAKE LAYERS

MARSHMALLOW CREAM FROSTING

1 cup sugar	¼ teaspoon cream of tartar
1 cup marshmallow cream	⅛ teaspoon salt
2 egg whites	1 teaspoon vanilla extract
¼ cup water	

1. Combine all ingredients except extract in top of a double boiler. Place over boiling water and beat with a hand rotary or electric beater about 5 minutes, or until frosting holds soft peaks.
2. Remove from water and add extract. Beat until frosting is cool before spreading on cake.

ENOUGH TO FILL AND FROST ONE 9-INCH 2-LAYER CAKE

DIVINITY FROSTING

2½ cups sugar	¼ cup marshmallow cream
½ cup water	
½ cup light corn syrup	1½ teaspoons lemon extract
¼ teaspoon salt	
2 egg whites	

1. Put the sugar, water, corn syrup, and salt into a deep 2-quart saucepan. Bring to boiling; cover pan and boil for 3 minutes.
2. Uncover pan, set candy thermometer in place, and cook gently to 248°F (firm-ball stage).
3. Meanwhile, beat egg whites in a large bowl until stiff, not dry, peaks are formed.
4. Remove syrup from heat and stir in the marshmallow cream.
5. Continue beating the egg whites, pouring the hot syrup in a thin stream over them. Beat at medium speed until frosting is cool and loses its shine. This may be speeded up by setting the bowl of frosting over another bowl of cold water. While beating, add extract. *Use the frosting right away, as it starts to set up quickly.*

ENOUGH TO FILL AND FROST ONE 9-INCH 3-LAYER CAKE

NOTE: If frosting becomes too stiff, beat in a little hot water until frosting is of spreading consistency. If frosting is too soft from undercooking, put it into double boiler top over boiling water until of proper consistency.

BUTTER CREAM FROSTING I

6 egg yolks	2 teaspoons vanilla extract
¾ cup sugar	
½ teaspoon cornstarch	1½ cups firm unsalted butter
¾ cup cream	

1. In top of a double boiler, beat the egg yolks until very thick. Gradually add a mixture of sugar and cornstarch, beating constantly. Gradually add the cream, stirring until well blended. Set over boiling water and cook, stirring constantly, until thickened, about 15 minutes.
2. Remove from heat and stir in the extract. Cover; cool slightly. Set in refrigerator to chill.
3. Put butter into a large mixer bowl. Beginning with medium speed of electric mixer, and as soon as possible increasing to high, beat butter until fluffy. Gradually add the chilled mixture to the creamed butter, beating until just blended after each addition. If necessary, set frosting over ice and water until firm enough to spread. If frosting should curdle, beat again until just smooth.
4. This frosting will keep several days, tightly covered, in the refrigerator. Beat just until smooth before using.

ENOUGH TO FROST SIDES AND TOPS OF THREE 9-INCH TORTE LAYERS

HAZELNUT BUTTER CREAM FROSTING: Grate ½ *cup (about 2½ ounces) hazelnuts* (filberts). Follow recipe for Butter Cream Frosting. Blend the grated nuts into the frosting after blending in the chilled mixture.

MOCHA BUTTER CREAM FROSTING: Dissolve *1¾ teaspoons instant coffee in 1 teaspoon boiling water.* Set aside to cool. Follow recipe for Butter Cream Frosting. Omit extract. Blend cooled coffee into the butter.

CHOCOLATE-MOCHA BUTTER CREAM FROSTING: Melt *1½ ounces (1½ squares) unsweetened chocolate* and set aside to cool. Follow recipe for Mocha Butter Cream Frosting. Gradually blend chocolate into whipped butter after adding coffee.

Frostings & Fillings

BROWNIE CARAMEL FROSTING

1¼ cups sugar	1 teaspoon vanilla extract
⅔ cup cream	
¾ cup lightly packed brown sugar	

1. Combine the sugar and cream in a medium-sized saucepan. Stir over low heat until sugar is dissolved. Increase heat and bring mixture to boiling. Set candy thermometer in place. Cook to 234°F (soft-ball stage). Using a pastry brush dipped in water, wash down crystals from sides of pan during cooking.
2. Meanwhile, heat the brown sugar in a heavy skillet; with back of wooden spoon, gently keep sugar moving toward center of skillet until sugar is melted. Stir melted brown sugar rapidly into the syrup. Boil again to soft ball stage (do not overcook).
3. Remove from heat. Set aside to cool to 110°F, or until just cool enough to hold pan on palm of hand.
4. Blend in extract and beat until creamy and of spreading consistency. Place frosting over hot water if it becomes too stiff while spreading on cake.

ENOUGH TO FROST SIDES AND TOPS OF TWO 8-INCH CAKE LAYERS OR 2 DOZEN CUPCAKES

FUDGE FROSTING

2 oz. (2 sq.) unsweetened chocolate, grated or cut in pieces	1 cup cream
	⅛ teaspoon salt
	1 teaspoon vanilla extract
2 cups sugar	

1. Put chocolate, sugar, cream, and salt into a heavy saucepan. Stir over low heat until sugar is dissolved and chocolate is melted.
2. Increase heat and bring mixture to boiling. Set candy thermometer in place. Continue cooking, stirring occasionally to prevent scorching, until mixture reaches 234°F (soft-ball stage). Using a pastry brush dipped in water, wash down crystals from sides of pan from time to time during cooking.
3. Remove from heat. Set aside to cool to 110°F, or until just cool enough to hold pan on palm of hand. Do not stir.
4. When cooled, blend in the extract. Beat vigorously just until mixture loses its gloss and is of spreading consistency. If frosting becomes too thick, beat in a small amount of *cream*.

ENOUGH TO FILL AND FROST ONE 9-INCH 2-LAYER CAKE

VANILLA FUDGE FROSTING

A wonderful frosting for lemon cake.

2¼ cups sugar	1½ tablespoons butter
¾ cup milk	¾ teaspoon vanilla extract
¼ teaspoon cream of tartar	1 to 2 tablespoons cream
¼ teaspoon salt	

1. Combine the sugar, milk, cream of tartar, and salt in a 2-quart saucepan. Stir over low heat until sugar is dissolved.
2. Increase heat and bring mixture to boiling. Set candy thermometer in place. Cook, stirring occasionally, to 234°F (soft-ball stage). Using a pastry brush dipped in water, wash down crystals from sides of saucepan from time to time during cooking.
3. Remove from heat. Set aside to cool to 110°F, or until just cool enough to hold pan on palm of hand. Do not stir.
4. When cooled, blend in butter and extract. Mix in enough cream for spreading consistency.

ENOUGH TO FILL AND FROST ONE 8-INCH 2-LAYER CAKE

HONEY-CHOCOLATE FROSTING

The hint of honey in this frosting gives it an intriguingly "different" flavor.

½ cup butter or margarine	⅛ teaspoon salt
	⅓ cup honey
2 oz.(2 sq.) unsweetened chocolate, cut in pieces	¼ cup cream or rich milk
	2 egg yolks, slightly beaten
½ cup sugar	

1. Combine all ingredients except egg yolks in the top of a double boiler and place over boiling water. When chocolate is melted, blend well with hand rotary or electric beater.
2. Vigorously stir about 3 tablespoons of the hot mixture into the egg yolks. Immediately blend into the mixture in top of double boiler.
3. Cook over boiling water, stirring constantly. When slightly thickened (about 2 minutes), remove from heat; set double boiler top in ice and water; beat frosting until of spreading consistency.

ENOUGH TO FILL AND FROST ONE 8-INCH 2-LAYER CAKE

Uncooked Frostings

BASIC BUTTER FROSTING

6 tablespoons butter
1½ teaspoons vanilla extract
3 cups confectioners' sugar
1½ tablespoons milk or cream

1. Cream butter with extract. Add confectioners' sugar gradually, beating thoroughly after each addition.
2. Stir in milk and beat until frosting is of spreading consistency. ENOUGH TO FILL AND FROST ONE 8- OR 9-INCH 2-LAYER CAKE

LEMON BUTTER FROSTING: Follow recipe for Basic Butter Frosting. Substitute *lemon juice* for milk and add *1½ teaspoons grated lemon peel*. If desired, add a few drops *yellow food coloring*.

MOCHA BUTTER FROSTING: Follow recipe for Basic Butter Frosting. Sift *1½ teaspoons instant coffee* with the confectioners' sugar. Melt and cool *3 ounces (3 squares) unsweetened chocolate* and blend in after adding sugar.

CHOCOLATE BUTTER FROSTING: Follow recipe for Basic Butter Frosting. Melt and cool *3 ounces (3 squares) unsweetened chocolate* and blend in after adding sugar.

RAISIN-RUM BUTTER FROSTING: Follow recipe for Basic Butter Frosting. Decrease vanilla extract to ½ teaspoon and add *1 teaspoon rum*. Increase milk to about 3 tablespoons and add *1 drop red food coloring* and *¼ cup finely chopped golden raisins*.

ORANGE BUTTER FROSTING: Follow recipe for Basic Butter Frosting. Substitute *1½ teaspoons grated orange peel* for the vanilla extract and *1½ to 2½ tablespoons orange juice* for the milk. If a deeper orange color is desired, mix *4 drops red food coloring* and *3 drops yellow food coloring* with orange juice.

BLACK WALNUT BUTTER FROSTING: Follow recipe for Basic Butter Frosting. Cream *2 teaspoons grated orange peel* with butter and extract. Stir in ¼ *cup finely chopped black walnuts*.

CREAM CHEESE BUTTER FROSTING: Follow recipe for Basic Butter Frosting, doubling recipe and creaming *3 ounces softened cream cheese* with the butter.

WHITE VELVET FROSTING

¼ cup butter or margarine
1½ teaspoons vanilla extract
⅛ teaspoon salt
1 egg yolk
3 cups confectioners' sugar
3 tablespoons milk or cream

1. Cream butter with extract, salt, and egg yolk until light and fluffy.
2. Alternately add confectioners' sugar and milk, beating after each addition. Beat until frosting is of spreading consistency.
ENOUGH TO FILL AND FROST ONE 8- OR 9-INCH 2-LAYER CAKE

LEMON VELVET FROSTING: Follow recipe for White Velvet Frosting. Substitute *1 teaspoon lemon extract* for vanilla extract.

BROWN VELVET FROSTING: Melt and cool *2 ounces (2 squares) unsweetened chocolate*. Follow recipe for White Velvet Frosting. Stir chocolate into frosting after addition of egg yolk.

CREAMY PEANUT BUTTER FROSTING

6 tablespoons butter
1½ tablespoons peanut butter
¾ teaspoon vanilla extract
2½ cups confectioners' sugar
1 egg yolk
1½ tablespoons milk

1. Cream butter with peanut butter and extract.
2. Gradually add the confectioners' sugar, beating well after each addition. Beat in the egg yolk.
3. Beat in enough of the milk until frosting is of spreading consistency. ENOUGH TO FROST ONE 8- OR 9-INCH SQUARE CAKE

CARAMEL MOCHA FROSTING

½ cup butter or margarine
1 tablespoon vanilla extract
2 teaspoons cocoa
3½ cups confectioners' sugar
1 egg yolk
3 tablespoons strong coffee

1. Cream butter with extract. Blend in cocoa. Gradually add confectioners' sugar, beating until smooth. Beat in the egg yolk.
2. Blend in the coffee a small amount at a time and beat until frosting is of spreading consistency.
ENOUGH TO FILL AND FROST ONE 9-INCH 2-LAYER CAKE

Frostings & Fillings

POURED CHOCOLATE FROSTING

5 tablespoons milk
¼ cup butter or margarine
2 cups confectioners' sugar
6 tablespoons cocoa
⅛ teaspoon salt
⅛ teaspoon vanilla extract

1. Put milk and butter into a heavy saucepan. Set over low heat until butter is melted and milk is scalded.
2. Remove from heat and beat in a mixture of the confectioners' sugar, cocoa, and salt. Blend in extract. Cool.
3. Pour frosting (frosting will be thin) in center of cake, spreading and working with spatula over top and sides of cake until frosting sets in desired swirls. ENOUGH TO FROST TOP AND SIDES OF TWO 8-INCH CAKE LAYERS

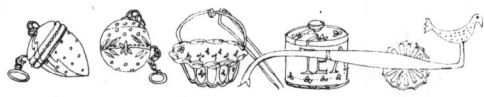

CHOCO-MARSHMALLOW FROSTING

6 tablespoons butter or margarine
6 tablespoons cocoa
½ cup milk
3 cups confectioners' sugar
1 teaspoon vanilla extract
½ cup golden raisins, rinsed and coarsely chopped
½ cup walnuts, coarsely chopped
⅔ cup (about 1 oz.) miniature marshmallows

1. Melt butter in a heavy saucepan over low heat. Blend in the cocoa, then the milk. Stirring constantly, cook until mixture thickens, about 3 minutes.
2. Remove from heat. Add confectioners' sugar gradually, stirring until smooth after each addition. Stir in the remaining ingredients.
ENOUGH TO FROST ONE 13x9-INCH CAKE

CREAM CHEESE FROSTING

3 oz. cream cheese, softened
1½ cups confectioners' sugar
1 teaspoon vanilla extract

Cream all ingredients together until fluffy.
ENOUGH TO FROST ONE 8x4-INCH LOAF CAKE

GLOSSY VANILLA ICING

½ cup sugar
½ cup cream
1 tablespoon light corn syrup
1 tablespoon butter or margarine
3⅓ cups confectioners' sugar
2½ teaspoons vanilla extract

1. Combine sugar, cream, corn syrup, and butter in a heavy saucepan. Set over low heat and stir until butter is melted.
2. Remove from heat and gradually add confectioners' sugar, blending until smooth. Mix in extract. If frosting is too stiff, blend in *cream*.
3. With spatula, spread frosting on top of cake, allowing it to drip slightly down sides of cake.
ENOUGH TO FROST TOP OF LOAF CAKE OR TOPS OF TWO 8- OR 9-INCH CAKE LAYERS

GLOSSY CHOCOLATE ICING: Follow recipe for Glossy Vanilla Icing. Melt *1 ounce (1 square) unsweetened chocolate* in butter mixture.

FLUFFY HONEY FROSTING

1 cup honey
Few grains salt
2 egg whites

1. Bring honey to boiling in a small saucepan over low heat.
2. Add salt to egg whites and beat until stiff, not dry, peaks are formed. Beating constantly, pour the hot honey very slowly in a thin stream over the egg whites. Continue beating 2 to 3 minutes, or until frosting forms rounded peaks.
ENOUGH TO FILL AND FROST ONE 8- OR 9-INCH 2-LAYER CAKE

Glazes & Toppings

FUDGE GLAZE

2 oz. (2 sq.) unsweetened chocolate
3 tablespoons butter
¼ cup cream
1¼ cups confectioners' sugar
⅛ teaspoon salt

1. Melt the chocolate and butter together; set aside.
2. Beat cream and mix with confectioners' sugar and salt. Add the melted chocolate and butter; stir vigorously until glaze is smooth. Spread over top of cake. ENOUGH TO GLAZE ONE 9-INCH CAKE LAYER

Frostings & Fillings

SWEETENED WHIPPED CREAM

1 cup chilled heavy cream
3 tablespoons confectioners' sugar
1 teaspoon vanilla extract

1. Beat the cream until it stands in soft peaks. With final few strokes, beat in the confectioners' sugar and extract until blended.
2. Set in refrigerator if not used immediately. If whipped cream is not stiff enough when ready to use, beat again. ABOUT 2 CUPS WHIPPED CREAM

ALMOND WHIPPED CREAM: Follow recipe for Sweetened Whipped Cream. Substitute ¼ teaspoon almond extract for vanilla extract. Fold in ½ cup toasted slivered blanched almonds.

COCOA WHIPPED CREAM I: Follow recipe for Sweetened Whipped Cream. Omit sugar, and add ¼ cup instant cocoa.

DUTCH COCOA WHIPPED CREAM: Follow recipe for Sweetened Whipped Cream. Mix *3 tablespoons Dutch process cocoa* with the sugar.

COINTREAU WHIPPED CREAM: Follow recipe for Sweetened Whipped Cream. Decrease sugar to 4 teaspoons and substitute *2 tablespoons Cointreau* for the extract.

CRÈME DE CACAO WHIPPED CREAM: Follow recipe for Sweetened Whipped Cream. Omit sugar and extract and add *3 tablespoons creme de cacao*.

CRÈME DE MENTHE WHIPPED CREAM: Follow recipe for Sweetened Whipped Cream. Decrease sugar to 2 tablespoons and substitute *2 tablespoons crème de menthe* for the extract.

MOCHA WHIPPED CREAM: Follow recipe for Sweetened Whipped Cream. Mix *1 teaspoon instant coffee* with the sugar.

MOLASSES WHIPPED CREAM: Follow recipe for Sweetened Whipped Cream. Omit sugar and add *2 tablespoons molasses* and a few grains *salt*.

ORANGE WHIPPED CREAM: Follow recipe for Sweetened Whipped Cream. Omit extract; beat in *1 teaspoon grated orange peel* and *¼ cup orange juice* with the sugar. Blend in *8 drops yellow food coloring* and *1 drop red food coloring*.

RUM WHIPPED CREAM: Follow recipe for Sweetened Whipped Cream. Substitute *1 to 1½ tablespoons rum* for extract.

STRAWBERRY WHIPPED CREAM: Follow recipe for Sweetened Whipped Cream, preparing 1½ times recipe. Slice *2 pints rinsed, hulled, fresh strawberries* (reserve a few whole berries for garnish, if desired). Fold berries into the cream.

COCOA WHIPPED CREAM II

5 tablespoons sugar
3 tablespoons cocoa
¼ teaspoon salt
1 cup heavy cream
2 teaspoons vanilla extract

1. Mix ingredients in order in a bowl. Chill, covered, 2 hours or longer.
2. Whip chilled mixture until cream stands in peaks. ENOUGH TO FILL ONE 15x10-INCH CAKE ROLL OR FILL AND FROST ONE 8-INCH 2-LAYER CAKE

COFFEE WHIPPED CREAM

1 cup chilled heavy cream
⅓ cup light corn syrup
1 tablespoon instant coffee
1 teaspoon vanilla extract

1. Combine the cream, corn syrup, and coffee in a large bowl. Cover; refrigerate about 1 hour.
2. Beat chilled mixture with electric mixer at medium speed until it thickens slightly. Add extract and continue beating until soft peaks form. ABOUT 2 CUPS WHIPPED CREAM

MOCHA GINGER CREAM

1 cup sugar
½ cup strong coffee
3 egg yolks
1 cup heavy cream, whipped
½ cup (about 3 oz.) chopped candied ginger

1. Combine sugar and coffee in a 1-quart saucepan. Set over low heat and stir until sugar is dissolved. Increase heat and bring mixture to boiling. Cover saucepan and boil gently for 5 minutes to dissolve any crystals that may have formed.
2. Uncover and set candy thermometer in place. Cook, stirring occasionally, to 234°F (soft-ball stage; remove from heat while testing). During cooking, wash down crystals from sides of pan with pastry brush dipped in water.
3. Using electric mixer, beat the egg yolks at high speed until very thick. Gradually pour syrup over beaten egg yolks, beating constantly. Continue beating until very stiff. Chill in refrigerator.
4. Gently fold the whipped cream into the chilled mixture along with the chopped ginger.
5. Serve as a topping for gingerbread or other cake. ABOUT 1 QUART TOPPING

Frostings and Fillings

MOCHA MAPLE CREAM: Follow recipe for Mocha Ginger Cream. Add *3 tablespoons maple syrup* to ingredients in saucepan. Fold *½ teaspoon maple extract* in with whipped cream. Omit candied ginger.

MOCHA-MALLOW WHIPPED CREAM

16 (4 oz.) marshmallows
⅓ cup strong coffee (dissolve 4 teaspoons instant coffee in ⅓ cup boiling water)
2 cups heavy cream

1. Heat the marshmallows and coffee together in top of a double boiler over boiling water until marshmallows are melted; stir occasionally.
2. Remove from heat. Cool; chill in refrigerator until mixture thickens.
3. Whip cream to soft peaks. Fold into chilled mixture.   ENOUGH TO FILL AND FROST ONE 8- OR 9-INCH 2-LAYER CAKE

BROILER FUDGE TOPPING

2 tablespoons butter or margarine, softened
½ cup lightly packed brown sugar
2 tablespoons cocoa
2 tablespoons cream
½ cup nuts, coarsely chopped

1. Cream butter, brown sugar, and cocoa until fluffy. Beat in the cream. Stir in nuts.
2. Spread lightly over cake after it has cooled in pan 10 to 15 minutes.
3. Place under broiler with top about 4 inches from source of heat. Broil about 1 minute, or until frosting bubbles; watch closely to avoid scorching.   ENOUGH TO FROST TOP OF ONE 8-INCH SQUARE CAKE

SPICED HONEY TOPPING

½ cup honey
1 teaspoon thick sweetened applesauce
⅛ teaspoon ground ginger
⅛ teaspoon ground cloves
⅛ teaspoon salt
1 egg white, unbeaten

Combine all ingredients in a bowl. Using hand rotary beater or electric mixer, beat until topping is of spreading consistency, about 5 minutes.
ENOUGH TO FROST TOP AND SIDES OF TWO 8-INCH CAKE LAYERS

Fillings

CREAM FILLING I

3 tablespoons flour
6 tablespoons sugar
¼ teaspoon salt
½ cup cold milk
1½ cups milk, scalded
4 egg yolks, fork beaten
1 teaspoon vanilla extract

1. Combine the flour, sugar, and salt in the top of a double boiler; mix well. Add the cold milk, stirring to blend thoroughly.
2. Gradually add the scalded milk, stirring to blend. Set over low heat and bring mixture to boiling, stirring constantly; cook about 2 minutes.
3. Vigorously stir about 3 tablespoons hot mixture into the egg yolks. Immediately return to mixture in double-boiler top.
4. Set over boiling water about 5 minutes, stirring to keep mixture cooking evenly. Remove from heat and pour into a bowl. Stir in the extract. Cover and cool slightly. Chill before spreading between layers.
2 CUPS FILLING

CREAMY VANILLA FILLING

⅓ cup sugar
2½ tablespoons flour
¼ teaspoon salt
1½ cups cream
3 egg yolks, slightly beaten
1 tablespoon butter or margarine
2 teaspoons vanilla extract
¼ teaspoon almond extract

1. Mix sugar, flour, and salt in a heavy saucepan. Stir constantly while gradually adding the cream. Bring to boiling; stir and cook 3 minutes.
2. Vigorously stir about 3 tablespoons of the hot mixture into the egg yolks; immediately blend into cream mixture. Stir and cook about 1 minute.
3. Remove from heat and blend in the remaining ingredients. Press a circle of waxed paper onto top (this prevents a crust from forming). Cool slightly, then chill.   ABOUT 1½ CUPS FILLING

CREAMY CHERRY FILLING: Follow recipe for Creamy Vanilla Filling. Omit almond extract. Mix in *1 to 2 tablespoons maraschino cherry syrup.* Mix *½ cup chopped maraschino cherries* into chilled filling.

CREAMY CHOCOLATE FILLING: Follow recipe for Creamy Vanilla Filling. Increase sugar to *½ cup.* Add *1½ ounces (1½ squares) unsweetened chocolate* to cream mixture.

* *Cape Cod Turkey Salad (214)*

PINEAPPLE CREAM FILLING: Follow recipe for Creamy Vanilla Filling. Drain contents of *1 can (8½ ounces) crushed pineapple.* Mix crushed pineapple into chilled filling.

VANILLA CREAM FILLING

½ cup sugar
2½ tablespoons flour
¼ teaspoon salt
½ cup cream
½ cup cream, scalded
3 egg yolks, slightly beaten
1 tablespoon butter or margarine
2 teaspoons vanilla extract
½ cup dairy sour cream

1. Mix sugar, flour, and salt in the top of a double boiler. Blend in the cold cream. Gradually add the scalded cream, stirring constantly. Bring to boiling over direct heat and cook 3 minutes, stirring constantly.
2. Remove from heat. Stir about 3 tablespoons of the hot mixture into beaten egg yolks; immediately blend into mixture in double boiler. Set over boiling water and cook about 5 minutes, stirring constantly.
3. Remove from heat. Blend in butter, extract, and sour cream. Cover and cool slightly; chill.

ABOUT 1½ CUPS FILLING

VANILLA CUSTARD FILLING

½ cup sugar
2 tablespoons cornstarch
¼ teaspoon salt
½ cup cold milk
1 cup milk, scalded
4 egg yolks, beaten
2 teaspoons vanilla extract

1. Mix sugar, cornstarch, and salt together in the top of a double boiler. Blend in the cold milk, stirring until mixture is smooth. Add scalded milk gradually, stirring constantly. Bring mixture rapidly to boiling over direct heat and cook 3 minutes, stirring constantly.
2. Remove from heat. Stir about 3 tablespoons of the hot mixture into egg yolks; immediately blend into mixture in double boiler. Set over boiling water and cook about 5 minutes, stirring constantly.
3. Remove from heat; blend in the extract. Cool slightly; refrigerate until ready to use.

ABOUT 1½ CUPS FILLING

CHOCOLATE FILLING

1 cup sugar
¼ cup cornstarch
½ teaspoon salt
¼ cup cold water
¾ cup boiling water
2 oz. (2 sq.) unsweetened chocolate, melted
¼ cup butter or margarine
2 teaspoons vanilla extract

1. Thoroughly blend the sugar, cornstarch, and salt in the top of a double boiler. Add the cold water and blend well. Gradually add the boiling water.
2. Stirring gently and constantly, bring mixture to boiling over direct heat, and cook 3 minutes. Place over simmering water; cover and cook 12 minutes, stirring 3 or 4 times.
3. Remove from heat; stir in melted chocolate, butter, and extract. Cool slightly.

ABOUT 1 CUP FILLING

CHOCOLATE-ALMOND FILLING
An especially delicious filling for devil's food cake. If this filling recipe is doubled, it will fill and frost an 8-inch 2-layer cake.

¼ cup sugar
3 tablespoons flour
⅛ teaspoon salt
¾ cup milk
1 oz. (1 sq.) unsweetened chocolate, grated
1 tablespoon butter or margarine
1½ teaspoons vanilla extract
Few drops almond extract
½ cup chilled heavy cream, whipped to soft peaks
½ cup toasted blanched almonds, finely chopped

1. Mix together sugar, flour, and salt in a heavy saucepan. Gradually add the milk and grated chocolate, stirring constantly. Cook and stir until the mixture is thick and smooth.
2. Remove from heat. Stir in butter and extracts. Set in refrigerator to chill thoroughly.
3. Spread the whipped cream and nuts over the chocolate mixture and gently fold together. Chill.

ABOUT 2 CUPS FILLING

SEMISWEET CHOCOLATE FILLING

1 pkg. (6 oz.) semisweet chocolate pieces
1½ cups milk
2 teaspoons instant coffee
⅛ teaspoon salt
2 tablespoons cornstarch
2 tablespoons cold water
2 eggs, beaten
1 teaspoon vanilla extract

1. Put chocolate pieces, milk, instant coffee, and

---

* *Salade Niçoise (page 217)*

Frostings and Fillings

salt into double-boiler top; heat over boiling water, stirring constantly until chocolate is melted.
2. Mix a blend of cornstarch and cold water and stir into eggs; stir about ½ cup of the melted chocolate mixture into eggs and blend thoroughly. Stir into mixture in double boiler and cook over boiling water, stirring constantly until very thick and smooth.
3. Remove from heat and stir in extract; cool thoroughly. (If a slightly sweeter filling is desired, blend in 1 to 2 tablespoons sugar.)

ABOUT 2¼ CUPS FILLING

SWEET CHOCOLATE FILLING

6 oz. sweet chocolate
2 tablespoons confectioners' sugar
2 tablespoons water
3 egg yolks, well beaten
3 egg whites
¼ teaspoon vanilla extract

1. Melt chocolate in the top of a double boiler over hot (not simmering) water. Stir in confectioners' sugar, water, and egg yolks. Cook, stirring constantly, until thickened. Remove from water and cool.
2. Beat egg whites until stiff, not dry, peaks are formed. Fold egg whites and extract into chocolate mixture.

1½ CUPS FILLING

LEMON FILLING I

3 egg whites
1 cup sugar
3 tablespoons lemon juice
1 teaspoon grated lemon peel
3 egg yolks, slightly beaten

1. Combine all ingredients except egg yolks in double-boiler top and beat slightly with hand rotary or electric beater.
2. Place over simmering water. Cook about 5 minutes, or until thickened, stirring constantly.
3. Vigorously stir about 3 tablespoons of hot mixture into the egg yolks. Immediately blend into mixture in double boiler. Cook over simmering water 10 minutes; stir slowly to keep mixture cooking evenly. Remove from heat and cool thoroughly.

ABOUT 1 CUP FILLING

ORANGE FILLING I

½ cup sugar
2½ tablespoons cornstarch
⅛ teaspoon salt
½ cup water
½ cup orange juice
1 egg yolk, slightly beaten
1 tablespoon lemon juice
1 tablespoon grated orange peel
2 teaspoons butter or margarine

1. Mix sugar, cornstarch, and salt together in the top of a double boiler. Blend in water and orange juice. Stirring gently and constantly, bring to boiling over direct heat and cook for 3 minutes. Cover and cook over simmering water 12 minutes, stirring 3 or 4 times.
2. Vigorously stir about 2 tablespoons hot mixture into egg yolk. Immediately blend into mixture in double boiler. Cook over simmering water 3 to 5 minutes, stirring slowly and constantly to keep mixture cooking evenly.
3. Remove from heat and blend in lemon juice, orange peel, and butter. Cool filling before spreading on the cake.

ABOUT 1 CUP FILLING

ORANGE FILLING II

¾ cup orange juice
½ cup sugar
1 tablespoon grated orange peel
2 egg whites
¼ cup sugar

1. Combine orange juice, sugar, and orange peel; set aside.
2. Beat egg whites until frothy; gradually add ¼ cup sugar, beating well. Continue beating until stiff peaks are formed.
3. Gently fold orange mixture into meringue.

ENOUGH TO FILL ONE 9-INCH LAYER CAKE

LEMON FILLING II: Follow recipe for Orange Filling II. Substitute *lemon juice* and *lemon peel* for orange juice and peel.

Chapter 12
PIES

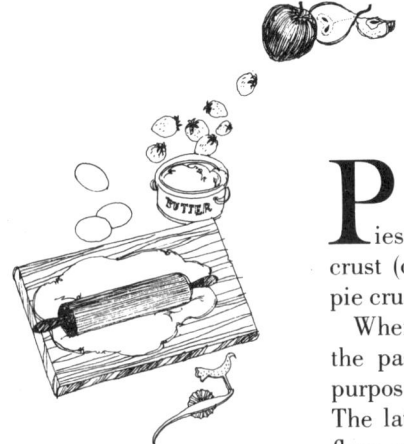

Pies offer an endless variety of textures and flavors in both the pie crust (or shell) and the filling. It is essential that the pastry for the pie crust be tender, digestible, and pleasing to the eye.

When making pastry it is advisable to work quickly and handle the pastry dough as little as possible. For the homemaker, all-purpose flour and cake flour are available for making pastry. The latter makes a very tender, but crumbly, pie crust. All-purpose flour makes a more flaky crust and also a tender one, providing sufficient fat is used and the dough is not overhandled.

While most pie shells are made using flour as the main ingredient, many "crumb" crusts are made using crushed wafer-type cookies, crackers, or ready-to-eat dry cereals. Meringue pie shells are also made using egg whites as their main ingredient. Baked meringue shells are usually filled with custard or fruit fillings or with ice cream.

Basic (plain) pastry may be prepared using several methods:

Method I — Cold shortening (lard, vegetable or all-purpose shortening, butter or margarine, or a combination of several shortenings) is cut into a mixture of flour and salt, using a pastry blender or two knives. Then only enough water is added to hold the mixture together to form a ball.

Method II — Cooking or salad oil (not olive oil) is thoroughly beaten with icy-cold water, then combined with flour and salt, mixing only until flour is moistened enough to hold mixture together and shape into a ball.

Method III — Boiling water is added to cold shortening (not oil), mixing with a fork until mixture is creamy and thickened. Flour with salt is added, stirring only until mixture can be shaped into a ball.

Today's homemaker has available on her grocers' shelves a number of packaged pie crust mixes. These are not only timesavers, but their uniformity aids the homemaker in making excellent pastry products.

TECHNIQUES FOR MAKING PIES
(Read also *Use Correct Techniques, page 2.*)
Assemble utensils — A pastry blender cuts shortening into flour evenly and quickly. A pastry canvas and a stockinet-covered rolling pin help prevent pastry from sticking to surface when rolling it out. A floured canvas also requires less flour for rolling out the dough than when rolling on a floured board.
Select pie pans of proper size — Measure inside from rim to rim.
To measure dry ingredients, liquids, and fats, see *page 2.*
Use only enough water to hold dough together to form a smooth ball. Too much moisture tends to cause shrinkage in the pie shell and also results in a less tender pastry. Avoid overmixing.
Chill pastry dough in refrigerator. This is especially advisable if the room is warm. Chilling will aid in insuring a more tender pastry.
To roll pastry for 1-crust pie, shape the dough into a slightly flattened ball. Put onto floured surface and gently roll with rolling pin from center to edge, keeping dough the same thickness throughout. Test the thickness of dough by pressing with finger; it should make only a slight dent. Roll into a circle about 1½ inches larger in diameter than the diameter of pie pan (measuring from outer rim of pan). Fold dough in half; transfer to pie pan; unfold and fit loosely into pan, pressing gently against bot-

tom and sides to remove any air bubbles. Do not stretch the dough. Handle carefully to avoid tearing dough. If cracks or tears do occur, mend them by pressing the pastry together or by patching with another piece of dough. Cracks in the bottom permit the filling to soak through and cause the pie to stick to the pan. Allowing 1 inch pastry beyond rim of pan, trim evenly with kitchen shears. Fold the overhung pastry back and under, then press to itself to form a stand-up edge.

Flute the edge by pressing index finger on edge of pastry and pinch pastry with thumb and index finger of other hand. Lift fingers and repeat procedure to flute around entire edge.

Prick pastry shell thoroughly with a fork before baking to prevent buckling and large blisters from forming while pie shell is baking. If blisters do occur during first few minutes of baking, prick them. Omit pricking if the pie filling is to be baked with the pie shell.

To roll pastry for a 2-crust pie, divide the dough almost in half, leaving the slightly larger portion for the top crust. Refrigerate the larger portion until ready to roll out. Roll the bottom crust, following directions for 1-crust pie, except do not allow the extra pastry for tucking under itself; instead, trim the crust even with edge of pan.

To complete 2-crust pie, add the filling and moisten the edge of bottom crust with water. Roll the remaining dough into a circle about 1 inch larger in diameter than diameter of pan. Fold in half and place carefully over filling; gently press edges of top and bottom crust together. Tuck the extra pastry under edge of bottom crust. Seal by fluting edges together or press edges with a fork. Cut enough slits in top crust to allow steam to escape while pie is baking.

HELPFUL HINTS ABOUT PIES

- To prevent juice from cooking out of pies into the oven, place a strip of dampened cloth or pastry tape around the edge of the pie or place a tiny funnel or 4-inch stick of uncooked macaroni in the center of the pie.
- To avoid shrinkage of a pastry crust, roll out the pastry, place in a pie pan without stretching, and set aside about 5 minutes before fluting the edge. Or place a second pie pan on the pastry before baking. Remove the second pan after about 10 minutes of baking to allow the pastry shell to brown on the inside.
- To make a crunchy topping for a 2-crust pie, combine 1 tablespoon butter or other shortening, 1 tablespoon sugar, 1/8 teaspoon grated lemon peel, few grains salt, and 3 tablespoons flour; mix until consistency of coarse crumbs. Brush top of unbaked pie with milk, then sprinkle with the crumb mixture. Bake pie as directed in recipe.

PASTRY CRUSTS

PASTRY I FOR 1-CRUST PIE

1 cup sifted all-purpose flour
½ teaspoon salt
⅓ cup lard, vegetable shortening, or all-purpose shortening
2 to 3 tablespoons cold water

1. Sift flour and salt together into a bowl. Cut in shortening with pastry blender or two knives until pieces are the size of small peas.
2. Sprinkle the water over mixture, a teaspoonful at a time, mixing lightly with a fork after each addition. Add only enough water to hold pastry together. Work quickly; do not overhandle. Shape into a ball and flatten on a lightly floured surface.
3. Roll from center to edge into a round about ⅛ inch thick and about 1 inch larger than overall size of pan.
4. Loosen pastry from surface with spatula and fold in quarters. Gently lay pastry in pan and unfold it, fitting it to pan so it is not stretched.
5. Trim edge with scissors or sharp knife so pastry extends about ½ inch beyond edge of pie pan. Fold extra pastry under at edge, and flute.
6. Thoroughly prick bottom and sides of shell with a fork. (Omit pricking if filling is to be baked in shell.)
7. Bake at 450°F 10 to 15 minutes, or until crust is light golden brown.
8. Cool on rack.   ONE 8- OR 9-INCH PIE SHELL

PASTRY FOR 2-CRUST PIE: Double the recipe for Pastry I. Divide pastry into halves and shape into a ball. Roll each ball as in Pastry I. For top crust, roll out one ball of pastry and cut 1 inch larger than pie pan. Slit pastry with knife in several places to allow steam to escape during baking. Gently fold in half and set aside while rolling bottom crust. Roll second ball of pastry and gently fit pastry into pie pan; avoid stretching. Trim pastry with scissors or sharp knife around edge of pan. Do not prick. Fill as directed in specific recipe. Moisten edge with water for a tight seal. Carefully arrange top crust over filling. Gently press edges to seal. Fold extra top pastry under bottom pastry. Flute or complete with desired *pastry edging*.

PASTRY FOR 1-CRUST 10-INCH PIE: Follow recipe for Pastry I. Increase flour to 1⅓ cups, salt to ¾ teaspoon, shortening to ½ cup, and water to about 3 tablespoons.

PASTRY FOR LATTICE-TOP PIE: Prepare pastry as in recipe for Pastry for 2-Crust Pie. Divide pastry into halves and shape into two balls. Follow directions in Pastry I for rolling pastry. Roll one pastry ball for bottom crust; fit gently into pie pan. Roll the second pastry ball into a rectangle about ⅛ inch thick and at least 10 inches long. Cut pastry with a sharp knife or pastry wheel into strips that are about ½ inch wide. Fill pastry shell as directed in specific recipe. *To Make a Lattice Top:* Cross two strips over the pie at the center. Working out from center to edge of pie, add the remaining strips one at a time, weaving the strips under and over each other in crisscross fashion; leave about 1 inch between the strips. Or, if desired, arrange half the strips over top, twisting each strip several times. Repeat using remaining pastry strips and placing them diagonally to first strips. Trim the strips even with the edge of the pastry. Moisten the edge of pastry shell with water for a tight seal. Fold edge of bottom crust over ends of strips. Flute or complete with desired *pastry edging*. Bake as directed in specific recipe.

PASTRY FOR LITTLE PIES AND TARTS: Prepare recipe for Pastry I. Roll pastry ⅛ inch thick and cut about ½ inch larger than overall size of pans. Carefully fit rounds into pans without stretching. Fold excess pastry under at edge. Flute or complete with desired *pastry edging*. Prick bottom and sides of shell with fork. (Omit pricking if filling is to be baked in shell.) Bake at 450°F 8 to 10 minutes, or until light golden brown. Cool on wire rack.
THREE 6-INCH PIES, SIX 3½ INCH TARTS, OR NINE 1½-INCH TARTS

PASTRY FOR ROSE-PETAL TARTS: Double recipe for Pastry I. Roll pastry ⅛ inch thick. Cut pastry into rounds, using 2½-inch round cutter. Place one pastry round in bottom of each 2¾-inch muffin-pan well. Fit 5 pastry rounds around inside of each well, overlapping edges. Press overlapping edges together. Prick bottom and sides well with fork. Bake at 450°F 8 to 10 minutes, or until light golden brown. Cool on wire rack. Carefully remove from pans.
SIX 2¾-INCH TARTS

SPICE PASTRY FOR 1-CRUST PIE: Follow recipe for Pastry I. Sift *2 tablespoons sugar, ¼ teaspoon cinnamon, ⅛ teaspoon ginger, and ⅛ teaspoon cloves* with flour and salt. Substitute *orange juice* for cold water.

CHEESE PASTRY FOR 1-CRUST PIE: Follow recipe for Pastry I. Cut in *½ cup (2 ounces) finely shredded Cheddar cheese* with the lard or shortening.

CHEESE PASTRY FOR 2-CRUST PIE: Follow recipe for Pastry for 2-Crust Pie. Cut in *1 cup (4 ounces) finely shredded Cheddar cheese* with the lard or shortening.

ROLLED OAT PASTRY FOR 1-CRUST PIE: Follow recipe for Pastry I. Mix *½ cup uncooked rolled oats* with the flour. Increase shortening to ½ cup. Bake at 400°F 15 minutes or until crust is lightly browned.

PASTRY TOPPING: Follow recipe for Pastry I. Roll out pastry 1 inch larger than overall size of baking dish or casserole and cut slits near center to allow steam to escape. Bake as directed in specific recipe.

PASTRY FOR HIGH-COLLARED 1-CRUST PIE

1⅓ cups sifted all-purpose flour	½ cup all-vegetable shortening (not oil)
½ teaspoon salt	2½ tablespoons cold water

1. Sift the flour and salt together into a bowl. Cut in shortening with pastry blender or two knives until particles resemble coarse crumbs.
2. Proceed as directed in *Pastry I for 1-Crust Pie, page 252*, through step 6, except roll pastry 1½ inches larger than pan. Flute edge forming a high collar.
ONE 9-INCH PIE SHELL

PEANUT BUTTER PASTRY

1½ cups sifted all-purpose flour
½ teaspoon salt
½ cup vegetable shortening or all-purpose shortening
3 tablespoons peanut butter
2 to 3 tablespoons cold water

1. Sift flour and salt together into a bowl. Add a blend of shortening and peanut butter. Proceed as in *Pastry I for 1-Crust Pie, page 252,* using a 9- or 10-inch pie pan.
2. Bake at 450°F 10 minutes.

ONE 9- OR 10-INCH PIE SHELL

SOUR CREAM PASTRY

1 cup sifted all-purpose flour
½ teaspoon salt
¼ cup butter or margarine, chilled and cut in pieces
4½ tablespoons dairy sour cream
1 tablespoon butter or margarine, cut in small pieces

1. Sift flour and salt together into a bowl. Using pastry blender or two knives, cut ¼ cup butter into flour until pieces are the size of peas.
2. Blend in sour cream, a little at a time, until pastry holds together; mix lightly with a fork after each addition. Add only enough sour cream to hold pastry together; do not overhandle.
3. Shape pastry into a ball and flatten on a lightly floured surface. Roll into a rectangle about ½ inch thick.
4. Dot two thirds of the pastry with the 1 tablespoon butter. Cover the center third of dough with the unbuttered third; fold remaining third over to form three thicknesses.
5. Roll into a rectangle ¼ inch thick and repeat folding to form three thicknesses. Chill thoroughly, about 30 minutes.
6. Proceed as in *Pastry I for 1-Crust Pie, page 252.*

ONE 8- OR 9-INCH PIE SHELL

BUTTER PASTRY FOR TARTS

1½ cups sifted all-purpose flour
⅛ teaspoon salt
½ cup butter
1 egg yolk
2 to 3 tablespoons cold water

1. Combine flour and salt in a bowl. Using a pastry blender or two knives, cut in butter as for pastry; mix in the egg yolk.
2. Add water gradually, mixing with a fork until pastry holds together. Shape dough into a ball; wrap and refrigerate until thoroughly chilled.
3. Using one half of dough at a time, roll about ⅛ inch thick on a lightly floured surface. Using a scalloped cookie cutter, cut out 3-inch rounds of dough.
4. Gently fit pastry rounds into 1¾-inch muffin pan wells; prick pastry with a fork.
5. Bake at 375°F about 15 minutes or until lightly browned.

ABOUT 2 DOZEN TART SHELLS

PIE SHELLS

GRAHAM CRACKER CRUMB CRUST

1⅓ cups graham cracker crumbs (16 to 18 crackers)
¼ cup sugar
¼ cup butter or margarine, softened

1. Mix cracker crumbs with sugar. Using a fork or pastry blender, blend butter evenly with crumb mixture.
2. With back of spoon, press crumb mixture firmly into an even layer on bottom and sides of an 8- or 9-inch pie pan. Level edges of the pie shell.
3. Bake at 375°F 8 minutes. Cool thoroughly before filling.

ONE 8- OR 9-INCH PIE SHELL

10-INCH GRAHAM CRACKER CRUST: Follow recipe for Graham Cracker Crumb Crust. Increase crumbs to 1⅔ cups, sugar to 5 tablespoons, and butter to 5 tablespoons. Press into a 10-inch pie pan.

NUT-CRUMB CRUST: Follow recipe for Graham Cracker Crumb Crust. Decrease graham cracker crumbs to 1 cup and mix in *½ cup finely chopped nuts.*

COOKIE CRUMB CRUST: Follow recipe for Graham Cracker Crumb Crust. Substitute *1⅓ cups cookie crumbs (about twenty-four 2⅛-inch cookies, such as vanilla or chocolate wafers)* for graham cracker crumbs. Omit sugar. Bake vanilla crumb crust at 375°F 8 minutes; bake chocolate crumb crust at 325°F 10 minutes. *For a 10-inch cookie crumb crust:* Increase cookie crumbs to 1¾ cups and butter to 5 tablespoons.

GRAHAM CRACKER TART SHELLS: Follow recipe for Graham Cracker Crumb Crust. Line eight 2½-inch muffin-pan wells with paper baking cups. Using back of spoon, press crumb mixture firmly into an even layer on bottom and sides of the paper cups. Bake at 375°F 6 minutes. Cool thoroughly on wire rack; remove paper baking cups.

CEREAL CRUMB CRUST

4 cups ready-to-eat high protein cereal, finely crushed
¼ cup butter or margarine, softened
2 tablespoons sugar

1. Blend all ingredients until well mixed. Reserve 2 tablespoons mixture for topping. Turn crumb mixture into a 9-inch pie pan and press firmly and evenly on bottom and sides. Chill.
2. Fill as desired and sprinkle with reserved crumbs.   ONE 9-INCH PIE SHELL

COCONUT-CEREAL CRUMB CRUST: Follow recipe for Cereal Crumb Crust. Stir ½ *cup flaked coconut* into crumb mixture.

CHOCOLATE-COCONUT CRUST

2 oz. (2 sq.) unsweetened chocolate
2 tablespoons butter or margarine
2 tablespoons hot milk
⅔ cup confectioners' sugar
¾ cup flaked coconut, toasted
¾ cup corn flakes

1. Heat chocolate and butter in a small heavy saucepan over low heat, stirring until well blended.
2. Stir the hot milk into the confectioners' sugar; blend into the chocolate. Mix in the coconut and corn flakes evenly.
3. Spread on the bottom and sides of a buttered 8-inch pie pan. Chill until firm.   ONE 8-INCH PIE SHELL

FILBERT CRUST

1¼ cups unblanched filberts, finely ground
¼ cup sugar
¼ cup butter or margarine

1. Mix the filberts and sugar in a bowl. Cut in the butter with a pastry blender or two knives. Turn mixture into a 9- or 10-inch pie pan; press firmly against the bottom and sides of pan.
2. Bake at 375°F 5 minutes, until lightly browned. Cool and chill.   ONE 9- OR 10-INCH PIE SHELL

BRAZIL NUT CRUST: Follow recipe for Filbert Crust. Substitute *1¼ cups unblanched Brazil nuts* for the filberts.

SALTED PEANUT CRUST: Follow recipe for Filbert Crust. Substitute *1¼ cups salted peanuts*, coarsely ground, for the filberts.

MERINGUE SHELL

4 egg whites
½ teaspoon cream of tartar
1⅓ cups sugar
½ teaspoon cider vinegar

1. Beat egg whites with cream of tartar until frothy; gradually add about one half of the sugar, beating constantly. Blend in the vinegar and gradually add remaining sugar, continuing to beat until stiff peaks are formed.
2. Spread a 1-inch layer of meringue on bottom of a lightly greased 9-inch pie pan.
3. Pile remaining meringue around edge of pan and swirl with a spatula to form the sides of the shell.
4. Bake at 250°F about 2¼ hours, or until meringue is dry.
5. Cool meringue in pan on a rack; store, if desired, in an airtight container.
   ONE 9-INCH MERINGUE SHELL

ALMOND MERINGUE SHELL: Follow recipe for Meringue Shell. Blanch, toast, and grate *½ cup almonds*; fold into stiffly beaten egg white mixture.

10-INCH MERINGUE SHELL: Follow recipe for Meringue Shell. Increase egg whites to 6, cream of tartar to ¾ teaspoon, sugar to 2 cups, and vinegar to ¾ teaspoon.

PIES

APPLE PIE

Pastry for 2-crust pie
6 to 8 tart cooking apples
1 tablespoon lemon juice
1 cup sugar
3 to 3½ tablespoons flour
1 teaspoon ground cinnamon
¼ teaspoon ground nutmeg
⅛ teaspoon salt
2 tablespoons butter or margarine

1. Prepare a 9-inch pie shell; roll out remaining pastry for top crust. Set aside.
2. Wash, quarter, core, pare, and thinly slice the apples. Turn into a bowl and drizzle with lemon juice. Toss lightly with mixture of sugar, flour, cinnamon, nutmeg, and salt.
3. Turn mixture into unbaked pie shell. Dot apples with butter. Complete as for a 2-crust pie.
4. Bake at 450°F 10 minutes; reduce oven temperature to 350°F and bake about 40 minutes, or until crust is lightly browned. Serve warm or cold.

ONE 9-INCH PIE

VICTORIA PIE

A recipe from Rickey Restaurant Studio Inn, Palo Alto, California.

5 large tart apples, cut in eighths, pared, and cored
½ cup water
½ cup dark seedless raisins
⅓ to ½ cup sugar
½ teaspoon ground cinnamon
1 unbaked 10-in. pie shell
½ cup sugar
4 oz. (½ cup) almond paste
6 egg yolks, beaten
⅓ cup heavy cream
Few grains salt

1. Combine apples and water in a saucepan; cover and cook until apples are just tender.
2. Add raisins and a mixture of ⅓ to ½ cup sugar and cinnamon; stir until sugar is dissolved. Cool slightly.
3. Turn apple-raisin mixture into pie shell.
4. Bake at 400°F 20 minutes.
5. Meanwhile, add the ½ cup sugar to almond paste gradually, beating thoroughly; add beaten egg yolks in thirds, beating well after each addition. Blend in the cream and salt.

6. Remove pie from oven; reduce oven temperature to 350°F. Spread almond mixture evenly over top. Return pie to oven and bake 10 to 15 minutes, or until top is lightly browned.
7. Remove to wire rack. Cool pie completely.

ONE 10-INCH PIE

FRESH APRICOT PIE

Pastry for Lattice-Top Pie, *page 253*
1 cup sugar
⅓ cup all-purpose flour
⅛ teaspoon ground nutmeg
4 cups fresh apricots, halved and pitted
2 tablespoons butter or margarine
2 tablespoons orange juice

1. Prepare a 9-inch pie shell and lattice strips for top crust; set aside.
2. Combine sugar, flour, and nutmeg; spoon some into pie shell. Arrange apricots, cut side up, over bottom of shell. Sprinkle with remaining sugar mixture. Dot with butter and drizzle with orange juice. Complete as directed for lattice-top pie.
3. Bake at 450°F 10 minutes; reduce oven temperature to 350°F and bake 30 to 35 minutes.

ONE 9-INCH PIE

APRICOT-APPLE PIE

1 cup dried apricots, cut in small pieces
⅔ cup water
4 large apples, pared, quartered, cored, and sliced (5 cups)
1⅓ cups sugar
¼ cup sifted all-purpose flour
1 teaspoon ground nutmeg
Salt
Double Crust Pastry *page 252*
2 tablespoons butter or margarine

1. Combine apricots and water in a small saucepan; heat to boiling. Simmer 5 minutes, or until water is absorbed. Combine apricots with apples in a large bowl. Sprinkle sugar, flour, nutmeg, and a dash of salt over fruit mixture; toss lightly to mix.
2. Preheat oven to 400°F.
3. Prepare Double Crust Pastry or make piecrust from your favorite mix. Roll out half to a 12-inch round on a lightly floured cloth; fit into a 9-inch pie plate; trim overhang to ½ inch. Spoon apple mixture

into crust; dot butter over top.
4. Roll out rest of pastry to an 11-inch round; cut several slits near center to let steam escape; place over filling. Trim overhang to ½ inch; turn top and bottom edges under flush with rim of pie plate; pinch to make a stand-up edge; flute. Sprinkle sugar lightly over top crust if you like.
5. Bake 50 minutes, or until filling bubbles up and pastry is golden. Cool on a wire rack. Serve warm or cold. 9-INCH PIE

FRESH RED RASPBERRY PIE

Pastry for 2-crust pie
5 cups red raspberries
1 tablespoon orange juice
1 cup sugar
⅓ cup flour
¼ teaspoon salt

1. Prepare an 8-inch pie shell; roll out remaining pastry for top crust. Set aside.
2. Gently toss raspberries with orange juice and a mixture of the remaining ingredients.
3. Turn into unbaked pie shell, heaping slightly at center. Complete as directed for 2-crust pie.
4. Bake at 450°F for 10 minutes; reduce oven temperature to 350°F and bake 25 to 30 minutes, or until pastry is lightly browned. ONE 8-INCH PIE

FRESH BLUEBERRY PIE

Pastry for 2-crust pie
4 cups fresh blueberries
4 teaspoons lemon juice
¾ cup sugar
¼ cup flour
½ teaspoon ground cinnamon
¼ teaspoon ground nutmeg
⅛ teaspoon salt
1 teaspoon grated lemon peel
2 tablespoons butter or margarine

1. Prepare an 8-inch pie shell; roll out remaining pastry for top crust; set aside.
2. Rinse and drain blueberries. Toss gently with lemon juice, then with a mixture of the sugar, flour, cinnamon, nutmeg, salt, and lemon peel.
3. Turn into unbaked pie shell, heaping berries slightly at center; dot with butter. Complete as directed for 2-crust pie.
4. Bake at 450°F 10 minutes; reduce oven temperature to 350°F and bake 30 to 35 minutes, or until crust is lightly browned. Serve warm or cool. ONE 8-INCH PIE

CRANBERRY-MINCE PIE

2½ cups fresh cranberries, stemmed
1¼ cups sugar
¼ cup water
1 can (22 ozs.) mincemeat pie filling
1 tablespoon lemon juice
Double Crust Pastry recipe on *page 252*

1. Combine cranberries, sugar, and water in a medium saucepan; heat, stirring several times, to boiling. Simmer 5 minutes, or until cranberries start to pop; stir in pie filling and lemon juice; cool.
2. Preheat oven to 400°.
3. Prepare Double Crust Pastry or make piecrust from your favorite mix. Roll out two-thirds to a 12-inch round on a lightly floured cloth; fit into a 9-inch pie plate; trim overhang to ½ inch. Spoon cranberry mixture into crust.
4. Roll out rest of pastry to a rectangle 12x5 inches; cut lengthwise into ten ½-inch-wide strips with a pastry wheel or knife. Lay 5 strips evenly over filling in pie plate. Weave remaining 5 strips, over and under, at right angles to those on pie to make a crisscross top. Trim strips even with overhang of bottom crust; fold bottom edge up over strips and pinch to make a stand-up edge; flute. Brush strips lightly with milk and sprinkle with sugar if you like.
5. Bake 40 minutes, or until filling bubbles up and pastry is golden. Cool pie on a wire rack. Serve plain or with vanilla ice cream if you like. 1 9-INCH PIE

GLAZED STRAWBERRY PIE

1 qt. strawberries, rinsed and hulled
6 tablespoons sugar
1½ tablespoons cornstarch
6 tablespoons water
1 teaspoon lemon juice
3 or 4 drops red food coloring
3 oz. cream cheese
1 tablespoon orange juice
1 baked 9-in. pie shell

1. Reserve 2 cups whole strawberries. Crush remaining strawberries with a fork; set aside.
2. Mix sugar and cornstarch thoroughly in a saucepan. Blend in the water. Stirring constantly, bring to boiling and boil for 3 minutes, or until clear.
3. Remove from heat; stir in crushed strawberries, lemon juice, and food coloring. Cool mixture slightly by setting pan in a bowl of ice and water. Cover and set aside.

4. Beat the cream cheese until softened, then beat in the orange juice until blended. Spread over bottom of baked pie shell. Turn whole strawberries into shell. Pour cooled strawberry mixture over berries. Chill in refrigerator.
5. If desired, serve with a *cream topping.*

ONE 9-INCH PIE

STRAWBERRY CRUMB PIE

6 cups halved fresh strawberries	Pastry for High-Collared 1-Crust Pie, *page 253*
¾ cup sugar	¼ cup packed light brown sugar
¼ cup quick-cooking tapioca	½ teaspoon ground cinnamon

1. Toss strawberries with sugar and tapioca; set aside.
2. Prepare pastry, reserving about ½ cup crumbs for topping, and make the pie shell. Turn strawberry mixture into shell. Cut an 8-inch round of aluminum foil and lay over filling.
3. Bake at 400°F 35 minutes.
4. Meanwhile, blend reserved flour mixture with brown sugar and cinnamon. Remove foil and sprinkle flour mixture evenly over pie. Continue baking 25 minutes, or until crust and topping are browned.
5. Cool on wire rack. Serve with *whipped cream.*

ONE 9-INCH PIE

STRAWBERRY MAPLE CHEESE PIE

Pastry for High-Collared 1-Crust Pie, *page 253*	3 tablespoons maple syrup
4 oz. cream cheese, softened	½ cup dairy sour cream
	4 cups halved fresh strawberries

1. Prepare pie shell, bake, and cool.
2. Blend cream cheese with maple syrup; stir in sour cream. Pour into cooled pie shell, cover filling with waxed paper, and chill about 3 hours.
3. Drizzle strawberries generously with maple syrup; chill.
4. Top cheese filling with strawberries.

ONE 9-INCH PIE

LATTICE-TOP CHERRY PIE

¾ to 1 cup sugar	¼ teaspoon almond extract
2½ tablespoons cornstarch	4 or 5 drops red food coloring
⅛ teaspoon salt	Pastry for Lattice-Top Pie, *page 253*
2 cans (16 oz. each) pitted tart red cherries, drained (reserve ¾ cup liquid)	1 tablespoon butter or margarine
1 teaspoon lemon juice	

1. Combine sugar, cornstarch, and salt in a heavy saucepan; stir in the reserved cherry liquid. Bring to boiling and boil 2 to 3 minutes, stirring constantly.
2. Remove from heat; stir in lemon juice, extract, and food coloring, then the cherries. Set aside.
3. Meanwhile, prepare an 8-inch pie shell and lattice strips for top crust; set aside.
4. When filling is cool, spoon into unbaked pie shell. Dot with butter. Complete as directed for lattice-top pie.
5. Bake at 450°F 10 minutes; reduce oven temperature to 350°F and bake about 35 minutes, or until pastry is lightly browned.
6. Remove pie to wire rack to cool. ONE 8-INCH PIE

FRESH FIG PIE

½ to ¾ lb. fresh figs	1 unbaked 9-in. pie shell
¾ cup sugar	2 tablespoons butter or margarine
1 tablespoon grated orange peel	
3 tablespoons lemon juice	

1. Peel and slice figs (enough for 3 cups). Stir sugar, orange peel, and lemon juice into figs. Turn fruit into unbaked pie shell. Dot with butter.
2. Bake at 450°F 10 minutes; reduce oven temperature to 350°F and bake about 25 minutes.

ONE 9-INCH PIE

GRAPE ARBOR PIE

Pastry for Lattice-Top Pie, *page 253*	1 tablespoon orange juice
3 cups Concord grapes	1 tablespoon lemon juice
1 cup sugar	
3 tablespoons cornstarch	1 tablespoon butter or margarine
¼ teaspoon salt	
2 teaspoons grated orange peel	

1. Prepare an 8-inch pie shell and lattice strips for top crust; set aside.
2. Rinse and drain the grapes; slip off skins and chop; set aside in a bowl.
3. Bring skinned grapes to boiling in a saucepan; lower heat and simmer 5 minutes, or until seeds are loosened.
4. Drain pulp, reserving juice. Force pulp through fine sieve or food mill into bowl with chopped grape skins; set aside. Discard the seeds.
5. Thoroughly mix sugar, cornstarch, and salt in a saucepan. Stir in the reserved grape juice until well blended. Bring mixture to boiling; stir and cook 3 minutes.
6. Remove from heat; stir in the pulp mixture, orange peel, and the juices. Turn filling into unbaked pie shell. Dot with butter. Complete as directed for lattice-top pie.
7. Bake at 450°F 10 minutes; reduce oven temperature to 350°F and bake 20 to 25 minutes, or until pastry is lightly browned.
8. Cool on wire rack.

ONE 8-INCH PIE

FRESH PEACH-PLUM PIE

Pastry for 2-crust pie
2 cups sliced peeled ripe peaches
2 cups sliced ripe purple plums
2 to 4 teaspoons lemon juice
¼ teaspoon almond extract
1½ cups sugar
3 tablespoons quick-cooking tapioca
1 teaspoon grated lemon peel
¼ teaspoon salt
2 tablespoons butter or margarine

1. Prepare a 9-inch pie shell; roll out remaining pastry for top crust. Set aside.
2. Gently toss peaches and plums with the lemon juice and extract, then with a mixture of the sugar, tapioca, lemon peel, and salt.
3. Turn into unbaked pie shell, heaping slightly at center; dot with butter. Complete as directed for 2-crust pie.
4. Bake at 450°F 10 minutes; reduce oven temperature to 350°F and bake about 35 minutes, or until crust is lightly browned.
5. Serve warm.

ONE 9-INCH PIE

FRESH PEACH PIE: Follow recipe for Fresh Peach-Plum Pie. Increase peaches to 4 cups and omit plums. Omit almond extract. Use 1¼ cups sugar.

FRESH PLUM PIE: Follow recipe for Fresh Peach-Plum Pie. Increase plums to 5 cups and omit the peaches. Omit almond extract. Decrease sugar to 1 cup; add ¼ cup firmly packed dark brown sugar. Decrease lemon peel to ½ teaspoon.

GLAZED PEACH PIE

2½ cups fresh peach slices
1 tablespoon lemon juice
¼ cup sugar
½ cup sugar
3 tablespoons cornstarch
2 tablespoons butter or margarine
⅛ teaspoon salt
⅛ teaspoon almond extract
1 baked 8-in. pie shell

1. Turn peach slices into a bowl. Drizzle lemon juice over them and mix lightly. Add ¼ cup sugar and toss gently. Set aside 1 hour.
2. Drain peaches, reserving syrup in a 1-cup measuring cup for liquids. Add enough water to syrup to measure 1 cup liquid.
3. Combine the ½ cup sugar and cornstarch in a saucepan. Stir in the reserved peach liquid until thoroughly blended. Stirring constantly, bring mixture to boiling; boil 3 minutes, or until thick and clear. Remove from heat.
4. Blend in the butter, salt, and extract. Add the peach slices and mix gently. Turn into baked pie shell; cool. If desired, serve with *whipped cream.*

ONE 8-INCH PIE

PRALINE PINEAPPLE-PEACH PIE

1 can (20 ozs.) pineapple chunks in juice
1 can (29 ozs.) cling peach slices in syrup
¼ cup granulated sugar
3 tablespoons quick-cooking tapioca
Double Crust Pastry
page 252
3 tablespons butter or margarine
⅓ cup firmly packed light brown sugar
¼ cup chopped pecans
1 tablespoon light cream

1. Drain juice from pineapple; measure ¾ cup and combine with pineapple in a large bowl. Drain syrup from peaches and save for fruit punch. Add peaches, granulated sugar, and tapioca to pineapple; mix lightly. Let stand while making pastry.

2. Preheat oven to 400°F.
3. Prepare Double Crust Pastry or make piecrust from your favorite mix. Roll out half to a 12-inch round on a lightly floured cloth; fit into a 9-inch pie plate; trim overhang to ½ inch. Spoon fruit mixture into crust; dot 1 tablespoon of the butter over top.
4. Roll out rest of pastry to an 11-inch round; cut several slits near center to let steam escape; place over filling. Trim overhang to ½ inch; turn top and bottom edges under flush with rim of pie plate; pinch to make a stand-up edge; flute.
5. Bake 40 minutes, or until pastry is lightly golden.
6. While pie bakes, melt remaining 2 tablespoons butter in a small saucepan. Stir in brown sugar, pecans, and cream; spread over top of hot pie. Bake 10 minutes longer, or until topping bubbles. Cool pie on a wire rack.   9-INCH PIE

FRESH PEAR PIE

Pastry for 2-crust pie
¾ cup sugar
3 tablespoons cornstarch
½ teaspoon ground nutmeg
Few grains salt
2 tablespoons lemon juice
4 large ripe pears, washed, quartered, cored, pared, and sliced (about 4 cups)
2 tablespoons butter or margarine

1. Prepare an 8-inch pie shell; roll out remaining pastry for top crust. Set aside.
2. Mix the sugar, cornstarch, nutmeg, and salt.
3. Sprinkle lemon juice over sliced pears and mix lightly; toss gently with the sugar mixture. Turn filling into pastry shell. Dot top with butter. Complete as directed for a 2-crust pie.
4. Bake at 450°F 10 minutes; reduce oven temperature to 350°F and bake 30 to 35 minutes, or until crust is light golden brown.
5. Cool pie on wire rack.   ONE 8-INCH PIE

STRAWBERRY TART GLACE

1 package piecrust mix
4 tablespoons sugar
1 egg
1 cup milk
4 packages (3 ozs. each) cream cheese, softened
3 tablespoons curacao
1 package (3¾ ozs.) vanilla-flavored instant pudding mix
2 pints strawberries, washed and hulled
¼ cup currant jelly

1. Preheat oven to 400°F.
2. Combine piecrust mix and 2 tablespoons of the sugar in a medium bowl. Beat egg well in a small bowl; stir into piecrust mixture until evenly moist. (If mixture seems too dry to roll, stir in about 1 tablespoon ice water.)
3. Roll out pastry to a 13-inch round on a lightly floured cloth; fit into a 9-inch round layer-cake pan; trim edge even with rim of pan. Prick shell well all over with a fork. (Use any pastry trimmings to make a smaller shell for another dessert or to turn into nibbles for the children.)
4. Bake shell 12 minutes, or until golden. Cool completely on a wire rack, then remove carefully from pan and place on a large flat serving plate.
5. Blend milk and cream cheese until smooth in a medium bowl; beat in remaining 2 tablespoons sugar and 2 tablespoons of the curaçao. Add pudding mix; beat 1 minute; spread evenly in pastry shell. Chill while fixing strawberry topping.
6. Arrange strawberries, pointed ends up, over filling in a shell to cover completely.
7. Heat jelly until melted in a small saucepan; stir in remaining 1 tablespoon curaçao; cool slightly. Brush over berries to glaze. Chill tart until glaze is firm or until serving time.   8 SERVINGS

ROSY RHUBARB PIE

Pastry for 2-crust pie
1 tablespoon quick-cooking tapioca
1¾ lbs. fresh rhubarb
¼ cup grenadine
¾ cup sugar
½ cup flour
¼ teaspoon salt
1 teaspoon grated orange peel
2 tablespoons butter or margarine
Egg white, beaten
2 teaspoons sugar

1. Prepare a 9-inch pie shell; roll out remaining pastry for top crust. Sprinkle tapioca over bottom of pie shell. Set aside.
2. Wash rhubarb, trim off leaves and ends of stems, and cut into 1-inch pieces to make 6 cups. (Peel only if skin is tough.)
3. Toss rhubarb with grenadine, then with a mixture of sugar, flour, salt, and orange peel. Turn into pie shell, heaping slightly in center; dot with butter. Complete as directed for a 2-crust pie.
4. Brush top lightly with egg white, then sprinkle with the 2 teaspoons sugar.
5. Bake at 450°F 15 minutes; reduce oven temperature to 375°F and bake 20 to 25 minutes, or until golden brown.   ONE 9-INCH PIE

CREAM PIE

¾ cup sugar
3 tablespoons cornstarch
2 tablespoons flour
½ teaspoon salt
3 cups milk
3 egg yolks, slightly beaten
1 tablespoon butter or margarine
1½ teaspoons vanilla extract
1 baked 9-in. pie shell or crumb crust

1. Mix sugar, cornstarch, flour, and salt in a 1½-quart saucepan. Stir in one half of the milk, then a blend of remaining milk and egg yolks. Bring to boiling over medium heat, stirring vigorously. Reduce heat; stir and cook about 5 minutes.
2. Remove from heat; blend in butter and extract. Cool slightly.
3. Turn filling into the pie shell. Chill.

ONE 9-INCH PIE

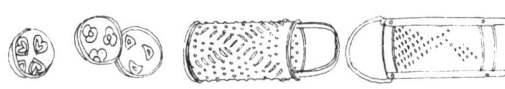

ALMOND MACAROON PIE

9 (1¾ in.) almond macaroon cookies
1 cup sugar
3 tablespoons flour
⅛ teaspoon salt
¼ cup cold milk
1 cup cream, scalded
3 egg yolks, slightly beaten
2 tablespoons butter or margarine
1 teaspoon almond extract
1 baked 9-in. pie shell
¼ cup blanched almonds, finely chopped

1. Heat cookies on a baking sheet in a 325°F oven for about 15 minutes; cool. Crush to make about ¾ cup fine crumbs.
2. Combine sugar, flour, and salt in top of double boiler; mix well and stir in the cold milk. Gradually add the scalded cream, stirring constantly. Bring to boiling and cook 3 minutes.
3. Stir about ½ cup of hot mixture into beaten egg yolks; immediately blend into mixture in double boiler. Place over boiling water and cook about 5 minutes, or until thickened, stirring occasionally.
4. Remove from water. Blend in butter, extract, and macaroon crumbs; cool to lukewarm.
5. Turn filling into pie shell. To complete pie, top with *sweetened whipped cream* and sprinkle with chopped almonds.

ONE 9-INCH PIE

BANANA BUTTERSCOTCH PIE

¾ cup firmly packed brown sugar
5 tablespoons flour
½ teaspoon salt
2 cups milk
2 egg yolks, slightly beaten
2 tablespoons butter or margarine
1 teaspoon vanilla extract
3 ripe bananas
1 baked 9-in. pie shell

1. Mix the brown sugar, flour, and salt together in the top of a double boiler. Add milk gradually, stirring until mixture is thoroughly blended.
2. Place over boiling water and cook, stirring constantly until thickened.
3. Vigorously stir about 3 tablespoons of the hot mixture into egg yolks, then blend into mixture in double-boiler top. Cook over boiling water about 5 minutes, stirring constantly. Remove from water. Blend in butter and extract; set aside.
4. Turn half of the lukewarm filling into the pastry shell. Cut bananas into crosswise slices and arrange over filling. Turn remaining filling over bananas. Top with *whipped cream*.

ONE 9-INCH PIE

RAINBOW FRUIT PIE

Single Crust Pastry, page 252
1 envelope unflavored gelatin
½ cup sugar (for filling)
Dash of salt
2 eggs, separated
½ cup milk
1 package (8 ozs.) cream cheese
1 teaspoon grated orange rind
1 cup orange juice
½ cup whipping cream
1 tablespoon sugar (for glaze).
1½ teaspoons cornstarch
1 pint strawberries, washed, hulled and halved
1 large banana
½ cup blueberries

1. Preheat oven to 400° F.
2. Prepare Single Crust Pastry or make piecrust from your favorite mix. Roll out to a 12-inch round on a lightly floured cloth; fit into a 9-inch pie plate. Trim overhang to ½ inch; turn edge under flush with rim of pie plate; flute to make a high edge. Prick shell well all over with a fork.
3. Bake 12 minutes, or until golden; cool shell completely on a wire rack.
4. Mix gelatin, ¼ cup of the sugar, and salt in a small saucepan.
5. Beat egg yolks with milk in a small bowl; stir into

gelatin mixture. Cook slowly, stirring constantly, until gelatin dissolves; cut up cream cheese and stir in until melted, keeping saucepan over very low heat, if needed. Pour mixture into a medium bowl; beat until smooth; stir in orange rind and ½ cup of the orange juice. Chill 30 minutes, or until mixture mounds softly.

6. While gelatin mixture chills, beat egg whites in a small bowl until foamy; slowly beat in remaining ¼ cup sugar until meringue forms soft peaks. Beat cream in a small bowl until stiff. Fold meringue, then whipped cream into gelatin mixture until no streaks of white remain. Spoon into prepared pastry shell, spreading top even. Chill 2 hours, or until firm.

7. Mix the 1 tablespoon sugar and cornstarch in a small saucepan; stir in remaining ½ cup orange juice. Cook slowly, stirring constantly, until mixture thickens and boils 1 minute; cool just until lukewarm.

8. Arrange enough strawberry halves, overlapping, on cream layer to form a circle around edge of shell. Peel banana and slice; overlap slices in a circle next to strawberries. Place blueberries in several rings next to bananas; arrange remaining strawberries in center. Brush cooled orange mixture over fruits to glaze generously. Chill pie until glaze sets.   9-INCH PIE

CANDIED PECAN PUMPKIN PIE

Single Crust Pastry (recipe on page 252
3 eggs
1 can (16 ozs.) pumpkin
1 cup granulated sugar
⅓ cup firmly packed brown sugar
2 teaspoons pumpkin-pie spice
1 teaspoon salt
1 tall can evaporated milk (1⅔ cups)
½ cup coarsely broken pecans
½ teaspoon vanilla
1½ cups whipping cream

1. Prepare Single Crust Pastry or make piecrust from your favorite mix.
2. Roll out to a 12-inch round on a lightly floured cloth; fit into a 9-inch pie plate. Trim overhang to ½ inch; turn edge under flush with rim of pie plate; pinch to make a stand-up edge; flute.
3. Preheat oven to 425°F.
4. Beat eggs in a medium bowl until blended; stir in pumpkin, ½ cup of the granulated sugar, brown sugar, **pumpkin-pie spice, salt, and evaporated milk until blended**; pour into prepared crust.
5. Bake 15 minutes; lower temperature to 350°F. Bake 25 minutes longer, or until filling is almost set but still soft in center. Cool completely on a wire rack.
6. While pie cools, measure remaining ½ cup granulated sugar into a small heavy skillet. Heat slowly, stirring constantly with a wooden spoon, until sugar melts and syrup turns golden. Quickly stir in pecans and vanilla. Spread on a foil-lined cookie sheet. (Work fast; mixture hardens quickly.) Let stand until cool and firm. Break into small pieces with a mallet.
7. When ready to serve pie, beat cream until stiff in a medium bowl; pile onto center. Sprinkle pecan brittle over cream.   9-INCH PIE

BLACK BOTTOM PIE

½ cup sugar
4 teaspoons cornstarch
½ cup cold milk
1½ cups milk, scalded
4 egg yolks, slightly beaten
1 env. unflavored gelatin
¼ cup cold water
1 tablespoon rum extract
1½ oz. (1½ sq.) unsweetened chocolate, melted and cooled
2 teaspoons vanilla extract
1 baked 10-in. pie shell
4 egg whites
¼ teaspoon salt
¼ teaspoon cream of tartar
½ cup sugar
1 cup heavy cream, whipped
½ oz. (½ sq.) unsweetened chocolate

1. Blend ½ cup sugar and cornstarch in a saucepan. Stir in the cold milk, then the scalded milk, adding gradually. Bring rapidly to boiling, stirring constantly. Cook 3 minutes.
2. Turn mixture into a double-boiler top and set over boiling water. Vigorously stir about 3 tablespoons of hot mixture into egg yolks. Immediately blend into mixture in double boiler. Cook over simmering water, stirring constantly, 3 to 5 minutes, or until mixture coats a metal spoon. Remove double-boiler top from hot water immediately.
3. Soften gelatin in the cold water. Remove 1 cup of the cooked filling and set aside. Immediately stir softened gelatin into mixture in double boiler until completely dissolved. Cool until mixture sets slightly. Blend in rum extract.
4. Blend the melted chocolate and vanilla extract into the 1 cup reserved filling. Cool completely; turn into the baked pie shell, spreading evenly over bottom. Chill until set.
5. Beat egg whites with salt until frothy. Add cream of tartar and beat slightly. Gradually add

remaining ½ cup sugar, beating well after each addition; continue beating until stiff peaks are formed. Spread over gelatin mixture and gently fold together. Turn onto chocolate filling in pie shell. Chill until firm.

6. Spread whipped cream over pie, swirling for a decorative effect. Top with chocolate curls shaved from the ½ ounce unsweetened chocolate. Chill until ready to serve.   ONE 10-INCH PIE

BUTTERSCOTCH-BANANA PIE

Single Crust Pastry (recipe on page 252)
2 cups milk
¾ cup firmly packed dark brown sugar
⅓ cup flour
⅛ teaspoon salt
3 eggs, separated
3 tablespoons butter or margarine
1 teaspoon vanilla
3 medium-sized firm ripe bananas
¼ teaspoon cream of tartar
6 tablespoons granulated sugar

1. Preheat oven to 400°F.
2. Prepare Single Crust Pastry or make piecrust from your favorite mix. Roll out to a 12-inch round on a lightly floured cloth; fit into a 9-inch pie plate. Trim overhang to ½ inch; turn edge under flush with rim fo pie plate; pinch to make a stand-up edge; flute. Prick shell all over with a fork.
3. Bake 12 minutes, or until pastry is golden; cool shell completely on a wire rack. Lower oven temperature to 350°F.
4. Scald milk in the top of a double boiler.
5. Mix brown sugar, flour, and salt in a small bowl; slowly stir into scalded milk. Cook, stirring constantly, until mixture thickens; cover. Continue cooking, stirring once or twice, 10 minutes longer.
6. Beat egg yolks well in a small bowl; slowly stir in about half of the hot mixture, then stir back into top of double boiler. Cook, stirring constantly, 2 minutes; remove from hot water. Stir in butter and vanilla.
7. Peel bananas and slice; layer half into pastry shell; top with half of the butterscotch mixture; repeat layers.
8. Beat egg whites with cream of tartar in a medium bowl until foamy; slowly beat in granulated sugar until meringue forms firm peaks. Pile onto butterscotch filling, spreading to edge of crust.
9. Bake 20 minutes, or until meringue is golden. Cool pie on a wire rack at least 4 hours before cutting.
   9-INCH PIE

TOASTED COCONUT PIE

¾ cup sugar
¼ cup flour
¼ teaspoon salt
2 cups milk, scalded
3 egg yolks, fork beaten
2 tablespoons butter or margarine
1 teaspoon vanilla extract
1 cup toasted flaked coconut*
1 baked 9-in. pie shell
Meringue, page 278

1. Combine the sugar, flour, and salt in a heavy saucepan. Add scalded milk gradually, stirring constantly until mixture is thoroughly blended. Cook, stirring vigorously over medium heat until mixture thickens and comes to boiling; boil 1 to 2 minutes, stirring constantly.
2. Stir about ½ cup of the hot mixture into egg yolks; blend thoroughly and return to saucepan. Reduce heat; stir and cook about 5 minutes.
3. Remove from heat; stir in butter until thoroughly blended. Mix in the extract and toasted coconut; set aside to cool.
4. Turn filling into baked pastry shell; top with meringue and bake as directed in meringue recipe. Or, instead of meringue, spread with *whipped cream* before serving.   ONE 9-INCH PIE

*To toast coconut, spread in a shallow baking pan; heat in a 350°F oven about 10 minutes, or until coconut is golden brown, stirring occasionally.

TOASTED COCONUT-BANANA PIE: Follow recipe for Toasted Coconut Pie. Decrease coconut to ¾ cup. Spread about one-third of cooled filling in bottom of pastry shell; slice *1 medium-sized banana* over filling and cover with another third of filling. Slice a second banana over filling and cover with remaining filling. Top with meringue and bake as directed until lightly browned.

LEMON-LIME MERINGUE PIE

2 bottles (7 oz. each) lemon-lime carbonated beverage
¾ cup sugar
¼ cup cornstarch
¼ cup flour
½ teaspoon salt
3 egg yolks
⅓ cup sugar
⅓ cup lemon juice
¼ cup lime juice
1 teaspoon grated lemon peel
2 tablespoons butter or margarine
1 baked 9-in. pie shell
Meringue, page 278

1. Heat lemon-lime carbonated beverage to boiling.

2. Combine the ¾ cup sugar, cornstarch, flour, and salt in a saucepan; add the hot beverage slowly, stirring until blended. Bring to boiling over medium heat, stirring constantly. Reduce heat; stir and cook 10 minutes.
3. Beat egg yolks and ⅓ cup sugar together. Stir about ½ cup of hot mixture into the egg yolks. Then blend into mixture in saucepan.
4. Add lemon and lime juices and cook over low heat until thickened, stirring constantly.
5. Remove from heat; stir in lemon peel and butter. Turn filling into pie shell; cool slightly.
6. Top with meringue and bake as directed in meringue recipe. ONE 9-INCH PIE

KEY LIME PIE
This popular pie originating in the Florida Keys takes on its piquant flavor from those small, yellow-green Key limes.

1 can (14 oz.) sweetened condensed milk
3 egg yolks
⅔ cup lime juice
1 or 2 drops green food coloring
1 baked 9-in. pie shell
3 egg whites
⅓ cup sugar

1. Mix the condensed milk, egg yolks, lime juice, and food coloring until blended. Chill.
2. Turn mixture into baked pie shell.
3. Beat egg whites until frothy; add sugar gradually, beating well after each addition. Beat until stiff peaks are formed; spread the meringue over pie filling to edge of pastry.
4. Set in a 450°F oven about 5 minutes, or until meringue is delicately browned. ONE 9-INCH PIE

REFRIGERATOR RASPBERRY PIE

¼ cup light corn syrup
2 tablespoons sugar
1 tablespoon butter or margarine
3 cups cornflakes
1 package (10 ozs.) frozen raspberries, thawed
Water
1 package (3 ozs.) raspberry-flavored gelatin
1 pint vanilla ice cream
½ cup whipping cream
2 tablespoons confectioners' powdered sugar

1. Combine corn syrup, sugar, and butter in a medium saucepan. Heat slowly, stirring several times, until mixture starts to bubble; remove from heat. Stir in cornflakes until evenly coated. Press mixture firmly over bottom and up side of an 8-inch pie plate to form a shell with a high edge. Chill shell while preparing filling.
2. Drain raspberry syrup into a 1-cup measure; add water to make 1 cup. Heat to boiling in a small saucepan; pour over gelatin in a medium bowl; stir until gelatin dissolves. Stir in ice cream until melted and mixture is smooth.
3. Chill 10 minutes, or until partly thickened; fold in raspberries. Pour into prepared shell; chill several hours, or until firm.
4. Just before serving, beat cream with confectioners' sugar until stiff in a small bowl; spoon onto center of pie. 8-INCH PIE

NESSELRODE TARTLETS

1 package (12 ozs.) semisweet chocolate pieces
2 tablespoons shortening
½ cup sugar
1 envelope unflavored gelatin
¼ teaspoon salt
3 eggs, separated
1¼ cups milk
1 jar (10 ozs.) Nesselrode dessert sauce
½ teaspoon rum extract
¼ teaspoon cream of tartar
1 cup whipping cream
1 square unsweetened chocolate, grated

1. Place sixteen 2½-inch foil baking cups in medium muffin-pan cups.
2. Combine chocolate pieces and shortening in a medium saucepan. Heat very slowly, stirring constantly, until melted; measure 2 scant tablespoons into each cup. Chill 10 minutes, or until mixture starts to harden.
3. Using the back of a spoon, spread chocolate mixture up sides of cups to coat evenly. Chill until firm. Very carefully peel foil from each shell; stand shells on a cookie sheet; keep chilled while making filling.
4. Mix ¼ cup of the sugar, gelatin, and salt in a medium saucepan. Beat egg yolks with milk in a small bowl; stir into gelatin mixture. Cook over low heat, stirring constantly, until gelatin dissolves and mixture coats a spoon. Stir in Nesselrode sauce and rum extract; pour into a large bowl.
5. Set bowl in a large pan of ice and water to speed setting. Chill mixture, stirring several times, just until

it starts to thicken.

6. While gelatin mixture chills, beat egg whites with cream of tartar in a medium bowl until foamy. Slowly beat in remaining ¼ cup sugar until meringue forms stiff peaks. Beat ½ cup of the cream until stiff in a small bowl. Fold meringue, then whipped cream into gelatin mixture. Spoon about ⅓ cup into each chocolate shell; chill until firm.

7. Just before serving, beat remaining ½ cup cream until stiff in a small bowl; spoon a dollop in center of each tartlet. Sprinkle grated chocolate over cream.

16 TARTLETS

TALBOTT INN ORANGE PIE
From Talbott Tavern, Bardstown, Kentucky.

¾ cup sugar	2 tablespoons lemon juice
½ cup flour	1 tablespoon orange extract
¼ teaspoon salt	
1¾ cups reconstituted frozen orange juice	1 baked 8-in. pie shell
2 egg yolks, slightly beaten	2 egg whites
	½ cup sugar
	2 tablespoons water

1. Mix sugar, flour, and salt in the top of a double boiler. Stir in orange juice and cook over direct heat until thickened, stirring constantly.
2. Add a small amount of hot mixture to egg yolks; blend well and return to double boiler. Cook over boiling water about 5 minutes, or until mixture is thick. Remove from heat; add lemon juice and orange extract. Chill and turn into baked pie shell.
3. Beat egg whites, sugar, and water in top of double boiler until blended. Place over boiling water and beat 1 minute. Remove from heat and beat until meringue stands in peaks.
4. Pile over the pie and garnish with *orange sections* and *flaked coconut*.   ONE 8-INCH PIE

CARAMEL APPLE PIE

Double Crust Pastry page 252	6 medium-sized tart apples, pared, quartered, cored, and sliced (6 cups)
¾ cup firmly packed light brown sugar	
2 tablespoons all-purpose flour	¼ cup butter or margarine
1 teaspoon ground cinnamon	Milk

1. Prepare Double Crust Pastry or make piecrust from your favorite mix. Roll out half to a 12-inch round on a lightly floured cloth; fit into a 9-inch pie plate; trim overhang to ½ inch.
2. Preheat oven to 425°F.
3. Mix brown sugar, flour, and cinnamon in a small bowl; sprinkle over apples in a large bowl; toss lightly to mix. Spoon into crust; dot butter over top.
4. Roll out rest of pastry to an 11-inch round; cut several slits near center to let steam escape; place over filling. Trim overhang to ½ inch; turn top and bottom edges under flush with rim of pie plate; pinch to make a stand-up edge; flute. Brush top lightly with milk; sprinkle with sugar if you like.
5. Bake 45 minutes, or until filling bubbles up and pastry is golden. Cool pie on a wire rack. Serve warm or cold, plain or with ice cream.   9-INCH PIE

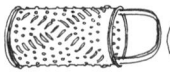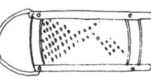

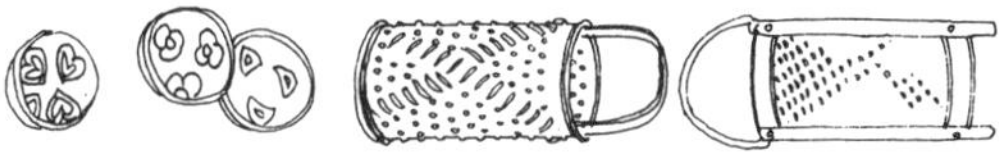

CUSTARD PIE

4 eggs	¾ cup cream, scalded
½ cup sugar	1 teaspoon vanilla extract
½ teaspoon nutmeg	
¼ teaspoon salt	1 unbaked 8-in. pie shell
1½ cups milk, scalded	

1. Beat the eggs slightly; add sugar, nutmeg, and salt and beat just until blended. Gradually add the scalded milk and cream, stirring constantly. Mix in the extract. Strain mixture into pie shell.
2. Bake at 450°F 10 minutes; reduce oven temperature to 350°F and bake 15 to 20 minutes, or until a knife inserted in custard halfway between center and edge comes out clean.
3. Cool on wire rack. Place in refrigerator until ready to serve.   ONE 8-INCH PIE

SLIPPED CUSTARD PIE: Follow recipe for Custard Pie for amounts of ingredients. Prepare, bake, and set pie shell aside to cool. Lightly butter a second 8-inch pie pan. Prepare custard and strain into the pan. Set in pan of hot water. Bake at 325°F 25 to 30 minutes, or until custard tests done. Remove from water and cool. Run tip of knife around edge of pan; hold pan level and shake gently to loosen custard. Hold pan at a slight angle and slip the custard carefully into pie shell. Work quickly to avoid breaking custard. Set aside a few minutes.

Pies

FRAU MOYER'S CHEESE CUSTARD PIE
This delicious pie is of Pennsylvania Dutch origin.

1 cup large-curd creamed cottage cheese	¼ teaspoon ground nutmeg
1 cup cream	5 egg yolks, slightly beaten
½ cup confectioners' sugar	¼ cup butter, melted
¼ teaspoon salt	5 egg whites
	1 unbaked 9-in. pie shell

1. Force cottage cheese through a fine sieve into a bowl. Stir in the cream, confectioners' sugar, salt, nutmeg, beaten egg yolks, and melted butter.
2. Beat egg whites until stiff, not dry, peaks are formed. Fold into cheese mixture until blended. Turn into the pie shell.
3. Bake at 450°F 10 minutes. Reduce oven temperature to 350°F; bake about 20 minutes, or until custard tests done. Serve warm. ONE 9-INCH PIE

STRAWBERRY-GLAZED CHEESE PIE

8 oz. cream cheese	½ cup heavy cream, whipped
½ cup sweetened condensed milk	1 baked 10-inch Graham Cracker Crumb Crust, page 254
¼ teaspoon vanilla extract	1 pkg. (16 oz.) frozen strawberries, thawed and drained (reserve syrup)
1 teaspoon grated lemon peel	
2 tablespoons lemon juice	2 teaspoons cornstarch

1. Soften cream cheese in a bowl; beat in condensed milk, extract, and lemon peel and juice until thoroughly blended. Fold in the whipped cream. Turn mixture into baked pie shell; chill.
2. Stir ¾ cup of the reserved strawberry syrup into cornstarch in a saucepan. Cook and stir over medium heat until mixture comes to boiling; cook 3 minutes longer, or until mixture is clear. Cool about 10 minutes.
3. Gently mix in strawberries; spoon glaze over pie; chill thoroughly. ONE 10-INCH PIE

SOUR CREAM-RAISIN PIE

½ cup sugar	1 egg, well beaten
2 tablespoons flour	1½ cups dairy sour cream
½ teaspoon ground cinnamon	1½ cups dark seedless raisins
¼ teaspoon ground nutmeg	1 unbaked 9-in. pie shell
¼ teaspoon salt	

1. Combine sugar, flour, spices, and salt.
2. Combine the egg with sour cream; gradually add dry ingredients, blending thoroughly. Stir in raisins. Turn filling into unbaked pie shell.
3. Bake at 450°F 10 minutes; reduce oven temperature to 350°F and bake 20 to 25 minutes, or until a knife inserted near center comes out clean.
4. Serve slightly warm. ONE 9-INCH PIE

SOUR CREAM-DATE PIE: Follow recipe for Sour Cream-Raisin Pie. Omit spices and raisins. Stir *1 teaspoon grated lemon peel* into sugar mixture. Mix *2 cups date pieces* and *⅓ cup coarsely chopped pecans* into sour cream mixture.

KENTUCKY CHESS PIE
Here is a popular recipe from the Beaumont Inn in Harrodsburg, Kentucky.

1 cup sugar	½ cup butter, melted
1 tablespoon flour	1 unbaked 8- or 9-in. pie shell
¼ teaspoon salt	
2 egg yolks	Meringue:
1 whole egg	2 egg whites
3 tablespoons water	2 tablespoons sugar
1 teaspoon white vinegar	

1. Mix the sugar, flour, and salt thoroughly.
2. Beat egg yolks with egg; beating constantly, slowly add the water, vinegar, and melted butter. Add dry ingredients and mix well. Turn into unbaked pie shell.
3. Bake at 350°F about 35 minutes, or until filling is "set."
4. Meanwhile, prepare meringue. Beat egg whites until foamy; add the sugar gradually, beating constantly until stiff peaks are formed.
5. Remove pie from oven; top with meringue and return to oven. Bake 12 to 15 minutes, or until meringue is lightly browned. ONE 8- OR 9-INCH PIE

HEAVENLY LEMON PIE

4 egg yolks	4 egg whites
2/3 cup sugar	1/4 teaspoon salt
1 tablespoon grated lemon peel	1/2 cup sugar
1/3 cup lemon juice	1 baked 10-in. pie shell

1. In the top of a double boiler, beat the egg yolks with the 2/3 cup sugar until thoroughly blended; beat in the lemon peel and juice.
2. Cook and stir over simmering water 12 to 15 minutes, or until mixture is very thick. Turn into a bowl; cool.
3. Beat egg whites with salt until frothy; gradually add the 1/2 cup sugar, beating constantly until stiff peaks are formed.
4. Carefully spread egg-white mixture over the cooled lemon mixture and gently fold together. Turn filling into baked pie shell.
5. Bake at 450°F 5 minutes, or until filling is puffy and lightly browned. Serve while warm.

ONE 10-INCH PIE

MINCE PIE

Pastry for a 2-crust pie	1 teaspoon grated lemon peel
3½ cups moist mincemeat	1 tablespoon lemon juice
1¼ cups chopped apple	

1. Prepare a 9-inch pie shell; roll out remaining pastry for top crust. Set aside.
2. Blend mincemeat and remaining ingredients in a saucepan; heat thoroughly. Cool slightly.
3. Turn filling into unbaked pie shell. Complete as directed for 2-crust pie.
4. Bake at 425°F 35 minutes. Cool on wire rack.

ONE 9-INCH PIE

SHOOFLY PIE

Pennsylvania Dutch in origin, this old-fashioned pie has found favor in other sections of our country.

1 cup all-purpose flour	5 tablespoons molasses
2/3 cup firmly packed dark brown sugar	1 tablespoon dark brown sugar
1/4 teaspoon salt	1/2 teaspoon baking soda
5 tablespoons butter or margarine	1 unbaked 8-in. pie shell
2/3 cup very hot water	

1. Combine flour, 2/3 cup brown sugar, and salt in a bowl. Cut in butter until particles resemble rice kernels; set aside.
2. Blend hot water with the molasses, 1 tablespoon brown sugar, and baking soda.
3. Reserving 3 tablespoons crumb mixture for topping, stir molasses mixture into remaining crumb mixture. Pour into unbaked pie shell. Sprinkle reserved crumbs over filling.
4. Bake at 350°F 35 to 40 minutes, or until top springs back when touched lightly.

ONE 8-INCH PIE

BUTTERNUT PIE

A favorite at Vermont House, Newbury, Vermont.

3 eggs	1 cup maple syrup
1 cup sugar	1 cup coarsely chopped butternuts*
1 teaspoon salt	
1 teaspoon vanilla extract	1 unbaked 9-in. pie shell

1. Beat the eggs, sugar, salt, and extract together until thick and piled softly. Beat in the maple syrup, then stir in butternuts. Pour the filling into unbaked pie shell.
2. Bake at 350°F about 40 minutes, or until a knife inserted near center comes out clean.

ONE 9-INCH PIE

*If butternuts are not available, substitute walnuts.

APPLE-PECAN PIE

Awarded a blue ribbon by apple-growers at their annual Apple Smorgasbord in Grand Rapids, Michigan.

2 tablespoons butter or margarine	1 cup coarsely chopped pecans
1 teaspoon vanilla extract	3/4 cup dark corn syrup
	1/2 cup thick applesauce
1 cup firmly packed light brown sugar	Few grains cinnamon
3 eggs	1 unbaked 9-in. pie shell

1. Cream butter with extract until softened; gradually add brown sugar, beating thoroughly. Add eggs, one at a time, beating thoroughly after each addition.
2. Blend in the pecans, corn syrup, applesauce, and cinnamon. Turn filling into unbaked pie shell.
3. Bake at 450°F 10 minutes; reduce oven temperature to 350°F and bake 35 to 40 minutes.
4. Cool on wire rack.

ONE 9-INCH PIE

BRIDGE PIE

¾ cup butter or margarine
¾ cup sugar
2 egg yolks
¼ cup milk
¾ cup chopped pecans
1 cup coarsely chopped dates
2 egg whites
1 unbaked 9-inch Graham Cracker Crumb Crust, *page 254*

1. Cream butter; gradually add sugar, beating thoroughly until light and fluffy. Add egg yolks and beat until smooth. Blend in the milk. Stir in pecans and dates.
2. Beat egg whites until stiff, not dry, peaks are formed; spread over date mixture and gently fold together. Turn filling into crust; spread evenly.
3. Bake at 350°F 35 to 40 minutes, or until "set."
4. Serve with *whipped cream*.   ONE 9-INCH PIE

APRICOT-NUT CHIFFON PIE

Apricot-Nut Pastry, *below*
1 env. unflavored gelatin
½ cup sugar
⅛ teaspoon salt
¼ cup cold water
¼ cup orange juice
1¼ cups apricot nectar
1 tablespoon lemon juice
1 can (16 or 17 oz.) apricot halves, drained and sieved
½ cup heavy cream, whipped
⅔ cup chopped nuts

1. Prepare and bake Apricot-Nut Pastry; set aside.
2. Thoroughly mix gelatin, sugar, and salt in a saucepan. Blend in cold water and orange juice. Stir over low heat until gelatin is dissolved. Remove from heat. Blend in apricot nectar and lemon juice.
3. Chill mixture until slightly thicker than consistency of thick, unbeaten egg white. Beat with hand rotary or electric beater until light and fluffy. Blend in the sieved apricots. Fold in the whipped cream and nuts; turn filling into pastry shell. Chill until firm.
4. Serve topped with *whipped cream*, if desired.
ONE 9-INCH PIE

APRICOT-NUT PASTRY

7 tablespoons butter or shortening
3 tablespoons apricot nectar, heated
1 teaspoon milk
1¼ cups sifted all-purpose flour
½ teaspoon salt
¼ cup chopped nuts

1. Combine butter, hot apricot nectar, and the milk in a bowl; whip with a fork until mixture is smooth.
2. Sift flour and salt together into the butter mixture; stir quickly to a smooth dough.
3. Shape dough into a flat round and roll out between two 12-inch squares of waxed paper into a round about ⅛ inch thick.
4. Peel off top piece of paper and sprinkle dough with 2 tablespoons of the nuts, leaving a 1-inch border plain. Cover with the paper and gently roll nuts into dough.
5. Turn pastry over and repeat step 4.
6. Peel off top paper and fit pastry into a 9-inch pie pan; remove other piece of paper.
7. Flute pastry edge and generously prick shell with a fork.
8. Bake at 450°F 8 to 9 minutes, or until pastry is lightly browned; cool.   ONE 9-INCH PIE SHELL

MOCHA-NOG PIE

2 env unflavored gelatin
½ cup cold water
⅔ cup sugar
½ teaspoon ground nutmeg
2 cups strong coffee
3 egg yolks, slightly beaten
3 egg whites
1 cup chilled heavy cream, whipped
1½ teaspoons vanilla extract
1 baked 10-in. pie shell
½ oz. (½ sq.) unsweetened chocolate

1. Soften gelatin in cold water; set aside.
2. Mix sugar, nutmeg, and coffee in top of double boiler. Bring to boiling. Remove from heat; add the gelatin and stir until gelatin is dissolved.
3. Stir about ½ cup hot coffee mixture into egg yolks, then blend into mixture in double boiler top. Cook over simmering water, stirring constantly, until mixture is slightly thickened. Remove from water; cool.
4. Chill until mixture is partially set.
5. Beat egg whites until stiff, not dry, peaks are formed. Spread beaten egg whites and a blend of whipped cream and extract over gelatin mixture and fold together. Turn filling into pie shell. Chill until firm.
6. Top with chocolate curls made by pulling the chocolate across a shredder.   ONE 10-INCH PIE

REGAL MOCHA-NOG PIE: Follow recipe for Mocha-

Nog Pie. Omit nutmeg and extract. When gelatin mixture is slightly thicker, blend in *½ cup brandy* or *¼ cup crème de cacao*. If brandy is used, beat egg whites until frothy; add *3 tablespoons sugar* gradually, continuing to beat until rounded peaks are formed.

CHOCOLATE CHIFFON PIE

Single Crust Pastry (recipe on page *252*)
¼ cup finely chopped California walnuts
1 envelope unflavored gelatin
1 cup sugar
¼ teaspoon salt
3 eggs, separated
1 cup milk
3 squares unsweetened chocolate
1 teaspoon vanilla
⅛ teaspoon cream of tartar
2 cups whipping cream
¼ cup semisweet chocolate pieces
½ teaspoon shortening

1. Preheat oven to 400° F.
2. Prepare Single Crust Pastry or make pastry from your favorite mix, stirring walnuts into flour mixture before adding water. Roll out to a 12-inch round on a lightly floured cloth; fit into a 9-inch pie plate. Trim overhang to ½ inch; turn edge under flush with rim of pie plate; pinch to make a stand-up edge; flute. Prick shell all over with a fork.
3. Bake 12 minutes, or until pastry is golden; cool shell completely on a wire rack.
4. Mix gelatin, ½ cup of the sugar, and salt in a medium saucepan. Beat egg yolks in a small bowl; stir into gelatin mixture with milk; add chocolate squares. Heat slowly, stirring constantly, until gelatin dissolves and chocolate melts; pour into a large bowl; stir in vanilla.
5. Place bowl in a pan of ice and water to speed setting. Chill, stirring several times, until mixture starts to thicken.
6. While gelatin mixture chills, beat egg whites with cream of tartar in a medium bowl until foamy; slowly beat in remaining ½ cup sugar until meringue forms firm peaks. Beat 1 cup of the cream until stiff in a medium bowl.
7. Keeping gelatin mixture over ice, beat until smooth; fold in meringue, then whipped cream; continue folding until mixture mounds softly. Spoon into pastry shell. Chill several hours, or until firm.
8. Melt chocolate pieces with shortening in a cup over hot water; pour onto a foil-lined cookie sheet; spread into a rectangle 6x3 inches. Chill 15 minutes, or just until firm enough to cut. Using a truffle cutter or knife, cut chocolate into fan shapes; chill again until firm; peel off foil.
9. Just before serving, beat remaining 1 cup cream in a medium bowl until stiff. Spoon onto center of pie; trim with chocolate fans. 9-INCH PIE

FILBERT BLACK-TOP PIE

½ cup chopped filberts
1 cup graham cracker crumbs
3 tablespoons sugar
⅓ cup butter or margarine, melted
1 env. unflavored gelatin
¼ cup cold water
2 egg yolks
¼ cup sugar
1 teaspoon rum flavoring
1½ cups milk
2 egg whites
2 tablespoons sugar
Chocolate Icing, *below*

1. Mix filberts, crumbs, 3 tablespoons sugar, and butter; press firmly into a 9-inch pie pan.
2. Bake at 350°F for 12 minutes; cool.
3. Soften gelatin in cold water; dissolve over boiling water.
4. Beat egg yolks with ¼ cup sugar and rum flavoring until thick.
5. Gradually add milk, beating well. Continue beating while adding dissolved gelatin. Chill until mixture is partially set.
6. Beat egg whites until frothy; add 2 tablespoons sugar and beat until stiff peaks are formed.
7. Beat gelatin mixture until fluffy; fold into beaten egg whites. Turn filling into pie shell. Chill until firm.
8. Spread Chocolate Icing over top of pie. Sprinkle with *½ cup chopped toasted filberts*. Chill until icing is set. ONE 9-INCH PIE

CHOCOLATE ICING: Melt *½ cup semisweet chocolate pieces* in the top of a double boiler over hot water. Add *¼ cup confectioners' sugar, 1 tablespoon butter or margarine*, and *2 to 4 tablespoons cream*. Stir until smooth. ABOUT ⅔ CUP ICING

GRAPE CHIFFON PIE

1 env. unflavored gelatin
½ cup cold water
1 can (6 oz.) frozen grape juice concentrate, thawed
½ cup grapefruit juice
2 tablespoons sugar
Few grains salt
1½ cups chilled heavy cream
1 baked 8-in. pie shell

1. Soften gelatin in cold water; stir over low heat until gelatin is dissolved.
2. Remove from heat and blend in the concentrate. Stir in grapefruit juice, sugar, and salt until sugar is dissolved. Chill until slightly thickened.
3. Beat 1 cup cream until it piles softly. Spread whipped cream over gelatin and fold together. Turn filling into pie shell; chill until firm.
4. To serve, beat remaining cream to soft peaks. Pile lightly on top of pie and swirl gently with back of a spoon. ONE 8-INCH PIE

LIME CHIFFON PIE

1 env. unflavored gelatin	½ cup lime juice
¼ cup cold water	¼ teaspoon salt
4 egg yolks, slightly beaten	2 to 3 drops green food coloring
⅔ cup sugar	4 egg whites
2 teaspoons grated lime peel	½ cup sugar
	1 baked 9-in. pie shell

1. Soften gelatin in cold water; set aside.
2. Mix the egg yolks, sugar, lime peel and juice, and salt together in top of a double boiler. Cook over simmering water, stirring constantly, until mixture is slightly thickened.
3. Remove from water and blend in gelatin, stirring until gelatin is dissolved. Mix in the food coloring. Cool. Chill until mixture is partially set.
4. Beat egg whites until frothy; gradually add ½ cup sugar, beating constantly until stiff peaks are formed. Spread over gelatin mixture and fold together. Turn into pie shell. Chill until firm.
ONE 9-INCH PIE

LEMON CHIFFON PIE: Follow recipe for Lime Chiffon Pie. Substitute *lemon peel and juice* for lime peel and juice. Substitute *yellow food coloring* for green.

DAKKERI CHIFFON PIE: Follow recipe for Lime Chiffon Pie. Use an 8-inch pie pan. Decrease egg yolks and egg whites to 3. Blend ⅓ *cup light rum* into cooled gelatin mixture. Garnish with thin slices of *lime*.

ORANGE CHIFFON PIE: Follow recipe for Lime Chiffon Pie. Substitute *2 tablespoons lemon juice* for 2 tablespoons of the water. Substitute *orange peel and juice* for lime peel and juice. Omit food coloring.

ORANGE-BLOSSOM CHIFFON PIE

1 env. unflavored gelatin	1 cup chilled heavy cream
⅓ cup cold water	2 tablespoons confectioners' sugar
2 egg yolks	1 teaspoon vanilla extract
1 cup water	
¼ teaspoon salt	2 egg whites
1 can (6 oz.) frozen orange juice concentrate, partially thawed	¼ cup sugar
	1 baked 9-in. pie shell

1. Sprinkle gelatin over ⅓ cup water in top of a double boiler to soften. Beat egg yolks, 1 cup water, and salt together. Blend into gelatin. Cook over boiling water, stirring constantly, until gelatin is dissolved and mixture is slightly thickened, about 5 minutes.
2. Immediately remove from heat, add orange juice concentrate, and stir until blended. Chill, stirring occasionally, until mixture mounds when dropped from a spoon (or chill over ice and water, stirring frequently).
3. Meanwhile, whip cream until soft peaks are formed. With final few strokes, beat in confectioners' sugar and extract; set in the refrigerator.
4. Using a clean beater, beat egg whites until frothy. Gradually add sugar, continuing to beat until rounded peaks are formed. Fold in the gelatin mixture and then the whipped cream.
5. Turn into a baked pie shell. Using the back of a spoon swirl top. Chill thoroughly. Decorate with *orange sections* and *pastry cutouts*. ONE 9-INCH PIE

AVOCADO-ORANGE CHIFFON PIE

1 env. unflavored gelatin	1¼ cups orange juice
2 tablespoons cold water	⅓ cup sugar
2 tablespoons lemon juice	¼ teaspoon salt
	1 large ripe avocado
¼ teaspoon grated orange peel	1 cup heavy cream, whipped
	1 baked 9-in. pie shell

1. Soften gelatin in a mixture of the cold water and lemon juice; dissolve over hot water.
2. Mix together orange peel and juice, sugar, and salt until sugar is dissolved; blend in dissolved gelatin. Chill until slightly thickened.
3. Meanwhile, cut into halves, pit, and peel avocado; force enough avocado through sieve or food mill

PEACHY PARFAIT PIE

6 almond macaroon cookies (1¾ in. each)	2 tablespoons sugar
1¼ cups boiling water	Few drops almond extract
1 pkg. (3 oz.) lemon-flavored gelatin	⅔ cup (about 3 oz.) salted almonds, coarsely chopped
1 pt. vanilla ice cream	1 baked 9-in. pie shell, or Graham Cracker Crumb Crust, page 254
2 medium-sized (about ½ lb.) firm ripe peaches	

1. Place cookies on a baking sheet and heat in a 325°F oven 15 minutes, or until cookies are dry. Cool on a wire rack; then crush enough to make ½ cup crumbs.
2. Pour boiling water over gelatin in a large bowl; stir until gelatin is dissolved. Add ice cream by heaping spoonfuls, blending well after each addition. Chill about 15 minutes, or until mixture mounds when dropped from a spoon.
3. Meanwhile, dip peaches into boiling water, then into cold water; slip off skins. Halve the peaches and remove pits. Chop enough of the peaches to yield about 1 cup. Sprinkle with sugar, add extract, and mix lightly.
4. Blend cookie crumbs, almonds, and peaches into thickened gelatin mixture. Turn filling into pie shell. Chill until set, 45 to 60 minutes.

ONE 9-INCH PIE

PIE OF GOLD: Follow recipe for Peachy Parfait Pie. Omit cookies, almonds, peaches, sugar, and extract. Substitute *orange-flavored gelatin* for the lemon-flavored gelatin and *1 pint orange sherbet* for the ice cream. Mix *2 cups orange sections*, cut in pieces, and *½ cup flaked coconut* into thickened gelatin. Proceed as directed.

DOUBLE STRAWBERRY PARFAIT PIE: Follow recipe for Peachy Parfait Pie. Omit cookies, almonds, peaches, sugar, and extract. Substitute *1 pint strawberry ice cream* for the vanilla ice cream. Mix *2 cups fresh ripe strawberries*, cut in pieces, into thickened gelatin. Proceed as directed.

PRUNE CHIFFON PIE

Coffee-Coconut Pie Shell, *page 271*	1 env. unflavored gelatin
1 cup chopped plumped prunes*	½ cup packed light brown sugar
⅓ cup bottled prune juice	¼ cup sugar
2 tablespoons grated orange peel	½ teaspoon salt
3 eggs	1 cup dairy sour cream
	1 cup chilled heavy cream

1. Prepare pie shell; bake and set aside.
2. Combine chopped prunes, prune juice, and orange peel in a heavy saucepan; mix well.
3. Beat eggs; add a mixture of the gelatin, sugars, and salt and blend thoroughly. Stir in the sour cream, then combine with the prune mixture. Cook, stirring constantly, over medium heat until thickened, about 10 minutes. Cool to lukewarm.
4. Beat ½ cup cream until it piles softly. Fold into prune mixture. Turn filling into pie shell. Chill until firm.
5. Just before serving, beat remaining ½ cup cream. Decorate pie with the whipped cream, plumped *prune halves*, and *maraschino cherries*.

ONE 9-INCH PIE

*To plump dried prunes, steam them in a colander over a pan of boiling water for 30 minutes or until prunes are well plumped.

COFFEE-COCONUT PIE SHELL: Combine *1 can (3½ ounces) flaked coconut* and *1 cup double-strength coffee*; let stand 30 to 40 minutes. Drain coconut; spread on absorbent paper and pat dry. Spread *2 tablespoons softened butter or margarine* over a 9-inch pie pan; sprinkle coconut evenly over buttered surface and press against bottom and sides. Bake at 350°F 10 to 12 minutes, or until coconut is crisp.

ENGLISH TOFFEE PIE

2 teaspoons unflavored gelatin	1 teaspoon vanilla extract
¼ cup cold water	2 egg whites
1 cup chilled heavy cream	⅛ teaspoon salt
¼ cup confectioners' sugar	½ lb. English toffee, coarsely crushed (about 1⅔ cups)
	1 baked 8-in. pie shell

1. Soften gelatin in cold water; stir over low heat until gelatin is dissolved. Set aside.
2. Beat cream until frothy; gradually add gelatin, beating continually until cream piles softly. Beat in confectioners' sugar and extract and continue to beat until cream stands in peaks.
3. Beat egg whites and salt until stiff, not dry, peaks are formed. Spread over whipped cream, add crushed toffee, and fold together. Turn filling into pie shell. Chill until firm.　　ONE 8-INCH PIE

VOODOO PIE

The name of this pie acknowledges the West Indian source of its chocolate-and-lime flavor.

2 eggs	1 pint chocolate ice
½ cup sugar	cream, softened
1 cup heavy cream	1 baked 10-in Chocolate
⅓ to ½ cup lime juice	Cookie Crumb
1 tablespoon grated lime peel	Crust, page 254
1 or 2 drops green food coloring	Grated unsweetened chocolate

1. Beat eggs and sugar until thick and piled softly.
2. Stir in cream and lime juice and peel until well blended; tint pale green with food coloring. Turn into refrigerator tray; freeze until mushlike in consistency.
3. Beat until smooth and return to refrigerator tray. Freeze until almost firm.
4. Spread ice cream over bottom of pie shell; spoon lime mixture over ice cream. Garnish top of pie with grated chocolate. Freeze until firm.
　　ONE 10-INCH PIE

STRAWBERRY ICE-CREAM PIE

2 pints vanilla ice cream, slightly softened	2 drops red food coloring
1 baked 9- or 10-in. pie shell	2 egg whites
	¼ teaspoon salt
16 large marshmallows	¼ cup sugar
2 tablespoons crushed ripe strawberries	1 cup ripe strawberries, rinsed, hulled, and sliced
½ teaspoon vanilla extract	

1. Spoon ice cream into cooled pastry shell and spread evenly. Set in freezer until very firm.
2. Combine the marshmallows and crushed strawberries in a heavy saucepan. Set over low heat, folding until marshmallows are half melted. Remove from heat and continue folding until mixture is smooth and foamy. Blend in the extract and food coloring; set aside to cool.
3. Beat egg whites and salt until frothy; gradually add the sugar, beating constantly until stiff peaks form.
4. Combine meringue with marshmallow mixture, folding until evenly blended. Remove filled pastry shell from freezer; cover with sliced strawberries. Top with meringue, sealing to edges.
5. Place pie on a wooden board and set under broiler with top of meringue about 4 inches from source of heat until meringue is lightly browned. Serve immediately. Or, return to freezer until ready to serve.　　6 TO 8 SERVINGS

TARTS

CREAMY COCONUT PETAL TARTS

1 pkg. (3 oz.) lemon-flavored gelatin	½ cup coarsely chopped walnuts
¼ cup sugar	1¼ cups (about 3½ oz.) flaked coconut
1 cup boiling water	
1 can (8½ oz.) crushed pineapple, drained (reserve syrup)	1 cup heavy cream, whipped
	12 baked Rose Petal Tart Shells, page 253
¼ cup sliced maraschino cherries, well drained	

1. Combine the gelatin and sugar in a bowl; add the boiling water. Stir until gelatin is dissolved.
2. Measure the reserved pineapple syrup; if necessary add enough water to measure ½ cup liquid; stir into the gelatin.
3. Chill until mixture is slightly thickened, and then mix in the pineapple, cherries, walnuts, and coconut. Fold in whipped cream. Spoon filling into tart shells.
4. Chill until firm. Decorate with *maraschino cherries* (with stems).　　12 TARTS

Chapter 13

DESSERTS & DESSERT SAUCES

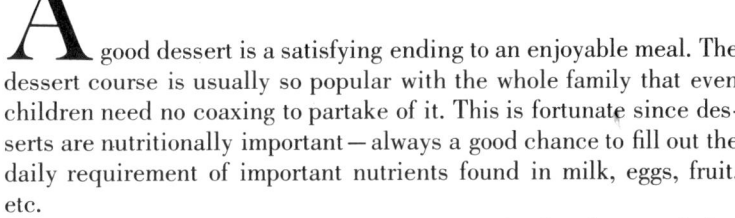

A good dessert is a satisfying ending to an enjoyable meal. The dessert course is usually so popular with the whole family that even children need no coaxing to partake of it. This is fortunate since desserts are nutritionally important — always a good chance to fill out the daily requirement of important nutrients found in milk, eggs, fruit, etc.

Following are desserts for every occasion; for luncheon and dinner menus, for the sole refreshment at a party, an afternoon tea or bridge game, a morning coffee, and numerous other occasions. Included are simple and elaborate desserts, light desserts to end hearty meals, and hearty desserts to conclude light meals.

Innumerable quick-and-easy packaged preparations are available to homemakers today. They include instant type gelatin desserts and puddings of many flavors, some requiring no cooking to thicken and others requiring a short cooking period after the addition of milk or other liquid. Canned, refrigerated, and frozen ready-to-serve puddings are available in a variety of flavors.

Cake Desserts

LUSCIOUS LEMON CHEESE CAKE

2⅔ cups zwieback crumbs (about 24 slices)
½ cup confectioners' sugar
1½ teaspoons grated lemon peel
½ cup butter or margarine, softened
2½ lbs. cream cheese, softened
1¾ cups sugar
3 tablespoons flour
1½ teaspoons grated lemon peel
½ teaspoon vanilla extract
4 eggs, slightly beaten
2 egg yolks
¼ cup heavy cream

1. Butter bottom and sides of a 9-inch springform pan.
2. Mix the crumbs, confectioners' sugar, and lemon peel in a bowl. Using a fork, mix in the butter. Reserve ¾ cup of the mixture for topping. Turn remainder into prepared pan; press crumbs firmly into an even layer on bottom and sides of pan. Set aside.
3. Combine the cream cheese, sugar, flour, lemon peel, and extract in a bowl. Beat until smooth and fluffy. Add the eggs and egg yolks in thirds, beating thoroughly after each addition. Blend in the cream.
4. Turn mixture into prepared crust, spreading evenly. Sprinkle reserved crumb mixture over top.
5. Bake at 250°F 2 hours. Turn off heat. Let cake stand in oven about 1 hour.
6. Remove to a wire rack to cool completely. Refrigerate several hours or overnight.
7. To serve, remove springform rim. Cut cake into wedges. ONE 9-INCH CHEESE CAKE

PURPLE PLUM COBBLER

2 cans (16 ozs. each) purple plums
2 tablespoons cornstarch
¼ teaspoon ground nutmeg
2 tablespoons butter or margarine
1½ cups sifted all-purpose flour
¼ cup sugar
3 teaspoons baking powder
¼ teaspoon salt
⅓ cup shortening
1 egg
½ cup milk
Light cream

Cake Desserts

1. Drain syrup from plums into a small bowl. Pit plums and place in a 2-quart shallow baking dish.
2. Mix cornstarch and nutmeg in a small saucepan; stir in plum syrup. Cook, stirring constantly, until mixture thickens and boils 1 minute; stir in butter until melted; pour over plums.
3. Preheat oven to 400°F. Place baking dish in oven to keep hot as oven preheats.
4. Sift flour, 2 tablespoons of the sugar, baking powder, and salt into a medium bowl; cut in shortening with a pastry blender until mixture forms fine crumbs.
5. Beat egg with milk until blended in a small bowl; add all at once to flour mixture; stir just until mixture is evenly moist. Drop by small spoonfuls over hot plum mixture to cover completely. Sprinkle remaining 2 tablespoons sugar over topping.
6. Bake 25 minutes, or until puffed and golden. Cool at least a half hour on a wire rack. Spoon into serving dishes; serve warm with cream. 6 SERVINGS

CHOCOLATE-MINT CHEESE CAKE

1 env. unflavored gelatin	¾ teaspoon peppermint extract
½ cup cold water	1 can (14½ oz.) evaporated milk
½ cup boiling water	
3 sq. (3 oz.) semisweet chocolate	1⅓ cups chocolate wafer crumbs (about 28 wafers)
8 oz. cream cheese	¼ cup butter, melted
1 cup sugar	3 tablespoons lemon juice
1½ teaspoons vanilla extract	

1. Soften gelatin in cold water in a bowl; add boiling water and stir until gelatin is completely dissolved. Set aside to cool.
2. Melt chocolate over hot water.
3. Meanwhile, cream the cream cheese, sugar, and extracts together. Blend in the melted chocolate. Add the gelatin gradually, blending thoroughly. Chill until mixture begins to gel.
4. Meanwhile, chill evaporated milk in a refrigerator tray in freezer until ice crystals begin to form around edge.
5. Mix wafer crumbs and melted butter.
6. Line the sides of a 9-inch springform pan with a double layer of waxed paper. Turn two-thirds of crumb mixture into the pan (remainder is for topping) and press into an even layer on bottom.
7. When chocolate mixture begins to gel, beat icy evaporated milk and lemon juice together until very stiff. Fold into chocolate mixture until thoroughly blended. Turn into the pan.
8. Sprinkle remaining crumbs in border around edge. Chill until set, 2 to 3 hours. 10 TO 12 SERVINGS

CHERRY CHEESECAKE

1½ cups graham-cracker crumbs	2 teaspoons grated lemon rind
⅓ cup melted butter or margarine	1 teaspoon vanilla
2 cups sugar	5 eggs
5 packages (8 ozs. each) cream cheese	2 egg yolks
	¼ cup whipping cream
3 tablespoons all-purpose flour	1 can (21 ozs.) cherry pie filling
	1 teaspoon grated orange rind

1. Blend graham-cracker crumbs with melted butter and ¼ cup of the sugar in a medium bowl; press over bottom of a 9-inch springform pan.
2. Preheat oven to 500°F.
3. Beat cream cheese until fluffy-light in a large bowl; beat in remaining 1¾ cups sugar, flour, lemon rind, and vanilla.
4. Beat in eggs and egg yolks, one at a time, until mixture is fluffy again; stir in cream. Pour into prepared pan.
5. Bake 10 minutes; lower oven temperature to 200°F. Bake 1 hour; turn off heat. Let cake stand in oven 2 to 3 hours, or until cool. Chill 4 hours, or overnight.
6. Loosen cake around edge in pan with a knife; release spring and carefully lift off side of pan. Place cake, on its metal base, on a serving plate.
7. Mix cherry pie filling and orange rind in a small bowl; spoon over top of cake. Chill until serving time. 12 SERVINGS

STRAWBERRY SHORTCAKE

1¾ cups all-purpose flour	½ teaspoon salt
	½ cup lard, chilled
2 tablespoons sugar	¾ cup milk
1 tablespoon baking powder	Sweetened sliced ripe strawberries

1. Blend the flour, sugar, baking powder, and salt in a bowl. Cut in the lard with a pastry blender or two knives until particles are about the size of coarse cornmeal. Make a well in the center and add

milk all at one time. Stir with a fork 20 to 30 strokes.
2. Turn dough out onto a lightly floured surface and shape it into a ball. Knead lightly with the fingertips about 15 times.
3. Divide dough into halves. Roll each half about ¼ inch thick to fit an 8-inch layer cake pan. Place one round of dough in pan and brush with *melted butter or margarine*. Cover with the other round. Brush top with *milk*.
4. Bake at 425°F 15 to 18 minutes, or until top is delicately browned.
5. Split shortcake while hot and spread with *butter or margarine*. Arrange half of the strawberry slices over bottom layer. Spoon *whipped dessert topping, dairy sour cream*, or *sweetened whipped cream* over berries. Cover with top layer and arrange remaining berries over it. Spoon additional topping over all. ABOUT 6 SERVINGS

NOTE: *Orange or lemon marmalade* or *strawberry jam* may be thinly spread over layers before adding strawberries and topping.

PEACH SHORTCAKE: Follow recipe for Strawberry Shortcake. Substitute sweetened *fresh peach slices* for strawberries.

SUNSHINE SHORTCAKE: Follow recipe for Strawberry Shortcake. Substitute *orange sections*, sliced *banana*, and *confectioners' sugar* for strawberries.

PLUM KUCHEN

2 cups sifted all-purpose flour	1 egg
3 teaspoons baking powder	¾ cup milk
½ teaspoon salt	2 lbs. plums, quartered and seeded (4 cups)
1 cup sugar	1 teaspoon ground cinnamon
½ cup butter or margarine	½ teaspoon ground nutmeg

1. Preheat oven to 400° F.
2. Sift flour, baking powder, salt, and ¼ cup of the sugar into a large bowl; cut in 6 tablespoons of the butter with a pastry blender until mixture forms fine crumbs.
3. Beat egg with milk in a small bowl; stir into flour mixture until well blended. Pour into a greased baking pan, 13x9x2 inches. Arrange plum quarters, overlapping, in rows on top. Melt remaining 2 tablespoons butter in a small skillet; drizzle over plums.
4. Mix remaining ¾ cup sugar, cinnamon, and nutmeg in a small bowl; sprinkle over plums.
5. Bake 40 minutes, or until plums are tender and a wooden pick inserted into center comes out clean. Cool at least 30 minutes in pan on a wire rack. Cut into squares; serve warm or cold, either plain or with soft vanilla ice cream if you like. 12 SERVINGS

CHANTILLY PEACH SHORTCAKE

1 ¼ cups sifted cake flour	¼ cup milk
1 teaspoon baking powder	1 teaspoon vanilla
¼ teaspoon salt	½ cup coarsely chopped California walnuts
½ cup butter or margarine	1 ½ cups whipping cream
1 ¼ cups granulated sugar	2 tablespoons confectioners' sugar
4 eggs, separated	
½ teaspoon almond extract	3 firm ripe peaches, peeled, pitted, and sliced

1. Preheat oven to 350°F. Grease two 8-inch round layer-cake pans; dust lightly with flour.
2. Sift flour, baking powder, and salt onto waxed paper.
3. Cream butter with ¾ cup of the granulated sugar in a medium bowl until fluffy-light; beat in egg yolks until fluffy again; stir in almond extract and milk. Stir in flour mixture, part at a time, until well blended. Spread batter evenly into prepared pans.
4. Beat egg whites in a medium bowl until foamy; beat in remaining ½ cup sugar, 1 tablespoon at a time, until meringue stands in firm peaks; beat in vanilla. Spread evenly over batter in pans; sprinkle walnuts over meringue.
5. Bake 35 minutes, or until golden. (Meringue will crack slightly during baking and seem to overflow pans, but will settle and smooth out as it cools.)
6. Cool layers 15 minutes in pans on wire racks. Loosen around edges with a knife; carefully turn out each layer onto the palm of one hand, then place, meringue side up, on racks; cool layers completely.
7. Just before serving, combine cream and confectioners' sugar in a medium bowl; beat until stiff. Place one cake layer on a serving plate; top with half of the cream and peaches, then second layer, rest of cream, and rest of peaches. To serve, cut into wedges.
8 TO 10 SERVINGS

MARBLE CHOCOLATE FREEZE

The irregularity of the cake slices creates a marbled effect in this dessert.

2 tablespoons cocoa	2 cups confectioners' sugar
1 pkg. angel food cake mix	6 egg yolks, well beaten
1 cup unsalted butter	3 oz. (3 sq.) unsweetened chocolate, melted and cooled
4 teaspoons vanilla extract	
	6 egg whites

1. Blend cocoa with flour portion of cake mix. Prepare, bake, and cool cake according to directions on package for a 10-inch tubed cake.
2. Cream butter with extract until butter is softened. Add confectioners' sugar gradually, beating constantly until light and fluffy. Add egg yolks in thirds, beating well after each addition. Blend in the cooled chocolate.
3. Beat egg whites until stiff, not dry, peaks are formed. Fold into chocolate mixture.
4. Slice the cooled cake into ½-inch wedges (measured at outer edge). Layer bottom of a 9x9x2-inch baking pan with a third of cake wedges.
5. Spread half of filling over cake. Repeat layers, ending with cake. Press lightly until top layer is even with edge of pan. Cover and freeze at least 8 hours.
6. Let stand at room temperature about 10 minutes before serving.   ABOUT 12 SERVINGS

Pastries

CREAM PUFF OR CHOUX PASTE
(Pâte à Choux)

Since this pastry puffs up in baking, it is used in many interesting ways by French pastry cooks. A popular use is for cream puffs and éclairs which are delightful in taste and appearance. These crisp, hollow shells also may be filled with a salad mixture or any hot, creamed food. To insure crispness, fill just before serving.

1 cup hot water	½ teaspoon salt
½ cup butter	1 cup all-purpose flour
1 tablespoon sugar	4 eggs

1. Put hot water, butter, sugar, and salt into a saucepan and bring to a rolling boil.
2. Add the flour all at one time. Beat vigorously with a wooden spoon until mixture leaves sides of pan and forms a smooth ball. Remove from heat.
3. Add eggs, one at a time, beating until smooth after each addition. Continue beating until mixture is thick and smooth.
4. Dough may be shaped and baked at once, or wrapped in waxed paper and stored in refrigerator overnight.
5. Complete as directed in any one of the following variations.   1 DOZEN LARGE OR 4 DOZEN MINIATURE PUFFS OR ÉCLAIRS

CREAM PUFFS (Choux à la Crème): Prepare recipe for Cream Puff or Choux Paste. Force dough through a pastry bag or drop by tablespoonfuls 2 inches apart onto a lightly greased baking sheet. Bake large puffs at 450°F 15 minutes; reduce oven temperature to 350°F and bake 20 to 25 minutes longer, or until golden in color. Bake small puffs at 450°F 10 minutes; reduce oven temperature to 350°F and bake 5 minutes longer, or until golden in color. Remove to rack and cool. Cut off tops of cream puffs, pull out any soft, moist dough, and fill shells with *French Pastry Cream*, or *Cocoa or Strawberry Filling, below.* Replace tops and sprinkle with *sifted confectioners' sugar.*

ÉCLAIRS (Éclairs de Crème au Chocolat): Follow recipe for Cream Puffs, forming dough into oblongs 1x4½ inches. When cool, cut a slit in the side of each éclair and pull out any soft, moist dough; force filling into éclair. Fill with *French Pastry Cream.* Frost with *Chocolate Glaze, below.*

Chocolate Glaze (Cooked): Melt *1 ounce (1 square) unsweetened chocolate.* Mix in heavy saucepan ¾ *cup confectioners' sugar, 1 teaspoon dark corn syrup, 1 tablespoon cream,* melted chocolate, *2 teaspoons boiling water,* and *1 teaspoon butter.* Place over low heat and stir constantly until butter melts. Remove from heat and add ½ *teaspoon vanilla extract.* Cool slightly. Spread evenly over tops of éclairs.

Chocolate Glaze (Uncooked): Blend *1½ cups confectioners' sugar* into *1 egg white.* Add ¾ *teaspoon vanilla extract* and *1½ ounces (1½ squares) unsweetened chocolate,* melted. Mix thoroughly and spread over tops of éclairs.

CREAM PUFF CHRISTMAS TREE: Prepare recipe for Cream Puff or Choux Paste. Force dough through a pastry bag and tube, or drop by spoonfuls 2 inches apart onto lightly greased baking sheets. Bake at 425°F 20 minutes, or until golden brown. Turn off oven. Prick puffs with a fork and return to oven for 20 minutes. Remove puffs to wire racks and cool completely. Cut off tops of puffs. Spoon about 3 tablespoons of *Custard Filling, page 278*, into each shell. Replace tops. On a serving plate, arrange puffs to form a tree. 18 TO 24 CREAM PUFFS

STRUDEL

4 cups sifted all-purpose flour	Lukewarm water (80° to 85°F)
1 egg, fork beaten	Melted butter
1 tablespoon melted butter	Flour
	Fine dry bread crumbs
1 tablespoon cider vinegar	Strudel Fillings, *below*

1. Put flour into a large bowl and make a well in center; add egg and butter. Put vinegar into a measuring cup and fill with lukewarm water to the 1-cup line. Gradually add to ingredients in bowl, mixing until all flour is moistened.
2. Turn dough onto a lightly floured pastry board and knead. Hold dough high above board and hit it hard against the board 100 to 125 times, or until dough is smooth and elastic and small bubbles appear on the surface. Knead dough occasionally during the hitting process. Shape dough into a smooth round ball and put onto a lightly floured board. Lightly brush top of dough with melted butter. Cover dough with an inverted bowl and allow to rest 30 minutes.
3. Cover a table (about 48x30 inches) with a clean cloth and sprinkle the cloth evenly with *½ cup flour*.
4. Place dough on center of cloth and sprinkle very lightly with flour. Roll dough into a rectangle ¼ to ⅛ inch thick.
5. Clench the fists, tucking the thumbs under the fingers. With the palm-side of fists down, reach under the dough to its center (dough will rest on back of hands). Being careful not to tear dough, stretch the center of the dough gently and steadily toward you as you slowly walk around the table. (Dough should not have any torn spots, if possible, but such perfection will come with practice.)
6. As the center becomes as thin as paper, concentrate the stretching motion closer to the edge of the dough. Continue until dough is as thin as tissue paper and hangs over edges of table. With kitchen shears, trim edges leaving about 2 inches of dough overhanging on all sides.
7. Allow stretched dough to dry about 5 minutes, or until it is no longer sticky. Avoid drying dough too long since it will become brittle.
8. Sprinkle melted butter and bread crumbs over dough. Cover dough with one of the *Strudel Fillings, below*.
9. Fold the overhanging dough on all sides over the filling, making strudel even with edge of table. Beginning at one narrow end of table, grasp the cloth with both hands; slowly lift cloth and fold over a strip of dough about 3 inches wide. Pull cloth toward you; again lift cloth and slowly and loosely roll dough, making roll about 3 inches wide. Brush off excess flour from the roll; cut roll into halves and place on a buttered 15x10x1-inch jelly roll pan. Brush top and sides with fork-beaten *egg*.
10. Bake at 350°F about 40 minutes, or until strudel is golden brown. Remove to wire rack. Sift *confectioners' sugar* over top of strudel. Cut into 2½-inch slices and serve warm or cooled.

1 DOZEN SLICES

Strudel Fillings

CHERRY FILLING: Drain *2 cans (20 ounces each) pitted tart red cherries*. Put cherries between layers of absorbent paper and pat gently to remove any excess liquid. Mix *¾ cup chopped toasted blanched almonds, 1 cup sugar*, and *½ teaspoon ground cinnamon*. Sprinkle prepared strudel dough with cherries and almond mixture.

POPPY SEED FILLING: Mix *½ pound freshly ground poppy seed, 1 cup sugar, ½ cup raisins*, and *2 teaspoons grated lemon peel* and spoon over prepared strudel dough.

APPLE AND CURRANT FILLING: Core and pare *1½ pounds tart apples*. Cut apples into ⅛-inch slices. Spoon apple slices and *½ cup currants or raisins* over prepared strudel dough. Sprinkle with a mixture of *¾ cup sugar, 1 teaspoon ground cinnamon, ⅛ teaspoon nutmeg*, and *1 teaspoon grated lemon or orange peel*.

COTTAGE CHEESE FILLING: Beat *2 egg yolks, ¼ cup sugar*, and *¼ teaspoon salt* until thick. Add *1 pound dry cottage cheese* gradually to egg mixture, beating well. Stir in *¼ cup raisins, ½ teaspoon vanilla extract*, and *½ teaspoon grated lemon peel*. Spoon filling in small mounds on prepared strudel dough; spread evenly, then roll as directed.

DRIED FRUIT FILLING: Mix *1 cup finely chopped dried apricots, 1 cup finely chopped prunes, 1 teaspoon grated orange peel, 2 tablespoons orange juice, ½ cup sugar*, and *2 tablespoons honey*, warmed. Spread over prepared strudel dough. Sprinkle *½ teaspoon ground nutmeg* before rolling.

CHOPPED NUT FILLING: Mix ½ *pound blanched almonds*, finely ground, *4 egg yolks*, *½ cup sugar*, and *1 teaspoon grated lemon peel* to form a paste. Spread in rows on prepared strudel dough. Drizzle with *¼ cup melted butter* before rolling.

RAISIN AND CHERRY FILLING: Mix *4 cups ground raisins*, *1 jar (8 ounce) maraschino cherries*, *4 cups chopped filberts*, *2 cups sugar*, *2 cups ground bread or cake crumbs*, and *¼ cup lemon juice.* Place on prepared strudel dough in rows fairly close together. Cut *Turkish paste* into small cubes and wedge into rows every few inches. (Or use *orange marmalade* and drop half teaspoonfuls into rows.) Roll as for other strudels. When cut, the colors of the paste or marmalade show through filling.

JELLY FILLING: Sprinkle prepared strudel dough generously with *cinnamon* and *sugar*. Mix *¾ cup chopped nuts*, *1 cup golden raisins*, *1 pint cherry, plum, or watermelon preserves*, *1 cup fine bread crumbs*, and *1 teaspoon grated lemon peel.* Place a row of filling on dough every few inches; roll.

MERINGUES

6 egg whites	1½ cups sugar
¼ teaspoon salt	Custard Filling, *below*
¾ teaspoon cream of tartar	Cherry-Cinnamon Sauce, *page 286*

1. Beat egg whites with salt and cream of tartar until frothy. Gradually add sugar, continuing to beat until stiff peaks are formed and sugar is dissolved.
2. Shape meringue shells with a spoon or force through a pastry bag and tube onto a baking sheet lined with unglazed paper.
3. Bake at 250°F 1 hour.
4. Transfer meringues from paper to wire racks to cool.
5. When ready to serve, spoon Custard Filling into meringue shells and top with Cherry-Cinnamon Sauce.   12 MERINGUE SHELLS

CUSTARD FILLING

½ cup sugar	6 egg yolks, beaten
2 teaspoons flour	1 teaspoon vanilla extract
¼ teaspoon salt	
2 cups milk	

1. Blend sugar, flour, and salt in a heavy saucepan. Stir in the milk. Bring to boiling; stir and cook 1 to 2 minutes.
2. Add a small amount of the hot mixture to egg yolks, stirring constantly. Blend into mixture in saucepan. Cook 1 minute.
3. Remove from heat and cool immediately by pouring custard into a chilled bowl and setting it in refrigerator or pan of cold water. Blend extract into cooled custard. Chill until serving time.
   ABOUT 2½ CUPS FILLING

CHOCOLATE MERINGUE SHELLS

4 egg whites	¼ teaspoon salt
¼ teaspoon cream of tartar	1 cup sugar
	¼ cup sifted cocoa

1. Lightly grease seven 4¼-inch tart pans. Flatten paper baking cups. Place one in each pan, pressing it to fit the pan. Set aside.
2. Beat the egg whites, cream of tartar, and salt until frothy; add gradually ½ cup of the sugar, beating constantly. Continue beating 5 minutes after the last addition.
3. Add remaining sugar gradually, beating constantly until very stiff peaks are formed. Quickly sprinkle cocoa over meringue and beat just until blended. (As the meringue tends to lose volume when the cocoa is added, it is important to incorporate the cocoa as quickly as possible.)
4. Spread meringue ¼ inch thick over the liner on bottoms of pans. Spread remaining meringue on sides of pans and ½ inch above rim; keep meringue within pan rim for ease of removal.
5. Bake at 250°F about 2 hours, or until shells are dry. To assure even drying of meringues, turn pans occasionally.
6. Remove from oven; cool completely on rack. (If the meringue shells are to be stored, keep them in an airtight container so that the meringue will not absorb moisture and become soft.) The shells should be crisp and dry and fine textured.
7. Remove cooled meringues from pans. Carefully peel off papers. Spoon desired cream filling or ice cream into shells just before serving.
   7 MERINGUE SHELLS

MERINGUE TORTE
(Schaumtorte)

6 egg whites (about ¾ cup)	½ teaspoon almond extract
2 teaspoons vinegar	¼ teaspoon salt
1 teaspoon vanilla extract	2 cups sugar

1. Grease bottoms only of two 9-inch layer cake pans with removable bottoms. (If using solid bottom pans, line with unglazed paper cut to fit bottoms.) Set aside.
2. Beat egg whites until frothy; beat in vinegar, extracts, and salt. Gradually add sugar, continuing to beat until stiff peaks are formed. Turn meringue into prepared pans and spread evenly to edges.
3. Bake at 300°F 40 minutes. Turn off oven, open oven door about 1 or 2 inches and allow torte layers to dry in oven 30 minutes.
4. Cool torte layers completely on wire racks before removing from pans. (It is likely that top surfaces may become slightly cracked when torte is being removed from pans.)
5. Fill layers with *Sweetened Whipped Cream, page 247* ONE 9-INCH TORTE

Custards & Puddings

FLOATING ISLAND

Soft Custard, *below*	⅛ teaspoon salt
Poached Meringues:	¼ teaspoon vanilla extract
2 cups milk or water	
2 egg whites	¼ cup sugar

1. Prepare Soft Custard, substituting *2 egg yolks* for 1 of the eggs. Pour custard into a serving bowl or individual dessert dishes; chill.
2. Scald milk or heat water to boiling in a large heavy skillet or saucepan.
3. Beat egg whites, salt, and extract until frothy; add sugar gradually, beating constantly until stiff peaks are formed.
4. Drop egg white mixture by tablespoonfuls, forming 8 mounds, onto scalding milk or boiling water. Cook, uncovered, over low heat about 5 minutes, or until "set."
5. Remove meringues with a slotted spoon to waxed or absorbent paper.
6. To serve, put poached meringues, "floating islands," onto chilled custard. If desired, top each meringue with a *strawberry* and accompany with additional strawberries. 4 SERVINGS

NOTE: If desired, poach the meringues in the scalded milk and use the milk for preparing custard.

SOFT CUSTARD

¼ cup sugar	2 cups milk, scalded
⅛ teaspoon salt	2 teaspoons vanilla extract
3 eggs, slightly beaten	

1. Add sugar and salt to beaten eggs and beat just until blended. Stirring constantly, gradually add scalded milk.
2. Strain mixture into a double-boiler top and cook, stirring constantly, over simmering water until custard coats a metal spoon.
3. Remove from heat and cool to lukewarm over cold water. Stir in extract. Chill. 4 SERVINGS

TRIFLE

Day-old pound cake (enough to line bottom of casserole)	5 egg yolks, slightly beaten
½ cup brandy or rum	½ cup sugar
1 env. unflavored gelatin	1½ cups milk, scalded
	3 egg whites
¼ cup cold water	¼ cup heavy cream, whipped

1. Cut the pound cake into 1-inch pieces. Arrange over bottom of a 2-quart shallow casserole. Pour brandy over cake pieces.
2. Soften gelatin in the cold water. Combine egg yolks with ¼ cup of the sugar in top of a double boiler. Add the scalded milk gradually, blending well. Cook over simmering water, stirring constantly until mixture coats a metal spoon. Immediately remove from heat and stir in gelatin until dissolved. Cool and chill until mixture becomes slightly thicker.
3. Beat the egg whites until frothy; gradually add the remaining ¼ cup sugar, beating constantly until stiff peaks are formed.
4. Spread egg whites and whipped cream over gelatin mixture and gently fold together. Turn into the casserole. Chill until firm.
5. When ready to serve, garnish with *candied cherries, slivered almonds*, and pieces of *angelica*. If desired, garnish with a border of *sweetened whipped cream* forced through a pastry bag and star decorating tube. ABOUT 12 SERVINGS

Custards & Puddings

PLANTATION PUDDING

2¼ cups sifted all-purpose flour
¾ cup firmly packed light brown sugar
1 teaspoon ground cinnamon
½ teaspoon ground nutmeg
¼ teaspoon salt
½ cup butter or margarine
1 cup light molasses
1 cup water
1 teaspoon baking soda
Lemon Sauce (recipe on page 302)
2 containers (4 ozs. each) whipped cream cheese
1 tablespoon granulated sugar

1. Preheat oven to 350°F.
2. Combine flour, brown sugar, cinnamon, nutmeg, and salt in a medium bowl; cut in butter with a pastry blender until mixture forms fine crumbs.
3. Mix molasses, water, and baking soda in a 1-quart measure.
4. Spread 1½ cups of the crumb mixture into a greased baking pan, 8x8x2 inches; pat down lightly to make an even layer. Drizzle half of the molasses mixture over top. Repeat layers, using two thirds of the remaining crumb mixture and all of the molasses mixture; sprinkle remaining crumb mixture on top.
5. Bake 45 minutes, or until a wooden pick inserted into center comes out clean. Cool pudding completely in pan.
6. Make Lemon Sauce and cool.
7. When ready to serve, mix cream cheese and granulated sugar in a bowl.
8. Cut pudding into squares; place in dessert dishes. Top each with a spoonful of cheese mixture; pour Lemon Sauce over top.   9 SERVINGS

rack to cool; chill thoroughly.
4. Before serving, sift brown sugar evenly over top. Place under broiler with top at least 5 inches from source of heat; broil until sugar is melted. Watch carefully so sugar will not burn.
5. Cool and refrigerate until ready to serve.
6. Serve plain or with *greengage plums* as an accompaniment.   ABOUT 6 SERVINGS

MAPLE FLAN

4 tablespoons maple-blended pancake syrup
5 eggs
⅔ cup sugar
1 teaspoon vanilla
3 cups milk, scalded

1. Preheat oven to 325°F.
2. Measure ½ tablespoon of the syrup into each of eight 6-oz. custard cups; tilt and turn cups until syrup coats sides.
3. Beat eggs in a medium bowl just until blended; stir in sugar and vanilla; slowly stir in scalded milk. Strain mixture and pour over syrup in cups. For easy handling, set cups in a baking pan, 13x9x2 inches; place pan on oven shelf. Pour very hot water into pan to within ½ inch of tops of cups.
4. Bake 40 minutes, or until a knife inserted into custard halfway between edge and center comes out clean. Remove cups from water; cool on a wire rack, then chill.
5. When ready to serve, run a knife around inside edges of cups to loosen custards; invert into serving dishes. Serve plain or with whipped cream if you like.
8 SERVINGS

CRÈME BRÛLÉE

4 egg yolks, slightly beaten
¼ cup sugar
2 cups heavy cream, scalded
2 teaspoons vanilla extract
½ cup firmly packed brown sugar

1. Combine egg yolks with sugar; blend thoroughly. Gradually add hot cream, stirring until sugar is dissolved. Strain into a 1-quart baking dish.
2. Blend in extract. Place baking dish in a shallow pan with hot water and bake at 325°F 50 minutes, or until a knife inserted in custard comes out clean.
3. Remove from oven and set baking dish on wire

CHOCOLATE CUSTARD

1 cup (6-oz. pkg.) semisweet chocolate pieces
3 tablespoons cream
3 cups milk
3 eggs
1 teaspoon vanilla extract
⅓ cup sugar
¼ teaspoon salt

1. Melt ⅔ cup of the chocolate pieces with the cream in the top of a double boiler over hot (not boiling) water. Stir until smooth; spoon about 1 tablespoon into each of 8 custard cups or 10 soufflé dishes. Spread evenly. Put cups into a shallow pan; set aside.
2. Scald milk. Melt remaining ⅓ cup chocolate

and, adding gradually, stir in scalded milk until blended.
3. Beat eggs, extract, sugar, and salt together. Gradually add milk mixture, stirring constantly. Pour into chocolate-lined cups.
4. Set pan with filled cups on oven rack and pour boiling water into pan to a depth of 1 inch.
5. Bake at 325°F about 25 minutes, or until a metal knife inserted halfway between center and edge of custard comes out clean.
6. Set cups on wire rack to cool slightly. Refrigerate and serve when thoroughly cooled. Unmold if desired. Garnish with *whipped cream rosettes*.

8 TO 10 SERVINGS

BRAZILIAN PUDIM MOKA WITH CHOCOLATE SAUCE

3 cups milk
1 cup cream
5 tablespoons instant coffee
2 teaspoons grated orange peel
4 eggs
1 egg yolk
½ cup sugar
½ teaspoon salt
1 teaspoon vanilla extract
Chocolate Sauce, 303
1 cup coarsely chopped Brazil nuts

1. Combine milk and cream in the top of a double boiler and heat over simmering water until scalded.
2. Add the instant coffee and orange peel and stir until the coffee is dissolved. Remove from simmering water and set aside to cool about 10 minutes.
3. Beat eggs and egg yolk slightly. Blend in sugar and salt.
4. Add coffee mixture gradually, stirring constantly; mix in extract. Strain through a fine sieve into eight 6-ounce custard cups. Sprinkle with *ground nutmeg*. Set cups in a pan of hot water.
5. Bake at 325°F 25 to 30 minutes, or until a knife inserted in center of custard comes out clean.
6. Cool and chill. To serve, invert each custard onto an individual serving plate. Pour Chocolate Sauce over top and sprinkle with Brazil nuts.

8 SERVINGS

LEMON SPONGE

1 cup sugar
3 tablespoons flour
Few grains salt
2 egg yolks, slightly beaten
2 teaspoons grated lemon peel
2 tablespoons lemon juice
1 tablespoon butter, melted
1 cup milk
2 egg whites

1. Combine the sugar, flour, and salt in a bowl; add a mixture of the beaten egg yolks, lemon peel and juice, and melted butter; mix well. Stir in the milk.
2. Beat egg whites until stiff, not dry, peaks are formed. Fold into first mixture. Pour into 6 custard cups.
3. Bake in a pan with hot water in a 350°F oven about 35 minutes, or until golden brown on top. Serve slightly warm.

6 SERVINGS

NOTE: If desired, this sponge may be turned into an unbaked 8-inch pie shell and baked at 350°F 35 to 40 minutes, or until filling is set.

BLUEBERRY-ORANGE PARFAITS

2 tablespoons cornstarch
1 cup sugar
¼ to ½ teaspoon salt
2 cups orange juice
2 eggs, beaten
¼ teaspoon grated lemon peel
½ teaspoon vanilla extract
2 tablespoons sugar
2 cups fresh blueberries, sorted and rinsed

1. Mix cornstarch, sugar, and salt in a double-boiler top. Add a small amount of the orange juice and blend until smooth. Stir in remaining orange juice. Bring to boiling over direct heat and cook, stirring constantly, 3 to 5 minutes. Remove from heat.
2. Immediately blend about 3 tablespoons of the hot mixture into the beaten eggs; stir egg mixture into the orange juice mixture.
3. Set over simmering water and cook 3 to 5 minutes, or until thickened, stirring constantly. Remove from water and cool. Stir in lemon peel and extract. Chill.
4. Meanwhile, sprinkle the 2 tablespoons sugar over blueberries and let stand at least 30 minutes.
5. Spoon alternate layers of orange mixture and blueberries into parfait glasses, beginning with a

layer of orange mixture and ending with blueberries. Top with *sweetened whipped cream.*

ABOUT 6 SERVINGS

LEMON STREUSEL BREAD PUDDING

10 small slices French bread, cut ½-inch thick
4 cups milk
¼ cup butter or margarine
4 eggs
½ cup sugar (for custard)
¼ teaspoon salt
¼ teaspoon ground nutmeg
2 teaspoons grated lemon rind
2 tablespoons sugar (for topping)

1. Preheat oven to 325°F.
2. Place 4 slices of the bread in a single layer in a 1½-quart shallow baking dish; overlap remaining slices on top.
3. Scald milk in a medium saucepan; stir in butter until melted.
4. Beat eggs slightly in a large bowl; stir in the ½ cup sugar, salt, and nutmeg, then slowly stir in hot milk mixture; pour over bread in dish.
5. Mix lemon rind and the 2 tablespoons sugar in a cup; sprinkle on top.
6. Place dish in a large shallow pan; pour boiling water into pan to a 1-inch depth.
7. Bake 35 minutes, or until almost set in center. Remove from water; cool on a wire rack. Serve warm, plain or with cream. 6 SERVINGS

COFFEE TAPIOCA PARFAIT

2 egg whites
¼ cup sugar
2 egg yolks, slightly beaten
3 cups milk
⅓ cup sugar
⅓ cup quick-cooking tapioca
2 tablespoons instant coffee
¼ teaspoon salt
1 teaspoon vanilla extract
Salted pecans or almonds, chopped
Whipped cream

1. Beat egg whites until frothy; gradually add ¼ cup sugar, beating until stiff peaks are formed.
2. Combine egg yolks with milk in a saucepan. Add ⅓ cup sugar, tapioca, instant coffee, and salt; mix well. Let stand 5 minutes.
3. Cook and stir over medium heat until mixture comes to a full boil; do not overcook.
4. Remove from heat and immediately stir a small amount of the hot mixture into egg white mixture.

Then quickly blend in the remaining hot mixture, extract, and nuts. Cool, stirring once after 15 minutes. Chill.
5. To complete parfait, spoon one third of the tapioca into bottom of chilled parfait glasses; spoon on a layer of whipped cream, sprinkle with *instant coffee*, then *shaved unsweetened chocolate, ground cinnamon*, and *grated orange peel*. Repeat layering two more times, ending with a swirl of whipped cream sprinkled with instant coffee, chocolate, cinnamon, and orange peel. ABOUT 8 SERVINGS

GLAMOUR PUDDING 'N' PEACHES

Plump, juicy peaches filled with fruit and nuts rest on beds of creamy pudding in this dessert.

1 pkg. vanilla pudding and pie filling mix
1½ cups milk
½ cup white grape juice
Chilled heavy cream, whipped to soft peaks and sweetened
1 can (29 oz.) cling peach halves, drained
½ cup chopped candied orange peel
2 tablespoons diced roasted almonds

1. Prepare pudding according to package directions using the 1½ cups milk.
2. Turn pudding into a bowl and cool slightly, stirring occasionally. Stirring constantly, gradually add grape juice to pudding. Fold in the desired amount of sweetened whipped cream.
3. Divide mixture equally among dessert dishes. Place a peach half, cut side up, in each.
4. Mix the remaining ingredients and spoon some onto each peach. Chill. 6 TO 8 SERVINGS

PEANUT ROCKY ROAD CUPS

1 can (18 ozs.) prepared chocolate pudding
3 tablespoons creamy peanut butter
1 container (4½ ozs.) frozen whipped topping, thawed
½ cup tiny marshmallows
Peanuts

1. Combine pudding and peanut butter in a medium bowl; beat until blended and smooth.
2. Set aside about ½ cup of the whipped topping for garnish; fold the rest into pudding mixture with marshmallows. Spoon into dessert dishes. Garnish each with a spoonful of remaining topping and several peanuts. Chill ½ hour, or until serving time. 6 SERVINGS

Custards & Puddings

APPLE CREAM

6 cups sliced apples (about 2 lbs.)
½ cup sugar
1 teaspoon ground cinnamon
1 teaspoon ground nutmeg
¼ cup butter
⅔ cup sugar
1 egg
½ cup flour
½ teaspoon baking powder
½ teaspoon salt
1 cup heavy cream

1. Toss the apple slices with a mixture of the ½ cup sugar, cinnamon, and nutmeg. Spread evenly in bottom of a buttered 9x9x2-inch baking dish.
2. Cream butter and ⅔ cup sugar together thoroughly. Add egg and continue beating until mixture is light and fluffy.
3. Blend flour, baking powder, and salt; beat into creamed mixture until just blended. Spread evenly over apples in baking dish.
4. Bake at 350°F 30 minutes. Remove from oven and pour cream evenly over surface. Return to oven and bake 10 minutes, or until topping is golden brown.
5. Serve warm with cream, if desired.

ABOUT 8 SERVINGS

CRANBERRY PUDDING WITH BUTTER SAUCE

1½ cups sifted all-purpose flour
¾ cup sugar
3 teaspoons baking powder
3 tablespoons butter, melted and cooled
1½ cups (about 6 oz.) fresh cranberries, rinsed and coarsely chopped
⅔ cup milk
Butter Sauce, *below*

1. Sift the flour, sugar, and baking powder into a bowl. Make a well in center and add the melted butter, cranberries, and milk. Stir just until dry ingredients are moistened.
2. Turn mixture into a greased 1-quart casserole.
3. Bake at 350°F 55 minutes. Serve warm with Butter Sauce. ABOUT 6 SERVINGS

BUTTER SAUCE: Melt *½ cup butter* in the top of a double boiler. Gradually add *2 cups sugar* and *¾ cup light cream*, stirring constantly. Place over simmering water and cook, stirring frequently, until sugar is completely dissolved, about 15 minutes. Serve with warm pudding. ABOUT 2 CUPS SAUCE

PEACHES 'N' CREAM KUCHEN

2 cups all-purpose flour
2 tablespoons sugar
½ teaspoon salt
¼ teaspoon baking powder
½ cup butter or margarine
9 fresh peach halves, peeled
¾ cup sugar
1 teaspoon ground cinnamon
2 egg yolks, slightly beaten
1 cup dairy sour cream

1. Combine the flour, 2 tablespoons sugar, salt, and baking powder in a bowl; mix well. Using a pastry blender or two knives, cut in butter until mixture resembles cornmeal.
2. Turn mixture into an 8x8x2-inch baking pan. Pat mixture evenly over bottom and halfway up sides of the pan.
3. Place peach halves, cut side up, in pan. Sprinkle a mixture of the ¾ cup sugar and cinnamon over the peaches.
4. Bake at 400°F 15 minutes. Combine the egg yolks and sour cream; mix thoroughly. Pour over peaches and bake 25 minutes longer. 6 SERVINGS

INDIAN PUDDING

One of many versions of an old New England pudding.

3 cups milk
½ cup yellow cornmeal
¼ cup sugar
1 teaspoon salt
1 teaspoon ground cinnamon
½ teaspoon ground ginger
1 egg, well beaten
½ cup molasses
2 tablespoons butter
1 cup cold milk

1. Scald the 3 cups milk in the top of a double boiler. Stirring constantly, slowly blend into milk a mixture of the cornmeal, sugar, salt, cinnamon, and ginger. Stir in a blend of the egg and molasses.
2. Cook and stir over boiling water 10 minutes, or until very thick. Beat in the butter.
3. Turn into a well-buttered 1½-quart casserole. Pour cold milk over top.
4. Bake at 300°F 2 hours, or until browned.

ABOUT 6 SERVINGS

PEACH TRIFLE

- 1 package (3 ⅛ ozs.) vanilla pudding and pie filling mix
- 2¼ cups milk
- ½ of a frozen 11-oz. plain poundcake, thawed
- 2 tablespoons dry white wine
- ¼ cup seedless raspberry preserves
- 1 can (16 ozs.) cling peach slices, drained
- ½ cup whipping cream
- 2 tablespoons toasted slivered almonds

1. Prepare pudding mix with milk as label directs; pour into a bowl. Press a sheet of transparent wrap directly onto pudding; chill until cold.
2. Cut poundcake into 4 slices; place on a cookie sheet. Drizzle wine over each, then spread preserves on top. Cut each crosswise into thirds.
3. Stand strips around edge in a deep glass serving bowl; spoon in pudding mixture. Arrange peach slices in a pretty pattern over pudding. Chill.
4. Beat cream until stiff in a small bowl; spoon over peaches; garnish cream with almonds.

6 SERVINGS

MILK CHOCOLATE SOUFFLÉ

- ¾ cup sugar
- 1 envelope unflavored gelatin
- ¾ cup water
- 1 package (6 ozs.) semisweet chocolate pieces
- 4 eggs, separated
- 2 tablespoons curacao
- 1 teaspoon vanilla
- 1½ cups whipping cream

1. Fold a 22-inch-long strip of regular foil in half lengthwise. Wrap around a straight-sided 1-quart dish to make a 2-inch stand-up collar; hold in place with cellophane tape.
2. Mix ¼ cup of the sugar and gelatin in the top of a double boiler; stir in water and chocolate pieces; place over simmering water. Heat, stirring constantly, until gelatin dissolves, chocolate melts, and mixture is smooth.
3. Beat egg yolks in a small bowl; slowly stir in a few spoonfuls of the hot chocolate mixture, then stir back into top of double boiler. Cook, stirring constantly, 3 minutes; remove from heat. Pour into a large bowl; stir in curaçao and vanilla. Place bowl in a pan of ice and water to speed setting. Chill, stirring several times, until mixture starts to thicken.
4. While chocolate mixture chills, beat egg whites in a medium bowl until foamy; slowly beat in remaining ½ cup sugar until meringue stands in firm peaks. Beat 1 cup of the cream in a medium bowl until stiff. Fold meringue, then whipped cream into thickened chocolate mixture until no streaks of white remain. Spoon into prepared dish. Chill at least 4 hours or overnight until firm.
5. Just before serving, beat remaining ½ cup cream in a small bowl until stiff. Carefully remove foil collar from soufflé; spoon cream in a ring on top. Garnish with maraschino cherry halves if you like.

6 SERVINGS

BLANCMANGE WITH ORANGE SAUCE

This glamorous dessert is one of Arlene Dahl's favorites.

- 1½ cups blanched almonds
- 2 cups water
- 1⅓ cups lump sugar
- 4 oranges
- 4 teaspoons unflavored gelatin
- ½ cup water
- 1 cup heavy cream, whipped
- 1 cup sugar
- ¾ cup water
- 4 teaspoons kirsch
- ½ cup apricot preserves

1. Chop almonds in a food chopper; continue crushing almonds in a mortar, gradually adding the 2 cups water. When completely crushed, press through a cheesecloth and squeeze out the liquid, about 1¾ cups. Set aside. Discard the almonds.
2. Rub sugar lumps over the surface of the oranges so that the orange peel flavor will be absorbed. Add to almond liquid and stir occasionally to dissolve.
3. Soften gelatin in ½ cup water in a saucepan. Stir over low heat until gelatin is dissolved. Add to the almond liquid-sugar mixture. Chill in refrigerator until mixture is slightly thickened, stirring occasionally.
4. Fold in the whipped cream. Turn into a 1-quart mold. Chill until firm.
5. Combine 1 cup sugar and ¾ cup water in a saucepan. Bring to boiling and boil 10 minutes. Remove from heat and stir in the kirsch.
6. Meanwhile, remove the peel from oranges and cut into natural sections. (Be sure all peel and

membrane have been removed.) Soak sections in the syrup about 1½ hours.
7. Unmold blancmange onto a chilled plate and garnish with flavored orange sections.
8. Heat the apricot preserves and strain. Spoon over the orange sections just before serving.

6 SERVINGS

SNOW PUDDING

1 env. unflavored gelatin	1¼ cups water
½ cup plus 2 tablespoons sugar	¼ cup strained lemon juice
⅛ teaspoon salt	3 egg whites

1. Mix the gelatin, sugar, and salt in a saucepan. Stir in the water. Stir over low heat until gelatin and sugar are dissolved. Remove from heat and stir in the lemon juice.
2. Chill until mixture is slightly thickened, stirring occasionally.
3. When gelatin is of desired consistency, beat egg whites until stiff, not dry, peaks are formed.
4. Beat gelatin mixture until frothy. Fold into the beaten egg whites. Turn into a 1½-quart fancy mold. Chill until firm, about 3 hours.
5. Unmold onto a chilled serving plate and serve with *lingonberries* or *Raspberry Sauce, page 304*.

ABOUT 6 SERVINGS

HONEYDEW CREAM

1 small honeydew melon	½ cup water
2 tablespoons lime juice	1 teaspoon grated lime rind
2 envelopes unflavored gelatin	1 container (4½ ozs.) frozen whipped topping, thawed
½ cup sugar	Green food coloring

1. Cut honeydew in half; scoop out seeds. Wrap half and chill for garnish. Pare remaining half; cut in small chunks.
2. Combine a few honeydew chunks with lime juice in an electric-blender container; cover. Beat until smooth. Add remaining chunks and beat to make 2½ cups purée.
3. Mix gelatin and sugar in a small saucepan; stir in water. Heat, stirring constantly, until gelatin dissolves; pour into a large bowl. Stir in the 2½ cups honeydew purée and lime rind. Chill at least 50 minutes, or until mixture is as thick as unbeaten egg white; beat until fluffy. Fold in whipped topping and a few drops food coloring to tint a delicate green. Spoon into a 1¼- or 1½-quart mold. Chill at least 4 hours, or until firm.
4. Just before serving, cut remaining honeydew into balls with a melon-ball cutter or ¼ teaspoon of a measuring spoon set.
5. Loosen dessert around edge with a knife; dip mold quickly in and out of warm water; invert onto a serving plate; lift off mold. Arrange honeydew balls in a ring around dessert. Garnish with a few sprigs of mint if you like.

6 SERVINGS

CREAMY CHERRY MOLD

1 can (29 oz.) pitted dark sweet cherries, drained (reserve syrup)	1 pkg. (3 oz.) cherry-flavored gelatin
	2 cups dairy sour cream

1. Add enough water to reserved cherry syrup to make 2 cups liquid. Heat 1 cup of the liquid to boiling and pour over the gelatin. Stir until dissolved. Stir in remaining liquid. Chill until mixture is slightly thickened, stirring occasionally.
2. Stir in the sour cream.
3. Halve the cherries and stir into gelatin mixture. Turn into a 1½-quart mold and chill until firm.
4. Unmold onto a chilled serving plate.

8 TO 10 SERVINGS

MOCHA-CARAMEL BAVARIAN

1 cup sugar	½ teaspoon vanilla extract
¾ cup boiling water	⅛ teaspoon salt
1 env. unflavored gelatin	1 cup undiluted evaporated milk, chilled and whipped
½ cup cold double-strength coffee	

1. Melt the sugar in a heavy light-colored skillet over low heat, gently moving it with wooden spoon toward center. Heat until golden brown.
2. Remove from heat and, stirring constantly, add the boiling water, a very small amount at a time. Return to low heat and continue stirring until bubbles are the size of dimes.
3. Meanwhile, soften gelatin in cold coffee. Gradually add the cooked syrup to the softened gelatin, stirring constantly; stir until gelatin is dissolved.
4. Stir the extract and salt into the gelatin mixture. Chill until mixture is slightly thickened, stir-

ring occasionally.
5. Gently fold whipped evaporated milk into chilled gelatin mixture. Turn into a 1-quart mold. Chill until firm.
6. Unmold onto a chilled serving plate or spoon into chilled sherbet glasses. 6 SERVINGS

LEMON EGG FLUFF

3 env. unflavored gelatin
½ cup sugar
Few grains salt
1 cup water
10 egg yolks, beaten

1 can (6 oz.) frozen lemonade concentrate, thawed
10 egg whites
½ cup sugar
Cherry-Cinnamon Sauce, *below*

1. Thoroughly blend gelatin, sugar, and salt in a heavy saucepan. Mix in water. Stir over low heat until gelatin is dissolved.
2. Gradually add a small amount of hot gelatin mixture to egg yolks, stirring constantly. Blend into mixture in saucepan; cook and stir 2 minutes without boiling.
3. Remove from heat. Stir in lemonade concentrate. Chill until mixture is slightly thickened.
4. Beat egg whites until frothy. Gradually add sugar, continuing to beat until stiff peaks are formed; fold in gelatin mixture. Turn into a 2½-quart tower mold and chill until firm.
5. Unmold onto a chilled serving plate and serve with Cherry-Cinnamon Sauce. 12 SERVINGS

CHERRY-CINNAMON SAUCE: Combine *½ cup sugar* and *2 tablespoons cornstarch* in a saucepan; mix thoroughly. Drain *1 can (about 16 ounces) tart red cherries*, reserving the liquid. Add cherry liquid and *3 tablespoons red cinnamon candies* to sugar mixture. Bring to boiling, stirring constantly; continue cooking until mixture is thickened and clear. Remove from heat. Stir in *1 tablespoon lemon juice* and the cherries. Cool. ABOUT 2¼ CUPS SAUCE

MELON-DUET MOLD

2 env. unflavored gelatin
⅓ cup sugar
¼ teaspoon salt
¾ cup chilled lemon-lime carbonated beverage

3 cups sieved watermelon (6 cups, diced)
⅓ cup lemon juice
2 cups cantaloupe balls
1 cup orange sections, cut in halves

1. Combine gelatin, sugar, and salt in a saucepan; mix in carbonated beverage. Stir over low heat until gelatin is dissolved.
2. Remove from heat and stir in sieved watermelon and lemon juice. Chill until mixture is slightly thickened, stirring often.
3. Stir in the cantaloupe balls and orange sections. Turn into a 5½-cup ring mold. Chill until firm.
4. Unmold onto a chilled serving plate. Fill center of mold with additional melon balls.
8 to 10 SERVINGS

CITRUS MOLD MARASCHINO

1 env. unflavored gelatin
1¼ cups cold water
½ cup quartered maraschino cherries
½ cup drained mandarin oranges
½ cup small seedless green grapes

3 env. unflavored gelatin
⅔ cup sugar
1 cup maraschino cherry syrup
⅔ cup grapefruit juice
⅔ cup lemon juice
⅔ cup orange juice
½ cup lime juice

1. Soften 1 envelope gelatin in ½ cup of the cold water in a small saucepan. Stir over low heat until gelatin is dissolved. Mix in remaining water and pour one half of the gelatin into a 2-quart charlotte mold or soufflé dish; chill until almost set, but not firm. Set remaining gelatin aside.
2. Lightly mark gelatin layer into quarters with a wooden pick. Arrange cherries in two opposite quarters, mandarin oranges in third, and grapes in fourth. Carefully pour remaining dissolved gelatin over fruits and chill until almost set, but not firm.
3. Meanwhile, combine 3 envelopes gelatin and the sugar in a saucepan. Mix well and stir in the remaining ingredients. Set over low heat until sugar and gelatin are dissolved, stirring constantly.
4. Turn into a bowl and set over ice and water, stirring frequently, until mixture is slightly thickened. Then beat with a hand rotary or electric beater until very light and fluffy.
5. Turn into mold, covering fruit layer. Chill until firm, about 3 hours.
6. Unmold onto a chilled serving plate. Garnish the plate with *stemmed maraschino cherries* and *green grapes*. If a glaze for cherries and grapes is desired, lightly brush each with *light corn syrup*.
8 TO 10 SERVINGS

MOLDED PINEAPPLE-COCONUT CREAM

1 can (8½ oz.) crushed pineapple, drained (reserve syrup)	2 teaspoons grated lime peel
1 pkg. (3 oz.) lime-flavored gelatin	½ cup lime juice
	1 pt. vanilla ice cream
	¾ cup flaked coconut

1. Add enough water to reserved pineapple syrup to make 1 cup liquid. Heat to boiling.
2. Mix gelatin and a *few grains salt* in a bowl. Add boiling liquid and stir until completely dissolved. Mix in lime peel and juice. Add ice cream by spoonfuls; blend until smooth. Chill until mixture is slightly thickened, stirring occasionally.
3. Mix in pineapple and coconut. Turn into a 5-cup mold. Cover; chill until firm, about 2 hours.
4. To serve, unmold onto a chilled plate and garnish with half slices of *lime*. ABOUT 8 SERVINGS

MOLDED RASPBERRY CRÈME

4 oz. (about 16) large marshmallows	1 cup boiling water
¼ cup grenadine	2 pkgs. (3 oz. each) raspberry-flavored gelatin
1⅓ cups dairy sour cream	1 cup cold water

1. Combine marshmallows and grenadine in the top of a double boiler. Heat over boiling water, stirring frequently, until marshmallows are melted. Remove from heat and blend in sour cream.
2. Pour boiling water over gelatin in a bowl, stirring until dissolved. Add the cold water.
3. Add gelatin slowly to sour cream mixture, stirring until well blended. Turn into a 1-quart mold or 6 individual tower molds. Chill until firm, about 3 hours.
4. To serve, unmold dessert and accompany with *a fresh red raspberry sauce*, if desired. 6 SERVINGS

ELEGANT STRAWBERRY CREAM

1½ tablespoons unflavored gelatin	½ teaspoon vanilla extract
¾ cup sugar	1 pkg. (16 oz.) frozen sliced strawberries, thawed
¼ teaspoon salt	
1 cup cream	
½ cup water	1 cup dairy sour cream

1. Mix the gelatin, sugar, and salt in a saucepan. Stir in the cream and water. Set over low heat and stir until sugar and gelatin are dissolved. Remove from heat and stir in the extract.
2. Cool slightly, then chill until mixture is slightly thickened, stirring occasionally.
3. Beat gelatin with hand rotary beater until light and fluffy. Add the strawberries and sour cream and stir lightly until blended. Turn into a 1-quart fancy mold and chill until firm.
4. Unmold dessert onto a chilled serving plate.
 ABOUT 6 SERVINGS

NOTE: *Frozen raspberries* may be substituted for strawberries, if desired.

Refrigerator Desserts

REGAL CHOCOLATE DESSERT

22 ladyfingers, split in halves	1½ teaspoons vanilla extract
3 oz. (3 sq.) unsweetened chocolate	2½ cups confectioners' sugar
⅓ cup sugar	6 egg whites
3 tablespoons water	⅓ cup sugar
6 egg yolks, well beaten	1 cup heavy cream, whipped
2 tablespoons light rum	
1½ cups unsalted butter	1 cup almond macaroon crumbs*

1. Line the bottom of a 9-inch springform pan with about 18 ladyfinger halves; set aside.
2. Combine the chocolate, ⅓ cup sugar, water, and a *few grains salt* in the top of a double boiler; heat over boiling water, stirring until smooth.
3. Stir about 3 tablespoons of the chocolate mixture into egg yolks. Immediately blend into mixture in double boiler top and cook over boiling water, stirring constantly, about 5 minutes. Remove from water and set aside to cool. Stir in the rum.
4. Cream the butter with the extract; add the confectioners' sugar, a small amount at a time, beating until light and fluffy after each addition. Blend in the chocolate mixture; set aside.
5. Beat egg whites until frothy; gradually add the remaining ⅓ cup sugar, beating constantly until stiff peaks are formed.
6. Fold whipped cream into chocolate mixture, then spread meringue over chocolate mixture; fold together. Fold in the macaroon crumbs.
7. Pour one half of the mixture into the springform pan over the layer of ladyfingers. Arrange 18 ladyfinger halves over the chocolate mixture and cover with remaining one half of mixture.
8. Chill until firm, 12 hours or overnight.

Refrigerator Desserts

9. Remove ring from springform pan and set cake on serving plate. Press remaining ladyfinger halves onto sides of mold. Garnish with *unsweetened whipped cream* and coarsely shredded *unsweetened chocolate*.

12 TO 16 SERVINGS

*If macaroons are moist, dry and toast them slightly in a 325°F oven before crushing.

CHOCOLATE REFRIGERATOR CAKE

4 oz. (4 sq.) unsweetened chocolate	1½ cups butter or margarine
½ cup sugar	¾ lb. confectioners' sugar (about 3 cups)
¼ cup water	
6 egg yolks, well beaten	18 ladyfingers, split
1 tablespoon vanilla extract	6 egg whites
	6 tablespoons sugar

1. Combine the chocolate, ½ cup sugar, and water in the top of a double boiler over boiling water. Cook and stir until mixture is smooth.
2. Stir about 3 tablespoons hot mixture into well-beaten egg yolks. Return to mixture in a double-boiler top. Cook and stir over boiling water about 5 minutes. Remove from heat and set aside to cool slightly. Stir in the extract.
3. Cream the butter with the confectioners' sugar until light and creamy. Beat in the chocolate mixture until thoroughly blended. Set aside.
4. Line the sides and bottom of a 9-inch springform pan with the ladyfingers; set aside.
5. Beat the egg whites until frothy; gradually add the 6 tablespoons sugar, beating constantly until stiff peaks are formed. Fold into the cooled chocolate mixture until evenly blended. Spoon into ladyfinger-lined pan. Chill at least 24 hours.
6. Serve with *whipped cream*.

ONE 9-INCH CAKE

DESIR DE LA POMPADOUR WITH ENGLISH CREAM

A recipe from Lasserre Restaurant, Paris, France.

30 ladyfingers	½ cup sieved apricot jam
2 egg yolks	
2 tablespoons sugar	⅓ cup toasted chopped almonds
½ cup butter, softened	
4 oz. (4 sq.) unsweetened chocolate, melted and cooled	English Cream, *next column*

1. Line the bottom of an 8-inch springform pan with 10 ladyfingers. Cut 10 ladyfingers in halves, crosswise, and arrange around side of pan; set aside.
2. Beat the egg yolks and sugar in a bowl until thick. Gradually blend in the butter, beating well. Blend in the melted chocolate.
3. Spread the chocolate mixture over the layer of ladyfingers. Arrange the remaining ladyfingers over the chocolate layer. Spread a thin layer of apricot jam over the top. Sprinkle with almonds. Chill 2 hours.
4. Serve in wedges topped with English Cream.

8 SERVINGS

ENGLISH CREAM

1⅓ cups milk	3 egg yolks, slightly beaten
1 piece (2 in.) vanilla bean, split lengthwise	6 tablespoons sugar
	2 tablespoons kirsch

1. Heat the milk with vanilla bean in a heavy saucepan until scalded. Set aside.
2. Blend the egg yolks and sugar in the top of a double boiler. Remove vanilla bean from milk and gradually add the milk to egg yolk mixture, stirring constantly.
3. Cook and stir over boiling water until mixture coats a metal spoon; do not overcook. Remove from boiling water and cool to lukewarm over cold water. Blend in the kirsch.
4. Set in the refrigerator until ready to serve.

ABOUT 1½ CUPS SAUCE

CRANBERRY CLOUD DESSERT

1 env. unflavored gelatin	3 tablespoons lemon juice
½ cup cold water	15 ladyfingers, split in halves
2 cups cranberries, finely chopped	1 can (14½ oz.) evaporated milk, chilled, *page 12*
1¼ cups sugar	
1 teaspoon grated lemon peel	1 tablespoon lemon juice

1. Soften gelatin in cold water in a saucepan. Stir over low heat until gelatin is dissolved.

2. Combine cranberries with the sugar, lemon peel, and 3 tablespoons lemon juice. Stir in the gelatin. Chill until mixture is thickened, but not set.
3. Meanwhile, arrange ladyfinger halves in bottom and around sides of a 9-inch springform pan.
4. Beat chilled evaporated milk until stiff; add 1 tablespoon lemon juice and beat until mixture is very stiff.
5. Blend cranberry-gelatin mixture into whipped evaporated milk, folding gently until blended. Turn filling into ladyfinger-lined pan.
6. Decorate top with green and red *maraschino cherry pieces* to form a wreath. Chill about 8 hours or overnight.   ABOUT 12 SERVINGS

LEMON BISQUE

The term "bisque" commonly refers to thick French soups, however it sometimes refers to creamy refrigerator or frozen desserts.

1¼ cups boiling water	3 tablespoons lemon juice
1 pkg. (3 oz.) lemon-flavored gelatin	1 can (14½ oz.) evaporated milk, chilled and whipped, *page 12*
⅓ cup honey	
⅛ teaspoon salt	
2 teaspoons grated lemon peel	2 cups crushed vanilla wafers (about ½ lb.)

1. Pour boiling water over gelatin in a bowl; stir until dissolved. Add honey, salt, and lemon peel and juice; cool. Chill until mixture is slightly thickened, stirring occasionally.
2. Add thickened gelatin to whipped evaporated milk and blend thoroughly.
3. Spread half of the crushed vanilla wafers in bottom of a 13x9x2-inch pan. Pour lemon mixture over crumbs and spread evenly. Top with remaining half of crumbs. Chill overnight.
4. Cut and serve with *sweetened whipped cream*.
   12 SERVINGS

CHARLOTTE À L'ORANGE

Ladyfingers decorate the edge and form the base for this orange chiffon dessert.

22 single ladyfingers	½ cup water
Chocolate Glaze, *below*	1 can (6 oz.) frozen orange juice concentrate, thawed
1 env. unflavored gelatin	
⅔ cup sugar	1 cup undiluted evaporated milk
⅛ teaspoon salt	

1. Line the bottom of a 9-inch pie pan with 5 ladyfingers. Dip remaining ladyfingers into the Chocolate Glaze to coat about one-fourth of each. Arrange chocolate-tipped ladyfingers around edge of pie pan. Drizzle half of remaining glaze over ladyfingers in pan. (Reserve rest of glaze for topping.) Set aside.
2. Combine gelatin, sugar, and salt in a saucepan. Stir in water. Set over low heat, stirring constantly, until gelatin is dissolved.
3. Remove from heat and blend in undiluted orange juice concentrate. Chill until mixture is slightly thickened, stirring occasionally.
4. Pour evaporated milk into a refrigerator tray and place in freezer until ice crystals form around edge. Turn into a chilled bowl and beat until very stiff; fold into gelatin.
5. Turn filling into the pie pan. Drizzle top with remaining Chocolate Glaze. Chill until firm, about 3 hours.   ONE 9-INCH PIE

CHOCOLATE GLAZE: Partially melt *2 ounces (2 squares) semisweet chocolate* and *2 tablespoons butter* over simmering water, being careful not to overheat. Remove from water and stir until chocolate is completely melted. Cool slightly.

PINEAPPLE REFRIGERATOR DESSERT

1 env. unflavored gelatin	2 cups heavy cream, whipped
1 can (20 oz.) crushed pineapple, drained (reserve syrup)	40 graham crackers
	¼ cup finely chopped crystallized ginger

1. Soften gelatin in ½ cup pineapple syrup in a saucepan. Stir over low heat until gelatin is dissolved. Blend into crushed pineapple. Chill until mixture is slightly thickened, stirring occasionally.
2. Fold half of the whipped cream into chilled gelatin mixture until evenly blended.
3. Spread a thin layer of the gelatin mixture on each graham cracker; turn crackers on end and press together to form a loaf.
4. Spread with remaining whipped cream; garnish with ginger. Chill about 3 hours.
5. To serve, cut into diagonal slices.
   ABOUT 10 SERVINGS

DANISH RASPBERRY PUDDING

2 pkgs. (10 oz. each) frozen raspberries	Peel of ½ lemon, cut in pieces
3 cups water	½ cup sugar
1 piece (3 in.) stick cinnamon	6 tablespoons cornstarch

1. Combine in a saucepan the raspberries, water, stick cinnamon, and lemon peel. Bring rapidly to boiling; break up block of frozen raspberries with a fork. Boil 5 minutes. Remove from heat. Strain, pressing out liquid. Return liquid to saucepan.
2. Mix the sugar with cornstarch. Blend in ½ *cup water*. Stir into raspberry liquid. Bring to boiling, stirring constantly. Boil 1 minute.
3. Pour mixture into a serving dish. Set aside to cool. Cover; chill thoroughly 3 to 4 hours.
4. Spoon chilled dessert into individual serving dishes and serve with *sugar* and *cream*.

ABOUT 10 SERVINGS

PASHKA
A traditional Russian Easter dessert.

2 pkgs. (8 oz. each) cream cheese, softened	1 tablespoon finely shredded orange peel
1 cup large-curd creamed cottage cheese	1 teaspoon vanilla extract
½ cup butter, softened	⅓ cup chopped candied red cherries
½ cup sugar	¼ cup golden raisins
1 tablespoon finely shredded lemon peel	2 tablespoons diced candied pineapple
	¼ cup chopped toasted almonds

1. Combine cheeses, butter, sugar, lemon and orange peels, and extract; beat until smooth. Mix in remaining ingredients.
2. With a moistened piece of cheesecloth, line a thoroughly cleaned flowerpot (5½ inches across top and 5½ inches high) having a drainage hole.
3. Spoon cheese mixture into flowerpot. Place pot on a rack in a shallow pan. Cover and chill overnight or longer, to allow flavors to blend.
4. Unmold and garnish with whole *candied cherries*.

10 TO 12 SERVINGS

HEAVENLY HASH PARFAITS

1 package (3 ozs.) cherry-flavored gelatin	1 can (8 ozs.) crushed pineapple in syrup, drained
1 cup boiling water	½ cup tiny marshmallows
¾ cup cold water	¼ cup chopped drained maraschino cherries
1 package (3⅝ ozs.) vanilla pudding and pie filling mix	½ cup cooked rice
1½ cups milk	1 cup thawed frozen whipped topping

1. Dissolve gelatin in boiling water in a medium bowl; stir in cold water. Pour into a shallow pan, 8x8x2 inches. Chill until firm.
2. Prepare pudding mix with milk as label directs; pour into a medium bowl; press a sheet of waxed paper directly onto surface of pudding. Chill until completely cold. Fold in remaining ingredients.
3. Rice gelatin mixture with a fork.
4. Spoon half of the pudding mixture into 8 parfait glasses to make a layer in each; spoon all of the gelatin on top; spoon rest of pudding mixture over gelatin. Chill until serving time.
5. Serve as is or garnish each parfait with more whipped topping and a maraschino cherry. 8 SERVINGS

AVOCADO MOUSSE

1½ cups mashed ripe avocado	8 drops green food coloring
1 teaspoon grated lemon peel	1 env. unflavored gelatin
2 tablespoons lemon juice	½ cup milk
2 tablespoons orange juice	¼ cup confectioners' sugar
¼ teaspoon salt	1½ cups heavy cream, whipped

1. Blend the avocado, lemon peel and juice, orange juice, salt, and food coloring; set aside.
2. Soften gelatin in milk in a small saucepan. Stir over low heat until dissolved. Blend into the avocado mixture. Chill about 45 minutes, or until mixture becomes slightly thicker.
3. Blend confectioners' sugar into whipped cream. Fold into the avocado mixture. Turn into a 5-cup fancy mold. Freeze until firm.
4. To serve, unmold on a chilled serving plate and allow to stand about 1 hour to soften slightly.

10 TO 12 SERVINGS

BEAU NASH DELIGHT

A recipe from the Pump Room of the Hotel Ambassador East, Chicago, Illinois.

6 oz. semisweet chocolate	½ cup hazelnuts (filberts)
1 cup egg yolks (about 12)	1 tablespoon kirsch
½ cup sugar	1 teaspoon vanilla extract
Pinch salt	Heavy cream, whipped (for decoration)
2 cups heavy cream, whipped	

1. Melt the chocolate in the top of a double boiler. Cool slightly and use it to line 6 to 10 paper baking cups, swirling the chocolate with a teaspoon to coat them evenly. Chill the cups until the chocolate is hard, then peel off the paper.
2. Beat egg yolks, sugar, and salt in top of a double boiler over hot water. Stir mixture constantly with wire whip until it is warm and very light. Cool over crushed ice, beating constantly.
3. Fold in the whipped cream, nuts, kirsch, and extract. Spoon mixture into the chocolate baskets. Place in freezer for several hours or until firm. To serve, top with whipped cream.   6 TO 10 SERVINGS

MACAROON MOUSSE

This towering Christmas dessert stands as its own monument to delicate, delectable flavor.

½ cup butter or margarine	1 teaspoon unflavored gelatin
1 teaspoon vanilla extract	¼ cup cold water
¾ cup sugar	1 cup icy cold water
4 eggs, well beaten	1 cup instant nonfat dry milk
1¾ cups fine almond macaroon crumbs*	2 tablespoons lemon juice

1. Cream butter with extract until softened. Gradually beat in the sugar until thoroughly blended. Add the eggs in thirds, beating thoroughly until light and fluffy.
2. Add the macaroon crumbs and beat at high speed with electric mixer about 5 minutes.
3. Soften gelatin in ¼ cup cold water. Stir over low heat until dissolved. Set aside to cool.
4. Mix the 1 cup cold water and dry milk in a bowl. Beat until soft peaks are formed, 3 to 4 minutes. Very gradually add the dissolved gelatin, beating constantly. Add the lemon juice and beat until stiff peaks are formed, 3 to 4 minutes.
5. Fold macaroon mixture into whipped milk and turn into a 1½-quart mold which has been rinsed with cold water. Freeze overnight or until firm.
6. Unmold onto a chilled serving plate and garnish plate as desired. Serve immediately.

8 TO 10 SERVINGS

*If macaroons are moist, dry and toast them slightly in a low oven before crushing. Crumbs may be prepared in an electric blender, crushing a portion at a time.

PARFAIT GRAND MARNIER

A recipe from Pavilion, Henry the Fourth, in Paris.

1½ cups sugar	2 tablespoons Grand Marnier
½ cup water	
6 egg yolks, beaten	1 cup heavy cream, whipped

1. Bring sugar and water to boiling in a saucepan; cook rapidly 5 minutes.
2. Gradually beat the syrup into egg yolks, using a hand rotary or electric beater. When thoroughly blended, return mixture to the saucepan. Simmer over low heat (do not boil), stirring constantly until thick and smooth.
3. Strain mixture through a fine sieve into a bowl. Place over cracked ice and stir until cold.
4. Blend in the Grand Marnier and fold in the whipped cream.
5. Turn mixture into a parfait mold, seal tightly, and freeze in a mixture of ice and salt for 2 to 3 hours.   ABOUT 6 SERVINGS

PEANUT BRITTLE MOUSSE

1 pkg. (10½ oz.) miniature marshmallows	¼ cup cold water
	1 egg white
	¾ cup crushed peanut brittle
1 cup milk	
½ cup strong coffee	1 cup heavy cream, whipped
1 teaspoon unflavored gelatin	

1. Combine marshmallows, milk, and coffee in top of a double boiler. Heat over boiling water until marshmallows are melted; stir occasionally.
2. Soften gelatin in water in a saucepan. Stir over low heat until gelatin is dissolved.

3. Remove marshmallow mixture from heat and stir in gelatin. Cool slightly and chill until slightly thickened, stirring occasionally.
4. Beat egg white until stiff, not dry, peaks are formed. Gently fold peanut brittle, beaten egg white, and whipped cream into marshmallow mixture. Turn into a 1½-quart mold rinsed with cold water.
5. Freeze until firm, but not solid. Before serving time, place mold in refrigerator 45 to 60 minutes to soften slightly. ABOUT 12 SERVINGS

NESSELRODE PUDDING

2 egg yolks
½ cup sugar
⅓ cup confectioners' sugar
1¼ teaspoons vanilla extract
1¾ cups heavy cream, whipped
2 egg whites
⅛ teaspoon salt
1 jar (10 oz.) Nesselrode mixture

1. Beat egg yolks with sugar until very thick.
2. Blend confectioners' sugar and extract into whipped cream.
3. Beat egg whites with salt until stiff, not dry, peaks are formed.
4. Blend Nesselrode mixture into egg yolk mixture. Spread whipped cream and egg whites over egg yolk mixture; gently fold together. Spoon into a 1½-quart mold or refrigerator trays. Freeze until firm.
5. If desired, garnish with *nut* and *maraschino cherry halves*. 8 SERVINGS

FROZEN DESSERT ROYALE

3 cups vanilla wafer crumbs (about 12 oz.)
6 tablespoons sugar
¾ cup butter, softened
2 tablespoons sugar
1 pt. fresh strawberries, rinsed, drained, and hulled
2 cups undiluted evaporated milk
1 pkg. (10½ oz.) miniature marshmallows
1 can (20 oz.) crushed pineapple, drained
2 cups small date pieces
2 cups chopped walnuts
1 can (6 oz.) frozen lemonade concentrate, thawed
1 tablespoon finely chopped crystallized ginger

1. Mix crumbs and 6 tablespoons sugar in a bowl. Blend in butter with a fork or pastry blender. Reserve ¾ cup crumb mixture for topping.
2. Using back of spoon, press crumb mixture firmly into an even layer on bottom and sides of a 9-inch springform pan.
3. Sprinkle 2 tablespoons sugar over strawberries in a bowl; set aside, stirring occasionally, until sugar is dissolved.
4. Combine evaporated milk and marshmallows in the top of a double boiler. Heat over boiling water, stirring occasionally, until marshmallows are just melted. Remove from water and cool completely.
5. Blend strawberries, drained pineapple, dates, walnuts, lemonade concentrate, and crystallized ginger into cooled marshmallow mixture.
6. Turn into crumb-lined pan. Sprinkle reserved crumb mixture evenly over top.
7. Freeze just until firm. ABOUT 12 SERVINGS

Ice Cream Desserts

BAKED ALASKA

1 qt. chocolate ice cream
1 qt. strawberry ice cream
Pound cake, sponge cake, or ladyfingers
5 egg whites
½ teaspoon vanilla extract
¼ teaspoon salt
¾ cup sugar

1. Line a chilled 2-quart melon mold with chocolate ice cream. Pack firmly against sides of mold. Fill center of mold with strawberry ice cream, packing firmly. Freeze until firm.
2. Cut a layer of cake about ¼ inch larger than mold and about 1¼ inches thick. Place on a wooden board or on a baking sheet lined with 2 sheets of heavy paper; set aside.
3. Beat egg whites with extract and salt until frothy; gradually add sugar, beating constantly until stiff peaks are formed.
4. Unmold ice cream onto center of cake. Working quickly, completely cover ice cream and cake with meringue, spreading evenly and being careful to completely seal bottom edge. With spatula, quickly swirl meringue into an attractive design and, if desired, garnish with *maraschino cherries*.
5. Set in a 450°F oven 4 to 5 minutes, or until meringue is lightly browned. Quickly slide onto a

chilled serving plate, slice and serve immediately. (If not ready to serve immediately, place baked Alaska in freezer so ice cream does not melt.)

12 to 16 SERVINGS

NOTE: If desired, a layer of *fresh fruit* (orange, mandarin orange, or grapefruit sections, sliced peaches, etc.) may be arranged over cake slice before unmolding ice cream over it.

BAKED ALASKA LOAF: Follow recipe for Baked Alaska. Substitute *1-quart brick ice cream* for molded ice cream. Cut cake about ¼ inch larger than mold on all sides.

INDIVIDUAL BAKED ALASKAS: Follow recipe for Baked Alaska. Decrease ice cream to 1½ pints chocolate, strawberry, or vanilla. Omit cake. Chill *8 canned pineapple slices.* Pat dry with absorbent paper and arrange on a thick wooden board. Quickly place 1 scoop of very firm ice cream in center of each slice. Completely cover ice cream with meringue, spreading evenly. Be careful to completely seal bottom edge to pineapple slice. Set in a 450°F oven about 4 minutes, or until meringue is lightly browned. Serve immediately. (Place in freezer if not ready to serve immediately.)   8 SERVINGS

FROZEN CHERRY EASTER EGG

This attractive mold should rate "four stars" for glamor appeal.

3 pts. vanilla ice cream, softened	3 tablespoons maraschino cherry syrup
1½ cups chopped candied red cherries	1 tablespoon vanilla extract
¾ cup chopped toasted filberts	1 env. (2 oz.) dessert topping mix, prepared according to pkg. directions
¼ cup finely chopped flaked coconut	

1. Mix into the softened ice cream the cherries, filberts, and coconut, then a blend of the syrup and extract. Pack mixture into a 1½-quart melon mold, which has been rinsed with cold water and drained. Cover and freeze until firm, about 3 hours.
2. Invert the mold on a chilled plate. Dip a clean towel in hot water, quickly wring it almost dry, and wrap it around the mold for a few seconds; lift off mold. If mold cannot be lifted off immediately, repeat. If necessary, set in freezer before frosting.
3. Frost the egg with the whipped dessert topping. Decorate, using a cake decorating set (aerosol cans of tinted frosting with decorating tips) or your favorite decorating frosting and pastry bag with decorating tubes. Pipe frosting onto frozen egg in an attractive design. Garnish with whole *candied red cherries.* Set in freezer until ready to serve.

10 TO 12 SERVINGS

CHERRY ALASKAS

1½ pints cherry-vanilla ice cream	6 packaged dessert shells
6 tablespoons cherry preserves	3 egg whites
	6 tablespoons sugar
	1 teaspoon vanilla

1. Scoop ice cream into 6 balls; place on a cookie sheet. Freeze several hours, or until very firm.
2. Spread 1 tablespoon of the cherry preserves on each dessert shell; place on a cookie sheet.
3. Preheat oven to 450°F.
4. Beat egg whites in a medium bowl until foamy; very slowly beat in sugar until meringue forms firm peaks; beat in vanilla.
5. Place an ice-cream ball on each dessert shell; quickly frost with meringue, spreading to bottom to seal in ice cream. (If kitchen is warm and ice cream starts to melt, return to freezer until firm again. Meringue-covered shells may also be placed in freezer until all are finished.)
6. Bake 4 minutes, or until meringue is tipped with gold. Place on dessert plates. Serve at once.

6 SERVINGS

Ice Creams, Sherbets, & Ices

PHILADELPHIA ICE CREAM

¾ cup sugar	1 teaspoon vanilla extract
⅛ teaspoon salt	
2 cups light cream, scalded	2 cups heavy cream, whipped

1. Stir the sugar and salt into the scalded cream; set aside to cool. Blend in the extract.
2. Pour mixture into refrigerator trays and freeze until mushy.
3. Remove from freezer and turn into a chilled large bowl. Beat with a rotary beater just until smooth. Fold in the whipped cream. Return to trays and freeze until firm, about 2 hours.

ABOUT 2 QUARTS ICE CREAM

STRAWBERRY ICE CREAM: Follow directions for

Philadelphia Ice Cream through step 2, omitting vanilla extract. Force *3 cups fresh strawberries* through a food mill; add ¾ *cup sugar* to pulp and let stand about 20 minutes. Stir into beaten mixture before final freezing.

BANANA-PECAN ICE CREAM

3 medium-sized firm ripe bananas	1 teaspoon vanilla extract
1 tablespoon lemon juice	2 egg whites
½ cup sugar	1 cup heavy cream, whipped
¼ teaspoon salt	½ cup chopped pecans
⅓ cup milk	
2 egg yolks	

1. Cut bananas into pieces and put into a blender container with lemon juice, sugar, salt, milk, egg yolks, and extract; blend until smooth.
2. Beat egg whites until stiff, not dry, peaks are formed. Fold whipped cream into egg whites and blend thoroughly. Stir in the banana mixture.
3. Turn into refrigerator trays; freeze until mixture begins to thicken, about 1½ hours (do not freeze solid).
4. Turn into a chilled bowl and beat until creamy and smooth. Stir in the pecans and return to trays. Freeze until firm, about 2 hours.

ABOUT 1 QUART ICE CREAM

HAITIAN ICE CREAM

2 cups milk	¼ teaspoon ground cloves
2 oz. (2 sq.) unsweetened chocolate	3 egg yolks, slightly beaten
1 cup sugar	2 cups cream
1 tablespoon flour	2 teaspoons vanilla extract
¼ teaspoon salt	

1. Combine milk and chocolate in top of a double boiler; heat over boiling water until milk is scalded and chocolate is melted.
2. Combine sugar, flour, salt, and cloves; add gradually to milk mixture, blending well. Cook and stir over direct heat 5 minutes.
3. Remove from heat and vigorously stir about 3 tablespoons of the hot mixture into the egg yolks; immediately stir into hot mixture. Cook over boiling water 10 minutes, stirring constantly, until mixture coats a metal spoon.
4. Remove from heat; cool. Stir in cream and extract. Pour into refrigerator trays and freeze until mushy.
5. Turn into a chilled bowl and beat with hand rotary or electric beater until smooth and creamy. Return mixture to trays and freeze until firm.

ABOUT 1½ QUARTS ICE CREAM

CHOCOLATE-MOCHA ICE CREAM

1 pkg. chocolate pudding and pie filling (instant or regular)	1 cup undiluted evaporated milk, chilled and whipped, *page 12*
½ cup dark corn syrup	½ cup chopped walnuts
½ teaspoon vanilla extract	

1. Prepare pudding according to directions on package, substituting ½ *cup double-strength coffee* for ½ cup of the milk. Add the corn syrup and extract to pudding and blend well.
2. Pour into refrigerator trays and freeze until mushy, about 1 hour.
3. Turn into a chilled bowl and beat until smooth. Fold in the whipped evaporated milk and walnuts.
4. Return to trays and freeze until firm, 3 to 4 hours, stirring several times.

ABOUT 1½ QUARTS ICE CREAM

FROZEN CRANBERRY CREAM

2 cups fresh cranberries, rinsed	Few grains ground cloves
½ cup water	Few grains ground nutmeg
1 cup sugar	1 cup heavy cream, whipped
⅛ teaspoon ground cinnamon	

1. Combine cranberries and water in a saucepan. Bring to boiling over medium heat and cook until skins pop. Force cranberries through a sieve or food mill.
2. Add the sugar, cinnamon, cloves, and nutmeg and stir until sugar is dissolved. Cool; chill about 1 hour.

3. Fold whipped cream into the cranberry mixture and turn into a refrigerator tray. Freeze until mixture is mushy.
4. Turn ice cream mixture into a chilled bowl and beat with a hand rotary or electric beater until smooth. Return to tray and freeze until firm.

ABOUT 1 QUART ICE CREAM

LEMON-CHEESE ICE CREAM

6 oz. cream cheese
2/3 cup sugar
2 cups cream
2 tablespoons lemon juice
1 teaspoon grated lemon peel
1/4 teaspoon vanilla extract

1. Using an electric beater, beat the cream cheese until softened. Gradually add the sugar, beating until fluffy.
2. Add cream slowly, mixing well. Beat in remaining ingredients until thoroughly mixed. Pour into a refrigerator tray and freeze until mushy.
3. Turn mixture into a chilled bowl and beat with a hand rotary or electric beater until smooth. Return to refrigerator tray and freeze until firm.

ABOUT 1 QUART ICE CREAM

PEACH ICE CREAM SUPERB

12 medium-sized (about 3 lbs.) fully ripe peaches, peeled and pitted
2¾ cups sugar
1 tablespoon lemon juice
1½ qts. chilled heavy cream
¼ teaspoon salt
1 teaspoon vanilla extract
1 teaspoon almond extract

1. Wash and scald cover, container, and dasher of a 4-quart ice cream freezer. Chill thoroughly.
2. Force peaches through a sieve or food mill. Stir the sugar and lemon juice into peaches and set aside 20 minutes.
3. Combine the cream, salt, and extracts; mix with peaches until blended.
4. Fill freezer container two thirds full with ice cream mixture. Cover tightly. Set in freezer tub. (For electric freezer, follow manufacturer's directions.)
5. Fill tub with alternate layers of 8 parts crushed ice and 1 part rock salt. Turn handle slowly 5 minutes. Add crushed ice and rock salt as necessary.
6. Wipe cover free of ice and salt. Remove dasher and pack down ice cream. Cover with moisture-vaporproof material. Replace cover and plug opening for dasher. Repack freezer with alternate layers of ice and salt, using 4 parts ice and 1 part rock salt. Cover with heavy paper or cloth. Let stand 2 to 3 hours to ripen.

ABOUT 3 QUARTS ICE CREAM

FRESH PURPLE PLUM ICE CREAM

This elegant ice cream will add a regal touch to many a commonplace luncheon or dinner.

24 fresh purple plums, pitted and quartered
1 cup sugar
½ cup light corn syrup
1½ cups water
2 teaspoons unflavored gelatin
⅓ cup cold water
2 tablespoons lemon juice
2 teaspoons vanilla extract
2 cups heavy cream, whipped

1. Mix the plums, sugar, corn syrup, and water in a saucepan. Simmer, uncovered, over low heat until fruit is very tender, about 25 minutes. Force plum mixture through a sieve or food mill.
2. Soften gelatin in the cold water. Immediately add gelatin to hot sieved mixture, stirring until completely dissolved. Blend in lemon juice. Chill until mixture is thick and syrupy.
3. Blend extract into whipped cream and fold into plum gelatin mixture. Pour into refrigerator trays and freeze until mushy.
4. Turn into a chilled bowl and beat until smooth; return to trays and freeze until firm.

ABOUT 2 QUARTS ICE CREAM

FROZEN STRAWBERRY CRÈME

1 cup sugar
4 egg yolks, slightly beaten
1 cup milk, scalded
2 cups crushed ripe strawberries, slightly sweetened
2 cups heavy cream, whipped to medium consistency
1 tablespoon lemon juice
½ teaspoon almond extract
Salted toasted almonds

1. Combine sugar with egg yolks and beat until thoroughly blended. Slowly add scalded milk, stirring constantly. Strain the mixture into a double-

boiler. Place over simmering water; stirring frequently, cook until mixture coats a metal spoon.
2. Remove from heat and chill immediately in ice and water, stirring the custard occasionally.
3. Add crushed berries to custard and fold in a blend of whipped cream, lemon juice, and extract.
4. Pour into refrigerator trays and set in freezer until mixture is partially frozen. Top with almonds and freeze until firm. ABOUT 1½ QUARTS CRÈME

CHOCOLATE-CHIPPED TORTONI

2 tablespoons sugar	1 egg white
1½ teaspoons vanilla extract	2 tablespoons sugar
½ cup almond macaroon crumbs*	3 oz. (½ cup) semisweet chocolate pieces
1 cup heavy cream, whipped	1 tablespoon vegetable shortening

1. Fold 2 tablespoons sugar, extract, and macaroon crumbs into the whipped cream until blended.
2. Beat egg white until frothy; gradually add 2 tablespoons sugar, beating constantly until stiff peaks are formed. Fold into whipped cream mixture. Turn into refrigerator tray and set in freezer until mixture begins to freeze, about 1 hour.
3. Place six 2-inch paper baking cups in muffin-pan wells.
4. About 20 minutes before removing mixture from freezer, melt chocolate pieces in the top of a double boiler over hot (not steaming) water. When melted, blend in the shortening.
5. Turn partially frozen mixture into a chilled bowl. Quickly crush and stir with a spoon until smooth but not melted. Stir constantly while pouring in a thin stream of melted chocolate. (The chocolate forms thin, firm pieces or "chips" as it is blended into the cold mixture.) Immediately spoon mixture into paper cups. Return to freezer and freeze until firm, about 2 hours.
6. Decorate with *whipped cream rosettes* or a border of *whipped cream*. 6 SERVINGS

*If macaroons are moist, dry and toast them slightly in 325°F oven before crushing.

LEMON SHERBET
Serve this versatile sherbet atop chilled fruit juice as a shrub, on individual fruit salads for a luncheon entrée, as an accompaniment for a main dish, or as a cooling dessert to end a warm weather meal.

| 2 cups sugar | ⅓ cup lemon juice |
| 1½ teaspoons grated lemon peel | 1 qt. milk |

1. Blend sugar and lemon peel and juice in a bowl. Add milk slowly, stirring until sugar is dissolved. Pour into two refrigerator trays, cover, and freeze until mixture becomes firm around edges.
2. Turn into a chilled bowl and beat until smooth. Return to trays and cover. Freeze until firm.
ABOUT 2½ PINTS SHERBET
NOTE: If desired, add a few drops of *yellow food coloring* to mixture before freezing.

PEACH-LIME SHERBET

1 can (29 oz.) cling peach slices	1 qt. milk
1½ to 2 cups sugar	Green food coloring (about 4 drops)
1½ teaspoons grated lime peel	1 cup chopped salted almonds or pecans
⅓ cup lime juice	

1. Using an electric blender, chop peaches in syrup.
2. Mix sugar and lime peel and juice. Add milk gradually, stirring until sugar is dissolved. Blend in the desired amount of food coloring. Mix in peaches and syrup.
3. Turn into refrigerator trays and set in freezer, stirring occasionally until partially frozen.
4. Press nuts onto surface. Freeze until firm.
ABOUT 2 QUARTS SHERBET

CRANBERRY ICE

4 cups (1 lb.) cranberries	1¾ cups water
2 cups water	½ cup orange juice
2 cups sugar	2 teaspoons grated lemon peel
2 teaspoons unflavored gelatin	¼ cup lemon juice

1. Rinse the cranberries (discarding imperfect berries) and drain. Cook in 2 cups water until skins pop. Force cranberries through a sieve or food mill.

Immediately stir a mixture of sugar and gelatin into hot pulp until sugar is dissolved.

2. Blend in remaining ingredients; pour into refrigerator tray. Freeze until mixture is firm, stirring several times.   1 QUART ICE

BOYSENBERRY ICE

2 cans (16 oz. each) boysenberries, drained (reserve syrup)
2 teaspoons unflavored gelatin
¼ cup sugar
¾ cup water
1 tablespoon lemon juice

1. Force drained boysenberries through a fine sieve; set aside.
2. Mix the gelatin and sugar in a saucepan. Stir in the water and set over low heat until gelatin and sugar are dissolved, stirring constantly.
3. Remove from heat and stir in 1½ cups of the reserved syrup, boysenberries, and lemon juice.
4. Pour into a 1-quart refrigerator tray and freeze until firm, stirring several times.
5. Serve in chilled sherbet glasses.

ABOUT 1 QUART ICE

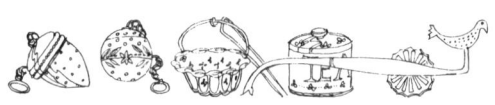

GREENGAGE PLUM ICE

2 teaspoons unflavored gelatin
½ cup sugar
⅛ teaspoon salt
1 cup water
2½ cups (20 oz. can) greengage plums and syrup
1 cup orange juice
2 tablespoons lemon juice
1 or 2 drops green food coloring

1. Combine the gelatin, sugar, and salt in a saucepan. Stir in the water and set over low heat until gelatin and sugar are dissolved, stirring constantly. Set aside to cool.
2. Cut plums into halves, pit, and force through a sieve or food mill (about 2¼ cups purée). Combine with cooled gelatin and the orange and lemon juices. Stir in the food coloring.
3. Pour into an 8-inch square pan and freeze until firm, stirring several times.   ABOUT 1 QUART ICE

Fruit Desserts

WENATCHEE VALLEY APPLE CRISP

5 large apples, pared, quartered, cored, and sliced thin (6 cups)
⅓ cup granulated sugar
½ cup instant nonfat dry milk
⅔ cup quick-cooking rolled oats
¼ cup firmly packed light brown sugar
¼ cup flaked coconut
2 tablespoons presweetened wheat germ
2 teaspoons sesame seeds
¼ cup sliced almonds
½ teaspoon ground cinnamon
¼ teaspoon ground nutmeg
4 tablespoons butter or margarine, melted
Vanilla ice cream

1. Preheat oven to 400°F.
2. Combine apple slices, granulated sugar, and nonfat dry milk in a large bowl; toss lightly to mix. Spoon into a shallow 1½-quart baking dish.
3. Combine rolled oats, brown sugar, coconut, wheat germ, sesame seeds, almonds, and spices in a medium bowl. Stir in melted butter until mixture is evenly moist; sprinkle evenly over apple mixture in dish.
4. Bake 30 minutes, or until apples are tender and topping is browned. Cool in dish on a wire rack at least 30 minutes.
5. Spoon into serving dishes; serve warm with ice cream.   6 SERVINGS

SWEDISH APPLECAKE WITH VANILLA SAUCE
(Äpplekaka med Vaniljsås)

13 rusks (4 oz.), finely crushed (about 2 cups crumbs)
¼ cup sugar
⅓ cup butter or margarine, melted
2½ cups thick applesauce
¼ cup butter or margarine
¼ cup confectioners' sugar
Vanilla Sauce, *next page*

1. Blend the crumbs and sugar in a bowl. Toss lightly with the melted butter until crumbs are evenly coated.
2. Generously grease a 1-quart casserole. Add one third of the crumbs and press them firmly into an even layer on bottom and sides of dish. Spoon one half of the applesauce into the dish. Dot with one half the remaining butter and sprinkle with one half the remaining crumbs. Repeat layering, ending with crumbs.

3. Bake at 350°F 30 to 40 minutes, or until crumbs are golden brown.
4. Cool completely and chill.
5. To form a design on top of cake, sift confectioners' sugar through a lacy paper doily placed on cake, then carefully lift off doily.   8 SERVINGS

VANILLA SAUCE: Cream ⅓ *cup butter or margarine* until softened; add ½ *cup sugar* gradually, beating thoroughly. Add *6 egg yolks* gradually, beating constantly until fluffy. Stir in ¾ *cup boiling water* very gradually. Pour mixture into the top of a double boiler. Cook over simmering water, stirring, until thickened. Blend in *1 teaspoon vanilla extract.* Cool; chill in refrigerator.   ABOUT 2 CUPS SAUCE

APPLE CHARLOTTE

6 thin slices white bread
½ cup butter, melted
2 tablespoons butter
6 large apples, quartered, cored, and pared
¼ cup sugar
2 tablespoons lemon juice
1 cup golden raisins
½ cup coarsely chopped pecans

1. Remove crusts from bread slices; cut each into 3 strips. Dip into melted butter; line bottom of a 1½-quart deep glass casserole or ovenproof bowl with strips, then arrange remaining strips upright around sides.
2. Heat the 2 tablespoons butter in a skillet; add the apples and cook until apples are tender but not mushy. Sprinkle with sugar and lemon juice. Lightly mix in raisins and pecans. Turn mixture into bread-lined casserole.
3. Bake at 350°F about 40 minutes, or until bread is golden brown.
6. Cool; unmold and serve with *whipped cream.*
   6 TO 8 SERVINGS

BANANAS FOSTER BRENNAN'S
A specialty of Brennan's in New Orleans.

1 tablespoon butter
2 teaspoons brown sugar
Dash ground cinnamon
1 firm ripe banana, cut crosswise in 4 pieces
2 tablespoons warm rum
1 teaspoon warm banana liqueur

1. Heat butter, brown sugar, and cinnamon in a chafing dish; add banana and sauté until tender.
2. Pour rum and banana liqueur over banana and flame the spirit.   1 SERVING

FRESH BLUEBERRY "COBBLER"

¾ cup firmly packed light brown sugar
3 tablespoons quick-cooking tapioca
¼ teaspoon salt
¼ teaspoon ground cinnamon
Few grains ground cloves
2 pts. fresh blueberries, rinsed and drained
1 tablespoon lemon juice
2 tablespoons butter or margarine
Pastry for 2-crust pie

1. Combine the brown sugar, tapioca, ¼ teaspoon salt, cinnamon, and cloves; mix well. Toss with blueberries until thoroughly mixed. Drizzle lemon juice over berries. Turn into a 10-inch plate. Dot with butter; set aside.
2. Prepare pastry. Shape into a ball and flatten on a lightly floured surface. Roll into a rectangle about ⅛ inch thick. Cut pastry diagonally into strips with a pastry wheel or knife, cutting one long strip 2 inches wide to use around edge of plate; cut remaining strips ½ inch wide.
3. Form a lattice design over berries. Arrange wider strip around edge so that it extends about ½ inch beyond rim of plate. Fold edge of wide strip under and flute pastry.
4. Bake at 425°F about 30 minutes, or until golden brown.
5. Serve warm or cool. If desired, garnish cobbler with additional fresh berries placed between lattice strips.   6 TO 8 SERVINGS

CHANTILLY CHERRY CUPS

1 carton (8 ozs.) whipped cream cheese
⅓ cup sifted confectioners' sugar
1 teaspoon vanilla
10 packaged dessert shells
1 cup flaked coconut
⅛ teaspoon almond extract
1 can (21 ozs.) cherry pie filling

1. Combine cream cheese, confectioners' sugar, and vanilla in a medium bowl; beat until smooth.
2. Spread around sides of dessert shells, using a generous 1½ tablespoons for each; roll shells in coconut on waxed paper; place on a tray or large flat plate.
3. Stir almond extract into cherry pie filling; spoon into shells. Chill.   10 SERVINGS

GRECIAN GLAZED ORANGES

Using a shredder, remove the peel from *oranges* (allow one per serving). Pour freshly *boiling water* over peel to cover, let stand 10 minutes, and drain. Repeat twice, being sure that the water is boiling each time it is poured over peel. Meanwhile, cut off and discard all the white underskin from oranges. Prepare a sugar syrup allowing for each orange *⅓ cup water* and *⅓ cup sugar*; boil for 10 minutes. Tint with a *few drops yellow or orange food coloring*. Pour boiling syrup over oranges; let stand about 15 minutes. Stir in the peel and pour over oranges; cool. Stack oranges pyramid fashion in a serving dish and pour syrup over them to glaze.

PEACHES WITH LIME CREAM

1 can (29 oz.) peach halves, drained (reserve ½ cup syrup)	2 tablespoons confectioners' sugar
⅓ cup firmly packed brown sugar	Few drops vanilla extract
Few grains salt	1 tablespoon lime juice
⅓ cup orange juice	½ cup heavy cream, whipped
2 tablespoons lime juice	1 teaspoon grated lime peel

1. Combine reserved peach syrup, brown sugar, salt, orange juice, and 2 tablespoons lime juice in a heavy skillet. Stirring constantly, cook over low heat until sugar is dissolved.
2. Add peach halves and simmer 15 minutes, turning peaches several times.
3. Blend confectioners' sugar, extract, and 1 tablespoon lime juice into whipped cream.
4. Spoon warm peaches and syrup into individual serving dishes. Top with the whipped cream and sprinkle with lime peel. ABOUT 6 SERVINGS

PEACHES 'N' CORNBREAD, SHORTCAKE STYLE

¾ cup plus 2 tablespoons all-purpose flour	1 egg, well beaten
½ teaspoon baking soda	½ cup buttermilk
¼ teaspoon salt	⅓ cup dairy sour cream
1 cup yellow cornmeal	Butter
¾ cup firmly packed light brown sugar	Sweetened fresh peach slices

1. Combine the flour, baking soda, salt, cornmeal, and brown sugar in a bowl; set aside.
2. Beat the egg, buttermilk, and sour cream together until well blended. Make a well in center of dry ingredients and add liquid all at one time. Stir until just smooth (do not overmix).
3. Turn into a greased (bottom only) 11x7x1½-inch pan and spread batter evenly to corners and sides of pan.
4. Bake at 425°F about 20 minutes, or until a cake tester or wooden pick inserted in center comes out clean.
5. While still warm, cut cornbread into serving-sized pieces, remove from pan, and split into two layers. Spread butter generously between layers. Top with peach slices. 9 TO 12 SERVINGS

PLUM COMPOTE

1 can (16 ozs.) orange and grapefruit sections in syrup	1 can (30 ozs.) purple plums in syrup
	⅓ cup sugar
	½ teaspoon mace

1. Drain syrup from orange and grapefruit sections into a 2-cup measure. Drain syrup from plums, adding enough to orange syrup to make 1¼ cups. Arrange fruits in a shallow serving bowl.
2. Combine the 1¼ cups syrup with sugar and mace in a small saucepan. Heat, stirring several times, to boiling; simmer 5 minutes; pour over fruits. Let stand ½ hour to season. Serve warm. 6 SERVINGS

PEAR BACON CRISP

6 cups sliced firm ripe pears	1 teaspoon ground cinnamon
2 tablespoons lemon juice	½ teaspoon ground nutmeg
½ cup flaked coconut	6 slices bacon, diced and fried until crisp (reserve 2 tablespoons drippings)
½ cup all-purpose flour	
¼ cup sugar	
¼ cup packed brown sugar	2 tablespoons butter or margarine
¼ teaspoon salt	

Fruit Desserts

1. Sprinkle pears with lemon juice. Toss with coconut. Put half of the pears into a greased 2-quart casserole.
2. Mix flour, sugars, salt, cinnamon, and nutmeg. Blend in reserved drippings and butter. Stir in bacon. Sprinkle half the mixture over pears, add remaining pears, and sprinkle with flour mixture.
3. Bake at 350°F 50 minutes, or until tender.
4. Garnish each serving with *flaked coconut*.

8 SERVINGS

PINEAPPLE WITH RUM CARAMEL SAUCE

3 tablespoons butter or margarine
1 can (20 oz.) pineapple slices, drained (reserve 1 tablespoon syrup)
¼ cup firmly packed light brown sugar
1 teaspoon lemon juice
1 tablespoon rum

1. Heat 2 tablespoons of the butter until foamy in a small saucepan. Stir in reserved pineapple syrup, brown sugar, and lemon juice. Cook 3 to 4 minutes, stirring constantly; remove from heat. Stir in the rum.
2. Meanwhile, heat remaining 1 tablespoon butter in a large skillet. Brown pineapple slices lightly on both sides.
3. Transfer slices to serving plates. Spoon rum caramel sauce over each.

5 SERVINGS

BAKED RHUBARB WITH PASTRY TOPPING

1½ lbs. tender pink rhubarb, cut in 1-in. pieces (about 6 cups)
1¼ to 1½ cups sugar
¾ teaspoon ground cinnamon
1½ teaspoons grated lemon peel
1 tablespoon lemon juice
Pastry Topping, *page 253*
2 tablespoons sugar
½ teaspoon ground cinnamon

1. Toss rhubarb with 1¼ to 1½ cups sugar, cinnamon, and lemon peel in a 1½-quart shallow baking dish. Drizzle with lemon juice.
2. Moisten rim of dish with cold water. Carefully place Pastry Topping over rhubarb and trim edge, allowing ½ inch to hang over. Fold edge under and press gently to seal. Flute edge. Sprinkle entire surface with a mixture of remaining ingredients.
3. Bake at 450°F 10 minutes; reduce temperature to 325°F and bake 15 minutes.
4. Serve warm with *whipped dessert topping*.

6 TO 8 SERVINGS

RHUBARB CRUNCH

1¼ lbs. rhubarb, trimmed and cut in ½-inch pieces (4 cups)
¾ cup sifted all-purpose flour
½ cup honey
¾ cup firmly packed light brown sugar
¾ cup cornflake crumbs
½ cup butter or margarine
Vanilla ice milk

1. Preheat oven to 350°F.
2. Combine rhubarb and ¼ cup of the flour in a medium bowl; toss to mix well; spoon into a 1½-quart shallow baking dish. Drizzle honey over top; cover.
3. Bake 25 minutes; uncover; stir well.
4. While rhubarb bakes, combine remaining ½ cup flour, brown sugar, and cornflake crumbs in a medium bowl; cut in butter with a pastry blender until fine crumbs form. Spoon evenly over hot rhubarb mixture.
5. Bake, uncovered, 30 minutes, or until topping is golden. Cool at least ½ hour on a wire rack. Spoon into serving dishes; top each serving with a spoonful of ice milk.

6 SERVINGS

PRUNE COBBLECAKE

2 cups sifted all-purpose flour
2 teaspoons baking powder
½ teaspoon salt
¾ cup milk
3 tablespoons butter or margarine
3 eggs
2 cups firmly packed light brown sugar
1 teaspoon vanilla
2 cups plain granola-type cereal
1 cup cut-up dried pitted prunes
1 teaspoon ground cinnamon
½ cup melted butter or margarine

1. Sift flour, baking powder, and salt onto waxed paper.
2. Scald milk with the 3 tablespoons butter in a small saucepan; set aside.
3. Beat eggs until fluffy and thick in a large bowl; slowly beat in 1½ cups of the brown sugar until mixture is fluffy again; beat in vanilla until blended.
4. Stir in flour mixture until blended, then scalded milk mixture. Pour into a greased baking pan, 13x9x2 inches.

5. Preheat oven to 350° F.
6. Mix cereal, remaining ½ cup brown sugar, prunes, and cinnamon in a medium bowl; drizzle melted butter over top; toss until well blended. Sprinkle over batter in pan.
7. Bake 35 minutes, or until golden and a wooden pick inserted into center comes out clean. Cool in pan on a wire rack. Serve warm or cold.   12 SERVINGS

GLAZED STRAWBERRY TART

A crown of glazed strawberries tops the creamy filling in this scrumptious tart.

Pastry for 1-crust 9-in. pie	½ teaspoon grated lemon peel
⅓ cup sugar	½ teaspoon vanilla extract
3 tablespoons cornstarch	¼ cup white grape juice
¼ teaspoon salt	2 pts. ripe strawberries, rinsed, hulled, and thoroughly dried
⅓ cup instant nonfat dry milk	
1½ cups milk	⅓ cup currant jelly
2 eggs, beaten	1 tablespoon sugar

1. Line tart or pie pan with pastry; bake and set aside on wire rack to cool completely.
2. Combine the ⅓ cup sugar with the cornstarch and salt in a heavy saucepan; mix well.
3. Blend the nonfat dry milk with the milk and stir into the cornstarch mixture until smooth. Bring mixture to boiling, stirring constantly; boil 2 to 3 minutes, continuing to stir.
4. Vigorously stir about 3 tablespoons of the hot mixture into the eggs; return to mixture in saucepan. Cook and stir over low heat about 3 minutes, or until very thick.
5. Remove from heat and stir in the lemon peel and extract. Cool slightly, then beat in the white grape juice with a hand rotary or electric beater until blended.
6. Spread the cooled filling in the baked shell and refrigerate until thoroughly chilled. Top with the strawberries; set aside.
7. Heat jelly until melted and continue to cook about 5 minutes. Spoon over strawberries on the tart filling. Just before serving, sprinkle remaining 1 tablespoon sugar over the tart.   ONE 9-INCH TART

GLAZED MIXED FRUIT

1 pkg. (about 12 oz.) mixed dried fruits	½ cup light corn syrup
	½ cup dark corn syrup
3 cups water	¼ teaspoon ground cinnamon
½ cup orange juice	
⅓ cup quick-cooking tapioca	¼ teaspoon ground nutmeg
2 tablespoons sugar	⅛ teaspoon salt

1. Combine fruit and water in a saucepan; bring to boiling and cook, uncovered, until fruit is tender. Remove from heat.
2. Remove fruit with a slotted spoon and arrange on a serving platter. Set aside.
3. Add orange juice to the cooking liquid in saucepan. Stir in a blend of tapioca and sugar. Set over low heat and bring to boiling; cook until mixture thickens and tapioca becomes transparent.
4. Stir in corn syrups and a mixture of the remaining ingredients; blend thoroughly. Remove the saucepan from heat and pour glaze over fruit. Let stand until glaze is set.
5. Serve in sauce dishes either warm or chilled and garnish with *whipped cream*, if desired.

ABOUT 8 SERVINGS

CANTALOUPE COUPE

3 small cantaloupes	3 tablespoons curacao
1 pint strawberries, hulled and cut in half	1 pint orange-pineapple ice cream
1 cup seedless green grapes	⅔ cup flaked coconut
	2 medium-sized firm ripe bananas
3 tablespoons sugar	

1. Cut cantaloupes in half crosswise; scoop out seeds. Cut fruit from rind in large pieces, leaving ¼-inch-thick shells. Turn shells upside down to drain, then wrap and chill.
2. Cut cantaloupe fruit into bite-sized pieces; combine with strawberries and grapes in a medium bowl. Sprinkle sugar and curaçao over top; toss lightly to mix; cover and chill.
3. Scoop ice cream into 6 small balls; roll each in coconut on waxed paper. Place on a plate and return to freezer.
4. When ready to serve, place each cantaloupe shell on a dessert plate. (If needed, trim a thin slice from rounded base so shell will sit flat on plate.)
5. Peel bananas and slice; stir into fruit mixture;

spoon into cantaloupe shells. Top each with an ice-cream ball.
6 SERVINGS

NOTE: To cut cantaloupe basket as pictured, draw a line around the middle of the whole melon with a knife point, or mark with wooden picks. Then make even sawtooth cuts into cantaloupe above and below line, cutting to center. Gently pull halves apart.

DESSERT SAUCES

VANILLA SAUCE

1 cup sugar
2 tablespoons cornstarch
¼ teaspoon salt
2 cups boiling water
¼ cup butter or margarine
2 teaspoons vanilla extract

1. Combine the sugar, cornstarch, and salt in a saucepan. Mix well and add boiling water gradually, stirring constantly. Continue to stir, bring to boiling and simmer 5 minutes.
2. Remove from heat and blend in butter and extract. Serve warm.
ABOUT 2 CUPS

LEMON SAUCE: Follow recipe for Vanilla Sauce. Substitute *3 tablespoons lemon juice* and *2 teaspoons grated lemon peel* for extract.

BRANDY SAUCE: Follow recipe for Lemon Sauce. Decrease lemon juice to 1 tablespoon and stir in *3 tablespoons brandy.*

GOLDEN SAUCE

This rich, delicately flavored sauce is delightful served over Snow Pudding, vanilla or chocolate pudding, steamed fruit pudding, or slices of cake.

3 tablespoons butter
¼ cup sugar
3 egg yolks, slightly beaten
⅓ cup boiling water
1 teaspoon vanilla extract

1. Cream the butter and beat in the sugar until fluffy. Gradually add the egg yolks, blending well. Very gradually add the boiling water while stirring. Turn mixture into the top of a double boiler; stir and cook over simmering water until thickened.
2. Remove from heat and blend in the extract. Cool; chill.
ABOUT 1 CUP

ALMOND BUTTERSCOTCH SAUCE

1¼ cups firmly packed light brown sugar
⅔ cup heavy cream
⅔ cup light corn syrup
¼ cup butter or margarine
⅛ teaspoon salt
½ cup toasted blanched almonds, chopped

1. Combine all ingredients except almonds in a 2-quart heavy saucepan; stir over low heat until sugar is dissolved and butter is melted. Increase heat to medium and bring to boiling; stir occasionally.
2. Set a candy thermometer in place. Cook without stirring until thermometer registers 226°F.
3. Remove from heat and cool slightly. Stir in the almonds. Serve warm.
ABOUT 2½ CUPS

NOTE: Sauce may be stored in a tightly covered container in the refrigerator and reheated before using.

LUSCIOUS BUTTERSCOTCH SAUCE

1 cup firmly packed light brown sugar
⅓ cup butter
⅓ cup cream
Few grains salt

1. Combine all ingredients in a small heavy saucepan; stir over low heat until sugar is dissolved.
2. Increase heat to medium and bring mixture to boiling, stirring occasionally. Boil 5 minutes without stirring. Serve warm.
ABOUT 1¼ CUPS SAUCE

SPICY CHERRY SAUCE
(Kirschsosse)

1 can (20 oz.) pitted tart red cherries (2½ cups)
2 whole cloves
3½ tablespoons corn syrup
4 teaspoons butter or margarine

1 piece (2 in.) stick
  cinnamon
4 teaspoons sugar
4 teaspoons cornstarch
¼ teaspoon salt
4 teaspoons cold water
1½ teaspoons lemon
  juice
¼ teaspoon almond
  extract
1 drop red food coloring

1. Combine cherries, cloves, and stick cinnamon in a covered saucepan. Cook 5 minutes. Remove from heat and discard spices. Force cherries through a sieve or food mill into a saucepan.
2. Combine the sugar, cornstarch, and salt in a small bowl. Blend in the water and corn syrup and stir into the hot cherry mixture. Bring rapidly to boiling; cook and stir about 3 minutes.
3. Remove from heat and stir in the remaining ingredients. Serve hot with steamed puddings.

ABOUT 1¾ CUPS

SEMISWEET CHOCOLATE SAUCE

2 oz. semisweet
  chocolate
½ cup butter
2 eggs, beaten
½ cup sugar

1. Melt chocolate and butter together in a heavy saucepan over low heat; stir occasionally.
2. Meanwhile, combine eggs and sugar in the top of a double boiler and cook over simmering water, stirring constantly until mixture is amber colored, about 10 minutes.
3. Slowly add egg mixture to chocolate mixture, stirring constantly until blended.
4. Cool, stirring occasionally, and chill.
5. Serve over *ice cream*.   ABOUT 1½ CUPS

NOTE: For a chocolate frosting or filling, blend *confectioners' sugar* into the sauce until of spreading consistency.

HOT FUDGE SAUCE

¼ cup butter or
  margarine
2 oz. (2 sq.) unsweet-
  ened chocolate
¾ cup sugar
¼ cup cocoa
½ cup undiluted
  evaporated milk
1 teaspoon vanilla
  extract
Few grains salt

1. Heat butter and chocolate together in a heavy saucepan or top of a double boiler over low heat until melted, stirring to blend.
2. Remove from heat and stir in a mixture of the sugar and cocoa.
3. Blend in the remaining ingredients and return saucepan to low heat (place double boiler top over boiling water) and cook until sauce is thickened; stir constantly.

1⅓ CUPS

CUSTARD SAUCE

⅓ cup sugar
1 teaspoon flour
⅛ teaspoon salt
2 eggs
1 egg yolk
1½ cups milk
1½ teaspoons vanilla
  extract

1. Combine sugar, flour, and salt in the top of a double boiler. Add the eggs and egg yolk; mix thoroughly. Blend in ¼ cup of the milk.
2. Heat remaining milk just until hot. Blend into mixture in double-boiler top. Stirring constantly, cook over simmering water until mixture coats a metal spoon, about 10 minutes.
3. Remove from water; stir in extract. Cool; chill at least 3 hours.   ABOUT 2 CUPS

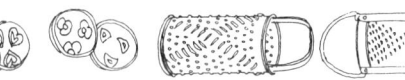

ZESTY LEMON SAUCE

½ cup butter
1 cup sugar
¼ cup water
1 egg, well beaten
3 tablespoons lemon
  juice
1 tablespoon grated
  lemon peel

Combine all ingredients in a saucepan. Cook over medium heat, stirring constantly, just until mixture comes to boiling. Remove from heat and serve warm.   ABOUT 1½ CUPS SAUCE

GRECIAN ORANGE SAUCE

6 oranges
Water
3 cups sugar
¼ cup currant jelly

1. Wash oranges; remove thin orange-colored top of the peel in small pieces with vegetable parer. Put peel in saucepan with *2 cups water*; bring to boiling. Boil 15 minutes; drain.

2. Cut oranges into eighths; reserve juice. Measure juice and add water, if necessary, to make 1 cup; combine in saucepan with sugar and jelly. Stir and bring to boiling; cook 25 minutes.
3. Add cooked peel and continue cooking until a candy thermometer registers 230°F.
4. Remove from heat and add orange sections. Cover and refrigerate at least 8 hours.
ABOUT 4 CUPS

PEANUT CRUNCH SAUCE

1 cup light corn syrup
½ cup crunchy peanut butter
¼ cup butter or margarine
1 teaspoon vanilla extract

Combine the corn syrup, peanut butter, and butter in a small heavy saucepan. Cook over low heat, stirring occasionally, until blended. Remove from heat and stir in extract. Serve hot. ABOUT 1¾ CUPS

FRESH RASPBERRY SAUCE

2 cups fresh raspberries, rinsed and thoroughly drained
½ cup sugar
1 tablespoon cold water
1½ teaspoons cornstarch

1. Force raspberries through a sieve into a small heavy saucepan. Blend in sugar.
2. Mix water into cornstarch to make a smooth paste. Thoroughly blend with berry mixture.
3. Stirring gently and constantly, bring rapidly to boiling. Continue to stir and boil about 3 minutes. Set aside to cool. Store in refrigerator. ABOUT 1 CUP
NOTE: For strawberry sauce, use rinsed and hulled *strawberries*.

ROSY GINGER SAUCE

Enhance sponge cake or ice cream with this quick sauce for a sophisticated spring dessert.

1 lb. fresh rhubarb
1 pt. fresh strawberries
½ cup sugar
2 teaspoons cornstarch
½ teaspoon ground allspice
½ cup sugar
2 tablespoons finely chopped preserved ginger

1. Cut rhubarb into ¾-inch slices (do not peel, if tender). Rinse and slice strawberries.
2. Combine rhubarb and ½ cup sugar in a heavy saucepan; cover tightly and cook until rhubarb is tender, about 5 minutes.
3. Meanwhile, mix together cornstarch, allspice, and remaining ½ cup sugar. Stirring constantly, gradually add to rhubarb and cook until mixture boils and thickens slightly.
4. Add strawberries and ginger. Cook 2 to 3 minutes, stirring occasionally. Cool. ABOUT 3 CUPS

FOAMY VANILLA SAUCE

¼ cup butter
1 teaspoon vanilla extract
1½ cups confectioners' sugar
2 egg whites

1. Cream butter with extract; add sugar gradually, beating until well blended.
2. Beat egg whites until stiff, not dry, peaks are formed; spread over butter-sugar mixture. Fold together until well blended. ABOUT 1½ CUPS

VANILLA HARD SAUCE

⅔ cup butter or margarine
2 teaspoons vanilla extract
2 cups confectioners' sugar
Few grains salt
2 teaspoons cream

1. Cream butter with extract. Add confectioners' sugar with salt gradually, beating until fluffy after each addition. Beat in the cream.
2. Chill until mixture is stiff enough to force through a pastry bag and tube. ABOUT 1⅓ CUPS
NOTE: If desired, press hard sauce evenly into an 8-inch square baking pan. Chill until firm and cut into fancy shapes.

ALMOND HARD SAUCE: Follow recipe for Vanilla Hard Sauce. Substitute ½ *teaspoon almond extract* for the vanilla extract and mix in ½ *cup finely chopped almonds*.

BRANDY HARD SAUCE: Follow recipe for Vanilla Hard Sauce. Substitute ¼ *cup brandy* for the vanilla extract. Increase confectioners' sugar if necessary and omit cream.

Chapter 14
COOKIES

The unknown person who originated the first cookies probably was unaware of the importance of her (or his) creation. Throughout the years this food item has had special appeal to people all around the world. It continues to be the perfect treat not only for children, but for the child in all of us that never grows up. On these pages are treasured recipes for all types of cookies, including the everyday variety appropriate for filling the cookie jar and the special-occasion type used for entertaining and for gifts.

BAR COOKIES

DUTCH ALMOND COOKIES

2 cups sifted all-purpose flour
1 teaspoon baking powder
¼ teaspoon salt
1 cup firmly packed dark brown sugar
½ teaspoon ground nutmeg
¼ teaspoon ground cinnamon
1 cup butter
½ cup milk
½ lb. blanched almonds, ground
1 cup sugar
1 tablespoon grated lemon peel
1 egg, slightly beaten

1. Blend flour, baking powder, salt, brown sugar, nutmeg, and cinnamon; cut in butter until particles are the size of rice kernels. Add milk and stir until blended.
2. Spoon half of mixture into an ungreased 11x7x1½-inch baking pan and spread evenly; set aside.
3. Mix remaining ingredients well. Turn mixture onto waxed paper and shape into an even layer the size of the pan. Invert over layer in pan and peel off paper. Spoon remaining mixture over almond layer and spread evenly.
4. Bake at 350°F 45 minutes.
5. Cut into bars while warm; cool completely before removing from pan.   ABOUT 2 DOZEN COOKIES

ARISTOCRATS
A distinctive pecan topping is the praise-winning feature of these apricot cookies of French origin.

¾ cup butter
1 teaspoon vanilla extract
⅔ cup sugar
1 egg
2 cups sifted cake flour
⅔ cup apricot preserves
Pecan Topping

1. Cream butter with extract; add sugar gradually, creaming until fluffy. Add egg and beat thoroughly.
2. Add flour in fourths, mixing until blended after each addition.
3. Turn dough into a lightly greased 11x7x1½-inch baking pan and spread evenly. Spread the apricot preserves over dough.
4. Bake at 350°F 20 to 25 minutes, or until edges are lightly browned. Remove pan to wire rack (do not remove cookie layer from pan).

Bar Cookies

5. Prepare Pecan Topping and spread evenly over cooled cookie layer. Chill 2 to 3 hours.
6. Cut into strips, about 2½x¾-inch. Place strips about ½ inch apart on cookie sheets.
7. Bake at 375°F 15 minutes, or until topping is delicately browned. ABOUT 4 DOZEN COOKIES

PECAN TOPPING: Beat *1 egg white* with ⅛ *teaspoon salt* until frothy. Add ⅔ *cup sugar* and *2 teaspoons flour* gradually, beating thoroughly after each addition. Beat until stiff peaks are formed. Fold in ⅔ *cup pecans*, finely chopped.

APRICOT SOURS

This cookie makes a delicious dessert when cut into large squares and topped with sweetened whipped cream.

⅔ cup butter, chilled
1½ cups sifted all-purpose flour
1 egg
½ cup firmly packed light brown sugar
¼ teaspoon vanilla extract
½ cup finely snipped apricots, cooked*
½ cup pecans, chopped
Lemon Glaze, *below*

1. Cut butter into flour until particles are the size of rice kernels. Press mixture evenly and firmly into a 13x9x2-inch baking pan.
2. Bake at 350°F 15 minutes.
3. Meanwhile, beat egg, brown sugar, and extract until thick; stir in a mixture of apricots and pecans.
4. Spread evenly over partially baked layer in pan.
5. Return to oven and bake about 20 minutes, or until lightly browned.
6. Remove from oven and immediately spread Lemon Glaze over top. When cool, cut into bars. ABOUT 4 DOZEN COOKIES

*Put snipped apricots into a heavy saucepan with a small amount of water (3 to 4 tablespoons). Cover tightly and cook over low heat about 10 minutes, or until apricots are soft and liquid is absorbed. Cool.

NOTE: If packaged dried apricots are extremely soft, it may not be necessary to cook the apricots.

LEMON GLAZE: Blend ¾ *cup confectioners' sugar* with *2 tablespoons lemon juice.*

CHEWY BUTTERSCOTCH BARS

Topping, *below*
1⅓ cups sifted cake flour
2 teaspoons baking powder
1 teaspoon salt
2 cups firmly packed brown sugar
½ cup corn oil
2 teaspoons vanilla extract
2 eggs
1 cup coarsely chopped pecans
1 cup flaked coconut

1. Prepare Topping; set over simmering water.
2. Sift flour, baking powder, and salt together; set aside.
3. Beat brown sugar, corn oil, and extract; add eggs, one at a time, beating thoroughly after each addition.
4. Stir in flour mixture until blended. Mix in pecans and coconut.
5. Turn into a well-greased 15x10x1-inch jelly roll pan and spread into corners. Drizzle hot topping over entire surface.
6. Bake at 350°F 30 minutes.
7. Cool 30 minutes in pan, cut into bars, and remove from pan. ABOUT 2½ DOZEN COOKIES

TOPPING: Blend ¾ *cup firmly packed brown sugar, 2 tablespoons butter, 3 tablespoons cream or evaporated milk,* and ¼ *cup dark corn syrup* in a saucepan. Cook over medium heat, stirring occasionally, to 234°F. Remove from heat; blend in *1 teaspoon vanilla extract.* ABOUT ⅔ CUP

FUDGY BROWNIES

Fudge Sauce, *below*
½ cup butter
1½ oz. (1½ sq.) unsweetened chocolate
2 eggs
1 cup sugar
¾ cup sifted all-purpose flour
½ teaspoon baking powder
⅛ teaspoon salt
¾ cup pecans, coarsely chopped

1. Prepare Fudge Sauce; set aside.
2. Melt butter and chocolate together; set aside to cool.
3. Beat eggs and sugar until thick and piled softly; add cooled chocolate mixture and beat until blended.
4. Sift together flour, baking powder, and salt; add in halves to chocolate mixture, mixing until blended after each addition.
5. Turn half of batter into a greased 9x9x2-inch baking pan and spread evenly.

6. Pour half of Fudge Sauce evenly over batter; remove remaining sauce from heat but allow to stand over hot water.
7. Spread remaining batter evenly over sauce.
8. Bake at 350°F 35 to 40 minutes.
9. Set on wire rack 5 minutes; top with remaining sauce; sprinkle with pecans.
10. Broil 4 inches from source of heat 1 to 2 minutes, or until entire top is bubbly; do not allow sauce to burn. Cool completely before cutting into squares. 3 DOZEN COOKIES

FUDGE SAUCE

1/3 cup undiluted evaporated milk	1 1/2 teaspoons butter
1/3 cup sugar	1/4 teaspoon vanilla extract
4 teaspoons water	1/8 teaspoon salt
1/2 oz. (1/2 sq.) unsweetened chocolate, grated	

1. Combine evaporated milk, sugar, and water in the top of a double boiler; stirring constantly, bring to boiling. Boil 3 minutes.
2. Remove from heat; blend in remaining ingredients.
3. Set over simmering water until needed.
ABOUT 1/2 CUP SAUCE

DOUBLE CHOCOLATE SQUARES: Follow recipe for Fudgy Brownies. Omit Fudge Sauce. Increase chocolate to 2 ounces (2 squares). After final addition of ingredients stir in pecans. Omit broiling; cool completely. If desired, spread with *Chocolate Glaze (Cooked)*, *page 276*, decreasing butter to 1 tablespoon; arrange pecan halves on top. Leave in pan until glaze has become firm.

LUXURY MALLOW-NUT BROWNIES: Follow recipe for Double Chocolate Squares. Omit Chocolate Glaze and pecan halves. Melt *12 ounces semisweet chocolate pieces* and *2 tablespoons butter*. Cut *12 marshmallows* into quarters (or use *1 1/3 cups miniature marshmallows*) and stir into melted chocolate with *1/2 cup coarsely chopped salted nuts*, such as pecans, pistachios, filberts, or almonds. Immediately spread over the baked brownies; cool.

SOUTHERN BROWNIES

Mrs. Andy Griffith, wife of the well known TV star, contributed this recipe.

3 tablespoons shortening	1 teaspoon vanilla extract
2 oz. (2 sq.) unsweetened chocolate	1 cup sugar
2 egg yolks, well beaten	1/2 cup all-purpose flour
	1/2 cup chopped nuts
	2 egg whites

1. Melt shortening and chocolate together in a large saucepan; cool.
2. Stir in egg yolks, then extract, sugar, flour, and nuts.
3. Beat egg whites until stiff, not dry, peaks are formed. Blend into chocolate mixture.
4. Spread batter in a well-greased 8x8x2-inch pan.
5. Bake at 350°F 30 minutes, or until a wooden pick comes out clean.
6. Cool completely before cutting.
ABOUT 2 DOZEN COOKIES

SURPRISE BARS

A crunchy, nutty-rich top layer disguises a delectable bottom layer . . . the surprise element of this cookie bar.

1 oz. (1 sq.) unsweetened chocolate	1/2 cup sugar
1/2 cup graham cracker crumbs	1 egg
2 tablespoons butter, melted	3/4 cup sifted all-purpose flour
1/2 cup butter or margarine	1/8 teaspoon baking soda
1/2 teaspoon vanilla extract	1/8 teaspoon salt
	1/4 cup dairy sour cream
	3/4 cup walnuts, coarsely chopped

1. Melt chocolate and set aside to cool.
2. Blend crumbs and melted butter; set aside.
3. Cream the 1/2 cup butter with the extract; add sugar gradually, beating until fluffy. Add egg and beat thoroughly.
4. Sift flour, baking soda, and salt together; add alternately to creamed mixture with sour cream, mixing until blended after each addition.
5. Divide mixture in half; blend cooled chocolate into one portion.
6. Turn chocolate mixture into a greased 8x8x2-inch baking pan and spread evenly. Cover with the crumbs and press lightly.
7. Stir walnuts into remaining portion; drop by spoonfuls over crumbs and carefully spread evenly.
8. Bake at 375° 25 to 30 minutes.
9. While warm, cut into bars. 2 1/2 DOZEN COOKIES

GRAHAM SENSATIONS

1¼ cups graham cracker crumbs
¼ cup sifted all-purpose flour
¼ teaspoon salt
1 can (14 oz.) sweetened condensed milk
¾ teaspoon vanilla extract
½ teaspoon grated lemon peel
½ cup flaked coconut
¾ cup coarsely chopped pecans
½ cup semisweet chocolate pieces

1. Blend crumbs, flour, and salt. Add condensed milk, extract, and lemon peel; mix well. Stir in remaining ingredients. Turn into a greased 13x9x2-inch baking pan and spread evenly.
2. Bake at 325°F 30 minutes.
3. While warm, cut into bars.

About 4 dozen cookies

FRUITY POLISH MAZUREK

Delightful small colorful cookie squares—fruity, nutty, and chock-full of wonderful citrus flavor.

2 cups sifted all-purpose flour
1 cup sugar
½ teaspoon salt
½ cup butter or margarine
1 egg
¼ cup cream
1⅔ cups seedless raisins, chopped
1½ cups pitted dates, chopped
1¼ cups dried figs, chopped
1 cup chopped walnuts
⅓ cup sugar
2 eggs
½ cup orange juice
3 tablespoons lemon juice

1. Sift flour, 1 cup sugar, and salt together into a bowl. Cut in butter.
2. Beat egg and cream together and add to flour mixture. Mix lightly with a fork until mixture forms a ball.
3. Spread dough in a greased 15x10x1-inch jelly roll pan.
4. Bake at 350°F about 30 minutes, or until dough is lightly browned around edges.
5. Meanwhile, prepare fruit topping by combining the chopped fruits and walnuts with a mixture of the ⅓ cup sugar, 2 eggs, and fruit juices; mix thoroughly. Spread over partially baked dough in pan.
6. Return to oven and bake 20 minutes.
7. Remove to wire rack; cool. If desired, garnish with *candied fruit* such as candied cherries, candied pineapple, and/or candied orange peel. Cut in 2x1-inch pieces.

About 6 dozen cookies

LUSCIOUS LEMON BARS

1 cup sifted all-purpose flour
¼ cup confectioners' sugar
½ cup butter, chilled
1 cup sugar
2 tablespoons flour
½ teaspoon baking powder
3 eggs, well beaten
½ cup unstrained lemon juice

1. Blend the 1 cup flour and confectioners' sugar in a bowl. Cut in the butter until blended. Firmly and evenly press into an ungreased 9x9x2-inch baking pan.
2. Bake at 350°F about 15 minutes.
3. Meanwhile, combine sugar, 2 tablespoons flour, and baking powder; blend into beaten eggs along with the lemon juice.
4. Pour mixture over crust in pan. Return to oven and bake 25 minutes.
5. Remove to wire rack to cool. Spread with a thin *confectioners' sugar icing* and top with *toasted sliced almonds*. Cut into bars.

About 3 dozen cookies

LEMON-COCONUT SOURS

⅓ cup butter, chilled
¾ cup sifted all-purpose flour
2 eggs
1 teaspoon grated lemon peel
½ teaspoon vanilla extract
1 cup firmly packed light brown sugar
¾ cup flaked coconut
½ cup pecans, coarsely chopped
Lemon Glaze, *page 306*

1. Cut butter into flour until thoroughly blended. Press evenly and firmly into an ungreased 13x9x2-inch baking pan.
2. Bake at 350°F 10 minutes.
3. Meanwhile, beat eggs, lemon peel, extract, and brown sugar until thick. Stir in coconut and pecans. Spread evenly over partially baked layer in pan.
4. Return to oven and bake about 20 minutes.
5. Immediately spread Lemon Glaze evenly over top. When cool, cut into bars or squares.

About 4 dozen cookies

PINEAPPLE BARS: Follow recipe for Lemon Coconut Sours. Substitute *unblanched almonds*, toasted and chopped, for pecans. Omit lemon peel and Lemon Glaze. Fold in *⅓ cup drained crushed pineapple* with coconut and almonds. Bake about 25 minutes.

PEANUT BUTTER DREAMS

¼ cup butter
½ cup peanut butter
½ cup firmly packed light brown sugar
1 cup sifted all-purpose flour
2 eggs
1 teaspoon vanilla extract
1 cup firmly packed light brown sugar
⅓ cup sifted all-purpose flour
½ teaspoon baking powder
¾ cup flaked coconut
6 oz. semisweet chocolate pieces

1. Cream butter with peanut butter thoroughly; add ½ cup brown sugar gradually, beating until fluffy.
2. Add 1 cup flour in halves, mixing until blended after each addition. Press evenly into greased 9x9x2-inch baking pan.
3. Bake at 350°F 10 to 15 minutes, or until lightly browned.
4. Meanwhile, beat eggs, extract, and 1 cup brown sugar until thick. Add a mixture of ⅓ cup flour and the baking powder; beat until blended.
5. Stir in coconut and chocolate pieces. Spread evenly over partially baked layer in pan.
6. Return to oven and bake 30 minutes.
7. Cool completely and cut into squares or bars.   ABOUT 2 DOZEN COOKIES

GOLDEN NUT BARS

1 cup finely crushed round scalloped crackers
½ cup pecans, finely chopped
1 cup sugar
1 teaspoon baking powder
3 egg whites
¼ teaspoon salt

1. Blend crumbs, pecans, sugar, and baking powder.
2. Beat egg whites and salt until stiff, not dry, peaks are formed; fold in the crumb mixture, a small amount at a time.
3. Turn into an ungreased 11x7x1½-inch baking pan and spread evenly.
4. Bake at 350°F 25 minutes.
5. Cool completely before cutting into bars.
          ABOUT 3 DOZEN COOKIES

ENGLISH TOFFEE BARS

1 cup butter
1 cup sugar
1 egg yolk
2 cups sifted all-purpose flour
1 teaspoon ground cinnamon
1 egg white, slightly beaten
1 cup chopped pecans
2 oz. (2 sq.) semisweet chocolate, melted

1. Cream butter; add sugar gradually, beating until fluffy. Beat in egg yolk.
2. Sift the flour and cinnamon together; gradually add to creamed mixture, beating until blended.
3. Turn into a greased 15x10x1-inch jelly roll pan and press evenly. Brush top with egg white. Sprinkle with pecans and press lightly into dough.
4. Bake at 275°F 1 hour.
5. While still hot, cut into 1½-inch squares. Drizzle with melted chocolate. Cool on wire rack.
          5 TO 6 DOZEN COOKIES

DROP COOKIES

CRISP SUGAR COOKIES

2½ cups sifted all-purpose flour
2 teaspoons cream of tartar
1 teaspoon baking soda
½ teaspoon salt
1 cup butter
1 teaspoon vanilla extract
1 cup sugar
2 eggs

1. Sift flour, cream of tartar, baking soda, and salt together; set aside.
2. Cream butter with extract; add sugar gradually, beating until fluffy. Add eggs, one at a time, beating thoroughly after each addition.
3. Add dry ingredients in fourths, mixing until blended after each addition.
4. Chill dough in refrigerator 1 hour.
5. Shape small balls by dropping small amounts of dough from a teaspoon 2 inches apart onto lightly greased cookie sheets. For glaze (this glaze is very important) dip bottom of a glass in *water;* then dip in *sugar.* Flatten each ball with sugar-coated glass.
6. Bake at 375°F 10 minutes.
          ABOUT 2 DOZEN COOKIES

RICH CHOCOLATE FILLING

1½ oz. (1½ sq.) unsweetened chocolate	2 egg yolks, slightly beaten
2 tablespoons sugar	½ teaspoon vanilla extract
1 tablespoon water	½ cup butter
⅛ teaspoon salt	1 cup confectioners' sugar

1. Heat chocolate, sugar, water, and salt over boiling water, stirring until mixture is smooth.
2. Blend egg yolks into mixture in double-boiler top and cook 3 to 5 minutes, stirring constantly. Stir in extract; set aside to cool.
3. Cream butter; add confectioners' sugar gradually, beating until fluffy.
4. Add chocolate mixture gradually, beating well; cover and chill.
5. Before using, beat filling with a spoon to soften slightly.   ABOUT 1¼ CUPS

FLORENTINES
(Echte Florentiner)

An Austrian cookie despite its Italian sounding name.

¼ cup butter	¾ cup sifted cake flour
⅓ cup firmly packed light brown sugar	¼ teaspoon salt
2 tablespoons honey	1 cup slivered blanched almonds
2 tablespoons light corn syrup	3 oz. candied orange peel, finely chopped
1 tablespoon heavy cream	Chocolate Glaze I, *page 276*; triple recipe

1. Cream butter; add brown sugar gradually, creaming until fluffy. Add honey, corn syrup, and cream gradually, beating well after each addition.
2. Sift flour and salt together; add in thirds to creamed mixture, mixing until blended after each addition. Mix in almonds and candied peel.
3. Drop by level tablespoonfuls 3 inches apart onto greased and lightly floured cookie sheets; spread into 2-inch rounds.
4. Bake at 350°F about 7 minutes. (Cookies should be delicately browned and about 3 inches in diameter with a slightly lacy appearance.)
5. Cool 2 to 3 minutes on cookie sheets. Carefully remove cookies to wire racks; turn flat side up and cool completely.
6. Evenly spread bottom of each cookie with about 1½ teaspoons Chocolate Glaze I. When chocolate is almost set, draw wavy lines through glaze.   ABOUT 2 DOZEN COOKIES

LACY ALMOND CRISPS

⅓ cup blanched almonds, grated	3 tablespoons butter or margarine
¼ cup sugar	1 tablespoon milk
2 teaspoons flour	

1. Mix almonds, sugar, and flour in a bowl. Blend in butter and milk.
2. Drop batter by teaspoonfuls about 4 inches apart onto greased and lightly floured cookie sheets.
3. Bake at 350°F 6 to 7 minutes, or until golden brown.
4. Let set about 1 minute; carefully remove with a spatula to a wire rack. Cool completely. Store in an airtight container.   ABOUT 2 DOZEN 3-INCH COOKIES

LACY FILBERT CRISPS: Follow recipe for Lacy Almond Crisps. Substitute ⅓ *cup filberts*, grated, for the almonds. Add ¼ *teaspoon ground mace*.

BANANA-BRAN COOKIES

¾ cup sifted all-purpose flour	⅛ teaspoon ground cloves
½ teaspoon baking powder	1 cup bran flakes
¼ teaspoon baking soda	½ cup mashed banana
¼ teaspoon salt	⅓ cup butter
½ teaspoon ground cinnamon	½ cup sugar
⅛ teaspoon ground allspice	1 egg
	¼ cup coarsely chopped pecans

1. Sift flour, baking powder, baking soda, salt, and spices together; set aside.
2. Combine bran flakes and the banana; set aside.
3. Cream butter; add sugar gradually, beating until fluffy. Add egg and beat thoroughly.
4. Add dry ingredients to creamed mixture alternately with the banana mixture, mixing until blended after each addition. Stir in pecans.

5. Drop by slightly rounded teaspoonfuls onto greased cookie sheets.
6. Bake at 375°F 10 to 12 minutes.

ABOUT 4 DOZEN COOKIES

CHOCOLATE-BANANA-BRAN COOKIES: Follow recipe for Banana Bran Cookies. Stir in *½ cup semisweet chocolate pieces* with the nuts.

BANANA SPICE COOKIES: Follow recipe for Banana Bran Cookies. Increase flour to ¾ cup plus 2 tablespoons. Decrease cinnamon to ¼ teaspoon. Omit allspice and bran flakes. Substitute *vegetable shortening* for butter. Increase pecans to ½ cup. Drop by tablespoonfuls onto the cookie sheets. If desired, frost cooled cookies with a *butter cream frosting* flavored with a few drops *banana extract*.

BRAN FLAKE DROPS: Follow recipe for Banana Bran Cookies. Increase baking powder to 1 teaspoon; omit baking soda. Omit banana; combine bran flakes with *¼ cup milk*.

CHOCOLATE MERINGUES

3 egg whites
¾ cup sugar
¾ teaspoon cider vinegar
¾ teaspoon vanilla extract
3 tablespoons Dutch process cocoa

1. Beat egg whites until frothy, using medium speed of electric mixer.
2. Add half of sugar gradually, beating constantly; beat 5 minutes after last addition of sugar.
3. Beat in vinegar and extract. Add remaining sugar gradually, beating constantly. Increase speed to high; beat until very stiff peaks are formed, about 3 minutes. Do not overbeat.
4. Sift cocoa evenly over meringue; using a flexible spatula, carefully fold in the cocoa until almost blended. (Mixture will be streaked.)
5. Force meringue through a pastry bag and star decorating tube, or drop meringue by heaping teaspoonfuls onto cookie sheets covered with unglazed paper; swirl to form rosettes.
6. Bake at 250°F 1½ hours.

ABOUT 2 DOZEN COOKIES

MINT MERINGUES: Follow recipe for Chocolate Meringues. Beat *6 drops of red or green food coloring* with egg whites. Omit vanilla extract and cocoa; add *¼ teaspoon peppermint extract*. Bake at 200°F 1½ hours.

WHITE MERINGUES: Follow recipe for Chocolate Meringues. Omit cocoa. Bake at 200°F 1½ hours.

COCONUT MACAROONS DE LUXE

7 oz. flaked coconut, finely chopped (in blender, if desired); about 2½ cups, chopped
¾ cup (about 6) egg whites, unbeaten
1 cup sugar
1 tablespoon cornstarch
¼ teaspoon almond extract

1. Put all ingredients into a 2-quart saucepan and mix thoroughly. Set over very low heat and stir until mixture is thickened and sugar is dissolved, about 20 minutes; keep temperature of mixture just below 150°F.
2. Remove from heat; cool 5 minutes.
3. Force through pastry bag and No. 7 star tube, which has been opened entirely, or drop by heaping teaspoonfuls directly onto cookie sheets lined with unglazed paper.
4. Press a *candied cherry piece* onto top of each.
5. Bake at 350°F 20 minutes.
6. Remove cookies to wire racks. (If necessary, slightly moisten underside of paper directly under each macaroon to remove.) ABOUT 3 DOZEN COOKIES

CHOCOLATE MACAROONS: Follow recipe for Coconut Macaroons de Luxe. Add *2 ounces (2 squares) unsweetened chocolate*, grated, to saucepan with coconut. Heat mixture to 120°F about 5 minutes.

MOUNT SHASTA COOKIES

Each cookie is baked with a mounded topping of coconut meringue, reminding one of a Western mountain peak.

½ cup shortening
1 teaspoon vanilla extract
½ cup sugar
½ cup firmly packed brown sugar
1 egg yolk
1½ cups sifted all-purpose flour
¾ teaspoon salt
3 tablespoons milk
1 cup walnuts, chopped
1 egg white
½ cup sugar
1 cup flaked coconut

1. Cream shortening with extract; add ½ cup sugar and brown sugar gradually, beating until fluffy. Add egg yolk; beat thoroughly.
2. Blend flour and salt; add to creamed mixture alternately with milk, mixing until blended after each addition. Stir in walnuts.
3. Drop by rounded teaspoonfuls onto ungreased cookie sheets, flatten slightly. Set aside.

Drop Cookies

4. Beat egg white until frothy; add ½ cup sugar gradually, beating constantly until stiff peaks are formed. Blend in coconut.
5. Top each cookie round with a teaspoonful of coconut meringue, shaping into a peak.
6. Bake at 375°F 10 to 12 minutes.

About 4½ dozen cookies

CURRANT CAKES
A Pennsylvania Dutch Christmas cookie.

2 cups butter	6 eggs, well beaten
2 teaspoons grated lemon peel	3¼ cups sifted all-purpose flour
2 tablespoons lemon juice	¼ teaspoon salt
2¼ cups sugar	½ lb. (1½ cups) currants

1. Cream butter with lemon peel and juice; add sugar gradually, beating until fluffy. Add eggs in thirds, beating thoroughly after each addition.
2. Blend flour and salt; add to creamed mixture in thirds, mixing until blended after each addition. Mix in the currants.
3. Drop by teaspoonfuls onto large well-greased cookie sheets, spreading batter for each cookie very thinly.
4. Bake at 350°F 10 minutes.

About 7½ dozen cookies

GINGERSNAPS

3 cups sifted all-purpose flour	½ teaspoon ground cinnamon
3 teaspoons baking soda	1 cup butter
3 teaspoons ground ginger	1 cup sugar
	½ cup molasses
	1 egg

1. Sift flour, baking soda, ginger, and cinnamon together; set aside.
2. Cream butter; add sugar gradually, beating until fluffy. Blend in molasses. Add egg and beat thoroughly.
3. Add dry ingredients in thirds, mixing until blended after each addition.
4. Drop by teaspoonfuls about 3 inches apart onto ungreased cookie sheets; sprinkle generously with *sugar*.
5. Bake at 350°F 10 to 12 minutes.

About 6 dozen cookies

QUEEN BEES

½ cup butter	½ teaspoon salt
½ cup sugar	¼ cup sherry
½ cup honey	1 cup chopped toasted blanched almonds
1 egg	½ cup finely chopped crystallized ginger
1¾ cups sifted all-purpose flour	
1 teaspoon baking powder	

1. Cream butter; add sugar gradually, then honey, creaming until fluffy. Add egg and beat thoroughly.
2. Sift flour, baking powder, and salt together; add to creamed mixture alternately with sherry, mixing until blended after each addition. Stir in a mixture of almonds and ginger.
3. Chill dough thoroughly.
4. Drop by teaspoonfuls 2 inches apart onto lightly greased cookie sheets.
5. Bake at 400°F about 10 minutes.

About 4½ dozen cookies

CHOCOLATE BEES: Follow recipe for Queen Bees. Omit crystallized ginger; use *½ cup finely chopped chocolate-coated crystallized ginger.*

ORANGE CANDY CRISPS

⅔ cup sifted all-purpose flour	¾ cup butter or margarine
½ teaspoon baking powder	½ teaspoon vanilla extract
¼ teaspoon baking soda	½ cup sugar
⅛ teaspoon salt	½ cup firmly packed brown sugar
½ lb. (about 1¼ cups) jellied candy orange slices, cut in small pieces	1 egg
	¾ cup uncooked rolled oats
3 tablespoons flour	½ cup flaked coconut

1. Sift ⅔ cup flour, baking powder, baking soda, and salt together; set aside.
2. Mix candy orange pieces with the 3 tablespoons flour; set aside.
3. Cream butter with extract; add the sugars gradually, beating until fluffy. Add the egg and beat thoroughly.
4. Add dry ingredients in halves, mixing until blended after each addition. Stir in the candy orange pieces, rolled oats, and coconut.

* *Black Forest Torte (page 241)*

5. Drop by teaspoonfuls 2 inches apart onto greased cookie sheets.
6. Bake at 375°F 10 to 12 minutes.
7. If necessary, cool cookies slightly before transferring to wire racks.   ABOUT 7 DOZEN COOKIES

NUT COLONELS
These salted peanut cookies are sure to please all.

1 egg	1½ cups salted peanuts
½ cup sugar	or cashews, coarsely
¼ teaspoon vanilla	chopped
extract	2 teaspoons flour

1. Beat egg, sugar, and extract until thick. Add nuts and flour gradually, folding in after each addition.
2. Drop by teaspoonfuls 2 inches apart onto greased cookie sheets.
3. Bake at 350°F 10 to 12 minutes.
   ABOUT 3 DOZEN COOKIES

PEANUT CRINKLES

1¾ cups sifted all-purpose flour	½ cup firmly packed light brown sugar
½ teaspoon baking soda	1 egg
¼ teaspoon salt	⅓ cup milk
½ cup regular wheat germ	2 cups cornflakes, finely crushed (½ cup crumbs)
1 cup butter or margarine	Peanuts
⅔ cup peanut butter	

1. Sift flour, baking soda, and salt into a medium bowl; stir in wheat germ.
2. Cream butter with peanut butter and brown sugar in a large bowl until fluffy-light; beat in egg and milk. Stir in flour mixture to make a soft dough. Chill at least an hour.
3. Preheat oven to 350°F.
4. Pinch off dough, a heaping tablespoon at a time, and roll into balls; roll each in cornflake crumbs to coat completely. Place, 2 inches apart, on greased cookie sheets. Flatten each ball slightly with fingertips. Decorate top of each with several peanuts.
5. Bake 15 minutes, or until balls are puffed and lightly crackled. Remove from cookie sheets to wire racks. Cool completely.   ABOUT 2½ DOZEN

* *Rainbow Fruit Pie (page 261)*

AUSTRIAN PECAN COOKIES

2 tablespoons plus 2 teaspoons butter	2 eggs, well beaten
1½ teaspoons vanilla extract	½ cup sifted cake flour
	1 teaspoon baking powder
2 cups firmly packed light brown sugar	½ teaspoon salt
	1½ cups chopped pecans

1. Cream butter with extract; add brown sugar gradually, blending well. Add beaten eggs in halves, beating thoroughly after each addition.
2. Sift cake flour, baking powder, and salt together; add to creamed mixture in halves, mixing until blended after each addition. (Batter will be thin.) Stir in pecans.
3. Drop by teaspoonfuls at least 2 inches apart onto cookie sheets lined with baking parchment.
4. Bake at 375°F about 6 minutes.
5. Cool completely, then remove from paper.
   ABOUT 10 DOZEN COOKIES

PLANTATION CRISPS

¼ cup butter	½ cup sifted all-purpose flour
½ teaspoon vanilla extract	¼ teaspoon salt
1 cup firmly packed dark brown sugar	1 cup pecans, coarsely chopped
1 egg	

1. Cream butter with extract; add brown sugar gradually, beating until fluffy. Add egg and beat thoroughly.
2. Blend flour and salt; add to creamed mixture in halves, mixing until blended after each addition. Stir in the pecans.
3. Drop by teaspoonfuls 3 inches apart onto ungreased cookie sheets; bake about 6 cookies at one time (they are difficult to remove when cooled).
4. Bake at 350°F 10 to 12 minutes.
5. Immediately remove cookies to wire racks to cool.   ABOUT 3½ DOZEN COOKIES

HERMITS
These old-fashioned spicy raisin cookies are a part of our New England heritage.

1 cup dark seedless raisins	½ teaspoon ground nutmeg

2½ cups sifted all-purpose flour	⅛ teaspoon ground cloves
¾ teaspoon baking soda	¾ cup butter
½ teaspoon salt	1½ cups firmly packed brown sugar
1 teaspoon ground cinnamon	3 eggs
	1 cup walnuts, chopped

1. Pour *2 cups boiling water* over raisins in a saucepan and bring to boiling; pour off water and drain raisins on absorbent paper. Coarsely chop raisins and set aside.
2. Sift flour, baking soda, salt, and spices together and blend thoroughly; set aside.
3. Cream butter; add brown sugar gradually, beating until fluffy. Add eggs, one at a time, beating thoroughly after each addition.
4. Add dry ingredients in fourths, mixing until blended after each addition. Stir in raisins and walnuts.
5. Drop by teaspoonfuls 2 inches apart onto lightly greased cookie sheets.
6. Bake at 400°F about 7 minutes.

ABOUT 8 DOZEN COOKIES

MOLDED COOKIES

MOJI PEARLS

¾ cup butter	1½ cups sifted all-purpose flour
½ teaspoon vanilla extract	⅛ teaspoon salt
⅓ cup sugar	

1. Cream butter with extract; add sugar gradually, beating until fluffy.
2. Blend flour and salt; add in thirds to creamed mixture, mixing until blended after each addition. Chill dough until easy to handle.
3. Shape into 1-inch balls or into crescents (if desired, roll in sesame seed). Place about 2 inches apart on ungreased cookie sheets.
4. Bake at 325°F 20 minutes.
5. If desired, while still warm, roll in *Vanilla Confectioners' Sugar, Spiced Confectioners' Sugar, or Cinnamon Sugar.*

ABOUT 3 DOZEN COOKIES

PECAN POOFS: Follow recipe for Moji Pearls. Substitute *¼ cup confectioners' sugar* for sugar. Decrease flour to 1 cup. Mix in *1 cup pecans*, finely chopped. Shape dough into balls or pyramids.

SPANISH BUTTER WAFERS
(Mantecaditos)

½ cup butter	1 teaspoon vanilla extract
½ cup lard	1¼ cups sugar
1½ teaspoons grated lemon peel, or 1 teaspoon anise seed (or both)	2 eggs
	1¾ cups sifted all-purpose flour
	½ teaspoon salt

1. Cream butter and lard with lemon peel and extract. Add sugar gradually, beating until fluffy. Add eggs, one at a time, beating thoroughly after each addition.
2. Blend flour and salt; add to creamed mixture in thirds, mixing until blended after each addition. Chill dough several hours, or until easy to handle.
3. Removing a small portion of dough at a time from refrigerator, shape into ¾- to 1-inch balls and place 1½ inches apart on an ungreased cookie sheet.
4. Bake at 350°F 8 to 10 minutes.

6 TO 7 DOZEN COOKIES

SNOWBALL MELTAWAYS
These melt-in-your-mouth morsels truly live up to their name.

1 cup butter	2½ cups sifted all-purpose flour
½ cup confectioners' sugar	½ cup finely chopped pecans
1 teaspoon vanilla extract	

1. In a heavy saucepan over low heat, melt and heat butter until light brown in color. Pour into a small mixing bowl; chill until firm.
2. Cream browned butter with confectioners' sugar and extract until light and fluffy. Gradually add flour, mixing until blended. Stir in the pecans. Chill several hours for ease in handling.

3. Shape into 1-inch balls. Place on ungreased cookie sheets.
4. Bake at 350°F about 20 minutes.
5. Remove to wire racks. While still hot, dust with *confectioners' sugar*.   ABOUT 4 DOZEN COOKIES

SWEDISH COFFEE FINGERS
(Mördegspinnar)

½ cup butter
1 teaspoon almond extract
2 tablespoons sugar
1¼ cups sifted all-purpose flour
Egg white, slightly beaten
½ cup finely chopped blanched almonds
3 tablespoons sugar

1. Cream butter with extract; add 2 tablespoons sugar gradually, beating until fluffy.
2. Add flour in fourths, mixing until blended after each addition. Chill dough thoroughly.
3. Shape small amounts of dough into fingers 2½ inches long and ¼ inch thick.
4. Brush each finger of dough with the egg white, then roll in mixture of the almonds and the remaining sugar.
5. Bake on ungreased cookie sheets at 350°F 10 to 12 minutes.
6. Carefully remove cookies to wire racks.
ABOUT 5 DOZEN COOKIES

CHERRY JEWELS

½ cup butter
1 teaspoon vanilla extract
¼ cup sugar
1 egg
1 teaspoon grated lemon peel
1 tablespoon lemon juice
1¼ cups sifted all-purpose flour
¾ cup finely chopped pecans
18 candied cherries, halved

1. Cream butter with extract and sugar until light and fluffy. Add the egg and lemon peel and juice; beat thoroughly. Gradually add flour, mixing until blended. Chill.
2. Shape dough into 1-inch balls, roll in chopped pecans and place on greased cookie sheets. Press a cherry half onto center of each ball.
3. Bake at 350°F 10 to 12 minutes.
4. Cool on wire racks.   3 DOZEN COOKIES

COCOA BUTTER STICKS
(Chokladbröd)
This delectable cookie is a Swedish specialty.

1½ cups sifted all-purpose flour
2 tablespoons cocoa
1 teaspoon baking powder
½ teaspoon salt
¾ cup butter or margarine
¾ cup sugar
1 egg, slightly beaten
1 tablespoon cold water
3 tablespoons finely chopped blanched almonds
2 tablespoons sugar

1. Sift flour, cocoa, baking powder, and salt together; set aside.
2. Cream butter; add ¾ cup sugar gradually, beating until fluffy. Reserve 1 tablespoon egg; blend remainder into butter mixture, beating thoroughly.
3. Add dry ingredients in fourths, mixing until blended after each addition. Chill dough thoroughly.
4. Divide dough into 4 portions; shape each into a roll ¾ inch in diameter.
5. Place rolls 4 inches apart on ungreased cookie sheets; flatten each until ¼ inch thick with a fork dipped in flour; smooth dough at edges.
6. Combine water with reserved egg; brush top of dough lightly.
7. Sprinkle a mixture of almonds and 2 tablespoons sugar over dough.
8. Bake at 400°F 8 to 10 minutes.
9. Cool 1 minute; cut crosswise into 1-inch pieces and remove to wire racks.   5 TO 6 DOZEN COOKIES
NOTE: For additional chocolate flavor, increase cocoa to ¼ cup and decrease salt to ¼ teaspoon.

COCOA BUTTER BALLS: Follow recipe for Cocoa Butter Sticks. Shape dough into ¾-inch balls; place about 2 inches apart on cookie sheets and flatten each with a fork. Brush tops with egg; sprinkle with almond-sugar mixture.

GINGER COOKIES

2 cups sifted all-purpose flour
1 teaspoon baking powder
½ teaspoon baking soda
½ teaspoon salt
1 teaspoon ground cinnamon
½ teaspoon ground cloves
½ teaspoon ground mace
1 cup butter
1 cup firmly packed brown sugar
¼ cup dark molasses

Molded Cookies

| 1 teaspoon ground ginger | 1 egg |

1. Sift flour, baking powder, baking soda, salt, and spices together; set aside.
2. Cream butter; add brown sugar gradually, beating until fluffy. Blend in molasses. Add egg and beat thoroughly.
3. Add dry ingredients in fourths, mixing until blended after each addition. Chill thoroughly.
4. Shape dough into 1-inch balls and dip in *sugar*. Place 2 inches apart on ungreased cookie sheets.
5. Bake at 350°F 10 to 15 minutes.

ABOUT 6 DOZEN COOKIES

MOLASSES BUTTER BALLS

1 cup butter	2 cups sifted all-purpose flour
½ teaspoon vanilla extract	½ teaspoon salt
¼ cup molasses	2 cups pecans, finely chopped

1. Cream butter with extract; add molasses and beat well.
2. Blend flour and salt; add in fourths to creamed mixture, mixing until blended after each addition. Stir in the pecans.
3. Shape dough into 1-inch balls; place on lightly greased cookie sheets.
4. Bake at 350°F 12 to 15 minutes.
5. Cool slightly; roll in *confectioners' sugar*.

ABOUT 5 DOZEN COOKIES

SPICY GINGER CRUNCHIES

2¼ cups sifted all-purpose flour	½ teaspoon ground cloves
2 teaspoons baking soda	¾ cup butter
1 teaspoon salt	1 teaspoon vanilla extract
1 teaspoon ground cinnamon	1 cup sugar
¾ teaspoon ground ginger	1 egg
	¼ cup molasses

1. Sift flour, baking soda, salt, and spices together; set aside.
2. Cream butter with extract; gradually add sugar, beating until light and fluffy. Add egg and molasses; beat thoroughly.
3. Gradually add dry ingredients to creamed mixture, mixing until blended. Chill several hours.
4. Shape dough into ¾-inch balls, roll in *sugar* and place 2 inches apart on greased cookie sheets.
5. Bake at 375°F 7 to 8 minutes.
6. Immediately remove to wire racks to cool.

6 TO 7 DOZEN COOKIES

NORWEGIAN CONES
(Krumkaker)

This traditional Christmas confection is extremely fragile, so handle and store it carefully.

1½ cups sifted all-purpose flour	1 cup butter
½ cup cornstarch	1¼ cups sugar
1½ teaspoons ground cardamom	3 egg yolks
	3 egg whites
	⅛ teaspoon salt

1. Blend flour, cornstarch, and cardamom.
2. Cream butter; add sugar gradually, beating until fluffy. Add egg yolks, one at a time, beating thoroughly after each addition.
3. Add dry ingredients in fourths, mixing until blended after each addition.
4. Beat egg whites and salt until stiff peaks are formed; gently fold into batter.
5. Heat krumkake iron (usually available in the housewares section of department stores) following manufacturer's instructions until a drop of water "sputters" on hot surface.
6. For each, spoon 1½ to 2 teaspoons batter onto hot iron; close the iron and bake on each side for a few minutes, or until lightly browned.
7. Using a spatula, immediately remove wafer and roll into cone. Cool completely.

ABOUT 4 DOZEN COOKIES

DANISH PEPPERNUTS
(Pebernødder)

The Danes have achieved an especially fine blend of flavors with sugar and spices and good Danish butter in this version of Pebernødder.

4 cups sifted all-purpose flour	1 teaspoon ground ginger
1 teaspoon crushed ammonium carbonate (available at your pharmacy)	¾ cup butter
	4 teaspoons finely shredded lemon peel
1½ teaspoons ground cinnamon	1¼ cups sugar
	2 eggs
1 teaspoon white pepper	¾ cup finely chopped almonds

REFRIGERATOR COOKIES

1. Thoroughly blend flour, ammonium carbonate, cinnamon, white pepper, and ginger; set aside.
2. Cream butter with lemon peel. Add sugar gradually, beating until fluffy. Add eggs, one at a time, beating well after each addition. Stir in almonds.
3. Add dry ingredients in thirds, mixing until blended after each addition. Chill about 1 hour.
4. Shape dough into ¾- to 1-inch balls; place on ungreased cookie sheets.
5. Bake at 350°F 12 or 13 minutes.

ABOUT 12 DOZEN COOKIES

OVERNIGHT COOKIES
(Hoide Kager)
A Danish cookie.

2¼ cups sifted all-purpose flour	¼ teaspoon vanilla extract
1 cup sugar	⅛ teaspoon lemon extract
1 cup butter	
½ cup cream	

1. Sift flour and sugar together; cut in butter until particles are the size of rice kernels.
2. Combine cream and extracts; add gradually to flour mixture, mixing with a fork until well blended.
3. Chill dough until easy to handle.
4. Shape into two 1½-inch rolls. Wrap and chill overnight.
5. Cut each roll into ⅛- or ¼-inch slices. Transfer slices to ungreased cookie sheets.
6. Bake at 350°F 9 to 12 minutes.

6 to 8 DOZEN COOKIES

BROWN WAFERS
Spices and orange peel lend a pleasing flavor blend to this Danish cookie.

1 cup butter	½ teaspoon ground cloves
1¼ cups sugar	
½ cup light corn syrup	½ cup slivered almonds
2½ teaspoons crushed ammonium carbonate (available at your pharmacy)	½ cup finely shredded orange peel
	4 cups sifted all-purpose flour
3 tablespoons ground cinnamon	

1. Heat butter, sugar, and corn syrup to boiling in a heavy saucepan; stir to blend. Cool.
2. Stir a small amount of *cold water* (about 1 teaspoon) into the ammonium carbonate. Blend into cooled butter mixture.
3. Add the spices, almonds, and orange peel, stirring only enough to blend the ingredients.
4. Add the flour in thirds, stirring until blended after each addition; mix well.
5. Shape the dough into four 2¼-inch rolls. Wrap in moisture-vaporproof material; chill overnight or longer.
6. Cut each roll into thin slices. Transfer slices to greased cookie sheets.
7. Bake at 350°F 5 to 7 minutes.
8. Store cookies in a loosely covered container.

ABOUT 8 DOZEN COOKIES

WHEAT SCOTCHIES

1½ cups sifted all-purpose flour	¾ cup butter or margarine
1 teaspoon baking soda	½ teaspoon vanilla extract
½ teaspoon cream of tartar	1 cup firmly packed dark brown sugar
½ teaspoon salt	1 egg
½ cup finely crushed shredded wheat	½ cup raisins

1. Sift flour, baking soda, cream of tartar, and salt together; mix in crushed shredded wheat and set aside.
2. Cream butter with extract; add brown sugar gradually, beating until fluffy. Add egg and beat thoroughly.
3. Add the dry ingredients in fourths, mixing until well blended after each addition. Stir in the raisins.
4. Shape into 1½-inch rolls. Wrap each roll and chill several hours or overnight.
5. Cut each roll into ⅛-inch slices. Place about 1 inch apart on ungreased cookie sheets.
6. Bake at 375°F 6 to 8 minutes.

ABOUT 9 DOZEN COOKIES

NOTE: If desired, lightly brown the finely crushed shredded wheat in *1 tablespoon butter or margarine*, stir occasionally.

ROLLED COOKIES

HUNGARIAN BUTTER COOKIES

2¾ cups sifted all-purpose flour
3 teaspoons baking powder
¼ teaspoon salt
1½ cups unsalted butter chilled
4 egg yolks, slightly beaten
1 cup dairy sour cream
¼ cup sugar
1 egg white, slightly beaten

1. Sift flour, baking powder, and salt together into a bowl. Cut in butter until particles are the size of rice kernels.
2. Add a mixture of egg yolks, sour cream, and sugar, mixing until blended.
3. Knead until a smooth dough is formed.
4. Roll dough ¼ inch thick on a lightly floured surface; cut with a 2½-inch round cutter.
5. With a sharp knife make a crisscross pattern on top of each; brush with egg white and sprinkle lightly with *vanilla granulated sugar*. Place on ungreased cookie sheets.
6. Bake at 400°F 5 minutes. Reduce oven temperature to 350°F and bake about 14 minutes.

ABOUT 4 DOZEN COOKIES

SAND TARTS

This particular recipe is a Pennsylvania Dutch favorite. However, variations of the butter-rich cookie appear in several European countries, and in England and Scotland, where it is known as shortbread.

2 cups butter
2½ cups sugar
2 eggs
4 cups sifted all-purpose flour
1 egg white, slightly beaten

1. Cream butter; add sugar gradually, beating until fluffy. Add eggs one at a time, beating thoroughly after each addition.
2. Add flour in fourths, mixing until well blended after each addition. Chill dough overnight.
3. Removing from refrigerator only amount needed for a single rolling, roll dough about 1/16 inch thick on a floured surface; cut with 2-inch round or fancy cutter. Brush tops with egg white; sprinkle with a mixture of *½ cup sugar* and *2 teaspoons ground cinnamon*.
4. Transfer to ungreased cookie sheets; press a quarter of *pecan* onto center of each cookie.
5. Bake at 350°F about 9 minutes.

ABOUT 17½ DOZEN COOKIES

SCOTTISH SHORTBREAD

2 cups sifted all-purpose flour
6 tablespoons sugar
2 tablespoons cornstarch
¾ cup butter

1. Sift flour, sugar, and cornstarch into a bowl. Cut in butter until mixture becomes a soft dough (requires working beyond the stage when particles are the size of rice kernels).
2. Shape dough into a ball; knead lightly with fingertips until mixture holds together.
3. Roll half of the dough at a time ¼ to ½ inch thick on a floured surface.
4. Cut into 1½x½-inch strips, or use fancy cutters. Place on ungreased cookie sheets.
5. Bake at 350°F 25 to 30 minutes; do not brown.

2½ TO 4 DOZEN COOKIES

PETTICOAT TAILS: Follow recipe for Scottish Shortbread. Roll dough about ¼ inch thick; cut out 5- or 6-inch rounds and cut a 2½-inch round from the center of each. (Bake centers for samplers.) Cut each ring into 8 pieces; crimp all edges of each piece and prick the surface with a fork; bake as directed.

GRASMERE SHORTBREAD: Follow recipe for Scottish Shortbread. Blend *½ teaspoon ground ginger* with dry ingredients. After addition of butter, stir in *½ cup finely chopped crystallized ginger*. Roll a fourth of dough at a time ⅛ inch thick on a floured surface; cut with a 2-inch fluted round cutter. Bake on ungreased cookie sheets at 350°F 12 minutes. Cool. Spread *Ginger Filling, below*, over bottoms of half the cooled cookies; cover with remaining cookies.

ABOUT 3 DOZEN COOKIES

Ginger Filling: Cream *¼ cup butter* and *1 teaspoon vanilla extract*; add *2 cups confectioners' sugar* gradually, beating until fluffy. Stir in *1 tablespoon milk* until of spreading consistency. Stir in *2 tablespoons grated crystallized ginger*.

ABOUT ⅔ CUP

DANISH KNOTS
(Kringler)

2¼ cups sifted all-purpose flour	½ cup firm butter
1 tablespoon sugar	1 cup chilled heavy cream, whipped
1 teaspoon baking powder	Crushed loaf sugar

1. Sift flour, sugar, and baking powder together into a bowl. Cut in butter until particles are the size of rice kernels.
2. Mix in cream with a fork and knead lightly with fingertips until mixture makes a ball.
3. Roll a fourth of dough at a time into a 6x4-inch rectangle ¼-inch thick on a floured surface. Sprinkle crushed loaf sugar over the dough, pressing in lightly. Cut into 6x¼-inch strips. Form into figure eights or loose knots to resemble pretzels. Place on ungreased cookie sheets.
4. Bake at 400°F about 12 minutes.

ABOUT 5 DOZEN COOKIES

MELTING SNOWFLAKES

⅓ cup butter, chilled	½ teaspoon almond extract
1 cup sifted all-purpose flour	Egg white, slightly beaten
2 egg yolks	
1 teaspoon cream	

1. Cut butter into flour until particles are the size of rice kernels.
2. Beat egg yolks, cream, and extract until very thick. Using a fork, blend into flour mixture in halves, mixing well after each addition. Chill dough thoroughly.
3. Roll dough ¼ inch thick on a floured surface; fold lengthwise in half, then crosswise in half; chill 1 hour.
4. Again roll dough ¼ inch thick. Cut with 1¼-inch round cutter. Transfer to ungreased cookie sheets. Brush rounds with egg white.
5. Bake at 350°F about 20 minutes.
6. Remove cookies to wire racks and sift with *Vanilla Confectioners' Sugar*.

ABOUT 2 DOZEN COOKIES

SCANDINAVIAN SPRINGERLE

Unlike the firm anise-flavored German Springerle, this delicately spiced cookie is pleasingly tender.

2 cups sifted all-purpose flour	1 cup butter
½ teaspoon ground cardamom	1 cup confectioners' sugar
½ teaspoon ground cinnamon	¾ cup blanched almonds, finely chopped

1. Sift flour and spices together; set aside.
2. Cream butter; add confectioners' sugar gradually, beating until fluffy. Add flour mixture in fourths, mixing until well blended after each addition. Stir in almonds. Chill dough thoroughly.
3. Roll dough ¼ inch thick on a floured surface or between sheets of waxed paper. Press lightly floured springerle rolling pin firmly into dough, rolling carefully to make clear designs; or press individual springerle molds firmly into dough.
4. Brush surface of dough gently with a soft brush to remove excess flour; cut the frames apart. Transfer to ungreased cookie sheets.
5. Bake at 350°F 10 minutes.

ABOUT 2½ DOZEN COOKIES

AUSTRIAN NUT BUTTER COOKIES

Rich Chocolate Filling, *page 310*	¼ teaspoon ground cloves
2 cups sifted all-purpose flour	¾ cup unblanched almonds, grated
⅔ cup sugar	1¼ cups butter, chilled
½ teaspoon ground cinnamon	Glossy Chocolate Frosting, *page 320*

1. Prepare Rich Chocolate Filling.
2. Sift flour, sugar, and spices together; mix in almonds.
3. Cut in butter until mixture becomes a soft dough (requires working beyond the stage when particles are the size of rice kernels). Using fingertips, shape into a ball.
4. Roll a third of dough at a time ⅛ inch thick on a floured surface; cut with 2½-inch round cutter.
5. Bake on ungreased cookie sheets at 325°F 12 minutes; do not brown.
6. When cool, sandwich cookies together with filling. Lightly spread top of each double cookie with sieved *apricot jam*, then with Glossy Chocolate Frosting; top each with a *pecan half* or *slivered almond piece*.

ABOUT 2½ DOZEN COOKIES

GLOSSY CHOCOLATE FROSTING

½ cup sugar
2 tablespoons cornstarch
¼ teaspoon salt
½ cup boiling water
1 oz. (1 sq.) unsweetened chocolate, cut in pieces
2 tablespoons butter or margarine
1 teaspoon vanilla extract

1. Mix sugar, cornstarch, and salt in a saucepan; stir in the water and chocolate.
2. Cook over medium heat until mixture thickens, stirring frequently.
3. Remove from heat; stir in butter and extract. Spread while frosting is warm.   ABOUT 1 CUP

ISCHL COOKIES

These regal Tyrolean cookies originated at Franz Josef's famous summer residence.

Follow recipe for Austrian Nut Butter Cookies. Omit filling, frosting, and nuts for garnish. After cutting out rounds, place half on cookie sheets and bake. From remainder, cut out from each round 3 small rounds ¼ to ½ inch in diameter; bake. When cookies are cool, spread each plain cookie with about ½ *teaspoon currant jelly.* Cover with cookies having holes.

ALMOND FLAKES NORMANDY

⅔ cup butter
1¼ cups sifted all-purpose flour
½ cup toasted blanched almonds, grated or finely chopped
¾ cup confectioners' sugar
Few grains salt
1 egg white
½ teaspoon almond extract
1 egg yolk, slightly beaten
3 to 4 tablespoons sugar

1. Cut butter into flour until particles are the size of rice kernels.
2. Blend in almonds, confectioners' sugar, and salt.
3. Beat the egg white and extract until frothy; add to flour-sugar mixture, mixing until a soft dough is formed.
4. Shape dough into a ball; knead lightly with fingertips until mixture holds together. Chill dough thoroughly.
5. Roll a third of dough at a time ⅛ inch thick between sheets of waxed paper. Cut with a 2-inch round cutter.
6. Transfer to ungreased cookie sheets; brush tops with egg yolk and sprinkle each with ¼ teaspoon sugar.
7. Bake at 300°F 18 to 20 minutes.
ABOUT 3 DOZEN COOKIES

BASLER BRUNSLI

As appropriate to Christmas as it is uniquely Swiss (Basler translates "from Basle"), this rich cookie will be one of your great joys of the season.

1 lb. unblanched almonds, grated* (5 cups)
4 to 4½ oz. (4 to 4½ sq.) unsweetened chocolate, grated*
2½ cups sugar
1 teaspoon ground cinnamon
1 tablespoon kirsch
4 egg whites (about ⅔ cup)

1. Thoroughly blend almonds and chocolate with a mixture of sugar and cinnamon. Drizzle with the kirsch.
2. Beat the egg whites until stiff, not dry, peaks are formed. Blend into nut mixture. Chill thoroughly.
3. Roll a fourth of the mixture at a time ½ inch thick on a lightly sugared surface. Cut with 1¼-inch round cutter. Place on lightly greased cookie sheets.
4. Bake at 300°F 15 minutes. Cool on wire racks.
ABOUT 10 DOZEN COOKIES
*Blender grating speeds the job.

CHOCOLATE-ALMOND CRESCENTS

2½ cups sifted all-purpose flour
¼ cup sugar
½ teaspoon salt
1 cup butter, chilled and cut in pieces
1 cup blanched, toasted almonds, finely chopped
⅓ cup semisweet chocolate pieces, grated
2 egg yolks, slightly beaten
Confectioners' sugar

1. Blend flour, sugar, and salt in a bowl. Cut in the butter with pastry blender or two knives until particles are the size of rice kernels.
2. Mix in the almonds and chocolate. Add the egg yolks gradually, mixing thoroughly with a fork.

Gather dough into a ball, working with fingertips until mixture holds together. Chill dough thoroughly.
3. Sift confectioners' sugar lightly and evenly over a flat surface. Roll a third of the dough about ¼ inch thick on the sugared surface. Cut with a lightly floured crescent-shaped cookie cutter. Transfer to lightly greased cookie sheets. Repeat for remaining dough.
4. Bake at 350°F about 7 minutes.
5. Immediately remove cookies to wire racks.
ABOUT 7 DOZEN COOKIES

CINNAMON STARS
(Zimtsterne)
The rich blend of almond and cinnamon flavor adds a touch of distinction to this star-shaped confection, a German-Swiss holiday favorite.

⅓ cup plus 1 tablespoon egg whites
1 cup confectioners' sugar
1 teaspoon grated lemon peel
¾ teaspoon ground cinnamon
2 cups unblanched almonds, grated

1. Lightly grease 2 cookie sheets, sprinkle with *flour*, and shake off excess; set aside.
2. Using an electric beater, beat egg whites until stiff, not dry, peaks are formed. Add confectioners' sugar gradually, beating 5 minutes at medium speed. Remove ⅓ cup of meringue and set aside.
3. Into remaining meringue, beat the lemon peel and cinnamon. Fold in the almonds.
4. Turn almond mixture onto a pastry canvas sprinkled with *confectioners'* or *granulated sugar*. Gently roll ¼ to ⅜ inch thick. Lightly sprinkle with sugar. Cut with a 2-inch star-shaped cookie cutter dipped in confectioners' sugar.
5. Transfer to cookie sheets; drop about ½ teaspoonful of reserved meringue onto each star and spread out evenly onto points. Set aside in a warm place (about 80°F) 1½ hours.
6. Bake at 375°F 5 minutes.
ABOUT 3 DOZEN COOKIES

JAN HAGEL
These Dutch delicacies are popular throughout the holiday season and particularly on the feast day of Saint Nicholas.

1 cup butter
1 cup sugar
1 egg yolk
2 cups sifted all-purpose flour
¼ teaspoon salt
1 egg white
4 pieces loaf sugar, finely crushed
½ teaspoon ground cinnamon
½ cup finely chopped nuts

1. Cream butter; add sugar gradually, beating until fluffy. Add egg yolk and beat well.
2. Blend flour and salt; add in fourths to creamed mixture, mixing until blended after each addition.
3. Divide dough into halves and roll each on an ungreased cookie sheet into a 12x10-inch rectangle.
4. Beat egg white slightly with a small amount of *water*; brush lightly over dough. Mix crushed sugar with cinnamon and nuts; sprinkle over each rectangle.
5. Bake at 375°F 15 minutes.
6. Trim the edges and cut into bars while warm.
ABOUT 4 DOZEN COOKIES

KOLACKY COOKIES

1 cup butter
8 oz. cream cheese, softened
¼ teaspoon vanilla extract
2¼ cups sifted all-purpose flour
½ teaspoon salt
Cherry preserves, apricot preserves, or prune filling

1. Cream butter and cream cheese with extract until fluffy.
2. Blend flour and salt; add in fourths to creamed mixture, mixing until blended after each addition. Chill dough thoroughly.
3. Roll dough ¼ inch thick on a floured surface; cut with 2-inch round cutter or fancy-shaped cutters. Transfer to ungreased cookie sheets, make a small indentation in center of each round, and fill with ½ teaspoon preserves.
4. Bake at 350°F 10 to 15 minutes, or until delicately browned.
ABOUT 3½ DOZEN COOKIES

Rolled Cookies

SHREWSBURY BISCUITS

Americans would call these tender, currant-flecked treats cookies, but being an English favorite, they're biscuits.

¾ cup butter	1 egg
2 teaspoons grated lemon peel	1¾ cups sifted all-purpose flour
2 tablespoons lemon juice	½ teaspoon baking powder
¾ cup sugar	¼ teaspoon salt
	1 cup currants

1. Cream butter with lemon peel and juice; add sugar gradually, beating until fluffy. Add egg and beat thoroughly.
2. Sift flour, baking powder, and salt together; add in fourths to creamed mixture, mixing until blended after each addition. Mix in currants. Chill dough thoroughly.
3. Roll a third of dough at a time ¼ inch thick on a floured surface. Cut with 2½-inch fluted cutter. Brush cutouts with *milk*; sprinkle with *sugar*. Transfer to ungreased cookie sheets.
4. Bake at 350°F 12 to 15 minutes.

ABOUT 2½ DOZEN COOKIES

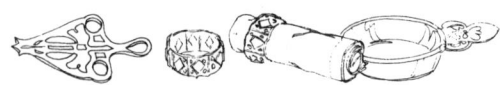

BUTTER STICKS

¼ cup sugar	¼ teaspoon almond extract
3 hard-cooked egg yolks, sieved	2¼ cups sifted all-purpose flour
1 cup butter, softened	

1. Add sugar gradually to sieved egg yolks, mixing well after each addition.
2. Add butter, a small amount at a time, beating until fluffy after each addition. Mix in extract.
3. Add flour in fourths, mixing until blended after each addition. Knead lightly with fingertips and form into a ball.
4. Roll a fourth of dough at a time ¼ inch thick on a floured surface.
5. Brush dough with slightly beaten *egg white*; sprinkle with a mixture of *ground cinnamon* and crushed *loaf sugar*. Cut into 4x¼-inch strips. Transfer to ungreased cookie sheets.
6. Bake at 350°F 8 to 10 minutes.

ABOUT 10 DOZEN COOKIES

GINGER SHORTBREAD

1½ cups sifted all-purpose flour	½ cup butter or margarine
1 teaspoon ground ginger	⅓ cup firmly packed brown sugar
¼ teaspoon salt	1 tablespoon heavy cream

1. Sift flour, ginger, and salt together; set aside.
2. Cream butter; add brown sugar gradually, beating well. Add flour mixture gradually, mixing until well blended. Stir in cream.
3. Divide dough into halves. Place on an ungreased cookie sheet. Flatten into rounds about ½ inch thick. Mark into wedges. Flute the edges and prick centers with a fork.
4. Bake at 350°F about 20 minutes.
5. While still warm, cut into wedges.

2 SHORTBREAD ROUNDS

SWEDISH GINGERSNAPS
(Pepparkakor)

It is the pride of Swedish cooks to roll wafer-thin the rich, spicy dough of their traditional Christmas Pepparkakor.

1½ cups sifted all-purpose flour	½ cup butter
1 teaspoon baking soda	¾ cup sugar
1½ teaspoons ground ginger	1 egg
1 teaspoon ground cinnamon	1½ teaspoons dark corn syrup
¼ teaspoon ground cloves	Whole blanched almonds, cut in small pieces

1. Sift flour, baking soda, and spices together; set aside.
2. Cream butter; add sugar gradually, beating until fluffy. Add egg and corn syrup and beat thoroughly.
3. Blend in dry ingredients in fourths, mixing thoroughly after each addition. Refrigerate dough several hours.
4. Using a portion of the dough at a time, roll about 1/16 inch thick on a lightly floured surface. Cut with lightly floured cookie cutters into various shapes. Transfer to ungreased cookie sheets. Place one almond piece in the center of each.
5. Bake at 375°F 6 to 8 minutes.

ABOUT 7 DOZEN COOKIES

SWISS CHRISTMAS COOKIES
(Mailaenderli)

¾ cup butter
½ teaspoon grated lemon peel
¼ teaspoon lemon juice
¾ cup sugar
1 egg
1 egg yolk
2¾ cups sifted all-purpose flour
⅛ teaspoon salt
1 egg yolk, beaten

1. Cream butter with lemon peel and juice; add sugar gradually, beating until fluffy. Add egg and 1 egg yolk, beating thoroughly after each addition.
2. Add a mixture of flour and salt in fourths, mixing until well blended after each addition. Chill dough thoroughly, at least 1 hour.
3. Roll a third of dough at a time about ¼ inch thick on a floured surface; cut with fancy cookie cutters. Transfer to lightly greased cookie sheets; brush tops with beaten egg yolk.
4. Bake at 375°F 10 to 12 minutes.

ABOUT 6 DOZEN COOKIES

GERMAN MOLASSES COOKIES

1 cup butter
1¼ cups light molasses
¾ cup firmly packed light brown sugar
4 cups sifted all-purpose flour
1 teaspoon baking soda
1 teaspoon salt
2 teaspoons ground ginger
1 teaspoon ground cinnamon
½ to ¾ teaspoon ground cloves

1. Melt butter in a saucepan; add molasses and brown sugar and heat until sugar is dissolved, stirring occasionally. Pour into a bowl; cool.
2. Sift remaining ingredients together; add to cooled mixture in fourths, mixing until blended after each addition.
3. Turn dough onto a floured surface and knead until easy to handle, using additional flour if necessary.
4. Wrap in moisture-vaporproof material; refrigerate and allow dough to ripen one or two days.
5. Roll one fourth of dough at a time about ⅛ inch thick on a floured surface; cut with a 3-inch round cutter or fancy cutters. Transfer to ungreased cookie sheets.
6. Bake at 350°F about 7 minutes.

ABOUT 8 DOZEN COOKIES

NOTE: For gingerbread men, roll dough ¼ inch thick and cut with a gingerbread-man cutter. Bake about 13 minutes.

BROWN MORAVIAN COOKIES
A Pennsylvania Dutch cookie.

4 cups sifted all-purpose flour
¼ teaspoon baking soda
¼ teaspoon salt
1 teaspoon ground cinnamon
½ teaspoon ground cloves
¼ teaspoon ground ginger
1 cup firmly packed light brown sugar
½ cup butter
½ cup lard*
1½ cups light molasses
½ teaspoon cider vinegar

1. Sift flour, baking soda, salt, and spices together into a large bowl. Add brown sugar; mix well.
2. Cut in butter and lard. Add molasses and vinegar gradually, mixing well. Chill dough thoroughly.
3. Using a small amount of dough at a time, roll out about ⅛-inch thick on a lightly floured surface. Cut with fancy cookie cutters. Transfer to greased cookie sheets.
4. Bake at 350°F 8 to 10 minutes.

ABOUT 6 DOZEN COOKIES

*Use butter, if desired, but then cookie will not be authentic.

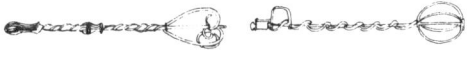

ITALIAN BUTTER COOKIES
(Canestrelli)

4 cups sifted all-purpose flour
1 cup sugar
2½ teaspoons grated lemon peel
1 tablespoon rum
4 egg yolks, beaten
1 cup firm unsalted butter, cut in pieces
1 egg white, slightly beaten

1. Combine flour, sugar, and lemon peel in a large bowl; mix thoroughly. Add rum and then egg yolks in fourths, mixing thoroughly after each addition.
2. Cut butter into flour mixture with pastry blender until particles are fine. Work with fingertips until a dough is formed.
3. Roll one half of dough at a time about ¼ inch thick on a lightly floured surface. Cut into desired shapes. Brush tops with egg white. Transfer to lightly greased cookie sheets.
4. Bake at 350°F about 15 minutes.

ABOUT 6 DOZEN COOKIES

LOVE LETTERS
(Szerelmes Levél)

Rich pastry squares folded like envelopes, with a nut-meringue filling inside, become Hungarian "love letters."

2 cups sifted all-purpose flour	½ cup coarsely chopped walnuts
2 tablespoons sugar	1 teaspoon grated lemon peel
¼ teaspoon salt	2 egg whites
¾ cup butter, chilled	¼ cup sugar
4 egg yolks, slightly beaten	½ teaspoon ground cinnamon

1. Blend flour, sugar, and salt. Cut in butter until particles are the size of rice kernels.
2. Add egg yolks gradually, blending with a fork (mixture will be crumbly). Knead lightly with fingertips and shape into a ball.
3. Divide dough into halves; wrap in waxed paper and chill 1 hour.
4. Mix walnuts and lemon peel; set aside.
5. Fifteen minutes before chilling time is ended, beat egg whites until frothy. Add a mixture of sugar and cinnamon gradually, beating well after each addition; beat until stiff peaks are formed.
6. Gently fold in nut mixture; set aside.
7. Roll one half of dough at a time ⅛ inch thick on a floured surface; cut into 3-inch squares.
8. Put about 2 teaspoons of filling onto center of each square; bring opposite corners together, overlapping slightly at center; repeat with other two corners.
9. Transfer to ungreased cookie sheets. Brush tops with slightly beaten *egg*.
10. Bake at 350°F about 20 minutes.
11. Cool cookies on wire racks. Sift a mixture of *2 to 3 tablespoons confectioners' sugar* and *½ to 1 teaspoon ground cinnamon* over cooled cookies.

ABOUT 2½ DOZEN COOKIES

APRICOT CRESCENTS

1 pkg active dry yeast	2½ cups sifted all-purpose flour
¼ cup warm water	3 egg yolks
1 cup softened butter	Confectioners' sugar
2 tablespoons sugar	¾ cup apricot preserves
1 teaspoon vanilla extract	
¼ teaspoon salt	
¼ cup cream, scalded	

1. Soften yeast in the warm water; set aside.
2. Mix in a large bowl the butter, sugar, extract, and salt. Add scalded cream and stir to blend. Thoroughly beat in ½ cup of the flour.
3. Add yeast to butter mixture; mix thoroughly. Add the egg yolks, one at a time, beating thoroughly after each addition. Add about half of the remaining flour and beat until very smooth. Beat in enough flour to make a soft dough.
4. Sift confectioners' sugar lightly and evenly over a flat surface. Roll a fourth of the dough at a time into a 12-inch round on the sugared surface. Cut into 16 wedge-shaped pieces. Spread wide end of each wedge with about ½ teaspoon filling. Roll up each wedge, beginning at the wide end; place with point down on an ungreased cookie sheet. Curve into crescents.
5. Cover with waxed paper and a clean towel; let stand 20 minutes (cookies will rise only slightly).
6. Bake at 350°F 15 to 20 minutes, or until lightly browned.
7. Remove cookies to wire racks and cool slightly. Sift Confectioners' sugar over tops. 5 DOZEN COOKIES

FATTIGMANN

A traditional Norwegian Christmas favorite.

10 egg yolks	5 cups sifted all-purpose flour
2 egg whites	2 teaspoons ground cardamom
¾ cup sugar	Lard for deep frying
¼ cup brandy	
1 cup heavy cream	

1. Beat egg yolks, egg whites, sugar, and brandy until very thick. Add cream slowly, stirring well.
2. Sift flour and cardamom together; add about ½ cup at a time to egg mixture, mixing thoroughly after each addition. Wrap and chill overnight.
3. Heat lard to 365° to 370°F in a deep saucepan.
4. Roll dough, a small portion at a time, ¹⁄₁₆ inch thick on a floured surface.
5. Using a floured knife or pastry wheel, cut into diamond shapes, 5x2 inches; make a lengthwise slit in the center of each diamond. Pull the tip of one end through each slit and tuck back under itself.
6. Deep fry 1 to 2 minutes, or until golden brown, turning once. Drain and cool.
7. Sprinkle cookies with *confectioners' sugar*. Store in tightly covered containers.

ABOUT 6 DOZEN COOKIES

Chapter 15

BEVERAGES—Hot & Cold

All over the world people have their favorite beverages. Here in the United States we are inclined to have many favorites and seem to have no truly national beverage. Americans usually judge the rightness of a drink by the occasion for which it is intended. But there is almost universal agreement among Americans that the day properly starts with coffee—coffee brewed the regular way from finely or coarsely ground coffee beans or coffee made the quick way by dissolving instant-type coffee in water.

For those who prefer starting the day with tea, there is the brew made from dried tea leaves, or the faster way—dissolving the "instant" product in water.

Beverage Syrups

COCOA SYRUP

2 cups sugar
1 cup cocoa
½ teaspoon salt
1 cup cold water
1 cup hot water
2 teaspoons vanilla extract

Combine the sugar, cocoa, and salt in a saucepan. Stir in cold water to make a paste. Blend in hot water. Simmer 4 to 6 minutes, stirring until thick and smooth. Cool and stir in the extract. Store in a tightly covered container in refrigerator.
ABOUT 3 CUPS
NOTE: For a chocolate eggnog, allow 3 tablespoons of the syrup per serving.

CHOCOLATE SYRUP

5 oz. (5 sq.) unsweetened chocolate
2 cups sugar syrup
½ teaspoon salt
2 cups hot water
2 teaspoons vanilla extract

Combine the chocolate, sugar syrup, and salt in a saucepan. Stir in the hot water. Simmer 4 to 6 minutes, stirring until thick and smooth. Cool. Stir in extract. Store, tightly covered, in refrigerator.
ABOUT 4 CUPS
NOTE: For each serving of chocolate milk shake, allow 2 to 3 tablespoons of the syrup.

CARAMEL SYRUP

1 cup sugar   1 cup boiling water

Melt the sugar in a heavy light-colored skillet over low heat, stirring constantly. When sugar becomes a golden brown syrup, remove from heat. Add the boiling water carefully and very gradually, stirring constantly. (Be careful so steam does not burn hand.) Return to low heat and continue to stir about 10 minutes, or until of syrup consistency. Cool and store, tightly covered, in refrigerator. ABOUT 1 CUP
NOTE: To flavor an 8-oz. serving of milk, stir in 2 tablespoons or more of the syrup.

LEMON SYRUP

1½ cups sugar
1 cup water
1 tablespoon grated lemon peel
½ cup lemon juice

1. Combine sugar, water, and lemon peel in a saucepan. Set over low heat and stir until sugar is dissolved. Cover, bring to boiling, and boil 5 minutes.

2. Remove from heat and stir in lemon juice. Set aside to cool. Chill thoroughly. Store covered in refrigerator. Use to sweeten iced tea. ABOUT 1½ CUPS

LIME SYRUP: Follow recipe for Lemon Syrup. Substitute *lime peel and juice* for the lemon.

MINT SYRUP: Follow recipe for Lemon Syrup. Decrease sugar to 1 cup. Omit lemon peel and juice. Stir ¼ *teaspoon mint extract* into syrup when removed from heat.

HOT BEVERAGES

DRIP COFFEE
Preheat a drip coffee maker by filling it with boiling water. Drain. For each standard measuring cup of water, using standard measuring spoon, measure *2 tablespoons drip grind coffee.* Put into filter section of drip coffee maker or in cone with filter paper. Pour measured freshly *boiling water* into upper container or cone. Cover, depending on type of pot used. Allow all of water to drip through coffee, keeping coffee maker over low heat 5 to 8 minutes, or as long as coffee is dripping. Do not let coffee boil at any time. Remove coffee compartment; stir and cover the brew. Place coffee maker over low heat. Stir before serving.

PERCOLATED COFFEE
Use *regular grind coffee.* Follow Drip Coffee recipe for amount to use. Put into strainer basket of coffee maker. Measure freshly drawn *cold water* into bottom of percolator. Place basket in coffee maker. Cover. Place over heat. When percolating begins, reduce heat to low so that percolating will be gentle and slow. Timing varies from 5 to 10 minutes after percolation starts. It's wise to experiment to determine exact timing for the amount of coffee generally made in your percolator. Larger amounts of coffee require the longer timing. Remove coffee basket, cover coffee maker, and keep coffee hot over low heat. Do not let coffee boil.

STEEPED COFFEE
Use *regular grind coffee.* Follow Drip Coffee recipe for amount to use. Put into coffee maker. To clarify coffee, mix in *1 teaspoon slightly beaten egg* for each 2 tablespoons coffee used. Measure and add freshly drawn *cold water.* Bring very slowly to boiling, stirring occasionally. Remove from heat at once. Pour ¼ *cup cold water* down spout to settle grounds. Let stand 3 to 5 minutes without heat. Strain through a fine strainer into a server which has been preheated with boiling water. Let coffee stand over low heat.

VACUUM-DRIP COFFEE
Use *drip or vacuum grind coffee.* Follow Drip Coffee recipe for amount to use. Specific directions for making vary according to the type of coffee maker used. Usually, freshly drawn *cold water* is measured and poured into the decanter or lower bowl. Coffee is measured into upper bowl. Cover. Place coffee maker over moderate to low heat. When all but a small amount of water has risen to upper bowl, remove coffee maker from heat. Remove top bowl when the brew has run into decanter. Cover. Serve immediately or keep hot over very low heat. Do not boil at any time.

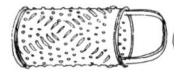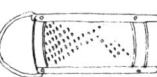

DEMITASSE
(After-Dinner Coffee)

Using ½ measuring cup water per serving, prepare Drip Coffee or any variation. Serve hot in demitasse or after-dinner cups.

CAFÉ L'ORANGE

2 medium-sized oranges, sliced
Whole cloves
8 cups (coffee-cup size) hot coffee
Sweetened whipped cream
Brown sugar
Ground cinnamon

1. Stud each orange slice with 4 cloves; pour hot coffee over them and allow to steep for 30 minutes. Discard orange slices and cloves.
2. Reheat coffee. Pour coffee into a handsome coffeepot or carafe.
3. Accompany with bowls of the whipped cream and brown sugar and a shaker of cinnamon so that guests may flavor their coffee as desired.

8 SERVINGS

CAFE AU LAIT

For each cup of freshly brewed *coffee*, scald an equal measure of rich *milk*. Simultaneously pour hot coffee and hot milk into each cup. Sweeten if desired.

BOSTON COFFEE: Serve *coffee* and *cream* in equal proportions.

VIENNA COFFEE: Serve *coffee* with *whipped cream*.

HOT TEA

Heat teapot thoroughly by filling with boiling water. Pour off water; put into pot *1 rounded teaspoon loose black tea* or *1 tea bag* for each cup of tea to be brewed, or use 1 large tea bag for about 4 cups tea. For each cup of tea, pour *1 cup briskly boiling freshly drawn water* into the teapot. Cover pot and allow tea to steep 3 to 5 minutes. Stir the brew and strain the tea into each teacup as it is poured or remove tea bag or bags before pouring.

HOT GINGER TEA

4 tea bags
2 pieces (3 in. each) stick cinnamon
8 whole cloves
2 large pieces crystallized ginger, cut in very thin slices
3 to 4 tablespoons sugar
6 cups boiling water

1. Put the tea bags, cinnamon sticks, cloves, crystallized ginger, and sugar into a large teapot. Pour on boiling water; allow to steep 3 minutes. Remove tea bags and steep for 5 minutes.
2. To serve, pour tea into cups and float a quarter slice of *orange* in each cup. ABOUT 8 SERVINGS

HOT COCOA

5 to 6 tablespoons cocoa, sieved
5 to 6 tablespoons sugar
¼ teaspoon salt
1 cup water
3 cups milk
½ teaspoon vanilla extract

1. Mix cocoa, sugar, and salt in a heavy saucepan. Blend in the water. Boil gently 2 minutes over direct heat, stirring until slightly thickened.
2. Stir in the milk, heating slowly until scalding hot. Remove from heat. Cover and keep hot, if necessary, over hot water.
3. Just before serving, mix in the extract. Beat with hand rotary or electric beater until foamy. Serve steaming hot, plain or with *whipped cream, marshmallow cream*, or *marshmallows*. 6 SERVINGS

HOT CHOCOLATE

2½ cups milk, scalded
2 oz. (2 sq.) unsweetened chocolate, quartered
¼ cup sugar
1 teaspoon vanilla extract
Dash salt

1. Rinse an electric blender container with hot water.
2. Put into container about ½ cup scalded milk, chocolate, sugar, extract, and salt. Cover and blend about 1 minute, or until smooth and color is even throughout.
3. Add remaining scalded milk and blend until thoroughly mixed. Serve immediately. 4 SERVINGS

MEXICAN CHOCOLATE

4 oz. sweet chocolate
4 cups milk
1 teaspoon ground cinnamon

1. Combine all ingredients in a heavy saucepan. Cook over medium heat, stirring frequently, until chocolate is melted and mixture is heated.
2. Beat with a hand rotary beater or mix in an electric blender until frothy, about 1 minute. Serve steaming hot. 6 TO 8 SERVINGS

HOT SPICED CIDER

2 qts. apple cider
1 teaspoon whole cloves
1 teaspoon whole allspice
2 pieces (3 in. each) stick cinnamon
½ cup firmly packed light brown sugar
Few grains salt

Bring all ingredients to boiling in a large saucepan; simmer, covered, 30 minutes. Remove spices. Serve hot, garnished with slices of unpared *red apples*.

ABOUT 2 QUARTS

COLD BEVERAGES

ICED COFFEE

For stronger flavor pour over coffee ice cubes. Using ½ measuring cup water per standard measure of coffee, prepare *Drip Coffee, page 326,* or any variation. Fill tall glasses to brim with ice cubes. Pour the hot coffee over the ice. Serve with *granulated* or *confectioners' sugar, sugar syrup, cream,* or *whipped cream* sprinkled with *ground cinnamon*.

CHOCOLATE JAVA

3 oz. (3 sq.) unsweetened chocolate
3 cups strong coffee
½ cup sugar
2 cups milk
4 egg yolks
¼ cup sugar
4 egg whites
¼ cup sugar

1. Combine chocolate, coffee, and ½ cup sugar in a saucepan. Set over low heat and stir constantly until chocolate is melted. Bring rapidly to boiling, stirring constantly. Reduce heat; cook and stir 3 minutes.
2. Remove from heat. Stir in the milk; chill thoroughly.
3. Beat egg yolks and ¼ cup sugar together until very thick. Gradually blend in the chilled chocolate mixture.
4. Beat egg whites until frothy; gradually add ¼ cup sugar, beating until rounded peaks are formed. Turn onto the chocolate mixture and slowly beat together until just blended. Chill. Serve topped with *Mocha Whipped Cream, page 247.*

ABOUT 10 SERVINGS

ICED CINNAMON COFFEE

4 cups strong coffee
  (use 2 to 4 teaspoons instant coffee to 1 cup boiling water)
1 piece (3 in.) stick cinnamon, broken in pieces
½ cup heavy cream
Coffee Syrup, *below*

1. Pour hot coffee over cinnamon pieces; cover and let stand about 1 hour.
2. Remove cinnamon and stir in the cream. Chill thoroughly.
3. To serve, pour into ice-filled glasses. Stir in desired amount of Coffee Syrup. If desired, top with *sweetened whipped cream* and sprinkle with *ground cinnamon.* Use *cinnamon sticks* as stirrers.

ABOUT 4 SERVINGS

COFFEE SYRUP

1 cup sugar
¾ cup water
1 teaspoon instant coffee
¼ cup boiling water

1. Combine sugar and the ¾ cup water in a saucepan. Stir over low heat until sugar is dissolved. Cover, bring to boiling, and boil 5 minutes. Remove from heat.
2. Dissolve instant coffee in boiling water. Stir into syrup. Cool; store covered in refrigerator.

ABOUT 1 CUP

ICED ORANGE MOCHA

4 cups strong coffee
  (use 4 tablespoons instant coffee to 4 cups hot water)
2 medium-sized oranges, sliced
6 tablespoons sugar
3 tablespoons Dutch process cocoa
2 cups cold milk

1. Pour coffee over orange slices. Let stand 30 minutes.
2. Remove orange slices; thoroughly chill the coffee.
3. Combine the sugar and cocoa. Add ¼ cup of the milk; stir until smooth. Bring to boiling over direct heat and cook 1 to 2 minutes. Remove from

heat. Add remaining milk gradually, blending well. Cover and chill until ready to use.

4. To serve, mix the chilled coffee and cocoa. Top each serving with *sweetened whipped cream*, sprinkled with a mixture of shaved *unsweetened chocolate* and grated *orange peel*.   6 TO 8 SERVINGS

ICED TEA

Fruit kabobs—lime quarters, pineapple chunks, and whole strawberries threaded onto skewers—make attractive stirrers for tall iced drinks.

COLD-WATER METHOD: For each ¾ cup (6 ounces) cold water use *3 teaspoons tea* or *3 tea bags*. Measure tea into quart jar or other glass or china container; add measured cold water. Cover; set in refrigerator for 12 to 24 hours. Strain; pour over ice.

HOT METHOD I: Use *6 teaspoons (2 tablespoons) tea* or *6 tea bags* for each *1 pint (16 ounces) water*. Measure tea into quart jar or other glass or china container. Pour measured boiling water on top; let stand in warm place 5 minutes, strain, pour over ice.

HOT METHOD II: Use *3 teaspoons tea* or *3 tea bags* for each *1½ cups boiling water*. Make as directed under Hot Method I, let stand 5 minutes, strain, cover, and let cool for 2 to 3 hours without refrigeration before pouring over ice.

To serve with tea—Lemon wedges, crosswise slices of orange with whole cloves stuck in edges, fresh mint leaves, preserved ginger, or brandied cherries.

LEMONADE

| 1 cup sugar | 4 cups cold water |
| 1 cup water | ¾ cup lemon juice |

1. Mix the sugar and 1 cup water in a saucepan. Stir over low heat until sugar is dissolved. Increase heat, cover, and boil 5 minutes. Remove from heat; cool.
2. Mix the cold water and lemon juice with the cooled syrup. Pour over chipped ice or ice cubes in tall glasses.   ABOUT 1½ QUARTS

LIMEADE: Follow recipe for Lemonade. Substitute *¾ cup lime juice* for lemon juice.

ORANGEADE: Follow recipe for Lemonade. Decrease lemon juice to ¼ cup (or substitute ¼ cup lime juice for lemon juice), decrease cold water to 1 cup, and mix *3 cups orange juice*.

GINGER ICE COOLER

| 1 can (6 oz.) frozen lemonade concentrate, partially thawed | ⅔ cup light corn syrup |
| | 1 qt. ginger ale, chilled |

1. Blend lemonade concentrate with corn syrup, then ginger ale.
2. Pour into individual glasses over ginger ice (freeze additional ginger ale in ice cube trays and finely crush the ice).   1½ QUARTS

RASPBERRY DELIGHT: Purée partially thawed *frozen red raspberries*. Blend with desired amount of Ginger Ice Cooler mixture. Strain if necessary. Serve thoroughly chilled in 4-ounce stemmed glasses. Omit ginger ice.

LEMON-CRANBERRY NECTAR

1 cup chilled cranberry juice cocktail	1 can (6 oz.) frozen lemonade concentrate (not reconstituted)
¾ cup chilled apricot nectar	
¾ cup water	Fresh ripe strawberries

1. Blend thoroughly the cranberry juice, apricot nectar, and water. Stir in lemonade concentrate until melted.
2. Pour into tall glasses over ice cubes or crushed ice.   ABOUT 3¼ CUPS

LIME-ROSEMARY ZING

1½ tablespoons crushed rosemary leaves	1½ cups apricot nectar
2½ tablespoons sugar	¾ cup lime juice
⅛ teaspoon salt	3 cups ginger ale, chilled
⅓ cup water	

1. Combine rosemary, sugar, salt, and water in a small saucepan; simmer 2 minutes. Cool; strain. Blend with apricot nectar and lime juice; chill.
2. Blend ginger ale with chilled fruit juice mixture. Pour over crushed ice in tall glasses. Garnish each serving with spiral strips of *lime peel*.
   ABOUT 5 CUPS

PURPLE PLUM COOLER

2 cups purple plum juice*
2 cups sugar
1½ teaspoons cider vinegar
2⅔ cups sparkling water, chilled

1. Combine plum juice and sugar in a saucepan. Set over low heat and stir until sugar is dissolved; increase heat and simmer 10 minutes. Remove from heat and stir in vinegar. Cool; chill thoroughly.
2. Just before serving, pour sparkling water into chilled mixture. ABOUT 5¼ CUPS

Plum Juice: Rinse fresh *purple plums.* Cut into halves and remove pits. Put in kettle with *cold water,* allowing ¼ cup cold water to 1 quart firmly packed plums. Cover. Bring to boiling. Simmer at least 10 minutes, or until plums are soft. Strain through a jelly bag. Allow to hang several hours. Reserve the pulp for preparing purée. This juice may be frozen and used for jellymaking or may be sweetened for beverage use, such as the shrub.

PEACH JULEP

½ cup sugar
1 tablespoon light brown sugar
2 tablespoons honey
1 cup water
2 whole cloves
1 piece (3 in.) stick cinnamon
1 cup coarsely chopped peaches, puréed in an electric blender or forced through food mill or sieve
½ cup lemon juice
2 cups orange juice

1. Combine the sugars, honey, water, cloves, and cinnamon stick in a saucepan; heat, stirring constantly, until sugar is completely dissolved. Cool; remove cloves and cinnamon.
2. Blend peach purée, lemon juice, and orange juice into the cooled sugar syrup. Chill.
3. Serve in stemmed glasses. ABOUT 12 SERVINGS

RASPBERRY AND LIME SWIZZLE

1 cup sugar
2 cups ripe red raspberries
1 cup lime juice
Lemon-lime carbonated beverage, chilled
Watermelon Sherbet, *below*
Thin lime slices

1. Sprinkle sugar over berries in an electric blender container; let stand 1 hour. Blend thoroughly.
2. Add lime juice and chill at least 2 hours. Strain through a sieve.
3. Pour ¼ cup of the raspberry syrup into each glass; add ½ cup lemon-lime carbonated beverage and stir. Top with a small scoop of Watermelon Sherbet. Garnish each glass with a thin slice of lime. ABOUT 10 SERVINGS

WATERMELON SHERBET: Mix *4 cups diced watermelon, ¼ cup lemon juice, 1 cup sugar,* and *⅛ teaspoon salt* together; chill 30 minutes; force through a sieve into a bowl. Soften *1 envelop unflavored gelatin* in *½ cup cold water* in a small saucepan. Set over low heat until dissolved, stirring constantly. Stir into watermelon mixture. Turn into refrigerator trays and freeze until firm, stirring once.
ABOUT 3 CUPS SHERBET

MINTED CHOCOLATE REFRESHER

3 oz. (3 sq.) unsweetened chocolate
1 cup boiling water
¾ cup sugar
16 large marshmallows
½ teaspoon peppermint extract
1 quart milk
Mint sprigs

1. Melt chocolate in boiling water. Add sugar and stir until dissolved; pour into an electric blender container. Add marshmallows and extract; cover and blend until smooth.
2. Mix into milk; chill thoroughly.
3. Mix well before pouring over ice cubes in tall chilled glasses. Garnish each serving with a mint sprig. ABOUT 6 CUPS

CHOCOLATE-BANANA SHAKE

8 ripe bananas
6 cups cold milk
1 cup instant chocolate-flavored drink mix
1 teaspoon vanilla extract
1½ pts. vanilla ice cream

1. Cut about one third of bananas into large pieces and put into an electric blender container. Add one third of each of the remaining ingredients; blend thoroughly. Pour into a chilled large pitcher. Repeat twice with remaining ingredients.
2. Pour into glasses and, if desired, top each with scoop of *vanilla ice cream.* 10 TO 12 SERVINGS

FROSTED COFFEE SHAKE

2 cups cold milk
2 tablespoons sugar
1 tablespoon instant coffee

½ pt. vanilla or chocolate ice cream

Put milk, sugar, and instant coffee into an electric blender container. Cover and blend thoroughly. Add ice cream by spoonfuls and blend until mixed.

ABOUT 3 CUPS

SPANISH LEMON AND LIME

1 cup instant nonfat dry milk
1 qt. icy cold milk
⅓ cup sugar

⅔ cup lime juice
1 pt. lemon sherbet
1 qt. crushed ice

1. Stir the dry milk into the cold milk until blended. Stir in the sugar until dissolved. Add the lime juice and sherbet and beat with hand rotary or electric beater until foamy.
2. Pour foamy beverage into a pitcher or individual glasses over part of the crushed ice. Garnish with *lemon and/or lime slices* and fresh *mint leaves*, along with the remaining ice. Serve with straws.

ABOUT 2 QUARTS

STRAWBERRY SHAKE

1 pt. strawberries, rinsed
1⅓ cups cold milk

¼ cup sugar
2 scoops vanilla or strawberry ice cream

Combine strawberries with the milk and sugar in an electric blender container. Cover and blend thoroughly. Add the ice cream and blend a few seconds.

3 SERVINGS

APRICOT WHIRL

1 can (12 oz.) apricot nectar
1 pt. vanilla ice cream

¼ cup instant natural-flavored malted milk powder
2 tablespoons lemon juice

1. Pour apricot nectar into refrigerator tray; freeze until mushy.
2. Spoon apricot nectar and ice cream into an electric blender container; add malted milk powder and lemon juice. Cover and blend until smooth and creamy.
3. Pour into chilled glasses and serve immediately with straws.

ABOUT 3¾ CUPS

HOMEMADE CHOCOLATE SODA

1 small scoop chocolate or vanilla ice cream
2 to 4 tablespoons sweetened chocolate syrup

½ cup cold milk
½ cup sparkling water or ginger ale
1 or 2 scoops softened ice cream

1. For each soda, blend a small scoop of ice cream and the chocolate syrup in a tall glass.
2. Add milk and sparkling water; mix thoroughly.
3. Float scoops of ice cream on top. Serve with straws and long-handled spoon.

1 SERVING

HOMEMADE LEMON SODA: Follow recipe for Homemade Chocolate Soda. Use *vanilla ice cream* and substitute *2 tablespoons thawed frozen lemonade concentrate* for the chocolate syrup.

HOMEMADE PEACH SODA: Follow recipe for Homemade Chocolate Soda. Use *vanilla ice cream* and substitute *⅓ cup mashed, sweetened ripe fresh peaches* for the chocolate syrup.

HOMEMADE PINEAPPLE SODA: Follow recipe for Homemade Chocolate Soda. Use *vanilla ice cream* and substitute *¼ cup canned or frozen crushed pineapple* for the chocolate syrup.

HOMEMADE RASPBERRY OR STRAWBERRY SODA: Follow recipe for Homemade Chocolate Soda. Use *vanilla ice cream* and substitute *¼ cup crushed, sweetened red raspberries or strawberries* for the chocolate syrup.

PUNCHES

SPARKLING PUNCH

Here's an easy-to-make punch for a Halloween party, a fine go-along with cake — refreshments to please guests of all ages.

2 qts. apple cider	4 bottles (12 oz. each) lemon-lime carbonated beverage, chilled
8 whole cloves	
2 pieces stick cinnamon	
6 whole allspice	
1 can (6 oz.) frozen pineapple-orange juice concentrate	

1. Refrigerate 1 quart of the cider and pour remaining 1 quart into a saucepan with the spices. Cook 15 minutes and strain to remove spices.
2. Combine the spiced and chilled cider and fruit juice concentrate in a chilled punch bowl; blend well. Slowly pour in the carbonated beverage.
3. Add ice cubes or a fancy ice mold.

ABOUT 3 QUARTS PUNCH

FOUR-FRUIT REFRESHER

4 cups apple juice	2 teaspoons vanilla extract
2 cups cranberry juice cocktail	¼ cup sugar
2 cups orange juice	2 cups ginger ale, chilled
¼ cup lemon juice	

1. Combine all ingredients except ginger ale; stir until sugar is completely dissolved. Chill thoroughly.
2. When ready to serve, pour fruit juice mixture into a chilled punch bowl, add ginger ale, and stir gently to blend.

ABOUT 2½ QUARTS PUNCH

SPICY CRANBERRY PUNCH

4 pieces (3 in. each) stick cinnamon, broken in pieces	3 qts. cranberry juice cocktail
8 whole allspice	1 orange, sliced
18 whole cloves	6 bottles (7 oz. each) lemon-lime carbonated beverage, chilled

1. Tie spices together in cheesecloth bag.
2. In a large saucepan, combine the cranberry juice cocktail, orange slices, and spice bag. Bring to boiling, reduce heat, and simmer about 20 minutes. Set aside to cool; discard spice bag and orange; chill cranberry juice.
3. Just before serving, pour into chilled punch bowl; add lemon-lime carbonated beverage and stir to blend. If desired, garnish with additional *orange slices.*

ABOUT 17 CUPS

LOGANBERRY-LEMONADE PUNCH

4 cans (6 oz. each) frozen lemonade concentrate	3 cups cold water
	3½ cups sparkling water, chilled
2 cups loganberry, blackberry, or raspberry juice	3½ cups ginger ale, chilled

1. Mix thoroughly the lemonade concentrate, berry juice, and water. Set in refrigerator to chill thoroughly.
2. When ready to serve, pour mixture into a chilled punch bowl. Add the sparkling water and ginger ale; stir to blend. If desired, a decorative ice block may be floated in the punch bowl.

ABOUT 3¾ QUARTS

SPARKLING GOLDEN COOLER

1 cup sugar	1 can (12 oz.) pineapple juice
1½ cups water	
2 medium-sized oranges	2 qts. ginger ale, chilled
1 lemon	
1 lime	Fresh strawberries
2 medium-sized bananas, cut in pieces	

1. Combine sugar and water in a saucepan; stir over low heat until sugar is dissolved. Increase heat and bring to boiling; boil 3 minutes. Cool.
2. Meanwhile, extract the juice from oranges, lemon, and lime. Put juice into an electric blender container with the bananas; blend until smooth. Mix with syrup and pineapple juice. Freeze in refrigerator trays until firm, about 3 hours.
3. To serve, scoop frozen crush into a large bowl; stir in ginger ale. Serve at once, garnished with fresh strawberries.

20 SERVINGS

SPARKLING FRUIT REFRESHER

1 can (6 oz.) frozen orange juice concentrate, thawed
1 can (6 oz.) frozen lemonade concentrate, thawed
3 cups cold water
2 drops red food coloring
1 bottle (12 oz.) ginger ale, chilled
1 pkg. (16 oz.) frozen whole strawberries, just thawed
1 pt. orange sherbet

Combine concentrates and water in a punch bowl; stir until well blended. Mix in food coloring and ginger ale. Add strawberries (including syrup). Float scoops of sherbet on punch. Serve immediately. ABOUT 12 SERVINGS

RASPBERRY FRUIT PUNCH

3 env. raspberry-flavored instant soft drink mix
3 env. grape-flavored instant soft drink mix
2¼ cups sugar
3 cans (6 oz. each) frozen pineapple-orange juice concentrate, thawed
1½ teaspoons red food coloring
½ teaspoon almond extract
12 bottles (7 oz. each) lemon-lime carbonated beverage, chilled

1. Mix thoroughly in a large bowl the soft drink mixes and sugar. Add *6 quarts water* gradually, stirring constantly until soft drink mixes and sugar are dissolved. Stir in the pineapple-orange juice concentrate, food coloring, and extract; stir until well blended.
2. Chill thoroughly.
3. Just before serving, stir in the chilled lemon-lime beverage. ABOUT 8 QUARTS PUNCH

GOLDEN PUNCH

1½ cups sugar
3 cups water
3 cups freshly prepared tea (cool at room temperature)
3 cups unsweetened pineapple juice
1½ cups lime juice
1 can (6 oz.) frozen orange juice concentrate, thawed
3 cups ginger ale, chilled

1. Combine sugar and water in a saucepan. Set over low heat and stir until sugar is dissolved. Increase heat, cover, and boil 5 minutes. Remove from heat; set aside to cool.
2. Combine in a large bowl the tea, pineapple juice, lime ice, and orange juice concentrate. Stir to blend ingredients. Chill in refrigerator.
3. When ready to serve, pour chilled fruit juice mixture into a chilled punch bowl. Pour in the sugar syrup and chilled ginger ale; stir to blend thoroughly. If desired, a decorative ice block may be floated in the punch. ABOUT 3 QUARTS PUNCH

SUMMER STRAWBERRY BOWL

4 pts. fresh strawberries, rinsed and hulled
2 cups icy cold water
½ cup lemon juice, strained
2 cups instant nonfat dry milk
¾ cup sugar
1 qt. vanilla ice cream, softened
2 qts. crushed ice

1. Purée some of the strawberries in an electric blender; turn into a large bowl. Repeat with the remaining strawberries.
2. Mix the water and lemon juice into the purée. Stir in dry milk and sugar until thoroughly blended.
3. Pour half of the strawberry mixture into a bowl. Using an electric mixer, beat in half of the ice cream until well blended. Pour into a chilled large punch bowl.
4. Repeat the mixing of remaining strawberries and ice cream. Pour into punch bowl. Blend in part of the ice, then add remaining ice and serve.
ABOUT 3 QUARTS PUNCH

CHAMPAGNE STRAWBERRY BOWL: Follow recipe for Summer Strawberry Bowl. Blend *3 cups chilled champagne* into the cream strawberry mixture. Float *2 cups fresh strawberry halves* in the punch.

ROSÉ STRAWBERRY BOWL: Follow recipe for Summer Strawberry Bowl. Blend *3 cups chilled rosé wine* into the creamy strawberry mixture. Float *2 cups fresh strawberry halves* in the punch.

NOTE: Some tastes may prefer champagne or rosé wine added in equal amounts with the creamy strawberry mixture.

Punches

HOT AROMATIC PUNCH

4½ cups boiling water	¼ cup sugar
5 tea bags	2 to 3 tablespoons
1 qt. apple cider	rubbed sage

1. Pour boiling water over tea bags in a heated teapot. Let steep about 5 minutes; remove the tea bags.
2. Meanwhile, combine apple cider, sugar, and sage in a saucepan. Cover, bring to boiling, and simmer 5 minutes.
3. Add the tea to apple cider mixture and simmer 10 minutes longer. Strain.
4. Serve hot in mugs. Garnish each with a twist of *lemon*.   ABOUT 7½ CUPS PUNCH

HOT BUTTERED CRANBERRY PUNCH

Fresh cranberries, pineapple juice, and spices contribute to the happy blend of flavors in this tangy-sweet punch.

2 cups water	¼ teaspoon ground cloves
4 cups fresh cranberries, rinsed	⅛ teaspoon ground nutmeg
1½ cups water	⅛ teaspoon salt
⅔ cup lightly packed brown sugar	1 can (18 oz.) unsweetened pineapple juice
½ teaspoon ground cinnamon	Butter or margarine
¼ teaspoon ground allspice	

1. Combine the 2 cups water and cranberries in a saucepan. Bring to boiling and cook until skins pop. Force cranberries through a food or sieve to make a purée.
2. Meanwhile, bring to boiling in a saucepan the 1½ cups water, brown sugar, spices, and salt. Add the cranberry purée and pineapple juice. Return to heat and simmer 5 minutes. Keep hot over simmering water until serving time.
3. Ladle punch into serving cups or mugs and add dots of butter to each cup. Serve with *cinnamon stick* stirrers, if desired.   ABOUT 1½ QUARTS PUNCH

SAGE CIDER PUNCH

"Sage brew"*	1 cup sugar
"Tea brew"**	2 tablespoons lime juice
1 qt. apple cider	(1 small lime)

1. Prepare the sage and tea brews; set aside.
2. Meanwhile, combine cider and sugar in a saucepan; set over low heat and stir until sugar is dissolved. Cover saucepan and heat the cider to simmering.
3. Add the strained sage and tea brews and the lime juice; blend thoroughly. Cover and keep hot over low heat until ready to serve. (Do not boil.)
4. Serve in small glasses or mugs. If desired, float several *sage leaves* on each serving.

ABOUT 5½ CUPS PUNCH

*To prepare "sage brew," pour *1 cup boiling water* over *2 tablespoons leaf sage* in a small saucepan. Bring to simmering; cover tightly and remove from heat. Let stand about 10 minutes to brew. Strain through cheesecloth or a fine sieve.   ABOUT ⅔ CUP

**To prepare "tea brew," pour *1 cup boiling water* over *1 tea bag* in a small saucepan; cover tightly and let stand about 10 minutes. Remove tea bag.   ABOUT 1 CUP

SPICED LEMON TEA PUNCH

Accented with crystallized ginger and a generous amount of lemon juice, you'll agree . . . this tea drink is something extra-special.

3 cups freshly boiling water	1 cup sugar
	¼ to 1 cup lemon juice
6 tea bags or 6 rounded teaspoons black tea	6 cups freshly boiling water
2 pieces (2 in. each) stick cinnamon	2 pieces (2 in. each) crystallized ginger, cut lengthwise in halves
12 to 16 whole cloves	
2 to 3 teaspoons grated lemon peel	

1. Pour 3 cups boiling water over tea. Add cinnamon sticks, cloves, and lemon peel. Allow to steep for 5 minutes.
2. Remove tea bags; add sugar and stir until dissolved. Strain. Return cinnamon sticks to the tea. Add lemon juice, 6 cups boiling water, and ginger pieces; stir to blend. Ladle hot punch into serving cups.   ABOUT 2½ QUARTS PUNCH

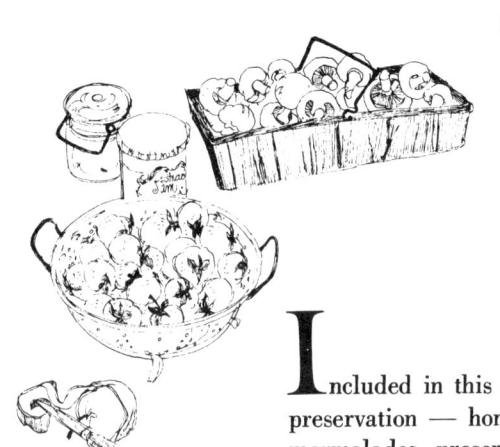

Bonus Chapter
PRESERVING, FREEZING

Included in this chapter are the following methods of home food preservation — home canning; preserving, *i.e.*, making jellies, jams, marmalades, preserves, conserves, and fruit butters; and also home freezing.

HOME CANNING OF FRUITS & VEGETABLES

To preserve foods by canning we must do two things — first, provide sufficient heat to destroy all microscopic life that will cause spoilage in food; second, provide a perfect seal which will prevent re-entrance of the micro-organisms.

The problems of preventing spoilage have been practically solved by improved methods of canning which are explained here. It must be remembered, however, that the process of canning never improves the product; it only preserves it for future use. Only the freshest produce should be canned.

METHODS OF CANNING

These methods refer to the manner in which food is prepared and packed into jars and must not be confused with methods of processing foods.

Open-Kettle — This method involves cooking the food completely and ladling it into hot sterilized jars (filling and sealing one jar at a time). Sterilized equipment and utensils should be used throughout.

With the open-kettle method there is always a possibility of spoilage through contamination of the food or jars since there is no period of sterilization after the jars have been sealed. Foods which are cooked in a thick syrup (jams, preserves, fruit butters, pickles, etc.) may be safely canned by this method. However, it is not recommended for canning fruits, juices, and tomatoes. Spoilage can result because the organisms (bacteria, yeast, and molds) which cause it are either not destroyed during cooking or they enter the jar before it is sealed.

Never use this method for canning vegetables or meat.

Cold (raw) Pack — This method involves packing the food firmly into clean hot jars and adding boiling liquid (syrup, water, or fruit juice), leaving some space between the packed food and the jar lid. Most raw fruits and vegetables shrink during processing so ½ inch space is usually sufficient. Exceptions are corn, lima beans, and peas which expand during processing. These should be packed loosely and about 1 inch of space allowed at top of jar. Enough boiling liquid should be added to completely cover the food.

Air bubbles are released from filled jars before adjusting lids. (Follow manufacturer's directions for the type of jars and lids being used.) The food is then cooked and sterilized simultaneously by processing in boiling water or in steam.

Fruits (except apples, pears, and pineapples) and tomatoes may be canned using the cold-pack method. Vegetables are packed raw into cans only if they are to be processed in a pressure canner.

Hot Pack — This method involves precooking the product a short time before packing it very hot into clean hot jars, then adding hot cooking liquid (or hot syrup or water), releasing air bubbles, sealing jars, and processing them.

Precooking food before packing causes it to shrink, thus allowing for slightly more to be packed into jars than when food is packed raw. Pack precooked foods loosely and allow about ½ inch headspace.

"Floating" (the rising of food to the top of jar during processing) can often be prevented by precooking before packing.

The hot-pack method is used for both vegetables and fruits.

EQUIPMENT

Glass Jars—Glass jars are sold with several types of caps or closures. Always use the correct size of closure (widemouth or regular) to fit your jars. When using a two-piece closure consisting of a metal screwband and flat metal lid with sealing compound, use the metal lid one time only. The band may be used again if it is in good condition. For a closure consisting of a porcelain-lined zinc cap with a rubber shoulder ring, always use clean, new rings of the right size for the jars. Do not test rings by stretching them.

Check jars and closures for nicks, dents, chips, or other defects. Use only perfect jars and closures.

Tin Cans—Tin cans may be purchased plain or with enamel linings of two types. *R-enamel type* cans have a bright gold lining and are recommended for certain fruits and vegetables to prevent discoloration of the food. Beets, red berries, red and black cherries, plums, pumpkin, rhubarb, and winter squash are canned in the R-enamel type. The *C-enamel type* has a dull gold lining and is used for corn and hominy.

The plain tin can is used for other fruits and vegetables and meat.

A mechanical sealer is necessary if tin cans are used. The sealer should be tested and adjusted each time before using it following manufacturer's directions.

Processing Equipment

Pressure Canner or Cooker—Vegetables (except tomatoes), meats, and other low-acid foods should be processed in steam in a pressure canner in order to destroy the spore-forming bacteria.

The pressure canner must be fitted with a rack in the bottom, a steam-tight cover, petcock, safety valve, and an accurate gauge or weight which measures definite pressures. The food processed in a canner reaches temperatures many degrees above the boiling temperature of water. Therefore, follow manufacturer's directions carefully for operating the canner.

Water-Bath Canner—Fruits and acid vegetables may be processed in a water-bath canner. This is available on the market but any large metal container with a tight-fitting cover may be used. It must be deep enough to allow 2 to 4 inches space above the jars for brisk boiling of the water. It must also have a wire or wooden rack in the bottom.

If a pressure canner is deep enough it may be used for a water-bath canner. When used for this purpose, cover the canner, but do not fasten, and leave the petcock open so that pressure does not build up inside.

Miscellaneous Equipment

Include several large kettles and pans, widemouthed funnel, colander, vegetable brushes, long-handled tongs and forks, a 1-quart measure, food chopper, jar lifter for lifting hot jars in and out of the canner, and cheesecloth.

CANNING PROCEDURE

Inspect and test equipment before beginning to prepare the product for canning.

Wash glass jars in hot soapy water and rinse thoroughly. Wash and rinse metal rings and bands and rubber rings (if used).

Sterilize jars if the open-kettle method of canning is used. To sterilize, put clean jars on a rack or folded dish cloth placed in bottom of a large kettle. Include a knife, spoon, and widemouthed funnel. Cover jars with boiling water and boil 15 minutes. Keep jars covered with water the entire time and leave in water until ready to use. Sterilization is unnecessary when food is cold- or hot-packed and processed in a water bath or pressure canner. Just wash and rinse the jars and leave in the hot rinsing water until ready to fill. Drain jars just before filling.

Follow manufacturer's directions for sterilizing jar closures. In some instances the jar caps are boiled 15 minutes along with the jars. Metal lids with sealing compounds may need to be submerged in boiling water for several minutes before using.

Prepare the product for canning—Use young, tender vegetables; use fresh, firm, not overripe fruits. Sort fruits and vegetables for size and ripeness or maturity so that the contents of each jar will be as nearly uniform as possible. Can the food before it loses its freshness. This is especially necessary with asparagus, peas, beans, and corn.

Wash the product thoroughly whether or not it is to be pared. Dirt contains some of the bacteria hardest to kill (spore forming) so wash foods under cold, running water or through several changes of water. Handle fruits and vegetables gently to avoid bruising. Do not let them soak in water before packing in jars.

Fill and seal jars — Pack the food to not more than ½ inch of top of jars. Exceptions are fruit juices, preserves, relishes, and some other foods which are not processed in the water bath or pressure canner. Only ¼ inch headspace is necessary for these.

Add salt to vegetables, if desired — 1 teaspoon per quart; ½ teaspoon per pint.

Add liquid to jars — boiling syrup, water, or extracted fruit juice for fruits; hot cooking liquid or water for vegetables.

Air bubbles will rise as the liquid is poured into jar. Assist the bubbles to come to the top and break them by running a knife or spatula down the side of jar. Add more hot liquid, if needed, to entirely cover the food in jar and leave the recommended amount of headspace at top of jar.

Wipe the rim of jar free of any food particles before adjusting lid. If the food is hot and processing is to be done in a water-bath canner, seal jar completely for any type of closure. Self-sealing lids are always sealed completely before processing the food in either the water-bath or pressure canner. If using rubber rings and the food is to be processed in a pressure canner, screw tops on tightly, then turn back ¼ inch. After processing, immediately tighten the tops (do not force them).

Process jars in pressure canner or water-bath as directed for specific foods. When processing in boiling-water bath, start counting the time after water has reached a full boil and keep it boiling for the entire time. Add more boiling water, if needed, to keep jars covered. Remove jars from water as soon as processing is completed.

When processing in pressure canner, have enough water in the canner to come up to the bottom of the rack (1 to 2 inches). Place filled jars or cans on rack, adjust cover of canner, and clamp down securely. Make sure that the petcock is open. Place canner over heat and when steam escapes from the petcock the specified number of minutes (follow manufacturer's directions), close petcock.

When the indicator on the canner registers the specific pressure start counting the processing time. Remove canner from heat as soon as processing is completed and allow to cool until pressure reaches zero. Then open petcock slowly; do not open canner until pressure is entirely released. Complete the seal if jars are only partially sealed.

Cool jars by placing them upright on folded towels or wire racks away from drafts. Inspect completely cooled jars for a perfect seal. Leakage or bubbles rising in jars means that the contents must be used or recanned at once.

Store jars in a cool, dry place after wiping with a damp cloth and labeling them. Boil home-canned vegetables (except tomatoes) 10 to 15 minutes before tasting or serving them.

SWEETENING FRUITS

Sugar helps canned fruit hold its shape, color, and flavor. Most fruits call for sweetening to be added in the form of a sugar syrup. For very juicy fruit packed hot, use sugar with no liquid added.

To prepare a sugar syrup — Boil sugar and water (or juice extracted from some of the fruit) together 5 minutes. Use a thin, medium, or heavy syrup depending on the sweetness of the fruit and individual tastes. To make syrup, combine water and sugar and boil 5 minutes.

PROPORTIONS

Cups Water (or juice)	Cups Sugar	Cups Syrup	Result
4	2	5	thin
4	3	5½	medium
4	4¾	6½	heavy

Keep syrup hot until needed but do not continue boiling after 5 minutes. A 1-quart jar of fruit requires 1 to 1½ cups syrup.

CANNING FRUITS USING BOILING-WATER BATH

Apples — Wash, pare, core, and cut into slices, quarters, or halves. To keep apples from darkening, immerse pieces in water containing 2 tablespoons each salt and vinegar per gallon of water. Drain fruit and boil 5 minutes in thin syrup (or water). Pack into jars and cover with the hot syrup (or water), leaving headspace; adjust lids. Process — pints 15 minutes; quarts 20 minutes.

Applesauce — Prepare applesauce and ladle hot into jars to within ¼ inch of top. Adjust lids and process — pints and quarts 10 minutes.

Apricots—Follow directions for Peaches except peel apricots or not, as desired.

Berries (except Strawberries)—Wash and sort berries. Can perfect berries and use imperfect ones in making the syrup. If packed into jars cold (uncooked), shake the jars to pack berries closely without crushing them. Fill jars to within 1 inch of top with hot thin or medium syrup. If berries are firm, the hot pack may be used, bringing berries to boiling in a medium or heavy syrup before packing. Cover berries in jars with hot syrup, leaving headspace; adjust lids. Process—pints 10 minutes; quarts 15 minutes for hot or cold pack.

Cherries, sweet—Wash, remove stems and pits. For hot pack, bring cherries to boiling in hot thin or medium syrup, then pack fruit into jars and fill jars with hot syrup, leaving headspace. Adjust lids. Process pints 10 minutes; quarts 15 minutes. For cold pack, pack cherries into jars and shake them down while filling jars to make a full pack. Pour medium or heavy syrup over fruit and proceed as for Cherries (sweet). Process—pints 20 minutes; quarts 25 minutes.

Cherries, tart—Follow directions for Cherries (sweet) using a heavy syrup.

Peaches—Immerse in boiling water until skins slip, then plunge into cold water and drain. Peel, halve, and pit the peaches. For cold pack, arrange peaches in jars, cut side down, packing firmly. Cover with medium syrup, leaving headspace at top of jar. For hot pack, bring fruit to boiling in medium syrup, then pack into jars and cover with syrup, leaving headspace. Adjust lids. (To prevent darkening of fruit during preparation, see Apples.) Process—pints 25 minutes; quarts 30 minutes for cold pack. Reduce processing time 5 minutes for hot pack.

Pears—Wash, pare, halve, and core fruit. Cook in medium syrup 3 to 5 minutes depending upon hardness of fruit. Pack hot into jars; cover with syrup, leaving headspace; adjust lids. Process—pints 20 minutes; quarts 25 minutes.

Plums—Wash fruit and prick several times with a needle to prevent bursting when heated. For cold pack, pack fruit firmly into jars and add hot medium syrup, leaving headspace. For hot pack, bring plums to boiling in medium or heavy syrup before packing into jars and adding the syrup. Process—pints 25 minutes; quarts 30 minutes for cold pack. Reduce processing time 5 minutes for hot pack.

Rhubarb—Wash and cut into ½ inch pieces. Add ½ cup sugar for each quart rhubarb and let stand several hours to draw out the juice. Then bring to boiling and pack hot into jars. Adjust lids. Process—pints and quarts 10 minutes.

Strawberries—Use firm, red-ripe strawberries. Strawberries tend to fade and lose color when canned. Hull, rinse, drain, and measure berries. Halve large strawberries, if desired. Use ½ to ¾ cup sugar for each quart strawberries. Gently toss with the sugar and let stand about 5 hours in a cool place. Heat slowly until sugar dissolves and strawberries are hot. Pack into hot jars and seal. Process—pints and quarts 20 minutes.

Tomatoes—Use firm, ripe, unblemished tomatoes. Scald them, plunge into cold water, drain, and peel. Pack closely into jars, pressing tomatoes down gently to fill all spaces. Add salt—½ teaspoon per pint, 1 teaspoon per quart. (Do not add water to tomatoes.) Adjust lids. Process—pints 35 minutes; quarts 45 minutes.

The hot-pack method of canning tomatoes is preferred by many. Quarter the peeled tomatoes and bring them to boiling in a kettle. Fill jars, leaving headspace. Add salt and adjust lids. Process—pints and quarts 10 minutes.

Tomato Juice—Cut peeled tomatoes into pieces and cook slowly in a kettle until soft. Put through a food mill or strainer. Add 1 teaspoon salt for each quart and bring to boiling in a kettle. Quickly ladle into jars, leaving headspace. Process—pints and quarts 10 minutes.

CANNING VEGETABLES USING PRESSURE CANNER

Vegetables are processed at 10 pounds pressure.

Asparagus—Wash, trim off scales and tough ends, and wash asparagus again. Cut into 1 inch pieces. For cold (raw) pack, pack asparagus firmly into jars to within ½ inch of top; add ½ teaspoon salt to pints; 1 teaspoon to quarts. Add boiling water, leaving headspace. Adjust lids. For hot pack, precook asparagus 2 to 3 minutes in boiling water before packing into jars. If the cooking liquid is free of grit use it to fill jars instead of boiling water. Adjust jar lids. Process—pints 25 minutes; quarts 30 minutes.

Beans, lima—Shell and wash beans, preferably

young, tender ones. For raw pack, follow directions for asparagus except increase headspace to 1 inch. For hot pack, cover shelled beans with boiling water and bring to boiling. Pack hot beans loosely into jar. Add salt and boiling water, leaving headspace. Adjust lids. Process—pints 40 minutes; quarts 50 minutes.

Beans, snap—Wash, remove ends and cut beans into even lengths. Proceed as for Asparagus. Process—pints 20 minutes; quarts 25 minutes.

Beets—Wash and sort beets for size; cut off tops, leaving about 1 inch of stem. Cook beets in boiling water 15 to 25 minutes, or until skins slip easily. Remove skins; leave small beets whole. Cube, slice, or quarter medium or large beets. Pack hot into jars and proceed as for Asparagus. Process—pints 30 minutes; quarts 35 minutes.

Carrots—Wash and scrape carrots; slice, dice, or leave whole if young and tender. For cold (raw) pack, see Asparagus. For hot pack, cook washed carrots in boiling water until skins slip off. Remove skins, slice, dice, or leave whole. Fill jars and process (see Asparagus).

Corn, cream style—Remove corn from cobs by cutting at about the center of kernel and scraping cobs using the dull edge of knife. Pack corn into jars (pints only) to within 1½ inches of top. Add salt and fill jars with boiling water to within ½ inch of top. Adjust lids and process 95 minutes. For hot pack, remove kernels from cobs (scraping cobs). To each quart of corn add 1 pint boiling water. (If desired, add a small amount of sugar.) Heat to boiling. Pack hot into jars (pints only) to 1 inch of top. Add salt; adjust lids. Process—85 minutes.

Corn, whole kernel—Husk corn and remove silk. Cut from cob at about ⅔ the depth of kernel. For cold (raw) pack, pack kernels into jars (do not press or shake down). Proceed as for Asparagus. Process—pints 55 minutes; quarts 85 minutes. For hot pack, cut kernels from cobs and for each quart of corn add 1 pint boiling water. Heat to boiling in a kettle and pack hot corn into jars. Cover with boiling hot cooking liquid, leaving 1 inch headspace. Add salt and adjust lids. Processing time (see cold-pack).

Peas, fresh green—Use tender, young peas. Shell, discarding blemished ones. Wash, cover with boiling water, and bring to boiling. Pack hot peas into jars and proceed as for Asparagus. Process—pints and quarts 40 minutes.

Spinach and other greens—Can only freshly picked, tender spinach. Remove tough stems and blemished leaves. Wash thoroughly (see *page 336*). Place about 2½ pounds spinach in a cheesecloth bag and steam 10 minutes or until leaves are wilted. Pack hot spinach loosely into jars; add ¼ teaspoon salt to pints; ½ teaspoon to quarts. Cover with boiling water, leaving headspace. Adjust lids. Process—pints 70 minutes; quarts 90 minutes.

Pumpkin (cubed)—Wash, remove seeds, and pare pumpkin. Cut into 1 inch cubes. Add just enough boiling water to cover and bring to boiling. Pack hot into jars. Add salt—½ teaspoon to pints; 1 teaspoon to quarts. Cover with hot cooking liquid, leaving headspace. Adjust jar lids. Process—pints 55 minutes; quarts 90 minutes.

Pumpkin (strained)—Steam the cubed pumpkin until tender, about 25 minutes. Put through a strainer or food mill. Cook slowly in a heavy saucepan until thoroughly heated, stirring to prevent sticking to bottom of pan. Ladle hot pumpkin into jars, allowing headspace. Add no salt or liquid. Adjust lids. Process—pints 65 minutes; quarts 80 minutes.

Squash, summer and zucchini—Wash thoroughly; do not pare. Cut into slices, halves, or quarters to make pieces of uniform size. Add just enough boiling water to cover and bring squash to boiling. Pack loosely into jars and proceed as for Asparagus. Process—pints 30 minutes; quarts 40 minutes.

Squash, winter, crookneck, Hubbard and banana—See Pumpkin, *above*.

PRESERVING

JELLIES

Jelly is made by combining fruit juice and sugar in the correct proportions and cooking until the mixture will "gel" when cool. A good jelly is clear and sparkling and free from sediment or crystals. It has the natural color and flavor of the fresh fruit. When turned from the glass it will hold its shape, but will quiver slightly. When cut, the edges are sharp and the jelly will cling to the knife.

Fruits Suitable for Jelly—To make a good jelly,

Preserving

fruit must be rich in both pectin and acid or it must be combined with another fruit which will supply whichever substance is lacking. Fruits which contain both pectin and acid in sufficient amounts are: apples (tart), blackberries, crab apples, currants, gooseberries, grapes, loganberries, plums, quinces, and raspberries.

Fruits lacking sufficient pectin are: cherries, peaches, pineapple, rhubarb, and strawberries.

Fruits lacking sufficient acid are: apples (sweet), blueberries, huckleberries, and pears.

Slightly underripe fruit usually contains more acid and pectin than fully ripe fruit but the flavor is not as good. A proportion frequently used is ¼ underripe fruit and ¾ ripe fruit. Fruits lacking in either pectin or acid are often combined with tart apples since apple juice affects color and flavor the least.

Use of Commercial Pectin—Juice from practically any fruit (overripe included) can be made into jelly by the addition of commercial pectin (liquid or powdered) and a large amount of sugar. Other advantages of this procedure are that less time is required to cook the jelly and, for the inexperienced, at least success is more certain.

If a commercial pectin is used, the directions provided with the product must be followed exactly.

Extracting Fruit Juice—Look over the fruit, removing stems and any signs of decay.

Cut up large fruit such as apples. Remove cores from quinces.

Crush juicy fruits and add no water or only a small amount. To less juicy fruits add only enough water to be seen through the pieces of fruit. If more water than necessary is added it must be evaporated from the juice later, which causes a dark color and loss of flavor. Cook the fruit, covered, until tender and the juice runs freely. (Avoid overcooking.) Pour into a jelly bag or through cheesecloth (see note) and set aside until the juice ceases to drip through into the bowl. For a clear jelly, do not squeeze the bag. More juice is obtained by squeezing, but the resulting jelly will be cloudy. If the bag is not squeezed the pulp in the bag may be forced through a food mill or sieve and made into jam or fruit butter.

NOTE: Purchase a jelly bag or prepare one in this manner: cut a double thickness of cheesecloth about 36 inches long; fold in half. Dip into hot water and wring as dry as possible. To strain the juice from pulp, put a large strainer or colander lined with the folded cheesecloth over a large bowl. Pour in the hot cooked fruit, gather up corners of cheesecloth and tie firmly.

Test for Pectin—To determine the proportion of pectin present in a fruit juice, combine 1 tablespoon extracted juice and 1 tablespoon grain alcohol; shake gently. If a large quantity of pectin is present it will appear in a single clot when poured from the glass. If pectin does not form into a clot, less sugar will be needed for the jelly. If pectin slips from glass in several clots, the quantity present is in good proportion and the usual amount of sugar will be needed.

Addition of Sugar—In general, ⅔ to ¾ as much sugar as fruit juice is sufficient. (Cane and beet sugar are equally suitable.) Too little sugar will cause the jelly to be firm; too much sugar will produce a syrupy jelly. The optimum amount of sugar needed will vary with the amount of pectin, acid, and water present and cannot be given exactly. When in doubt, it is better to use less sugar then more.

Cooking the Jelly—Use no more than 4 cups juice at a time to retain the best color, flavor, and texture in the jelly. Heat juice to boiling and add sugar gradually, stirring constantly. Boil rapidly until jellying stage is reached.

To make a jelly test—Dip a small amount of boiling liquid from saucepan with a spoon and slowly pour it back into saucepan from edge of spoon. If jelly is insufficiently cooked the liquid will run off in parallel drops. When jelly is sufficiently cooked, the drops will run together and fall from spoon in a sheet, leaving edge of spoon clean. Remove jelly from heat while testing. Avoid long cooking after the jelly test is obtained as mixture will become syrupy.

Skim jelly and pour into hot sterilized glasses to within ⅜ inch of top.

Pour melted paraffin over the surface of jelly at once, making a layer about ⅛ inch thick. Let this layer cool completely, then repeat with a second layer, tilting glass to distribute paraffin evenly over top and seal to edge of glass. When paraffin has cooled, place metal covers on the jelly glasses or cover securely with aluminum foil. (*Paraffin is unnecessary when glass jars with self-sealing lids are used.*)

Wipe glasses or jars with a damp cloth, label, and store in a cool, dry, dark place.

JAMS

Jams are made from whole small fruits which are either mashed or cooked to a pulp with sugar. Good jam is soft, tender, and jellylike in texture, bright and sparkling in color, and of the same consistency throughout the mixture.

HELPFUL HINTS FOR SUCCESSFUL JAMS

- Use some underripe fruit. Portions of fruit leftover from canning or broken fruit may be used for jam but at least a portion of the fruit should be underripe. Overripe fruit lacks pectin, the jellying substance so necessary for good jam.
- In order to develop the pectin substance, the fruit should be cooked a few minutes before the sugar is added. If fruit does not have sufficient juice, add just enough water to keep it from sticking to bottom of kettle. Cover the kettle. Avoid too much sugar. The best jam is made by using not more than ¾ pound sugar for each pound of fruit.
- Cook jam quickly and not too long. After the sugar is added to fruit, continue the cooking rapidly until jam has a jellylike appearance. It should hang in sheets from the spoon or set quickly if a portion is dropped onto a cold plate. It should be tender, not thick and tough. Jam thickens on cooling and an allowance must be made for this. Overcooking darkens the product. Cooking a small amount at a time is recommended, using enamel or porcelain cooking utensils if possible. Stir jam to prevent burning. It is a highly concentrated mass and will scorch easily unless the mass is lifted from bottom of kettle with a wooden spoon.

MARMALADES

Marmalade is made from fruits which have some jellymaking properties (both pectin and acid are present). Thin slices of fruit are used and the product shows a clear jelly or jellylike syrup in which the sliced or cut fruit is suspended. If a fruit is used lacking these jellying properties, they are often supplied by adding sliced orange or lemon, tart apple juice, or commercial pectin.

Marmalades are prepared in the same way as jams, except that the fruit remains in slices or cut portions and is not mashed. Marmalades should be clear and sparkling in color.

PRESERVES

Preserves are fruits in which the tissues have absorbed enough heavy syrup to replace the water in the tissues. Good preserved fruit is plump and tender in texture, bright in color, and filled with sweetness.

HELPFUL HINTS FOR SUCCESSFUL PRESERVES

- Precook hard fruits before combining with heavy syrup. Hard pears, underripe peaches, pineapples, apples, quinces, watermelon rind, and citron must be cooked in a small amount of water until fruit is just tender or soft enough so that the heavy syrup enters the cells of fruit. Hard fruit added to the syrup will result in preserves which are hard and tough instead of plump and tender.

Tender fruits (ripe peaches, plums, cherries, and berries) are added to the syrup immediately. Drain precooked fruits thoroughly before adding to the syrup.

Bring fruits to boiling rapidly in the syrup and continue the rapid cooking until fruit has a bright, clear, sparkling appearance, indicating that the syrup has permeated the fruit completely. Avoid overcooking as this results in a dark, stiff product. Plump the fruit for an extra fine quality of preserve. For plumping, add fruit to syrup and heat it only until mixture is bubbly. Then let stand overnight in a covered bowl or enamel preserving kettle. The next day continue the cooking. In this way more syrup is absorbed by the fruit. If desired, the heating and cooling processes may be repeated several times. Pears, peaches, green tomatoes, whole tomatoes, crab apples, citron, and melon rind are especially adapted to plumping. Fruit to be candied should be plumped.

- Seal preserves in clean hot jars (see *Open-Kettle method, page 335*). Jelly glasses may be used but melted paraffin must be poured over top of preserves before covering glasses with lids or with aluminum foil.
- If trouble has been experienced with molds appearing on preserves, it may be desirable to process the sealed jars (not glasses) in a boiling-water bath, *page 335*, about 5 minutes as an extra precaution. If filled jars are not to be processed, it is necessary to sterilize jars, closures, spoons, and any other utensil used.

CONSERVES

Conserves, like marmalades, may be made of large or small fruits. They differ in that several fruits are often combined and nuts are usually added. In this way it is possible to develop pleasing combinations of flavors and to combine fruits that have good acid and pectin content with fruits that lack these qualities. Add nuts, if used, at the end of cooking time.

FRUIT BUTTERS

Fruit Butters are among the most wholesome of fruit sweets and are easy to prepare. The whole fruit is cooked until tender, then put through a food mill or sieve. Sugar is added (also spice if desired) and the mixture is cooked until smooth and thick. Like jams, fruit butters must be watched carefully and not overcooked.

HELPFUL HINTS ABOUT PRESERVING

- To remove odors from jars and bottles, pour a solution of water and dry mustard into them and let stand several hours. Or use a dilute chlorine solution and rinse jars in hot water.
- When covering jelly with melted paraffin, pour a thin layer over top; place a strong piece of string on paraffin with end over edge of glass. Pour another layer of paraffin over string. Set aside until paraffin is firm. When jelly is to be used, lift off the paraffin layer by using the string.
- To open glass jars containing fruit easily, set them upside down in hot water for a few minutes.

Jellies

APPLE JELLY

| 4 lbs. tart apples | Sugar |
| 4 cups water | Paraffin |

1. Rinse, remove stem ends, and quarter apples. (Do not core or pare fruit.) Add the water to apples in a preserving kettle. Cover and cook gently until fruit is soft, stirring occasionally.
2. Strain fruit through a jelly bag, *page 340*. The pulp remaining in bag may be used to make apple butter, if desired.
3. To prepare jelly, measure not more than 4 cups of apple juice into saucepan. Measure ¾ cup sugar for each cup of juice. Heat the juice to boiling and stir in the sugar. Return to boiling and cook rapidly until mixture responds to jelly test, *page 340*.
4. Remove from heat; skim off foam. Ladle into hot sterilized glasses. Cover with melted paraffin, *page 340*.   FIVE 8-OUNCE GLASSES JELLY

QUICK SPARKLING JELLY

| 1 qt. bottled apple juice | 1 box powdered fruit pectin |
| ½ env. (about 1 tablespoon) strawberry-flavored soft drink mix | 4¼ cups sugar Paraffin |

1. Blend apple juice, drink mix, and pectin in a large heavy saucepot; stir over high heat until mixture comes to a full boil.
2. Add the sugar all at one time and blend thoroughly. Bring to a full rolling boil; boil 1 minute, stirring constantly.
3. Remove jelly from heat; let stand several minutes and skim off foam.
4. Pour jelly into hot sterilized glasses and seal with melted paraffin, *page 340*.
SEVEN 8-OUNCE GLASSES JELLY

BLUEBERRY JELLY

1 large lemon, sliced	Sugar (about 4½ cups)
3 qts. blueberries	Paraffin
3 lbs. tart apples	

1. Add enough water to lemon slices to just cover (about 1 cup). Cover and set aside 12 hours, or overnight.
2. Pick over blueberries, discarding blemished berries. Rinse and drain. Turn into a saucepot.
3. Wash apples; remove stems, blossom ends, and blemished portions. Quarter the apples and put into a kettle; cover with water (about 2½ cups). Cook, covered, over medium heat until apples are soft.
4. Drain the liquid from lemon slices and mix with blueberries (discard lemon peel). Cook gently until blueberries are soft and juice flows freely.
5. Pour both fruit mixtures into a jelly bag, *page 340;* let drain 6 to 12 hours. (There should be about 6 cups juice.)
6. To make jelly, measure half the juice into a 2-quart saucepan and bring rapidly to boiling. For

each cup of juice add ¾ cup sugar and stir until sugar is dissolved. Continue cooking rapidly until mixture responds to jelly test, *page 340*.
7. Remove from heat; skim off any foam. Pour jelly into hot sterilized glasses. Repeat step 6 using remaining juice.
8. Immediately cover jelly in glasses with melted paraffin, *page 340*.

ABOUT SEVEN 8-OUNCE GLASSES JELLY

CURRANT JELLY

| 4 lbs. (about 4 qts.) ripe red currants | 4 cups sugar Paraffin |
| 1 cup water | |

1. Rinse, remove leaves (not the stems), drain, and put currants into a kettle. Crush them thoroughly and stir in the water.
2. Bring rapidly to boiling; reduce heat and simmer, covered, 10 minutes. Strain through a jelly bag, *page 340*.
3. Measure 4 cups juice into a saucepan and bring rapidly to boiling. Add sugar and stir until dissolved; continue cooking rapidly until mixture responds to jelly test, *page 340*.
4. Remove from heat; skim off any foam. Pour jelly into hot sterilized glasses and seal with melted paraffin, *page 340*.

ABOUT SIX 8-OUNCE GLASSES JELLY

CRAB APPLE JELLY: Follow recipe for Currant Jelly. Omit currants. Rinse, remove stem ends, and cut into quarters enough *crab apples* to yield 3 quarts. (Do not core or pare the fruit.) Increase water to 3 cups and cook 20 minutes, or until apples are very tender. Decrease sugar to 3 cups.

BASIL GRAPE JELLY

½ cup boiling water	3½ cups sugar
1 tablespoon basil	½ bottle liquid fruit pectin
1½ cups bottled grape juice	Paraffin

1. Pour boiling water over basil in a small saucepan; cover tightly and set aside 10 to 15 minutes. Strain "herb brew" through fine strainer or cheesecloth into a 4-quart kettle or saucepan. Discard herb.
2. Add grape juice and sugar to the kettle; stir over medium heat until sugar is dissolved. Increase heat and bring mixture to boiling.
3. Stir in the pectin and return to boiling; boil rapidly 1 minute, stirring constantly. Remove from heat and skim off foam.
4. Pour into hot sterilized glasses and seal immediately with melted paraffin, *page 340*.

ABOUT FOUR 8-OUNCE GLASSES JELLY

SPICED GRAPE JELLY

3 lbs. Concord grapes	7 cups sugar
½ cup cider vinegar	½ bottle liquid fruit pectin
2 teaspoons ground cinnamon	Paraffin
1 teaspoon ground cloves	

1. Rinse grapes, discard stems and blemished grapes. Drain and put into a large kettle. Crush grapes thoroughly.
2. Mix vinegar and spices and blend with grapes. Bring rapidly to boiling; reduce heat, cover kettle, and simmer mixture 10 minutes. Strain through a jelly bag, *page 340*.
3. Measure 4 cups of the strained juice into a large saucepan; cook over high heat until very hot. Add the sugar and stir until dissolved. Bring rapidly to boiling and stir in the pectin. Boil vigorously 1 minute, stirring constantly.
4. Remove from heat; skim off foam. Pour into hot sterilized jelly glasses and cover with melted paraffin, *page 340*.

EIGHT 8-OUNCE GLASSES JELLY

SAVORY GRAPEFRUIT JELLY

½ cup boiling water	Few drops green food coloring
2 tablespoons savory	
1 cup unsweetened grapefruit juice	½ bottle liquid fruit pectin
3¼ cups sugar	Paraffin

1. Pour boiling water over savory in a small saucepan; cover tightly and set aside 10 to 15 minutes. Strain "herb brew" through fine strainer or cheesecloth into a measuring cup; add enough water to make ½ cup. Discard savory.
2. Pour liquid into a 4-quart kettle or saucepan. Add grapefruit juice and sugar; stir over medium heat until sugar is dissolved. Increase heat and bring mixture to boiling. Stir in food coloring and then pectin. Return to boiling; boil rapidly 1 minute, stirring constantly. Remove from heat and skim off foam.
3. Pour into hot sterilized glasses and seal immediately with melted paraffin, *page 340*.

ABOUT FOUR 6-OUNCE GLASSES JELLY

MINT-HONEY JELLY

For those who appreciate the distinctive flavor of honey this mint jelly, served with a lamb roast, will be sheer ambrosia.

¾ cup boiling water	Few drops green food coloring
2 tablespoons dried mint leaves	½ bottle liquid fruit pectin
2½ cups strained honey	Paraffin

1. Pour boiling water over mint in a saucepan; cover tightly and let stand 15 minutes. Strain and add enough water to make ¾ cup.
2. Add honey and heat to boiling. Stir in coloring to tint a light green. Add pectin, stirring constantly. Bring to full rolling boil. Remove from heat and skim off foam.
3. Pour jelly into hot sterilized glasses. Seal with melted paraffin, *page 340.*

FIVE 6-OUNCE GLASSES JELLY

GOLDEN JELLY

4 cups sugar	2 tablespoons lime juice
2 cups orange juice	½ bottle liquid fruit pectin
3 tablespoons lemon juice	Paraffin

1. Mix sugar and juices in a heavy 3-quart saucepan. Stir over medium heat until sugar is dissolved; bring to boiling.
2. Immediately stir in pectin and return to boiling; stir and boil rapidly 1 minute. Remove from heat; skim off any foam.
3. Ladle into hot sterilized glasses and seal with melted paraffin, *page 340.*

FOUR 8-OUNCE GLASSES JELLY

PINEAPPLE JELLY

2¼ cups unsweetened pineapple juice	4½ cups sugar
¼ cup lemon juice	1 bottle liquid fruit pectin

1. Measure pineapple juice and lemon juice into a large kettle; add sugar and mix well.
2. Bring to boiling rapidly, stirring constantly. Stir in pectin and bring to a full rolling boil; boil vigorously 1 minute, continuing to stir.
3. Remove from heat; skim off any foam. Pour into hot sterilized jelly glasses; seal with melted paraffin, *page 340.* (If jelly is to be used within 2 months, omit the paraffin.)
4. Cover glasses with lids, waxed paper, or aluminum foil, and store in refrigerator.

SEVEN 6-OUNCE GLASSES JELLY

PINEAPPLE-STRAWBERRY JELLY-JAM

2½ cups whole strawberries	3 tablespoons lemon juice
1 can (12 oz.) unsweetened pineapple juice	1 box powdered fruit pectin
	4 cups sugar

1. Wash, hull, and quarter berries; measure 2 cups.
2. Mix berries, juices, and pectin in a flat bottomed preserving kettle. Place over high heat and stir until mixture comes to a full boil. Stir in the sugar and return to rolling boil; boil vigorously 1 minute, stirring constantly.
3. Skim foam from surface and ladle into hot sterilized jars or glasses. Seal, *page 336.*

ABOUT SIX 8-OUNCE JARS JELLY-JAM

SPICED PLUM JELLY

4 lbs. fully ripe tart clingstone plums*	⅛ teaspoon ground allspice
1 cup water	½ bottle liquid fruit pectin
6½ cups sugar	Paraffin
½ teaspoon ground cinnamon	

1. Rinse, halve, pit, and crush plums (do not peel). Place in a large saucepan; add the water. Bring to boiling; reduce heat and simmer, covered, 10 minutes.
2. Ladle mixture into a jelly bag, *page 340,* and squeeze out juice. Measure 4 cups of the juice into a very large saucepan. Mix in a blend of sugar and spices.
3. Stir over high heat until mixture comes to a full boil. Immediately stir in fruit pectin and bring to a full rolling boil; boil rapidly 1 minute, stirring constantly.
4. Remove from heat and skim off foam. Pour at once into hot sterilized jelly glasses to within ½ inch of top. Immediately seal with melted paraffin, *page 340.*   ABOUT TEN 8-OUNCE GLASSES JELLY

*If using sweet plums or freestone purple plums, use 3½ cups prepared juice and add ¼ cup lemon juice.

* Chocolate Chiffon Pie (page 269)

Jams

ROSEMARY JELLY

1½ cups boiling water
2 teaspoons dried rosemary
3½ cups sugar
2 tablespoons cider vinegar
4 drops red food coloring
½ bottle liquid fruit pectin
Paraffin

1. Pour boiling water over rosemary in a small saucepan; cover tightly and set aside about 15 minutes.
2. Strain "herb brew" through a fine sieve or cheesecloth into a large saucepan. Add the sugar, vinegar, and food coloring.
3. Stir over medium heat until sugar is dissolved; increase heat and bring mixture to boiling. Add pectin, bring to boiling, and boil rapidly 1 minute, stirring constantly. Remove from heat; skim off foam.
4. Pour into hot sterilized glasses; seal with melted paraffin, *page 340*.

THREE 8-OUNCE GLASSES JELLY

TANGERINE JELLY

1 box powdered fruit pectin
2 cups water
¾ cup (6 oz.) undiluted frozen tangerine juice concentrate
½ teaspoon grated lemon peel
2 tablespoons lemon juice
3½ cups sugar
Paraffin

1. Combine the pectin and water in a large saucepan; mix well. Bring to full rolling boil and boil 1 minute, stirring constantly.
2. Reduce heat; add the undiluted tangerine juice concentrate, lemon peel and juice, and sugar. Stir and cook until sugar is completely dissolved. Do not boil.
3. Remove from heat and skim off foam. Ladle into hot sterilized jelly glasses and immediately seal with melted paraffin, *page 340*.

FOUR 8-OUNCE GLASSES JELLY

Strawberry Shortcake (page 274)

Jams

BLUEBERRY-LEMON JAM

1 qt. fresh blueberries, rinsed and drained
1½ tablespoons grated lemon peel
⅔ cup lemon juice
7 cups sugar
¼ teaspoon salt
¼ teaspoon ground cloves
½ bottle liquid fruit pectin

1. Put blueberries into a kettle and crush thoroughly. Add the lemon peel and juice, sugar, salt, and cloves and blend thoroughly.
2. Stir over medium heat until sugar is dissolved; bring to boiling; boil 1 minute without stirring.
3. Remove from heat and stir in the pectin; skim off any foam.
4. Ladle jam into hot sterilized jars and seal.

EIGHT ½-PINT JARS JAM

CHERRY-PLUM JAM

2 lbs. dark sweet cherries
10 medium-sized red plums
1 cup water
1 tablespoon lemon juice
Sugar
1 box powdered fruit pectin

1. Rinse, stem, halve, and pit the cherries. (There should be about 1 quart.)
2. Rinse, halve, and pit the plums. (There should be about 3½ cups.)
3. Mix fruits, water, and lemon juice in a kettle. Bring to boiling, stirring occasionally; reduce heat and cook gently 3 minutes.
4. Remove from heat; measure mixture and return to kettle. For each cup of cooked fruit, add an equal amount of sugar. Stir until thoroughly blended.
5. Stir in the pectin and return to heat. Bring rapidly to full rolling boil, stirring constantly; boil and stir 2 minutes.
6. Remove from heat; skim off any foam. Ladle into hot sterilized jars and seal, *page 336*.

TEN ½-PINT JARS JAM

ROSY BANANA-PEACH JAM

1 cup mashed fully ripe bananas (about 3 medium-sized)
½ cup drained chopped maraschino cherries

3¼ cups mashed fully ripe peaches (about 2 lbs. peaches, peeled)
2 tablespoons lemon juice
6 cups sugar
1 box powdered fruit pectin

1. Put prepared fruit and lemon juice into a large saucepan; mix.
2. Measure sugar into a bowl; set aside.
3. Mix pectin into fruit in saucepan. Stir and cook over high heat until mixture comes to a full rolling boil. Immediately add and stir in the sugar. Bring to a full rolling boil; stirring constantly, boil rapidly 1 minute.
4. Remove from heat; skim foam with metal spoon and then stir and skim for 5 minutes, to cool slightly and prevent floating fruit.
5. Immediately ladle into sterilized jars, filling to within ½ inch of top. Seal immediately following manufacturer's directions.

ABOUT EIGHT ½-PINT JARS JAM

PINEAPPLE-RHUBARB JAM

1 pkg. (16 oz.) frozen rhubarb, thawed
1 can (20½ oz.) crushed pineapple
1 teaspoon grated orange peel
½ teaspoon grated lemon peel
2 tablespoons lemon juice
6 cups sugar
½ bottle liquid fruit pectin
Few drops red food coloring

1. Combine rhubarb, pineapple, orange and lemon peels, and lemon juice in a large heavy saucepan. Add sugar and mix thoroughly. Bring to full rolling boil over high heat and boil rapidly 1 minute, stirring constantly.
2. Remove from heat; stir in pectin and food coloring. Skim foam, then stir about 10 minutes to cool jam slightly and keep fruit in suspension.
3. Ladle jam into hot sterilized jars and seal, *page 336.*

SEVEN ½-PINT JARS JAM

MIXED FRUIT JAM

You'll love the delicate harmony of color and flavors in this attractive jam.

½ orange juice
¼ cup lemon juice
1 cup coarsely chopped peaches
½ cup drained maraschino cherries, chopped
5 cups sugar
1 cup coarsely chopped pears
1 can (8¾ oz.) crushed pineapple
½ bottle liquid fruit pectin

1. Mix the juices, fruits, and sugar in a large heavy saucepan; let stand 1 hour. Bring to a full rolling boil and boil 1 minute.
2. Remove from heat and immediately blend in the pectin. Stir for 5 minutes.
3. Ladle into hot sterilized jars and seal, *page 336.*

SIX ½-PINT JARS JAM

BLACKBERRY JAM
(Refrigerator-Freezer Type)

3 cups mashed or sieved blackberries
5½ cups sugar
1 box powdered fruit pectin
1 cup water

1. Mix the berries and sugar in a bowl; let stand 20 minutes, stirring occasionally.
2. Blend the pectin and water in a large saucepan; bring to boiling and boil rapidly 1 minute, stirring constantly. Remove from heat; add the berry-sugar mixture and stir about 2 minutes.
3. Ladle into clean hot jars, cover, and let stand 24 to 48 hours, or until the jam is "set". Store, tightly covered, in freezer. (Jam will keep several weeks in refrigerator.)

SEVEN ½-PINT JARS JAM

PEACH-ROSEMARY JAM
(Refrigerator-Freezer Type)

¾ cup boiling water
2 tablespoons dried rosemary
1½ lbs. ripe peaches, peeled and pitted
Juice of ½ lemon (1½ to 2 tablespoons)
4¼ cups sugar
1 box powdered fruit pectin
Few drops yellow food coloring (optional)

1. Pour boiling water over rosemary in a small saucepan; cover tightly and set aside 10 minutes. Strain through cheesecloth and add water to make ¾ cup. Set aside.
2. Put peaches through food chopper, using medium blade. (There should be about 1¾ cups.)

3. In a large bowl, mix peaches and lemon juice; stir in the sugar; set aside about 20 minutes.
4. Meanwhile, combine the "herb brew" with the pectin in a small saucepan; bring to a rolling boil and boil 1 minute, stirring constantly.
5. Pour pectin mixture into fruit, stirring about 3 minutes, or until thoroughly blended. Stir in food coloring, if used.
6. Ladle jam into clean hot jars; seal immediately and set aside until jam is "set."
7. Store in refrigerator if used within 2 or 3 weeks. Store in freezer if kept longer.

FIVE ½-PINT JARS JAM

PEACH AND NUT JAM: Follow recipe for Peach-Rosemary Jam. Omit rosemary and use ¾ *cup cold water* with the pectin. Add *1 teaspoon almond extract* and *⅓ cup slivered blanched almonds* to peach-sugar mixture. SIX ½-PINT JARS JAM

SPICED PEACH JAM: Follow directions for Peach-Rosemary Jam. Omit rosemary and use ¾ *cup cold water* with the pectin. Add ¼ *teaspoon ground nutmeg* to peach-sugar mixture. SIX ½-PINT JARS JAM

STRAWBERRY JAM
(Refrigerator-Freezer Type)

4 cups sugar	¾ cup water
2 cups crushed ripe strawberries (about 2 pts.)	1 box powdered fruit pectin

1. Add sugar to crushed strawberries in a large bowl; mix well and set aside.
2. Combine the water and pectin in a small saucepan; blend well. Bring to boiling and boil 1 minute, stirring constantly. Stir into sweetened strawberries. Continue stirring about 3 minutes. (There will be some sugar crystals remaining.)
3. Quickly ladle jam into jars and cover with tight-fitting lids. Let stand until "set."
4. If used within 2 or 3 weeks store in refrigerator; if kept longer store in freezer.

FIVE ½-PINT JARS JAM

STRAWBERRY-MINT JAM: Follow recipe for Strawberry Jam. Add *1 or 2 drops mint extract* to each jar before filling. Stir quickly to blend. Cover immediately.

STRAWBERRY-CARDAMOM JAM: Follow recipe for Strawberry Jam. Mix *2 teaspoons ground cardamom* with the sugar and add to strawberries; blend well.

Marmalades

PEACH MARMALADE

3 lbs. firm ripe peaches (about 12 medium-sized)	1 orange 3 cups sugar

1. Plunge peaches into boiling water to loosen skins; plunge into cold water and gently slip off skins.
2. Halve and pit the peaches; coarsely chop enough to yield 4 cups.
3. Wash the orange; cut off ends and thinly slice; discard seeds.
4. Combine peaches, orange, and sugar in a large saucepot; stir over medium heat until sugar is dissolved. Increase heat and cook rapidly until clear and thick, stirring frequently to prevent sticking. (Cooking time will vary with degree of ripeness and type of peach.)
5. Remove marmalade from heat and skim off any foam. Immediately fill hot sterilized jars and seal, *page 336.* THREE ½-PINT JARS MARMALADE

CITRUS MARMALADE

1 large grapefruit	Sugar
2 medium-sized oranges	¼ cup fresh lemon juice
1 medium-sized lemon	

1. Wash the fruit. Slice into thin cartwheel slices. Cut grapefruit cartwheels into thirds, orange and lemon into halves.
2. Measure the fruit into a large kettle and add 1 cup water for each cup fruit. Bring to boiling; boil 20 minutes.
3. Remove from heat and measure the hot mixture; return to kettle and bring to boiling.
4. Remove from heat and add ¾ cup sugar for each cup of fruit and juice. Stir with a wooden spoon until thoroughly blended.
5. Return to heat and return to boiling. Boil 20 to 25 minutes, or until jellying stage is reached. (To test, remove marmalade from heat and spoon a small amount onto a cold saucer; chill quickly. If marmalade does not "set" to the proper consistency, cook a few minutes longer.)
6. Just before removing from heat, stir in lemon juice.
7. Ladle into hot sterilized glasses and cover marmalade with melted paraffin, *page 340*

EIGHT 6-OUNCE GLASSES MARMALADE

LIME MARMALADE

Lime lovers take note . . . the robust, tangy flavor of the fruit permeates this marmalade.

4 medium-sized limes
2 medium-sized lemons
Sugar

1. Wash and dry the fruit. Cut through peel and pulp into very thin slivers; discard seeds.
2. Measure the fruit and juice into a large bowl. (There will be about 2½ cups.) Add 3 times the amount of water. Cover and set aside overnight.
3. The next day, turn the mixture into a large kettle and bring rapidly to boiling; reduce heat and simmer about 30 minutes. Return to the bowl, cover, and set aside overnight.
4. The third day measure the mixture into a heavy saucepan or kettle. (There will be about 6 cups.) For each cup add ¾ cup sugar; mix well.
5. Cook gently over low heat until the mixture thickens. (To test, drop a teaspoon of marmalade onto a chilled saucer and chill quickly in refrigerator. If it is of marmalade consistency, remove from heat.)
6. Ladle into hot sterilized jars and seal, *page 336*.

FIVE ½-PINT JARS MARMALADE

Preserves

CANTALOUPE PRESERVES

1 large unripe cantaloupe
1 qt. water
2 cups sugar
½ lemon, thinly sliced
2 tablespoons thinly sliced crystallized ginger

1. Cut cantaloupe into wedges, discarding seedy portion. Pare wedges and cut pink portion into 1-inch pieces. (There should be 3½ to 4 cups cantaloupe pieces.)
2. Cover cantaloupe in a bowl with a *salt solution* (dissolve 1 tablespoon salt in 2 quarts cold water). Cover and let stand 8 hours, or overnight.
3. Drain cantaloupe in a colander and rinse with cold water. Put into a large saucepan and cover with boiling water; cook 8 to 10 minutes, or until cantaloupe is tender. (Do not cook until soft.) Drain thoroughly.
4. Meanwhile, mix the water and sugar in a saucepan. Bring to boiling, stirring until sugar is dissolved; boil, uncovered, about 5 minutes. Add the cantaloupe, lemon, and ginger. Cook rapidly until cantaloupe is translucent, 30 to 40 minutes. Remove from heat and let stand overnight.
5. The next day, reheat the preserves to boiling and ladle into hot sterilized jars. Seal immediately, *page 336*.

FOUR ½-PINT JARS PRESERVES

CHERRY BERRY PRESERVES

1 lb. dark sweet cherries, rinsed, stemmed, pitted, and halved (about 2½ cups)
1 pt. strawberries, sliced (about 2 cups)
3 cups sugar
¼ cup water
½ cup lemon juice
¼ teaspoon almond extract

1. Mix fruits, sugar, and water in a large saucepan. Cook and stir over low heat until sugar is dissolved.
2. Increase heat and bring to boiling, stirring occasionally. Stir in lemon juice and extract and boil 1 minute longer.
3. Remove from heat; skim off foam. Ladle preserves into hot sterilized glasses or jars. Cover preserves in glasses with melted paraffin; adjust lids on jars, *page 340*.

SEVEN 4-OUNCE GLASSES PRESERVES

FRESH PINEAPPLE PRESERVES

2 medium-sized fresh pineapples (about 2 lbs. each)
Sugar

1. Cut off spiny tops and rinse the pineapples. Cut into ½-inch crosswise slices. With a sharp knife, cut away and discard the rind and "eyes" from each slice. Cut out the core and cut slice into small wedges.
2. Measure 4 cups of the pineapple wedges and 3 cups sugar. Place half the fruit into a bowl and cover with half the sugar. Repeat with remaining fruit and sugar. Cover bowl tightly and set aside overnight.
3. The following day, drain the pineapple; reserve the syrup. Bring syrup to boiling in a saucepan and boil 1 minute. Remove from heat and add drained pineapple. Turn the mixture into a shallow heat-resistant dish and set aside to cool.
4. Ladle cooled preserves into hot sterilized jars and seal, *page 336*.

THREE ½-PINT JARS PRESERVES

LEBANON COUNTY RHUBARB PRESERVES

One of "seven sweets and seven sours" which comprise a typical Pennsylvania Dutch dinner menu.

2½ lbs. rhubarb	2 to 2½ tablespoons grated orange peel
1½ lbs. sugar	¾ cup orange juice

1. Wash rhubarb and cut into small pieces. (Peel stalks only if skin is tough.) Combine in a saucepan with the sugar and orange peel and juice.
2. Stir over low heat until sugar is dissolved, then bring to boiling over medium heat. Reduce heat and cook slowly until mixture thickens, about 30 minutes, stirring occasionally.
3. Ladle into hot sterilized jars and seal, *page 336*.

ABOUT 3 PINTS PRESERVES

PRIZE STRAWBERRY PRESERVES

3 cups fresh firm ripe strawberries	3 cups sugar

1. Rinse, hull, and drain berries thoroughly on absorbent paper. Halve the very large berries. Put into a heavy saucepan.
2. Add 1 cup sugar; stirring gently, bring to boiling. Boil 5 minutes, stirring constantly.
3. Repeat step 2 twice more, using remaining 2 cups sugar and boiling 5 minutes after each addition.
4. Turn into shallow glass dish, cover, and let stand 24 hours. Stir occasionally while cooling.
5. Ladle into hot sterilized jars and seal, *page 336*.

THREE ½-PINT JARS PRESERVES

HOLIDAY TREAT PRESERVES

4 cups (1 lb.) cranberries	1 can (14 oz.) pineapple tidbits, drained (reserve ¼ cup syrup)
2 cups diced pears (about 3 small)	½ cup water
	2 cups sugar

1. Wash, drain, and sort cranberries.
2. Rinse, halve, core, pare, and dice enough pears to yield 2 cups. Sprinkle reserved pineapple syrup over pears.
3. Mix water and sugar in a saucepan; stir over medium heat until boiling; cover and boil gently 5 minutes. Add the cranberries and cook, uncovered, until all the skins burst.
4. Add the pears with syrup and drained pineapple. Continue cooking until thick, about 20 minutes. Remove from heat; skim off any foam.
5. Ladle into hot sterilized jars and seal, *page 336*.

FIVE ½-PINT JARS PRESERVES

GINGER TOMATOES

Call these tomatoes a preserve, marmalade, or relish, whatever the name, they are irresistible as an accompaniment for meat or poultry or with toast for breakfast.

6 lbs. green tomatoes	3 lemons, thinly sliced
2 lbs. firm ripe tomatoes	1 teaspoon whole cloves
5 lbs. sugar	3 pieces (½ in. each) ginger root

1. Rinse tomatoes and cover with boiling water to loosen skins; plunge into cold water and remove skins and stem ends; quarter the small tomatoes and cut larger ones into eighths.
2. Combine tomatoes with sugar, lemon slices, cloves (tied in a spice bag), and ginger root in a large kettle; bring to boiling over medium heat. Reduce heat and cook slowly until mixture thickens, stirring occasionally to prevent sticking.
3. Ladle into hot sterilized jars (remove cloves and ginger root) and seal, *page 336*.

ABOUT 8 PINTS PRESERVES

BEST-EVER TOMATO PRESERVES

1 lb. tart green apples	2 lemon slices, ¼-in. thick
4 lbs. firm, ripe tomatoes	4 cups sugar

1. Wash, pare, quarter, core, and cut apples into small cubes. (There should be about 3 cups.)
2. Rinse, scald, peel, and cut tomatoes into small pieces. (There should be about 2 quarts.)
3. Mix apples, tomatoes, and lemon in a large preserving kettle. Bring to simmering over medium heat and stir in the sugar. Cook gently, uncovered, until of desired consistency, about 1½ hours. Stir occasionally as the mixture begins to thicken.
4. If desired, stir in several drops of *red food coloring* before ladling preserves into hot sterilized jars. Seal, *page 336*.

FOUR ½-PINT JARS PRESERVES

Conserves

GINGER-APRICOT CONSERVE

1 lb. dried apricots
2½ cups water
7 cups sugar
½ cup thinly sliced crystallized ginger
1 cup thinly sliced Brazil nuts

1. Cover apricots with the water in a heavy saucepan; set aside 1 hour. Stir in sugar and ginger.
2. Bring to a rolling boil over medium heat; reduce heat and cook gently 15 to 20 minutes, or until of desired consistency. Stir occasionally to prevent sticking.
3. Stir in the nuts and remove from heat; skim off any foam. Pour into hot sterilized jars; seal immediately, *page 336*. EIGHT ½-PINT JARS CONSERVE

CRANBERRY CONSERVE

4 cups (1 lb.) fresh cranberries
1 cup water
1 cup dark seedless raisins, chopped
2½ cups sugar
1 tablespoon grated orange peel
⅓ cup orange juice
1 cup coarsely chopped walnuts (or other nuts)

1. Wash and drain cranberries.
2. Put cranberries into a saucepan and add water; bring to boiling and cook, uncovered, 5 minutes, or until all the skins burst.
3. Force cranberries through a sieve or food mill. Combine purée in a saucepan with the raisins, sugar, and orange peel and juice; mix well. Stir over medium heat until sugar is dissolved, then continue cooking about 15 minutes, or until thick.
4. Remove from heat; stir in walnuts. Ladle into hot sterilized jars and seal, *page 336*.

THREE ½-**PINT** JARS CONSERVE

ORANGE CONSERVE

2 cups cold water
4½ cups thinly sliced oranges
1 lemon, thinly sliced
3 cups sugar
1 teaspoon vanilla extract
½ cup pecans or walnuts, chopped
¼ cup maraschino cherries

1. Pour cold water over oranges and lemon in a bowl. Let stand, covered, 8 hours or overnight.
2. Turn into a large kettle and cook gently, uncovered, 1½ hours, or until peel is tender.
3. Measure the mixture into a saucepan. (There should be about 3 cups.) Stir in 3 cups sugar (or use equal parts sugar and fruit). Cook gently until thickened, 1 to 1½ hours.
4. Add extract, nuts, and cherries several minutes before cooking time is ended.
5. Ladle into hot sterilized jars and seal, *page 336*.

THREE ½-PINT JARS CONSERVE

BEST-EVER PURPLE PLUM CONSERVE

5 to 6 lbs. firm purple plums, rinsed, pitted, and quartered crosswise (3 qts. cut-up plums)
8 cups sugar
1 tablespoon grated orange peel
1 tablespoon grated lemon peel
½ cup orange juice
¼ cup lemon juice
1 lb. dark seedless raisins (use half golden raisins, if desired)
1 cup walnuts, broken in coarse pieces (do not chop)

1. Mix plums with 4 cups of the sugar in a large bowl; set aside in a cool place several hours or overnight. Pour off the syrup which has formed into a heavy 3-quart saucepot.
2. Add the remaining sugar to syrup and bring to boiling; boil 5 minutes, stirring constantly.
3. Add plums and fruit peels and juices; cook gently about 30 minutes, reducing heat as the mixture thickens. Stir frequently with a wooden spoon.
4. Add raisins and continue cooking about 25 minutes, stirring gently from time to time (do not overcook).
5. Stir in the walnuts several minutes before cooking time is ended. (To test conserve, quickly chill a spoonful on a chilled saucer. It should be of spreading consistency.)
6. Ladle into hot sterilized jars and seal, *page 336*

TWELVE ½-PINT JARS CONSERVE

RHUBARB CONSERVE

2 pkgs. (16 oz. each) frozen sweetened rhubarb, thawed
1 large orange
1 cup water
½ cup golden raisins
3 tablespoons Ginger Brew, *next page*
2 tablespoons white vinegar
5½ cups sugar
¼ teaspoon salt
1 bottle liquid fruit pectin
½ cup chopped pecans

1. Put rhubarb with syrup into a large kettle.
2. Wash and halve the orange; remove seeds; cut through peel and pulp into fine slivers about ¾ inch long. Mix with the water in a saucepan and simmer until peel is almost tender, about 4 minutes; add to the rhubarb.
3. Stir in raisins, Ginger Brew, vinegar, sugar, and salt; blend well. Bring rapidly to boiling; boil vigorously 1 minute, stirring constantly.
4. Remove from heat; immediately stir in pectin. Skim off any foam. Add pecans; continue stirring 5 minutes to keep fruit and nuts in suspension.
5. Ladle into hot sterilized jars and seal, *page 336*.

NINE ½-PINT JARS CONSERVE

GINGER BREW: Combine *2 teaspoons crushed ginger root* with *½ cup water* in a small saucepan. Cover and bring to boiling; simmer over low heat 2 minutes. Remove from heat; let stand 5 minutes and strain.

CHERRY-TOMATO CONSERVE

4 large tomatoes, peeled and chopped
1½ cups sugar
1 medium-sized onion, chopped
1 green pepper, chopped
1 lemon, thinly sliced
1 teaspoon ground ginger
1 jar (8 oz.) red maraschino cherries, drained and chopped
½ cup nuts, chopped

1. Mix tomatoes and sugar together in a saucepan. Let stand 3 hours, or until sugar is dissolved; stir occasionally.
2. Add onion, pepper, lemon slices, and ginger; mix well. Bring to boiling. Reduce heat and simmer until thick, 1½ to 2 hours, stirring occasionally.
3. Remove from heat and mix in cherries and nuts. Ladle mixture into hot sterilized jars and seal immediately, *page 336*.

THREE ½-PINT JARS CONSERVE

Fruit Butters

MOSELEM SPRINGS APPLE BUTTER
A favorite Pennsylvania Dutch recipe.

16 medium-sized tart apples (about 6 lbs.)
2 qts. water
1½ qts. apple cider
1½ lbs. sugar
1 teaspoon ground cinnamon
1 teaspoon ground allspice
1 teaspoon ground cloves

1. Wash and cut the apples into small pieces. (There should be about 4 quarts.) Cover with the water in a large kettle and cook, covered, until apples are soft, stirring occasionally.
2. Press through a coarse sieve or food mill to remove skins and seeds.
3. Bring cider to boiling in a heavy saucepot; stir in the apple pulp and sugar. Cook and stir over medium heat until sugar is dissolved. Reduce heat and cook slowly until mixture thickens, stirring occasionally to prevent sticking.
4. Blend in a mixture of the spices and continue cooking until apple butter is of spreading consistency.
5. Ladle into hot sterilized jars and seal, *page 336*.

ABOUT 4 PINTS APPLE BUTTER

BANANA-PECAN BUTTER

3 cups crushed ripe bananas (6 to 7 medium sized)
1 teaspoon grated lemon peel
¼ cup lemon juice
6½ cups sugar
½ teaspoon butter or margarine
1 bottle liquid fruit pectin
1 cup pecans, chopped

1. Combine the bananas, lemon peel and juice, sugar, and butter in a large heavy saucepan; blend thoroughly.
2. Bring to boiling and boil 2 minutes, stirring constantly to prevent sticking on bottom.
3. Remove from heat; stir in pectin and chopped pecans. Ladle into hot sterilized jars and seal, *page 336*.

EIGHT ½-PINT JARS FRUIT BUTTER

GRAPE BUTTER

2 lbs. Concord grapes
4½ cups sugar

1. Rinse the grapes; discard stems and blemished grapes. Drain and put into a large heavy saucepot. Add sugar and mix thoroughly. Stir over medium heat until sugar is dissolved. Increase heat and cook rapidly 20 minutes, stirring frequently to prevent sticking.
2. Remove the grape mixture from heat and force through a coarse sieve or food mill.

3. Return the pulp to saucepot and bring to boiling over high heat, stirring constantly. Boil rapidly 1 minute.

4. Remove from heat and skim off any foam. Ladle into hot sterilized jars and seal, *page 336*.

ABOUT FIVE ½-PINT JARS BUTTER

FREEZING

Freezing as a way of preserving food is recognized by most modern homemakers as not only a simple, economical, and safe method, but one whereby the food undergoes remarkably little, if any, change in flavor, color, and texture. Research also seems to show that freezing retains vitamins and minerals in foods better than most other preserving methods. Frozen foods such as fruits and vegetables, which are frozen promptly after harvesting, often rate higher in nutritive values than the so-called fresh product purchased in the market hours, even days, after harvesting.

However, to insure perfect results and to help you get the most from your food freezer some basic rules pertaining to its operation and the preparation of the food to be stored are given here. Other sources of information are the freezer manufacturer's instruction booklet (usually supplied with the purchase of a freezer), bulletins from U.S. Department of Agriculture, Washington, D.C., your state university extension service, and manufacturers of freezer containers and wrapping materials.

PLAN YOUR FREEZER SPACE

Keep your freezer filled with food. The more food stored each year the less cost per pound. Keep in mind the foods which are perennial family favorites and freeze these in season when they are top quality. Don't overstock commercially-frozen foods which are always available. Watch for special bargains and reduced prices on these items and save on the food budget. But even at bargain prices, avoid overstocking any one item. This applies to home-frozen foods as well. You don't want to find yourself short of space when other desirable foods come into season.

Unless you have a very large freezer, don't freeze such foods as carrots, beets, etc., which are usually available all year around.

Allow freezer space for short-time storage of prepared dishes, baked goods, leftovers, lunch box meals, complete meals, and special party food. To accomplish this, use your freezer space for preserving seasonal foods such as fruits and vegetables when the supply is abundant and the price is moderate. When these foods (along with the meats and poultry) are consumed, use the space for cooked, baked, and ready-to-eat items.

When freezing seasonal foods, freeze only the amounts you will consume before they are in season again.

FOLLOW APPROVED FREEZING METHODS

Select varieties of fruits and vegetables which freeze best. Your state agricultural extension service is a good source for that information.
Freeze only high-quality foods. Remember that freezing retains quality but cannot improve it.
Freeze foods promptly. Garden products, especially vegetables, rapidly lose quality at room temperature. If it is impossible to freeze at once, refrigerate them.
Freeze foods in small amounts. Buy or prepare only the amounts that can be frozen at one time. Your own freezer instruction bulletin should be the best source of information for recommended amounts. Overloading your freezer should be avoided as it results in unduly raising the temperature of the foods already stored. Overloading also keeps the new items from freezing as rapidly as is necessary for optimum quality. A general rule is to add not more than 3 pounds of food per cubic foot of freezer space during any 24 hour period. If you have more than recommended amounts to freeze, have the food frozen at a locker plant, if one is available, then store it in your home freezer.
Process foods carefully. Before freezing, blanch or scald vegetables in boiling water, or steam to stop the chemical action caused by enzymes. If the enzymes remain active, the vegetable will develop undesirable flavors and become lower in quality during the freezer storage.
Package foods properly. Use moisture-vaporproof

materials which will protect the food from the air and also against loss of moisture. Make sure the packages and containers you use can be sealed tightly. When air reaches food during storage, the result is loss of moisture accompanied by a change in flavor. This condition is called "freezer burn."

Allow some headspace in containers and jars for expansion during freezing. For dry pack, allow about ½ inch; for liquids or semi-liquids, allow from ½ to 1½ inches, depending upon the width of the neck opening of container.

Some foods can be frozen loose on baking sheets or in shallow pans. Immediately after they are frozen they must be packed in moisture-vaporproof containers or bags. After packaging, freeze foods at once. If there must be delay, keep packages in refrigerator.

Label foods accurately. Write on label the date, name of product, weight (meat), and number of servings. It is helpful to add the "maximum-storage date" so food will be used before that time.

Freeze and store foods at 0°F or lower. Put unfrozen foods in the fastest freezing area of your freezer or in direct contact with freezer walls or shelves and away from already frozen foods. Leave some space between packages to permit circulation of air.

Keep a thermometer in the storage compartment and make sure the temperature remains at zero or below. Ice or snow inside the packages usually indicates fluctuations of temperatures above zero.

Foods frozen first should be used first. Always remember that freezing retards bacterial and enzymatic action but it cannot stop it entirely.

To help you with a normal turnover of foods in the freezer, set up a record or "checking account." Use a wall chart or book and as food is put into the freezer, record it. Then as packages are removed, check them off the record.

Refreezing completely thawed food is not recommended. Uncooked fruits and vegetables suffer loss of color, flavor, and texture even if thawed for a short time. Refreezing causes further loss of quality. However, if ice crystals remain in partially thawed fruits and vegetables it is probably safe to refreeze them. Completely thawed fruit and fruit juice concentrates which have reached room temperature may still be safe unless fermentation has already started making them inedible.

If prepared foods containing milk, eggs, fish, and meat have not thawed completely, they may be safe to use if they are thoroughly heated before serving.

Meats, poultry, and fish which have a normal odor are usually safe to use. When in doubt, discard.

The final decision on whether or not to refreeze should be based on the temperature of the thawed food as measured with a reliable thermometer. If the temperature of the food has risen about 40°F, discard it. According to the United States Department of Agriculture, "No health hazard is involved if the temperature of the food has not risen above ordinary refrigerator temperatures."

Maximum Time Limits

General time limits (in months except as noted) for storing frozen foods at 0°F or lower.

Baked and Cooked Foods

Breads, yeast, baked	2 to 3
bakery (in original wrap)	less than 1
quick, baked	1 to 3
unbaked	2 weeks
rolls, baked	2 to 3
brown and serve	2 to 3
unbaked	less than 1
Cakes, frosted	1 to 2
unfrosted	2 to 3
batters	less than 1
cupcakes	2 to 3
fruitcakes	12
Cookies, baked	9
dough	9
Pies, baked	2 to 3
unbaked	3 to 4
chiffon	1
pastry shells	2
Sandwiches	less than 1
Stews, soups, prepared main dishes	2 to 3
Leftover cooked foods	1

Fruits and Vegetables 8 to 12

Dairy Products

Creamery butter, Cheddar cheese	4 to 5
Cottage cheese (not creamed)	4 to 6
Cream (40%)	3 to 4
whipped	1
Eggs, whole and yolks	12
whites	9
Ice cream	1 to 2
Milk (homogenized)	1

Fish and Shellfish

Fish, lean	6 to 8
fatty	3 to 4
salmon	2 to 3
Shellfish	4 to 6

shrimp, cooked, peeled	2 to 3
cooked, unpeeled	4 to 6
Game	8 to 18
Game Birds	8 to 12
Poultry	
Chicken, whole	6 to 8
cut up	4 to 6
giblets	1 to 3
Duckling, turkey	6 to 8
Goose	3 to 4
Meats	
Fresh, beef	6 to 12
veal	6 to 9
lamb	6 to 9
pork	3 to 6
ground beef, veal, lamb	3 to 4
ground pork	1 to 3
variety meats	3 to 4
Smoked ham, whole	2
Corned beef	2 weeks
Cooked, leftover	2 to 3
meat pies	3
Swiss steak	3
stews	3 to 4
Prepared meat dinners	2 to 6
Nuts	
Salted	3
Unsalted	9 to 12

FREEZING FRUITS

Fruits including berries are prepared for freezing in one of three ways—packed dry with no sugar; with dry sugar; or with a sugar syrup (or a combination of sugar syrup and corn syrup).

Generally, the natural color and flavor are better retained if fruits are sweetened before freezing. However, there are a few fruits that freeze satisfactorily without sweetening and are used for pies, jam and jelly-making, and for special diets. Among them are blueberries, cranberries, pineapple, raspberries, and rhubarb. To freeze them, rinse and drain off excess water by spreading them on absorbent paper so they will not freeze in a solid mass. Then pack in moisture-vaporproof containers.

Dry-sugar pack—Sprinkle sugar over the fruit as it is put into the freezer container, coating the fruit well. Or mix the fruit and sugar together lightly in a bowl before filling containers.

The most commonly used ratio is 4 cups fruit to 1 cup sugar. For a sweeter product, use 3 cups fruit to 1 cup sugar. For a less sweet product, use 5 cups fruit to 1 cup sugar.

Syrup-pack—This method of sweetening is good from the standpoint of completely covering the fruit.

To prepare the syrup, combine sugar with water and stir until sugar is dissolved. Chill syrup thoroughly before using. About 1 cup syrup is needed for a 1 pound package of fruit.

Amounts of Sugar and Water Needed for Syrups

Syrup	Cups Sugar	Cups Water
Light (30%)	2	4
Medium (40%)	3-3½	4
Heavy (50%)	4-5	4

If you wish to substitute a dry-sugar pack for a sugar syrup, the following ratios of fruit and sugar, which closely correspond to the above syrup concentration, will be a helpful guide:

30% syrup—5 cups fruit to 1 cup sugar
40% syrup—4 cups fruit to 1 cup sugar
50% syrup—3 cups fruit to 1 cup sugar

If you wish to use corn syrup in combination with a sugar syrup, substitute ⅓ of the sugar in the above amounts with light corn syrup.

Preventing Discoloration of Fruits

There are several ways to prevent discoloration of apples, apricots, peaches, pears, and other fruits. The use of ascorbic acid is the recommended method. It is available in powdered or crystalline form and may be purchased at drugstores and locker plants. Use 1½ to 2 teaspoons for each gallon of chilled syrup and add just before using the syrup.

Commercially prepared mixtures containing some ascorbic acid are also available. They usually cost less than pure ascorbic acid, but a greater amount is needed to prevent discoloration. Follow package directions for their use.

Citric acid (or lemon juice) alone or in combination with ascorbic acid may be used for treating some fruits, but it is not as effective as ascorbic acid. Citric acid is available in powdered or crystalline form. Use ¼ teaspoonful per quart of water.

If using lemon juice, use 1 teaspoon per quart of water. Let the fruit stand in the acidified water for 2 minutes, then drain thoroughly before packaging with the syrup.

Preparing Fruits

Apples (sliced)—Wash, pare, core, and slice about ½ inch thick. To prevent discoloration during preparation, slice apples into a salt solution (1½ tablespoons salt for each quart water). When all the apples are sliced, rinse in cold water and drain thoroughly. To prevent discoloration during freezing, scald the apples in live steam for about 2 minutes. If apples are quite soft, add calcium chloride to water used for scalding (1 tablespoon for each 2 quarts water). Cool immediately in cold running water and drain. If apples are to be used for pies, the amount of dry sugar needed may be added before packaging.

A second method of preventing discoloration is to submerge the slices in a sodium bisulfite-water solution (1½ teaspoons per gallon cold water) for 5 minutes. Mix the solution in an earthenware, glass, stainless steel, or enameled container. Drain slices thoroughly and pack with or without sugar. For the sugar pack, sprinkle ½ cup sugar over each quart (1¼ pounds) of apple slices. For the syrup pack, use a 40% syrup with ½ teaspoon ascorbic acid added for each quart of syrup.

Apples (baked whole), Applesauce—Prepare as for serving; cool thoroughly. Put into containers and freeze immediately.

Apricots—Wash, peel, halve, and pit. Add dry sugar or 40% syrup which contains ascorbic acid.

Blackberries, boysenberries, raspberries, loganberries, dewberries, youngberries—Wash, discarding soft, mushy, and underripe fruit. Drain in a colander or on absorbent towels. For use in desserts, put berries into freezer containers and cover with 40% or 50% syrup. Or mix gently with dry sugar in a flat pan (¾ cup sugar per quart berries). For use in pies and other cooked products, sweeten with sugar or freeze unsweetened.

Blueberries, elderberries, huckleberries—Wash, sort, and drain, discarding stems and underripe berries. For use in fruit cups and other desserts, cover with cold 40% syrup. For use in pies, muffins, and other cooked products, freeze unsweetened.

Cherries—Wash, sort, stem, drain, and pit cherries. (If cherries are sweet, pitting is unnecessary.) Sweeten tart cherries for fruit pies with ¾ to 1 cup sugar per quart of pitted fruit. Pack sweet cherries directly into containers and cover with 40% syrup which contains 1 teaspoon ascorbic acid for each 4 quarts of syrup.

Cranberries—Wash, sort, and stem, discarding imperfect berries. Drain. Pack dry; no sugar is needed.

Cranberries purchased in sealed moisture-vaporproof bags may be frozen immediately. When ready to use, rinse the frozen berries in cold water and drain. Use as you would fresh berries. Thawing is unnecessary before chopping or grinding for preparations such as cranberry relish.

Citrus fruits (grapefruit, oranges)—Freeze firm, tree-ripened fruit. Wash and peel; divide into sections; remove all membrane and seeds (see *page 356*). Or slice oranges, if desired. Drain off the juice and sweeten it with dry sugar. Pack fruit into containers and pour sweetened juice over it. Or mix the juice with a 50% syrup, to which has been added ½ teaspoon ascorbic acid for each quart syrup, just before pouring over fruit in containers.

Grapes—Wash, sort, stem, and drain. If used for fruit cups, remove seeds and pack whole in 40% syrup. If grapes are to be used for jelly-making or jam, pack unsweetened.

Melons—Wash, halve, and remove seeds; cut into slices, cubes, or balls of uniform size. Pack into containers and cover with 30% syrup. If desired, pack cantaloupe balls with whole seedless grapes and cover with orange juice.

Peaches—Freeze only peaches ripe enough for immediate eating. To remove peel, plunge fruit into boiling water, then into cold running water. If fruit is ripe, the peel will slip off easily. Halve the fruit, remove pit with a spoon, and slice halves directly into containers which contain a 40% syrup. (Start with ½ cup syrup for a 1-pint container.) When container is filled, press fruit down and add more syrup if needed to cover fruit. To prevent darkening of the peaches, add ascorbic acid to syrup (½ teaspoon per quart) just before pouring over fruit. To keep fruit submerged in the syrup, place crumpled waxed paper on top of it. If desired, peaches may be sugar-packed, mixing dry sugar with ascorbic acid powder. Follow directions on package. Mix ⅔ cup sugar with each quart (1½ pounds) prepared peaches.

Pineapple—Freeze ripe pineapple of good flavor. Pare, remove "eyes," and core. Slice, dice, crush, or cut into wedges. Pack without sugar or cover with 30% or 40% syrup.

Plums, Prunes—Sort, wash, halve, and remove pits. Pack into containers and cover with 40% syrup containing ¾ to 1 teaspoon ascorbic acid for each 2 quarts syrup. Or sweeten fruit with sugar and pack.

Rhubarb—Wash, remove leaves, and cut stalks into 1-inch pieces. Pack unsweetened for pies, or sweeten with dry sugar, mixing 1 pound sugar with each 4 pounds of cut rhubarb. To help retain color and flavor, heat rhubarb in boiling water for 1 minute, cool quickly in icy cold water, drain thoroughly, and package with or without sugar. To freeze rhubarb sauce, prepare as you would for immediate use, package, and freeze.

Strawberries — Rinse in water with ice, then sort, hull, and halve the large berries. Small berries may be frozen whole, but cutting them helps preserve color and flavor. Gently mix with sugar, using ½ to ¾ cup with each quart berries. Medium-sized whole berries may be covered with a 40% or 50% syrup. For special diets, place whole berries in freezer containers and cover with water containing 1 teaspoon ascorbic acid for each quart water.

Juices (apple, berry, cherry, grape, plum, rhubarb) — Simmer fruits for 5 minutes in just enough water to prevent sticking. Drain through a sieve or a jelly bag, if clear juice is desired. Sweeten to taste, or, if juices are to be used later for making jelly, freeze without sugar. When freezing fruit juices, work quckly to save vitamin C. Exposure to air destroys this valuable nutrient.

To freeze citrus juices (orange, grapefruit, lemon, or lime), extract juices, strain, and sweeten to taste, or freeze without sugar.

Thawing Fruits

Thaw fruits in their containers in refrigerator, at room temperature, or under cold running water until pieces can be separated, but are still icy cold.

FREEZING VEGETABLES

Use young, barely mature vegetables. Overmature vegetables become starchy and do not freeze well.

Wash thoroughly in cold running water. Sort, trim, and cut vegetables into uniform pieces.

Blanch or scald in boiling water or live steam. For home freezing, the boiling water method is generally used. However, blanching in steam is recommended by some authorities. (For directions, see U.S. Department of Agriculture bulletins.)

Leafy vegetables should always be scalded in boiling water so that leaves heat uniformly and do not mat. On the other hand, steam-blanching is considered slightly better for broccoli.

To blanch in boiling water, use about 4 quarts boiling water for each 1 pound batch of vegetables. Put vegetables into a wire basket or cheesecloth bag and immerse in rapidly boiling water. Cover kettle and immediately start counting the blanching time. If water takes more than 60 to 75 seconds to return to boiling, reduce the amount of vegetables being blanched at one time.

Chill thoroughly in water with ice. Add ice cubes to keep water very cold. Chill vegetables about as long as they have been blanched. Drain thoroughly and package. Seal packages, label, and freeze at once.

Preparing Vegetables

The scalding or blanching times given below are for the boiling water method unless otherwise designated.

Asparagus — Freeze only the tender portion. Thoroughly wash the stalks. Dirt tends to lodge under scales. If asparagus is very gritty, snip off the scales or lift them to clean thoroughly. Sort stalks according to thickness and freeze them whole (cut to the size of the container) or cut in 1-inch pieces. Scald 2 to 3 minutes. Chill in icy cold water, drain, and package.

Beans, lima — Shell, wash, and discard discolored, split, white beans. Sort into large and small sizes. Scald 2 minutes for large beans, 1 minute for small. Chill in icy cold water, drain, and package.

Beans, snap — Wash, snip off ends, and sort into two or three sizes. Small beans may be packed whole, medium-sized beans sliced lengthwise (French style), and large ones cut in 1-inch lengths. Scald 1½ minutes for whole and French style, 2½ minutes for cut beans. Chill in icy cold water; package.

Broccoli — Trim off large leaves, wilted parts, and woody stem ends. Wash thoroughly. If there is evidence of insect damage, cover stalks with salted water (4 teaspoons salt to 4 cups water); let stand 30 minutes. Rinse in running cold water. Separate the heads into suitable pieces for serving. Slice very large stalks lengthwise into uniform pieces about 1½ inches in diameter. Scald in steam about 5 minutes, in boiling water about 3 minutes. Chill in icy cold water, drain, and package.

Brussels sprouts — Wash thoroughly; trim coarse leaves. If there is evidence of insect damage, let stand in salted water (see *Broccoli*). If sprouts are not uniform in size, sort as to size. Scald small sprouts 3 minutes, large ones 4 minutes. Chill, drain, and package.

Cauliflower — Trim off leaves. To remove foreign matter from heads of cauliflower, let stand in salted water (see *Broccoli*). Separate heads into florets and scald as for broccoli. Chill in icy cold water, drain, and package.

Corn-on-cob — Use freshly picked, young, tender ears. Husk, remove silk, wash, trim tips, and sort ears according to size. Scald 7 minutes for small ears, 9 minutes for medium, and 11 minutes for large. Chill in icy cold water. Pack in cartons or wrap ears individually in aluminum foil.

Corn, whole kernel — Prepare as for corn-on-cob, scalding ears 3 to 7 minutes, depending on size. After chilling, drain and cut kernels from cob. Avoid cutting into cob. Package and freeze.

Eggplant — Pare and slice or dice. Scald 4 minutes in boiling water containing 4½ teaspoons citric acid (or ½ cup lemon juice) per gallon of water. Chill in icy cold water, drain, and package.

Greens (spinach, kale, beet tops, mustard greens, etc.) — Use only tender, young leaves free from woody or fibrous stems. Wash thoroughly to remove all dirt and sand. Scald 3 minutes in 170°F water. Stir occasionally during scalding to keep leaves from matting. Chill in icy cold water, drain thoroughly, chop, if desired, and package.

Mushrooms — Sort for size. Wash; cut off stem ends. Slice mushrooms larger than 1 inch in diameter. To prevent darkening, before scalding mushrooms immerse them in a solution of 1 teaspoon lemon juice (or 1½ teaspoons citric acid) and 2 cups cold water for 5 minutes. Scalding by live steam is recommended — 3½ minutes for small, whole mushrooms, and 3 minutes for sliced mushrooms. Chill in icy cold water, drain, and package.

If desired, mushrooms may be cooked in hot butter or margarine about 5 minutes, then cooled quickly and packaged.

Peppers, green or red — Wash, cut out stems, cut peppers into halves, and remove seeds and fiber. If desired, cut into strips or rings. Scald 2 to 3 minutes. Chill in icy cold water, drain, and package.

Peppers to be used in uncooked foods are best frozen without scalding. No headspace is necessary when packaging.

If peppers are to be stuffed, freeze them whole without scalding.

Peas, green, blackeyed — Shell peas and discard overmature ones. Scald 1 minute for tender, immature peas, 2½ minutes for mature ones. Chill in icy cold water, drain, and package.

Squash, summer — Wash and cut into ½ inch slices. Scald 3 minutes. Chill in icy cold water, drain, and package.

Squash, winter, and pumpkin — Wash, cut into pieces, remove seeds and fiber. Cook until tender in pressure cooker or in 350°F oven. Scoop out pulp from rind and mash it or put through a food mill. Chill by setting the pan in water with ice. Package.

When freezing pumpkin to be used later for pie filling, the spices may be added before freezing.

Cooking Frozen Vegetables

Do not thaw vegetables before cooking (corn-on-cob is an exception). Cook covered in a small amount of boiling, salted water until just tender. They will cook in about one half the time required for the garden-fresh product since the scalding or blanching treatment previous to packaging them was a short precooking process.

Vegetables such as squash and pumpkin which have been entirely cooked before freezing should be reheated for serving in the top of a double boiler over boiling water or heated in the oven.

FREEZING MEATS

Freezing is the simplest and safest method of preserving meat and a highly satisfactory one, provided the basic rules of freezing are carefully observed.

Freeze only high quality meats. Meat from young beef which has been aged is recommended. Lamb and game are also improved in flavor and texture if allowed to age.

Package meat in portions to fit family needs. Be sure it is cut according to the way you plan to cook it. Remove the butcher's paper from meat purchased from the market. Also remove any moisture-absorbing labels or backing boards. These may give an off-flavor to frozen meat. Trim off excess fat and remove bones, when possible, to avoid wasting storage space. (Make soup stock from the bones and freeze it for future use.) Trim sharp edges from bones which cannot be removed from meat. (Sharp edges could puncture the outer wrap.) Wrap meat tightly in moisture-vaporproof material — waxed locker paper (use double thickness), freezer foil, or plastic film. When wrapping steaks, chops, and meat patties, place a layer of the wrap between individual pieces of meat to make separation easy without completely thawing out the meat when ready to use it.

Use enough wrapping material to allow for folding the edges down at least three times. Place the meat in center of the wrap, bring the two edges together above the meat, and fold down in ½ to 1 inch folds until the paper is tight against the meat.

Freezing

Fold the ends in the same manner. Press the wrap firmly against meat to squeeze out as much air in package as possible. Seal securely with freezer tape and label with the date, kind of meat, cut, and number of servings (or the weight). Freeze meat quickly and store at zero degrees or lower.

Thawing Frozen Meats

To completely thaw a large roast at room temperature allow 2 to 3 hours per pound; in refrigerator allow 4 to 7 hours per pound.

Thawing meat in water is recommended only if it is to be cooked in liquid.

To thaw a 1-inch steak at room temperature allow 2 to 4 hours; in refrigerator allow 12 hours.

Cooking Frozen Meats

Frozen meat which has been completely thawed may be cooked in the same way as meat not frozen. This is also true of meat cooked without thawing, except that a longer time is required.

Frozen roasts require a third to a half again as long for cooking as roasts which have been thawed.

The additional time for cooking steaks and chops will vary according to surface area and thickness of meat as well as the broiling temperature.

Broil thick frozen steaks, chops, and ground meat patties further from the heat than thawed ones so that the meat will be cooked to the desired degree of doneness without browning too much on the surface. If pieces of meat are dipped in egg and coated with crumbs or dipped in a batter before cooking, thaw the meat partially so that the coating will adhere to meat.

Panbroil frozen steaks and chops in a very hot skillet so that the meat has a chance to brown well before thawing on surface. (Thawing retards browning.) When sufficiently browned, reduce heat and continue cooking, turning meat occasionally so that it will cook in the center without becoming too brown on the outside.

FREEZING POULTRY

All poultry for freezing must be thoroughly cleaned and prepared so that they are ready for cooking when removed from freezer. Freeze whole or disjointed (cut in pieces).

To prepare whole birds, lock the wings and fold neck skin neatly over wings. If leg ends are sharp, wrap them to prevent puncturing the outer wrap. Then push the legs down and forward and tie them compactly against body of bird. Wrap the bird in moisture-vaporproof sheet wrapping, or use a plastic bag. Press out as much air as possible and seal tightly with freezer tape.

To prepare disjointed poultry, flatten the pieces and place double thicknesses of wrapping material between them so they can be easily separated while poultry is still frozen. If leg ends are sharp, wrap them. Then wrap and seal the pieces the same as for whole birds.

Package giblets (except livers) separately and use within three months. Package livers and use within one month.

Turkeys usually are packaged whole. However, halves and quarters of very large birds are often

DRUGSTORE WRAP FOR MEATS

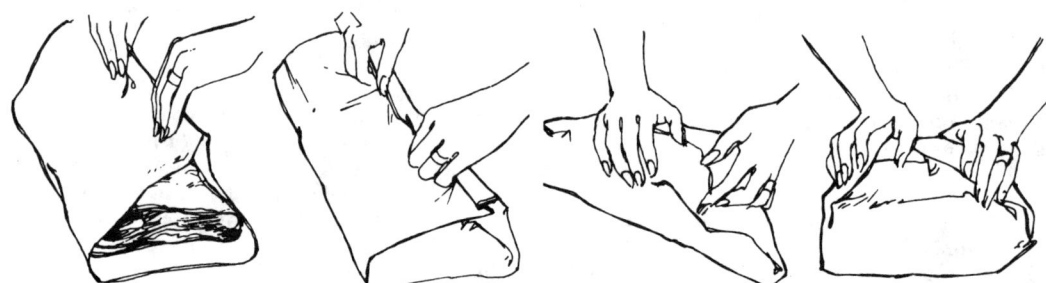

1. Place meat near center of sheet of freezer paper. Bring edges of paper together over meat.

2. Fold the paper over once; then fold again so that the second fold is tight against the meat.

3. Make top folds evenly. Smooth ends close to meat and fold into triangles. Invert package.

4. Fold ends under package away from top fold. Seal with freezer tape. Label and date.

more convenient than a whole bird and freeze well. *Do not stuff poultry before it is frozen.* A stuffed bird makes an excellent place for harmful bacteria to grow either while thawing at room temperature or in the oven before the internal temperature of the bird reaches cooking temperature. The stuffing is best if put into the bird just before it is put into the oven for roasting. This does not apply to commercially stuffed frozen birds however. They are perfectly safe to use as they are frozen under carefully controlled conditions which cannot be duplicated in the home.

To freeze leftover cooked poultry, cut meat from the bones and package in slices or pieces. Freezing slices in leftover gravy or cream sauce keeps air away from the meat and helps to retain its flavor.

Thawing Frozen Poultry

Thaw poultry in wrappings in the refrigerator or, if package is airtight, under running cold water. For a turkey, allow two to three days for a large (18 pounds or over) bird to thaw in refrigerator: allow several hours in running cold water.

Cook all poultry as soon as thawed and while extremely cold. Do not refreeze the uncooked poultry.

FREEZING GAME

When freezing game of any kind, be sure to check regulations in your state concerning length of time game may legally be stored and amount of each kind you may store.

In general, freeze game birds and animals just as you would either poultry or meat.

FREEZING FISH

Most fish freeze satisfactorily provided it is handled quickly and kept cold until frozen. (Fish is a highly perishable food.) If possible, freeze it on the day it is caught. Clean fish as you would for immediate serving. Freeze small ones whole, large ones in steaks and fillets.

To prepare lean fish (such as perch and halibut), a salt brine dip is recommended (½ cup salt dissolved in 1 quart cold water). Dip fish in brine 20 seconds. This firms the fish and reduces leakage or drip when fish is thawed.

To prepare fat fish such as lake trout, pink salmon, and mackerel, an ascorbic dip is recommended (2 teaspoons ascorbic acid to 1 quart cold water). Dip fish in the solution 1 minute.

To package fish, place double thicknesses of freezer wrap between each whole fish, fillet, or steak so they will separate easily before they are completely thawed. Put only enough fish for one meal in a package; wrap tightly in freezer wrap, seal with freezer tape, and label.

FREEZING SHELLFISH

To freeze oysters, clams, and scallops, rinse the sand from them before removing from shells; save the liquor. Wash shellfish in a salt brine (dissolve 1 cup salt in 1 quart cold water). Pack shellfish in their own liquor and freeze promptly.

To freeze crabs, remove the back shell (use only live crabs); eviscerate and wash them. Be sure to remove newly forming shell, a jelly-like substance which might discolor the body meat. Break the crabs in halves and cook them in boiling water for 15 minutes. Cool slightly and remove the meat, keeping the body meat and leg meat separate for packing. Pack the meat in freezer containers and cover with a salt brine (dissolve 1 tablespoon salt in 1 quart water). Seal and freeze promptly.

To freeze lobsters, drop them live in boiling salted water and cook 20 minutes. Lay them on their backs to cool. When cooled, remove edible meat from the shells. Package and freeze immediately.

To freeze shrimp, peel, clean and package. Or, if desired, freeze in the shell. (Cooking before freezing is not recommended as cooked shrimp has a tendency to toughen during storage.)

Thawing Frozen Fish and Shellfish

Thaw in wrappings in refrigerator and allow to thaw slowly. Fish may also be thawed at room temperature, but less leakage occurs with slow thawing. Once thawed, do not refreeze. Cook while still very cold.

Thaw seafood only long enough to separate it, then cook promptly.

FREEZING EGGS

Whole eggs — Gently mix whites and yolks (do not beat air into eggs). If used for desserts such as cake and custard, stir in 1 tablespoon sugar per cup eggs. If used for scrambling, omelets, or other kinds of cooking, stir in 1 teaspoon salt per cup eggs.

Yolks — Follow directions for whole eggs, increasing sugar or syrup to 2 tablespoons per cup. (Amount of salt remains the same.)

Whites — No special treatment is needed.

Thawing Frozen Eggs

Thaw in their container in refrigerator or at room

temperature. Thawing can be hastened by placing watertight containers of frozen eggs in a pan of cold water. Thawed whole eggs and yolks should be used at once. Whites alone will remain fresh in refrigerator two or three days.

Using Frozen Eggs in Cooking

Frozen eggs may be substituted in any recipe requiring fresh eggs.

The thawed whites, beaten when they have reached room temperature, give just as good volume as fresh egg whites, making them suitable for angel cakes, meringues, and fluffy icings.

To estimate the amount of thawed yolks, whites, or whole eggs to use for fresh eggs, use the following measurements:

1 to 1½ tablespoons yolk — 1 egg yolk
1½ to 2 tablespoon white — 1 egg white
2½ to 3 tablespoons yolks and whites — 1 egg

FREEZING DAIRY PRODUCTS

Butter — Overwrap the original waxed carton with aluminum foil or other freezer material. Butter is extremely sensitive to odors or flavors picked up from other foods, so be sure to use an odorproof wrap.

Cheese — Cottage cheese does not freeze very well. Cheddar-type cheeses may be frozen, but they have a tendency to crumble when thawed. Wrapped properly, they may be kept in the refrigerator for reasonable lengths of time so not much is gained by freezing them. Leftover grated or shredded cheese may be frozen, if desired.

Cream — Pasteurized cream with at least 40% butterfat may be frozen satisfactorily. For best results, add ⅓ cup sugar to 1 quart of cream before freezing. Cream may be frozen in the original carton if tightly sealed.

Mounds of whipped cream sweetened with confectioners' sugar may be frozen on a baking sheet, then wrapped and stored for as long as one month, to be used later for dessert topping. Mounds thaw quickly so place them on desserts just before serving.

Ice cream — One-half or one gallon cartons of ice cream are favorite items among store "specials." Freeze in original carton. When once opened, overwrap the carton with freezer wrap or put it into a plastic bag for extra protection. When purchased in gallon containers, it is advisable to repack the ice cream in several smaller containers before storing.

FREEZING BAKED PRODUCTS

Yeast breads, rolls, and coffee cakes — Use your favorite recipes. Prepare and bake yeast breads for freezing just as you would for immediate consumption. If preparing rolls for freezing, for best results use a generous amount of fat and sugar in recipe.

Cool baked products quickly, then wrap in aluminum foil or other moisture-vaporproof material. Overwrap commerically baked goods even though they are already packaged.

To prepare bread for serving, thaw the loaf in original wrap at room temperature, allowing 1 to 2 hours. If loaf is foil-wrapped, it may be heated in a 300°F oven, allowing 20 to 30 minutes.

Sliced bread may be toasted without thawing.

To prepare rolls for serving, thaw in original wrap at room temperature, allowing about 30 minutes; or place, unthawed and wrapped in foil, on baking sheet and heat in 250° to 300°F oven about 15 minutes.

To prepare coffee cake for serving, thaw at room temperature, allowing 1 to 2 hours depending upon size; or heat in oven (see rolls). If coffee cake is to be frosted, spread on frosting just before serving.

Quick breads — Biscuits, muffins, corn bread, doughnuts, nut breads, waffles, and popovers freeze well. When baked, cool product and wrap in moisture-vaporproof material. Use freezer foil if product is to be reheated in oven before serving.

Some quick breads, such as baking powder biscuits and muffins, are more satisfactorily frozen unbaked. They may be baked unthawed or thawed, allowing more time when baked in the frozen state.

Cakes — All kinds, including those made from mixes, may be frozen. If cakes are frosted, freeze the cake until frosting is set before wrapping. Butter frostings are best for freezing. Icings made with egg whites become frothy and spongy.

To prepare cakes for serving, thaw at room temperature. Unwrap frosted cakes; leave unfrosted cakes in wrapper. Cupcakes thaw in about 30 minutes, cake layers in 1 hour, loaf cakes in 2 to 3 hours.

Cookies (baked) — Cool, then package in sturdy containers (coffee or shortening cans are good). Pack in layers, separating each layer with sheet freezer wrap. Freeze fragile cookies; then wrap.

Thaw bar or crisp cookies in containers; unwrap others.

Cookie dough — For rolled cookies, cut out shapes from rolled dough and stack cutouts in layers, separating with sheet freezer wrap. When ready to use, place on cookie sheets and bake without thawing.

Shape refrigerator cookie dough into rolls and wrap in freezer foil. When ready to use, thaw the wrapped rolls of dough in refrigerator just enough to slice easily.

For drop cookies, drop the dough in mounds of desired size about ¼ inch apart on cookie sheets. Freeze until firm. Transfer mounds to containers, separating layers with sheet freezer wrap. Bake, unthawed, on cookie sheets.

If desired, cookie dough may be wrapped in a mass and frozen. When ready to use, thaw the dough until it can be handled easily, then prepare and bake as directed in the recipe.

Pies — In general, pies may be frozen baked or unbaked, whichever is more convenient. However, pies with fruit and berry fillings tend to have a crisper crust if frozen before baking.

Freezing custard-type and cream filled pies is not recommended. Meringue toppings should also be avoided as they toughen during freezing.

Fruit and mince pies — Prepare in the usual manner. If pie is to be frozen before baking, do not cut slits in top crust. (Do this before pie is put into oven.) To prevent soggy undercrust, brush it with melted fat, egg white, or spread inside of pie plate with a coating of 2 parts shortening creamed with 1 part flour. If using fresh fruit for pie filling, add lemon juice or ascorbic acid to the fruit to prevent darkening during freezing. If using frozen fruit, thaw it just enough to break apart. Thicken juice for filling with cornstarch or flour.

Chiffon pies — Prepare in the usual manner. Chill until filling is set before wrapping for freezing.

Pumpkin pie — Prepare and bake in usual manner; cool and wrap for freezing. If desired, filling may be prepared and frozen in containers. When ready to use, thaw filling, pour into unbaked pastry shell, and bake pie as usual.

To package pies, cool thoroughly (if they have been baked) and wrap in foil or other freezer material; slip pie into a plastic freezer bag, seal, and place in a flat carton for extra protection.

Pies that are too tender to wrap easily may be frozen until firm, then packaged immediately. Covering a pie with an inverted paper plate before wrapping will help protect the top crust.

To prepare an unbaked pie for serving, remove the wrapping and bake, unthawed, in a 425° to 450°F oven 15 to 20 minutes; reduce oven temperature to 350° to 375°F and complete the baking.

To prepare a baked pie for serving, thaw, wrapped, at room temperature 1 to 1½ hours if it is to be served cold. Remove wrapping and place pie in a 375°F oven 35 to 50 minutes if served warm.

To freeze pastry, prepare as usual and shape into a ball; freeze in plastic freezer bag. Or roll out pastry into rounds 2 to 3 inches larger than pie plates or pans. Stack the rounds on a stiff cardboard circle with layers of waxed paper between the rounds. Overwrap with freezer wrap or slip pastry rounds into freezer bags and seal.

To freeze pie shells, prepare in the usual manner in pie plates or pans. Then freeze, whether baked or unbaked, before wrapping. Frozen unbaked pie shells may be removed from pie pans and stacked before wrapping, putting several layers of crumpled waxed paper between each frozen shell.

To use a frozen baked pie shell, remove the wrap and place shell in 375°F oven 10 minutes. Or thaw the shell in the wrap at room temperature.

To use an unbaked pie shell, unwrap and bake at 450°F 5 minutes, then prick pastry with tines of a fork and bake about 15 minutes.

To use frozen unrolled pie dough, thaw overnight in refrigerator, or thaw at room temperature, then roll out as desired.

FREEZING SANDWICHES

Making sandwiches in quantities when it is convenient or whenever you have filling ingredients on hand, is a wonderful timesaver for homemakers with lunchbox toters in the family. But keep in mind the fact that although all kinds of fresh bread freeze well, not all fillings do. The following are some filling ingredients which do freeze well: peanut butter; finely chopped nut meats; cooked egg yolk; sliced or ground cooked or canned chicken, turkey, and fish; sliced or ground cooked meat; dried chopped fruit; chopped or sliced olives; crushed pineapple. Suitable ingredients which may be used to hold filling mixture together are lemon, orange, or pineapple juice, milk, dairy sour cream, and applesauce. Use mayonnaise and salad dressings sparingly as they tend to separate when frozen. Avoid very moist fillings such as egg salad.

Also avoid raw chopped, grated, or sliced vegetables, as they lose their crispness when frozen. Such ingredients as tomato slices, lettuce, celery, and carrots should be added to sandwiches just before eating.

Spread each slice of bread for sandwiches generously with softened butter or margarine. This will keep the filling from soaking into bread. For variety, season the butter with prepared horseradish or mustard, or chili sauce.

Wrap the filled sandwiches with moisture-vapor-proof material, each in its own individual wrap.

Freeze sandwiches no longer than two weeks. Thaw at room temperature in their wrappings.

FREEZING COOKED FOODS

Prepare your favorite recipes in double or triple amounts so there will be enough food to freeze after a family meal. Undercook rather than overcook foods that must be heated before serving. Meat should be tender but still firm and vegetables crisp-tender.

Cool foods quickly after cooking by placing the utensil in water with ice. Then package and freeze. Omit potatoes from stews and meat pies as they become mushy; add them before serving.

Avoid hard-cooked egg whites in frozen dishes as they change in texture and develop an off flavor.

Use as little fat as possible in gravies and sauces. Fats have a tendency to separate, but if used in smaller quantities they will recombine with the sauce when stirred while reheating. Fried foods are apt to become rancid after one or two months storage. Use seasonings sparingly as some of them change in flavor during storage (pepper, especially, gets stronger). Add most of the seasoning when reheating the food for serving.

Pack foods to be baked or reheated in oven in heat-resistant casseroles or baking dishes or foil freezer boxes so they may go directly from freezer to the oven.

Package in amounts suitable for family servings. Cooked foods, once reheated, should not be refrozen.

Pack cooked food which is to be reheated on surface of the range in straight-sided containers. To remove the food before thawing completely, dip container into warm water a few seconds and the food will slip out into saucepan or double boiler. Some containers may be peeled off and the contents removed.

Bonus Chapter
OUTDOOR COOKING

Grilling outdoors is a very ancient way of cooking food. It's a relatively easy way to entertain a large group, and besides, it's lots of fun for everyone. Outdoor cooking is a man's art and one distaff job that women are quite willing to relinquish to the men.

The essentials for grilling are few — a grill (of which there are many types), the fuel, the fire-starter, the tools, the food for the feast, and, if possible, an imaginative chef.

Fuel — Charcoal lumps or briquets are preferred by most experts. At times you may want to use fruit wood or hardwood such as apple or hickory chips. Dampened hickory chips tossed on a charcoal fire just before the meat is placed on the grill add an interesting flavor. Soft woods like pine are undesirable as they give food a tarry, sooty coating and also produce an unsatisfactory bed of coals.

To build a fire — Start with a bed of charcoal 2 to 3 inches deep. (It should last the entire cooking period.) Apply a liquid or solid-type lighter and ignite it. Start grilling when the coals have burned to a gray color with a ruddy glow underneath. (This requires about 30 minutes.) Another way to start the fire is by beginning the bed with a little paper and kindling, then adding a small amount of charcoal. When it is burning, build the entire bed as directed.

To control heat — The distance from the top of the coals to the food helps determine the degree of heat. More distance makes less heat and slower cooking. Many grills have adjustable fireboxes that can raise or lower the bed of coals. Hoods built on the back of some grills intensify the heat. Using this type of grill shortens cooking times slightly.

Length of cooking periods will vary with the size of firebox, degree of heat, amount and direction of the wind, and the type of grill used.

During cooking, when flare-ups occur (caused by fat dripping onto the coals), douse flames with a basting tube filled with water, or a water pistol.

Grill equipment — Besides the grill, there are many items available — some necessary, some useful, and others merely colorful gadgets. Useful additions are items such as: long-handled tools with heat-resistant handles (forks, spoons, turners, tongs), asbestos or well-padded mitts, a baster (which doubles as a douser if fat flares in the fire), a wooden cutting board, a sharp knife, a pot for a marinade or basting sauce, a basting brush, and paper towels. Long metal skewers, a steak broiler, and a spit attachment for the grill all aid in developing one's outdoor culinary skills.

The chef who wants to grill out-of-doors, but demands all the conveniences which are associated with indoor broiling, might find that preparing a fire of glowing charcoal is too much of a challenge to his patience. For him there is available the gas-fired grill with its easily controllable flame and special ceramic briquets which provide perfect radiant heat in a hurry and can be used again and again.

Marinades & Sauces

CAPER MARINADE: Mix $\frac{1}{2}$ cup cider vinegar, $\frac{1}{2}$ cup sweet pickle liquid, $\frac{1}{3}$ cup olive oil, 1 tablespoon dry mustard, 1 teaspoon salt, $\frac{1}{2}$ teaspoon pepper, and 2 tablespoons capers. Marinate lamb cubes for kabobs 6 hours.

CLARET MARINADE: Mix $\frac{3}{4}$ cup olive oil, $\frac{3}{4}$ cup claret, 3 large cloves garlic, crushed, 4 drops Tabasco, $\frac{1}{2}$ teaspoon dry mustard, 1 teaspoon ground nutmeg, and $\frac{1}{4}$ cup finely chopped pimiento-stuffed *olives.* Marinate steaks or beef cubes for kabobs 6 hours or overnight, turning occasionally.

HERB MARINADE: Blend 2/3 *cup cooking or salad oil,* 3/4 *cup lemon juice, 1 tablespoon prepared horseradish, 1 teaspoon seasoned salt,* 1/8 *teaspoon cayenne pepper,* 1/2 *teaspoon crushed savory,* 1/2 *teaspoon crushed tarragon leaves,* and *1 large clove garlic,* crushed. Mix well. Marinate raw shrimp several hours or overnight.

PINEAPPLE MARINADE: Blend *1 cup honey, 1 cup unsweetened pineapple juice, 2 cans (8½ ounces each) crushed pineapple,* 2/3 *cup red wine vinegar, 2 tablespoons soy sauce, 6 large cloves garlic,* crushed, *2 tablespoons ground ginger, 1 tablespoon ground coriander, 1 teaspoon salt,* and 1/2 *cup chopped onion* in a large skillet. Cook over medium heat, stirring occasionally, about 40 minutes, or until thickened. Reserve 1 cup to heat and serve with ribs. Marinate ribs (4 pounds) 24 hours.

BUTTER SAUCE: Heat *1 cup butter, 2 tablespoons lemon juice,* 1/4 *teaspoon salt,* 1/4 *teaspoon paprika,* 1/8 *teaspoon black pepper,* and 1/4 *cup chopped parsley* until butter is melted. Brush lobster tails with sauce. Serve remaining sauce hot with lobster.

MINT SAUCE: Stir together 1/2 *cup water,* 1/4 *cup lemon juice, 12 fresh mint leaves,* crushed, *2 split cloves garlic, 2 tablespoons chopped onion,* and *1 teaspoon rosemary.* Let stand overnight. Brush lamb chops with sauce.

ORANGE BASTING SAUCE: In a small saucepan mix *2 tablespoons light corn syrup, 1 teaspoon garlic salt, 1 teaspoon dry mustard,* 1/2 *teaspoon monosodium glutamate,* 1/2 *cup orange juice, few drops Tabasco,* and *2 tablespoons butter or margarine.* Heat until butter melts; stir to blend and brush chicken or pork while sauce is still warm. (If using chicken, coat pieces with cooking oil and let stand about 30 minutes.)

TOMATO BASTING SAUCE: Lightly brown 1/2 *cup chopped onion* in *1 tablespoon melted butter.* Blend in *1 cup ketchup,* 3/4 *cup cider vinegar,* 1/2 *cup water,* 1/2 *cup light molasses, 1 envelope garlic salad dressing mix,* and *2 beef bouillon cubes;* bring to boiling. Simmer 15 minutes. Brush chicken or scored frankfurters with sauce.

NOTE: *Sake* may be substituted for vinegar and *French salad dressing mix* for garlic dressing mix.

PIQUANT TOMATO SAUCE: Mix *1 cup ketchup,* 1/4 *cup lemon juice, 1 tablespoon soy sauce, 2 tablespoons brown sugar, 1 tablespoon prepared horseradish mustard, 1 tablespoon grated onion,* 1½ *teaspoons salt,* 1/2 *teaspoon black pepper,* 1/4 *teaspoon oregano,* 1/4 *teaspoon Tabasco,* and *1 split clove garlic.* Simmer 10 minutes. Brush on ribs.

MEATS ON THE GRILL

How to Grill Meats

STEAKS (Porterhouse, sirloin, T-bone, or rib): Have steaks cut 1½ inches thick. Marinate in *Claret Marinade, page 363,* if desired. Grill 3 inches from coals (brushing frequently with marinade, if used). When well browned, turn and season or continue brushing. Total grilling time: 12 minutes for rare. For medium or well done, increase distance from coals and grilling time.

KABOBS (beef or lamb): Marinate meat cubes, 1 to 1½ inches, in *Claret Marinade* (for beef) or *Caper Marinade* (for lamb), *page 363.* Thread marinated meat cubes onto skewers. Place rather close together for rare meat or separate slightly for well done. Grill about 3 inches from coals 15 to 20 minutes, or until tender and browned, turning and brushing frequently with marinade.

SPARERIBS AND BACK RIBS: Marinate in *Pineapple Marinade, above,* if desired. Place on a rack in a large shallow pan. Cover with aluminum foil; partially cook in a 350°F oven 30 minutes. (If done in advance and refrigerated, return to room temperature.) To grill, place 6 to 8 inches from coals and brush with marinade or sauce. Grill 40 to 50 minutes, or until meat is done, turning and brushing frequently. (To grill ribs without precooking, grill over a drip pan about 2 hours, turning occasionally. Turn and brush frequently with marinade or sauce last 40 minutes.)

SINGLE RIBS FOR APPETIZERS: Have meat dealer saw spareribs (unnecessary for back ribs) across rib bones, if desired. Precook as directed above. Cut into individual ribs. Arrange in a broiler basket and brush with marinade or sauce. Grill 6 inches from coals 40 to 50 minutes, turning and brushing frequently.

LAMB CHOPS: Have chops cut 1½ inches thick. Grill 4 inches from coals (brushing often with *Mint Sauce, page 364*, if desired). When well browned, turn and season or continue brushing. Total grilling time: 16 minutes for medium done.

FRANKFURTERS: Score frankfurters and grill 3 inches from coals 5 to 6 minutes, or until browned, turning frequently (and brushing with *Tomato Basting Sauce, page 364*, or bottled barbecue sauce, if desired).

MARINATED BLACK PEPPER STEAK

The amount of crushed peppercorns used depends entirely on personal taste. As a guide, try two teaspoonfuls for each side of a large steak.

Purchase a *sirloin steak*, cut 1½ to 2 inches thick. (Allow ¾ to 1 pound per person.) Put steak in a large shallow pan and cover with *Steak Marinade, below*; allow to marinate several hours or overnight, turning occasionally. Before grilling, remove steak from marinade and press coarsely crushed *peppercorns* liberally into both sides of steak. Grill 3 to 4 inches from coals, allowing about 15 minutes for total grilling time; turn once. (Test doneness by slitting meat near bone and noting color of meat.) To serve, cut steak diagonally into thin slices.

STEAK MARINADE

1 cup red wine vinegar	¼ teaspoon salt
½ cup salad oil	¼ teaspoon marjoram
⅓ cup firmly packed brown sugar	¼ teaspoon rosemary
	¾ cup chopped onion
Few drops Tabasco	1 clove garlic, minced

Combine all ingredients in a screw-top jar. Shake well to blend. ABOUT 2 CUPS

GRILLED STEAK WITH GARDEN BUTTER SAUCE

Place *4 pounds beef steak*, such as sirloin, porterhouse, T-bone, or rib, cut 1½ inches thick, on a lightly greased grill about 3 inches from coals. Grill about 6 minutes, or until first side is browned. Turn with tongs and season with *salt* and *black pepper*. Grill second side about 6 minutes, or until done. (To test doneness, slit meat near bone and note color of meat.) Season second side of steak. Remove from grill to serving plate and slice. Serve with *Garden Butter Sauce, below*. ABOUT 4 SERVINGS

GARDEN BUTTER SAUCE: Melt ¼ cup butter in a skillet or saucepan. Add ¼ cup finely chopped parsley, 2 tablespoons finely chopped watercress, 2 tablespoons finely chopped celery tops, ¼ teaspoon crushed tarragon, and 1 cup beef bouillon (dissolve 1 beef bouillon cube in 1 cup boiling water); mix well. Add *10 sliced pimiento-stuffed olives* and stir gently. Set skillet on edge of grill to keep warm. ABOUT 1½ CUPS

HERBED BEEF STEAK

Sprinkle *steak* generously on both sides with *garlic salt*. Pour ¼ cup cooking or salad oil into a shallow pan or dish. Put steak into pan and turn to coat with oil. Allow to stand 1 hour, turning occasionally. Grill to desired degree of doneness, brushing frequently with *Herbed Vinegar, below*.

HERBED VINEGAR: Combine ½ cup tarragon vinegar, ½ teaspoon dill weed, crushed, ¼ teaspoon thyme, crushed, and 1 tablespoon finely chopped parsley.

FULL-FLAVORED STEAK

To marinate is to glamorize the flavor of the king of American meats . . . steak.

2½ tablespoons brown sugar	1 tablespoon tarragon vinegar
1½ tablespoons sugar	3 lbs. beef steak (sirloin, porterhouse, T-bone, or rib), cut 1½ inches thick
1 tablespoon ground ginger	
1 clove garlic, crushed	
½ cup soy sauce	

1. Combine the sugars, ginger, garlic, soy sauce, and vinegar.
2. Put meat into a large shallow dish and pour soy sauce mixture over meat. Allow to marinate at least 30 minutes, basting frequently and turning once or twice.
3. When ready to grill, remove meat from marinade, reserving marinade.

4. Place steak on grill about 3 inches from coals. Brushing frequently with marinade, grill about 6 minutes, or until one side is browned. Turn and grill other side about 6 minutes, or until done. (To test doneness, slit meat near bone and note color of meat.) Serve immediately.   4 TO 6 SERVINGS

RIB STEAKS, WESTERN STYLE

1 cup hot bacon drippings
3 tablespoons butter or margarine
⅓ cup lemon juice
3 tablespoons Worcestershire sauce
2 tablespoons ketchup
1 tablespoon paprika
½ cup finely chopped onion
½ clove garlic, crushed
1½ bay leaves
2 teaspoons prepared horseradish
½ teaspoon salt
⅛ teaspoon pepper
4 rib steaks, cut about 1-in. thick (each steak about 1 lb.)

1. Mix all ingredients except steaks thoroughly. Pour over steaks and allow to stand about 30 minutes at room temperature for flavors to blend. Remove bay leaves.
2. Lightly grease grill with cooking oil. Place steaks on grill about 3 inches from coals. Grill about 4 minutes, or until first side is browned. Turn with tongs; grill second side about 4 minutes, or until done. (To test doneness, slit meat near bone and note color of meat.) During grilling, baste frequently with the sauce. Serve at once.   4 SERVINGS

GRILLED SIRLOIN STEAK JULIANA

1 cup tomato juice
1 cup orange juice
½ cup minced onion
½ cup finely chopped pimiento-stuffed olives
2 cloves garlic, crushed
1 tablespoon soy sauce
1 teaspoon salt
1 teaspoon paprika
¼ teaspoon cayenne pepper
Sirloin steak, cut about 2 in. thick (allow ½ to ¾ lb. per person)

1. Combine the juices, onion, olives, garlic, and soy sauce; stir in a mixture of the salt, paprika, and cayenne pepper.
2. Pour sauce over steak in a shallow dish; allow to stand about 1 hour at room temperature, turning occasionally.
3. Transfer steak from sauce to grill and brown quickly on both sides close to hot coals. Continue grilling about 4 inches from coals, basting occasionally with sauce. Allow about 30 minutes total grilling time, depending upon desired doneness of meat. (Test doneness by slitting meat near bone and noting color of meat.) To serve, cut steak diagonally into thin slices and serve with remaining heated sauce.   1 STEAK

GRILLED BURGERS WITH CHEESE SAUCE

2 lbs. ground beef
2 teaspoons salt
¼ teaspoon pepper
½ teaspoon monosodium glutamate

1. Lightly mix all ingredients and shape into 8 patties. Place in a greased broiler basket or on a greased grill. Grill about 3 inches from coals 10 to 15 minutes, turning once.
2. Serve on toasted *hamburger buns* with *Lightning Cheese Sauce, below*.   8 BURGERS
NOTE: For variety, mix in one or more of the following: *½ cup chopped onion, 1 cup chopped green onion, ¼ cup chopped green pepper, ¼ cup chopped pimiento-stuffed olives,* or *1 teaspoon dill weed.*
BLACK PEPPER BURGERS: Mix in *1 tablespoon Worcestershire sauce* with the seasonings and press about *¾ teaspoon coarsely crushed peppercorns* onto top and bottom of each patty before grilling.
LIGHTNING CHEESE SAUCE: Blend *1 can (10¾ ounces) condensed Cheddar cheese soup, 1 tablespoon lemon juice, ½ teaspoon prepared mustard,* and a *few grains cayenne pepper* in a saucepan. Heat thoroughly.   ABOUT 1⅓ CUPS

SAUCY ROQUEFORT BURGERS

Make a large depression in the center of each 1-inch thick *hamburger*. Fill with *2 teaspoons crumbled Roquefort cheese* and *½ teaspoon olive oil*. Reshape burgers to seal in filling. Grill in broiler basket or on a greased grill 4 to 5 inches from coals, brushing frequently with *bottled barbecue sauce*. When browned, turn and season or continue brushing. Total grilling time: 10 minutes for medium done.

GRILLED GROUND BEEF "FRANKS" IN BUNS

1 lb. ground beef
1 egg, fork beaten
3 tablespoons fine dry bread crumbs
½ teaspoon salt
⅛ teaspoon pepper
¼ teaspoon ground nutmeg
¼ teaspoon crushed thyme
¼ cup chopped onion
2 tablespoons chopped green pepper
¼ cup snipped parsley
½ cup finely diced sharp Cheddar cheese

1. Combine ground beef and a mixture of egg, crumbs, salt, pepper, nutmeg, and thyme. Add onion, green pepper, parsley, and cheese; mix lightly but thoroughly.
2. Divide meat mixture into 6 equal portions and shape each into a 6-inch long "frankfurter." Wrap each with *bacon* to cover completely; fasten ends of bacon with wooden picks.
3. Thread each "frankfurter" lengthwise onto a skewer. Grill about 4 inches from coals until meat is of desired doneness, about 20 minutes, turning occasionally.
4. Serve in hot toasted buttered *frankfurter buns*.

6 SERVINGS

APPETIZER SPARERIBS

These ribs not only awaken the appetite—they tantalize the nose, delight the eye, and reward the palate.

Put *4 pounds spareribs*, meaty side up, in a shallow roasting pan. Rub with *1 cut clove garlic* and sprinkle with *salt*. Roast in a 350° oven 1½ hours or until done, draining off excess fat as it accumulates. Cut ribs apart. Dip in either *Tangy Plum Sauce* or *Sweet-Sour Apricot Sauce, below*; grill about 3 inches from coals until well browned, turning frequently.   APPETIZERS FOR 10 TO 12

TANGY PLUM SAUCE: Drain *1 can (16 ounces) purple plums*, reserving ¼ cup syrup. Pit plums and force through a sieve or food mill into a bowl. Blend in the reserved syrup, *½ cup thawed frozen orange juice concentrate*, and *½ teaspoon Worcestershire sauce*. Store, covered, in refrigerator until ready to use.   ABOUT 1½ CUPS

SWEET-SOUR APRICOT SAUCE

2 cans (30 oz. each) apricot halves, drained
½ teaspoon salt
Few grains white pepper
2 tablespoons cider vinegar
½ cup drained crushed pineapple
½ cup honey
½ cup brown sugar
2 large cloves garlic, quartered

1. Force apricots through a sieve or food mill into a saucepan. Stir in a mixture of pineapple, honey, brown sugar, salt, white pepper, and vinegar, then garlic.
2. Bring mixture to boiling, reduce heat to medium, and cook 10 minutes, stirring occasionally. Remove garlic. Cool and store, covered, in refrigerator until ready to use.   ABOUT 2½ CUPS

BARBECUED RIBS

4 lbs. back ribs
3 cloves garlic, crushed
¼ cup cooking or salad oil
1 cup chopped onion
1 can (8 oz.) tomato sauce
½ cup water
¼ cup lemon juice
3 tablespoons Worcestershire sauce
¼ cup firmly packed brown sugar
1 teaspoon salt
¼ teaspoon pepper

1. Rub ribs with crushed garlic; cut into serving-sized pieces. Place the ribs in a large shallow pan; set aside.
2. Heat oil in a skillet; add onion and cook until tender, stirring occasionally. Blend in tomato sauce, water, lemon juice, Worcestershire sauce, brown sugar, salt, and pepper; bring to boiling, reduce heat, and simmer 5 minutes.
3. Pour sauce over ribs and marinate 2 hours at room temperature, or overnight in refrigerator.
4. Remove ribs from marinade (reserve for brushing) and put on grill or in a broiler basket 5 inches from coals. Grill 1 hour or until done, turning and brushing frequently with the marinade.

ABOUT 6 SERVINGS

STUFFED PORK TENDERLOIN PATTIES

8 pork tenderloin patties
4 slices bacon
16 medium-sized mushrooms, chopped (about 1⅓ cups)
¼ cup chopped onion
2 tablespoons ketchup
¼ teaspoon salt
Orange Basting Sauce, *page 364*

1. Remove excess fat from patties and flatten to

about ¼ inch thickness. Set patties aside.

2. To make stuffing, cook bacon in a skillet until crisp; drain on absorbent paper, crumble, and set aside. Pour off all but 3 tablespoons bacon fat and add mushrooms and onion to skillet. Cook until mushrooms are lightly browned and onion is soft, stirring frequently. Remove from heat and mix in bacon, ketchup, and salt.

3. Sprinkle meat lightly with *salt*. Spoon stuffing equally onto half of the patties. Top with remaining flattened patties.

4. Brush outside surfaces of meat with *cooking or salad oil*.

5. Grill in a broiler basket or on grill about 6 inches from coals 25 to 30 minutes, turning frequently and brushing with Orange Basting Sauce.

4 GENEROUS SERVINGS

GINGER-GLAZED LAMB CHOPS

Season double *loin lamb chops* with *salt, monosodium glutamate,* and *pepper*. Brush with *Ginger Glaze, below,* and grill 5 to 6 inches from coals 12 to 15 minutes on each side; brush frequently with glaze. Meanwhile, put *canned yams* into small aluminum foil pans and spoon some of glaze over them. Set on grill; turn and baste with glaze until thoroughly heated.

GINGER GLAZE: Mix thoroughly *1 cup ginger marmalade, ¼ cup butter or margarine, 2 tablespoons lemon juice,* and *1 teaspoon soy sauce*.

MINTED LAMB CHOPS

¼ cup finely chopped mushrooms, lightly browned in butter or margarine	¼ cup firmly packed brown sugar
	1 teaspoon dry mustard
	½ teaspoon salt
2 tablespoons crushed fresh mint leaves, or 1 tablespoon dry mint leaves	2 tablespoons wine vinegar
	8 loin or rib lamb chops, cut 1½ to 2 in. thick

1. Combine mushrooms, mint, brown sugar, dry mustard, salt, and vinegar; toss gently to mix.

2. Grill chops about 4 inches from coals 8 to 10 minutes on one side. Turn chops and spoon mushroom mixture over surface of each; grill second side 8 to 10 minutes, or until done.

8 SERVINGS

BARBECUED BOLOGNA ROLL

4 lb. bologna roll	1 teaspoon prepared horseradish
1½ tablespoons prepared mustard	1 cup chili sauce
1½ teaspoons brown sugar	3 tablespoons cider vinegar

1. Score bologna roll on one side, making cuts ½- to 1-inch deep and 1 inch apart. Secure roll on a long skewer.

2. Mix mustard, brown sugar, and horseradish. Spread into cuts.

3. Place roll directly on grill about 3 inches from coals. Baste well with a mixture of chili sauce and vinegar. Turning frequently, grill 15 to 20 minutes or until roll is thoroughly heated and browned.

4. Remove skewer and slice meat.

16 SERVINGS

BACON-WRAPPED FRANKS

Slit *frankfurters* almost through lengthwise. Spread cut surfaces with about *1 teaspoon process blue cheese spread*. Starting at one end, wrap *1 slice bacon* around each frankfurter; secure ends with *whole cloves*. Put in a hot-dog roaster or on the grill. Grill about 3 inches from coals, turning often, until bacon and frankfurters are lightly browned. (If desired, partially cook bacon before wrapping around franks.)

MARINATED FRANKS

For 1¼ cups marinade, in a shallow dish mix *½ cup soy sauce, ⅓ cup ketchup, ¼ cup salad oil, ¼ cup cider vinegar, 1 teaspoon prepared horseradish, ½ teaspoon dry mustard,* and *¼ teaspoon thyme*. Cut gashes in *frankfurters*. Put the frankfurters into marinade and let stand about 3 hours, turning frequently to coat well. Drain and reserve marinade. Put frankfurters in roaster or on grill. Grill about 10 minutes, turning often and basting with reserved marinade.

DOUBLE TREAT FRANK-BURGERS

2 lbs. ground beef	6 strips (½ in. each) Cheddar cheese
2 teaspoons salt	
2 tablespoons ketchup	3 dill pickles, cut in quarters lengthwise
6 frankfurters, cut in halves lengthwise	Bottled barbecue sauce

1. Lightly toss the ground beef, salt, *pepper*, and ketchup together. Form into twelve flat patties.
2. Place 2 frankfurter halves, cut side down, on each of 6 patties; place a strip of cheese and two pickle strips between the frankfurter halves. Brush lightly with barbecue sauce. Top with remaining patties and brush with sauce.
3. Place frank-burgers, sauce side down, in a broiler basket. Brush tops with sauce and close broiler basket. Grill about 3 inches from coals 10 to 15 minutes, frequently turning and brushing with barbecue sauce. 6 SERVINGS

GLAZED BEEF-FRUIT KABOB DUO

3 lbs. boneless beef (sirloin, rib or tenderloin), cut in 1½-in. cubes	Spicy Apricot-Lime Sauce, *below* Glazed Fruit Kabobs, *below*

1. Thread beef cubes onto eight 5-inch skewers, separating pieces slightly. Brush with Spicy Apricot-Lime Sauce. Place on a greased grill and cook 4 to 5 inches from coals, turning and brushing frequently with the sauce until meat is the desired degree of doneness, 12 to 15 minutes.
2. Arrange beef and fruit kabobs on fluffy cooked rice, if desired. Serve immediately with the remaining hot sauce. 8 SERVINGS

GLAZED FRUIT KABOBS: Thread alternately onto eight 4-inch skewers, 16 large orange wedges (4 large oranges, peeled), 16 lime slices (2 large limes cut in ¼-inch slices), and 16 honeydew melon slices, 2¾ inches each. Brush with Spicy Apricot-Lime Sauce, *below*; and grill or broil 4 to 5 inches from source of heat about 10 minutes, turning and brushing frequently with the sauce until fruit is heated and well glazed.

SPICY APRICOT-LIME SAUCE

1 cup apricot preserves	1 teaspoon ground cinnamon
½ cup light corn syrup	
½ cup butter	¼ teaspoon ground cloves
¼ cup lime juice	

Combine all ingredients in a saucepan. Stirring occasionally, bring slowly to simmering and cook until slightly thicker, about 10 minutes. 2 CUPS

BEEF KABOBS WITH ORIENTAL SAUCE

¾ cup cooking or salad oil	1½ teaspoons garlic powder
¼ cup soy sauce	1½ teaspoons finely chopped green onion
3 tablespoons honey	
2 tablespoons cider vinegar	1½ lbs. boneless sirloin steak, cut in 1½-in. cubes
1½ teaspoons ground ginger	

1. Combine oil, soy sauce, honey, vinegar, ground ginger, garlic powder, and chopped green onion in a large shallow dish. Add the meat cubes; turn until pieces are coated. Set in refrigerator to marinate for at least 4 hours, turning several times.
2. Remove meat from marinade with a slotted spoon and drain. Reserve marinade for basting.
3. Thread three meat cubes onto each 6-inch skewer. Place meat close together for rare; separate cubes slightly for well done.
4. Grill kabobs on a greased grill about 3 inches from coals, turning often for even browning. Baste frequently with marinade. Grilling period ranges from 10 to 20 minutes, or until meat is done to the desired stage. (Test for doneness by cutting a slit in meat and noting internal color.) ABOUT 4 SERVINGS

MARINATED LAMB KABOBS

½ cup soy sauce	1½ lbs. boneless lamb (leg or shoulder), cut in 1½-in. cubes
1 clove garlic, crushed	
1 teaspoon chopped candied ginger	Mushroom caps
3 tablespoons sugar	1-in. green pepper squares
	Pimiento-stuffed olives

1. Combine the soy sauce, garlic, ginger, and sugar in a shallow dish. Add the meat cubes and turn until pieces are coated. Refrigerate at least 6 hours, turning several times.
2. Remove meat from marinade with a slotted spoon and drain; reserve marinade for basting.
3. Alternately thread onto four 16-inch skewers

mushrooms, lamb, green pepper, and olives, ending each skewer with a mushroom and olive.
4. Basting generously and frequently, grill kabobs on a greased grill about 3 inches from coals about 20 minutes, or until meat is tender and rich brown.

ABOUT 4 SERVINGS

HAM 'N' PICKLE KABOBS

1 jar (10 oz., about 1 cup) currant jelly	Leftover cooked ham (about 1½ lbs.), cut in 1-in. cubes
1/3 cup prepared mustard	8 to 10 canned peach halves, each cut in 3 wedges
2 tablespoons light corn syrup	Pickle slices

1. Melt jelly in a saucepan. Blend in mustard and corn syrup until well blended; boil 2 minutes.
2. Stir in ham cubes; reduce heat and simmer, covered, 20 minutes. Gently stir in peaches and pickle slices; cover and heat 10 minutes. Drain sauce from ham, peaches, and pickles and reserve for brushing on kabobs.
3. Alternately thread ham cubes, pairs of pickle slices, and peach wedges onto skewers, starting and ending with ham. Brush kabobs with sauce.
4. Grill about 4 inches from coals until ham is thoroughly browned, turning and brushing frequently with sauce; allow about 30 minutes grilling time.

ABOUT 8 KABOBS

HELP-YOURSELF APPETIZER KABOBS

Arrange a Lazy Susan or tray with individual bowls of *canned Vienna sausage*, cut in halves, thick slices of *banana* (having green-tipped peel), *pineapple chunks*, pitted large *ripe olives*, *canned green chilies*, cut in large pieces, and *bottled sweet and sour sauce*. Spear morsels (your choice) on a 6-inch skewer, coat generously with the sauce, and grill 2 to 3 inches from coals until sauce is bubbly and tidbits begin to brown.

QUICKIE KABOBS

Allowing ¼ pound meat per serving, cut *canned luncheon meat* or *bologna* into 1- to 1½-inch cubes; cut *green pepper* and *bacon* into 1- to 1½-inch pieces. Alternately thread onto skewers along with *pitted olives*. Grill on greased grill about 3 inches from coals about 5 minutes, turning and brushing constantly with your favorite *salad dressing* (bottled or prepared from a mix) or a *bottled barbecue sauce*.

CHICKEN ON THE GRILL

LEMON-DIPPED CHICKEN
Pick up your chicken and eat it out of hand.

1 cup lemon juice	1 teaspoon Tabasco
½ cup cooking or salad oil	2 broiler-fryers (1 to 1½ lbs. each), split lengthwise
2 tablespoons molasses	
2 teaspoons salt	

1. Mix together in a large shallow dish the lemon juice, oil, molasses, salt, and Tabasco. Add chicken halves; turn until pieces are coated. Set in refrigerator to marinate for at least 4 hours, turning several times.
2. Drain and reserve marinade for basting. Place chicken halves on greased grill or in a greased steak broiler; brush with marinade. Grill, cut side down, about 3 inches from coals. Turn every 5 minutes to brown and cook evenly. Brush frequently with the reserved marinade.
3. Grill about 20 minutes, or until chickens test done. (Chicken is done when meat on thickest part of drumstick cuts easily.)

ABOUT 4 SERVINGS

SAUCY CINNAMON CHICKEN

¾ cup lemon juice	1 tablespoon ground cinnamon
¾ cup cooking or salad oil	1½ teaspoons curry powder
6 tablespoons light corn syrup	1½ teaspoons salt
1 small clove garlic, crushed	2 broiler-fryers (1½ to 2 lbs. each), split lengthwise

1. Combine the lemon juice, oil, corn syrup, and garlic; stir in a mixture of the cinnamon, curry powder, and salt.
2. Pour mixture over chickens in a shallow pan. Cover and refrigerate several hours or overnight to marinate, turning and basting chickens occasionally.
3. Drain chickens, reserving marinade for basting sauce. Grill about 4 inches from coals, basting frequently with marinade and turning occasionally to brown evenly. Grill about 35 minutes, or until breast meat near wing joint is fork-tender.

4 SERVINGS

GLAZED GRILLED CHICKEN

Split *2 broiler-fryers* (1½ to 2 pounds each) into halves lengthwise. Put chicken halves, cut side down, on a greased grill 3 to 5 inches from coals. Turn and brush with *Barbecue Sauce* or *Currant-Mustard Glaze, page 374*, every 5 minutes for even cooking and browning. Grill about 20 minutes, or until chicken tests done. (Chicken is done when meat on thickest part of drumstick cuts easily.)   4 SERVINGS

NOTE: Chicken halves, quarters, or pieces may also be brushed with *Tomato Basting Sauce, page 364, Tangy Plum Sauce, page 367, Pineapple Marinade, page 364,* or a *lemon-flavored butter* and placed in a greased steak broiler. Brush frequently with sauce and turn every 5 minutes until chicken tests done.

FISH & SHELLFISH ON THE GRILL

GRILLED TROUT
A sportsman's contribution to outdoor cooking.

6 cleaned fresh trout (about 5 to 6 oz. each)
⅔ cup olive oil
¼ cup lemon juice
2 tablespoons water
2 tablespoons grated onion
2 tablespoons minced parsley
2 teaspoons salt
½ teaspoon black pepper
1 teaspoon curry powder
½ teaspoon celery flakes
½ teaspoon tarragon

1. Remove heads and fins from trout, if desired; rinse trout under cold running water and pat dry with absorbent paper. Put in a shallow dish.
2. Combine remaining ingredients in a screw-top jar. Shake well to blend. Pour over trout, cover, and set in refrigerator to marinate at least 2 hours, turning occasionally.
3. Drain and reserve marinade. Put trout on greased grill or in a greased broiler basket; brush with marinade. Grill 3 inches from coals about 4 minutes; turn, brush with marinade, and grill second side about 4 minutes, or until fish flakes easily. Serve immediately.   6 SERVINGS

NOTE: Other fresh-water fish may be prepared this way.

GRILLED ROCK LOBSTER TAILS

6 frozen South African rock lobster tails, thawed
¾ cup pineapple juice
½ cup packed brown sugar
¼ cup cider vinegar
2½ teaspoons dry mustard

1. Cut underside membrane of lobster tails around edges and remove. Insert skewers lengthwise through meat to keep tails flat during cooking.
2. Place on grill about 4 inches from coals, flesh side down, 3 to 5 minutes. Turn, brush meat with a mixture of pineapple juice and remaining ingredients, and continue grilling until meat is opaque and tender. Brush meat several times during cooking and just before serving. Serve with remaining sauce and *lemon wedges*.   6 SERVINGS

NOTE: *Butter Sauce, page 364,* may be substituted for the pineapple mixture.

GRILLED LOBSTER TAILS ITALIANO
Cooking with garlic presents no olfactory problems when it's done outdoors.

4 South African rock lobster tails (about 6 oz. each)
2 tablespoons snipped parsley

Fish & Shellfish on the Grill

1/3 cup butter or
  margarine, melted
1 tablespoon grated
  onion
1 clove garlic, crushed
1/2 teaspoon basil,
  crushed
1/4 teaspoon oregano,
  crushed
1/4 cup shredded
  Parmesan cheese

1. Thaw rock lobster tails according to package directions. Cut underside membrane around edges and remove. To prevent curling, hold tail in hands and bend it toward shell side to crack in three places; or insert skewer lengthwise through meat to keep tail flat.
2. Blend butter with onion, garlic, and a mixture of the parsley and herbs. Brush flesh side of lobster tails with the seasoned butter.
3. Grill lobster tails, shell side down, about 4 inches from coals 5 minutes, brushing flesh side generously with seasoned butter. Turn and continue broiling until meat is opaque and tender when tested with a fork. Turn flesh side up and sprinkle each lobster tail with about 1 tablespoon cheese; heat until cheese is melted. Transfer lobster tails to heated serving platter and serve with remaining butter sauce. 4 SERVINGS

ROCK LOBSTER TAILS WITH ORANGE-BUTTER SAUCE

1 can (6 oz.) frozen
  orange juice
  concentrate, undiluted
1/4 cup lemon juice
1/2 teaspoon dry mustard
1/4 teaspoon rosemary
1/2 teaspoon celery salt
1/2 teaspoon onion powder
1/2 teaspoon salt
1/4 teaspoon Angostura
  bitters
1/2 cup butter or
  margarine
12 frozen South African
  rock lobster tails
  (2 pkgs., 1 1/2 lbs. each)

1. For sauce, combine all ingredients except butter and lobster in a saucepan; heat slowly, stirring constantly, until mixture comes to a boil; boil 1 minute.
2. When ready to grill, melt butter in a small saucepan over fire; add sauce, stirring to blend thoroughly; use to brush rock lobster tails during grilling and serve remaining sauce for dipping.
3. Let frozen rock lobster tails thaw gradually; when ready to cook, slit thin underside membrane down center and peel open; insert tails on long skewers. (If tails are cooked flat on grill, prevent curling by bending tails backward to crack sharply in several places.)

4. Grill tails, shell side down, about 4 inches from coals 5 minutes, brushing occasionally with butter sauce; turn tails and grill 5 minutes longer, or until meat is opaque and creamy white.
5. Serve with remaining sauce. 8 SERVINGS

GRILLED SHRIMP APPETIZERS

Shell fresh *shrimp*, leaving tails; devein and rinse under running cold water; put into a large bowl. Partially cover with *bottled Italian salad dressing*; cover bowl and refrigerate at least 2 hours, turning shrimp several times. Drain shrimp, reserving marinade. Allow guests to thread onto metal or bamboo skewers (soak bamboo skewers in water before using): *shrimp, cherry tomatoes, green pepper squares,* and *avocado pieces*. Grill 3 inches from coals about 3 minutes, or until shrimp are done, turning and brushing with marinade.

MARINATED GRILLED SHRIMP

Cut each *raw shrimp* through shell along back; remove black vein. Carefully spread shell open; rinse and drain well. Marinate in *Herb Marinade, page 364,* several hours or overnight. Put shrimp, one layer deep, in a broiler basket. Turning occasionally, grill 3 inches from coals 15 minutes, or until shrimp are done.

GRILLED SHRIMP IN SHELLS

Serve this exotic shrimp piping hot as an appetizer. Plenty of paper napkins are a necessity as well as a convenience.

2 lbs. jumbo-sized
  shrimp or prawns,
  fresh or thawed frozen
  (about 24)
1 cup olive oil
1/2 cup lemon juice
2 tablespoons soy sauce
1/2 teaspoon salt
1 large clove garlic,
  crushed
2 tablespoons chopped
  parsley
1/2 teaspoon thyme,
  crushed
1/2 teaspoon marjoram,
  crushed
1/2 teaspoon celery
  seed

1. Using scissors, cut through shell at the back of each raw shrimp; remove the black vein. Wash shrimp with shells thoroughly; drain on absorbent

paper. Put the shrimp into a large bowl.
2. Combine remaining ingredients; mix well and pour over shrimp. Cover and refrigerate at least 2 hours, turning shrimp several times.
3. Arrange the shrimp in a hinged steak broiler or broiler basket. Grill about 3 inches from coals until shells are slightly charred. Turn broiler and grill shrimp several minutes longer. Serve immediately.
ABOUT 6 SERVINGS

NOTE: If desired, substitute *1 tablespoon chopped onion* for garlic. Omit thyme, marjoram, and celery seed. Add *4 teaspoons crushed tarragon*, *½ teaspoon chervil*, and *¼ teaspoon basil*.

SPIT COOKERY

ROAST LOIN OF PORK
(Schweinebraten)

For a traditional German dinner, serve this succulent pork roast with sauerkraut and apples.

3½-lb. (8 ribs) pork loin roast	½ teaspoon marjoram, crushed
1½ teaspoons onion salt	¼ teaspoon pepper

1. Rub roast with a mixture of the salt, marjoram, and pepper. Secure roast on spit. Insert meat thermometer. Adjust spit about 8 inches above prepared coals, placing aluminum foil pan under pork to catch drippings. If using a gas-fired grill, adjust flame size following manufacturer's directions.
2. Roast until meat thermometer registers 170°F. or until meat is tender. About 30 minutes before roast is done, score surface.
3. Place roast on a warm serving platter. Garnish with *parsley*.
8 SERVINGS

NOTE: To roast in the oven, place pork loin, fat side up, on a rack in a shallow roasting pan. Roast, uncovered, at 325°F about 2½ hours.

HAM ON A SPIT

Center a *canned ham* on a motor-driven spit following grill manufacturer's directions. Roast until thoroughly heated and browned, brushing with a blend of *apricot preserves* and *fruit juices*, or with one of *Glazes for Ham, page 103*.

LAMB BARBACOA

6-lb. boned leg or shoulder of lamb, rolled and tied	8 to 10 drops Tabasco
	2 medium-sized tomatoes, diced
1 cup water	1 medium-sized green pepper, diced
1 cup port wine	1 medium-sized onion, sliced
½ cup olive oil	
1 tablespoon salt	½ cup coarsely chopped parsley
1 teaspoon freshly ground black pepper	
⅛ teaspoon marjoram	3 cloves garlic, minced
⅛ teaspoon dry mustard	

1. Insert a skewer at intervals to make small holes all over lamb. Set lamb in a large shallow pan.
2. Combine and thoroughly blend the remaining ingredients and pour over the lamb. Cover and marinate about 24 hours in refrigerator; baste frequently, turning the lamb occasionally.
3. When ready to grill, remove the lamb from the marinade (reserve) and secure roast on spit, making sure it is evenly balanced. Insert meat thermometer so tip does not touch the spit or rest in fat; put drip pan in place and start motor.
4. Basting frequently with the liquid from the marinade, rotate on spit 2½ to 3 hours, or until meat thermometer registers 175°F for medium done or 180°F for well done.
5. Serve hot with the cold vegetable marinade as a relish.
8 TO 12 SERVINGS

BARBECUED CHICKEN ON A SPIT

2 broilers-fryers (1½ to 2 lbs. each)	Barbecue Sauce or Currant-Mustard Glaze, *next page*
2 teaspoons salt	

1. Remove spit from grill before building fire.
2. Clean chickens; rinse and pat dry with absorbent paper. Rub cavities of birds with salt. Skewer neck skin to back; tuck wings under. Carefully insert spit lengthwise through both birds. Be sure they are well balanced on spit for even turning. Tie

drumsticks to spit. Brush chickens with Barbecue Sauce or glaze.

3. Grill 8 inches from coals, turning frequently. Baste often with the sauce. (Hold a pan under the chickens while basting to catch any drippings.) Grill until a drumstick twists out of joint easily, about 1 hour. Serve with remaining sauce.

4 SERVINGS

BARBECUE SAUCE

1 can (8 oz.) tomato sauce
1 can (6 oz.) tomato paste
⅓ cup chopped onion
1 clove garlic, crushed
1 tablespoon Worcestershire sauce
⅛ teaspoon Tabasco
1 teaspoon salt
⅛ teaspoon pepper
½ teaspoon celery salt
¼ cup firmly packed brown sugar
¼ cup cider vinegar
½ teaspoon dry mustard
½ teaspoon chili powder

Combine all ingredients in a heavy saucepan. Bring to boiling, stirring until brown sugar is dissolved. Reduce heat, cover, and simmer about 20 minutes. ABOUT 1½ CUPS

NOTE: This sauce keeps well and may be stored in the refrigerator for days before using. Heat before serving.

CURRANT-MUSTARD GLAZE: Combine *1 jar (8 ounces) red currant jelly, ⅓ cup prepared mustard,* and *½ teaspoon Tabasco* in a small saucepan. Set over low heat until well blended and jelly is melted, stirring occasionally. ABOUT 1 CUP

COOKING IN ALUMINUM FOIL

Cooking in aluminum foil over an open fire of hot coals becomes increasingly more popular — and no wonder. The method is convenient, quick and easy, and a marvelous way of retaining the natural flavors and juices in the food. And best of all, foil packets take relatively little space on an outdoor grill.

Individual packets — Cut 8- to 12-inch squares of heavy-duty aluminum foil. Spoon equal amounts of a suggested vegetable mixture onto each square. Wrap loosely and seal securely, using the drugstore wrap. Place on grill 5 inches from coals. Turning packets occasionally, cook 15 to 20 minutes, or until vegetables are tender.

Large packets — Using 18-inch squares of foil, wrap, seal, and cook vegetables as for individual packets, allowing 20 to 35 minutes. Mix gently before serving.

NOTE: Try to combine foods in packets which require approximately the same cooking time.

FISH DINNER DE LUXE IN FOIL

½ cup butter or margarine
½ cup chopped celery
½ cup chopped onion
2 cups coarsely crumbled saltines
¼ cup finely snipped parsley
½ lb. fresh mushrooms, sliced
½ teaspoon salt
¼ teaspoon pepper
2 teaspoons Worcestershire sauce
6 fish fillets (sole or flounder)
6 tomatoes
6 ears sweet corn, husked and brushed with melted butter

1. Heat the butter or margarine in a skillet. Add celery, onion, and mushrooms; cook 5 minutes or until mushrooms are lightly browned, stirring occasionally.
2. Mix in the salt, pepper, and Worcestershire sauce, then the crumbled saltines and parsley; blend thoroughly.
3. Form a ring with each fish fillet, overlapping ends and fastening with wooden picks. Place each rolled fillet on an 18-inch square of heavy-duty aluminum foil.
4. Fill each fillet with stuffing, reserving 6 tablespoons. Cut out stem end from each tomato and fill with 1 tablespoon of the stuffing. Add a tomato and an ear of corn to each packet. Sprinkle each ear of corn lightly with *salt*.
5. Wrap packets securely, using drugstore wrap. Place on grill 3 inches from coals and cook 10 minutes. Turn packet and cook 10 minutes longer, or until fish and vegetables are done. 6 PACKETS

SHRIMP-GREEN PEPPER PACKETS

1 lb. shrimp, peeled, deveined, and rinsed	1 teaspoon salt
	1/8 teaspoon pepper
1/2 cup bottled barbecue sauce	1/2 teaspoon ground ginger
1 large green pepper, cut in long 1/4-in. strips	1/2 teaspoon dry mustard
	1/4 cup lime juice
	1 tablespoon honey
1 clove garlic, minced	8 drops Tabasco
1 teaspoon grated onion	
1/2 cup butter	

1. Combine shrimp and barbecue sauce; turn shrimp to coat well with sauce. Set aside.
2. Divide green pepper equally on center of 4 large pieces of heavy-duty aluminum foil. Bring edges of foil up slightly to hold sauce.
3. Stir garlic and onion into hot butter in a skillet; cook 2 minutes. Remove from heat and blend in a mixture of salt, pepper, ginger, and dry mustard, then the remaining ingredients. Pour the seasoned butter over green pepper.
4. Divide the shrimp and sauce equally among the 4 packets. Bring edges of foil up over mixture and seal tightly, using drugstore wrap.
5. Place on grill 3 to 4 inches from coals and cook about 20 minutes; turn packets over once to cook shrimp evenly. 4 PACKETS

MACE-FLAVORED GREEN BEANS IN PACKET

2 pkgs. (9 oz. each) frozen cut green beans, partially thawed	1 teaspoon salt
	1/8 teaspoon pepper
	1/4 teaspoon ground mace
1/2 lb. sliced fresh mushrooms	1/4 cup butter or margarine
1/4 cup chopped onion	

1. Put beans, mushrooms, and onion onto center of a large square of heavy-duty aluminum foil. Break beans apart, if necessary.
2. Sprinkle a mixture of seasonings over vegetables and dot with butter. Bring foil up over contents and seal tightly, using drugstore wrap.
3. Place packet on grill about 5 inches from coals and cook about 35 minutes, or until beans are just tender; turn packet over once during the cooking period.
4. If desired, before serving, top with or blend in chopped *salted almonds*. ABOUT 8 SERVINGS

WAX BEAN PACKET

1 pkg. (9 oz.) frozen wax beans, partially thawed	1/2 teaspoon salt
	1/8 teaspoon freshly ground black pepper
1/2 medium-sized green pepper, cut in strips	1/4 teaspoon paprika
	1/2 clove garlic, minced
1/4 cup sliced green onions with tops	3 tablespoons butter or margarine, cut in pieces
1/4 lb. fresh mushrooms, sliced	

1. Put the beans, green pepper, onion, and mushrooms in center of a large square of heavy-duty aluminum foil. Sprinkle with a mixture of salt, pepper, and paprika. Mix in garlic. Top with butter. Wrap and seal.
2. Cook on grill until tender. ABOUT 4 SERVINGS

CARROT-CELERY-GREEN PEPPER PACKET

2 cups raw carrot slices (1/4 in.)	1/4 cup cooking or salad oil
2 cups diagonally cut celery slices (1/2 in.)	2 teaspoons salt
	1/8 teaspoon black pepper
2 cups green pepper pieces (1/2 in.)	1 teaspoon dill weed

1. Measure all ingredients onto a large square of heavy-duty aluminum foil; wrap and seal.
2. Cook on grill 35 minutes. 8 SERVINGS

CORN IN FOIL

Remove husks, silk, and blemishes from ears of *corn*. Place each ear on a piece of heavy-duty aluminum foil. Brush generously with *Golden Glow Butter, below*. Wrap foil around ears, sealing edges with double folds. Cook on grill about 15 minutes, turning frequently. Partially unwrap and serve corn in foil with a bowl of Golden Glow Butter and a shaker of *salt*.

CORN ON THE GRILL: Loosen husks only enough to remove silks and blemishes from ears of *corn*. Dip ears in *water*. Shake well. Rewrap husks around corn. Plunge into water again and let stand until husks are soaked, about 1 hour. Place ears over coals and roast, turning frequently, until tender, about 15 minutes. Immediately husk the corn, brush with

Golden Glow Butter or Perky Butter Sauce, below, and sprinkle with salt.

GOLDEN GLOW BUTTER: Heat together ½ cup butter or margarine, 2 tablespoons sieved pimiento, ½ teaspoon onion juice, ¼ teaspoon paprika, ⅛ teaspoon salt, and a few grains black pepper.

PERKY BUTTER SAUCE: Heat together ½ cup butter or margarine, ½ teaspoon dry Italian salad dressing mix, ½ teaspoon paprika, and ¼ teaspoon chili powder. Serve hot.

DILLED ONION PACKET

1 large Bermuda onion
1 teaspoon butter or margarine
½ teaspoon dill weed
Seasoned salt

1. Peel and partially core the onion (allow 1 for each serving). Put the butter and dill weed into cavity; sprinkle generously with the seasoned salt. Wrap in a square of heavy-duty aluminum foil.
2. Cook on grill 1 to 1½ hours. Serve topped with *dairy sour cream*.
1 SERVING

GRILLED WHOLE ONIONS: Leave dry outer skins on *Spanish or Bermuda onions*. Wet thoroughly and place on grill about 50 minutes, or until onions are black outside and soft and creamy inside. Roll occasionally to cook evenly.

ROASTED POTATOES IN FOIL

Scrub, dry, and rub *potatoes* with *fat*. Wrap in aluminum foil, sealing edges with double folds. Place on grill about 1 hour, or until potatoes are soft when pressed with glove-protected fingers. Turn several times. Loosen foil, cut a cross in top each potato, and pinch open. Spoon *Herb Butter, below*, into each potato. Rewrap; grill to melt cheese.

HERB BUTTER: Blend ½ cup softened butter with *2 teaspoons minced parsley, 1 teaspoon crushed sweet basil*, and *1 teaspoon crushed tarragon*. Top with *grated cheese*.

POTATOES BAKED IN COALS: Wash and scrub large baking potatoes and bury in the coals for 45 minutes to 1 hour. Potatoes are done when they can be easily pierced with a fork.

DILLED POTATOES IN PACKETS

6 medium-sized potatoes, pared
½ cup butter or margarine, softened
2 tablespoons snipped parsley
1 tablespoon dill weed

1. Cut each potato crosswise into 1-inch slices and place on an individual square of heavy-duty aluminum foil. Sprinkle slices generously with *salt* and spread with butter. Sprinkle evenly with snipped parsley and dill weed.
2. Put slices together to reassemble each potato; wrap in foil, sealing tightly.
3. Place on grill 3 inches from coals and cook about 35 minutes, or until potatoes are tender. Turn packets occasionally to cook evenly.
6 SERVINGS

RICE AND PEAS IN A POUCH

6 cups cooked rice
1 pkg. (10 oz.) frozen green peas, partially thawed
1 can (5 oz.) water chestnuts, drained and sliced
½ cup chopped green onion with tops
2 medium-sized tomatoes, cut in thin wedges
¾ cup butter or margarine
1½ teaspoons seasoned salt
Freshly ground black pepper
1½ teaspoons basil, crushed

1. Make 8 pouches from 18x12-inch pieces of heavy-duty aluminum foil by pressing each sheet of foil into a small bowl; remove from bowl.
2. Divide all ingredients equally among the 8 pouches. Seal each pouch securely. Place on grill over hot coals until mixture is thoroughly heated, 15 to 20 minutes.
4. Open foil and fluff with a fork before serving.
8 SERVINGS

TOMATOES IN FOIL

4 large tomatoes
Salt
Freshly ground black pepper
8 teaspoons butter or margarine
¼ cup chopped parsley
⅓ cup chopped green onion with tops
1 teaspoon basil, crushed
1 teaspoon tarragon, crushed
1 clove garlic, crushed

1. Halve tomatoes crosswise. Sprinkle cut sur-

faces generously with salt and pepper; top each with 1 teaspoon butter.
2. Mix remaining ingredients and mound equally on each tomato half. Set four tomato halves on each of 2 large pieces of heavy-duty aluminum foil; wrap and seal tightly. Grill 3 inches from coals about 10 minutes, or until just tender (not mushy). 8 SERVINGS

CHEESE-TOPPED TOMATOES IN PACKETS

Large ripe tomatoes, cut crosswise into halves	Chopped chives Creamy Roquefort or blue cheese salad dressing
Seasoned salt	

1. Place each tomato half in the center of a 6-inch square of heavy-duty aluminum foil. Sprinkle cut surfaces of tomatoes with salt and chives. Top with dressing. Bring corners of foil up over tomatoes.
2. Cook on grill 3 to 5 minutes.

1 TOMATO HALF PER SERVING

ZUCCHINI PACKET

6 small zucchini, cut crosswise in ¼-in. slices	1 tablespoon brown sugar
1 medium-sized onion, halved and thinly sliced	1 beef bouillon cube, crushed
½ teaspoon salt	¼ teaspoon crushed fennel seed
¼ teaspoon pepper	3 tablespoons butter or margarine, cut in pieces

1. Put zucchini and onion onto center of a large square of heavy-duty aluminum foil. Sprinkle with salt, pepper, brown sugar, bouillon cube, and fennel seed, then dot with butter. Wrap and seal.
2. Cook 20 minutes, or until tender.

4 TO 6 SERVINGS

FENNEL-FLAVORED VEGETABLE PACKET

2 tomatoes, cut in wedges	1 beef bouillon cube, crushed
1 cup finger-sized pieces eggplant	½ teaspoon salt
1 medium-sized onion, sliced	⅛ teaspoon pepper
2 zucchini, sliced	¼ teaspoon crushed fennel seed
1 tablespoon brown sugar	3 tablespoons butter, cut in pieces

1. Toss all ingredients lightly in a bowl. Put onto center of a large square of heavy-duty aluminum foil. Seal packet securely, using drugstore wrap.
2. Place on grill 5 inches from coals and cook about 30 minutes, turning packet over once.

ABOUT 4 SERVINGS

HERBED VEGETABLE MEDLEY

4 medium-sized zucchini, cut crosswise into ½-in. slices	¼ teaspoon marjoram
	½ teaspoon salt
1 or 2 large tomatoes, cut in pieces	Few grains freshly ground black pepper
1 medium-sized onion, thinly sliced	¼ cup highly-seasoned French dressing (preferably with wine vinegar)
½ teaspoon basil	
¼ teaspoon thyme	

1. Put the zucchini, tomatoes, onion, and a mixture of remaining ingredients in the center of a large square of heavy-duty aluminum foil. Bring corners of foil up over vegetables; seal tightly.
2. Cook on grill about 20 minutes, or until zucchini is tender but not mushy. Sprinkle with *seasoned salt* before serving.

6 TO 8 SERVINGS

VEGETABLE MEDLEY IN FOIL

3 medium-sized zucchini, cut in ½-in. slices	8 large pimiento-stuffed green olives, sliced
7 large mushrooms, sliced lengthwise through caps and stems	3 tablespoons olive oil
	1 clove garlic, crushed
	1 teaspoon parsley flakes
1 large tomato, cut in pieces	½ teaspoon sweet basil
3 medium-sized onions, thinly sliced	1 teaspoon salt
	Freshly ground black pepper

1. Toss the vegetables and olives together in the center of a large square of heavy-duty aluminum foil; gently mix in remaining ingredients. Bring edges of foil up over mixture and seal tightly to avoid leakage when packet is turned.
2. Place on grill about 3 inches from coals and cook 15 to 20 minutes, or until zucchini is tender. Turn packet over occasionally to cook vegetables evenly.

4 TO 6 SERVINGS

ZUCCHINI-TOMATO PACKET

6 small zucchini, cut crosswise in ¼-in. slices
1 medium-sized onion, halved and thinly sliced
2 tomatoes, cut in small pieces
¼ cup shredded Cheddar cheese
1 teaspoon salt
Few grains black pepper
3 tablespoons butter or margarine, cut in pieces
2 tablespoons soy sauce

1. Mix all ingredients and put onto center of a large square of heavy-duty aluminum foil; wrap and seal.
2. Cook on grill 20 minutes, or until tender.

4 TO 6 SERVINGS

CHEESY ENGLISH MUFFIN SPLITS

¼ cup butter or margarine
2 tablespoons snipped chives
¼ teaspoon garlic salt
¼ teaspoon oregano
1 teaspoon Worcestershire sauce
2 drops Tabasco
15 oz. (3 jars) pasteurized process cheese spread
14 grilled, buttered, large English muffin halves

1. Cream the butter with chives, salt, oregano, Worcestershire sauce, and Tabasco; beat in the cheese. Spread on the grilled English muffins.
2. Heat on aluminum foil on grill.

14 MUFFIN HALVES

SKILLET COOKING

CHILI-ETTI

1 can (14 to 17 oz.) chili with beans
1 can (15¼ oz.) spaghetti in tomato sauce with cheese
1 tablespoon instant minced onion
2 tablespoons grated Parmesan cheese

1. Turn chili and spaghetti into a heavy skillet. Mix in the onion.
2. Put skillet on back of grill and cook slowly 8 to 10 minutes, stirring occasionally until mixture is thoroughly heated. When ready to serve, sprinkle with the Parmesan cheese.

4 SERVINGS

CRAZY DOGS

1 teaspoon fat
¼ cup chopped onion
1½ lbs. lean ground beef
1 can (1 lb.) chili with beans
8 frankfurters, cut diagonally in ½-in. pieces
⅔ cup condensed tomato soup
½ cup ketchup
½ teaspoon salt

1. Heat fat in a skillet on the grill. Add onion and cook until transparent, occasionally moving and turning with a spoon. Add the ground beef and cook until lightly browned, breaking into small pieces with a spoon.
2. When meat is browned, mix in the remaining ingredients.
3. Put skillet on back of grill and cook slowly about 45 minutes, stirring occasionally. Spoon bean mixture onto *Toasted Buns, below.*

ABOUT 12 SERVINGS

TOASTED BUNS: Cut *buns* into halves and brush the cut side with *melted butter*. Place on grill and toast buttered side. Serve hot.

PORK AND BEANS ON THE GRILL

4 slices bacon
½ cup finely chopped onion
¼ cup chopped green pepper
2 cans (14 to 17 oz. each) pork and beans with tomato sauce
1 tablespoon dark molasses
2 teaspoons Worcestershire sauce
3 tablespoons dark brown sugar
½ teaspoon salt
⅛ teaspoon pepper
¼ teaspoon oregano

1. Fry bacon in a skillet; reserve 2 tablespoons drippings. Crumble bacon and set aside.
2. Heat the reserved drippings in skillet. Add onion and green pepper and cook about 5 minutes, stirring occasionally.
3. Turn beans into a 1½-quart heat-resistant casserole. Mix in onion, green pepper, bacon, molasses, Worcestershire sauce, and a mixture of remaining ingredients.
4. Cover and set on top of grill until thoroughly heated.

ABOUT 6 SERVINGS

Index

Index

A

Accompaniments
  lemon sherbet, 296
Acorn squash, baked, 192
  corn-filled, 191
  stuffed w/ham and apple, 192
À la Creole, Brennan's gumbo, 31
  shrimp, 166
À la king, shrimp, 166
À la Mexicana, cheese ball casserole, 127
All-American scallop, 72
All-seasons macaroni salad, 214
Almond(s)
  au gratin, celery and, 177
  butterscotch sauce, 302
  cake, 223
  cookies,
    Dutch, 305
  creamed spinach w/, 191
  crescents, chocolate, 320
  crisps, lacy, 310
  filling, 47
    chocolate, 249
  flakes Normandy, 320
  hard sauce, 304
  icing, 223
  macaroon pie, 261
  meringue shell, 255
  paste, 234
    filling, 48
  ringlet croustades, 62
  stuffed eggs, curry, 69
  whipped cream, 247
À l'orange, charlotte, 289
  duckling, 147
Amande, chicken, 142
Amandine,
  eggplant, 178
Anadama bread, 37
Angel dessert, mocha, 236
Angel food & sponge cakes, 236
  cake, 236
    cherry-nut, 236
    cocoa, 236
    rainbow, 236
    toasty-coconut, 236
Antoine's chicken Creole, 142
Appetizer(s)—hot & cold 13-24
  cold, 18
  canapés & hors d'oeuvres, 21
    butter tarts w/ mushroom cream, 22
    carciofi alla Greca George's, 21
    cheesy sesame-stuffed celery, 21
    crab-avocado, 22
      avocado spread, 22
    cucumber-chicken, 21
    deviled ham, 22
    wine-cheese, 21
    lobster tidbits, 22
    sardine cartwheel, 23
      herbed mayonnaise, 23
  savory miniature croustades, 22
  dip-its, 18
    blue cheese, w/mushrooms, 18
    chili and bean, 18
    cucumber, 19
    multi-cheese blendip, 18
    shrimp crisps, 20
    tuna sensation, 19
  spreads, 19
    Braunschweiger canapé, 19
    Camembert mousse, 20
    cheese ball, 20
    guacamole, 19
    homemade pot cheese, 19
    liver pâté exceptionale, 21
    nut-coated cheese log(s), 19
    pungent pâté, 19
  garnishes for canapés, 14
  hot, 14
    avocado toast fingers, 15
    bacon-wrapped shrimp, 18
    boiled bacon buns, 16
    broiled bacon-cheese canapés, 16
    date, 16
    Cheddar puffs, 16
    flash un kas, 15
    Fontainebleau hors d'oeuvre pie, 14
    grilled shrimp, 372
    ham-cheese puffs, 17
    help-yourself kabobs, 370
    mushroom, 17
    olive bites, 17
    on-the-wing, 16
    sardine finger canapés, 17
    saucy cocktail franks, 16
    shrimp Ernie, 164
    single ribs for, 364
    si si pastries, 17
    spareribs, 367
    Swiss cheese pastry morsels, 15
    teriyaki, 15
    "veal-lets" Parmigiana, 18
    zesty kraut pastry
    snacks, 124
  planning, 13
  canapés, 14
  hors d'oeuvres, 13
  sit-down, 23
    lomi lomi salmon, 24
    oysters piquante in the half shell, 163
      Rockefeller, 23
    rosy sauce, 24
    salde Siciliano, 215
    shrimp cocktail, Seviche style, 24
      remoulade, 24
Apple(s)
  and buttons, 103
  and currant filling, 277
  butter, Moselem Springs, 351
  spice cake, 228
  Dutch, 52
  charlotte, 298
  cream, 283
  crisp, Wenatchee Valley, 297
  jelly, 342
    crab, 343
  kraut stuffed spareribs, 101
  kraut w/, 188
  pie(s), 256
    pecan, 267
  raisin dressing, heart w/, 120
  sauce, 68
  stuffed pork chops, 99
  stuffing, 149
Applecake w/vanilla sauce, Swedish, 297
Applekaka med vanilljsas, 297
Applesauce cake, chocolate, 231
Apricot
  bread, 51
  conserve, ginger, 350
  crescents, 324
  glaze, 103
  nut pastry, 268
  fresh, 256
  pie
    nut chiffon, 268
  sauce
    lime, spicy, 369
    sweet-sour, 367
  rice stuffing, 150
  sours, 306
  spread, 47
  stuffed roast pork, 97
  upside-down cake, 232
  whirl, 331
Aristocrats, 305
Armenian meatballs, 129
Artichoke(s)
  how to cook, 170
  in mushroom cream, 170
  Milanese, 170
  Seville, 171
  Véronique, 169
Asparagus
  supreme, 171
  vinaigrette, 202
Aspic(s)
  vegetable, 213
Au gratin
  celery and almonds, 177
  crab meat, 160
  eggs, 65
  potatoes, 184
  skillet, 186
Au lait, café, 327
Austrian recipes
  echte Florentiner, 310
  fish fillets Viennese, 152
  Ischl cookies, 320
  nut butter cookies, 319
  pecan cookies, 313
  veal Viennese w/sour cream, 115
Au vin, le coq, 143
Avocado
  canapés, crab, 22
  chicken casserole, 144
  mousse, 206
  orange chiffon pie, 479
  salad, shrimp and, 217
  soup, 33
  spread, 22
  toast fingers, 15

B

Bacon
  and cream cheese scramble, 66
  broiled buns, 16
  crisp, pear, 299
  nut corn sticks, 54
  omelet, 68
  stuffed eggs, dilly, 69
  w/mustard sauce, Canadian-style, 102
  wrapped franks, 368
    shrimp appetizers, 18
Bahmie goreng, 100
Baked
  acorn squash, 192
  Alaska, 292
  cherry, 293
  individual, 293
  loaf, 293
  cheese fondue, 140
  fish, 151
    w/shrimp stuffing, 151
  ham slice w/curried fruit, 104
  potatoes, 183
  Restigouche salmon Breval, 152
  rhubarb w/pastry topping, 300
  tomatoes, Genoa style, 193

Index

hash stuffed, 194
tomato halves w/Danish blue cheese, 193
Baking powder biscuits, 55
Balkan lamb and eggplant casserole, 130
Banana(s)
  bran cookies, 310
    chocolate, 311
  bread, 51
    oat flake, 51
  cake, jelly squares, 224
    royale, 224
  cornbread, 60
  corn muffins, 60
  cupcakes, 240
  Foster, Brennan's, 298
  peach jam, rosy, 345
  pecan butter, 351
    ice cream, 294
  pie, butterscotch, 261
    toasted coconut, 263
  shake, chocolate, 330
  spice cookies, 311
Barbecue(d)
  bologna roll, 368
  chicken on a spit, 373
  lamb shanks, 110
  ribs, 367
  sauce, 374
    orange, 198
  spareribs, 101
Barbecuing, *see* OUTDOOR COOKING
Bar cookies, 305
Basic butter frosting, 245
Basil grape jelly, 343
Basler Brunsli, 320
Basting sauce, orange, 364
  tomato, 364
Bavarian cabbage, 175
Bayou Chowder, 29
Bean(s)
  buckaroo, 172
  chili and, 125
  dip, chili and, 18
  Green Beans Gruyère, 172
  Lima Bean Bake, 173
  Mexican, 171
  refried, 171
  on the grill, pork and, 378
  packet, wax, 375
  soup, Cuban black, 27
Béarnaise sauce, 83, 197
Beau Nash delight, 291
Béchamel sauce, 196
Beef, 80, *see also* MEATS
  and broccoli skillet, 91
  and kidney pie, 119
  balls Orientale, sauced walnut, 123
  bouillon w/broiled orange, 26

brisket, cooked corned, 93
  w/horseradish sauce, 89
  Burgundy style, 92
chow mein, 85
eggplant patties in casserole, 126
"franks" in buns, grilled ground, 367
fruit kaboob duo, glazed, 369
kabobs w/Oriental sauce, 369
Lindstrom, 122
noodle scallop, ground, 180
pasties, kraut and, 124
Polynesian, 125
pot roast à la Province, 87
Saigon, 91
soup, 27
steak, herbed, 365
stock, 26
stroganoff, 84
tacos, 124
tongue w/tomato sauce, 118
tournedos Orlando, prime, 81
Wellington, 80
  w/onions, 92
Yorkshire pie, 124
Beet(s)
  à la Russe, 174
  in orange sauce, 174
  salad, spinach, 204
Beignets, 49
Belgian
  carrots phantasie, 175
Bercy sauce, 196
Bernaise sauce, 197
Best-ever Brussels sprouts, 175
  purple plum conserve, 350
  tomato preserves, 349
Beverage(s) —hot & cold, 325-334
  cold, 328
    apricot whirl, 331
    chocolate-banana shake, 330
    java, 328
    frosted coffee shake, 331
    ginger ice cooler, 329
    raspberry delight, 329
    homemade soda(s)
      chocolate, 331
      lemon, 331
      peach, 331
      pineapple, 331
      raspberry or strawberry, 331

iced
  coffee, 328
  cinnamon, 328
  syrup, 328
  orange mocha, 328
  tea, cold-water method, 329
    hot method I, 329
    II, 329
lemonade, 329
limeade, 329
orangeade, 329
lemon-cranberry nectar, 329
lime-rosemary zing, 329
minted chocolate refresher, 330
peach julep, 330
purple plum cooler, 330
raspberry and lime swizzle, 330
watermelon sherbet, 330
Spanish lemon and lime, 331
strawberry shake, 331
hot, 326
café au lait, 327
  Boston coffee, 327
  Vienna coffee, 327
café l'orange, 327
chocolate, 327
demitasse, 326
drip coffee, 326,
  percolated, 326
  steeped, 326
  vacuum-drip, 326
ginger tea, 327
Mexican chocolate, 327
spiced cider, 328
tea, 327
punch(es), 332
  four-fruit refresher, 332
  golden, 333
  hot aromatic, 334
  buttered cranberry, 334
  loganberry-lemonade, 332
  raspberry fruit, 333
  sage cider, 334
  sparkling, 332
    fruit refresher, 333
    golden cooler, 332
  spiced lemon tea, 334
  spicy cranberry, 332
  summer strawberry bowl, 333
    champagne, 333
    rosé, 333
syrups, 325
  caramel, 325
  chocolate, 325
  cocoa, 325

  coffee, 328
  lemon, 326
  lime, 326
  mint, 326
Beverage syrups, 325
Biscuit(s)
  baking powder, 55
  buttermilk, 55
  double onion, 60
  mace 'n' cheese, 60
  Shrewsbury, 322
Blackberry jam, 346
Black bottom pie, 262
Black Forest torte, 241
Black pepper burgers, 366
Black walnut butter frosting, 245
Blancmange w/orange sauce, 284
Blitzkuchen, 53
Blueberry
  "cobbler," fresh, 298
  coffee cake, 53
  jelly, 342
  lemon jam, 345
  muffins, 56
  orange parfaits, 281
  pie, fresh, 257
Blue cheese, baked tomato halves w/Danish, 193
  dip w/mushrooms, 18
Blue ribbon potato-onion salad, 204
Bobotie, 130
Boeuf Bourguignon, 92
"Boiled" dinner, 93
Bologna, roll, barbecued, 368
Booky baked crab, 161
Bordelaise sauce, 196
Borsch, jellied, 33
Boston coffee, 327
Bouillon, 26
  w/broiled orange, beef, 26
Boysenberry ice, 297
Bran
  bread, granny's Texas, 37
  cookies, banana, 310
    chocolate-banana, 311
  flake drops, 311
  puffs, 55
Brandy hard sauce, 304
  sauce, 302
Braunschweiger canapé spread, 19
Brazilian pudim moka w/chocolate sauce, 281
Brazil nut crust, 255
Bread(s) —yeast, quick & the kind you buy, 35-62
  from mixes, 56
    biscuit mix, 57
    frosted brown sugar

Index

bubble loaf, 57
coffee glaze, 58
hot cross fruit muffins, 59
frosting, 59
new moon yeast rolls, 58
crescent cheese rolls, 59
Parmesan quick bread, 58
Cheddar cheese quick bread, 58
peachy rich breakfast slices, 59
quick 'n' easy jam braid, 58
sesame seed twists, 59
hot roll mix, 56
fruit-filled coffee ring, 56
orange glaze, 57
miniature butter cream loaves, 57
butter cream filling, 57
petite orange-currant loaves, 57
other mixes, 60
banana cornbread, 60
corn muffins, 60
helpful hints about, 35
quick, 50
biscuits & muffins, 55
baking powder, 55
buttermilk, 55
bran puffs, 55
ginger-date muffins, 56
blueberry muffins, 56
Irish scones, 55
Italian cheese, 55
orange-prune, 56
Stouffer's pumpkin muffins, 56
coffee cakes, tea breads &, 51
cornbreads, 54
bacon-nut corn sticks, 54
corn-cheese twists, 54
Hermitage spoon bread, 54
johnnycake, 54
muffins, biscuits &, 55
tea breads & coffee cakes, 51
apricot, 51
banana, 51
blueberry, 53
orange cream icing, 53
California fruit nut, 52
cheese-cranberry, 51
Dutch apple cake, 52
Irish soda, w/currants, 52
lemon nut, 52
oat flake banana, 51
quick, 53
Swiss whipped cream-nut loaf, 52
toasted filbert, 53
topping, 54
storage, 35
techniques for making, 50
things to do w/refrigerated doughs & bakers' breads, 60
bakers' breads, 61
buttered French bread, 62
seasoned butters, 62
French toast, 61
cinnamon-orange, 62
Oahu, 62
orange toast "blintzes," 62
ringlet croustades, 62
almond, 62
sesame, 62
refrigerated doughs, 60
cornmeal-kist biscuits, 60
double onion biscuits, 60
flaky cheese-filled rolls, 61
mace 'n' cheese biscuits, 60
watercress biscuits, 60
orange sticky buns, 61
pan o' rolls, 60
pineapple-pecan coffee cake, 61
yeast, 36
coffee cakes, sweet breads &, 41
dinner roll(s), 44
butter semmels, 46
buttery yeast, 44
crescent, 45
herbed Parmesan, 46
rolls, 44
sesame sticks, 46
doughnuts, sweet rolls &, 47
loaves, 36
Anadama, 37
candied fruit cobble cake, 40
cherry/coconut babka, 39
Easter egg, 40
granny's Texas bran, 37
julekake, 38
old-fashioned herb, 36
raisin-oatmeal, 38
Sally Lunn, 39
w/strawberries, 40
Swedish rye, 38
white, (basic), 36
white (straight dough method), 36
rolls, dinner, 44
sweet breads & coffee cake(s), 41
cinnamon pinwheel loaf, 42
coffee rings, 41
glaze, 41
tea rings, 41
Danish pastry, 41
honey bun coffee ring, 42
kulich, 43
Luci-buns, 37
Norwegian Christmas, 43
raisin/nut loaf, 42
Stollen, 43
sweet rolls & doughnuts, 47
Creole doughnuts, 49
Danish pastry, 47
almond paste filling, 48
shapes, 48
combs, 48
crescents, 48
envelopes, 48
vanilla cream filling, 47
miniature orange, 49
orange glaze, 49
pumpkin, 49
semlor, 48
hot cross buns, 48
sweet-tooth breakfast, 47
fillings, 47
almond, 47
apricot spread, 47
marmalade spread, 47
orange cube, 47
pineapple spread, 47
Breaded veal cutlets, 114

Bread stuffing, 135
Brennan's gumbo à la Creole, 31
Bringal Bertie Green, 178
Broccoli
ring, 174
sauce, tangy, cheese, 156
skillet, beef and, 91
w/horseradish cream, 174
w/mustard cream, 174
w/provolone sauce, yams and, 193
Brochette de foie de veau Zurichoise, 117
Broiled
bacon buns, 16
bacon-cheese canapés, 16
date appetizers, 16
fish, 153
trout, 153
Broiler fudge topping, 248
Brown
gravy, 199
Moravian cookies, 323
or espagnole sauce, 196
roux, 195
sauce, espagnole, 117
stock, 26
sugar,
frosted bubble loaf, 57
glaze for ham, 103
velvet frosting, 245
wafers, 317
Brownie(s)
caramel frosting, 244
fudgy, 306
luxury mallow-nut, 307
Southern, 307
Brussels sprouts
best-ever, 175
w/chestnuts, 174
Buckaroo beans, 172
Budget parmigiano, 116
Buns
hot cross, 48
orange sticky, 61
toasted, 378
Burgers
black pepper, 366
double treat frank, 368
saucy Roquefort, 366
w/cheese sauce, grilled, 366
Burgoo, 93
Butter(s),
apple, Moselem Springs, 351
balls, cocoa, 315
molasses, 316
banana-pecan, 351
cookies, Austrian nut, 319
Hungarian, 318
cream
filling, 57
frosting, 243

Index

chocolate-mocha, 243
hazelnut, 243
mocha, 243
loaves, miniature, 57
frosting
basic, 245
black walnut, 245
chocolate, 245
cream cheese, 245
lemon, 245
mocha, 245
orange, 245
raisin-rum, 245
fruit, 351
golden glow, 376
grape, 351
herb, 376
herb-garlic, 138
lemon, 138
pastry for tarts, 254
rosemary, herb, 138
sauce, 283, 364
garden, 365
perky, 376
rock lobster tails w/ orange, 372
seasoned, 62
semmels, 46
sponge cake, 238
sticks, 322
cocoa, 315
tarragon, 138, 199
tarts, w/mushroom cream, 22
wafers, Spanish, 314
Buttered
French bread, 62
raisins, cinnamon, 206
Buttermilk biscuits, 55
Butternut cake, maple, 226
pie, 267
Butterscotch
banana pie, 263
bars, chewy, 306
pie, banana, 261
rich dark, 261
sauce, almond, 302
Buttery, pastry, 81
Buttery yeast rolls, 44

C

Cabbage
in orange sauce, new, 175
rolls, stuffed, 132
slaw
Chinese, 28
Cacciatore, chicken, 142
Café au lait, 327
l'orange, 327

Cake
desserts, 273
Dutch apple, 52
Cakes & tortes, frostings & fillings, 221
cake(s), 222
angel food & sponge, 236
angel food, 236
cherry nut, 236
cocoa, 236
mocha angel dessert, 236
rainbow, 236
toasty coconut, 236
butter sponge, 238
French pastry, 238
small fancy, 238
daffodil torte, 238
sponge, 236
ring dessert, 238
sunshine, 237
lemon layer, 237
lemon squares, 237
chiffon, 239
cocoa, 239
orange, 239
conventional, 222
chocolate, 229
applesauce, 231
Jerry Lewis', 230
Mrs. Eisenhower's devil's food, 230
old-fashioned, 229
Wellesley fudge, 230
pound cakes & fruitcakes, 233
old Williamsburg-style fruitcake, 234
almond paste, 234
pound, ring, 233
citrus glaze, 233
special-flavor, 231
crunch-top raisin, 233
maraschino datenut, 233
pineapple upsidedown, 232
apricot, 232
cranberry, 232
lemon, 231
peachy nut, 233
strawberry-lime, 232
spice, 228
apple butter, 228
old-fashioned molasses, 229
pumpkin, 229

miniatures, 229
soft gingerbread, 228
w/praline frosting, 228
white, 222
delicate, 222
rich coconut fruit filling, 222
Lincoln's favorite, 223
yellow, 223
almond, 223
rosette, 226
icing, 223
banana, jelly squares, 224
royale, 224
gold, 223
honey, 225
maple syrup, 226
butternut, 226
marbleized tubed, 227
orange blossom, 226
praline carrot, 225
caramel syrup, 225
cooked carrots, 225
salted peanut, 227
turban, 224
cupcakes & cakelets, 239
banana cupcakes, 240
chocolate-coated party, 240
chocolate cupcakes, 239
French pastry, 238
ladyfingers, 241
peanut butter cupcakes, 240
pumpkin miniatures, 229
small fancy, 238
helpful hints about, 222
one-bowl & quick, 234
caraway, 235
merrie companie, 234
quick cocoa, 235
whipped cream, 235
sponge, angel food &, 236
fillings, 248
cherry, 241
chocolate, 249
almond, 249
cream I, 248
creamy vanilla, 248
cherry, 248

chocolate, 248
pineapple cream, 249
lemon I, 250
II, 250
orange,
I, 250
II, 250
rich chocolate, 310
rich coconut fruit, 222
semisweet chocolate, 249
sweet chocolate, 250
vanilla cream, 249
dustard, 249
frostings, 242
cooked, 242
brownie caramel, 244
butter cream I, 243
chocolate mocha, 243
hazelnut, 243
mocha, 243
divinity, 243
fruit 'n' nut white mountain, 242
fudge, 244
glossy chocolate, 320
honey chocolate, 244
marshmallow cream, 243
seafoam, 242
seven-minute, 242
chocolate, 242
marshmallow, 242
mocha, 242
orange, 242
peppermint, 242
pistachio, 242
vanilla fudge, 244
glazes & toppings, 246
broiler fudge topping, 248
chocolate glaze, 224, 276, 289
citrus glaze, 233
cocoa whipped cream II, 247
coffee glaze, 58
whipped cream, 247
fudge glaze, 246
lemon glaze, 306
mocha ginger cream, 247
mallow whipped cream, 248
maple cream, 248
orange glaze, 49
spiced honey topping, 248
sweetened whipped cream, 247
almond, 247
cocoa I, 247

Cointreau, 247
crème de cacao, 247
crème de menthe, 247
Dutch cocoa, 247
mocha, 247
molasses, 247
orange, 247
rum, 247
strawberry, 247
uncooked, 245
almond icing, 223
basic butter, 245
black walnut, 245
burnt-sugar, 245
chocolate, 245
cream cheese, 245
lemon, 245
mocha, 245
orange, 245
raisin-rum, 245
caramel, mocha, 245
chocolate icing, 269
choco-marshmallow, 246
cream cheese, 246
creamy peanut butter, 245
fluffy honey, 246
vanilla, 246
chocolate, 246
orange cream icing, 53
poured chocolate, 246
white, velvet, 245
brown, 245
lemon, 245
tortes, 241
Black Forest, 241
cherry filling, 241
Calf's liver Matius, 117
on skewers, Zurich style, 117
California fruit nut bread, 52
Calypso steak sticks, 84
Camembert mousse, 20
Canadian style bacon w/mustard sauce, 102
Canapé(s) & hors d'oeuvres, 21
broiled bacon buns, 16
broiled bacon-cheese, 16
crab-avocado, 22
cucumber-chicken, 21
deviled ham, 22
sardine finger, 17
supread, Braunschweiger, 19
Canard aux olives, 148
Can-can stroganoff, 84

Candied
fruit cobble cake, 40
pecan-pumpkin pie, 262
Candy crisps, orange, 312
Canestrelli, 323
Canned & frozen fish dishes, 155
Canned & ready-to-eat meats, 368
Cannelloni alla Piemontese "maison," 131
Canning fruits using boiling-water bath, 337
procedure, 336
vegetables using pressure canner, 338
Cantaloupe
coupe, 301
preserves, 348
Cape Cod turkey, 214
Caper(s)
celery root w/mushrooms and, 177
(sauce), 83
Caramel(s)
Bavarian, mocha, 285
frosting, brownie, 244
mocha, 245
sauce, pineapple w/rum, 300
raisin, ham 'n' yams in, 106
syrup, 225, 325
Caraway cake, 235
sauerkraut w/, 188
Carciofi alla Greca George's, 21
Cardamom
jam, strawberry, 347
Caribbean turkey, 146
Carrot(s)
cake, praline, 225
celery-green pepper, packet, 375
cooked, 225
phantasie, Belgian, 175
spiced, 176
stuffing, lamb breast w/, 109
w/grapes, herbed, 176
Carving meats & poultry, see end papers
Casserole(s)
au gratin potatoes, 184
avocado-chicken, 144
Balkan lamb and eggplant, 130
beef and kidney pie, 119
beef-eggplant patties in, 126
cauliflower supreme, 176
celery and almonds au gratin, 177
cheese ball, à la Mexicana, 127

cheese, royale, 71
chicken
crab meat rosemary, 144
corn pudding, 177
crab meat au gratin, 160
creamy green bean, 172
dessert, see DESSERTS
eggplant amandine, 178
eggs farci, 70
green bean-pork chop supper, 98
green rice, 187
ground beef-eggplant, 126
Hermitage spoon bread, 54
lasagne, 189
lima bean bake, 174
lima beans au gratin, 173
mushroom-ham, 105
onion, 182
potatoes Anna, 184
scalloped corn, 178
oysters, 163
potatoes, 184
tomatoes, 193
Spanish rice, 187
sweet potato pudding, 192
zucchini Provençale, 194
Cauliflower supreme, 176
Celebrity recipes
Abraham Lincoln: Lincoln's favorite cake, 223
Andrew Jackson: Hermitage spoon bread, 54
Arlene Dahl: blancmange w/orange sauce, 284
Barbara Stanwyck: steak à la Barbara Stanwyck, 82
David Janssen: beef, Burgundy style, 92
James Shigeta: Eenyhow, 99
Jerry Lewis: Jerry Lewis' chocolate cake, 230; scrambled eggs w/cheese, 66
Lyndon B. Johnson: banana bread, 51
Martha Hyer: oysters up, 82
Mrs. Andy Griffith: Southern brownies, 307
Mrs. Dwight D. Eisenhower: Mrs. Eisenhower's devil's food cake, 230
Mrs. Hubert Humphrey: beef soup, 27; scalloped

corn, 178
Polly Bergen: Spanish rice casserole, 187
Robert Taylor: shrimp à la Creole, 166
Tennessee Ernie Ford: red eye gravy, 200
Walt Disney: chili and beans, 125
William McKinley: old fashioned chocolate cake, 229
Celery
and almonds au gratin, 177
cheesy sesame-stuffed, 21
green pepper packet, carrot, 375
herbed peas and, 183
Celery root
w/mushrooms and capers, 177
Celery seed
cream dressing, 215
Cereal
crumb crust, 255
coconut, 255
Chafing dish recipes
calf's liver Matius, 117
ham à la cranberry, 105
Champagne strawberry bowl, 333
Chantilly cherry cups, 298
Charlotte à l'orange, 289
Cheddar
cheese
quick bread, 58
puffs, 16
Cheese
ball, 20
casserole à la Mexicana, 127
biscuits, mace 'n', 60
blendip, multi, 18
bread, cranberry, 51
quick, Cheddar, 58
broccoli sauce, tangy, 156
cake
chocolate-mint, 274
luscious lemon, 273
canapés, broiled bacon, 16
casserole royale, 71
croquettes Dutch, 71
dip, w/mushrooms, blue, 18
dishes, 71
dressing, Roquefort, 220
filled rolls, flaky, 61
ice cream, lemon, 295
log, nut-coated, 19
mousse, Danish blue, 213
pastry, 457
for 1-crust pie, 253

Index

for 2-crust pie, 253
pie
  custard, Frau Moyer's, 266
  strawberry-glazed, 266
    maple, 258
puffs, ham, 17
rolls, crescent, 59
Italian, 55
salad, orange-crowned, 208
sauce,
  grilled burgers w/, 366
  lightning, 366
  Normandy, 196
  scrambled eggs w/, 66
soufflé, 76
  Swiss, 76
tart,
  spinach, 191
topped
  tomatoes in packets, 377
twists,
  corn, 54
wine, 21
Cheeseburgers, garlic, 122
Cheesy
  English muffin splits, 378
  sesame-stuffed celery, 21
Chef's fruit salad, 206
Cherry(ies)
  Baked Alaska, 293
  berry preserves, 348
  cinnamon sauce, 286
  coconut balka, 39
  cottage cheese salad mold, 207
  Easter egg, frozen, 293
  filling, 241, 277
    creamy, 248
    raisin and, 278
  jewels, 315
  mold, creamy, 285
  nut cake, 236
  pie, lattice-top, 258
  plum jam, 345
  sauce,
    spicy, 302
  tomato conserve, 351
Chess pie,
  Kentucky, 266
Chestnut(s)
  Brussels sprouts w/, 174
  stuffing, 149
Chewy butterscotch bars, 306
Chicken, 135, see also POULTRY
  amande, 142
  amandine, rice and, 187
  and dumplings, 143
  and sweet potatoes in cream, 136
  appetizer, 34

broiled, 138
cacciatore, 142
canapés, cucumber, 21
casserole, avocado, 144
crab meat casserole rosemary, 144
Creole, Antoine's, 142
empress, 140
flavor-full broiled, 138
fricasse, 143
glazed grilled, 371
gravy, turkey or, 200
kumquat, 136
lemon-dipped, 370
on a spit, barbecued, 373
  the grill, 370
orange-glazed, 135
Oriental,
  oven-fried, 137
oven-barbecued, 136
Pennsylvania Dutch roast, 135
pie, old-fashioned, 143
salad filling,
  party, 215
saucy cinnamon, 370
Swiss-capped glazed, 140
tangerine, 144
w/pineapple piquant good fortune, 141
Chicken liver(s),
  omelet, 68
  paste, eggs stuffed w/, 69
Chiffon cakes, 239
  pies, 268
Chili
  and bean dip, 18
  and beans, 125
  conqueso beef roast, 81
  dip, 18
  etti, 378
  sauce,
    onion, 83
Chinese
  beef and pea pods, 86
  cabbage soup, 28
  sizzled meatballs w/ vegetables and rice, 127
Chipped beef and potato boats, 188
Choco-marshmallow frosting, 246
Chocolate
  almond crescents, 320
  filling, 249
  applesauce cake, 231
  banana-shake, 330
  bees, 312
  butter frosting, 245
  cake(s), 229
    Jerry Lewis', 230
    old-fashioned, 229
  chipped tortoni, 29
  coated party cakes, 240
  coconut crust, 255
  cupcakes, 239

custard, 280
dessert
  regal, 287
filling(s), 249
  creamy, 248
  rich, 310
  semisweet, 249
  sweet, 250
freeze, marble, 276
frosting(s),
  glossy, 320
  honey, 244
  poured, 246
glaze, 224, 276, 289
hot, 327
icing, 269
  glossy, 246
java, 328
macaroons, 311
meringue shells, 278
Mexican, 327
mint cheese cake, 274
mocha butter cream frosting, 243
  ice cream, 294
pie, 269
refresher, minted, 330
refrigerator cake, 288
sauce, 303
  Brazilian pudim moka w/, 281
  semisweet, 303
seven-minute frosting, 242
soda, homemade, 331
soufflé, milk, 284
squares, double, 307
syrup, 325
Chokladbröd, 315
Chop
  supper, green bean-pork, 98
Chopped nut filling, 278
Chops
  en brochette, lamb, 109
  gourmet, pork, 97
  party pork, 99
  skillet orange pork, 98
  stuffed pork, 98
  rib lamb, 109
Choux à la crème, 276
  paste, cream puff or, 276
Chowder(s) & fish soups, 31, see also SOUPS
  New England clam, 32
  salmon, 33
  shellfish, 32
Chow mein, beef, 85
Christmas
  bread, Norwegian, 43
  cookies, Swiss, 323
  recipes
    Basler Brunsli, 320
    cinnamon stars, 321
    currant cakes, 312
    fattigmann, 324
    Jan Hagel, 321

macaroon mousse, 291
Norwegian cones, 316
Chunky corn chowder, 28
Cider
  glaze, 103
  hot spiced, 328
  punch, sage, 334
Cinnamon
  buttered raisins, 206
  chicken, saucy, 370
  coffee, iced, 328
  orange French toast, 62
  pinwheel loaf, 42
  sauce, cherry, 286
  stars, 321
Citrus
  glaze, 233
  marmalade, 347
  mold maraschino, 286
  omelet, 68
Clam(s), 158
  chowder, New England, 32
  pie, 159
Cock-a-leekie chowder, 29
Cocktail, see also APPETIZERS
  seviche style, shrimp, 24
Cocoa
  angel food cake, 236
  butter balls, 315
  cake, quick, 235
  sticks, 315
  chiffon cake, 239
  syrup, 325
  whipped cream I, 247
    II, 247
Coconut
  banana
    pie, toasted, 263
  cake
    toasty, 236
  cereal crumb crust, 255
  cream, molded pineapple, 287
  salad, 209
  crust, chocolate, 255
  curry, lamb and, 110
  fruit filling, rich, 222
  macaroons de luxe, 311
  petal tarts, creamy, 272
  pie, toasted, 263
  shell, coffee, 271
  sours, lemon, 308
Codfish cakes, 154
Coffee
  Boston, 327
  coconut pie shell, 271
  drip, 326
  fingers, Swedish, 315
  iced, 328
    cinnamon, 328
  percolated, 326
  shake, frosted, 331
  steeped, 326
  syrup, 328
  tapioca parfait, 282

Index

vacuum-drip, 326
Vienna, 327
whipped cream, 247
Coffee cake(s)
  blueberry, 53
  Danish pastry, 41
  glaze, 58
  pineapple-pecan, 61
  quick, 53
  ring, fruit-filled, 56
    honey bun, 42
  rings, 41
  toasted filbert, 53
Cointreau whipped cream, 247
Cold
  appetizers, 18
  beverages, 328
Cole slaw, crunchy peanut, 203, see also SLAW
Coliflor Acapulco, 202
Confectioners' Sugar Icing, 48
Conserve(s), 341, 350
  best-ever purple plum, 350
  cherry-tomato, 351
  cranberry, 350
  ginger-apricot, 350
  orange, 350
  rhubarb, 350
Consommé, 26
  madrilène, jellied, 33
Conventional cakes, 222
Cooked
  carrots, 225
  chicken dishes, 143
  corned beef brisket, 93
  frostings, 242
  pineapple salad dressing, 212
  shrimp, 164
Cookie crumb crust, 254
Cookies, 305-324
  bar(s), 305
    apricot sours, 306
      lemon glaze, 306
    aristocrats, 305
      pecan topping, 306
    chewy butterscotch, 306
      topping, 306
    Dutch almond, 305
    English toffee, 309
    fruity Polish mazurek, 308
    fudgy brownies, 306
      double chocolate squares, 307
      fudge sauce, 307
      luxury mallow-nut brownies, 307
    golden nut, 309
    graham sensations, 308
    lemon-coconut sours, 308
      pineapple, 308

luscious lemon, 308
peanut butter dreams, 309
Southern brownies, 307
  surprise, 307
deep-fried, 324
  fattigmann, 324
drop(s), 309
  Austrian pecan, 313
  banana-bran, 310
  banana spice, 311
    bran flake, 311
    chocolate-banana-bran, 311
  coconut macaroons de luxe, 311
    chocolate, 311
  crisp sugar, 309
  currant cakes, 312
  Florentines, 310
  gingersnaps, 312
  hermits, 313
  lacy almond crisps, 310
  filbert crisps, 310
  Mount Shasta, 311
  nut colonels, 313
  orange candy crisps, 312
  peanut crinkles, 313
  plantation crisps, 313
  queen bees, 312
    chocolate bees, 312
  molded, 314
    cherry jewels, 315
    cocoa butter sticks, 315
      cocoa butter balls, 315
    Danish peppernuts, 316
    ginger, 315
    moji pearls, 314
      pecan poofs, 314
    molasses butter balls, 316
    Norwegian cones, 316
    snowball meltaways, 314
    Spanish butter wafers, 314
    spicy ginger crunchies, 316
    Swedish coffee fingers, 315
  refrigerator, 317
    brown wafers, 317
    overnight, 317
    wheat scotchies, 317
  rolled, 318
    almond flakes Normandy, 320
    apricot crescents, 324
    Austrian nut butter, 319

glossy chocolate frosting, 320
Ischl cookies, 320
Basler Brunsli, 320
brown Moravian, 323
butter sticks, 322
chocolate-almond crescents, 320
cinnamon stars, 321
Danish knots, 319
German molasses, 323
ginger shortbread, 322
Hungarian butter, 318
Italian butter, 323
Jan Hagel, 321
kolacky, 321
love letters, 324
melting snowflakes, 319
sand tarts, 318
Scandinavian springerle, 319
Scottish shortbread, 318
  Grasmere shortbread, 318
    ginger filling, 318
    petticoat tails, 318
Shewsbury biscuits, 322
Swedish gingersnaps, 322
Swiss Christmas, 323
Cooking in aluminum foil, 374
Cooler
  ginger ice, 329
  purple plum, 330
  sparkling golden, 332
Corn
  and onion stuffing, 150
  cheese twists, 54
  filled acorn squash, 191
  in foil, 375
  muffins, banana, 60
  on the grill, 375
  pudding, 177
  scalloped, 178
  sticks, bacon-nut, 54
  w/mushrooms, 178
Cornbread(s)
  banana, 60
  shortcake style, peaches 'n', 299
  stuffing, old-fashioned, 150
Cornmeal
  crusted mountain trout, 155
  dumplings, 143
  fried onion rings, lacy, 182
Cottage cheese
  filling, 277
  salad mold, cherry, 207
Crab(s) & crab meat, 159
  avocado canapés, 22

Booky baked, 101
divan, 160
Louis, 216
Ebake, 164
ravigote, 160
stuffed eggs, 69
sole, 155
soufflé, 160
strata, 161
Crab apple(s)
  jelly, 343
Crab meat
  à la Sardi, 159
  au gratin, 160
  casserole rosemary, chicken, 144
  flounder stuffed w/, 152
  salad, 212
Cranberry
  bread, cheese, 51
  cloud dessert, 288
  conserve, 350
  cream, frozen, 294
  ham à la, 105
  ice, 296
  mince pie, 257
  nectar, lemon, 329
  pudding w/butter sauce, 283
  punch,
    hot buttered, 334
    spicy, 332
  salad, 207
  upside-down cake, 232
Crazy dogs, 378
Cream
  almond whipped, 247
  cheese
    butter frosting, 245
    frosting, 246
    scramble, bacon and, 66
    ham and, 66
  cocoa whipped I, 247
    II, 247
  coffee whipped, 247
  Cointreau whipped, 247
  crème de cacao whipped, 247
  crème de menthe whipped, 247
  dressing, celery seed, 215
  Dutch cocoa whipped, 247
  filling I, 248
  gravy, 132
  icing, orange, 53
  loaves, miniature butter, 57
  mocha ginger, 247
    mallow whipped, 248
  maple, 248
  whipped, 247
  nut loaf, Swiss whipped, 52
  of turkey soup, 31

Index

orange whipped, 247
pies, 261
puff Christmas tree, 276
  or choux paste, 276
puffs, 276
rum whipped, 247
  sauce, 115
strawberry whipped, 247
sweetened whipped, 247
Creamed
  ham and sweetbreads, 118
  spinach w/almonds, 191
  sweetbreads, 119
  tomatoes, 193
Creamy
  cherry filling, 248
    mold, 285
  chocolate filling, 248
  coconut petal tarts, 272
  French dressing, 219
  green bean casserole, 172
  lemon
    mayonnaise, 220
  mushroom soup, 29
  peanut butter frosting, 248
  vanilla filling, 248
Crème
  brûlée, 280
  de cacao, whipped cream, 247
  de menthe whipped cream, 247
  Senegalese, 34
Creole
  cod, 158
  doughnuts, 49
  shrimp à la, 166
  tripe, 120
Crêpes,
  farcie, 181
  ham-olive, 106
Crescents
  apricot, 324
  cheese rolls, 59
  chocolate-almond, 320
  rolls, 45
Crisp sugar cookies, 309
Croissants, 45
Croquettes
  Dutch cheese, 71
Croustade(s)
  almond ringlet, 62
  ringlet, 62
  savory miniature, 22
  sesame ringlet, 62
Croutons, 26
  herb, 204
Crumb crust
  cereal, 255
  coconut-cereal, 255
  cookie, 254
  nut, 254
Crunchies, spicy ginger, 316
Crunch-top raisin cake, 233
Crunchy

peanut cole slaw, 203
wax beans, 173
Crust
  Brazil nut, 255
  cereal crumb, 255
  chocolate-coconut, 255
  coconut-cereal crumb, 255
  cookie crumb, 254
  filbert, 255
  graham cracker crumb, 254
  nut-crumb, 254
  salted peanut, 255
  10-inch graham cracker, 254
Cuban black bean soup, 27
Cucumber
  chicken canapés, 21
  dip, 19
  mold, exquisite, 210
  salad bowl, 202
  sauce, 199
  soup, 29
    Danish style, 34,
Culinary know-how, 1
  culinary terms, 5
  equipping your kitchen, 1
  foreign words & phrases, 9
  helpful hints for the cook, 9
  high altitude cooking, 7
  how to do it, 11
  ingredients, 3
  measurements & equivalents, 2
  oven temperatures, 7
  use correct techniques, 2
Cumberland leg of lamb, 108
Cupcakes & cakelets, 239
Currant(s)
  cakes, 312
  filling, apple and, 277
  Irish soda bread w/, 52
  jelly, 343
  loaves, petite orange, 57
  mustard glaze, 374
Curried
  chicken, 218
  chicken salad, 218
  French dressing, 219
  fruit, 104
  lamb-prune burgers, 129
  prawns, 165
Curry
  almond-stuffed eggs, 69
  mayonnaise dressing, 208
  sauce, 83
  South African, 130
Custard
  chocolate, 280

388

filling, 278
  vanilla, 249
pies, 265
  Frau Moyer's cheese, 266
  slipped, 265
  sauce, 303
  soft, 279
Custards & puddings, 279

D

Daffodil torte, 238
Dakkeri chiffon pie, 270
Danish, *see also*
  SCANDINAVIAN
  blue cheese mousse, 213
  dinner, 96
  ham rolls in Samsoe cheese sauce, 107
  knots, 319
  meatballs, 127
  overnight cookies, 317
  pastry, 47
    coffee cake, 41
  peppernuts, 316
  potato platter, 210
  raspberry pudding, 290
  recipes
    brown wafers, 317
    frikadeller, 127
    hoide kager, 317
    kringler, 319
    pebernødder, 316
  style, cucumber soup, 34
    red cabbage, 175
    sugar-browned potatoes, 184
Date(s)
  appetizers broiled, 16
  muffins, ginger, 56
  nut
    cake maraschino, 233
  pie, sour cream, 266
Deep-fried
  codfish cakes, 154
  cookies, 324
  Dutch cheese croquettes, 71
  lacy cornmeal fried onion rings, 182
    French-fried onion rings, 182
Delicate white cake, 222
Deluxe scrambled eggs, 66
Demitasse, 326
Désir de la Pompadour w/ English cream, 288
Dessert(s) & dessert
  sauces, 273-304
  cake-desserts, 273
    cherry cheesecake, 274
    chocolate-mint cheese cake, 274
    luscious lemon, 273
  marble chocolate freeze, 276

plum kutchew, 275
shortcake,
  Chantilly peach, 275
  strawberry, 274
  peach, 275
  sunshine, 275
casseroles
  apple charlotte, 298
  baked rhubarb w/ pastry topping, 300
  pear bacon crisp, 299
  purple plum cobbler, 273
  compote, 299
custards & puddings, 279
  apple cream, 283
  blueberry-orange parfaits, 281
  Brazilian pudim moka w/chocolate sauce, 281
  chocolate custard, 280
  coffee tapioca parfait, 282
  cranberry pudding w/butter sauce, 283
    butter sauce, 283
  crème brûlée, 280
  floating island, 279
  glamour pudding 'n' peaches, 282
  Indian pudding, 283
  lemon sponge, 281
  lemon streusel bread pudding, 282
  maple flan, 280
  peaches 'n' cream kuchen, 283
  peanut rocky road cups, 282
  plantation pudding, 280
  soft custard, 279
  trifle, 279
  peach, 284
frozen, 290
  avocado mousse, 290
  Beau Nash delight, 291
  heavenly hash pairfaits, 290
  macaroon mousse, 291
  Nesselrode pudding, 292
  parfait Grand Marnier, 291
  peanut brittle mousse, 291
  royale, 292
fruit, 297
  charlotte, 298
  baked rhubarb w/ pastry topping, 300
  bananas Foster, Brennan's, 298
  cantaloupe coupe, 301
  Chantilly cherry cups, 298

Index

fresh blueberry "cobbler," 298
glazed mixed, 301
   strawberry tart, 301
Grecian glazed oranges, 299
peaches 'n' cornbread, shortcake style, 299
   w/lime cream, 299
pear bacon crisp, 299
pineapple w/rum caramel sauce, 300
purple plum cobbler, 273
   compote, 299
prune cobble cake, 300
rhubarb crunch, 300
Swedish applecake w/vanilla sauce, 297
Wenatchee apple crisp, 297
gelatin, 284
   blancmange w/orange sauce, 284
   citrus mold maraschino, 286
   cherry mold, 285
   elegant strawberry cream, 287
   honey dew cream, 285
   lemon egg fluff, 286
      cherry-cinnamon sauce, 286
   melon-duet mold, 286
   mocha-caramel Bavarian, 285
   molded pineapple-coconut cream, 287
      raspberry crème, 287
   snow pudding, 285
ice cream, 292
   baked Alaska, 292
   cherry, 293
      individual baked Alaska, 293
      loaf, 293
   frozen cherry Easter egg, 293
ice creams, sherbets & ices, 293
ice
   boysenberry, 297
   cranberry, 296
   greengage plum, 297
ice cream
   banana-pecan, 294
   chocolate chipped tortoni, 296
   mocha, 294
   fresh purple plum, 295
   frozen cranberry cream, 294
      strawberry crème, 295
   Haitian, 294

lemon-cheese, 295
peach superb, 295
Philadelphia, 293
   strawberry, 293
sherbet
   lemon, 296
   peach-lime, 296
   watermelon, 330
ices, ice creams, sherbets &, 293
meringue, 278
   chocolate meringue shells, 278
   meringues, 278
      custard filling, 278
   torte, 279
pastries, 276
   cream puff or choux paste, 276
   cream puffs, 276
   éclairs, 276
   strudel, 277
   fillings, 277
      apple and currant, 277
      cherry, 277
      chopped nut, 278
      cottage cheese, 277
      dried fruit, 277
      jelly, 278
      poppyseed, 277
      raisin and cherry, 278
puddings, custards &, 279
refrigerator, 287
   charlotte à l'orange, 289
      chocolate glaze, 289
   chocolate cake, 288
   cranberry cloud, 288
   Danish raspberry pudding, 290
   desir de la Pompadour w/English cream, 288
      English cream, 288
   lemon bisque, 289
   pashka, 290
   pineapple, 289
   regal chocolate, 287
sauces, 302
   almond butterscotch, 302
   butter, 283
   cherry,
   cinnamon, 286
   custard, 303
   English cream, 288
   foamy vanilla, 304
   fresh raspberry, 304
   golden, 302
   Grecian orange, 303
   hot fudge, 303
   luscious butterscotch, 302
   peanut butter crunch,

304
   rosy ginger, 304
   semisweet chocolate, 303
   spicy cherry, 302
   vanilla, 298, 302
      brandy, 302
      lemon, 302
   vanilla hard sauce, 304
      almond hard sauce, 304
      brandy hard sauce, 304
   zesty lemon, 303
sherbets & ices, ice creams, 293
soufflé(s)—hot & cold, 284
   milk chocolate, 284
Dessert sauces, 302
Dessert soufflés—hot & cold, 284
Deviled
   egg salad, 214
   eggs, 71
   ham canapés, 22
   salmon, 157
   steak, 83
Devil's food cake, Mrs. Eisenhower's, 230
Dilled
   mushroom sauce, 198
   onion packet, 376
   potatoes in packets, 376
Dilly bacon-stuffed eggs, 69
Dip, see also APPETIZERS
   blue cheese w/mushrooms, 18
   chili, 18
Divinity frosting, 243
Don Quixote Horcher, 115
Double
   chocolate squares, 307
   strawberry parfait pie, 271
   treat frank-burgers, 368
Doughnut(s)
   Creole, 49
Dressings, see STUFFINGS
Dressings, salad, see SALADS & SALAD DRESSINGS
Dried fruit filling, 277
Drink(s), see also BEVERAGES
Drip coffee, 326
Drop cookies, 309
Duckling, 147
   à l'orange, roast, 147
Ducks, wild
   w/olives, 148
Dumplings
   chicken and, 143
   cornmeal, 143
   potato, 88
Dutch
   almond cookies, 305

apple cake, 52
cheese croquettes, 71
cocoa whipped cream, 247
stewed potatoes, 186
Duxbury pork, 94

E

Easter
   egg bread, 40
Echte Florentiner, 310
Éclairs, 276
Eenyhow, 99
Egg(s)
   and treasure tuna bake, 71
   au gratin, 65
   Benedict, 66
   bread, Easter, 40
   drop soup, 30
   farci, 70
   fluff, lemon, 280
   salad
      deviled, 214
      stuffed w/chicken liver paste, 69
Egg & cheese dishes, 63-76
   about cheese, 64
   about eggs, 63
   helpful hints, 64
   cheese dishes, 71
      all-American scallop, 72
      casserole royale, 71
      Dutch, croquettes, 71
      green enchiladas, 72
      Monterey tamale busyday dinner, 72
   egg dishes, 65
      hard-cooked, 69
      crab-stuffed, 69
      deviled eggs, 71
      egg-and-treasure tuna bake, 71
      farci, 70
      perky stuffed, 69
      scotch, 70
      stuffed, sophisticate, 69
         curry-almond stuffed, 69
         dilly bacon-stuffed, 69
         stuffed w/chicken liver paste, 69
   omelet(s), 67
      French, 67
      bacon, 68
      chicken liver, 68
      citrus, 68
      Roquefort, 68
      mushroom, 68
      saucy ham, 68
      apple sauce, 68
      zucchini, 69
   poached, 65

Index

au gratin, 65
  Benedict, 66
  "Duchesse Anne," 65
  scrambled, 66
    bacon and cream-cheese scramble, 66
    ham and cream cheese scramble, 66
    chili-egg, 67
    de luxe, 66
    lemon custard French toast, 67
    golden apricot syrup, 67
    pisto à la "El Chico," 67
    w/cheese, 66
  soft-cooked, 64
  hard-cooked, 64
soufflé(s) frying pan, 76
  Swiss cheese, 76
  top hat shrimp, 76
Eggplant
  amandine, 178
  casserole, Balkan lamb and, 130
  ground beef, 126
  patties in casserole, beef, 126
  slims, Parmesan, 179
Elegant
  mayonnaise, 219
  strawberry cream, 287
Empress chicken, 140
English
  cream, 288
  muffin splits, cheesy, 378
  mustard sauce, 198
  toffee bars, 309
  toffee pie, 271
Epicurean beef à la Far East, 89
Espagnole, brown sauce, 117
  sauce, brown or, 196
Exquisite cucumber mold, 210

F

Fattigmann, 324
Fennel-flavored vegetable packet, 377
Fettuccine al burro Alfredo, 181
  Alfredo, 181
Fiesta roast pork, 94
Fig pie, fresh, 258
Filbert
  black-top pie, 269
  coffee cake, toasted, 53
  crisps, lacy, 310
  crust, 255
  roast chicken, honey-glazed, 135
  topping, toasted, 54
Filet mignon Stanley, 81
Filling(s), 248
  almond, 47
    paste, 48
  cherry, 241, 277
  chocolate, rich, 310
  cream, 248
  ginger, 318
  vanilla cream, 47
Finnish meatballs, 122
Fish, see also by name
  and chips, 158
  dinner de luxe in foil, 374
  soups, chowders &, 31
Fish & shellfish, 151-166
  fish, 151
    availability, 151
    baked, 151
      fillets Viennese, 152
      flounder dinner au gratin, 154
      flounder stuffed w/ crab meat, 152
      halibut parmesan, 154
      Restigouche salmon Breval, 152
      w/shrimp stuffing, 151
    broiled, 153
      pompano Florentine, 153
      trout, 153
    canned & frozen, dishes, 155
      Creole cod, 158
      fish and chips, 158
      deviled salmon, 157
      golden tuna florentine, 156
      palos verdes stew, 158
      savory salmon kabobs, 156
      tangy cheese-broccoli sauce, 156
      skillet tuna supreme, 156
      sole, crab-stuffed, 155
      stick special, 157
      tuna empandas, 157
      yankee double tuna bake, 157
    fried, 154
      codfish cakes, 154
      cornmeal-crusted mountain trout, 155
      fillets Mornay, 154
      smelts, 155
    frozen-fish dishes, canned &, 155
    on the grill, 371
    poached, 155
      salmon aromatic, 155
      scalloped haddock en coquilles, 155
      storage, 151
  shellfish, 158
    clam(s), 158
      paella, 159
      pie, 159
    crab(s) & crab meat, 159
      à la Sardi, 159
        Sardi sauce, 159
        sauce velouté, 160
      au gratin, 160
      Booky baked, 161
      divan, 160
      ravigote, 160
      soufflé, 160
      strata, 161
    lobsters & lobster meat, 161
      shrimp and lobster stew, 162
      tails, thermidor, 161
    oyster(s), 162
      piquante in the half shell, 162
      scalloped, 163
    scallops, 163
      coquilles Saint-Jacques, 164
      en Brochette with onion risotto, 163
      gourmet in patty shells, 163
    shrimp, 164
      à la Creole, 166
      à la king, 166
      cooked, 164
      curried prawns, 165
      Ernie, 164
      Indienne, 165
      jambalaya, 165
      Louis bake, 164
      scampi flamingo, 166
        sauce, 166
Flaky cheese-filled rolls, 61
Flash un kas, 15
Flavor blends for foil-baked ham, 104
Flavor-full broiled chicken, 138
Floating island, 279
Florentines, 310
Flounder, dinner au gratin, 154
  stuffed w/crab meat, 152
Fluffy honey, 246
Foamy sauce, vanilla, 304
Foil-baked flavor-glazed ham, 103-104
Fondue
  Bourguignonne, 83
  jiffy sauces for, 83
Fontainebleau hors d'oeuvres pie, 14
For a crowd
  baked Alaska, 292
  cranberry cloud dessert, 288
  curried chicken salad, 218
  Danish blue cheese mousse, 213
  lemon bisque, 289
    egg fluff, 286
  party-perfect salad molds, 208
  peachy rich breakfast slices, 59
  peanut brittle mousse, 291
  pineapple salad dressing, 220
  raspberry fruit punch, 333
  regal chocolate dessert, 287
  sparkling fruit refresher, 332
  spicy cranberry punch, 332
  super tuna ring, 212
Foreign recipes, see by country of origin
  words & phrases, 9
Four-fruit refresher, 332
Franconia potatoes, 183
Frank-burgers, double treat, 368
Frankfurter, see also HOT DOG
Franks
  bacon-wrapped, 368
  in buns, grilled ground beef, 367
  marinated, 368
  saucy cocktail, 16
Frau Moyer's cheese custard pie, 266
Freezing, 352
  baked products, 360
  cooked foods, 362
  dairy products, 360
  eggs, 359
  fish, 359
  fruits, 354
  game, 359
  meats, 357
  poultry, 358
  sandwiches, 361
  shellfish, 359
  vegetables, 356
French
  bread, buttered, 62
  dressing, 219
    creamy, 219
    curried, 219
    honey, 219
    lime, 219

Lorenzo, 219
tangy, 219
tomato soup, 219
fried potatoes, 185
omelet, 67
pastry cakes, 238
peas, 183
recipes
  canard aux olives, 148
  cream puff or choux paste, 276
  cream puffs, 276
  croissants, 45
  éclairs, 276
  gâteau génoise, 238
  oeufs gratines Laperouse, 65
  petits fours, 238
  ratatouille w/Spanish olives, 179
  salade Niçoise, 217
  salade Provençale, 204
  style green beans w/ water chestnuts, 172
  style leg of lamb, 108
toast, 61
  cinnamon-orange, 62
Fresh
  apricot pie, 256
  blueberry "cobbler," 298
    pie, 257
  fig pie, 258
  leg of pork w/exotic stuffing, 96
  mushroom sous cloche, 180
  peach-plum pie, 259
  pear pie, 260
  pineapple preserves, 348
  plum pie, 259
  purple plum ice cream, 295
  raspberry sauce, 304
    pie, red, 257
Fricassee, chicken, 143
Fricasseed & stewed chicken, 143
Fried
  fish, 154
  ham w/red gravy, 105
  rice, 126, 186
  smelts, 155
  tomatoes, 193
  turkey, 145
Frijoles, 171
  refritos, 171
Frikadeller, 127
Frosted
  brown sugar bubble loaf, 57
  coffee shake, 331
Frosting(s), 242
  see also ICINGS
  basic butter, 245
  black walnut butter, 245
  brownie caramel, 244

butter cream I, 243
caramel mocha, 245
chocolate butter, 245
  cream cheese, 246
  mocha butter cream, 243
  seven-minute, 242
choco-marshmallow, 246
cream cheese butter, 245
creamy peanut butter, 245
divinity, 243
fluffy honey, 246
fruit 'n' nut white mountain, 242
glossy chocolate, 320
hazlenut butter cream, 243
honey-chocolate, 244
lemon butter, 245
  cream cheese, 245
marshmallow, 242
  cream, 243
mocha butter, 245
  cream, 243
  seven-minute, 242
orange butter, 245
  seven-minute, 242
peppermint seven-minute, 242
pistachio seven-minute, 242
poured chocolate, 246
praline, spice cake w/, 228
raisin rum, 245
seven-minute, 242
vanilla fudge, 244
white velvet, 245
Frozen
  cherry Easter egg, 293
  cranberry cream, 294
  dessert royale, 292
  desserts, 290
  strawberry crème, 295
Fruit, see also by name
  butters, 341, 351
  compote salad, molded, 208
  curried, 104
  desserts, 297
  filled coffee ring, 56
  filling, dried, 277
    rich coconut, 222
  glazed mixed, 301
  jam, mixed, 346
  kabobs duo, glazed beef, 369
    glazed, 369
  muffins, hot cross, 59
  'n' nut white mountain frosting, 242
  nut bread, California, 52
  pies, 256
  punch, raspberry, 333
  refresher, four, 332
  salad(s), 205

chef's, 206
Fruitcake(s), pound cakes &, 233
  old Williamsburg-style, 234
Fruited lamb spareribs, 110
  lamb stew de luxe, 111
Fruity Polish mazurek, 308
Fudge
  cake, Wellesley, 230
  frosting
    vanilla, 244
  sauce, 307
    hot, 303
    topping, broiler, 248
Fudgy brownies, 306
Full-flavored steak, 365

G

Gala lobster salad, 217
Gallatin's mushrooms à la crème George, 179
Game hens
  lime-glazed, 149
  roast Rock Cornish, 149
  Rock Cornish, 148
  w/spicy stuffing, 148
Garden
  butter-sauce, 365
  potato salad, 204
Garlic
  butter, herb, 138
  cheeseburgers, 122
  green beans w/, 173
Gâteau génoise, 238
Gazpacho bowl, 203
Gelatin
  cubes, spicy, 211
  desserts, 284
  techniques, 206
German
  meatballs, 123
  molasses cookies, 323
  noodle ring, 180
  recipes
    Blitzkuchen, 53
    cinnamon stars, 321
    Kartoffelklosse, 88
    Kirschsosse, 302
    Koenigsberger Klops, 123
    Kraut mit Apfeln, 188
    Sauerbraten, 88
    Schaumtorte, 279
    Stollen, 43
    turban cake, 224
Giblet gravy, 200
Ginger
  apricot conserve, 350
  brew, 351
  cookies, 315
  cream, mocha, 247
  crunchies, spicy, 316
  date muffins, 56
  filling, 318

glaze, 368
glazed lamb chops, 368
gravy, 200
ice cooler, 329
sauce, rosy, 304
shortbread, 322
tea, hot, 327
tomatoes, 349
Gingerbread, soft, 228
Gingersnap(s), 312
  gravy, 88, 200
  Swedish, 322
Glamour pudding 'n' peaches, 282
Glaze(s) & toppings, 41, 103, 246
  apricot, 103
  brown sugar, 103
  chocolate, 224, 289
    cooked, 276
    uncooked, 276
  cider, 103
  citrus, 233
  coffee, 58
  currant-mustard, 374
  for ham, 103
  fudge, 246
  ginger, 368
  honey, 138
  jelly or jam, 103
  lemon, 306
  mustard, 103
  orange, 49
Glazed
  beef-fruit kabob duo, 369
  corned beef, 91
  fruit kabobs, 369
  grilled chicken, 371
  mixed fruit, 301
  onions, 181
  peach pie, 259
  pork sausage patties, 101
  roast ham, 103
  rolled leg of lamb, 108
  strawberry pie, 257
  tart, 301
Glossy
  chocolate frosting, 320
  icing, 246
  vanilla icing, 246
Gold cake, 223
Golden
  apricot syrup, 67
  barbecue sauce, 136
  glow butter, 376
  jelly, 344
  nut bars, 309
  punch, 333
  ragout, 116
  sauce, 302
  tuna Florentine, 156
Good fortune chicken w/ pineapple piquant, 141
Goose, 148
  roast, 148
Goulash, gypsy style, 93
  szekely, 101

Index

Gourmet salad dressing, 219
Graham cracker
 crumb crust, 254
  10-inch, 254
  sensations, 308
  tart shells, 255
Granny's Texas bran bread, 37
Grape(s)
 arbor pie, 258
 butter, 351
 chiffon pie, 269
 jelly, basil, 343
  spiced, 343
Grapefruit
 jelly, savory, 343
 lime mold, 207
Grasmere shortbread, 318
Gravy, 95, 148, 199
 brown, 199
 cream, 132
 giblet, 200
 gingersnap, 88
 orange, 147
 prune, 94
 red eye, 200
 special, 95
 turkey or chicken, 200
Grecian glazed oranges, 299
 orange sauce, 303
Green
 beans
  casserole, creamy, 172
  gruyere, 172
  in packet, mace-flavored, 375
  pork chop supper, 98
  w/garlic, 173
  w/water chestnuts, French-style, 172
 enchiladas, 72
 goddess salad dressing, 320
 grapes, herbed carrots w/, 176
 pepper packet, carrot-celery, 375
 packets, shrimp, 375
 rice, 187
Green & vegetable salads, 202
Greengage plum ice, 297
Grilled
 burgers w/cheese sauce, 366
 ground beef "franks" in buns, 367
 lobster tails Italiano, 371
 rock lobster tails, 371
 shrimp appetizers, 372
  in shells, 372
 sirloin steak Juliana, 366
 steak w/garden butter sauce, 365
 trout, 371

whole onions, 376
Grilling, *see* OUTDOOR COOKING
Ground beef, 121
 à la stroganoff, 126
 eggplant casserole, 126
 "franks" in buns, grilled, 367
 noodle scallop, 180
Ground meat cookery, 120
 tomato sauce w/, 190
 towers, saucy, 121
Guacamole, 19
Gumbo a la Creole, Brennan's, 31

H

Haitian ice cream, 294
Half-hour meal, 102
Halibut Parmesan, 154
Halloween
 sparkling punch, 332
Ham, 103, *see also* MEATS
 à la cranberry, 105
 and bananas, 105
 and cream cheese scramble, 66
 and sweetbreads, creamed, 118
 canapés, deviled, 22
 casserole, mushroom, 105
 cheese puffs, 17
 glazes for, 103
 jubilee, 106
 loaf, party, 128
 mousse, 211
 'n' pickle kabobs, 370
 'n' yams in raisin-caramel sauce, 106
 olive crêpes, 106
 omelet, saucy, 68
 on a spit, 373
 pinwheel ring, 128
 rolls in Samsoe cheese sauce, Danish, 107
 slice in orange sauce, 105
 veal loaf w/saucy topping, 128
Hamburgers, *see* BURGERS
Hard-cooked eggs, 69
Hard sauce, almond, 304
 brandy, 304
 vanilla, 304
Harvest pork, 97
Hash-stuffed tomatoes, 94
Hazelnut butter cream frosting, 243
Heart w/apple-raisin dressing, 120
Heavenly Hash parfaits, 270
Heavenly lemon pie, 267
Helpful hints
 about breads, 35

cakes, 222
eggs, 64
fruits, 205
pies, 252
preserving, 341
soups, 25
vegetables, 169
for
 successful jams, 341
 preserves, 341
Help-yourself appetizer kabobs, 370
Herb
 bread, old fashioned, 36
 butter, 376
 butters, 138
 croutons, 204
 garlic butter, 138
Herbed
 beef roulades, 86
 beef steak, 365
 carrots w/grapes, 176
 mayonnaise, 23
 Parmesan rolls, 46
 peas and celery, 183
 stuffing, 150
 tomato sauce, 121
 vegetable medley, 377
 vinegar, 365
Hermitage spoon bread, 54
Hermits, 313
Herring salad, 376
High altitude cooking, 7
Hints, *see* HELPFUL HINTS
 for fried chicken, 140
Hi-style spinach, 191
Hoide kager, 317
Holiday treat preserves, 349
Hollandaise sauce, 197
Home canning of fruits & vegetables, 335
Homemade
 pot cheese, 19
 soda, chocolate, 331
 lemon, 331
 peach, 331
 pineapple, 331
 raspberry or strawberry, 331
Honey
 bun coffee ring, 42
 cake, 225
 chocolate frosting, 244
 chutney glaze, stuffed lamb shoulder roast w/, 108
French dressing, 219
frosting, fluffy, 246
glaze, 138
glazed filbert
 roast chicken, 135
jelly, mint, 344
lime French dressing, 219
topping, spiced, 248
Honeydew Cream gelatin

mold, 285
Hors d'oeuvre pie, Fontainebleau, 14
Hors d'oeuvres, *see* APPETIZERS
Horseradish
 cream, broccoli w/, 174
 onion-sauce, 83
 sauces, 83
Hot
 appetizers, 14
 aromatic punch, 334
 beverages, 326
 buttered cranberry punch, 334
 chocolate, 327
 cross buns, 48
 fruit muffins, 59
 fudge sauce, 303
 ginger tea, 327
 mushroom appetizers, 17
 ravigote sauce, 197
 spiced cider, 328
 tea, 327
Hot dog, *see also* FRANKFURTERS
How to
 blanch nuts, 11
 clarify fats, 11
 clean mushrooms, 11
 cook artichokes, 170
 wild rice, 11
 grill meats, 364
 make butter balls, 11
 curls, 11
 melt chocolate, 11
 plump raisins, 11
 prepare
  crumbs, 11
  garlic, 11
  quick broth, 12
  roast chestnuts, 12
 salt nuts, 12
 sour cream, 12
 milk, 12
 modify baking recipes for high altitude cooking, 8
 use an electric blender, 11
 whip cream, 12
 evaporated milk, 12
Hungarian
 butter cookies, 318
 recipes
  szerelmes levél, 324

I

Ice cream, *see also* DESSERTS
 banana-pecan, 294
 chocolate-mocha, 294

Index

desserts, 292
fresh purple plum, 295
Haitian, 294
lemon-cheese, 295
peach, superb, 295
Philadelphia, 293
pie(s), 272
strawberry, 272
strawberry, 293
Ice creams, sherbets & ices, 293
Iced
coffee, 328
cinnamon, 328
orange mocha, 328
tea, 329
Icing(s), 234, see also FROSTING(S)
almond, 223
chocolate, 269
Confectioners' Sugar, 48
orange cream, 53
Indian pudding, 283
Individual baked Alaskas, 293
Indonesian lamb, 112
Irish scones, 55
soda bread w/currants, 52
Ischl cookies, 320
Italian
beef bake, 91
butter cookies, 323
meat patties, 122
recipes
canestrelli, 323
cannelloni alla piemontese "maison," 131
cheese rolls, 55
chicken cacciatore, 142
Easter egg bread, 40
fettuccine al burro Alfredo, 181
Alfredo, 181
linguine w/marinara sauce, 190
pomodori Genovese, 193
salsa Italiana, 198
rosata, 24
scampi flamingo, 166
skillet veal loaf Firenze, 130
tagliarini, 180
spaghetti sauce, 190

J

Jam(s), 341, 345
blackberry, 346
blueberry-lemon, 345
braid, quick 'n' easy, 58
cherry-plum, 345
mixed fruit, 346
peach and nut, 347
rosemary, 346
rosy banana, 345
spiced, 347
pineapple-rhubarb, 346
strawberry, 347
cardamom, 347
mint, 347
Jan Hagel, 321
Java, chocolate, 328
Jellied
borsch, 33
consommé madrilène, 33
Jellies, 339, 342
apple, 342
basil grape, 343
blueberry, 342
crab apple, 343
currant, 343
golden, 344
jam, pineapple-strawberry, 344
mint-honey, 344
pineapple, 344
quick sparkling, 342
rosemary, 345
savory grapefruit, 343
spiced grape, 343
plum, 344
tangerine, 345
Jelly
filling, 278
or jam glaze, 103
Jerry Lewis' chocolate cake, 230
Jiffy sauces for fondue Bourguignonne, 83
Johnnycake, 54
Julekake, 38, 43
Julep, peach, 330

K

Kabob duo, glazed beef-fruit, 369
Kabobs
calf's liver on skewers, Zurich style, 117
calypso steak sticks, 84
glazed fruit, 369
ham 'n' pickle, 370
help-yourself appetizer, 370
lamb,
lamb
marinated, 369
pineapple, 110
quickie, 370
savory salmon, 156
turkey, 145
w/Oriental sauce, beef, 369
Kåldolmar, 132
Kartoffelklösse, 88
Kentucky chess pie, 266
Key lime pie, 264
Kidney(s)
grill, lamb 'n', 119
pie, beef and, 119
Kolacky cookies, 321
Kraut, see also SAUERKRAUT
and beef pasties, 124
mit Apfeln, 188
pastry snacks, zesty, 124
stuffed spareribs, apple, 101
w/apples, 188
Kringler, 319
Krumkaker, 316
Kulich, 43
Kumquat chicken, 136

L

Lacy
almond crisps, 310
cornmeal fried onion rings, 182
filbert crisps, 310
French-fried onion rings, 182
Ladyfingers, 241
Lamb, 108, see also MEAT
and coconut curry, 110
Cassolet, 112
eggplant casserole, Balkan, 130
barbacoa, 373
breast w/carrot stuffing, 109
chops
en brochette, 109
ginger-glazed, 368
minted, 368
kabobs, marinated, 369
loaf w/curry sauce, 112
'n' kidney grill, 119
pineapple kabobs, 110
prune burgers, curried, 129
shanks, barbecued, 110
spareribs, fruited, 110
stew Picasso, 111
Lasagne, 189
shrimp, 189
Lattice-top cherry pie, 258
Lebanon County rhubarb preserves, 349
Le coq au vin, 143
Lemon
and lime, Spanish, 331
bisque, 289
butter, 138
frosting, 245
cake, upside-down, 231
cheese cake, luscious, 273
ice cream, 295
chiffon pie, 270
coconut sours, 308
cranberry nectar, 329
cream cheese frosting, 245
custard French toast, 67
dipped chicken, 370
egg fluff, 286
filling,
I, 250
II, 250
ginger carrots, 204
glaze, 306
jam, blueberry, 345
lime meringue pie, 263
mayonnaise, creamy, 220
nut bread, 52
olive meatballs, 221
pie, heavenly, 267
sauce, 302
velvet, 83
sherbet, 296
soda, homemade, 331
sponge, 281
streusel bread pudding, 282
sunshine cake squares, 237
layer cake, 237
syrup, 326
tea punch, spiced, 334
velvet frosting, 245
Lemonade, 329
punch, loganberry, 332
Lettuce, wilted, 204
Lightning cheese sauce, 366
Lima bean(s)
au gratin, 173
bake, 173
Lime
chiffon pie, 270
cream, peaches w/, 299
French dressing, honey, 219
glazed game hens, 149
marmalade, 348
meringue pie, lemon, 263
mold-grapefruit, 207
pie, Key, 264
rosemary zing, 329
sauce, spicy, apricot, 369
sherbet, peach, 296
Spanish lemon and, 331
swizzle, raspberry and, 330
syrup, 326
Limeade, 329
Limpa, 38
Lincoln's favorite cake, 223
Linguine,
w/marinara sauce, 190
Liver
à la Madame Begue, 118
and onions, Italian style, 117
chicken, omelet, 68
Matius, calf's, 117
Zurich style, calf's, 117
pâté exceptionale, 21

Index

Lobster & lobster meat, 161
  appetizer tidbits, 22
  elegance, molded, 212
  salad, gala, 217
  stew, shrimp, 162
  tails, grilled rock, 371
    Italiano, grilled, 371
  thermidor, 161
  w/orange-butter sauce, rock, 372
Loganberry-lemonade punch, 332
Lomi lomi salmon, 24
London broil, 86
L'orange, café, 327
Lorenzo French dressing, 219
Love letters, 324
Lucia buns, 37
Lumberjack burgoo, 28
Luscious
  butterscotch sauce, 302
  lemon bars, 308
  cheese cake, 273
Luxury mallow-nut brownies, 307

M

Macaroni
  salad, all seasons, 214
Macaroon(s)
  chocolate, 311
  de luxe, coconut, 311
  mousse, 291
  pie, almond, 261
Mace-flavored green beans in packet, 375
'n' cheese biscuits, 60
Madrilène jellied consommé, 33
Mailaenderli, 323
Main-dish salads, 214
Mallow-nut brownies, luxury, 307
Mancha manteles, 141
Maple
  butternut cake, 226
  cheese pie, strawberry, 258
  cream, mocha, 248
  flan, 280
  syrup cake, 226
Maraschino
  citrus mold, 286
  date-nut cake, 233
Marble chocolate freeze, 276
Marbleized tubed cake, 227
Marinade, 202
  caper, 363
  claret, 363
  herb, 364
  pineapple, 364
  steak, 365
Marinades & sauces, 363
Marinara sauce, linguine w/, 190
Marinated
  black pepper steak, 365
  franks, 368
  grilled shrimp, 372
  lamb kabobs, 369
Marmalade(s), 341, 347
  citrus, 347
  lime, 348
  peach, 347
  spread, 347
Marshmallow(s)
  frosting, 242
  choco, 246
  cream, 243
Mayonnaise, 219
  dressing, curry, 208
  elegant, 219
  herbed, 23
  sour cream, 220
  sauce, 199
Meal-in-a-kettle, 89
Meat, *see also by name*
  patties, Italian, 122
  ring, sauce-crowned, 121
  sauce, tomato, 190
Meatballs
  Armenian, 129
  chinese sizzled, w/ vegetables and rice, 127
  Danish, 127
  Finnish, 122
  German, 123
  Swedish, 123
Meats, 77-132
  beef, 80
  and broccoli skillet, 91
  "boiled" dinner, 93
  brisket w/horseradish sauce, 89
  Burgoo, 93
  Burgundy style, 92
  calypso steak sticks, 84
  can-can stroganoff, 84
  chili con queso beef roast, 81
  Chinese, and pea pods, 86
  chow mein, 85
  cooked corned beef brisket, 93
  deviled steak, 83
  epicurean, à la Far East, 89
  filet mignon Stanley, 81
  fondue Bourguignonne, 83
    jiffy sauces for fondue Bourguignonne, 83
    barbecue, 83
    béarnaise, 83
    caper, 83
    curry, 83
    horseradish, 83
    mustard, 83
    onion-chili, 83
    horseradish, 83
    paprika, 83
    rémoulade sauce, 84
    velvet lemon sauce, 83
  glazed corned beef, 91
  glazed fruit kabob duo, 369
  goulash, gypsy style, 93
    quick beef, 92
  ground, 121
  herbed beef roulades, 86
  herbed, steak, 365
  Italian beef bake, 91
  kabobs w/Oriental sauce, 369
  London broil, 86
  meal-in-a-kettle, 89
  mock pepper steak, 86
  oysters up, 82
  Parmesan steak, 82
  pot roast à la Provinçe, 87
  prime, tournedos Orlando, 81
  ragout w/piquant sauce, 92
  rippled steak, 85
  Saigon, 91
  Sauerbraten, 88
    gingersnap gravy, 88
    potato dumplings, 88
  savory pot roast, 87
  standing rib roast, 88
  rolled rib roast of, 80
  Yorkshire pudding, 80
  steak à la Barbara Stanwyck, 82
  steak Diane, 82
  stroganoff, 84
  stuffed beef pinwheel, 89
  stuffed steak rolls, 87
    stuffing, 87
  sukiyaki, 85
  Swiss steak in vegetable sauce, 90
  teriyaki beef rolls, 90
  tomato-smothered steak, 90
  Wellington, 80
    buttery pastry, 81
  w/onions, 92
canned & ready-to-eat, 368
  bacon-wrapped franks, 368
  barbecued bologna roll, 368
  marinated franks, 368
cooking frozen meats, 80
ground meat cookery, 120
  beef, 121
  à la stroganoff, 126
  black pepper burgers, 366
  chili and beans, 125
  double treat frankburgers, 368
  eggplant casserole, 126
    patties in casserole, 126
  Finnish meatballs, 122
  garlic cheeseburgers, 122
  German meatballs, 123
  grilled burgers w/ cheese sauce, 366
  lightning cheese sauce, 366
  grilled, "franks" in buns, 367
  Italian, patties, 122
  kraut and beef pasties, 124
  zesty kraut pastry snacks, 124
  Lindstrom, 122
  miniature, loaves Roquefort burgers, 366
  towers, 121
    herbed tomato sauce, 121
  Polynesian, 125
    fried rice, 126
  sauce-crowned, ring, 121
    topping, 121
  sauced walnut, balls Orientale, 123
    toasted soy walnuts, 124
  sheepherder's stew, 121
  sloppy Joe bake, 125
  Swedish meatballs, 123
  tacos, 124
  Yorkshire pie, 124
ham, 128
  party, loaf, 128
  pinwheel ring, 128
  sauce par excellence, 129
  veal loaf w/saucy topping, 128
    topping, 128

Index

lamb, 129
  Armenian meatballs, 129
  Balkan lamb and eggplant casserole, 130
  curried lamb-prune burgers, 129
  moussake, 129
  South African curry, 130
pork, 127
  cheese ball casserole à la Mexicana, 127
  Chinese sizzled meatballs w/ vegetables and rice, 127
  Danish meatballs, 127
veal, 130
  cannelloni alla Piemontese "maison," 131
  oyster loaf, 131
  party loaf w/sauce, 132
  sauce, 132
  skillet, loaf Firenze, 130
  spinach pinwheels, 131
  stuffed cabbage rolls, 132
ham, 103
  à la cranberry, 105
  baked, slice w/curried fruit, 104
  Danish ham rolls in Samsoe cheese sauce, 107
  foil-baked flavor glazed, 103-104
    and bananas, 105
    flavor blends for foil-baked ham, 104
    orange, 104
    pineapple, 104
    sherry or Madeira, 104
  sauces
    orange, 104
    pineapple, 104
    wine, 104
  "fried," w/red gravy, 105
  glazed roast, 103
  glazes for, 103
    apricot, 103
    brown sugar, 103
    cider, 103
    jelly or jam, 103
    mustard, 103
  ground, 128
  jubilee, 106
  mushroom-ham casserole, 105

'n' pickle kabobs, 370
'n' yams in raisin-caramel sauce, 106
olive crêpes, 106
on a spit, 373
potato/ham scallop, 107
slice in orange sauce, 105
timetable for baking ham in aluminum foil, 104
lamb, 108
  and coconut curry, 110
  barbacoa, 373
  barbecued, shanks, 110
  breast w/carrot stuffing, 109
  cassoulet, 112
  en brochette, 109
  fruited, spareribs, 110
  stew de luxe, 111
  noodle ring, 112
  ginger-glazed, chops, 368
  glazed rolled leg of, 108
  Indonesian, 112
  kabobs, marinated, 369
  loaf w/curry sauce, 112
  minted, chops, 368
  mock duck, 111
  Persian stew, 111
  pineapple kabobs, 110
  roast leg of,
    Cumberland, 108
    French style, 108
  stew Picasso, 111
  stuffed rib, chops, 109
  shoulder roast w/ honey chutney glaze, 108
  methods of cooking, 78-80
  on the grill, 364
pork, 94
  apple-kraut stuffed spareribs, 101
  apricot-stuffed roast, 97
  bahmie goreng, 100
  barbecued spareribs, 101
  Canadian-style bacon, w/mustard sauce, 102
  Cantonese, 100
  chops gourmet, 97
  apple-stuffed, 99
  Danish dinner, 96
  Duxbury, 94
  Eenyhow, 99
  fiesta roast, 94
  fresh leg of, w/exotic stuffing, 96
  glazed, sausage patties, 101

green bean-pork chop supper, 98
ground, 127
half-hour meal, 102
harvest, 97
mandarin, 100
Mandarin, 100
Midwestern, bake, 99
party, chops, 99
prune-stuffed, roast, 94
  prune gravy, 94
rack of Forum, 97
roast fresh leg of, 95
  Hawaiian, 95
  loin of, 373
  Pennsylvania Dutch style, 95
  w/olives and rice, 95
  saffron rice, 95
  special gravy, 95
sausage links, 102
schnitz un knepp, 103
skillet orange, chops, 98
smoked shoulder roll, 102
  w/mustard sauce, 102
stuffed, chops, 98
  tenderloin patties, 367
szekely goulash, 101
ready-to-eat, canned &, 368
  storage, 77
  time, 78
variety, 117
beef and kidney pie, 119
tongue w/tomato sauce, 118
calf's liver Matius, 117
  brown sauce espagnole, 117
calf's liver on skewers, Zurich style, 117
creamed ham and sweetbreads, 118
heart w/apple raisin dressing, 120
lamb 'n' kidney grill
liver à la Madame Begue, 118
  and onions, Italian style, 117
sweetbreads
  creamed, 119
  tripe Creole, 120
veal, 113
  birds w/mushroom stuffing, 116
  breaded, cutlets, 114
  budget parmigiano, 116
  Cordon Bleu, 114
  Don Quixote Horcher, 115
  cream sauce, 115
  Florentine "21," 113
  golden ragout, 116
  ground, 130
  paprika cream schnitzel, 115
  scaloppine
    alla Marsala, 114
    scaloppini el Presidente, 114
  stuffed breast of, 113
  tarragon, 116
  Viennese w/sour cream, 115
Meats on the grill, 364
Medium white sauce, 196
Melon dessert élégant, duet mold, 286
Meltaways, snowball, 314
Melting snowflakes, 319
Meringue(s), 278
  desserts, 278
  shell(s), 255
    10-inch, 255
  torte, 279
Merrie companie cake, 234
Methods of canning, 335
Mexican
  beans, 171
    refried, 171
  chocolate, 327
  recipes
    beef tacos, 124
    coliflor Acapulco, 202
    frijoles, 171
    refritos, 171
    guacamole, 19
    mancha manteles, 141
    soup Mexicana, 29
Milk chocolate
  soufflé, 284
  sauce, 284
Mince pie, 267
Miniature(s)
  butter cream loaves, 57
  orange sweet rolls, 49
Mint
  cheese cake, chocolate, 274
  honey jelly, 344
  jam, strawberry, 347
  sauce, 364
  syrup, 326
Minted
  chocolate refresher, 330
  lamb chops, 368
Mixed
  fruit jam, 346
  vegetable dishes, 377
Mocha
  angel dessert, 236
  caramel Bavarian, 285
  frosting,
    butter, 245
    cream, 243
      chocolate, 243
    caramel, 245

Index

ginger cream, 247
ice cream, chocolate, 294
iced orange, 328
mallow whipped cream, 248
maple cream, 248
nog pie, 268
  regal, 268
seven-minute frosting, 242
whipped cream, 247
Moji pearls, 314
  mock duck, 111
  mock pepper steak, 89
Molasses
  butter balls, 316
  cake, old-fashioned, 229
  cookies, German, 323
  whipped cream, 247
Molded
  cookies, 314
  fruit compote salad, 208
  lobster elegance, 212
  meat, chicken, fish, & shellfish salads, 211
  pineapple-coconut cream, 287
  raspberry crème, 287
  salads, 206
  vegetable salads, 210
Monterey tamale
  busy-day dinner, 72
Moravian cookies, brown, 323
Mödegspinnar, 315
Mornay sauce, 197
Moselem Springs apple butter, 351
Mount Shasta cookies, 311
Moussaka, 129
Mousse
  avocado, 206
  Camembert, 20
  Danish blue cheese, 213
  ham, 211
  macaroon, 291
  peanut brittle, 291
Mrs. Eisenhower's devil's food cake, 230
Muffins, 56
  banana corn, 60
  blueberry, 56
  ginger-date, 56
  hot cross fruit, 59
  orange-prune, 56
  Stouffer's pumpkin, 56
Multi-cheese blendip, 18
  à la crème George, Gallatin's, 179
  and capers, celery root w/, 177
  appetizers, hot, 17
  corn w/, 178
  cream, artichokes in, 170
    butter tarts w/, 22
  ham casserole, 105
  omelet, 68
  sauce, dilled, 198

soup, creamy, 29
sous cloche, fresh, 180
stuffing
  veal birds w/, 116
  wild rice w/, 188
Mustard
  glaze, 103
  currant, 374
  sauce, 83
    Canadian-style bacon w/, 102
    English, 198
    smoked shoulder roll w/, 102

N

Nesselrode tortlets, 264
  pudding, 292
New cabbage in orange sauce, 175
  moon yeast rolls, 58
New England
  clam chowder, 32
  recipes
    hermits, 313
    Indian pudding, 283
    Johnnycake, 54
    maple syrup cake, 226
Nicoise buffet platter, 216
Noodle(s)
  dishes, 180
  ring, 112
  German, 180
  scallop, ground beef, 180
Normandy sauce, 196
Norwegian
  Christmas bread, 43
  cones, 316
  recipes
    fattimann, 324
    julecake, 43
    krumaker, 316
Novelty
  molded salads, 213
Nut(s), *see also by name*
  bars, golden, 309
  bread
    California fruit, 52
    lemon, 52
    brownies, luxury mallow, 307
    buttercookies, Austrian, 319
  cake, cherry, 236
    maraschino date, 233
  chiffon pie, apricot, 268
  coated cheese log, 19
  colonels, 313
  corn sticks, bacon, 54
  crumb crust, 254
  filling
    chopped, 278
  jam, peach and, 347
  loaf, Swiss whipped cream, 52
  pastry, apricot, 268

raisin, loaf, 52
upside-down cake, peachy, 233

O

Oahu toast, 62
Oat flake banana bread, 51
Oatmeal
  raisin bread, 38
O'Brien potatoes, 185
Oeufs gratines Laperouse, 65
Old fashioned
  chicken pie, 143
  chocolate cake, 229
  cornbread stuffing, 150
  herb bread, 36
  molasses cake, 229
  Williamsburg-style fruitcake, 234
Olive(s)
  and rice, pork roast w/, 95
  bites, 17
  crêpes, ham, 106
  duck w/, 148
  ratatouille w/Spanish, 179
Omelet
  bacon, 68
  chicken liver, 68
  citrus, 68
  French, 67
  mushroom, 68
  Roquefort, 68
  saucy ham, 68
  zucchini, 69
One-bowl & quick cakes, 234
Onion(s)
  beef w/, 92
  casserole, 182
  chili, 83
  glazed, 181
  grilled whole, 376
  horseradish, 83
  Italian style, liver and, 117
  packets, dilled, 376
  rings, lacy cornmeal fried, 182
    French-fried, 182
  salad, blue ribbon potato, 204
  soup, Les Halles, 27
  sour cream dressing, 204
  superb, 182
  w/lemon butter, peas and, 182
Orange
  barbecue sauce, 198
  basting sauce, 364
  blossom cake, 226
  chiffon pie, 270
  butter
    carrots, 176

frosting, 245
sauce, rock lobster tails w/, 372
candy crisps, 312
charlotte à l', 289
chiffon cake, 239
  pie, 270
  avocado, 270
conserve, 350
cream cheese
  icing, 53
crowned cheese salad, 208
cube, 47
currant loaves, petite, 57
filling,
  I, 250
  II, 250
flavor blend, 104
French toast, cinnamon, 62
glaze, 49
gravy, 147
mocha, iced, 328
parfaits, blueberry, 281
pie, Talbott Inn, 265
pork chops, skillet, 98
prune, muffins, 56
salad dressing, 219
sauce(s), 104
  beets in, 174
  blancmange w/, 284
  Grecian, 303
  ham slice in, 105
  seven-minute frosting, 242
  sticky buns, 61
  sweet rolls, miniature, 49
  toast "blintzes," 62
  whipped cream, 247
Orangeade, 329
Oranges, Grecian glazed, 299
Oriental
  oven-fried chicken, 137
  sauce, beef kabobs w/, 369
Outdoor cooking, 363-378
  chicken on the grill, 370
    glazed grilled, 371
    lemon-dipped, 370
    saucy cinnamon, 370
  cooking in aluminum foil, 374
    carrot-celery-green pepper packet, 385
    cheese-topped tomatoes in packets, 377
  cheesy English muffin splits, 378
  corn in foil, 375
    golden glow butter, 376
    corn on the grill, 375

Index

perky butter sauce, 376
dilled onion packets, 376
  grilled whole onions, 376
dilled potatoes in packets, 376
fennel-flavored vegetable packet, 377
fish dinner de luxe, 374
herbed vegetable medley, 377
mace-flavored green beans in packet, 375
potatoes, roasted in foil, 376
  baked in coals, 376
  herb butter, 376
rice in peas in a pouch, 376
shrimp-green pepper packet, 375
tomatoes in foil, 376
vegetable medley in foil, 377
wax bean packet, 375
zucchini packet, 377
tomato, 378
fish & shellfish on the grill, 371
  grilled
    lobster tails Italiano, 371
    rock lobster tails, 371
    shrimp appetizers, 372
    in shells, 372
    marinated, 372
    trout, 371
  rock lobster tails w/orange-butter sauce, 372
marinades & sauces, 363
  butter sauce, 364
  caper marinade, 363
  claret marinade, 363
  herb marinade, 364
  mint sauce, 364
  orange basting sauce, 364
  pineapple marinade, 364
  piquant tomato sauce, 364
  tomato basting sauce, 364
meats on the grill, 364
  appetizer spareribs, 367
    sweet-sour apricot sauce, 367
    tangy plum sauce, 367
  bacon-wrapped franks, 368

barbecued bologna roll, 368
  ribs, 367
beef kabobs w/ Oriental sauce, 369
double treat frankburgers, 368
full-flavored steak, 365
ginger-glazed lamb chops, 368
  ginger glaze, 368
glazed beef-fruit kabob duo, 369
  glazed fruit kabobs, 369
  spicy apricot-lime sauce, 369
grilled burgers w/ cheese sauce, 366
  black pepper burgers, 366
  lightning cheese sauce, 366
grilled ground beef "franks" in buns, 367
grilled sirloin steak Juliana, 366
grilled steak w/garden butter sauce, 365
  garden butter sauce, 365
ham 'n' pickle kabobs, 370
help-yourself appetizer kabobs, 370
herbed beef steak, 365
  herbed vinegar, 365
how to grill, 364
  frankfurters, 365
  kabobs, 364
  lamb chops, 365
  single ribs for appetizers, 364
  spareribs and back ribs, 364
  steaks, 364
marinated black pepper steak, 365
  steak marinade, 365
marinated franks, 368
lamb kabobs, 369
minted lamb chops, 368
quickie kabobs, 370
rib steak, Western style, 366
saucy Roquefort burgers, 366
stuffed pork tenderloin patties, 367
sauces, marinades, 363
shellfish on the grill, fish &, 371
skillet cooking, 378
  chili-etti, 378
  crazy dogs, 378
  toasted buns, 378
  pork and beans on the

    grill, 378
  spit cookery, 373
    barbecued chicken on a spit, 373
    barbecue sauce, 374
    currant-mustard glaze, 374
  ham on a spit, 373
  lamb barbacoa, 373
  roast loin of pork, 373
Oven
  barbecued chicken, 136
  browned potatoes, 183
  fried or baked chicken, 136
  temperatures, 7
Oyster(s), 162
  loaf, veal, 131
  piquante in the half shell, 162
  Rockefeller, 23
  scalloped, 163
Oysters up, 82

P

Paella, 159
Palos Verdes stew, 158
Pan o' rolls, 60
Paper frills, 145
Paprika
  cream schnitzel, 115
  sauce, 83
Parfait Grand Marnier, 291
Parmesan
  eggplant slims, 179
  quick bread, 58
  rolls, herbed, 46
  steak, 82
Party
  cakes, chocolate-coated, 240
  chicken salad, 215
  ham loaf, 128
  perfect salad molds, 208
  pork chops, 99
  veal loaf w/sauce, 132
Pashka, 290
Pasta e fagroli, 30
Pastas & rice dishes, 180
  noodle dishes, 180
    crêpes farcie, 181
    fettuccine
      alburro Alfredo, 181
      Alfredo, 181
    German, ring, 180
    ground beef-noodle scallop, 180
    ring, 112
    tagliarini, 180
  rice dishes, 186
    and chicken amandine, 187
    and peas in a pouch, 376
    dumplings, 198

    fried, 126, 186
    green, 187
    pilaf, 187
    Spanish casserole, 187
    wild, w/mushrooms, 188
  spaghetti dishes, 188
    lasagne, 189
    shrimp, 189
    linguine w/marinara sauce, 190
    supreme, 188
    turkey parmazzini, 189
    w/tuna-tomato sauce, 188
  spaghetti sauces, 190
    Italian, 190
    seafood, 190
    tomato meat, 190
Pastries, 276
  si si, 17
Pastry
  buttery, 81
  crusts, 252
  Danish, 47
  for 1-crust pie, 252
    cheese, 253
    high-collared, 253
    lattice-top pie, 253
    little pies and tarts, 253
    rolled oat, 253
    rose-petal tarts, 253
    spice, 253
    10-inch pie, 253
    2-crust pie, 252
    cheese, 253
  morsels, Swiss cheese, 15
  topping, 253
Pâté à choux, 276
  pungent, 19
Pea(s)
  and celery, herbed, 183
  and onions w/lemon butter, 182
  French, 183
  in a pouch, rice and, 376
  pods, Chinese beef and, 86
  soup
    w/pork, yellow, 30
Peach(es)
  glamour pudding 'n', 282
  ice cream superb, 295
  jam, nut, 347
  rosemary, 346
  rosy banana, 345
  spiced, 347
  julep, 330
  lime sherbet, 296
  marmalade, 347
  melba salad, 209
  mold, sparkling fresh, 208
  'n' cornbread, shortcake style, 299
  'n' cream kuchen, 283

Index

pie, 259
  glazed, 259
plum pie, fresh, 259
shortcake, 275
soda, homemade, 331
trifle, 284
  w/lime cream, 299
Peachy nut upside-down cake, 233
  parfait pie, 271
  rich breakfast slices, 59
Peanut
  brittle mousse, 291
  cake, salted, 227
  cole slaw, crunchy, 203
  crunch sauce, 304
Peanut butter
  cupcakes, 240
  dreams, 309
  frosting, creamy, 245
  pastry, 254
  rocky road cups, 282
Pear(s)
  bacon crisp, 299
  pie, fresh, 260
Pebernødder, 316
Pecan
  butter, banana, 351
  coffee cake, pineapple, 61
  cookies, Austrian, 313
  ice cream, banana, 294
    apple, 267
  poofs, 314
  topping, 306
Pennsylvania Dutch recipes
  brown Moravian cookies, 323
  butter semmels, 46
  currant cakes, 312
  Dutch stewed potatoes, 186
  flash un kas, 15
  Frau Moyer's cheese custard pie, 266
  Lebanon County rhubarb preserves, 349
  lemon sponge, 281
  Moselem Springs apple butter, 351
  paprika cream schnitzel, 115
  sand tarts, 318
  sauerkraut w/caraway, 188
  schnitz un knepp, 103
  shoofly pie, 267
  smoked shoulder roll, 102
  wilted lettuce, 204
  roast chicken, 135
  style, roast pork, 95
Pepparkakor, 322
Pepper(s)
  packet, carrot-celery-green, 375
    shrimp-green, 375

steak, marinated black, 365
  stuffed, 179
Peppermint
  seven-minute frosting, 242
Peppernötter, 316
Peppernuts, Danish, 316
Percolated coffee, 326
Perky butter sauce, 376
  stuffed eggs, 69
Persian stew, 111
Petite
  orange-currant loaves, 57
Petits fours, 238
Petticoat tails, 318
Philadelphia ice cream, 293
Pickle
  kabobs, ham 'n', 370
Pie of gold, 271
  shells, 254
Pies, 251-272
  chiffon, 268
    apricot-nut, 268
    pastry, 268
    avocado-orange, 270
    chocolate, 269
    English toffee, 271
    filbert black-top, 269
      chocolate icing, 269
    grape, 269
    lime, 270
    dakkeri, 270
    lemon, 270
    orange, 270
    mocha-nog, 268
    regal, 268
    orange blossom, 270
    peachy parfait, 271
    double strawberry parfait, 271
    pie of gold, 271
    prune, 271
    coffee-coconut pie shell, 271
  cream, 261
    almond macaroon, 261
    banana butterscotch, 261
    black bottom, 262
    butterscotch-banana, 263
    candied pecan-pumpkin, 262
    cream, 261
    Key lime, 264
    lemon-lime meringue, 263
    Nesselrode tartlets, 264
    rainbow fruit, 261
    refrigerator raspberry, 264
    Talbott Inn orange, 265
    toasted coconut, 263

banana, 263
crusts, pastry, 252
  caramel, 265
  custard, 265
  slipped custard, 265
  Frau Moyer's cheese, 266
  sour cream
    raisin, 266
    date, 266
    strawberry-glazed cheese, 266
fruit, 256
  apple, 256
  cranberry-mince, 257
  fresh, 256
    apple, 256
    apricot, 256
    blueberry, 257
    fig pie, 258
    peach, 259
    plum, 259
    pear pie, 260
    red raspberry, 257
  glazed peach, 259
  glazed strawberry, 257
  grape arbor, 258
  lattice-top cherry, 258
  praline-pineapple-peach, 259
  rosy rhubarb, 260
  strawberry crumb, 258
    maple cheese, 258
    strawberry tart glacé, 260
  Victoria, 256
helpful hints about, 252
ice-cream, 272
  strawberry, 272
  voodoo, 272
pastry crusts, 252
  apricot-nut pastry, 268
  butter pastry for tarts, 254
  pastry I for 1-crust pie, 252
    cheese, 253
    for 2-crust pie, 253
    for lattice-top pie, 253
    for little pies and tarts, 253
    for rose-petal tarts, 253
    for 10-inch pie, 253
    for 2-crust pie, 252
    rolled oat, 253
    spice, 253
    topping, 253
  pastry for high-collared 1-crust pie, 253
  peanut butter pastry, 254

sour cream pastry, 254
pie shells, 254
  cereal crumb crust, 255
  coconut-cereal crumb crust, 255
  chocolate-coconut crust, 255
  coffee coconut, 271
  filbert crust, 255
    Brazil nut crust, 255
    salted peanut crust, 255
  graham cracker crumb crust, 254
    cookie crumb crust, 254
  graham cracker tart shells, 255
  nut-crumb crust, 254
  10-inch graham cracker crust, 254
  meringue shell, 255
    almond, 255
    10-inch, 255
    special, 266
  apple-pecan, 267
  bridge, 268
  butternut, 267
  heavenly lemon, 267
  Kentucky chess, 266
  mince, 267
  shoofly, 267
  tarts, 272
    creamy coconut petal tarts, 272
  techniques for making, 251
Pilaf, rice, 187
Pineapple
  bars, 308
  coconut cream, molded, 287
  cream filling, 249
  flavor blend, 104
  jelly, 344
  kabobs, lamb, 110
  pecan coffee cake, 61
  piquant, good fortune chicken w/, 141
  preserves, fresh, 348
  refrigerator dessert, 289
  rhubarb jam, 346
  salad dressing, 220
    cooked, 212
  sauce, 104
  soda, homemade, 331
  spread, 47
  strawberry jelly-jam, 344
  upside-down cake, 232
  w/rum caramel sauce, 300
Pistachio seven-minute frosting, 242
Pisto à la "El Chico," 67
Plantation crisps, 313
  pudding, 280
Plum(s)

conserve, best-ever purple 350
cobbler, purple, 273
compote, purple, 299
cooler, purple, 330
ice cream, fresh purple, 295
ice, greengage, 297
jam, cherry, 345
jelly, spiced, 344
juice, 330
kuchen, 275
pie, fresh, 259
  fresh peach, 259
sauce,
  for poultry, tangy, 199
  rosemary, 199
  tangy, 367
Poached
  eggs, 65
    "Duchesse Ann," 65
  fish, 155
  salmon aromatic, 155
Pomodori Genovese, 193
Pompano Florentine, 153
Poppy seed cake, sunny, 393
  dressing, 382
  filling, 277
  strudel, 277
Pork, 94, *see also* MEAT 378
  and beans on the grill, 378
  chop 'n',
    green bean, supper, 98
  chops
    gourmet, 97
    party, 99
    skillet orange, 98
    stuffed, 98
  mandarin, 100
  midwestern bake, 99
  roast loin of, 373
    w/olives and rice, 95
  sausage links, 102
  tenderloin
    patties, stuffed, 367
Potato(es)
  Anna, 184
  au gratin, 184
  baked, 183
    in coals, 376
  dumplings, 88
  Dutch stewed, 186
  franconia, 183
  French-fried, 185
  ham scallop, 107
  in foil, roasted, 376
  in packets, dilled, 376
  O'Brien, 185
  onion salad, blue ribbon, 204
  patties, superb hash-brown, 185
  roesti, 185
  salad
    garden, 204

mold, 210
scalloped, 184
stuffed, 183
sugar-browned, 184
Pot cheese, homemade, 19
Pot roast
  à la Provinçe, beef, 87
  savory, 87
Poultry & stuffings, 133-150
  see also by name
  chicken, 135
    baked chicken, oven-fried or, 136
    broiled,
      flavor-full, 138
      herb butters, 138
      herb-garlic, 138
      rosemary, 138
      tarragon, 138
      honey glaze, 138
      lemon butter, 138
    cooked-chicken dishes, 143
      avocado-chicken casserole, 144
      crab meat casserole rosemary, 144
      old-fashioned pie, 143
      tangerine, 144
    fricasseed & stewed, 143
    fricassee, 143
      cornmeal dumplings, 143
      dumplings, 143
    le coq au vin, 143
    fried, 140
      amande, 142
      Antoine's Creole, 142
      cacciatore, 142
      empress, 140
      good fortune, w/ pineapple piquant, 141
      hints for, 140
      mancha manteles, 141
      Swiss-capped glazed, 140
    oven-fried or baked, 136
      and sweet potatoes in cream, 136
      Benedict, 139
      Cantonese, 137
      Ceylonese, 139
      chef's, 136
      dieter's Kiev, 138
      Dixie pie, 139
      easy bake, 140
      herbed, 138
      kumquat, 136
      Oriental, 137
      oven-barbecued, 136
        golden barbecue sauce, 136

sesame, 137
roast, 135
  honey-glazed filbert, 135
  orange-glazed, 135
  Pennsylvania Dutch, 135
    bread stuffing, 135
  stewed, fricasseed & 143
classes, 133
cooking, 134
duckling, 147
  à l'orange, 147
    orange gravy, 147
  duck w/olives, 148
game hens, Rock Cornish, 148
goose, 148
  roast, 148
    gravy, 148
Rock Cornish game hens, 148
  lime-glazed, 149
  roast, 149
  w/spicy stuffing, 148
storage, 134
stuffings for, 149
  apple, 149
  apricot rice, 150
  chestnut, 149
  corn and onion, 150
  herbed, 150
  old-fashioned cornbread, 150
  wild rice, 150
styles, 133
turkey, 145
  Caribbean, 146
  divan, 147
  fried, 145
  kabobs, 145
  mole poblano, 146
  roast, 145
  tarragon, rolls, 146
Pound cake(s) & fruit-cakes, 233
  ring, 233
Poured chocolate frosting, 246
Praline
  carrot cake, 225
  frosting, spice cake w 228
Prawns, curried, 165
Preserves, 341, 348
  best-ever tomato, 349
  cantaloupe, 348
  cherry berry, 348
  fresh pineapple, 348
  holiday treat, 349
  Lebanon County rhubarb, 349
  prize strawberry, 349
Preserving & freezing, 335-362
  canning fruits & vegetables, home, 335

Index

freezing, 352
  baked products, 360
  cooked foods, 362
  dairy products, 360
  eggs, 359
  fish, 359
  follow approved freezing methods, 352
  fruits, 354
  game, 359
  meats, 357
    drugstore wrap for meats, 358
  plan your freezer space, 352
  poultry, 358
  sandwiches, 361
  shellfish, 359
  vegetables, 356
home canning of fruits & vegetables, 335
  canning fruits using boiling-water bath, 337
  canning procedure, 336
  canning vegetables using pressure canner, 338
  equipment, 336
  methods of canning, 335
  sweetening fruits, 627
preserving, 339
  conserves, 341, 350
    best-ever purple plum, 350
    cherry-tomato, 351
    cranberry, 350
    ginger-apricot, 350
    orange, 350
    rhubarb, 350
    ginger brew, 351
  fruit butter(s), 341
    banana-pecan, 351
    grape, 351
    Moselem Springs apple, 351
  helpful hints about, 341
  jam(s), 341, 345
    blackberry, 346
    blueberry-lemon, 345
    cherry-plum, 345
    helpful hints for successful, 341
    mixed fruit, 346
    peach-rosemary, 346
    and nut, 347
    spiced, 347
    pineapple rhubarb, 436
    rosy banana peach, 345
Laperouse, Paris, France: eggs au gratin, 65

Index

strawberry, 347
   cardamom, 347
   mint, 347
jelly(ies), 339, 342
   apple, 342
   basil grape, 343
   blueberry, 342
   currant, 343
      crab apple, 343
   golden, 344
   mint-honey, 344
   pineapple, 344
      strawberry jelly-jam, 344
   quick sparkling, 342
   rosemary, 345
   savory-grapefruit, 343
   spiced grape, 343
   plum, 344
   tangerine, 345
marmalade(s), 341, 347
   citrus, 347
   lime, 348
   peach, 347
preserve(s), 341, 348
   best-ever tomato, 349
   cantaloupe, 348
   cherry berry, 348
   fresh pineapple, 348
   ginger tomatoes, 349
   helpful hints for successful, 341
   holiday treat, 349
   Lebanon County rhubarb, 349
   strawberry, prize, 349
Prime beef tournedos Orlando, 81
Prize strawberry preserves, 349
Provolone sauce, 197
Prune(s)
   burgers, curried lamb, 129
   chiffon pie, 271
   cobble cake, 300
   gravy, 94
   muffins, orange, 56
Pudding
   corn, 177
   Indian, 283
   'n' peaches, glamour, 282
   sweet potato, 192
   w/butter sauce, cranberry, 283
Pudding (cont'd)
   Yorkshire, 80
Puddings, custards &, 279
Puff(s)
   ham-cheese, 17
Pumpkin
   cake, 229
   miniatures, 229
   rolls, 49

Punch(es), 332
   golden, 333
   hot aromatic, 334
      buttered cranberry, 334
   loganberry-lemonade, 332
   raspberry fruit, 333
   sage cider, 334
   sparkling, 332
   spiced lemon tea, 334
   spicy cranberry, 332
Pungent paté, 19
Purple plum
   cobbler, 273
   compote, 299
   cooler, 330

Q

Queen bees, 312
Quick
   breads, 50
   cocoa cake, 235
   coffee cake, 53
   dishes
      fish stick special, 157
      garden potato salad, 204
      kraut w/apples, 331
      potato salad mold, 210
   'n' easy jam braid, 58
   soups to serve hot, 26
   sparkling jelly, 342
   tomato sauce, 198
Quickie kabobs, 370

R

Rack of Pork Forum, 97
Ragout
   w/piquant sauce, 92
Rainbow angel food, 236
Raisin
   and cherry filling, 278
   bread
      oatmeal, 38
   cake, crunch-top, 233
   caramel sauce,
      ham 'n' yams in, 106
   dressing, heart w/apple, 120
   nut loaf, 42
   pie, sour cream, 266
   rum butter frosting, 245
Raisins, cinnamon-buttered, 206
Raspberry
   and lime swizzle, 330
   crème, molded, 287
   delight, 329
   fruit punch, 333
   or strawberry soda, homemade, 331
   pie, fresh red, 257
   pudding, Danish, 290
   salad mold, 363
   sauce

      fresh, 304
Ratatouille w/Spanish olives, 179
Ravigote sauce
   hot, 197
Red
   cabbage, Danish style, 175
   eye gravy, 200
   gravy, "fried" ham w/, 105
   raspberry pie, fresh, 257
Refrigerator cookies, 317
   desserts, 287
Regal
   chocolate dessert, 287
   mocha-nog pie, 268
Rémoulade sauce, 84, 347
Restaurant recipes
   Alfredo's Rome Italy: fettucine al burro Alfredo; fettuccine, Alfredo, 181
   Antico Martini, Venice, Italy; rosy sauce, 24
   Antoine's New Orleans, Louisiana: Antoine's chicken Creole, 142; fresh mushroom sous cloche, 180; shrimp à la king, 166
   Aruba Caribbean Hotel-Casino, Aruba, Netherlands Antilles: bahmie goreng, 100; sweet potato pudding, 192
   Au Petit Jean Restaurant, Beverly Hills, California: crêpes farcie, 181
   Beaumont Inn, Harrodsburg, Kentucky: Kentucky chess pie, 266
   Ben Gross Restaurant, Irwin Pennsylvania: flounder stuffed w/crab meat 152
   Bookbinder's Sea Food House, Philadelphia, Pennsylvania: Booky baked crab, 161
   Bräe Loch Inn, Cazenovia, New York: beets in orange sauce, 174
   Brennan's, New Orleans, Louisiana: bananas Foster, Brennan's, 298; Brennan's gumbo à la Creole, 31; crab ravigote, 161; filet mignon Stanley, 81
   Caribe Hilton, San Juan, Puerto Rico: shrimp and lobster stew, 162
   Charlie's Cafe Exceptionale, Minneapolis,

Minnesota: liver pâté exceptionale, 21
Chocolate House, Edinburgh, Scotland: South African curry, 130
Condado Beach Hotel, San Juan, Puerto Rico: Cuban black bean soup, 27; salde Siciliano, 215
Copper Kettle, Aspen, Colorado: cucumber soup, 29
Danieli Royal Excelsior, Venice, Italy: scampi flamingo, 166; zuppa di pesce, Royal Danieli, 32
El Chico Spanish Restaurant, New York, New York: pisto à la "El Chico," 67
El Prado, Clift Hotel, San Francisco, California: curried prawns, 165
Fleur de Lis, San Francisco, California: Roquefort omelet, 68
Fontainbleau Hotel, Miami Beach, Florida: Fontainbleau hors d'oeuvre pie, 14
Gallatin's, Monterey, California: Gallatin's mushrooms à la crème George, 179
George's on Via Marche, Rome, Italy: carciofi alla Greca George's, 21
Grand Hotel de la Place, Dinan, France: poached eggs "Duchesse Anne," 65
Horcher's, Madrid, Spain: Don Quixote Horcher, 115
Hotel Aiglon, Menton, France: duck w/olives, 148
Hotel Limone, Limone Piemonte, Italy: cannelloni alla Piemontese "maison," 131
Idle Spurs, Barstow, California: Roquefort cheese dressing, 220
Imperial House, Chicago, Illinois: rice pilaf, 187
Jack and Charlie's "21," New York, New York: veal Florentine "21," 113
Jockey Club, Madrid, Spain: tomato cream, 30
Johnny Cake Inn, Ivoryton, Connecticut: apricot bread, 51

Index

La Rue, Los Angeles, California: prime beef tournedos Orlando, 81
La Scala, Beverly Hills, California: scaloppini el Presidente, 114
Lasserre Restaurant, Paris, France: desir de la Pompadour w/ English cream, 288
Latham's Cape Cod, Brewster, Massachusetts: celery and almonds au gratin, 177
Le Cremaillere, Banksville, New York: le coq au vin, 148
Lord Jeffery Inn, Amherst, Massachusetts: vichyssoise, 34
Old Southern Tea Room, Vicksburg, Mississippi: avocado toast fingers, 15
Pavilion, Henry the Fourth, Paris, France: parfait Grand Marnier, 291
Rickey Restaurant Studio Inn, Palo Alto, California: Victoria pie, 256
Rosellini's, Seattle, Washington: scaloppine alla Marsala, 114
Royal York Hotel, Toronto, Canada: baked Restigouche salmon Breval, 152
Sardi's New York, New York: crab meat à la Sardi, 159; Sardi sauce, 159; sauce Velouté, 160
71 Club Executive House, Chicago, Illinois: Belgian carrots phantasie, 175
Smokey Joe's Grecian Terrace, St. Louis, Missouri: beef w/ onions, 92
Talbott Tavern, Bardstown, Kentucky: Talbott Inn orange pie, 265
  The Astor Club, London, England: Bringal Berti Green, 178
The Forum of the Twelve Caesars, New York, New York: calf's liver Matius, 117; rack of pork Forum, 97
The Pump Room, Hotel Ambassador East, Chicago, Illinois: Beau Nash delight, 291

Veltliner-Keller, Zurich, Switzerland: liver on skewers, Zurich style, 117
Vermont House, Newbury, Vermont: beef bouillon, w/broiled orange, 26; butternut pie, 267
Ye Old College Inn, Houston, Texas: shrimp Ernie, 164
Rhubarb
  crunch, 300
  jam, pineapple, 346
  pie, rosy, 260
  preserves, Lebanon County, 349
  strawberry mold, 209
  w/pastry topping, baked, 300
Rib roast of beef, rolled, 80
  standing, 80
  steaks, Western style, 366
Ribs, barbecued, 367
  also SPARERIBS
  saucy, 101
Rice
  and chicken amandine, 187
  and peas in a pouch, 376
  casserole, Spanish, 187
  Chinese sizzled meatballs w/vegetables and, 127
  dishes, 186
  fried, 126, 186
  green, 187
  pork roast w/olives and, 95
  pudding
    saffron, 95
  salad, chicken, curried, 218
  stuffing
    apricot, 150
    wild, 150
    w/mushrooms, 188
Rich
  chocolate filling, 310
  coconut fruit filling, 222
Ringlet croustades, 62
Roast
  duckling à l'orange, 147
  goose, 148
  lamb, leg of, French style, 108
  of beef, rolled rib, 80
    standing rib, 80
  pork, fresh leg of, 95
    loin of, 373
    Pennsylvania Dutch style, 95
Rock Cornish game hens, 149

squab, 149
turkey, 145
Roasted potatoes in foil, 376
Rock Cornish game hens, 148
Rock lobster tails w/orange-butter sauce, 372
Roesti potatoes, 185
Rolled cookies, 318
  oat pastry for 1-crust pie, 253
  rib roast of beef, 80
Rolls
  crescent, 45
  cheese, 59
  flaky cheese-filled, 61
  herbed Parmesan, 46
  miniature orange sweet, 49
  new moon yeast, 58
  pan o', 60
  pumpkin, 49
  sweet-tooth breakfast, 47
  yeast, 44
Roquefort
  burgers, saucy, 366
  cheese dressing, 220
  omelet, 68
Rosemary
  brew, 199
  jam, peach, 346
  jelly, 345
  plum sauce, 199
  zing, lime, 329
Rosé strawberry bowl, 333
Rosette cake, 226
Rosy
  banana-peach jam, 345
  ginger sauce, 304
  rhubarb pie, 260
  sauce, 24
Roux, brown, 195
Rum
  butter frosting, raisin, 245
  caramel sauce, pineapple w/, 300
  whipped cream, 247
Russian dressing, 220
  recipes
    borsch
      jellied, 33
    kulich, 43
    pashka, 290
Rutabaga soufflé, 186
Rutabagas, whipped, 186
Rye bread, Swedish, 38

S

Saffron rice, 95
Sage cider punch, 334
Salad
  bowl w/shrimp-tomato aspic, Senate, 213

pointers, 201
Salad(s) & salad dressings, 201-220
  dressings, 217, 218
    celery seed
      cream, 215
    cooked pineapple, 212
      pineapple, 212
    creamy lemon mayonnaise, 220
    curry-mayonnaise, 208
    French, 219
      creamy, 219
      curried, 219
      honey, 219
      lime, 219
      Lorenzo, 219
      tangy, 219
      tomato soup, 219
        gourmet, 219
    green goddess, 220
    hot, 380
    mayonnaise, 219
      elegant, 219
      Russian, 220
      sour cream, 220
      Thousand Island, 220
    onion-sour cream, 204
    orange, 219
    pineapple, 220
    Roquefort cheese, 220
  fruit, 205
    chef's, 206
      cinnamon-buttered raisins, 206
    helpful hints about, 205
    strawberry-pineapple crown, 205
    Waldorf, 205
  green & vegetable, 202
    asparagus vinaigrette, 202
    blue ribbon potato-onion, 204
    coliflor Acapulco, 202
      marinade, 202
    crunchy peanut cole slaw, 203
    cucumber salad bowl, 202
    garden potato, 204
    gazpacho bowl, 203
    lemon/ginger-carrots, 204
    piquant cucumber slices, 203
    salade Provençale, 204
    spinach-beet, 204
      herb croutons, 204
    tomato-cream slaw, 203
    varieties & preparations, 202
    wilted lettuce, 204
  main-dish, 214
    all-seasons macaroni, 214

Index

crab Louis, 216
curried chicken, 218
gala lobster, 217
ham mousse
  Veronique, 217
Niçoise buffet platter, 216
party chicken, 215
celery seed-cream
  dressing, 215
salade Niçoise, 217
  salad dressing, 217
salade Siciliano, 215
seafood, supreme, 216
shrimp and avocado, 217
molded, 206
aspic(s), 213
Senate salad bowl
  w/shrimp-tomato, 213
  vegetable, 213
fruit, 206
  avocado
    mousse, 206
  cherry-cottage
    cheese, mold, 207
  coconut-cream, 209
  cranberry, 207
  fruit, 206
    compote, 208
    curry-mayonnaise dressing, 208
  grapefruit-lime
    mold, 207
  orange-crowned
    cheese, 208
  party-perfect,
    molds, 208
  peach melba, 209
  rhubarb-strawberry
    mold, 209
  sparkling fresh
    peach mold, 208
  spiced peach
    crown, 209
gelatin techniques, 206
meat, chicken, fish &
  shellfish, 211
  crab meat, 212
    cooked pineapple,
      dressing, 212
  ham mousse, 211
    spicy gelatin
      cubes, 211
  lobster elegance, 212
  super tuna ring, 212
  tongue-vegetable,
    mold, 211
novelty, 213
  Cape Cod turkey, 214
  Danish blue cheese
    mousse, 213
  deviled egg, 214
  vegetable, 210
    Danish potato
      platter, 210
    exquisite cucumber
      mold, 210
    potato, mold, 210
  pointers, 201
  vegetable, green &, 202
Salade Niçoise, 217
Salade Provençale, 204
Salade Siciliano, 215
Sally Lunn, 39
  w/strawberries, 40
Salmon
  aromatic, poached, 155
  Breval, baked Restigouche, 152
  chowder, 33
  kabobs, 156
  lomi lomi, 24
Salsa Italiana, 198
  rosata, 24
Salted peanut cake, 227
  crust, 255
Sand tarts, 318
Sardine
  cartwheel, 23
  finger canapés, 17
Sardi sauce, 159
Sauce
  crowned meat ring, 121
  fudge, 307
Sauce(s) & gravies, 195-200
  brown roux, 195
  gravy(ies), 199
    brown, 199
    giblet, 200
    method I, 199
    II, 199
    cream, 132
    gingersnap, 88, 200
    orange, 147
    prune, 94
    red eye, 200
    special, 95
    turkey or chicken, 200
  sauce(s), 196
    apple, 68
    barbecue, 374
    Bearnaise, 197
    béchamel, 196
    Bercy, 196
    Bordelaise, 196
    brown, espagnole, 117, 196
    butter, 364
    cheese
      grilled burgers w/, 366
    dessert, see DESSERT
      SAUCES
    dilled mushroom, 198
    English mustard, 198
    for foil-baked ham, 104
    garden butter, 365
    golden barbecue, 136
    herbed tomato, 121
    hollandaise, 197
    hot ravigote, 197
    lightning cheese, 366
    marinara, linguine w/, 190
    mint, 364
    Mornay, 197
    Normandy, 196
      barbecue, 198
      basting, 364
      butter, rock lobster
        tails w/, 372
    Oriental, 198
    par excellence, 129
    perky butter, 376
    Provolone sauce, 197
    quick tomato, 198
    rémoulade, 84
    rosemary plum, 199
      brew, 199
      rosy, 24
    salsa Italiana, 198
    sour cream, 199
      cucumber, 199
      mayonnaise, 199
    spicy apricot-lime, 369
    sweet-sour apricot, 367
    tangy cheese-broccoli, 156
    plum, 367
    plum for poultry, 199
    tarragon butter, 199
    tartar, 199
    teriyaki, 199
    tomato basting, 364
    velouté, 160
    velvet lemon, 83
    white, medium, 196
      thick, 196
      thin, 196
Sauced walnut beef balls
  Orientale, 123
Saucy
  cinnamon chicken, 370
  cocktail franks, 16
  ground meat towers, 121
  ham omelet, 68
  ribs, 101
  Roquefort burgers, 366
Sauerbraten, 88
Sauerkraut, see also KRAUT
  w/caraway, 188
Sausage
  links, pork, 102
  patties, glazed pork, 101
  stuffed roesti, 185
Savory
  grapefruit jelly, 343
  miniature croustades, 22
  pot roast, 87
  salmon kabobs, 156
Scalloped
  corn, 178
  haddock en coquilles, 155
  oysters, 163
  potatoes, 184
  tomatoes, 193
Scallops, 163
  coquilles, St. Jacques, 164
  en Brochette
    w/Onion risotto, 163
  gourmet in patty shells, 163
Scaloppine alla Marsala, 114
Scaloppini el Presidente, 114
Scampi flamingo, 166
Scandinavian recipes
  beef Lindstrom, 122
  semlor, 48
Schaumtorte, 279
Schnitz un knepp, 103
Schweinebraten, 373
Scones, Irish, 55
Scotch eggs, 70
Scottish shortbread, 318
Scramble, bacon and cream
  cheese, 66
  ham and cream cheese, 66
Scrambled eggs, 66
  de luxe, 66
  mushroom, 746
  w/cheese, 66
Seafoam frosting, 242
Seafood, see also FISH &
  SHELLFISH
  bisque, 31
  salad supreme, 216
Seasoned
  butters, 62
  zucchini, 194
Semisweet chocolate filling, 249
  sauce, 303
Semlor, 48
Senate salad bowl w/
  shrimp-tomato aspic, 213
Sesame ringlet croustades, 62
  seed
    sticks, 46
    twists, 59
Seven-minute frosting, 242
  chocolate, 242
  marshmallow, 242
  mocha, 242
  orange, 242
  peppermint, 242
  pistachio, 242
Shake, chocolate-banana, 330
  frosted coffee, 331
  strawberry, 331
Sheepherder's stew, 121
Shellfish, 158
  chowder, 32
  clams, 158
  crab meat, 159
  crabs, 159
  lobster & lobster meats, 162
  scallops, 163

shrimp, 164
Sherbet
  lemon, 296
  peach lime, 296
  watermelon, 330
Sherry
  or Madeira (flavor blend), 104
Shoofly pie, 267
Shortbread, ginger, 322
  Grasmere, 318
  Scottish, 318
Shortcake
  Chantilly, 275
  peach, 275
  strawberry, 274
  sunshine, 275
Shrewsbury biscuits, 322
Shrimp, 164
  à la Creole, 166
  king, 166
  and avocado salad, 217
  lobster stew, 162
  appetizers, bacon-wrapped, 18
  crisps, 20
  grilled, 372
  cocktail, Seviche style, 24
  cooked, 164
  Indienne, 165
  Ernie, 164
  green pepper packets, 375
  in shells, grilled, 372
  jambalaya, 165
  lasagne, 189
  marinated grilled, 372
  remoulade, 24
  stuffing, baked fish w/, 151
  tomato aspic, Senate salad bowl w/ 213
Sirloin steak Juliana grilled 366
Si si pastries, 17
Sit-down appetizers, 23
Skillet
  cooking, 378
  orange pork chops, 98
  potatoes au gratin, 186
  tuna supreme, 156
  veal loaf Fiernze, 130
Slaw
  tomato-cream, 203
Slipped custard pie, 265
Sloppy Joe Bake, 125
Small fancy cakes, 238
Smelts, fried, 155
Smoked
  shoulder roll, 102
  w/mustard sauce, 102
Snowball meltaways, 314
Snow pudding, 285
Soda
  bread w/currants, Irish, 52

homemade chocolate, 331
  lemon, 331
  peach, 331
  pineapple, 331
  raspberry or strawberry, 331
Soft custard, 279
  gingerbread, 228
Soufflé(s)
  milk chocolate, 284
  rutabaga, 186
Soup(s)—hot & cold, 25-34
  fish, chowders &, 31
  garnishes, 25-26
  helpful hints about, 25
  quick, to serve hot, 26
    beef bouillon w/ broiled orange, 26
  to serve cold, 33
    avocado, 33
    jellied consommé madrilène, 33
  to serve cold (cont'd)
    crème Senegalese, 34
    cucumber, Danish style, 34
    jellied borsch, 33
    chicken appetizers, 34
    vichyssoise, 34
  to serve hot, 26
    beef, 27
    bouillon with broiled orange, 26
    stock, 26
    bouillon, 26
    brown, 26
    consommé, 26
    white, 26
  Chinese cabbage, 28
  chowders & fish, 31
  bayou, 29
    Brennan's gumbo à la Creole, 31
    New England clam chowder, 32
    salmon chowder, 33
    seafood bisque, 31
    shellfish chowder, 32
    zuppa di pesce:
      Royal Danieli, 32
  chunky corn, 28
  cream of turkey, 31
  cock-a-leekie, 31
  creamy mushroom, 29
  Cuban black bean, 27
  cudumber, 29
  egg drop, 30
  lumberjack burgoo, 28
  Mexicana, 29
  onion-Halles, 27
  pasta e fagroli, 30
  tomato cream, 30
  whole-meal barley broth, 27
  yellow pea, w/pork, 30
Sour cream

mayonnaise, 220
  onion, 204
  pastry, 254
pie
  date, 266
  raisin, 266
  sauce, 199
  mayonnaise, 199
  veal Viennese w/, 203
South African curry, 130
Southern
  brownies, 307
  recipes
    beaten biscuits, 55
    beignets, 49
    burgoo, 93
    Creole doughnuts, 49
    Key lime pie, 264
    shrimp jambalaya, 165
Spaghetti
  dishes, 188
    Italian, 190
    seafood, 190
    supreme, 188
    w/tuna-tomato sauce, 188
Spanish
  butter wafers, 314
  lemon and lime, 331
  recipes
    lamb stew Picasso, 111
    paella, 159
    Pisto à la "El Chico," 67
    tuna salad Granada, 378
  rice casserole, 187
Spareribs
  appetizer, 367
  apple-kraut stuffed, 101
  barbecued, 101
Sparkling
  fresh peach mold, 208
  fruit refresher, 333
  golden cooler, 332
  punch, 332
Special
  flavor cakes, 231
  gravy, 95
  pies, 266
Spice
  cake(s), 228
    apple butter, 228
    w/praline frosting, 228
  cookies, banana, 311
  pastry for 1-crust pie, 253
Spiced
  carrots, 176
  honey topping, 248
  jelly, grape, 343
  plum, 344
  lemon tea punch, 334
  peach jam, 209
  peach jam, 347
  short ribs w/cabbage, 175
Spicy

applesauce torte, 424
apricot-lime sauce, 672
cherry sauce, 551
cinnamon towers, 588
Spicy (cont'd)
  cranberry punch, 332
  gelatin cubes, 211
  ginger crunchies, 579
  stuffing
    game hens w/, 148
    whipped sweet potatoes, 192
Spinach
  beet salad, 204
  cheese tart, 191
  hi-style, 191
  pinwheels, veal, 131
  w/almonds, creamed, 191
Spit cookery, 373
Sponge cake, 236
  butter, 238
  ring dessert, 238
Spoon bread, Hermitage, 54
Spreads, 19, see also APPETIZERS
  apricot, 47
  avocado, 22
  Braunschweiger canapé, 19
  marmalade, 47
  pineapple, 47
  pungent paté, 19
Springerle
  Scandinavian, 319
Squash
  baked, 192
  corn filled, 191
  stuffed w/ham and apple, 192
Standing rib roast of beef, 80
Steak(s)
  à la Barbara Stanwyck, 82
  Diane, 82
  full-flavored, 365
  herbed beef, 365
  Juliana, grilled sirloin, 366
  marinated black pepper, 365
    steak marinade, 365
  rolls, stuffed, 87
  sticks, calypso, 84
  tomato-smothered, 90
  Western style, rib, 366
  w/garden butter sauce, grilled, 365
Steeped coffee, 326
Stew(s)
  beef
    Burgundy style, 92
    w/onions, 92
  burgoo, 93
  de luxe, fruit lamb, 111
  goulash, gypsy style, 93
  Persian, 111

Index

Picasso, lamb, 111
ragout w/piquant sauce, 92
shrimp and lobster, 162
szekely goulash, 101
Sticks, bacon-nut corn, 54
butter, 322
Stifado, 92
Stock, beef, 26
brown, 26
white, 26
Stollen, 43
Strawberry(ies)
bowl, champagne, 333
rosé, 333
summer, 333
cardamom jam, 347
cream, elegant, 287
crème, frozen, 295
ice cream, 293
jam, 347
jelly-jam, pineapple, 344
jewel dessert, 520
lime cake, 232
mint jam, 347
mold, rhubarb, 209
pie
crumb, 258
glazed, 257
cheese, 266
ice cream, 272
maple cheese pie, 258
parfait, double, 271
pineapple crown salad, 205
preserves, prize, 349
shake, 331
shortcake, 274
soda, homemade raspberry or, 331
tart, glazed, 301
whipped cream, 247
Stroganoff, beef, 84
can-can, 84
ground beef à la, 126
Strudel, 277
Stuffed beef pinwheel, 89
breast of veal, 113
cabbage rolls, 132
eggs sophisticate, 69
lamb shoulder roast w/ honey chutney glaze, 108
peppers, 179
pork chops, 98
tenderloin patties, 367
potatoes, 183
rib lamb chops, 109
steak rolls, 87
zucchini, 194
Stuffing(s)
apricot rice, 150
baked w/shrimp, 151
for poultry, 149
game hens w/spicy, 148
veal birds w/mushroom, 116

wild rice, 150
Sugar
browned potatoes, 184
cookies
crisp, 309
Sukiyaki, 85
Summer strawberry bowl, 333
Sunshine
cake, 237
shortcake, 275
succotash, 173
Superb hash-brown potato patties, 185
Super tuna ring, 212
Surprise bars, 307
Swedish
applecake w/vanilla sauce, 297
coffee fingers, 315
gingersnaps, 322
meatballs, 123
recipes
äpplekaka med vaniljsas, 297
ärter med fläsk, 30
chokladbröd, 315
cocoa butter balls, 315
sticks, 315
kåldomar, 132
limpa, 38
mördegspinnar, 315
pepparkakor 322
rye bread, 38
Sweet
breads & coffee cakes, yeast, 41
chocolate filling, 250
potatoes
in cream, chicken and, 136
pudding, 192
spicy whipped, 192
rolls & doughnuts, yeast, 47
sour apricot sauce, 367
tooth breakfast rolls, 47
Sweetbreads
creamed, 119
creamed ham and, 118
Sweetened whipped cream, 247
Swiss
capped glazed chicken, 140
cheese
pastry morsels, 15
soufflé, 76
Christmas cookies, 323
recipes
Basler Brunsli, 320
brochette de foie de veau Zurichoise, 117
Mailaenderli, 323
roesti potatoes, 185
steak in vegetable sauce, 90

whipped cream-nut loaf, 52
Syrup(s)
beverage, 325
caramel, 225, 325
cocoa, 325
coffee, 328
lemon, 326
lime, 326
mint, 326
Szekely goulash, 101
Szerelmes levél, 324

T

Tacos, beef, 124
Tagliarini, 180
Talbott Inn
orange pie, 265
Tangerine jelly, 345
Tangy
cheese-broccoli sauce, 156
French dressing, 219
plum sauce, 367
for poultry, 199
Tarragon
butter, 138, 199
celery, 177
Tartar sauce, 199
Tarts
creamy coconut petal, 272
sand, 318
w/mushroom cream butter, 22
Tea(s)
hot, 327
ginger, 327
iced, 329
punch, spiced lemon, 334
rings, 41
Techniques for making
gelatin, 206
pies, 251
quick breads, 50
Teriyaki, 15
beef rolls, 90
sauce, 199
Thick white sauce, 196
Things to do with refrigerated doughs & bakers' breads, 60
Thin white sauce, 196
Thousand Island dressing, 220
Timetable(s) for
baking ham in aluminum foil, 104
Toast
"blintzes," orange, 62
avocado, 15
French, 61
Oahu, 61

Toasted
buns, 378
filbert coffee cake, 53
topping, 54
pie, banana, 263
coconut, 263
soy walnuts, 124
Toasty-coconut cake, 236
Toffee
bars, English, 309
pie, English, 271
Tomato(es)
Senate salad bowl w/ shrimp, 213
basting sauce, 364
conserve, cherry, 351
cream, 30
slaw, 203
creamed, 193
fried, 193
Genoa style, baked, 193
halves w/Danish blue cheese, baked, 193
in foil, 376
packets, cheese topped, 377
packet, zucchini, 378
preserves, best-ever, 349
sauce
beef tongue w/, 118
herbed, 121
meat, 190
quick, 198
spaghetti w/tuna, 188
scalloped, 193
smothered steak, 90
soup, French dressing, 219
Tongue
vegetable salad mold, 211
w/tomato sauce, beef, 118
Top hat shrimp soufflé, 76
Topping
broiler fudge, 248
pecan, 306
spiced honey, 248
toasted filbert, 54
Torte(s), 241
Black Forest, 241
Trifle, 279
Tripe Creole, 120
Trout
broiled, 153
cornmeal-crusted mountain, 155
grilled, 371
Tubed cake, marbleized, 227
Tuna
empanadas, 157
ring, super, 212
sensation, 19
supreme, skillet, 156
tomato sauce, w/ spaghetti, 188

Index

Turban cake, 224
Turkey, 145
  divan, 147
  fried, 145
  kabobs, 145
  mole poblano, 146
  or chicken gravy, 200
  parmazzini, 189
  roast, 145
  soup, cream of, 31
  tarragon, rolls, 146

U

Uncooked frostings, 245
Upside-down cake
  apricot, 232
  cranberry, 232
  lemon, 231
  peachy nut, 233
  pineapple, 232

V

Vacuum-drip coffee, 326
Vanilla
  filling
    cream, 47, 249
    creamy, 248
    custard, 249
  fudge frosting, 244
  hard sauce, 304
  icing, glossy, 246
  sauce, 298, 302
  foamy, 304
Variety meats, *see also* MEATS
Veal, *see also* MEATS
  birds, w/mushroom stuffing, 116
  cutlets, breaded, 114
  Florentine "21," 113
Veal (cont'd)
  lets Parmigiana, 18
  loaf
    Firenze, skillet, 130
    w/saucy topping, ham, 128
  oyster loaf, 131
  spinach pinwheels, 131
  stuffed breast of, 113
  tarragon, 116
  Viennese w/sour cream, 115
Vegetable
  aspic, 213
  medley, herbed, 377
    in foil, 377
  packet, fennel-flavored, 377
  salad
    mold, tongue, 211
Vegetables, *see also by name*

helpful hints about, 169
  mixed, dishes, 377
  fennel-flavored packet, 377
  medley in foil, 377
  preparation, 167
  selection, 167
  storage, 167
  A to Z, 167
acorn squash stuffed w/ham and apple, 192
artichokes
  in mushroom cream, 170
  how to cook, 170
  Milanese, 170
  véronique, 169
  Seville, 171
  supreme, 171
baked
  potatoes, 183
  tomatoes, Genoa style, 193
  tomatoes, hash-stuffed, 194
  tomato halves w/ Danish blue cheese, 193
Bavarian cabbage, 175
beets
  à la Russe, 174
  in orange sauce, 174
Belgian carrots phantasie, 175
Bringal Bertie Green, 178
broccoli
  ring, 174
  w/horseradish cream, 174
  w/mustard cream, 174
Brussels sprouts
  bestever, 175
  w/chestnuts, 174
buckaroo beans, 172
cauliflower
  supreme, 176
celery and almonds au gratin, 177
celery root w/mushrooms and capers, 177
chipped beef and potato boats, 184
corn
  filled acorn squash, 191
  baked acorn squash, 192
  pudding, 177
  w/mushrooms, 178
creamed
  spinach w/almonds, 191
creamy

green bean casserole, 172
crunchy wax beans, 173
Dutch stewed potatoes, 186
eggplant amandine, 178
Franconia potatoes, 183
French-fried potatoes, 185
  peas, 183
  style green beans w/water chestnuts, 172
fresh mushroom sous cloche, 180
fried tomatoes, 193
  creamed tomatoes, 193
Gallatin's mushrooms à la crème George, 179
glazed onions, 181
green beans gruyere, 172
  w/garlic, 173
herbed
  carrots w/grapes, 176
  peas and celery, 183
  vegetable medley, 377
hi-style spinach, 191
how to cook artichokes, 170
kraut w/apples, 188
lacy French-fried onion rings, 182
cornmeal fried onion rings, 182
lima bean bake, 173
  beans au gratin, 173
  sunshine succotash, 173
Mexican beans, 171
  refried beans, 171
new cabbage in orange sauce, 175
noodle dishes, 180
  crêpe farcie, 181
  fettucine al burro Alfredo, 181
  Alfredo, 181
  German ring, 180
  ground beef-noodle scallop, 180
  Tagliarini, 180
O'Brien potatoes, 185
onion casserole, 182
onions superb, 182
orange-butter carrots, 176
Parmesan-eggplant slims, 179
peas

and onions w/lemon butter, 182
French, 183
potato(es)
  Anna, 184
  roesti, 185
  sausage stuffed, 184
  ratatouille w/Spanish olives, 179
red cabbage, Danish style, 175
rice dishes, 186
  and chicken amandine, 187
  fried, 186
  green, 187
  pilaf, 187
  Spanish, casserole, 187
  wild, w/mushrooms, 188
rutabaga soufflé, 186
sauerkraut w/caraway, 188
scalloped corn, 178
  potatoes, 184
  tomatoes, 193
seasoned zucchini, 194
skillet potatoes au gratin, 186
spaghetti dishes, 188
  lasagne, 189
  shrimp, 189
  linguine w/marinara sauce, 190
  supreme, 188
  turkey parmazzini, 189
  w/tuna-tomato sauce, 188
spaghetti sauces, 190
  Italian, 190
  seafood, 190
  tomato meat, 190
spiced carrots, 176
spicy whipped sweet potatoes, 192
spinach cheese tart, 191
stuffed
  peppers, 179
  potatoes, 183
  zucchini, 194
sugar-browned potatoes, 184
superb hash-brown potato patties, 185
sweet potato pudding, 192
tarragon celery, 177
whipped rutabagas, 186
yams and broccoli w/provolone sauce, 193
zucchini
  Provençale, 194

Index

stuffed, 194
Vegetables and rice,
  Chinese sizzled meatballs
    w/, 127
Velvet lemon sauce, 83
Vichyssoise, 34
Victoria pie, 256
Vienna coffee, 327
Vinegar, herbed, 365
Voodoo pie, 272

W

Wafers, brown, 317
Waldorf salad, 205
Walnut
  beef balls Orientale,
    sauced, 123
  toasted soy, 124
Water chestnut(s)
  French-style green beans
    w/, 172
Watercress biscuits, 60
Watermelon sherbet, 330

Wax bean packet, 375
  cruchy, 173
Wellesley fudge cake, 230
Wenatchee Valley apple
  crisp, 297
Wheat scotchies, 317
Whipped cream
  almond, 247
  cake, 235
  cocoa, 247
    II, 247
  coffee, 247
  Cointreau, 247
  crème de cacao, 247
  crème de menthe, 247
  Dutch cocoa, 247
  mocha, 247
  mallow, 248
  molasses, 247
  nut-loaf, Swiss, 52
  orange, 247
  rum, 247
  strawberry, 247
  sweetened, 247
Whipped rutabagas, 186
White
  bread, basic, 36

straight dough
  method, 36
cake, delicate, 222
sauce, 196
stock, 26
velvet frosting, 245
Whole-meal barley broth,
  27
Wiener Schnitzel, 114
Wild rice stuffing, 150
  w/mushrooms, 188
Wilted lettuce, 204
Wine
  cheese (canapés), 21
  sauce, 104

Y

Yandee Doodle tuna bake,
  157
Yams and broccoli
  w/provolone sauce, 193
  in raisin-caramel
    sauce, ham 'n', 106
Yeast breads, 36

loaves, 36
rolls, 44
  new moon, 58
sweet breads & coffee
  cakes, 41
rolls & doughnuts, 47
Yellow
  cakes, 223
  pea soup w/pork, 30
Yorkshire pudding, 80

Z

Zesty kraut pastry snacks,
  124
Zimtsterne, 321
Zucchini
  omelet, 69
  packet, 377
  Provençale, 194
  seasoned, 194
  stuffed, 194
  tomato packet, 378
Zuppa di pesce: Royal
  Danieli, 32

Corned Beef

The brisket is usually three "faces," as shown here. Slices should be thin and they should be cut at a slight angle (referred to as diagonal slices). Slices are made in rotation so that the different "faces" will remain equal to each other in size. The meat fibers in the brisket are relatively long, but when thin slices are carved across the grain, the meat is very tender. Other cuts of corned beef are carved like the rolled rump. Keep in mind when carving the less tender cuts such as those used in making corned beef to make the slices very thin. It is better to serve two or three thin slices than one thick slice.

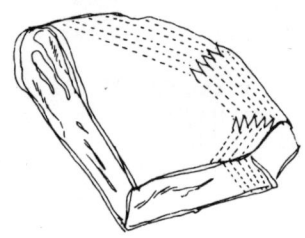

Lamb Leg Roast

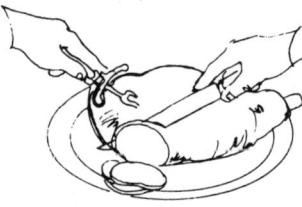 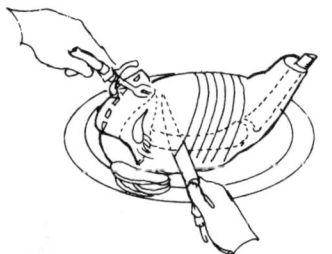 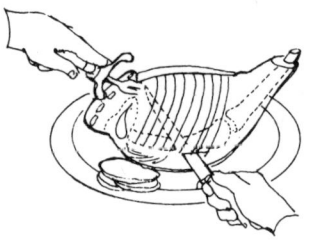

1. With lower leg bone to right, remove two or three lengthwise slices from thin side of leg. This side has the knee cap.

2. Turn roast up on its base and, starting where shank joins the leg, make slices perpendicular to leg bone or lift off cushion similar to method shown for picnic shoulder.

3. Loosen slices by cutting under them, following closely along top of leg bone. Lift slices to an auxiliary platter for serving.

Crown Roasts

1. The usual crown roast of lamb, pork, or veal contains about 14 ribs, but crowns with 40 or 50 ribs can be made. To facilitate carving and serving, the backbone should be completely removed in the market. Crown roasts may be garnished so elaborately that at first glance they may appear difficult to carve, but such is not the case. Remove from the center of the crown any garnish that might interfere with carving.

2. Slice down between the ribs, removing one rib chop at a time. Stuffing in the center of the crown, depending upon its consistency, may be either carved or removed with a spoon and served with the meat.

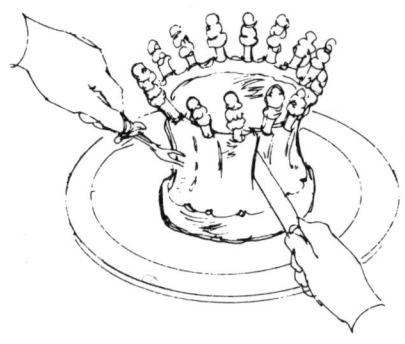

Courtesy National Live Stock and Meat Board